Early Childhood Education

Scott, Foresman Series in Education,
Theodore W. Hipple, Editor

Early Childhood Education

A Human Ecological Approach

David E. Day
University of Massachusetts, Amherst

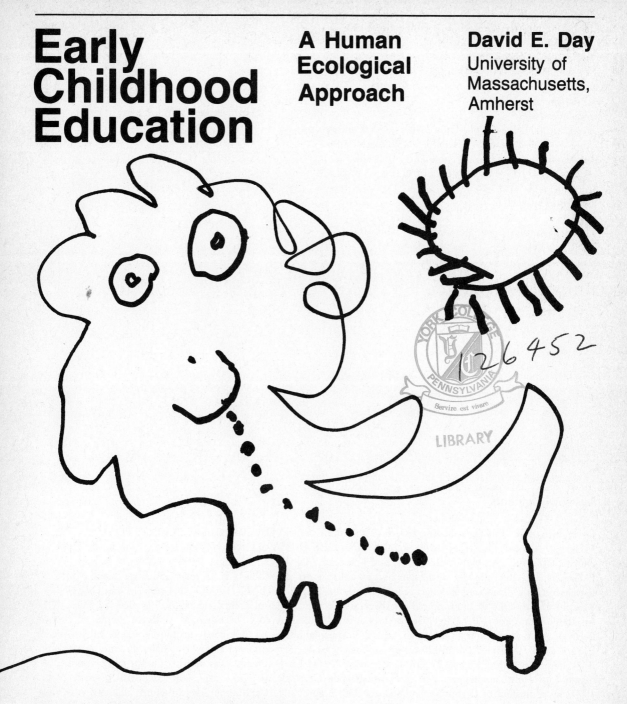

Scott, Foresman and Company

Glenview, Illinois   Dallas, Tex.   Oakland, N. J.   Palo Alto, Cal.
Tucker, Ga.   London, England

Library of Congress Cataloging in Publication Data

Day, David E., 1931–
    Early childhood education.

    Bibliography: p. 262
    Includes index.
    1. Education, Preschool—United States.   2. Education,
Primary—United States.   3. Compensatory education—
United States.   4. School environment.   I. Title.
LB1140.23.D39 1983   372'.21'0973   82-21528

ISBN 0-673-16029-7

Acknowledgments

Cover, title page, and part opening art courtesy of the Deerfield Day Care Center, Deerfield, Illinois. (**p. 79**)
Table 5.1: "Growth Gradients: Bodily Activity" from CHILD DEVELOPMENT: An Introduction to the Study of
Human Growth by Arnold Gesell, M. D. and Frances L. Ilg, M.D. Copyright 1949 by Harper & Row,
Publishers, Inc. Reprinted by permission of the publisher. (**p. 86**) Table 5.2: "Bereiter and Engelmann: Minimum
Preschool Goals" from Carl Bereiter, Seigfried Engelmann, TEACHING DISADVANTAGED CHILDREN IN
THE PRESCHOOL, © 1966, pp. 48–49. Reprinted by permission of Prentice-Hall, Inc., Englewood Cliffs, NJ.
(**p. 100**) Excerpt from "Behavioral Technology and Behavioral Ecology" by Edwin P. Willems, *Journal of Applied
Behavior Analysis*, Volume 7, 1974, pp. 152–153. Copyright 1974 by the Society for the Experimental Analysis of
Behavior, Inc. Reprinted by permission of the Society for the Experimental Analysis of Behavior, Inc. and Edwin
P. Willems. (**p. 105**) Figure 6.2: "Bronfenbrenner's Nested Environments" was designed by the author from
material in U. Bronfenbrenner, *The Ecology of Human Development*. Cambridge, MA.: Harvard University Press,
1979. By permission of U. Bronfenbrenner. (**p. 230**) Figure 11.1: "A Multipurpose Structure," Photo: Chris Vail
for Scott, Foresman and Company. (**p. 232**) Figure 11.2: "Outdoor Learning Centers" from SCHOOL ZONE by
Anne P. Taylor and George Vlastos. Copyright © 1975 by Van Nostrand Reinhold Company. Reprinted by
permission of the publisher. (**p. 242**) Figure 11.5: "Washington Elementary School Yard Before Redevelopment,"
Photo: Robin Moore. (**p. 243**) Figure 11.6: "Washington Elementary School Yard After Redevelopment," Photo:
Robin Moore.

Preface

Historians will one day characterize the years from 1960 to 1975 as a major epoch in early education. The vital shift in our view of the nature of human development, the rise in our concern for the education of racial minorities and the economically disadvantaged, and the emergence of the feminist movement all have had a significant impact on group child-care and early education practices. In less than a decade we became convinced that carefully designed group education experiences for preschool-aged children could contribute to their subsequent intellectual competence and social behavior. In addition, we dared to suggest that the group-care and preschool setting might support the development of some children better than the constant care and attention of their mothers. The rush to establish preschool, day-care, and compensatory primary school programs is well documented. It is becoming clear, as we review some of those programs, that we may have been too presumptuous in assuming that early education for selected groups of children was better than what they were experiencing at home and that it would enhance individual development and result in important social change. In retrospect, it seems clear that although early education needs careful consideration, it can be of value to children and their families. However, the task of developing the most appropriate program for any child remains a difficult, if not impossible, task for educators.

To address this issue, *Early Childhood Education: A Human Ecological Approach* focuses on ecological psychology. Its purpose is to offer clear guidelines and specific suggestions for employing human ecological theory and principles to improve the quality of group care and early education. It is written for practitioners and students preparing for careers in early childhood education. Day-care and preschool teachers, as well as teachers of children from kindergarten through third grade, should find it useful.

This textbook is designed for upper-division undergraduates who have had at least one practicum or student teaching experience and thus have a basic understanding of the dynamics of the early education classroom. It can be used in courses on the organization and curriculum design of early education and in seminars accompanying or following the major student teaching experience. *Early Childhood Education* is written, too, for use in graduate courses aimed at assisting practitioners in becoming more skilled at their craft. It should be particularly useful in supporting their examination of the environmental elements of their classrooms, in the analysis of activities and learning areas, and in the redesign of educational settings.

The human ecological perspective presented here is drawn from the theories and research of Kurt Lewin, Roger Barker, Paul Gump, and Urie Bronfenbrenner, among others. The book is based on an interactive psychology which assumes that development and learning are a function of the mutual effects of the person on his/her environment and of the environment on the person. It goes beyond most contemporary interactive psychologies, however, in giving special emphasis to the analysis of the environment, as well as to the behavior of the person. The influence of the environment on behavior is of particular importance in the discussion of early education presented here.

The book is divided into two parts. The first consists of a short history of childhood and early education in the western world. The materials presented in the first part set the stage for the ecological analysis of early childhood education practices, which forms the second and most important part of the text. Part Two treats three essential and interrelated features of quality early education. First, attention is given to three influential theories of human development and the ways in which each affects child care and early education practices. A second feature consists of an examination of the ecology of human behavior with particular emphasis on children in group settings. The third feature of this part is a series of chapters containing suggestions for ways in which practitioners can use principles of human ecology in programs for children.

It is often said that writing is a private and lonely process, and, to be sure, much of it is. However, I could never have completed this project without the support and assistance of many people. About ten years ago Rob Sheehan suggested a study of day-care programs, which resulted in my first attempt at ecological analysis. He continued to encourage my work and provided helpful comments on early versions of some chapters. All during the writing period students in the Early Childhood Education M.Ed. program at the University of Massachusetts provided me with regular critiques of my ideas and of the drafts of many chapters. Special thanks is due Professor Suzanne Krogh of the University of Florida for her perceptive and helpful review of the entire manuscript. Thanks also need to be given to Chris Jennison and Molly Gardiner of Scott, Foresman and Company: Chris for having faith in me, and Molly for her sage advice and patience. I should also like to express appreciation to Sue Krzanowski, who transformed a mountain of hand-written work into a readable manuscript. And last, to Jean, Jeff, and John, who created and maintained an environment entirely suited for writing: Without their support this book would never have been completed.

David E. Day

Contents

13

Introduction

When ecological theory and principles are applied to early education, as they are in *Early Childhood Education*, emphasis must fall on what Altman refers to as the "mutual and joint impact of environments on organisms and organisms on environments" *(The Environment and Social Behavior,* 1975, p. 205). This in turn suggests that the study of behavior—of development—cannot be divorced from the context in which it occurs, that individuals and the setting interact in ways which influence both the behavior exhibited there and the perceived nature and function of the setting. This textbook accepts Barker's assertion that the environment can coerce the behavior of the individual, as well as Bronfenbrenner's observation that the setting and the individual create a tension which produces change in both setting and organism.

Much of the work of Roger Barker (1968), Paul Gump (1975), and Urie Bronfenbrenner (1979) has been drawn upon in establishing the foundation for this text. Special attention is given to Barker's analysis of the behavior setting and the application of behavior setting principles to the creation of environments for young children. Walter Mischel's study of personality and social cognition (1968) is drawn upon in considering the role of the individual in an ecological system, and in developing applications from the concept of intra-individual differences for the structure of programs for children. An earlier study by Day and Sheehan (1975) indicated an interactive relationship between three environmental factors and children's behavior in day-care centers. These factors—the organization of physical space, the presentation of materials, and adult-child interaction—are given particular attention. Care has also been taken to identify and discuss principles of child development, and teaching procedures and techniques are presented in close connection with the discussion of ecological theory and human behavior. Moreover, generalizations useful in a variety of early education settings are tied to methods employed by teachers. In short, an effort has been made to integrate theory, knowledge, and effective practice wherever possible.

There are two parts to this book. The first part, Early Childhood Education: A Brief History, is comprised of four chapters which review the history of child care and early education. This section of the book is designed to place current early education practice in an historical context. Students might wish to use this section as a starting point for a more thorough study of the evolution of childhood and the social and political history of child care and education.

A second goal for Part One is to make readers aware of the influence of time, setting, and circumstance on the creation of attitudes towards children, their families, and their education. As Western civilization has developed over the past two thousand years, changes in our perception of what causes development to occur (or not to occur) have led to a better understanding of the ways in which environment and experience interact to influence what each of us becomes.

The first chapter, The Discovery of Childhood, traces the development of this concept of childhood from ancient times to the twentieth century. It is designed to introduce students to the idea that our contemporary conception of infancy and childhood is relatively new and compassionate. Chapter 2 deals with the history of early education in the United States from its European foundation, beginning with Froebel, to the rise of the American kindergarten and the advent of the nursery school movement. Chapters 3 and 4 address the interrelated issues of child care, education, and social reform. Special attention is given to the rise of the compensatory education movement in the 1960s, its historical antecedents in the progressive era, and the problems and issues attendant on the movement today. Day care is also discussed in terms of its purposes, sources of support, and contemporary problems.

Part Two, An Ecological Approach to Early Education, is the true heart of the book. The nine chapters in this part begin with a detailed introduction to and exposition of human ecology, developmental theory, and intra-individual differences. Chapter 5 includes the presentation and illustration of three alternative theories of human development which are important because of the role each plays in providing direction to early education programs. Basic principles of human ecological systems and the discussion of Barker's behavior setting analysis constitute the core of Chapter 6, Human Ecology and Early Childhood Education. Some implications for the practice of early education drawn from concepts of human ecology are discussed and illustrated.

Chapter 7 is an important part of the text, for it is here that the concept of intra-individual variability is introduced and related to the development of programs for young children. An ecological interpretation of interactionist theory suggests that we alter or adjust our behavior from setting to setting and time to time for reasons ranging from psychological need to perceptions of what the situation demands. This concept is treated in some detail along with three considerations practitioners must keep in mind as they develop programs for children.

Chapters 8 to 11 are concerned with more practical matters related to program design. Three environmental factors crucial to the creation of developmentally effective programs are presented and discussed in Chapters 8, 9, and 10. The physical setting and utilization of space is the topic of Chapter 8. Chapter 9 considers the selection, presentation and use of materials, and Chapter 10 addresses adult-child interaction. These important chapters are based on a study of child-care environments which revealed that the interactive effect of these three environmental factors was related to the behavior of the children. Where there was evidence that the staff had considered the organization of the space, the presentation and use of materials, and the role adults would play, there was an increase in the frequency with which children manifested developmentally appropriate behavior. Unfortunately, the converse was also seen: The absence of concern for these factors was related to the occurrence of growth-inhibiting behavior.

The out-of-doors is the subject of Chapter 11. The argument is made for considering the out-of-doors (mainly the play area) an integral part of the entire program. The idea of the play area as an extension of the indoor program is presented and argued. Suggestions are made for the application of the three environmental factors presented in the previous chapters to the out-of-doors; ecological principles are considered in relationship to the play area as well.

A text on early education cannot ignore common concerns about the subject matter or content of the program. Though typical curriculum elements are not discussed, matters of social and cultural values are treated in Chapter 12, The Curriculum. Proposals are made which should enable teachers of the primary grades in particular to meet the developmental needs of the children and at the same time to prepare them for the demands of the culture.

Finally, Chapter 13 presents an alternative evaluation procedure especially suited for the analysis of human behavior set forth in this text. It is based on the assumption that children's natural behavior in the day-to-day activities of the early education setting constitutes the most valid indication of their development, and includes an assessment of the context within which behavior is observed. Data obtained by procedures outlined in this chapter are useful in adjusting the environment of the early education setting so that it may more appropriately meet the needs of the children and the expectations for which it was established.

Part One Early Childhood Education: A Brief History

1 The Discovery of Childhood

The education of young children cannot be considered apart from the importance families and societies have placed on their care and rearing. The relationship between attitudes and beliefs about the importance of childhood and the establishment of schools has been demonstrated over and over in the brief history of the European settlement of North America. There appears to be a connection between a shift from the belief that children were born damned to one of salvation through devotion to God and the establishment of children's schools in New England communities; the early kindergartens of Boston seemed to reflect a conviction that children's social behavior could be shaped by appropriate early education; the reforms of the progressive era in the years from near 1890 to 1914 were reflected in the writings and teachings of John Dewey. Even very recently, the compensatory education epoch (1960–1970) was shaped as much by a commitment to an optimistic view of childhood as by any other factor. In short, it does seem that the reasons adults give for or against support for day care, preschool education, and kindergarten education are expressions of a set of beliefs about the nature, process, and the importance of the first few years to all of life which follows. Early childhood education is affected by contemporary and historical beliefs about the nature of human growth and development and the relationship of childhood to the well-being of the group, the society, and the culture.

The creation of Head Start in 1965 as the first national program of preschool education in the United States serves to illustrate further the relationship between child development values and beliefs, and education.[1] Head Start was begun in the summer of 1965 as a community action program designed to address health, nutrition, and education needs of poor families. Foremost among the purposes of Head Start, and perhaps its most widely recognized goal, was the education of children before they entered the elementary school in ways which might prevent school failure. It had become generally acknowledged that children of poverty had greater difficulty in meeting the requirements of the schools, and Head Start was considered by many as a program that might compensate for the consequences of an educationally impoverished childhood. The purposes and expectations of Head Start were based in considerable measure on a belief in the importance of the years from birth to age five to subsequent performance in school subjects such as reading and mathematics. More particularly, psychologists, educators, and politicians were able to convince parents that the outrageous frequency of school failure among poor and minority children was the consequence of the absence of intellectual stimulation, of extensive and elaborate conversation, and a dearth of culturally enriching experiences. An important assumption about development and education was inherent in this position: development was more a consequence of experience than inheritance, and carefully designed educational experiences could compensate for any deficit accruing from poverty and cultural isolation.

The perceived relationship of poverty and discrimination to performance in school marked an important shift in our collective belief about the contribution made to intellectual skill and school performance by events during the preschool years. Since early in the nineteenth century most Americans had been quite sure that a child's social behavior was the consequence of child-rearing practices in the home, the cultural group, and the community. Intellectual behavior, on the other hand, was not considered malleable. Many psychologists, educators, and parents were inclined to believe that how a child performed in school reflected *inherited* skills and abilities. It was generally believed that some children were born more or less brighter than other children; intellectual behavior was predetermined. Early in the 1960s this belief substantially changed (Hunt, 1962; Bloom, 1963; Fowler, 1965). More and more child-development research produced information which convincingly suggested that human intellect was not impervious to environmental influence, that experience could affect aspects of intellectual performance. Americans—educators, policymakers, parents—began to change their beliefs regarding the value and contribution of the early years to school performance and intellectual competence. This shift in attitude became a part of the rationale for expanding preschool education programs—and a justification for Head Start.

---

[1]Day care and nursery programs were established under the Work Progress Administration in the 1930s and again in 1941 under the Lanham Act. Though these were federally financed programs, they were created for reasons other than the promotion of child development. WPA nurseries created jobs for out-of-work teachers; day care programs established under the Lanham Act supported the war effort by freeing women for work in industry. Head Start is the first national early education program which was created primarily in support of child development. This will be explained more fully in chapters 3, 4, and 5.

Statements of the value of children and the importance of the early years have not always been as clear and positive as was the initial decision to fund Head Start.[2] Western civilization has a rather bleak history of concern for children in almost every way. It has only been since the sixteenth century that childhood has been considered an important period in human development. Considerable evidence exists that prior to the 1500s there was no real conception of childhood as a special and different period in life. The protective and supportive ethos which seems to characterize both personal attitudes and public policy today may not have existed in any significant way prior to 1800.

A detailed history of childhood is neither possible nor warranted in this text. In fact, there is the strong suggestion by scholars that the history of children cannot yet be written, for we have only recently begun the search for the story. Yet because of the assertion that child care and educational practices reflect society's values, and because the concept of childhood continues to evolve, it is important to discuss some historical views of childhood.

The Concept of Childhood

It was not until the thirteenth and fourteenth centuries that a European idea of childhood—the period from birth to seven or eight years—as special and important began to emerge. Evidence from family records, paintings, literature, and written histories suggests that prior to this time adults placed no particular importance on childhood. In fact, it may not be unfair to characterize adult behavior towards infants and young children as reflecting ambivalence, on the one hand, and abuse, on the other (deMause, 1974). It was almost as though life were divided into two periods, one important and the other only necessary. Infancy was necessary but unimportant, a period in which children were incapable of caring for themselves. Adulthood, on the other hand, began when a child was capable of moving away from a caretaker and could begin to assume a place and role in adult society.

But attitudes and beliefs did change. What began as an apparent lack of concern by parents has developed into a rather widespread assumption that parents are responsible for child development and are the cause of much of the behavior of their children. I should like to trace briefly some of the steps in the emergence of the concept of childhood from apathy and hostility to concern and nurturance.

Infanticide and Abuse

Sacrificing one's children to the gods was a widespread practice in ancient civilizations. Records indicate that such ritualistic sacrifice was practiced in Carthage, Phoenicia,

---

[2]Many people might question the assertion that Head Start is a positive statement of public support for poor children. The government has never provided funding for more than 25% of the children eligible for Head Start. Also, Head Start was subjected to a frontal attack by Nixon during the time in which he dismantled the Economic Opportunity Agency. More about this, however, in chapter 5.

and Ammon, if not in other ancient settlements. (deMause, 1974; Greenleaf, 1978). The firstborn male child has since antiquity held a special place in most families, but ironically, there does seem to be reason to believe that these children were very often sacrificed to indicate to the gods the extent of the adult's devotion.

Unfortunately, children were murdered in great numbers for reasons that had nothing to do with religious practices. DeMause (1974) takes one on a gruesome history of infanticide well into the fourth century. Unwanted infants in Greece and Rome, among other cultures, were simply abandoned on the hillsides to die. Usually this did not occur with firstborn males but was common practice with females and sons born later. It is not clear why healthy children were killed by abandonment, being thrown in the sea or a river to drown, or encased in large pots. It may have been a cruel method of controlling the population; it may have had something to do with status or simply have reflected economic crises. Whatever the reasons, it is important to remember that in early Western societies infants were not infrequently killed or abandoned by their parents with apparent impunity.

Children born with an infirmity—a twisted limb or distorted features, for example—or sickly and premature were almost without exception destroyed. It seems as though no value were placed upon an unhealthy, handicapped newborn; it may have been that beliefs about the cause of such birth defects prescribed that the children be destroyed. Furthermore, there is evidence that such states as Sparta carefully killed all but the very fit as one means of maintaining strength in the society. Yet there is evidence that in both Greece and Rome, healthy abandoned children were mutilated by adults who found them and subsequently taught them to beg. Greenleaf (p. 19) quotes Seneca's defense of such practices for the joy and laughter these poor unfortunate children brought to those who looked upon their grotesque shapes. Though infanticide became a punishable crime by the fourth century, deMause claims that evidence exists that such practices existed in some degree to the eighteenth and nineteenth centuries.

The history of children includes accounts of their being sold into bondage, of abandonment to children's homes, of sexual abuse, of beatings and similar cruel treatment from earliest times to the 1700s. Indeed, the exploitation of children below the age of ten in industry continued well into the twentieth century. A less obvious example of adults', especially parents', lack of attachment to children was the common practice of sending children away from the home soon after birth to be reared by a wet-nurse or another family. Very often such children did not return to their homes until after age six. There was, too, a significant amount of infant and child mortality, which, according to deMause, might have been the result of the care given the children in their foster homes.

The role and lack of influence of women may also have been a contributing factor in child abuse. Premodern societies were even more male-dominated than ours today. Women had few rights, and it seems that control over the destiny of their children was not one of them. Greenleaf describes ritualistic infant sacrifices at which women were subjected to a fine if they cried or in other ways protested the slaughter of their children. She also records a case of an Egyptian male commanding his wife to save male newborns but to "expose" female infants (p. 19). Had mothers had more influence in the affairs of the family, the state, and religion, less infanticide and abuse might have occurred.

In summary, it appears that children in Western civilization have been subjected to murder and cruel treatment for a longer period of time than they have been protected from adults by law. In large part, this may have been the consequence of the absence of a conception of childhood and an appreciation of the importance of the early years to adult behavior. It also seems clear that religious customs and beliefs for sometime contributed to child abuse.

Infant Mortality

Another reason why the idea of childhood as a special time in life did not emerge before the 1500s may have been the high rate of infant mortality. Aries (1962) suggests that parents were forced to maintain a psychological separation from their infants because of the very real possibility that the child would die early in life. In his study of children in early France, Aries noted that it was the custom of the Middle Ages to paint a portrait of the deceased on the tomb. This custom did not extend to infants and children; Aries could not find any tombs bearing paintings of dead children until late in the sixteenth century. When icons of children did appear on grave markers, it was not on their own but rather on that of a parent or elder sibling. Aries explains the absence of children's portraits within the context of high infant mortality.

"No one thought of keeping a picture of a child if that child had lived to grow to manhood or had died in infancy. In the first case, childhood was simply an unimportant phase of which there was no need to keep any record; in the second case, that of the dead child, it was thought that the little thing which disappeared so soon in life was not worthy of remembrance: there were far too many children whose survival was problematical" (p. 38).

Aries continues by suggesting that "the general feeling was . . . that one had several children in order to keep just a few" (p. 38). He describes a 1622 account of a conversation between two women, one who is the mother of six children, having just delivered her sixth. The helping neighbor assures her that there is no need to worry about rearing so many children by saying that "before they are old enough to bother you, you will have lost half of them, or perhaps all of them" (p. 38).

Though today we might be put off by the lack of compassion for the newborn expressed by this woman, we should recognize that by the seventeenth century the brutality of earlier times had all but disappeared. There is considerable evidence that children were nurtured and loved, if not always by their parents. There might have been a more pronounced recognition of newborn children had not the threat of death been so real. To illustrate this point we can examine the autobiography of Montaigne. Montaigne is remembered as one of the most passionate exponents of gentle care in child rearing in the sixteenth century. Nonetheless, he was very cautious in maintaining a degree of emotional distance from his infant children.

"Though I have lost two or three babes at nurse, if not without grief, at least without repining—yet there is hardly any accident which pierces nearer to the quick.

The generality and more solid sort of men look upon an abundance of children as a great blessing. I and some others think it is as great a benefit to be without them. As for that strong bond which, they say, attaches us to the future by reason of having children, I am—as it is—too much tied to the world and to life" (Montaigne, p. 158).

On June 28, 1570, Montaigne's first child was born. She died two months later. Only one daughter of six survived. His apparent ambivalence toward children may have been influenced by the death of four of his children before they had lived even six months. "In July 1573 was born my third daughter, Anne, who lived only seven weeks; in December 1754, a fourth girl, who died about three months later; in May 1577 the fifth child—a girl—who died within a month; and in February 1583 another girl, baptized Marie, who lived but a few days" (p. 158).

Aries does not find it surprising that childhood appears not to have been acknowledged until the seventeenth and eighteenth centuries in French cities and not until the nineteenth century in rural sections of Europe. The pervasiveness of infant mortality resulted in families losing more children than those who survived. Infant life in the 1500s and 1600s remained extremely precarious as demonstrated by Montaigne's lament. Aries found it somewhat surprising that a budding recognition of childhood should begin to emerge as early as it did, given the high incidence of death among young children.

The Emergence of Compassion

One index of the beginning of childhood was the seventeenth century change in the dress of male children. Among the more affluent families, boys were no longer dressed in adult-style clothing once they had emerged from the child's role. Rather, they began to wear specially designed breeches with child's hats; only later did they begin to dress as small men.[3] It can be suggested (Aries, pp. 51-61) that the introduction of particular dress for male children was an acknowledgement, however oblique, of the importance of age and of growth in the development cycle. It may also have represented the first spark of compassion for children.

The matter of child care, a very radical idea, was being considered in both France and England by the seventeenth century. Montaigne wrote about the compassionate way in which he was cared for by his father—though Montaigne was raised in another home. Nonetheless, he argued for gentleness in child care and the expression of love and concern by both fathers and mothers.

---

[3]Designing clothing for female children never seems to have been practical. Girls continued to wear clothing very much like that worn by adult females.

The Englishman John Locke confronted child-rearing practices much more directly in arguing against swaddling and in advocating the fostering of children's play. In the mid-1600s it was common practice to swaddle all infants. Newborns were wrapped in strips of cloth, often quite tightly, in a way which prevented movement of the limbs. Swaddling was considered a medically sound practice which protected the infant from disease. Children were kept wrapped for long periods of time, being changed only when the stench from soiling became overwhelming. The practice extended well beyond the first year of life. Locke was a physician who was convinced that swaddling did no good and might have harmed children. He told parents to refrain from this practice and to dress their children in robes and loose fitting dresses instead. Locke also counseled parents in the use of restraint in all child-rearing practices. He believed that giving children freedom to crawl and to play was important in supporting their development. Locke even went so far as to advocate the use of shame and the refusal to meet children's demands as disciplinary substitutes for physical punishment (Illick, 1974). Though Locke felt it important for adults to maintain control over the mind and body of the child, his suggestions were nonetheless revolutionary; he was a somewhat isolated advocate for the use of moderation, arguing from what appears to have been a compassionate view of infancy and childhood.

During the late sixteenth and seventeenth centuries there was a growing tendency among the gentry of France to find enjoyment in children. Children were played with, made to laugh and laughed at for their childish antics, and generally enjoyed in ways not common in earlier times (Aries, 1962). Children were accepted for the amusement and sense of well-being they were able to bring to their parents including, it should be noted, their fathers. At about the same time, families began to be concerned about the soul of the child. Aries said that "a new sensibility granted these fragile, threatened creatures a characteristic which the world had hitherto failed to recognize in them: as if it were only then that the common conscience had discovered that the child's soul too was immortal" (p. 43).

A compassionate concern for children, as well as adults, began to emerge in the sixteenth and seventeenth centuries. Mankind began to consider the effect that adult care and nurturance of growing and developing children could have on their well-being. The acknowledgement of childhood as a special time, the joy children could bring to life, and the spread of some Christian beliefs influenced the ways in which adults began to consider their relationship to children and the process of growing.

Parents' Responsibilities

The emergence of the concept of childhood was followed soon after by a struggle for the mind of the child and by a growing assumption of responsibility by parents in this regard. By the mid-1700s the realization that "the child is father of the Man" and that childhood was developmentally connected to adulthood had produced the belief that consideration should be given to the ways in which children were reared. Widespread ignorance of infants and children began to be replaced by a regimen of disciplined activity and tasks which were designed to foster an appropriate spirit, a fear of and respect for the Christian god and one's elders. A growing system for educating children, in secular and religious schools, accompanied the spread of these beliefs. The acknowledgement of childhood was followed by a zealous determination to shape the minds and the spirits of the children in ways that were influenced by religious beliefs. It was generally acknowledged that parents were largely responsible for ensuring that this education took place.

The Puritan fundamentalist belief in original sin included the belief that the child, too, had a soul which, though damned at birth, could be saved through devotion to God. In colonial Massachusetts it was especially important for children to begin their study of Christian doctrine early and, though the church was the center of such activity, it was considered the parents', particularly the father's, responsibility to ensure that children began in earnest the arduous trek to salvation.

The road to eternal life was harsh for children. Montaigne and Locke seem not to have had much impact on common child-rearing practices. Their counsel for gentleness and compassion was not heeded; a belief in the value of harsh disciplinary methods was very much the vogue. Moral and spiritual goodness were often taught with the support of the birch whip. Well into the nineteenth and twentieth centuries children were commonly beaten by adults for their transgressions. DeMause tells us that very often parents and teachers assured children that thrashing them hurt the adult more than the child but that it needed to be done to drive out the evil spirit. In short, it was done for the well-being of the child.

The Psychology of Child Development

Early Advocates

The Puritan's conception of child development, though perhaps the most widely accepted, was not the only important view. Locke and Montaigne were followed by Rousseau (1712–1778), one of western civilization's most outspoken champions of children's needs and rights. Rousseau presented a view of the child as one born without evil, who needed gentle care early in life and who became "bad" or evil as a consequence of life itself.

In *Emile,* one of Rousseau's most important statements, he argued for child-rearing and educational practices in which play and direct experience were to be exploited to the fullest extent possible. He asserted that play was the means by which children developed both understanding and character and that adults could best promote development by assisting the child's investigation of all things in his/her life experience. Giving the child freedom to explore on his/her own, said Rousseau, was the best way to ensure full and effective adult development. He spoke passionately against the use of harsh physical punishment of children as well as against an education system which stressed memorization and recitation. He was also very much against any curriculum which reflected the values of the church and aristocracy above his beliefs regarding the nature of development. Rousseau also included in *Emile* a description of the process of development emphasizing the value of childhood activity and interests for their own sake and the contributions they make to all subsequent behavior. His was a loud and radical voice of compassion and restraint.

Rousseau's teachings remain valuable today and are more easily accepted now than when he wrote. Yet he was not alone in his study of childhood or in his advocacy of new and more compassionate child-rearing techniques. From the mid-1700s to 1840 and the establishment of Froebel's kindergarten, there were several important voices raised in support of the study of childhood. Pestallozi (1746–1827) and Herbart (1776–1841) each designed a school for children based on carefully developed, though different, psychologies of child development. Froebel, whose work will be discussed in more detail in Chapter 2, created the kindergarten (child's garden) circa 1840. It has spread throughout the world and exists today much as it did then. Though we know Froebel primarily for this contribution to education and child development, his most important contribution may have been the description of the value of and necessity for play in the development of the child.

During this hundred-year period, the ideas of distinguished people from Montaigne to Froebel reflected concern for the role of childhood in human development and went against the conventional wisdom regarding appropriate procedures for adults to follow in shaping the lives of children. These men maintained that the care and education of children must be considered in relationship to their effect on the growing child and must be less concerned with the imposition of adult behavioral standards. A psychology of child development and learning began to emerge during this century which continues to influence both parents and students of children's development.

The Rise of Empathy

Sears (1975) by indirection suggests that the emergence of a psychology of child development may have resulted from a general liberalization of attitudes and beliefs regarding the rights of women and children. As early as the late eighteenth century questions began to be raised about the treatment of women, children, peasants, and the infirm as property. The belief that the common person should expect freedom from tyranny and have the opportunity to participate in political affairs grew, spurred on by the American and French revolutions.

Sears seems to suggest that this manifestation of respect and concern for all humankind, but particularly children, is in part explained by the appearance of an empathetic ethos, in which people began to acknowledge that they could feel what others were experiencing. The effects of maltreatment, such as slavery and child labor, the harsh and severe punishment of delinquents, for example, began to be considered inhumane. Sears (p. 5) identifies Pinel's 1792 claim that madness is an illness as a prime example of budding humanitarianism. Pinel, of course, wanted the mad to be treated by clinicians rather than locked away in crazy houses. We should remember, however, that although empathy began to be expressed, it has yet to touch fully the major institutions of western societies.

Yet within three to four hundred years we proceeded from a lack of a clear conceptualization of childhood to a recognition of the importance of the early years for human development. Furthermore, we progressed from the abolition of infanticide to the adoration, love, and protection of infant children, and from there to a concern for the well-being of all persons.

Nineteenth-Century America

Lest we become too enthusiastic, it should be pointed out that the evolution of thought from the absence of humanity to the conceptualization of empathy was just that, progress in ideas. The nineteenth century was certainly no heaven-on-earth for children of any age, and observers of the contemporary scene might suggest that our child care and rearing have not yet caught up with our rhetoric. Recognition of childhood, introduction of ideas for social reform, and a rise in concern for others did not lead directly to gentle and developmentally supportive child-rearing practices. For one thing, when the struggle for the minds and souls of children typical of colonial America, was confronted by the liberal ideas described above, much of society was divided on the issue of appropriate child-rearing practices.

In an earlier section it was stated that Puritan religious thought assumed that all children were born evil and capable of salvation only through devotion to God. Children were regularly punished for their transgressions, however slight, because the Puritans believed that antisocial and irreligious behavior was the work of the devil. Harsh disciplinary methods, including beatings and excessive work assignments, were not at all unusual. By the early 1800s the doctrine of original sin began to be eroded by a belief in the innate goodness of all newborn children. Much of traditional Christian thought was challenged by this new idea that mankind was not born evil but rather became so as a consequence of being reared. There were thus conflicting ideologies regarding the nature of God's role in behavior and that of the parents as well. Parents were being encouraged to nurture the free spirit of their children, to help them conquer their environment and live free and productive lives. This new approach, however, ran hard against those traditionalists who were certain that sparing both the rod and the Bible was to consign the young to moral and spritual decay, not to mention to a surefire trip to hell (Wishy, 1968).

By 1830 industrialism was very much a part of the eastern American scene. Also, and not unrelated to the growth of factories, the great immigration of Europeans to the northern cities began. There were also migrations by Americans away from the farms and rural settlements to the cities. Farmers were leaving the harsh and unceasing demands of the farm for what they believed to be the better and easier life of the city. The combination of foreign and domestic immigrants to the cities cast in high relief a conflict in child rearing, which, though not ideologically based, was nonetheless consonant with the debate described above. The European immigrant and his rural American counterpart did not share in the culture and tradition of those who had for so long controlled the cities and major institutions of America.

The established neo-Puritan citizen of the cities, God-fearing, hardworking, and self-controlled, was faced with the rough-and-tumble, hardworking citizen who had been forced to scratch life from the hostile interior and who had little time for and understanding of traditional American values. The newly arrived foreigners, too, were faced with the Herculean task of surviving. Together these groups had little time and less inclination to teach their children how to meet the established behavioral codes.

It was from this social reality—rapidly growing cities, heavily populated with families who were struggling to eke out an existence—that there came a movement to *save the children* and thereby maintain the integrity of the culture. Wishy describes the processes by which the concern for controlling children for God's sake came to be replaced by a system of education (not only in schools) in which the amoral and undisciplined children of both groups of new immigrants were to be taught ways of behaving so that society might be maintained as it had been. The important challenge to the doctrine of original sin and eternal damnation by liberal thought led to the concept that children different from those valued by church and state should be educated for the good of society.[4]

Neglect by Parents

One of the beliefs held by those who wanted to create institutions to save children was that parents were neglecting their child-rearing responsibilities. The assumption grew that wayward and slothful children were the products of parents who had failed in their responsibility to guide their youngsters to "good" citizenship. By the 1860s there existed a rather widespread conviction that children's personal and social behavior reflected the competence and attention given them by their parents. This was an important milestone in the evaluation of childhood, for it marked the acceptance of the belief that parents, not God, the devil, or social circumstances, were responsible for how their children behaved. It was to be some time before many began to question this assumption by raising the issue of what impact the larger culture and environment might have on behavior and development. Nonetheless, the shifting of responsibility to parents was not without significance.

The idea of parents' neglect contributed to the creation of social institutions designed to assume some of this responsibility. The early kindergartens—schools for children aged three and older—came to be considered an important supplement to the home. Many of the goals of these schools reflected a concern for the moral and social growth of children. Women were recruited and hired as teachers so that they might assume a mother-surrogate role. (Teaching had heretofore been considered a male occupation. Cremin, 1961.) Sunday schools were established so that the teachings of Christianity might be impressed on children from homes where such instruction had been neglected. Thus, there was the creation of "agencies to share parent's work" (Wishy, p. 68).

The Study of Human Development

By 1890 American society had begun to accept the idea that some people had greater knowledge and expertise in child development than did others. Foremost among the early experts was G. Stanley Hall, who began a child-study movement in 1891. Hall had been writing about children's school behavior since 1883 and began in 1891 a

---

[4]This theme is discussed in more detail in Chapter 2 in the section on the American kindergarten movement.

study of behavior from birth to adolescence. He enlisted the cooperation of hundreds of parents across the land, who provided him with a steady stream of information describing their children. He sent parents questionnaires designed to produce information about the emotional and intellectual behavior of children of all ages. Parents were also asked to keep a diary of their children's daily activity. From all of these data Hall developed both a theory of human development and principles of child rearing. In 1904 he published *Adolescence*, the culmination of his years of work.

Hall's theory, his research methods, and his instructions to parents and teachers were subjected to serious criticism by his peers. His theory of development was debunked; he lost most of his influence with teachers shortly after the turn of the century. Yet it must be recognized that Hall was a prime mover in the creation of the discipline of child study in society at large and the university in particular. He contributed greatly to making the study of human development important to parents, teachers, and university faculty. Furthermore, Hall trained Arnold Gesell and Louis Terman, who were to be so influential in education and child study that their works continue to exert a substantial influence today on how we explain human development (see Chapter 6).

The last decade of the nineteenth century was a period of considerable attention to matters of parents' responsibilities in child rearing. The issues were quite unlike those of earlier periods in the century; parents were gradually being asked to consider the schools and the larger society as partners in protecting and nurturing children. Following the Civil War, parents' manuals were introduced which presumed to advise parents on their role in fostering child development. These manuals were presumably based on the author's knowledge of development and were widely read by those adults who were growing in their concern for the well-being of their children.

In 1892 Kate Douglas Wiggen's *Children's Rights* was published. Like the manuals, it was an impassioned argument in support of providing for children's freedom (within very specific bounds) and for allowing them the opportunity to develop their own character. Wiggins reintroduced Rousseau but at a level of popular discourse. At the same time William James, one of our nation's most famous and influential psychologists, published his *Principles of Psychology* (1890), in which he argued that the child must be an active participant in his/her development, that the child contributed to his/her growth by participating actively in the environment. James was especially concerned with the educational practices common in most schools. John Dewey also began his long and distinguished career during the 1890s. He, of course, was a very forceful advocate of school reform, especially as it concerned the introduction of teaching procedures which freed the child from memorization and recitation. Dewey, like James, was convinced that learning occurred best when the child was actively engaged in producing his/her own knowledge. Dewey developed a formidable philosophy of knowledge and learning which continues to influence both educators and parents.

The point of this brief and incomplete overview of the study of human development in the later decades of the 1800s is that society was growing more and more receptive to ideas regarding the nature and causes of child behavior which were arising from the study of children. Futhermore, there was a growing acceptance by parents and school personnel of alternative child-rearing and educational practices. The impetus for all of this seems to have been the realization that character and some kinds of competence were formed after birth, an idea which implied that parents and the social institutions shared in the responsibility for child development. Contrast this, if you will, with the reception given to the ideas of Locke and Rousseau during their time: they were considered radicals and their ideas dangerous. Their influence on generations of educators and parents seems to have grown only after they had left the scene. Wiggins, James, Dewey, and Hall, by contrast, were read, considered, and accepted by large segments of society during the time in which they wrote.

The progressive era has not brought all good things to children and society. We continue to evolve both in our conception of childhood and in practices most beneficial to children and society. Yet it does seem clear that what began in the eighteenth century as a struggle for the mind and soul of the child had by the twentieth century been transformed to concern for those elements in the lives of children which most influenced their character, disposition, and competence.

Summary

The evolution of the concept childhood did not stop with the beginning of the twentieth century. The struggle to understand the nature of human development, particularly for young children, continues today at an accelerated pace. Important epochs in the 1900s will be discussed in the chapters to follow. This chapter has attempted to paint in very broad strokes a picture of Western civilization's attitudes and behaviors toward children over the past 2,000 years. The portrait is not one of which we should be proud. Children were early regarded with seeming indifference, as nonentities, and only recently as beings for whom society must provide protection and support. Sears has suggested that this history is perhaps a reflection of humanity's concern for one another and only with the introduction of empathetic ideals did we truly begin to make special provisions for all helpless beings, including our children.

Lest we be too critical of our European ancestors, we must understand that the rise of empathic thought was likely influenced by changes in society—changes in the way people were governed, in religious beliefs and customs, in the distribution of wealth, and in the provision of services to the common person. Montaigne's psychological separation from his infant children was, by his own admission, a reaction against the reality of epidemic infant mortality. Under the circumstances his behavior seems to be entirely understandable and even necessary lest he become emotionally paralyzed by the loss of so many of his infant daughters. Such psychological abandonment, when found in our society today, is commonly judged to be inexcusable and often constitutes sufficient reason for the state to remove children from the custody of their parents. Today there is no medical and little economic reason why parents should find it necessary to create distance between themselves and their newborn children. Circumstances have changed, as have expectations for children's survival and development and parents' behavior. It would seem to be essential that we maintain this distinction as we interpret the history of childhood in Europe and North America.

Table 1.1   **The History of Childhood**

    I No apparent conception of childhood
    To the 4th century A.D.: The Infanticide Mode
    The 4th to the 13th century: The Abandonment Mode

    II The emergence of the idea of childhood as a special period
    The 14th to the 17th century: The Ambivalent Mode

    III Parents begin to feel a responsibility for the soul of the child
    The 18th century: The Intrusive Mode

    IV Parents become responsible for training the child; a recognition of independence
    The 19th to the mid-20th century: The Socialization Mode

From deMause (1974, pp. 1–74)

DeMause identifies six periods in this history which may help conceptualize the growth of ideas regarding children. Five are summarized in Table 1.1.

Many of us may argue about deMause's assertion that we are now in a Helping Mode. He suggests that this mode assumes that the "child knows better than the parent what it needs at each stage of life, and fully involves both parents in the child's life as they work to empathize with and fulfill the expanding and particular needs" (p. 52). It may be too early to know if society will accept fully the implications of deMause's observation that the child is not helpless but a thinking, emotional, and responsive being who should be in control of his/her own development. It is interesting to contemplate, however, how far we have come in our ideas regarding children to have such a concept seriously considered. We shall all participate in proving deMause accurate or not.

References: Chapter 1

Altman, Irwin. *The environment and social behavior.* Monterey, CA: Brooks/ Cole, 1975.

Aries, Philippe. *Centuries of childhood.* New York: Alfred A. Knopf, 1962.

Barker, Roger G. *Ecological psychology.* Palo Alto, CA: Stanford University Press, 1968.

Bloom, Benjamin S. *Stability and change in human characteristics.* New York: Wiley, 1964.

Bronfenbrenner, Urie. *The ecology of human development.* Cambridge, MA: Harvard University Press, 1979.

Cremin, Lawrence A. *The transformation of the school.* New York: Alfred A. Knopf, 1961.

Day, David E., & Sheehan, Robert. Elements of a better school. *Young Children,* 1974, *30* (1), 15–23.

deMause, Lloyd. The evolution of childhood. In L. deMause (Ed.), *The history of childhood.* New York: The Psychohistory Press, 1974.

Fowler, William. Cognitive learning in infancy and early childhood. *Psychological Bulletin,* 1962, *59,* 116–152.

Greenleaf, Barbara Kaye. *Children through the ages: A history of childhood*. New York: McGraw-Hill, 1978.

Gump, Paul V. Intra-setting analysis: The third grade classroom as a special but instructive case. In E. Willems, & H. Rausch (Eds.), *Naturalistic viewpoints in psychological research*. New York: Holt, Rinehart and Winston, 1969.

Hunt, J. McV. *Intelligence and experience*. New York: Ronald Press, 1961.

Illick, Joseph E. Child-rearing in seventeenth century England and America. In L. deMause (Ed.), *The history of childhood*. New York: Psychohistory Press, 1974.

Lowenthal, Marvin (Ed.). *The autobiography of Michel de Montaigne*. New York: Vintage, 1960.

Mischel, Walter. *Personality and assessment*. New York: Wiley, 1968.

Sears, Robert R. Your ancients revisited: A history of child development. In E. Mavis Heatherington (Ed.), *Review of Child Development Research* (Vol. 5). Chicago: University of Chicago Press, 1975.

Wishy, Bernard. *The child and the Republic: The dawn of modern American child nurture*. Philadelphia: University of Pennsylvania Press, 1968.

2 Early Education in the United States

Soon after European settlers arrived in the New World they began to establish schools and to require the attendance of all children from about age six. The Massachusetts Bay Colony enacted a law in 1647 by which all communities of fifty households had to hire a teacher and open a school. In towns and villages with one hundred families, a Latin grammar school was to be established. There was no separation of church and school in Massachusetts; the schools were considered necessary in extending the fundamentalist values of the Calvinists. Children were taught to read so that they would better understand the message of the Bible. Other colonies made provisions for freedom of religious thought and some schools were established by religious groups. However, many private and locally sponsored schools were opened for any child who chose to attend. By the beginning of the eighteenth century most settlements in colonial America had made some provisions for the education of their children. It should be understood, however, that for children under the age of six or seven schooling was commonly deemed unnecessary and likely to be of little benefit. Many adults continued to believe that children from birth to age six or seven should stay with their mothers for succor and moral training. The belief among many Puritans that children were born damned and in need of the careful attention of the family was widespread.

It was not until after the Civil War that early childhood education as we know it today was introduced to the United States. In 1837 Frederick Froebel, a German educator, introduced a special program for children aged three to five; it was the kindergarten. In 1856 Mrs. Carl Schurz, a German emigrant, opened the first kindergarten in the United States. Not long after that in 1860, Elizabeth Peabody, a native of Massachusetts, opened a kindergarten in Boston. Both Schurz and Peabody patterned their kindergartens after that of Froebel, and thus began the movement to establish formal educational experiences for preschool-aged children in this country.

Kindergarten education began to spread across the land on a great wave of enthusiasm. There was a growing feeling of empathy for young children, especially the poor and urban slum dwellers. Immigrant families were settling in the cities and towns of the east coast in increasingly greater numbers, and the clash of cultures and values began to be felt. Many women, captured by the idealism of Froebel's kindergarten and their own sense of distress at the sight of young children left to grow on their own, began to organize kindergartens in order to achieve some degree of social change (see Lazerson, 1971).

At the same time leaders of the public schools were becoming convinced that a preschool experience might be an appropriate beginning for the process of formal education. The growth of public and private kindergartens from 1880 to 1900 was phenomenal. There seemed to be almost universal acknowledgment by parents, educators, and social reformers that some form of education for three- to five-year-olds was beneficial to child and society and perhaps necessary for child development.

The enthusiasm for kindergarten education influenced the creation of nursery schools and day-care programs. In this chapter I should like to describe in some detail the beginnings of the kindergarten and nursery school with emphasis on the ideas of Froebel, the introduction of his curriculum to the United States and its subsequent reform, and the advent of the nursery school movement. Day-care practices will be addressed in Chapter 3.

Any discussion of the origins of early education in the United States must be placed in the context of the profound changes which occurred during this time in our beliefs about the nature of development and the responsibility of society for its members. As was pointed out in Chapter 1, by 1850 there had been a shift in our attitude regarding the doctrine of original sin. Fewer and fewer people considered children to be born damned, believing instead that they grew to be "evil" or "good" primarily as a result of their upbringing. This change in belief placed the burden of making good citizens on the shoulders of parents but, more significantly, suggested that the early years were important because of their influence—positive and negative—on all subsequent development. The child was important now, if for no other reason than for what he/she could become.

We should note that from 1840 to 1914 there were great migrations of people within the United States to the industrial centers, especially in the northeast. This was also the period of European and Asian immigration. Hundreds of thousands of people left their homes and cultures to seek a better life in the United States. One important consequence of this was that North American culture was faced with numbers of persons who knew little about what was expected of them as citizens in the new land and who wanted to cling tenaciously to their beliefs, language, and other cultural traditions. There was a clash of cultures which might have been a major reason for the introduction of the kindergarten. Americans did not want to change to accommodate the immigrants. They sought ways of making all citizens in their own image. Social activists soon recognized the potential of the kindergarten as an effective means for achieving this goal. The situation was ripe for the introduction and spread of the kindergarten. More is presented on the kindergarten as an agency for social reform in a later section of this chapter.

We should also remember that by 1890 there was a growing national concern for the ways in which the poor of the cities and the newly arrived immigrants were being forced to exist. The progressive era began at about this time. Social critics such as Jacob Riis, who wrote *The Children of the Poor* (1905), and John Spargo (*The Bitter Cry of the Children*, 1905) deplored the conditions in which children and their families were compelled to live. Considerable efforts were made during this period to enact child labor laws, to establish clean milk distribution centers, and to provide for the nurturance of children whose parents needed to work. There was a feeling that our society should not tolerate economic, ethnic, and racial discrimination as had been the pattern for so many years. It seems important to keep in mind that the growth of early education in the United States was a part of and shaped by this progressive movement.[1]

Frederick Froebel's Kindergarten

Froebel (1782–1852) opened his kindergarten in 1837 after many years of study and thought about the nature of development and the relationship of children's activity to the achievement of understanding and knowledge. He became convinced that beauty and reason existed in all children, if only it could be released, and was sure that the kindergarten he had designed would contribute significantly to this end. He was a philosopher concerned with issues of morality and spiritual development and considered the growth of the moral person as an appropriate goal of education. Froebel believed in the unity of all things, real and spiritual, and in humanity's innate potential for morality based on self-awareness. His curriculum consisted of a series of activities designed to assist children in recognizing the unity of all things and their relationship to all they experienced.

Though a thorough examination of Froebel's philosophy and spiritual beliefs cannot be included in this chapter, it is necessary to understand that his kindergarten rested on a carefully developed idealism which assumed the potential for perfection in each child. His concern for the development of children was linked to his desire for a moral society. Froebel's garden for children was much more than a new or creative school for youngsters; it was a means by which his vision of the good person and the good society might be achieved.

In designing his curriculum Froebel borrowed a page from the work of both Rousseau and Pestallozi by asserting that children's play was a natural and necessary developmental activity. He believed that through play children manage to arrange the world in ways understandable to them. He was absolutely confident that his kindergarten would be successful to the degree that children's need to engage in active,

---

[1]See Lawrence A. Cremin, *Transformation of the Schools* (1961) for an excellent and compelling account of the interrelationship of progressive education and social reform. See also M. Lazerson, *Origin of the Urban School* (1971) for a more detailed account of what occurred in Massachusetts.

creative play could be channeled. Froebel did not accept Rousseau's belief in the value of natural, undirected play; he devised a program whereby children's tendency to play could be exploited.

There were two components of the Froebelian kindergarten curriculum. The first consisted of a series of ten "gifts" and four "occupations" which served as the major focus of the program. The "gifts" were carefully developed geometric shapes and three-dimensional materials which were to be played with in a structured and controlled sequence. The first "gift" consisted of six soft fabric balls, each a bit over one inch in diameter. This gift was to be offered by parent or kindergarten teacher early in the child's development. Froebel was confident that the child would gain an understanding of separateness, of grasping and releasing from careful play with the balls. Other gifts included a wooden ball, cylinder, and cube (second gift); eight rectangular blocks, $2 \times 1 \times \frac{1}{2}$ inch (fourth gift). Examples of gifts and some of the ways in which they were to be manipulated is presented in Figure 2.1. Froebel selected his gifts on the basis of his knowledge of children's interest in objects or shapes. For example, the ball was selected because "it had such extraordinary charm, such a constant attraction for early childhood" (Froebel, 1895, p. 33), and "The child will . . . retain . . . the ball as his beloved plaything" (p. 70). The sphere, cube, and triangle, and beans, seeds and pebbles were other objects selected as "gifts," all for much the same reason: the child's presumed natural affinity for them.

Though children's instincts were assumed to be the basis for the selection of the materials, children were not allowed to follow their natural inclinations in playing with the "gifts." Froebel offered very particular advice to teachers and parents about the introduction and use of the materials. Regarding the ball he said, "As soon as the child is sufficiently developed to perceive the ball as a thing separate from himself, it will be easy for you, dear mother, and you, dear nurse, having previously fastened a string to the ball which you give into the child's hand, to draw the ball gently by the string as if you wished to lift it out of the child's little hand" (p. 36). All of this direction was, of course, designed to support and enhance the child's understanding of self and his/her relationship to all things experienced. The benefits to be derived from the manipulation of the ball are as vague and abstract as they seem. Froebel's preciseness in describing the procedure for using the materials somehow got misplaced when he wrote about the benefits of his curriculum.

The "occupations" were a series of activities that children were to complete using materials representative of four geometric features—solids, surfaces, lines, and points. Children were to mold clay, fold paper, weave, and draw, and string beads in sequence. Children's enthusiasm and the "creative" use of these materials was limited in much the same ways as was the play with the "gifts." Teachers directed the children's "occupations," too.

It is important to note, too, that Froebel's pedagogy addressed the relationship of the individual to society. In his view of the affairs of mankind, the moral person was one who had learned to accommodate himself to the needs and desires of others. Froebel placed considerable emphasis on training the child to submit to the requirements of the group. This he referred to as cooperation, but there is little evidence that he was really interested in encouraging children to struggle with developing relationships with other

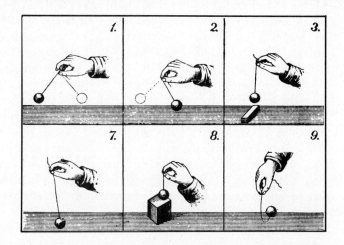

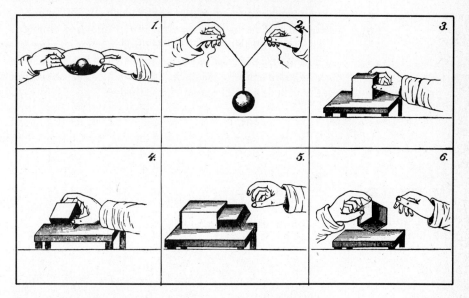

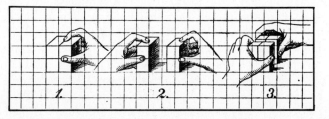

Figure 2.1   **Examples of Froebel's Kindergarten Gifts**

From Froebel (1895, Plates I, II, and III)

conducted in three Harlem schools. This project had the dual purposes of investigating the relationship of poor children's environment to intellectual and academic development, and of designing a curriculum which would prepare them for success in school (Deutsch, 1964).

Deutsch and his colleagues opened the prekindergarten classes with a curriculum especially designed to overcome the effects of deprivation based on racial separation and poverty. Particular emphasis was placed on language development—both the acquisition and use of language—but children were also schooled in prereading skills, concept formation, and inquiry techniques. This program for the preschool children was continued until they had completed the third grade.

The work of Gray and Klaus and of Deutsch and his associates marked a significant departure in the kind of curriculum offered to young children regardless of their circumstances. The program developed in Higher Horizons was basically one of enrichment: the children had a deprived childhood which needed to be compensated for by specialized instruction and by culturally broadening experiences. Though Gray and Deutsch also agreed that the life-experiences of the children contributed to their inability to perform well in school, they were much more precise in their analysis of the problem. Gray's focus on sensorimotor development and problem solving skills was derived from her observations of the aptitude of high school students. Deutsch believed that the language of the black child was inadequate because of syntactic irregularities, a dearth of description, and a lack of precision. Both Deutsch and Gray were convinced that the children needed to be taught in a carefully prescribed way if they were ever to achieve the potential both researchers were convinced they possessed. They had an important influence on early education because they dared to suggest that children under the age of six should have special academic training.

The Nature of Human Development   Psychologists were making important contributions to our understanding of the nature of human development during the early years of the compensatory education epoch. Three seem to have had a special impact on the revolution in early childhood education: J. McV. Hunt, Benjamin Bloom, and William Fowler.

In 1961 Hunt published *Intelligence and Experience*, one of the most important books of our time. In this exceptional volume Hunt argued convincingly against the widely accepted interrelated concepts of fixed intelligence and predetermined development. Conventional wisdom held that both intelligence and physical and motor abilities were established at the moment of conception and that what we became, intellectually and physically, could not be altered in any appreciable way after birth. The teachings of such influential students of child development as Arnold Gesell had led us to believe that prior experience accounted for little in the achievements of any person; the pattern of development written in the genes of our parents was inevitably played out in our lives. Hunt demonstrated through a careful review of research that the human organism could be significantly influenced by his/her environment, at least from the moment of birth and perhaps *in utero*. Hunt maintained that intelligence is a function of the interaction which occurs between the organism and his/her environment over the course of its life. More important, however, was the idea presented by Hunt that the earliest years—from birth to age six—were of special importance in laying the foundation for subsequent intellectual behavior.[3]

In 1964 Benjamin Bloom's *Stability and Change in Human Characteristics* supported and extended Hunt's thesis regarding the importance of experience in human development. Bloom reanalyzed previously published studies on learning and concluded that as much as 70% of intellectual aptitude as measured by IQ tests and about 50% of reading skill of young adults had been established between the fourth and ninth years. Bloom's results supported and extended Hunt's thesis regarding the importance of the early years. Bloom also gave educators reason to believe that the kinds of experiences children have in early-education settings were of particular importance in establishing the foundation for subsequent scholastic performance.

Almost from the moment their books were published, the ideas of Hunt and Bloom were captured by educators and psychologists as a major component in an argument for using early education as "an antidote to cultural deprivation" (Hunt, 1969). These educators, including Hunt, were confident that the cumulative effects of disadvantage could be ameliorated by providing poor children with an enriched program of early education. Enthusiasm grew among this group largely because they were confident that education, and preschool education in particular, could transform society. The key seemed to have been found for unlocking the potential hidden away in the lives of so many poor and minority children. The problem of creating the appropriate compensatory education curricula remained, but only time was necessary to discover the way.

William Fowler made an important contribution to the development of curricula by challenging conventional wisdom regarding the appropriate emphasis in early childhood education. Psychologists and educators, influenced by Freudian psychodynamic theory, were sure that the curriculum of the preschool should be concerned only with the social and emotional development of children. According to this belief, teachers were advised to provide experiences which would contribute to the socialization of children and to the development of their sense of self-worth and importance. This belief also held that emphasis placed on stimulating or challenging young children's intellect might damage their psychological development.

Fowler (1962) suggested that concept formation began during infancy; that children at six months of age were actively solving problems and by two years were able to cite elementary principles they had used in problem resolution. He found evidence that early verbal stimulation did appear to help the development of memory and knowledge acquisition, and advocated language stimulation because of evidence of a relationship between verbal ability and cognition.

The work of Hunt, Bloom, and Fowler struck at the heart of conventional knowledge about the nature of child development and early education. It had been commonly believed that the earliest years were rather benign, of little importance save

---

[3] Hunt's contributions to changes in our conception of human development are discussed in more detail in Chapter 5. The shift in our belief about the importance of experience in human development continues to exert influence over the design of early education programs.

in socializing children. In the past, educators and reformers considered early education an important means for influencing the *habits* of children and the child-rearing practices of their mothers. Slum children had been protected, fed, clothed, and initiated into the process of becoming American citizens in ways envisioned by a rather select group of citizens; however, it was never really considered appropriate or necessary to use the preschool and kindergarten as a means by which cognitive development might be enhanced. These three researchers suggested that the early years were important beyond social and personality development; that the foundation for intellectual and scholastic development might be even more influenced by early experience. Furthermore, there was in much of their writings encouragement for those who wished to use early education in transforming society.

The Role of the Federal Government

The third factor in the rise of compensatory education was the emergence of the federal government as the leader in the fight against racial discrimination and poverty in our society. One of the first and most significant activities of the government in this fight was passage in 1964 of the Economic Opportunity Act (EOA), commonly referred to as the "War on Poverty" legislation. This was an omnibus law providing funds for the design and implementation of training programs directed almost exclusively at the poor and the oppressed. Head Start was one of the show case programs provided for under this law.

Head Start was conceived as a community action program designed to provide medical, nutritional, and educational asistance to poor preschool children and their families. It was to be locally governed by a board which would include a fair representation of the parents of the children enrolled in the program. The locus of activity was to be a six-week summer school for children who were to enter kindergarten or first grade in September. While the children were in the preschool they would be given physical examinations and provided with medical and dental care. During the first year hundreds of thousands of teeth were filled, glasses prescribed, and operations performed—from the most simple to the most complex. Poor children were provided with at least one nutritious meal each day at the Head Start center; parents were provided with information about ways in which they could offer their families nutritious meals on meager incomes. Parents were hired as aides to the children's program and were taught, indirectly at least, skills in negotiating with government agencies.

Head Start began as a summer program in 1965 with an enrollment of approximately 560,000 children. Admission to the program was based on an index of poverty established by the original EOA legislation. In the winter of 1965–66 it was decided in Washington that the summer program, as good as it had been declared, was inadequate to the needs of the children. The educational program had been planned as a means by which these poor children could be prepared for the demands of entry into school; it was to be a compensatory education program with goals very much like those of Klaus and Gray, Deutsch, and the many projects begun under the aegis of the Great Cities School Improvement Program. On the basis of some rather meager evidence of the positive influence of the first summer's program and with some strong lobbying by politicians and influential educators, Head Start was expanded to a school-year program, paralleling the public school year. The six-week summer program was continued, too. Enrollment rose in 1966 to 570,000 children in the summer program and 160,000 during the school year. Until 1969 the total enrollment stayed at about 680,000 children. In 1970 the summer program was discontinued in favor of the full year program. The number of children served was reduced substantially so that by 1978 approximately 400,000 children were enrolled.

What began as a program to remediate the presumed consequences of poverty and discrimination soon became a highly valued, federally supported preschool for low income families. From time to time presidents and bureaucrats have tried to reduce the funds for the support of Head Start but with only marginal success. Parents (mothers of the poor children) have marched on Washington and lobbied their congressmen so effectively that today Head Start would appear to be as secure as any social program funded by the federal government.[4] Yet it is exceedingly important to understand that though Head Start can be found in nearly every community in the nation, the funds for the support of the children's program have never been sufficient for more than 20% of those eligible under the poverty guidelines. Parents and educators may have been successful in protecting Head Start and assuring its continued existence, but they have not been able to get Congress to appropriate the money necessary to meet fully the purposes for which the program was designed. It should also be noted that though Head Start was conceived as an important means by which the effects of discrimination could be reversed, the regulations governing admission to the program have produced an educational experience segregated by income. Head Start has been restricted to poor and handicapped children; parents who would pay tuition for their children to attend Head Start have found it nearly impossible to do.

As difficult as it has been to expand Head Start, it must be said that it has been the most significant impetus for change in the history of early education in the United States. This influence began to be felt in 1967, when a program was proposed by governmental officials for the continued education of the Head Start children through grade three. Project Follow Through was the name given to this program, and in the words of its first director, Robert Egbert, it was "designed to capitalize upon and to augment the gains poor children have made in the full year Head Start . . . or similar quality preschool programs" (Egbert, 1969). The plans to provide Follow Through for every Head Start graduate had to be changed before the project was initiated because sufficient funds were not appropriated by Congress. As a consequence, it was decided to create a research project to compare and contrast alternative early education programs.

In 1968 a few psychologists and educators who had been experimenting with early education programs (including Gray and Deutsch) were invited to prepare proposals for a national experiment in early education called Head Start Planned Variation and Follow Through. Each of the educators was developing an approach to early

---

[4] It must be understood that support for any program like Head Start can disappear over night. Though President Reagan has praised Head Start, his budget requests have called for sharp cuts in social programs, many of which benefit poor children.

education, often including the primary school grades, which would treat the problems attendant on poverty and school failure. In 1968 fourteen programs were begun which served 15,500 children in 91 school districts or Head Start centers. In 1969 there were 20 Follow Through sponsors in 148 schools serving 37,000 children. Follow Through was originally designed to last for four years; it was still operating in 1979–80 but with a stormy and controversial history.

Evaluations of Follow Through have not produced convincing evidence that the programs have had a significant and lasting influence on the educational performance of economically disadvantaged children. (See *Harvard Educational Review*, Vol. 48, 1978 for a presentation of the issues surrounding the evaluation of Follow Through.) Some curriculum models seem better able to raise scores on IQ tests than others, some programs prepare mothers for more effective work with their children, and some programs seem to be more adept than others in enhancing children's sense of self-worth. But none seems to have found the key to unlocking children's potential in the ways envisioned early in the compensatory education movement.

The most important effect of Head Start and Follow Through has been the creative attention given to the design and implementation of a variety of early education programs. Parents and educators now have a wide range of options from which to choose as they select programs for children. Many of these programs are based on beliefs about the purpose of education quite different from one another.

Head Start and Follow Through were only two of many programs initiated by the federal government during the 1960s which were designed to compensate for educational disadvantage. In 1965 Congress passed the Elementary and Secondary Education Act, which for the first time provided funds to school districts in support of locally designed educational programs. One part of this act, Title 1, was especially designed to support the creation of preschools for poor children to be directed by the schools. Other legislation was enacted which addressed such special problems as the education of non-English speaking children, the use of multicultural curriculum materials, the training of teachers for work with minority group children, and the teaching of "standard" English to children who speak dialects of American English. In retrospect, some of the programs semed to have been ill-conceived and not carefully implemented. Nonetheless, it must be acknowledged that the federal government played the major role in the creation of the compensatory education epoch. Furthermore, the influence of the efforts of the government were more strongly felt in early education than in any other aspect of the educational enterprise.

The End of Enthusiasm

The use of kindergarten education and day-care service as a means for transforming the children of poor and immigrant families to productive and socialized members of American society was described in chapter 2. Early education during the progressive era was an important instrument for accomplishing societal goals as well as for ministering to the needs of poor and displaced families. But the progressive era ended, and before 1914 educators, industrial leaders, and politicians were quite sure that all the attention given to early education really wasn't necessary (Lazerson, 1971). The flow of immigrants had subsided, industry no longer required the new workers it had three decades earlier, the nation was caught in an economic decline, and local school districts were looking for ways of reducing costs. Poverty didn't disappear nor did the matter of conflicting values; the melting-pot philosophy was very much alive. For all the reasons listed and more, there was a loss of interest in matters related to the lives of disadvantaged citizens. Much had been accomplished in twenty or thirty years: the kindergarten was established; day care was accepted even if only as social welfare; social work had emerged as a profession; and profoundly important labor laws were enacted which protected children and women from employer abuse, for example. But the zeal with which progressives had viewed the role of schooling as a means for social reform had been lost.

It is interesting, if not ironic, to note that much the same thing occurred with early education programs near the end of the 1960s. By 1969 some psychologists and many politicians were no longer enthusiastic about the role education, and particularly the preschool, could play in preventing school failure. There is no question that the compensatory education epoch ended before 1970 and that there was a movement among some educators and politicians to return to the ideas, beliefs, and practices which existed prior to 1960. I should like to describe some of the events which mark the end of the compensatory education epoch, with particular attention to two conflicting forces: (1) the attack against programs begun earlier in the decade and (2) the beginning of a period of reflection and reconsideration about the theories, goals, and practices of compensatory education.

The Westinghouse Report

The Westinghouse Learning Corporation and Ohio University were awarded a grant from the Office of Economic Opportunity to conduct an evaluation of the effectiveness of summer and full-year Head Start programs (Cicarelli, et al., 1969). Children who had attended summer Head Start in 1965, 1966 and 1967 and those enrolled in full-year programs in 1966 and 1967 were compared with a similar group of children who had not attended Head Start on measures of school achievement and aspects of personality. The purpose of this study was to determine what, if any, effect Head Start had had on the scholastic performance of the children.

The results of the Westinghouse study were very damaging to those who were sure that Head Start would make a difference. [5] As quickly as Head Start had been declared a success by President Johnson (in a premature statement at a press conference after the first summer), it was now judged to be a failure, for no differences in scholastic performance were found between the two groups of children. Congressmen and some

---

[5] In all fairness, it must be said that many of the pioneers in compensatory early education were not optimistic from the start. Head Start was hurriedly implemented before many people had a clear idea of the dimensions of educational disadvantage which were presumed to exist and, worse, of the kind of curriculum best suited for preparing children for school. Yet it must be said, too, that it was with some pain that these pioneers received the report of the Head Start evaluation.

government employees seized upon the data as evidence of the inadequacy of Head Start and early intervention and quickly began to suggest that appropriations be cut and the program be phased out. Advocates of Head Start found themselves hard pressed to counter the results of the study, though many worked hard at the task.

Head Start had clearly promised too much. The caution common to expressions of intent in most social-educational research had not been exercised in either the creation or control of this program. Those who carried the message to the citizens were unrealistic in their claims and unwise in their enthusiasm. Yet, it can also be said that by June, 1969, when the Westinghouse report became public, the political climate in the nation had undergone a severe change from the progressive attitude of 1965, when the program had begun. There was less concern for the problem of minorities, President Johnson had been driven from office by his commitment to the Vietnam war, the Democrats had lost a national election to the Nixon-led Republicans, and the nation was angry at young people who were violently demonstrating against the war in Vietnam. An attitude was prevalent which suggested that nearly a decade of reform was sufficient; that we had not been able to demonstrate our ability to remediate the lives of the poor and oppressed and it was unlikely we ever could. Anger and frustration were to be found at every turn, and Head Start, like other programs, became an easy, if not an appropriate, target.

The Jensen Essay

Arthur Jensen had, until 1969, been a highly respected educational psychologist who had made a substantial contribution to our understanding of the role experience played in human development. He had been especially prominent in the search for ways in which poverty and discrimination influenced intellectual performance. So it was noteworthy and important when he published an article in 1969 on social status and intelligence claiming that compensatory education had been tried and had failed (Jensen, 1969). Jensen said in this controversial manuscript that social science and education had been given massive amounts of financial support by the government exclusively for the purpose of assisting poor and minority children over the hurdles which kept them from entering the educational mainstream and had found the task beyond their reach. Jensen cited studies, including those of Head Start, to support his claim. Had this been all he had said, his stature in the academic community and respect among governmental officials would have been sufficient to cool the enthusiasm for special projects for disadvantaged children.

However, Jensen said much more than that compensatory education had failed. He claimed to have discovered evidence sufficient to explain why it had failed. His research on aspects of the intellectual performance of black and white students led him to claim that on one level of cognition there was no difference, but on another more abstract level, black children consistently scored below the level of competence of white students. Furthermore, Jensen asserted that this difference between the two groups appeared to be the effect of inherited potential and not, as had been widely believed, of discrimination and social status. In short, he was asserting that blacks were innately inferior to whites; that the black gene pool (the genetic history of the race) was not equal to that of whites. If Jensen's conclusion regarding the natural ability of black children was correct, it would follow that compensatory education would continue to fail, regardless of the efforts of educators.

As might be imagined, his article was immediately attacked by his colleagues. He had dared to suggest that all mankind, all races, were not equal in intellectual potential, a suggestion which ran hard against the prevailing beliefs. Most psychologists, educators, and policymakers had become certain that the age-old notion of racial and cultural superiority and inferiority had been laid to rest. We were quite confident in our knowledge that all races shared a potential for development on a scale equal with all other races. Furthermore, as a nation we had just worked our way through a period of considerable stress and turmoil as efforts were made to remove the legal yoke of oppression from all black Americans.

Jensen's article stirred the emotions of all of us; people immediately began to take sides. Jensen felt it necessary to defend himself and his work rather than to have it considered on its merits by his colleagues. The immediate effect was that his claims became much more than assertions rising from an investigation; they became political statements readily seized upon by those who would limit the government's role in extending the rights of citizenship to all Americans.

The Compensatory Education Thesis

Early in the 1970s social scientists and educators began to question the basic assumptions upon which compensatory education rested. These questions, by and large, were of a type much different from those raised by Jensen. The challenge by this group was, if anything, an attempt to introduce greater understanding and awareness of the dimensions of cultural variation in our society and a recognition of the ways in which such variety was expressed.

Michael Cole and Jerome Bruner (Cole & Bruner, 1972), very important psychologists too, suggested that compensatory education was a faulty concept, for it held that the lives of poor and minority children were inadequate and thus helped create *deficiencies* in their development. According to Cole and Bruner, such a conception led to our believing that the dialect of lower-status children, for example, was deficient or inadequate. Cole and Bruner drew upon the work of William Labov (1972) to suggest that we had confused being *different* with being *inferior*. Labov's research carefully described the speech patterns of lower-status blacks and showed in a convincing way that this language was at least equal in its potential to any other American dialect.

In 1970 Stephen and Joan Baratz argued against the concepts of cultural deprivation and compensatory education by suggesting they were creatures of racism which had become a pervasive force in American social science (Baratz & Baratz, 1970). The Baratzes were sure that the assessment of the developmental differences in poor children, so much a part of the start of compensatory education, reflected racist attitudes which equated cultural difference with inferiority. Their article was strident, harsh, and not always fair to those social scientists who were in the forefront of compensatory education. Yet they argued effectively for a reconsideration of our perceptions of the poor and minorities and the educational programs especially designed for them.

At the heart of the concerns expressed by both Cole and Bruner and the Baratzes was the theoretical basis for most of what was being done in the name of compensatory education. Head Start, special reading instruction, programs to teach problem-solving skills, and the myriad other compensatory education practices were based on the belief that poor and minority children suffered from a childhood deficient in experiences common among children who had little difficulty in meeting school expectations. It was further assumed that this deficiency existed because parents were unable or unwilling to provide the appropriate experiences or because the social setting in which the children lived was too hectic and disorganized. In short, it was generally assumed that these children were culturally deprived and in need of a special educational experience which would compensate for these earlier deficiencies.

By 1970 there was considerable doubt about the validity of the deficit theory, as shown by the writings of Cole and Bruner, and the Baratzes, but of a kind very different from that expressed by Jensen. These observers were concerned that the programs might contribute to stereotyping and social ranking which, if anything, would tend to close society more than it already was. Cole and Bruner, especially, thought that we needed to make sure we weren't imposing a set of beliefs about appropriate and necessary behavior on groups of people whose traditions were very different. They did not see racial inadequacy as had Jensen, but cultural difference which needed to be acknowledged and built upon.

It is difficult to believe that the designers of compensatory education programs were evil, as Baratz and Baratz suggested. The deficit theory, though terribly ethnocentric, was basically an optimistic theory; all poor and minority children could do well if only they had the appropriate cultural experiences. It seems quite clear that the early proponents of compensatory education wanted the programs to succeed and the children to do well in school. By 1970, however, it became obvious that we all had been unbelievably short-sighted and uninformed: theory and practice needed to be changed.[6]

Summary

One of the most striking features of the 1960s was the widespread enthusiasm and optimism shared by educators, psychologists, policy makers, and politicians about the role schooling, and early education in particular, could play in transforming society. Our rush to develop and implement compensatory early education projects was accompanied by an abiding faith in its potential success. I suggested in the introduction to this chapter that this faith has not entirely disappeared, that we still believe that early education can effect social change; the continued support for Head Start was cited as a

---

[6] I do not want to leave the reader with the impression that programs started during the compensatory education epoch have been halted. This is not the case at all. Head Start and Follow Through are operating; Title 1 programs can be found in most school districts; aid to public schools was increased in President Carter's 1981 budget.

manifestation of this faith. There is no question that practitioner's and researcher's certainty about the benefits of education for the structure and organization of society has been tempered by the difficulties encountered in the compensatory education epoch. By the same token, it can be argued that although we may have lost faith in particular programs which so captured our imagination during the 1960s, we have maintained our belief in the potential power of education to serve the individual and society.

It appears that one of the most significant things we have learned in the past twenty years is that, as important as the school or day-care center can be, education will be effective only to the degree that other human needs are also addressed. In the early 1960s we were quite certain that providing children of poverty with meals, health care, and a rich educational program could transcend the debilitating effects of an inadequate income. It was almost as though we believed that the experience of the preschool or elementary school could lift the spirit and the vision of children from the reality of their otherwise difficult existence. Today we have learned, if Bronfenbrenner (1974) is correct, that the effects of poverty and discrimination on children and their families are so pervasive and disabling that anything less than a comprehensive attack on all their aspects is bound to fail. Education is an essential part of the lives of young children. So too are the attitudes, self-concept, and perception of each child's parents. Bronfenbrenner has argued convincingly that it isn't sufficient to offer quality early education to poor children; rather, it is essential to find the ways and means of making life better in every way for every member of a poor family if they are live up to their potential in the schoolroom. It is essential to consider early education as an element in an ecological approach to the resolution of race and status problems in our society.

Thus, it is not that we have turned away from early education as a means of social reform but that we have matured in our perception of what it is possible for any public agency to accomplish alone. The ferment so much a part of the decade of the 1960s remains today, though in a different form. We are no longer building alternative curricula but evaluating, redesigning, and otherwise extending what was created earlier. We are also continuing to expand our knowledge of children's development and the ways in which group care and early education affect that development. This most recent history of early education has taught us how incomplete we were in our analyses and overconfident in projecting our successes. But, the process goes on, always with the view that the lives of children and their families should be enriched and enhanced by our efforts.

Building on the History

The most difficult and enduring task of any teacher is to create an educational environment which will be so appropriate for each child that he or she will flourish and develop as fully as possible during the time he/she is under the teacher's care. It should not be surprising that teachers and child-care workers search unendingly for techniques of classroom organization, and for materials and activities which offer them the promise of realizing this goal. The brief history reviewed in these first four chapters reveals the degree to which our evolving perception of children's development and the demands of societies have shaped our conception of what it is possible for children to achieve and necessary for them to acquire. We have over short periods of time changed both our perceptions of the possibility of childhood and what we expect of our schools; thus it is difficult for teachers to rely on the history of educational practice and child care to instruct them in creating the most appropriate educational and developmental setting.

But we can and must learn from the past. Perhaps the most important knowledge we can take from the events of the compensatory education epoch is that the school and day-care center exist as a part of an ecological system which, in toto, exerts profound influence over the development of each of us. Assuming as we did during the 1960s that the only important developmental differences between children of poverty and those of affluence were patterns of speech, experiences with written language, and visions of what was possible was to misunderstand what Altman describes as the impact of the individual on his/her environment and the influence of the environment on the whole person. It seems apparent today that we are affected by our environment—it does shape much of our behavior—but we also contribute to the form and content of our lives to the degree we find it necessary and possible. The child in poverty is not any less a pawn of his position in society than is the child of the suburb. To survive both must become engaged with those things which surround them and exert whatever influence they can on their settings as a means of enhancing life.

One of the most important implications to be drawn from this analysis is that the school, the classroom, and the day-care center or nursery must be considered a setting within which every child must accommodate himself *and* exert influence, as it seems warranted. That is, the Head Start or second grade classroom exists for each child as a contained environment which either supports the child's need to explore, manipulate, discover, and engage or it does not. The classroom—a defined space, a reason for being, a collection of materials, equipment and activities, and peopled by adults and children—will be a sound ecological unit and thus enhance children's growth by the degree to which it provides for children's influence and reflects their developmental needs. Perhaps this idea taken from the study of the history of childhood, child development, and early education will be useful for practitioners as they struggle to create the optimum educational environment.

Part II will address this issue. I shall develop more thoroughly the concept of an ecological system as it applies to early education and discuss in detail the place of the individual within such a system. I shall present an analysis of the early education context in terms of the kinds of provisions teachers should make to support children's natural and appropriate development. I hope that it will be clear that what is presented in Part II is based on what has been taught us all over the past years but particularly on the realization that the behavior of each of us must always be explained in large part by the context in which it occurs. The nursery school and first-grade classrooms do cause children to behave in particular ways—they either enhance or impede development—and the remainder of this book will deal with some ways in which that occurs and what we as teachers should learn from this realization.

**References:
Chapter 4**

Baratz, Stephen S., & Baratz, Joan C. Early childhood intervention: The social science base of institutional racism. *Harvard Educational Review*, 1970, 40, 29–50.

Bloom, Benjamin S. *Stability and change in human characteristics.* New York: Wiley, 1964.

Board of Education of the City of New York. *Fourth annual progress report 1959–60.* Demonstration Guidance Project, Bureau of Educational Research, New York City.

Bronfenbrenner, Urie. *Is early intervention effective? A report on longitudinal evaluations of preschool programs* (Vol. 2). Washington, DC: U.S. Department of Health, Education and Welfare, Office of Child Development, 1974.

Cicirelli, V. G., Evans, J. W., & Schiller, J. S. *The impact of Head Start: An evaluation of the effects on children's cognitive and affective-development* (2 vols.). Athens, Ohio: Ohio University-Westinghouse Learning Corp, 1969. (Mimeograph)

Cole, Michael, & Bruner, Jerome S. Preliminaries to a theory of cultural differences. In I. J. Gordon (Ed.), *Early childhood education. The seventy-first yearbook of the National Society for the Study of Education, Part II.* Chicago: University of Chicago Press, 1972.

Day, David E. Language instruction for young children: What ten years of confusion has taught us. *Interchange*, 1974, 5 (1), 59–71.

Deutsch, Martin. Facilitating development in the preschool child: social and psychological perspectives. *Merrill-Palmer Quarterly*, 1964, 10, 249–263.

Egbert, Robert L. *Individualizing instruction for young, disadvantaged children.* Paper presented at the Worldwide Conference on Individualizing Instruction and Learning, July 8, 1969. (Mimeograph)

Fowler, William. Cognitive learning in infancy and early childhood. *Psychological Bulletin*, 1962, 59, 116–162.

Gordon, Edmund W., & Wilkerson, Doxey A. *Compensatory education for the disadvantaged.* New York: College Entrance Examination Board, 1966.

Gray, Susan, & Klaus, Rupert. The early training project: A seventh year report. *Child Development*, 1970, 41, 909-924.

Gray, Susan, Ramsey, Barbara K., & Klaus, Rupert A. *From 3 to 20: The early training project.* Baltimore: University Park Press, 1982.

Harvard Educational Review. 1978, 48 (2).

Hunt, J. McV. *Intelligence and experience.* New York: Ronald Press, 1961.

Hunt, J. McV. *The challenge of incompetence and poverty.* Urbana, IL: University of Illinois Press, 1969.

Jensen, Arthur R. How much can we boost I.Q. and scholastic achievement? *Harvard Educational Review*, 1969, 39, 1–123.

Labov, William. *Language in the inner city.* Philadelphia: University of Pennsylvania Press, 1972.

Lazerson, Marvin. *Origins of the urban school.* Cambridge, MA: Harvard University Press, 1971.

Lazerson, Marvin. The historical antecedents of early childhood education. In I. J. Gordon (Ed.), *Early childhood education. The seventy-first yearbook of the National Society for the Study of Education, Part II.* Chicago: University of Chicago Press, 1972.

Schreiber, Daniel. *The Higher Horizons Program, first annual report.* New York: Board of Education of the City of New York, 1959, (Mimeograph)

Part Two An Ecological Approach to Early Education

5 Human Development Theory and Early Childhood Education

Chapter 1, The Discovery of Childhood, suggested directly that mankind has over the centuries been concerned with the nature of human development, particularly with the explanation of its causes. As was pointed out in that chapter, a belief that children were born miniature adults was widespread not too long ago. At other times we have believed the child was born an empty vessel into which the wisdom and the customs of the culture must be poured. Some of us have thought that adult behavior reflects the relationships that were established between children and parents; that what we become reflects our sense of competence, our freedom from feelings of guilt, and our belief that we alone control our life. The contemporary belief that human development is influenced markedly by the continuous accumulation of experience is relatively new.

We may choose to believe that changes in the conception of the nature of human development reflect increased knowledge of human behavior, but this is not altogether the case. History suggests that religious doctrines, medical discoveries, as well as advanced scientific theory and knowledge, have combined to shape our beliefs about how man grows and develops. For example, in Western Christian cultures modification of the concept of original sin allowed us to entertain the possibility that a child may be saved from eternal hell through devotion to God. The crack in the doctrine of eternal damnation allowed us to contemplate the possibility that our actions could influence our destiny. This was a significant event in our attempt to understand the course of human development from birth to adulthood.

Chapter 1 discussed Aires' (1962) study of the evolution of the concept of childhood in Western cultures and his conclusion that it was only after infant mortality had been reduced that childhood became an accepted idea. Apparently, when the chances of a newborn living to maturity were marginal, parents were unable to invest the psychological attachment to children now so common throughout the world. Parents had believed that an infant was only an infant, to be cared for by someone else if possible. Only when children were fairly autonomous and capable of providing some care for themselves did the parents fully recognize their existence, and only then as miniature adults. Children dressed as adults, played games adults played, and assumed as much of an adult role as they could.

A view of childhood more akin to contemporary ideas began to emerge when the care during delivery and the subsequent nurture of the newborn progressed to the point where parents could anticipate the survival of their children. The recognition of infanthood and childhood, even to the extent of naming children immediately after birth, transformed our basic attitudes about the first years. Children's games were developed; they were not now expected to engage in adult activities. The child's clothing was no longer the same as the adult's. The recognition and acceptance of the concept of childhood had a profound influence on the ways in which we conceived of the factors that affected growth.

Though there is widespread belief today that the early years are of crucial importance in a child's development to adulthood, the lack of certainty about the impact of many factors continues. Our concern about early childhood has not produced any consensus about the most appropriate child care or educational experiences for children. In many ways, the difficulty in achieving any agreement about the form and content of early childhood education reflects the conflict between explanations of the nature of human development mentioned here.

There are preschools and day-care centers in American society that operate on the assumption that the child's development will occur automatically if only he is left alone to grow. Other programs exemplify the belief in the importance of instructing the young in the ways of the culture, especially those related to achieving success in such institutions as the school and marketplace. We also are witness to the recent development of programs for young children that suggest that the child is a self-generating organism that exerts much control over its own development. This is a fairly new idea and certainly not fully developed. Yet this view too has its roots in the continuing struggle to gain insights into the mysteries of human development and behavior.

In this chapter I should like to discuss three of the most widely accepted theories of child development. It is important to know about these because they are so widely accepted and because they provide the rationale and justification for very divergent current early childhood education (ECE) practices. These three views of human development—predeterminism, environmentalism, and transactionism—will each be discussed in turn. [1] Examples of the kinds of early childhood programs based on each view will be presented as well. Wherever possible, I shall attempt to illustrate the

---

[1] Transactionism and interactionism are often used synonymously.

influence of each theory or view on the conduct of child care and education programs. In the course of explaining each theory and relating it to practice, I shall attempt to make clear my belief that the transactionist perspective provides us with the clearest and most comprehensive view.

Three Views of Human Development

The three views of human development—predeterminism, environmentalism, and transactionism—differ in important ways. However, it should be noted that the most significant point of disagreement is centered on the importance each theory gives to the role of heredity and environment in influencing human development. The predeterminist position is based in large part on the belief that inherited traits and characteristics determine one's development. The environmentalist differs from the predeterminist in assuming that environment or experience is far more important in determining development than inherited tendencies. The transactionist, as one might suspect, assumes that human development is a response to the interactive effects of both inheritance and experience.

Clearly, one's view of early education will depend on which explanation of human development one believes. Contemporary ECE practice does reflect acceptance or rejection of these theories.

Predeterminism

Perhaps no scientific theory has had more influence on our conception of human development than Darwin's theory of evolution. There is a clear connection between the first publication of his thesis in 1859 and the emergence of the belief that development is determined by inherited characteristics. American psychologists who advocated predeterminism—G. Stanley Hall, Arnold Gesell, and Louis Terman, among others—are in large part responsible for much of what we believe about the nature of human intelligence, the process of infant and child development, and the functional nature of intellectual behavior. Many programs for young children reflect their teachings.

Predeterminists believe that heredity is the single most important factor in human development. They maintain that human behavior is transmitted from generation to generation through the genes of parents; humans are alike because they are members of the same species. The continued similarity and lack of variation is the result of each parent's passing an equal number of human characteristics to each offspring. We are, according to the predeterminists, so much alike because of inherited characteristics. Our differences, too, can be accounted for in genetic construction. Hereditarians believe that the experiences we have with our environment contribute little to what we become.

The predeterminist view does recognize stages of development. Arnold Gesell (1940) has provided us with an extensive taxonomy of human development, carefully describing its many stages and the ages at which they should appear. These stages of

Table 5.1	Growth Gradients: Bodily Activity

2 Years: Runs without falling, and squats in play.
Rhythmical responses as bending knees in bouncing, swaying, swinging arms, nodding head, and tapping feet.

2½: Walks on tip toe; jumps on two feet.
Runs ahead or lags when walking on street.
Pushes toy with good steering.
Runs, gallops and swings to music.
Can carry breakable object.

3 Years: Walks erect and is sure and nimble on his feet.
Walks rather than runs. Can stand on one foot momentarily.
Throws a ball without losing his balance.
Gallops, jumps, walks and runs to music.

3½: Increased tension and may fall or stumble.

4 Years: Very active, covering more ground. Races up and down stairs.
Dashes on tricycle.
Enjoys activities requiring balance. Can carry cup of liquid without spilling.
Prefers large blocks and makes more complicated structures.
Throws a ball overhand.
In rhythms interprets and demonstrates own response.

5 Years: There is greater ease and control of general bodily activity, and economy of movement.
Posture is predominantly symmetrical and closely knit. May walk with feet pronate.
Control over large muscles is still more advanced than control over small ones.
Plays in one location for longer periods, but changes posture from standing, sitting, squatting.
Likes to climb fences and go from one thing to another. Jumps from table height.
Likes to activate a story. Runs, climbs onto and under chairs and tables.
Throws, including mud and snow and is beginning to use hands more than arms in catching a small ball but frequently fails to catch.
Alternates feet descending stairs and skips alternately.
Attempts to roller skate, jump rope, and to walk on stilts.
Likes to march to music.

From Gesell & Ilg (1949, p. 232).

development, such as beginning to walk alone, acquiring language, and learning consideration of others, are assumed to unfold naturally and in response to a genetic time clock ticking away within each of us. (Some examples from Gesell's work are included in Table 5.1.)

Any variation from the norms for developing behavior are considered to be a function of inheritance, too. If, for example, a child begins to talk in complete sentences at age two—earlier than the norms would suggest—we may assume that the combination of genes influencing speech development is such that the child has been endowed with an unusual gift. By the same token, if a physically healthy six-year-old child's speech does not conform to the syntactic rules of his/her speech community, we may assume that this is an inherited effect also. Unfortunately in this case, the child would probably be labeled congenitally retarded. In either case, the ultimate effect of accepting the predeterminist position is to assume that human behavior cannot be influenced markedly by experience. According to this view we are what we have been given by our parents; each of us should accept this and resign ourselves to the facts.

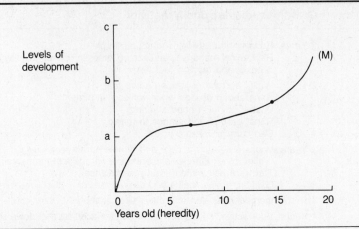

Figure 5.1   **Predeterminism**

Figure 5.1 depicts the predeterminist view of human development. The horizontal axis represents age in years or the influence of maturation determined by heredity. The vertical axis represents levels of development, with *a* being early or the first stage and *c* representing full development or the last stage.

Development begins with a rapid spurt at birth which continues until age seven or eight. At this time it slows considerably until puberty when once again there is very rapid growth. Full development or maturity M is attained in about 20 years and is the result of innate potential unfolding over time. Central to the hereditarian conception is the assumption that experience is relatively unimportant.

Predeterminists do not totally reject the influence of environment. Any growing organism, be it a hearty oak or an infant child, must be provided with proper nutrition, protection from the elements, and a large portion of tender love and care. The infant is helpless and needs support from adults in order to survive. But, by being given adequate care, the child will unfold as the petals of a rose—there is little we can do to influence what nature has put together.

Although predeterminism is considered by many to be an archaic theory, its influence is still very much alive in American early childhood education.[2] The traditional nursery school, established over the past six decades, is a good example of the application of hereditarian concepts to child care and education.

What would occur in a nursery school, day-care center, or kindergarten operating from such a point of view? One thing seems clear: promoting human development would not be a preoccupation of the staff, but maintaining an atmosphere within which development could occur would be important. This is more than a subtle distinction. In the traditional American nursery supporting development, a warm, supportive environment and an exciting and attractive play setting would be seen, as teachers

---

[2] This influence transcends program design as shown by the work of Arthur Jensen (1969) who attributes intellectual differences between races to inherited traits.

provided love and attention for each child. If growth and development are predetermined, the role of the teacher would be to provide the psychological support all adults should give children. Obviously, all of this should take place where children can enjoy themselves.

In the traditional early education setting, considerable attention is given to the selection of materials and activities, but the major criterion is their appeal to the interests of the children. Since young children enjoy painting, easels and fingerpaints would be provided; since children also enjoy visiting places such as the fire station or the local dairy, these would be scheduled. Teachers carefully consider each activity, each game and toy in terms of the children's reaction to the presentation. If the children were to express dissatisfaction with a story, the book might be put away. If a game, exciting though it might be, promotes what the teacher considers too aggressive behavior, it would not be played again. In short, the emphasis is on capturing the interests and the attention of the children, keeping them engaged and happy in their activities. Teachers spend much time observing the children's behavior in anticipation of changes from one stage to another.

In a predeterminist nursery school, the children play with the materials and each other, exploring the wonders of life and enjoying being with each other. It is assumed that children develop by *being* children. What adults need to do most of all is to provide psychological support, attend to the children's basic needs, and spend the remainder of the time out of their way. Quite obviously, this is a very *passive* view of child development.

There is one area of growth and development in which the predeterminist teachers feel a strong obligation to actively guide the child's behavior. Direct efforts are usually made to influence the socialization of the child. The predeterminist position has never been viewed as license to allow children to do anything they choose to. Children of every culture are socialized to the accepted code of conduct of that culture. How we behave towards one another, the roles of males and females, the acceptable responses to adult demands are not innate; they must be learned after birth. Whether or not a child excuses himself after bumping into someone else is not a function of inheritance, but learned in the context of his/her life. The traditional American nursery school has placed great emphasis on teaching children appropriate social responses, especially sharing with others and cooperating in group ventures. Although the goal may be to support development, until very recently *the emphasis in American early education has been on socialization*.

The traditional teacher of young children will likely eschew concern for the promotion of intellectual development or even large motor development. Intellectual development, often confused with such tasks as learning to read for example, will occur better later on when the child is ready. The larger muscles need to be exercised, and children enjoy being active, so this becomes part of the curriculum but not because it is necessary in order to insure proper development.

One important consequence of the acceptance of the predeterminist view is that teachers and parents believe that what children become is what they were determined to be. If a child seems incapable of sorting blocks into like groups at age five—a stage of development we have reason to believe normal five-year-olds achieve—we should wait a bit longer. If it does not appear by age six, we may assume that the child has not been born with the requisite abilities necessary to complete this task. We may take comfort from the belief that, unfortunate though it may be, nature doesn't distribute talent equally to all of us. There is frightfully little any of us can do to influence the natural course of events.

In summary, a predeterminist would suggest that the role of early childhood education is to support the natural growth process and to socialize the child to the culture. What each of us will become is written in our genes; environment plays an insignificant role in our development. Rather more than less, traditional American early childhood education programs have reflected a belief in the predeterminist position. The concept of readiness—waiting for a child to mature—coupled with the attitude that early instruction will have little lasting effect are but two illustrations of the ways this view of human development has influenced the practice of early childhood education.

Environmentalism

In the early 1900s, American psychologist J. B. Watson led an environmentalist reaction against predeterminism. Watson did not believe that human behavior was innate. He asserted that the common belief in the inheritance of capacity, talent, temperament, mental constitution, and personality characteristics was wrong. (Watson, 1925, p. 8) He maintained that man was shaped by his environment, that he learned and therefore developed. Watson boasted about his presumed ability to create any type of adult from any child through the use of proper training techniques. Watson's environmentalism was the forerunner of today's behaviorism.

Environmentalists maintain that development is basically learned behavior. It is the result of the association of experience with the consequent effect—pleasure or displeasure. A child will learn to stay away from a hot stove because of the pain resulting from touching it and being burned. By the same token, the environmentalist believes that if we find pleasure in the consequences of an act, we are more likely to repeat the act. For example, if a child is praised by a teacher for putting toys away and the child enjoys being complimented, the pleasure derived from receiving the praise will tend to prompt the child to put the toys away at some time in the future. The child will "learn" to put the toys away in anticipation of receiving more praise. To the environmentalist, what we are is the result of reactions to what we have experienced and not a consequence of our inheritance. According to environmentalism, the events of our life, from conception onward, shape us and make us what we are.

Environmentalists tend to view human development in terms of environmental inputs and action or response outputs. The organism's behavior is presumed to be the consequence of external stimulation and not the result of either genetically predetermined traits or internal psychological states of being. The concept of will plays no significant role in the environmentalist/behaviorist view of human development. Central to this theory of development is the assumption that the individual learns, or changes behavior, in direct response to systems of rewards and punishments. As illustrated in the preceding paragraph, actions that result in pleasure are more apt to be repeated than those that lead to displeasure. Also, acts that result in punishment, pain, or anguish are unlikely to be practiced often.

An environmentalist or behaviorist concept of development is also a theory of learning. Development is defined in terms of the human organism's acquisition of behaviors. How quickly a child acquires the behaviors (demonstrates the appropriate responses) is an indication of how well he or she has learned. This can be illustrated by drawing upon a behaviorist's explanation of speech development.

Children's speech is not a function of any innate predisposition on the part of the species to speak. Rather it is the consequence of three interrelated stimuli: the expectation society places on all of us to acquire language, the example set by those who can speak, and the rewards that accrue to even the most feeble attempts to imitate adult speech. Behaviorists would admit that even the most precocious child cannot speak immediately after birth. Some behaviors can appear only after the organism has gained sufficient control over those muscles and nerves necessary to activate the response. However, admitting the need for some maturation does not detract from the behaviorist's explanation that speech is a type of learned behavior resulting from appropriate external reinforcement.

If an environmentalist/behaviorist conception of development is also a learning theory, it should not surprise us that the goals of development are defined in terms of children's behavior. For example, if one developmental goal is to have all children speak in understandable sentences, it is necessary to define what this means, so that parents and teachers know what the successive steps in achieving this goal are. Behaviorists have been promoting such an approach to education and child development for years.

The environmentalist view is attractive on the one hand and frightfully unattractive on the other. In its favor, behaviorism has provided us with an alternative explanation for the gross inequities found in society. If a person is a product of experience, the commonly held view that status reflects innate talent no longer seems valid. Rather than assume the hereditarian perspective that position in life is a reflection of ability, the behaviorist would tend to search for societal factors such as racism, ethnic stratification, and other forms of discrimination to explain differences in achievement and status. To be very specific, some behaviorists have attributed the significantly high incidence of school failure of low-status and minority children to a lack of appropriate corollary experience. Failure in school is viewed as a consequence of inappropriate preschool experience and improper instruction in school. This explanation of children's school behavior rests on the belief that students have the potential but have simply not acquired the behaviors upon which learning in school is based. The solution lies in designing special instructional programs that will compensate for this lack of requisite behavior.

The response of a teacher to a child's inability to read may not be as dramatic as the example just given but may illuminate more clearly the logic of an environmentalist position. In the absence of data indicating a child has some malady, brain damage, serious illness, or other learning impairment, the teacher would assume that the child is not reading because of the use of inappropriate instructional materials and procedures. There would be no question regarding native intelligence; there would be

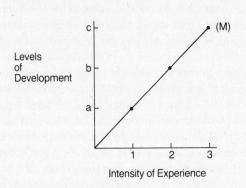

Figure 5.2   **Environmentalism**

The environmentalist position as illustrated in Figure 5.2 suggests an almost positive correlation between experience and development. The child achieves varying levels of development in direct response to the intensity of experience encountered. Intensity of experience refers to the demands adults, situations, or personal desire place on a child to develop new procedures for understanding and gaining control over the environment. This is an instructional model. A child develops as a consequence of having learned. Heredity is important only in that it influences physical growth which may inhibit some aspects of development.

an analysis of the task and the identification of appropriate alternative teaching methods. This approach is basically optimistic. The teacher would assume that in time and through careful analysis of the three behaviors of which reading is comprised a system of instruction could be devised that would teach the child. In summary, it can be said that environmentalists/behaviorists accept the premise that the absence of development (learning) is a function of inappropriate analyses of the behaviors and consequent reinforcement procedures (instructional methodology).

Though aspects of environmentalism are attractive, there is much about behaviorism that is frightening. The assumption that development is a response to experience fits nicely with the attitude many have regarding the basic equality of all mankind. It is troublesome, however, to accept the corollary belief that we are creatures that respond only to external stimulation. Our literature, our religious teachings, our beliefs about good and evil are permeated with the assumption that man has a will which helps in the development of a sense of what is right, just, and deserving. To suggest, as does B. F. Skinner, that individual will does not exist, that we simply respond to external stimulation and reinforcement, shakes many of our most tenaciously held beliefs to the core.

As if challenging the concept of internal motivation and will were not enough, behaviorists employ procedures that make it difficult to believe that behaviorism can be good in any way. If an organism has no will, if it learns (develops) as a consequence of the effect of behavior, then the procedures used in promoting development must be of the sort that brings either pleasure or pain to behavior. That is, if we want children to be able to recognize the letters of the alphabet, we must devise a teaching procedure that requires the children to recognize and speak the letters and to provide them with rewards which are satisfying. We must do all we can to select a reinforcer which will tend to promote the reoccurrence of this behavior. If we find a child who refuses to practice, we might design a reinforcement that would discourage him from avoiding the practice. In short, behavioral analysis techniques are designed to shape the behavior of children in ways determined well in advance of instruction. The child is conditioned by the effects of his or her behavior. The techniques of reinforcing human behavior include both token and social reinforcers, very much like those parents use quite naturally with their children, such as material rewards, special foods, and especially attractive social experiences. It should be noted that in most behavioral techniques, the use of punishment as reinforcement is avoided. Rather, children are rewarded for appropriate behavior and not rewarded for inappropriate behavior.

Environmentalism is a double-edged sword. Its rejection of hereditarianism leads to the belief in the potential of all persons and therefore is attractive. Not so that aspect of behaviorism which suggests that mankind is not in control of himself but rather is a responsive organism controlled by external stimuli. Many early childhood specialists become morally outraged at the thought that one must consciously shape the behavior of children in order to promote learning and development.

As unattractive as behavioristic principles might be, they are being applied in some contemporary child-care and development programs. The early childhood education program originally conceived by Carl Bereiter and Sigfried Engelmann (1966) is perhaps the most widely known, though it is only one among many. It is appropriate to examine briefly their approach, for it addresses the problems of school failure for the poor and minorities by, among other things, directly challenging the predeterminist's conception of human behavior.[3]

Bereiter and Engelmann built a strong argument for an environmental explanation of low IQ scores, academic underachievement, and school failure among lower-status and minority children. They attempted to demonstrate that intelligence test scores and school achievement were not a function of innate intelligence, but rather an artifact of discrimination, poor schooling, and inadequate upbringing. They used the facts that they had raised the IQ of preschoolers and that IQ is correlative with school success as the proof of their assertion.

The remedy for school failure, proposed by Bereiter and Engelmann, was compensatory education. Preschools were designed to overcome the cumulative effect of experiential deficit. The poor and minority children simply had not been taught what was needed to score well on IQ tests or to complete early school tasks.

Bereiter and Engelmann identified what they believed to be the most significant behaviors absent among poor children and present among those succeeding in school.

---

[3] Bereiter and Engelmann no longer collaborate. The program described here continues now under the direction of Engelmann and Wesley Becker.

Table 5.2	Bereiter and Engelmann: Minimum Preschool Goals

1. Ability to use both affirmative and *not* statements in reply to the question "What is this?" "This is a ball. This is not a book."

2. Ability to use both affirmative and *not* statements in response to the command "Tell me about this _____ (ball, pencil, etc.)." "This pencil is red. This pencil is not blue."

3. Ability to handle polar opposites ("if it is not _____, it must be _____") for at least four concept pairs, e.g., big-little, up-down, long-short, fat-skinny.

4. Ability to use the following prepositions correctly in statements describing arrangements of objects: on, in, under, over, between. "Where is the pencil?" "The pencil is under the book."

5. Ability to name positive and negative instances for at least four classes, such as tools, weapons, pieces of furniture, wild animals, farm animals, and vehicles. "Tell me something that is a weapon." "A gun is a weapon." "Tell me something that is not a weapon." "A cow is not a weapon." The child should also be able to apply these class concepts correctly to nouns with which he is familiar, e.g., "Is a crayon a piece of furniture?" "No, a crayon is not a piece of furniture. A crayon is something to write with."

6. Ability to perform simple if-then deductions. The child is presented a diagram containing big squares and little squares. All the big squares are red, but the little squares are of various other colors. "If the square is big, what do you know about it?" "It's red."

7. Ability to use *not* in deductions. "If the square is little, what else do you know about it?" "It is not red."

8. Ability to use *or* in simple deductions. "If the square is little, then it is not red. What else do you know about it?" It's blue *or* yellow."

9. Ability to name the basic colors, plus white, black, and brown.

10. Ability to count aloud to 20 without help and to 100 with help at decade points (30, 40, etc.).

11. Ability to count objects correctly up to ten.

12. Ability to recognize and name the vowels and at least 15 consonants.

13. Ability to distinguish printed words from pictures.

14. Ability to rhyme in some fashion to produce a word that rhymes with a given word, to tell whether two words do or do not rhyme, or to complete unfamiliar rhyming jingles like "I had a dog, and his name was Abel; I found him hiding under the _____."

15. A sight-reading vocabulary of at least four words in addition to proper names, with evidence that the printed word has the same meaning for them as the corresponding spoken word. "What word is this?" "Cat." "Is this a thing that goes 'Woof-woof'?" "No, it goes 'Meow'."

Bereiter and Engelmann (1966, pp. 48–49).

(See Table 5.2 for a listing of their minimum preschool goals.) An instructional program was then designed which incorporated behavioral principles. The teachers were instructed in what they should do during the entire preschool day. They were told how to teach, how to reinforce, how to isolate children who disrupted the process. The skills selected by Bereiter and Engelmann were carefully specified so as to allow precise evaluation. They were taught directly and reinforced consistently. The behavior of each child was carefully controlled; attempts to deter the progression toward the desired goals were thwarted.

By and large, the results of this program were what the authors had wanted. Short term evaluations indicated that IQ could be raised and initial achievement improved. The net effect of this approach over many years is not known; however, it does seem safe to suggest that if one believes that raising IQ and achievement levels is what is needed in order to improve the educational and life chances of disadvantaged children, then the approach of Bereiter and Engelmann has had success beyond many other compensatory early education programs.

There is a basic and profound difference between the behaviorism of Bereiter and Engelmann and the predeterminism of Gesell, for example. Bereiter and Engelmann believed that development was acquired/learned; Gesell assumed it to be innate. This difference is very evident in the assumption each makes about the source and the conception of IQ. Both Gesell and Bereiter and Engelmann could accept the idea that IQ consists of a collection of specific competencies. The behaviorists believed these to be learned; Gesell attributed them to inheritance. A Gesellian faced with the reality of a child's low IQ would attempt to design an educational program consonant with the established measures of intelligence. Bereiter and Engelmann, on the other hand, maintained that a depressed IQ was an indication of inadequate experience. Therefore, they would proceed to design an instructional program to teach the child those missing skills and behaviors. The desired effect would be to raise the IQ and, in the eyes of Bereiter and Engelmann, improve the chances for the child's success in school.

Many American early childhood educators have rejected the Bereiter and Engelmann approach in particular and behaviorism in general. It does not appear that this was done as a consequence of a belief in fixed development. Rather, it would appear that many cannot accept the assertion that the human organism, however young, is incapable of directing significant aspects of its own behavior. The notion that the lives of young children need to be carefully shaped is repulsive to many.[4]

Environmentalism as defined by contemporary behaviorists is not readily accepted for reasons more important than an emotional antipathy. The theory does not adequately deal with either the conception of internal motivation or that of variability in competence. Dismissing the idea of will as something unknown and unknowable is not an adequate explanation. To suggest that inheritance plays no significant role in human behavior is primitive, to say the least, and inaccurate.

Though environmentalism seems an incomplete description of human development, we cannot deny the evidence that social circumstance does influence what we become. That status and race are often used as measures of the worth of a person is hard for us to ignore. However each of us may resolve this unfortunate fact of life, belief in the importance of experience makes it necessary for adults to assume an active role in influencing the direction of children's development.

Transactionism

Arguments about the value of a predeterminist as contrasted with an environmentalist explanation of human development will invariably be reduced to a debate about the relative importance of inheritance and experience. It has been pointed out in earlier

---

[4] It should be noted that the application of behaviorism in ECE occurs most frequently in attempts to eliminate disruptive behavior and to increase on-task behavior among normal children and in instructing retarded or disturbed children—wherever it is judged that all learning must be carefully monitored and reinforced.

sections that Gesell and others who advocated a hereditarian view suggested that what a child may learn from practice or experience will have only marginal impact on subsequent development. The behaviorists, including Skinner, who believe that development is the consequence of learning, would discount the impact inborn, genetic predisposition could have on human behavior. In each case, the argument is polarized and dichotomous; growth and development arise from A or from B. There is little room in either of these positions for the possibility that what we become is the consequence of the interaction of inheritance and experience. Transactionism can be fairly defined as this third view. Central to it is the belief that development is the result of the effect experience can have on the human organism coupled with the particular ways in which this organism modifies, reorganizes, and interprets sensations and perceptions from the environment.

A transactionist view of child development is more than the mere sum of inheritance and experience. It is a dynamic theory based on principles of development which, together, present a picture of the human organism as one which contributes to its own growth. In a way somewhat similar to the predeterminist theory, transactionists accept the view that the human organism is born with particular competencies which, in many ways, serve to direct the course of development. The brain and central nervous system clearly serve as means by which sensory data are interpreted and used. It seems just as evident that though there may be great variability between individuals, most of mankind process these sensory data in similar ways. There is a great sameness about the activity of the human brain. At least some intellectual behavior would appear to be an innate feature of mankind, passed from generation to generation through the genes.

Transactionism is also, at times, consonant with aspects of behaviorism. It is recognized that some forms of human behavior assumed to be universal and innate will not appear without appropriate experience. Walking erect may be one such behavior. A study by Dennis (1960) revealed that children raised in an orphanage failed to crawl, sit alone, and walk at an age when children would normally demonstrate these behaviors. The children had spent most of their infant life alone in a crib with only infrequent adult stimulation and very little contact with other children. Once these nonwalking children were taken from the cribs and placed in a more normal environment, they began to develop locomotor skills equal to other children their age. Quite clearly, one cannot discount the very important influence of experience in human development.

As was said earlier, it is not simply the combination of inheritance and experience which explains the transactionist position. Dennis' studies suggest that waiting for the organism to mature would not be sufficient to provoke even the most prosaic of behaviors. Children aged three, healthy in every respect, were not walking. By the same token, Gesell provided us with a convincing argument against the strict environmental explanation of development by demonstrating that providing practice in a skill before a child was "ready" for it did not measurably affect performance (Gesell et al., 1940): young children were given instruction in climbing stairs before they were of the age when this would normally be expected of them; the training did not result in their gaining the skill earlier, nor were they superior to their peers when they were able to climb stairs. Though we know that both instruction (or experience) and inheritance influence development, this relationship is far more subtle than a simple, direct application would suggest.

What then does appear to be the explanation for the role nature and nurture play in human development? The writings of Jean Piaget[5] and Lev Vygotsky (1962 & 1978) help provide some answers to this question.

Piaget seems to have traced a progressive change in intellectual behavior from birth to adulthood resulting from a person's interaction with his/her environment. A process of adaptation and the organization of our perceptions and conclusions, Piaget believes, cause cognitive development to occur. He believes that all humans inherit a predisposition or tendency to understand and to organize most of what they experience. Adaptation and organization are not passive acts, however, but occur only when the organism actively engages in the process of trying to comprehend any experience and store some account of it in the memory or system for organizing knowledge. Clearly an infant's intellectual behavior is different from that of a ten-year-old and an adult. Piaget attributes this difference not to maturation or physical development, though he acknowledges the importance of the continuing growth of the brain. Rather he asserts that the intellectual behavior of the infant is of a kind different from that of the ten-year-old, who probably thinks in a way different from the adult. The major reason for the differences in patterns of thought among persons of different ages is that each of us must construct and reconstruct our own knowledge of the world. Piaget believes that construction—adaptation and organization—can only occur directly as we live and struggle in our world.

Piaget's view of the nature of the developmental process is very instructive, for it helps us to understand that a child who randomly arranges blocks with clearly different characteristics is demonstrating an intellectual operation of a different kind and magnitude than another child who arranges them by using a uniform criterion such as shape.

Vygotsky demonstrated this point in some provocative grouping experiments. He found that random sorting was in fact arranging objects without any apparent reason. In random sorting a child's behavior does not appear to be directed by anything save the instructions of an adult to place objects in groups. At a later stage of development, Vygotsky found that children were able to group blocks by means of a variety of techniques. These techniques were of varied complexity, but each seemed to be based on some attempt to establish a generalization for the action. These phases of grouping discovered by Vygotsky appeared to mark a new and different process by which perceptual stimuli were acted upon. Vygotsky's studies and those of Piaget suggest that a major feature of intellectual growth is a progressive change in the *kind* of cognitive behavior we employ in trying to understand what we are experiencing.

---

[5] Those who have not yet begun to read Piaget may find it appropriate to begin with *Six Psychological Studies* (1968) and should find Ginsburg and Opper (1979) unusually helpful in understanding Piaget's theory.

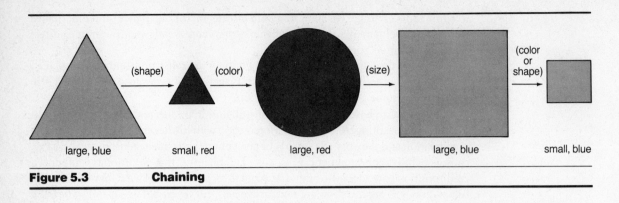

| | (shape) | | (color) | | (size) | | (color or shape) | |
| large, blue | | small, red | | large, red | | large, blue | | small, blue |

Figure 5.3   **Chaining**

Both Piaget and Vygotsky argue that development proceeds through a series of fixed stages. A child is born and begins to interact with his/her new environment. For years students of human development have charted the organism's growth from birth to maturity; it was Piaget, however, who had the most influence in helping us to understand that development, though continuous, must be seen as a succession of separate and different stages, each based on the one that preceded it. Piaget has identified four major cognitive stages of development. From most immature to mature they are sensorimotor, preoperational, concrete operational, and formal operational. According to Piaget, sensorimotor intelligence must precede the concrete operational stage of cognition. Though operations are dependent upon the ways in which a child organizes experience and perceptions at the preoperational level, the behavior of a child at each stage will be different. Also, though the stages are age related—sensorimotor, birth to 2 years; preoperational, 2-7; concrete operational, 7-11; and formal operational, 11 years and older—the age of the child is not necessarily descriptive of the stage of development. Normal, healthy, fully endowed children age eleven may not be operating at a formal operational level. Maturity alone is not sufficient for describing the reasons for development. Rather, it is a consequence of interaction.

The nature and effect of interaction can be more fully explained by drawing upon Vygotsky's studies of language and thought. Like Piaget, Vygotsky described development as a process of moving through increasingly complex stages of behavior. His characterization of the steps in achieving the use of generalization and conceptualization in classification of blocks illustrates interactive stage theory. Early in language acquisition, children begin to label or name objects in their surroundings. When this process starts, there appears to be some confusion in the child's mind about the name of the object *(cow)* and its attributes *(horns)*. A child may use the label *cow* for any animal having horns. The name signifies the attribute, i.e., *cow* equals *horns*. In relatively rapid progression, the child moves from confusion of label with attribute to the use of names as symbols for categories or classes of similar objects. *Cow* becomes the name given to a class of animals having multiple, similar attributes: it is a large, horned or unhorned animal which is often seen grazing in a field, from which we get milk, and which can "moo."

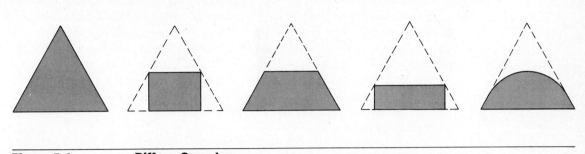

Figure 5.4   **Diffuse Complex**

Developing the sense that names can be used to signify categories arises from the effect language development and everyday experience have on each other. The child is struggling to acquire a more complete language system, one that is more elaborate in structure and meaning. This results, in large part, from the demands of living in a society wherein communication is largely dependent upon speech. The necessity to organize, describe, and share experience with others must serve as added incentives in the development of these cognitive and linguistic skills. We may learn to differentiate between cats and dogs or sheep and goats because we have an internal need to do so and the practical necessity so that communication may go forward.

According to Vygotsky, developing labels or names for objects provides the foundation for categorization. Once we are able to identify objects in our experience by name, we may then begin the process of organizing them into like and unlike classes. Initially, a child may sort objects randomly without the use of public or known criteria. The child may group a series of different shaped blocks only because they are near each other. There may be no general rule used, yet the process occurs. The child seems to know that it is possible to separate, classify, and organize experience but lack the cognitive system necessary to demonstrate how it should be done.

There is a significant leap in the grouping behavior of children when they no longer arrange objects in random fashion. Vygotsky has named the next stage the *complex stage*. Here a child arranges groups on the basis of a perceived relationship between objects. Chaining is one complex system. It is illustrated in Figure 5.3. Figure 5.3 depicts the result of a child's attempt to group an array of objects. The child began with the large blue triangle at the left of the figure. He then selected a small red triangle. The explanation for choosing the smaller triangle was the similarity of shape: they are both triangles. The child then selected a large, red circle. It has no relationship to the large triangle; it has been selected because it is of the same color as the triangle. The chain has started to be connected link by link. The large and small squares are added for similar reasons, though using different criteria.

Though we may suggest that chaining is only a marginal improvement over random sorting, there should be little doubt that it is an entirely different kind of behavior. It is grouping based on clear and public use of one criterion, though different at each link.

Diffuse complex is a name given by Vygotsky to a higher stage of categorization. At this level of development, a child will combine the use of multiple attributes, logical deduction, and visual imagery. The child will combine perceptual properties of objects with imagined characteristics to create a logical, though imaginary, class. For example, a child may group a square, triangle, parallelogram, rectangle, and semicircle on the basis of their all having properties of triangularity.
The child imagines that each shape may have been taken from a larger triangle; thus they are grouped because of presumed prior common properties. This behavior is illustrated in Figure 5.4.

Clearly, organization by diffuse complex is an entirely different kind or stage of behavior than simple random grouping. Though in each case the child is grouping objects, the processes by which this is completed are totally dissimilar. In addition, the end result is different. There are, as these examples illustrate, different stages or phases in a child's development of categorization behavior. The behavior in chaining is different from that in either random sorting or grouping by diffuse complex.

The appearance of any stage of development is the consequence of the interaction of internal need, cultural demands, and experience. They are all necessary, and each influences the rate and degree of development. Transactionists, as was pointed out earlier, can accept the belief that the human organism has specific characteristics passed from generation to generation without much variation. The need to develop an understanding of one's environment is one of these traits. It has been suggested that the child develops in large part because he is *curious* or desires to know and understand his world. We suggest that this is a *natural* behavior.

This innate need to achieve understanding is coupled with the demands any culture will place on its members to develop a system of behavior that is rule directed. A child learns how to interact with adults because the society demands that he/she do so. The rules become more and more complex and symbolic; becoming an adult member of a culture constitutes much more than growing older. Maturity, from a transactionist perspective, is defined as the development of systems of behavior appropriate for the acquisition of subsequent, more complex behavior.

Experience is central to both equilibration and learning the rules of culture. Transactionist's maintain that innate predispositions to know, to understand, to organize stimuli will not be developed in the absence of the appropriate stimuli. The Piagetian concept of equilibration assumes that the organism seeks understanding and that earlier understanding leads to subsequent needs to know. For example, understanding what categorization means sets both the stage and the need for grouping by chaining and diffuse complex. The existence of an internal, species-specific system of motivation is accepted by transactionists. However, it is also widely recognized that this innate system will not be activated in the absence of appropriate external stimuli from the culture. We may have an innate need to group, but it is unlikely that it would ever appear without the corresponding experience that living in a culture provides. Furthermore, the experience we have is organized in unique ways depending on how we as *individuals* interpret and internalize these stimuli. In this sense, we do not simply take in experience but process it carefully into units of understanding consonant with

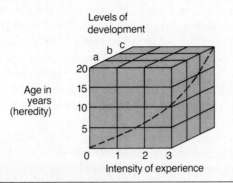

| Figure 5.5 | **Transactionism** |

The transactionist conception of human development is far more dynamic than either the environmentalist or the predeterminist position. The transactionist believes that growth to any point on the developmental spectrum is the result of the interaction that occurs between experience and heredity. At specific points along the development scale heredity or experience may be more influential. For example, this figure suggests that movement from birth to developmental level *a* is largely a function of age. Experience is important but less so at this point of development. However, the ratio changes as the child moves up the developmental scale. Level *c* can only be achieved as a result of optimum experience interacting with the maturity derived from the accumulation of experience which growing older allows.

our prior knowledge and experience. We thus participate actively in our own development; there is a *transactional* relationship between what we know and what we experience which very often results in new knowledge.

Ways in which transactionist developmental theory can be applied to educational practice can be drawn from Maria Montessori's work at the turn of the century (1964), John Dewey's progressive education curricula of the first half of the twentieth century, and, more recently, the educational practices of the English Infant School (Weber, 1971) and attempts to apply Piagetian theory to early education (Forman & Kushner, 1977; Kamii & DeVries, 1978).

Montessori's major goal was to promote movement along the developmental spectrum by providing children with carefully selected materials to be used in prescribed ways. The effect of the use of the materials would be the development of perception and cognition. Montessori believed that children developed by *doing*, or acting on their environment. However, she believed that the materials and experiences must be carefully selected, for every activity would not contribute to development.

Children in a Montessori classroom can be observed arranging cylinders in order of their size, tracing the shape of sand-paper letters and polishing silverware or shoes, for example. The teacher is unobtrusively guiding the activity of each child; children are working alone or with one or two others as they perform the exercises for which the materials were designed. As they completed one task—arranging pairs of identically sounding chimes, for example—they might choose to order an array of ten rectangular rods from smallest to largest. In any event, the choice of activity is the child's.

Activities in a Montessori nursery usually require children to perform operations on materials in prescribed ways. Montessori studied the use and effect of each material in her school to determine the consequences of its use for the child's development. Because she was sure of the growth that would result from a particular use of the materials, she insisted on limiting the ways in which children could manipulate them. Montessori believed that demanding, challenging, and focused activity is the means by which human potential develops.

Though many followers of Dewey and of Piaget would criticize Montessori's method, it cannot be doubted that she early perceived development as a function of the child's acting on materials and events in his/her environment. It was the child who was ultimately responsible for constructing his/her knowledge, and this was facilitated by her careful selection of materials and patterning of the ways in which they would be used.

Some of John Dewey's followers were very critical of Montessori's curriculum and method (Kilpatrick, 1914). They were especially concerned with the constraints placed on the child's freedom to explore a larger environment and with the restrictions Montessori placed on material use. Dewey was sure that children's knowledge of the world, a sense of moral commitment, and the acquisition of skills could be achieved only through active engagement in the affairs of society. Dewey argued for education designed around topics or issues of meaningful concern to children, in which they would identify questions needing to be addressed and then proceed to search for answers. His curriculum was no less demanding than Montessori's but more subject to the expressed needs of the children.

Dewey believed that children's education should reflect the values and the concerns of the larger society. Very often the curriculum would emerge from issues raised by the children and their teachers. The instructional mode, too, was different from Montessori. Dewey believed that inquiry—the search for truth—was the basis of all understanding and that teachers should conduct classes in a way which promoted inquiry. Furthermore, Dewey was quite sure that education should be considered in a social context; children should engage with each other in their search for knowledge. And so it was that children in Dewey's progressive schools worked together on units of study involving topics as wide ranging as the effect of heat, light, and water on the germination of seeds to the study of the contributions various community workers made to the well-being of society.

Many progressive educators seemed to be less concerned with the amount and completeness of the knowledge and understanding resulting from inquiry than with the attitudes and the skills derived from inquiry itself. Dewey and his supporters believed that the transactions occurring between children and the process of inquiry were far the more important factors in the educative process.

Beginning in 1967 Americans began to become aware of a design for educating young children being followed in some sections of England. Description of the English Infant School, as it came to be known, began to appear in the popular and professional literature (Featherstone, 1967, a, b, & c; Weber, 1971). This "new" procedure was in many ways akin to programs developed by Dewey. Children were provided with a carefully designed and stimulating environment consisting of activities and learning areas to which they would move fairly freely. The more common subjects of the primary grades were not neglected. Reading, writing, and mathematics were a major part of the curriculum but taught in quite a different way. The mathematical operations were learned as the children completed tasks in the math area. They manipulated scales, arranged metric rods, calculated multiples by using geometric blocks of various configurations. Reading might be taught by a teacher but to one or a few children at a time using materials from the children's library as well as the more common reader.

In the tradition of Dewey, children in the English Infant Schools were encouraged to become engaged with materials and to pursue their own investigative interests. It was assumed that the child's engagement with the material of the education setting would be the most productive way of furthering his/her intellectual, social, and educational development.

The English Infant School now has many American exponents, and programs based on this approach are found throughout the nation. More recently, these practices have become associated with the teachings of Jean Piaget. It is often assumed that the interactive process which is the essence of the English Infant School program is a sound manifestation of Piaget's theory of cognitive development.

Whether or not the English Infant School model is Piagetian in design, it is clear that many educators believe that his constructivist theory holds the greatest potential for use in designing transactionist early education programs. It is also quite widely recognized that translating Piaget's theory to curricula and teacher practices continues to be a most difficult task. Progress is, however, being made, as is demonstrated by the writings of Copple, Sigel, and Saunders (1979), Kamii and DeVries (1978), by Forman and Kuschner (1977), and Forman and Hill (1980). Kamii and DeVries have focused on Piaget's concept of physical knowledge—knowledge gained from interactions with materials in the environment—as it can be applied to preschool education. Forman and his colleagues also have addressed preschool education but considered the larger issue of constructivism as their major emphasis. Copple, Sigel, and Saunders emphasize representational behavior. In each case, the authors have described both the processes by which children construct meaning from their actions on materials and the procedures teachers should follow in designing an appropriate preschool setting and analyzing the children's behavior. The reader is encouraged to consult the work of these authors to get a clearer understanding of how Piaget is being translated into educational practice. (See Chapter 12 on the curriculum.)

Though there seem to be many interpretations of the way in which transactionist theory should be translated to educational practice, there is one common theme running throughout. Montessori, Dewey, the advocates of the English model, and the Piagetians all would agree that the primary function of the teacher is to prepare an environment in which children can become engaged in the process of constructing knowledge and understanding. Furthermore, the process of engaging child and environment is far the most important element in education; knowledge is quite relative and subject to changes in perception and perspective, not to mention changes in the process itself. Education based on transactionist theory would be active and personal, dynamic and idiosyncratic; a product of the child's engagement rather than maturity alone or response to carefully controlled stimuli.

Summary

The three views of human development outlined here comprise a fair representation of those important to early childhood educators. Each seeks not only to explain the causes of development but to provide guidelines so that teachers and parents can support the process. In this sense, they are all positive theories; each anticipates that every child will become everything he/she is capable of becoming.

It should be pointed out, too, that each theory has some basis in fact. Predeterminism reflects the influence of Darwin's theory of evolution on conceptions of human behavior. Watson's environmentalism was, among other things, a reaction against the rather simple conception of the effect of inheritance on growth, which was so much a part of hereditarianism. The transactionist position, in turn, is built on the efforts of both the environmentalists and the predeterminists to explain development.

John Dewey, Piaget, and the Russian Lev Vygotsky observed the influence of the interaction of maturity and experience on most aspects of human behavior. Quite separately they became convinced that gaining the ability to handle objects with ease, for example, provided the means by which a child could begin to arrange other objects in perceptually similar and dissimilar groups. The work of these men, among others, led them to believe that grouping objects, for example, could not be explained completely by either heredity or instruction. All children do not group the same objects similarly, nor do they get identical instruction prior to grouping. This universal phenomenon could only be explained on the basis of the child's creating a system for understanding the grouping task, carrying it out, and recognizing when it had been completed.

Though the science of human behavior has not yet become so exact as to allow us to embrace any theory with absolute certainty, it does seem clear that the transactionist position more nearly accounts for the striking similarity and wide diversity among us than either environmentalism or hereditarianism. The process of development, as depicted in Figure 5.6, results from the influence growth and maturation, learning, and experience have on each other. The transactionist view does not discount the effect of growing older or the influence of instruction. Rather, this view maintains that the fully developed person is one who has been responsible for the creation of increasingly more complex systems for organizing and understanding the events of life.

How, then, it might be asked, does one select a theory of development to provide guidance in the organization and presentation of early childhood programs? The answer rests with the goals we select. If we seek to *teach* children those behaviors we have identified as being important for survival, success, or adequate performance as adults, for example, it is likely that the environmentalist position would be the most appropriate. If we would rather allow the child to *grow* in a more or less *organic*

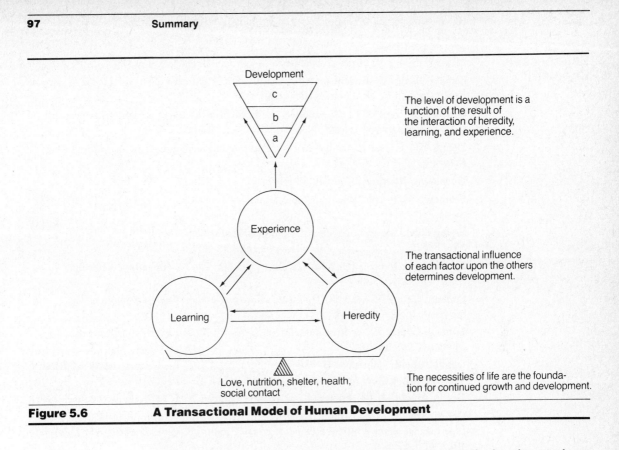

Figure 5.6   A Transactional Model of Human Development

fashion, to become whatever his/her predisposition dictates, the hereditarian theory would seem best. If, on the other hand, we recognize the influence and importance of both instruction and inheritance and yet maintain that the goal of child care and education is to assist the child in adapting to and integrating experience, the transactionist position is most appropriate.

An attempt has been made in this chapter to depict some of the ways in which each developmental theory might influence the design of educational programs for children. In subsequent chapters in this book we will turn our attention to another, related issue in understanding human behavior; the relationship of environmental settings to human behavior. I am convinced that each of us is profoundly influenced in the ways we act and think by the setting in which we find ourselves. For example, children will behave in a wading pool quite differently than in the classroom; the setting itself will provoke behaviors appropriate to that setting. I am also quite sure that each of us seeks an accommodation with each setting based on our knowledge and perception of what is appropriate and necessary, for our own well-being. This means that accommodating to a setting is a process in which the individual plays an important role; it is a transactional relationship. Teachers of young children must understand the influence of setting on behavior and consider this knowledge as they design and implement educational programs. A discussion of this behavior-environment interaction will begin in chapter 6, Human Ecology and Early Childhood Education.

References:
Chapter 5

Aries, Philippe. *Centuries of childhood.* New York: Alfred A. Knopf, 1962.

Bereiter, Carl, & Engelmann, S. *Teaching disadvantaged children in the pre-school.* Englewood Cliffs, NJ: Prentice-Hall, 1966.

Copple, C., Sigel, I. E., & Saunders, R. *Educating the young thinker: Classroom strategies for cognitive growth.* New York: D. Van Nostrand, 1979.

Dennis, W. Causes of retardation among institutional children: Iran. *Journal of Genetic Psychology,* 1960, *96,* 47–59.

Donaldson, Margaret. *Children's minds.* New York: Norton, 1979.

Featherstone, Joseph. How children learn. *The New Republic,* September 2, 1967, *157,* 17–21. (a)

Featherstone, Joseph. Schools for children: What's happening in British classrooms. *The New Republic,* August 19, 1967, *157,* 17–21. (b)

Featherstone, Joseph. Teaching Children to Think. *The New Republic,* September 9, 1967, *157,* 15–19. (c)

Forman, George E., & Hill, D. Fleet. *Constructive play: Applying Piaget in the preschool.* Monterey, CA: Brooks/Cole, 1980.

Forman, George E., & Kuschner, David S. *The child's construction of knowledge.* Monterey, CA: Brooks/Cole, 1977.

Gesell, Arnold, Halverson, H. M., Thompson, H., Ilg, F. L., Castner, B. M., & Bates, L. *The first five years of life.* New York: Harpers, 1940.

Gesell, Arnold, & Ilg, Frances L. Child development. New York: Harper & Row, 1949.

Gesell, Arnold, & Thompson, Helen. Learning and maturation in identical twins: An experimental analysis by the method of co-twin control. *Genetic Psychology Monographs,* 1929, *6,* 5–124.

Ginsburg, Herbert, & Opper, Sylvia. *Piaget's theory of intellectual development* (2nd ed.) Englewood Cliffs, NJ: Prentice-Hall, 1979.

Jensen, Arthur R. How much can we boost I.Q. and scholastic achievement? *Harvard Educational Review,* 1969, *39,* 1–123.

Kamii, Constance, & DeVries, Rheta. *Physical knowledge in preschool education.* Englewood Cliffs, NJ: Prentice-Hall, 1978.

Kilpatrick, William H. *The Montessori system examined.* Boston: Houghton Mifflin, 1914.

Montessori, Maria. *The Montessori method.* Cambridge, MA: Robert Bentley, 1964.

Piaget, Jean. *Six psychological studies.* New York: Vintage Books, 1968.

Vygotsky, Lev S. *Thought and language.* Cambridge, MA: MIT Press, 1962.

Vygotsky, Lev S. *Mind in society.* Cambridge, MA: Harvard University Press, 1978.

Watson, John B. *Behaviorism.* New York: People's Institute Publishing, 1925.

Weber, Lillian. *The English Infant School and informal education.* Englewood Cliffs, NJ: Prentice-Hall, 1971.

6 Human Ecology and Early Childhood Education

The transactionist theory of human development assumes that each of us influences and is influenced by our environment in very important ways. This assumption is so important that it is considered a cornerstone of transactionist psychology. Unlike behaviorists, however, most transactionists have spent little time studying the context of behavior. As in the case of Piaget and Kohlberg, there has been a devotion to the description of the stages or phases of human development and only a nod to the contribution environment makes to growth. Movement through the developmental stages is attributed to both inherited characteristics *and* life experiences though transactionists spend little time in the study of either of these two factors. Yet the application of the theory to child care and early education must rest as much on an understanding of the role of the environment in child development as it does on the knowledge of the natural progression of human behavior. One reason why there is so much confusion and difficulty attendant on the application of Piaget's stage theory to early childhood education may be that we have little more than the research context in which behaviors were observed to direct the creation of Piagetian-derived early-education programs.

These comments are not meant to suggest that transactionist theory is inadequate in explaining development. Rather, they suggest that practitioners may have to look beyond many of the studies of child development to understand the dynamic impact of environment on behavior. It would seem that the application of ecological principles to the study of human behavior might be an appropriate place to begin. The chapter will begin with a definition of ecological systems, followed by the presentation of the characteristics of such systems. Perhaps the most significant section for early childhood practitioners will be the discussion of the behavior settings taken from Roger Barker's work. The influence of setting on behavior will be emphasized throughout this book; however, it is important for the reader to remember that the individual influences the environment as well. An introduction to the ways in which this can occur will follow the discussion of the behavior setting. The chapter will end with a brief statement on the value of an ecological perspective.

Ecological Systems Defined

An ecological perspective on all behavior—human or not—involves the consideration of the interrelationship of the organism and the setting in which the behavior is observed. Perhaps this interrelationship can be made clear by recounting an English ornithologist's struggle to breed bearded titmice in captivity. The episode is described by Edwin Willems (1974).

"Armed with all the relevant information he could find about the tit, the ornithologist went to great pains to build the right setting. Introducing a male and female to the setting, he noted that, by all behavioral criteria, the birds functioned very well. Unfortunately, soon after the birds hatched babies, they shoved the babies out of the nest, onto the ground, where they died. This cycle, beginning with mating and ending with the babies dead on the ground, repeated itself many times.

The ornithologist tried many modifications of the setting, but none forestalled the infanticide. After many hours of direct observation of tits in the wild, the ornithologist noted three patterns of behavior that had missed everyone's attention. First, throughout most of the daylight hours in the wild, the parent tits were very active at finding and bringing food for the infants. Second, the infants, with whose food demands the parents could hardly keep pace, spent the same hours with their mouths open, apparently crying for food. The third pattern was that any inanimate object, whether eggshell, leaf, or beetle shell, was quickly shoved out of the nest by the parents. With these observations in mind, the ornithologist went back to observe his captive tits, and he found that during the short time a new brood of infants lived, the parents spent only brief periods feeding them by racing between the nest and the food supply, which the ornithologist had provided in abundance. After a short period of such feeding, the infants, apparently satiated, fell asleep. The first time the infants slept for any length of time during the daylight hours, the parents shoved them out of the nest. When he made the food supply less abundant and less accessible, and thereby made the parents work much longer and harder to find food, the ornithologist found the infants spent more daylight time awake, demanding food, and the tits then produced many families and cared for them to maturity" (pp. 152–153).

This illustration reflects the relationships which need to be considered in order to secure the continued existence of the captured titmouse population. The ornithologist's apparent concern for the creation of an appropriate aviary with ample food and nesting material was sufficient to support the life of the two adult birds.

However, the generosity of the scientist in providing much easily obtained food created a situation in which the parent birds actually could have destroyed their species (at least in the aviary). The birds reacted to the situation of their young in ways patterned by thousands of generations of titmice which had preceded them. One might suggest that these birds are compulsive nest-cleaners who find it necessary to remove any inanimate object. One can conjecture that they might have destroyed their young in the same way in the natural setting if they had happened upon an abundance of food. The point is that the birds did not react as the ornithologist had supposed, but in the only way they could under the circumstances. They did not simply accept the environment of the aviary and thrive, or reject it and die. Rather, they tried to continue their life-cycle and maintain a balance with the environment. The introduction of easily obtained food produced an effect which ultimately required an important adjustment in the environment by the ornithologist.

There are other examples of the interrelationship between organism and environment that come to mind. Many young children learn early in their school experience about the relationship between the survival of the hatching chicken and its need to struggle unassisted from the shell. Making it easier for the chick to emerge by breaking the shell away ensures that it will not survive. Another example concerns the affect of the use of DDT on the survival of the California brown pelican. The birds ingested DDT through their food chain. The DDT residue in the pelicans affected the strength of the egg shell so that the birds were laying soft-shelled eggs which did not mature. These examples are only a few of the many which could be cited as illustrations of the "mutual and joint impact of environments on organisms and organisms on environments" (Altman, 1975, p. 205). It is this interdependent impact which constitutes the structure of an ecological system.

The essence of an ecological system is that the behaviors of any organism are both influenced by the environment and, in turn, influence the environment. Bronfenbrenner (1977) suggested that such a system produces a reciprocal tension which over time changes both setting and organism. The application of this concept to early education can be illustrated in the following hypothetical example:

The setting is a nursery school, a literature or story alcove set apart from the remainder of the classroom. A teacher has invited seven children to join her to listen to a story. Our subject is a girl who enters the area and sits on the rug immediately in front of the teacher. She begins a conversation with a fellow classmate sitting nearby. Her friend responds, and the two engage casually in some conversation while the other children enter the area and occupy a space.

The teacher has selected a book and taken a position with the children arranged in front of her. She asks all of the children to end their conversation, to be quiet and focus on her, the teacher. She is about to begin and announces this by her call for quiet. The story is begun with all seven children attentive. This lasts for only a few moments when our subject shouts out a comment about an experience similar to that in the story being read. The teacher briefly and pointedly responds, asking the child to refrain from making more comments, and proceeds to continue reading.

Our young friend seems to be having none of this, she appears to be overflowing with a need to continue her tale, prompted by the book selected by the teacher. Our subject turns to her right and proceeds, once again, to relate her story to anyone other than the teacher. The teacher asks again for the child to be quiet and to listen to the story but to no avail. The child implores the teacher to hear her tale.

The teacher, for whatever reasons, relents, She closes the book and encourages the child to continue with her story. The subject's account of what happened to her interests the other children, many of whom become involved in tales of their own. Very soon there is an animated and enthusiastic discussion involving all of the children. There is much question asking, commenting, and a considerable amount of bragging.

The teacher begins to assert her role as leader once again by helping the children carry on the discussion. She asks for cooperation in taking turns; she asks questions and makes comments; she draws the children out and encourages each to maintain a focus on the topic introduced by our subject. The episode continues for ten minutes after which the group is dissolved. The book is put away for another time without the teacher's having finished and, more to the point, without her having imposed any sanctions on the children for not attending to what she had planned. The story time had been transformed into a group discussion in which the children and the teacher demonstrated respect, curiosity, and the desire to elaborate on the theme introduced by our subject.

The nature of the ecological system can be derived from this example. A group of seven children were gathered together for the purpose of listening to an adult read a story. Though the children and the teacher were part of a larger ecological unit (the nursery school), they occupied a section of the room (the reading area) especially designed for the activity which has been described. The story-reading milieu was located in a corner of the room, enclosed by a tall bookcase and the two abutting walls. (See the sketch in Figure 6.1). The teacher had covered the floor with a shagrug remnant and placed several floor pillows in the area. An old and attractive floor lamp stood in the corner. Pictures and posters, frequently changed, were mounted on the two room walls, the tops of which were no more than three feet off the floor. There were three shelves in the book case, on two of which were placed never more than 12 children's picture and story books. An asparagus fern sat on the top shelf. The area was large enough to accommodate the seven children and one adult comfortably but not more than this number. The floor dimensions were six by five feet.

Care has been taken in describing the physical setting of the reading area, for in many ways our behavior is influenced by our perception of what we think is expected of us in a given setting. The influence of environment on behavior will be described in detail in the next section of this chapter. However, it should be noted that locating the reading area away from the more active areas of the classroom, keeping it limited to approximately 30 square feet, carpeting it, and decorating with pillows and posters should suggest something about the kind of behavior expected in such a place. Furthermore, to add a special lamp and a display of a few children's books further

Figure 6.1   **The Reading Area**

clarifies the intended use of the area. The physical setting tells all who would enter that it is a place for a very few people at any time, one in which looking at books or listening to stories or talking about a book might occur.

In the situation described here, seven children have joined an adult for what was to be story reading. This is a very appropriate activity for the area but not one our young subject was content to accept. She almost immediately began to change the activity and particularly the behavior of the teacher by insisting on talking about an experience she had had, prompted by the story being read.

The youngster was a *disruptive* influence in the sense that she refused to accept the conditions established by the teacher and the setting (seven children seated in a fan-shaped array in front of the story-reading teacher). However, the child's behavior was *productive* in the sense that she sought not to destroy the gathering but only to modify the activity in a way that was consonant with the physical setting, as well as socially and educationally appropriate. The beginning of the reading provoked the recollection of a prior experience which became of consuming interest to the child. She was more intent on discussing her recollection than listening to the story.

The child had a profound influence on the story-listening milieu. She caused the activity to be changed in ways she wanted by convincing the teacher to alter the structure and the purpose of the activity. In turn, our subject was influenced by the actions of the teacher and the other children. The child remained in the group and became centrally involved in the activity. The teacher did not punish the child or otherwise make her adhere to the purpose and structure originally planned (though this might at times be necessary).

The events in this activity clearly reveal an interactive relationship between the environment of the story-reading area, the activity selected by the teacher, and the strength of purpose of our subject. The ecological segment described here includes such environmental factors as the physical setting, the announced purpose for drawing the children together, the behavior of our subject and that of the other children, and especially the behavior of the teacher. The account of the events in this microecological system describes the ways in which the child was influenced by the environment, and most importantly, how she became an agent for change.

Implicit in the account of this story-telling episode are two human factors which become central in any ecological system and should be explicitly discussed, if only briefly. One is the individual's perception of the situation and the other is volition or the exercise of will. Though it cannot be disputed that the physical setting will influence how we behave, it is our perception of what is allowed there which may be the ultimate deciding factor. The child here described may have perceived the purpose of the setting accurately—story-reading. She may also have believed that it was possible to influence what would transpire once events began to unfold. Volition cannot be separated from perception, for the exercise of will may have considerable influence on how an event or experience is perceived. Nonetheless, it does seem important to note that the child's strong will produced by the need to share with the group her prior experience contributed much to the shape of events as they unfolded. One could suggest that our subject was influenced to behave as she did because the setting brought forth feelings, memories, and thoughts which she needed to act upon. Our child may have been responding not only to the stimuli of the setting but also to some internal need aroused by the situation. Further, she apparently chose to act on this need by asserting her desire to engage the entire group in a discussion of her experience.

The needs aroused by our recollections may not always result in the same behavioral response. Our subject may at another time and in a very similar situation respond by withdrawing from the group, becoming lost in her own thoughts, or even announcing that she dislikes the story. It is important to note that whatever the response, it may best be considered in the context of the interactive relationship between the perceptions and needs of the child and the structure of the milieu.

Characteristics of Ecological Systems

Quite obviously there are various types of ecological systems. If the situation just discussed represents one, another would be the classroom within which the story reading actively occurred. And, the preschool comprises only one ecological system in the life of each child. Furthermore, for human development to occur there must be, as Bronfenbrenner suggests, a "progressive, mutual accommodation, throughout the life span, between a growing human organism and the changing immediate environments in which it lives" (1977, p. 514). The child in our discussion not only must

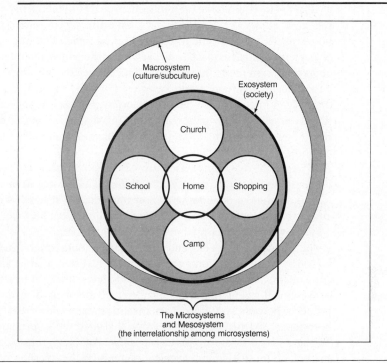

Figure 6.2   Bronfenbrenner's Nested Environments

Data from Bronfenbrenner (1977, pp. 513–531)

accommodate herself to the changes which occur in moving outside the preschool setting but to those with which she is faced within the program. Bronfenbrenner has built on the seminal thought of Kurt Lewin (1935) in describing four categories of environment in the lives of all of us. It will be helpful to outline and discuss briefly each category so that we may better understand the place of the early education setting in the life of the child.

Bronfenbrenner's four categories of environments actually represent different kinds of ecological systems, each of which exerts a different kind of influence on our behavior. These systems exist not independent of or adjacent to one another but rather are nested one within the other as depicted in the sketch in Figure 6.2.

The macrosystem is one's culture. As Bronfenbrenner suggests, the macrosystem is a set of value, customs, and beliefs, transmitted over generations, which influences perception, motivation, and the meaning of those things experienced in life.

The exosystem is the social structure within which we live. It is more formal than the macrosystem and much more immediate in its influence. It is the system of relationships that is established in a neighborhood, on the job, and the political arena, for example. It may be likened to what sociologists have traditionally referred to as the system for communicating and maintaining relationships within a social setting. In a word, it is society.

The microsystem is the most immediate and perhaps the most important ecological system. It consists of the day-to-day events and activities each person experiences at home, at school, or in the workplace, for example. The microsystem has particular characteristics such as place, time, action, participants, and role. Activities and events of the microsystem very likely have influence over and are affected by our behavior to a greater degree than any other ecological system. The mesosystem consists of several interrelated microsystems. The behavior in school is interrelated to that at home, on the way to school, and on the community playground. Yet each of these environments constitutes a microsystem. The relationship among and between these microsystems constitutes the mesosystem.

There is at least one reason why Bronfenbrenner's four-environment thesis is important to those who work with children. There is the implied suggestion that the microsystem—the environment most immediately at hand—is most influenced by and, in turn, exerts the most influence over individual behavior. Microsystem events are those which are clearly perceptible and which cannot be denied. By the same token, it would appear that society and culture exert a more general and diffuse influence on behavior. Values, customs, patterns of response certainly affect perceptions and consequent actions but more by inference than interaction. For example, conventional belief about the character of members of a different society would influence how one would approach meeting someone from that group. We might have been taught by members of our group that these other people were unfriendly and hostile, and to be avoided whenever possible. An initial, unavoidable first meeting with someone from this different society might raise the question of the accuracy of this traditional belief. The person might be friendly, interested in knowing about our culture, and not at all wary of becoming engaged in animated discussion. It is more likely in this case that one would respond more to the situation than to the prejudices and traditional beliefs handed down over the years. In fact, continued contact with this new person and others from his society might have the ultimate effect of bringing into question traditional cultural values.

One implication of the suggestion that the immediate environment has a major influence on behavior is that the search for primary explanations of behavior in the culture, the personality, the cognitive or emotional state of a person may be somewhat misdirected. It may be far more productive for us to study the milieu in which the behavior occurs, tempered of course by a knowledge of the culture and concern for the well-being of the child. We will return to this assertion again, and so it will not be fully discussed here. However, it should be said that the rather commonplace practice of attributing children's behavior largely to factors such as sex, race or ethnicity, family size, and wealth may need to be reconsidered.

Without question these factors contribute to our perceptions, motivation, and knowledge (Bronfenbrenner, 1977) but, perhaps, they influence the style and mode of our response more than determining whether or not we respond at all. To illustrate the point, we may recall that American Indian children are very often taught to avert their eyes when speaking to an elder, especially one who has been given unusual status in society. This cultural influence will be evident in schools; it should be known by teachers of Indian children so that a child's turning away from the gaze of a teacher during an instructional interchange may not be interpreted as lack of interest, involvement, as hostility, or as an indication of the child's scholastic ability. The reaction of the child, which might signify lack of interest to an unknowing adult, would, in this instance, be more a function of the situation established by the teacher than any other factor. And, to make the point once again, it may be more fruitful for those of us who care for and educate children to concentrate our search for explanations of their behavior in the context in which it occurs.

The Behavior Setting

Roger Barker's (1968) ecological studies of natural behavior in everyday situations led to what Jerome Bruner described as the ironic truism "that the best way to predict the behavior of a human being is to know where he is: in a post office he behaves post office, at church he behaves church" (Schoggen, 1978, p. 37). This obvious conclusion by Bruner suggests nothing more or less than in most settings our behavior is influenced more by factors of that milieu than by anything we might bring to it. We do conform to established behavior patterns in public institutions such as the post office. Furthermore, the arrangement of the environment must give us clues as to how we should behave. We are so affected by those clues that any obvious change in setting will set us about the task of determining what, if any, change in our behavior is called for. An illustration might make this clearer.

The post office in Amherst, Massachusetts, quite recently instituted an important change in the way in which one is to conduct business other than simply dropping mail in chute. In the past anyone entering the building would proceed to one of the postal clerks and purchase stamps, post packages, or complete whatever task brought them there. When there was a crowd, invariably one joined the shorter lined and waited his/her turn. Occasionally, patrons would hop from one line to another in the hope of shortening the waiting time. In brief, this describes what Bruner may have had in mind when he said that in the "post office we behave post office." All of this behavior has now been changed, and not by stages but all at once. No longer does the patron scan the lines upon entering the building; rather each enters a queuing-up space from which he/she moves to an open clerk, as someone else, having completed their business, moves away. The queuing-up space is marked by a series of posts and ropes very much like those used in theaters to control the movement of large groups of people. (see Figure 6.3). There is an "Enter" sign attached to the first post and another sign at the exit to this area which admonishes all to remain there until a clerk's station has been vacated.

This is a very different arrangement from that to which those who use this facility had been accustomed. Yet it seems quite clear that post office patrons have accommodated themselves to this demand for different behavior readily and without distress. Though I have not observed at great length, I have not yet seen anyone refusing to enter the queue or complaining about the procedure. Furthermore, all seem to have taken their cues from the setting without any need for special instruction. No one from the postal service has been standing by the door telling patrons how to behave.

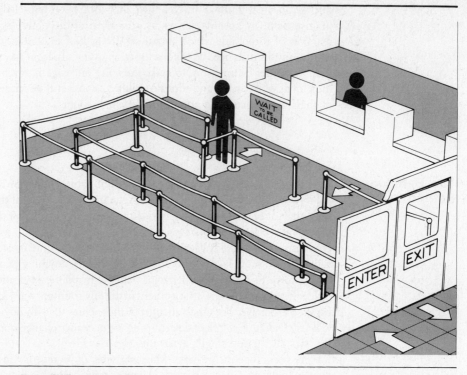

Figure 6.3   **Post Office Behavior**

Barker discovered more about the environment-behavior relationship among children that suggests an interaction effect in which behavior contributes to the maintenance of the setting. His observations led him to make three explanatory generalizations. First, a person's behavior changes from situation to situation. A child will act differently in the classroom, the playground, at church, or on the street. It might be added that those who experienced this new behavior in the post office do not look for a queue at the local stationery store. Second, the behavior of persons in the same setting tends to be more alike there than their behavior in another environment. Children may be quiet and reserved in a classroom and assertive and noisy on the playground. They will act alike in each setting rather than maintaining one type of behavior over all environments. The noisy child on the playground is very likely to temper his/her behavior when entering the classroom. Third, there is a consistency in a person's behavior within any behavior setting. Barker described a child's behavior in a drug store as wandering away from her mother, looking at merchandise, teasing for a soda, and spinning on a stool; though very different, the acts constituted appropriate drug store behavior. The child was interested in different parts of the drug store but maintained "drug store" behavior all the while she was there. This example suggests that there may be more than one appropriate behavior for any behavior setting. This observation will become very important in discussion near the end of this chapter.

Barker has analyzed behavior settings and identified several characteristics which are the fundamental features of a micro-ecological system. These characteristics help explain the interactive effect of behavior and environment. Four will be discussed here

Standing Patterns of Behavior

Barker's observations about the consistency of behavior among persons in a particular environment, such as the church, drug store, or post office, quite naturally led to the identification of *standing patterns of behavior* as a primary characteristic of behavior settings. Put very simply, standing patterns of behavior consist of all those discrete or complete actions commonly observed in any behavior setting regardless of who is there.[1] We all tend to do the same things in the store, post office, or classroom and when we leave, those who take our place generally do as we have done. A standing pattern of behavior is, therefore, something which transcends any one person; "it is an extra-individual behavior phenomenon" (Barker, 1968, p. 18).

The behavior setting does not have some supernatural behavior-shaping power. Barker is careful to suggest that the form and structure of the environment will influence how we act. For example, in their study of the behavior of people in a midwest town, Barker and Wright (1955) observed that most children would run, chase one another, play tag, or in other ways engage in exuberant running immediately upon being placed in an open field, large play area, or park. Barker and Wright attributed this, in part, to the setting itself; it certainly invited and fairly required this kind of behavior. By the same token; one can say that the new post office behavior in Amherst is largely prescribed by the posts, lines, and instructional signs.

We should not discount the effect of social pressure and learning on individuals' behavior in any setting. Parents in subtle and not so subtle ways spend much of their time with young children in "teaching" them how to behave in different environments. We are also taught to use our perceptual skills and good judgment in determining how to behave in any new or different situation. Hess and Shipman (1968) describe two kinds of instruction mothers gave to their children upon entering first grade. One message was for the children to be quiet, to listen and pay attention, to do what was asked of them because the teacher was going to teach them. Other children were told that their teacher was there to help them continue their learning which had started in kindergarten, pre-school, and the home. Children receiving this message were told that they were competent learners and that the school and teacher were going to support and maintain this competence. In each case, the parents were telling the children what to expect in this new environment and how to use their best judgment in deciding how to behave there. Interestingly enough, both groups of parents were right in their analysis of what kinds of behavior were acceptable in school. Quiet, pleasant, and submissive behavior is valued as is self-assertive, independent, and task-focused

---

[1]Complete actions, such as waving a greeting to a friend, are usually called *molar behaviors* by psychologists. The term *molar behavior* seems to have been taken from chemistry and is used to denote a whole action. In contrast, *molecular behavior* is part of a whole action. Eye blinks are *molecular behaviors*; picking up a block and placing it on a stack of other blocks is a *molar behavior*.

behavior. Though they are manifested in quite different ways, each meets the standing pattern of behavior for most first-grade classrooms. In summary, we behave as we do in all behavior settings largely because the physical structure of the setting, the consequences of enculturation and instruction, and our own skills in perceiving the requirements of the situation all combine to establish standing patterns of behaviors.

The ways in which people behave in any behavior setting can and will change over time. Standing patterns of behavior are not static; once established, they do not always remain constant and the same. Over the past decade there has been a marked change in the behavior of children and of teachers in some primary-grade settings. In about 1970 the influence of the infant school practices of Leicestershire County, England, began to be felt in the United States (Silberman, 1969; Featherstone, 1967; Weber, 1971). Though it is difficult to itemize the curricular structure of infant school practice, the essence seemed to be that children were to be engaged in the process of acquiring skills and discovering knowledge without always being directed by a teacher. One obvious consequence of programs of this kind was that the standing pattern of behavior for children began to include much more self-direction and activity involvement and less passive receipt of instruction by adults. Teachers spent much less time in group instruction and more on individual counseling and small-group guidance.

Several changes in adult and child behavior resulted from the introduction of infant school practices in the primary grades. Among the most prominent was a shift in attitude by teachers regarding appropriate learning behaviors for children. A belief seems to pervade the new practice that children should be given freedom to explore and to become engaged with one another and with materials. A second change has been the restructuring of the classroom setting. Infant school classrooms are often organized around discrete learning areas such as a science corner, creative play area, mathematics table, painting area, and a reading area, for example. In many cases, children are no longer assigned to seats or desks but have a container in which they deposit their work, and move from area to area and activity to activity as the day progresses, leaving the products of their activity in the container. This brief description of the behavior of children and teachers in the "new" English Infant School illustrates how standing patterns of behavior in old and established settings such as the classroom can and do change.

It is necessary to make one last comment about variability in standing patterns of behavior. Any behavior setting is likely to have a variety of behaviors that are appropriate and comprise the standing patterns for that setting. The standing patterns of behavior for a nursery school classroom can include solitary play, group activity, self-directed inquiry, wandering, and cooperative problem-solving, among others. Furthermore, any of these behaviors may appear in different ways. One time a child's inquiry may consist of engaging a teacher in answering a series of questions. At another time this child may be more reflective and rely on observation and trial-and-error manipulation to achieve answers to questions. The point is that each type of inquiry would be an appropriate demonstration of a standing pattern of behavior for the nursery school.

Milieu or Physical Structure

Milieu, briefly defined, means environment. As it is applied to the study of behavior settings, it means a particular space set apart from other environments by, among other things, its physical structure including the objects which are contained in the setting. The now-famous Amherst post office obviously has a particular milieu or physical structure designed for post office behavior; the building and everything in it constitute the milieu for post office behavior. A less obvious but nonetheless important milieu could be the front lawn of the town hall where local young people congregate to socialize with each other. The physical structure might consist of that section of the lawn on the south side of the building, bounded on two sides by a sidewalk, on one side by the building, and on the fourth side by a rose garden. Furthermore, the locus or center of this physical setting may be the trunk of the only maple tree in the yard. Characteristic of the examples given here and of all behavior settings, is that the physical structure or parts of the environment exist in the absence of people. The post office and all its properties remain after the close of the business day. So, too, do the features of the young people's gathering spot, even when wet with rain or covered with snow.

Obviously the permanent characteristics of the post office—the brick, mortar, locked and unlocked doors, and the rest—set it apart from expedient and possibly transitory behavior settings like the town lawn. I would like to suggest that teachers of young children create in their classrooms at least two kinds of milieu, one more permanent than the other, like the behavior settings described here.

A classroom, day-care setting, or nursery school would constitute the more permanent type of physical setting. It would be an enclosed area (or areas) set apart from adjacent areas by such factors as its purpose, the population of youngsters it is to serve, and its physical separation from everything which is not a part of the child-care/education setting. Parents, passers-by, health department inspectors, licensing and credentialing personnel, and others could refer to it as 2nd Avenue Head Start, the Mt. Warner Nursery and Kindergarten, or whatever name might be given to the program identifying it as a place with a particular purpose and reason for being. Furthermore, merely naming the place would allow most people to infer some of the behaviors that would be expected to take place there.

There is a second less permanent order of physical setting which exists within the child care/education setting. It is what Paul Gump (1975) refers to as segments or the structured units within a larger behavior setting. To be more precise, a segment is a learning area within the nursery or kindergarten which has been created by the staff for particular reasons. The block area is a segment if it is separated from adjacent areas by such barriers as shelves upon which the blocks are stored and a rug beyond which the blocks cannot be taken. Other segments could include the easels, a table-games area, the literature corner, and the circle-time rug. Each area is a behavior setting with standing patterns of behavior. It is important to stress here that a classroom consists of an array of segments, each of which should call for a rather unique kind of behavior. The block area is not a segment merely because it is physically separated from all other areas in the preschool, though this is important. It is a segment because children's behavior there will be somewhat different than it would be in the other areas of the classroom. This factor suggests a third characteristic of a behavior setting.

Consonance Between Milieu and Standing Patterns of Behavior

The physical setting of the typical housekeeping area in any kindergarten is designed to elicit and support role playing and other types of creative dramatics and fantasy play. A teacher would probably not anticipate children using the housekeeping area as a place to complete solitary activity such as working a puzzle. Nor would they be apt to think of children consistently refusing to engage in play with others in the housekeeping area. On the contrary, many educators would value the housekeeping area because it ought to promote and support cooperative activity among children. This simple illustration is designed to show that the behavior and the milieu of any behavior setting support one another, or, as Barker suggests, there must be an "essential fittingness between them" (1968, p. 19).

Milieu-behavior consonance is an essential characteristic of every behavior setting, and this becomes especially important as we examine the relationship of segments to the entire early education program. The standing patterns of behavior for circle time could include respecting the personal space of those children nearby, attending to the teacher and to any child who might be talking, joining in the conversation when encouraged to do so, and remaining seated. These behaviors may be very inappropriate in the block area, at the easel, or even in the housekeeping area. Each segment ought to call upon children to behave in a way somewhat different from other areas but always in a way which is supportive of the physical setting (and, by implication, of the purposes for which the setting was established).

The Interdependence of Behavior Settings

Every behavior setting, complex or simple, must exist in a larger interrelated environment. Barker illustrates this interdependence by suggesting that a church and 4-H Club would not schedule a bake sale on the same day in any small town. The leaders of each organization would know that to do so would jeopardize the effectiveness of each sale; there simply would not be enough customers for two sales on the same day. A much more dramatic illustration of the interdependence of behavior settings can usually be found in local news reports. In most communities, large or small, restrictions are placed on the type and size of businesses which may be opened in any neighborhood. Not infrequently newspapers will carry accounts of citizens petitioning the zoning board in an attempt to prevent the introduction of a business to their neigborhood which they feel would be incompatible with the quality of life in that area. Most residents would object to having a saloon or a gas station erected in their residential neighborhood, especially if there were now no businesses there. These same citizens might petition the town or city council in an attempt to have a recreation area constructed on unused land in the community. Parents might believe that a playground would substantially add to the quality of life in their neighborhood in a way that a saloon never could.

The interdependence of behavior settings primarily concerns the relationship of alternative patterns of behaviors in adjacent settings. At issue is the compatibility of behavior within any larger behavior setting and between adjacent behavior settings. The compatibility between different but proximate settings is the more obvious issue. On a very simple level, locating a saloon in a residential neighborhood, as in the illustration given above, brings into sharp relief the belief of residents that the behaviors consonant with a drinking establishment would interfere with those standing patterns of behavior common to the neighborhood as it now exists. Though the structure of the saloon would appear to contain the drinking behaviors (it would be a separate building from which no drinks could be taken), the residents of the neighborhood might *feel* that having such an enterprise in the area would introduce other behavior settings entirely compatible with a drinking establishment but detrimental to the community. It could be argued that patrons would come from areas far away from the neigborhood and create a hang-out outside of the saloon. Residents might also be concerned with the possibility that other businesses such as restaurants might want to be introduced there.

The issue in this example is not whether there should or should not be bars and restaurants and gasoline stations but whether they can exist side-by-side with any other behavior setting without introducing tension into the environment. Most citizens would agree that athletic fields and hospitals are both desirable for any community. Yet we would all very likely agree that to locate a football field next to a hospital would create considerable behavioral dissonance. The legitimate, noisy standing patterns of behavior of any athletic event—shouting, cheering, whistle-blowing—would be incompatible with the quiet, reserved behavior common to hospital settings.

Unfortunately, it is not apparent that child care providers and early child educators always consider the question of alternative behavior settings in selecting the location for nursery schools or day-care centers. It is rather widespread practice to use available physical facilities for preschool programs of any type. Day-care centers, Head Start classrooms, and cooperative nurseries are often found in the large, open basement rooms of churches or public halls, in reconverted office space or storefronts. There are examples of attractive ways in which these settings have been transformed to serve the needs of children. However, it is far more common to find a program for children located in a space which is considered by the major tenant to exist for very different reasons; this often has unfortunate consequences.

Consider the preschool housed in a combination auditorium and gymnasium. This space is over 100 feet long by 75 feet wide. The ceilings are very high, as would be expected in a gymnasium, and there is a large raised stage along one side. The hall is regularly used for basketball games, community meetings, and theatrical presentations. Most adolescents and adults consider the auditorium to be a valuable recreational facility; it is remembered only as an afterthought as the place in which a nursery school is housed. Each Friday afternoon and often during the week, all of the equipment and materials of the preschool must be removed to a small, connecting storage room. Every remnant of the program for children must be taken away so that the facility can assume the character for which it was constructed. It is not hard to see

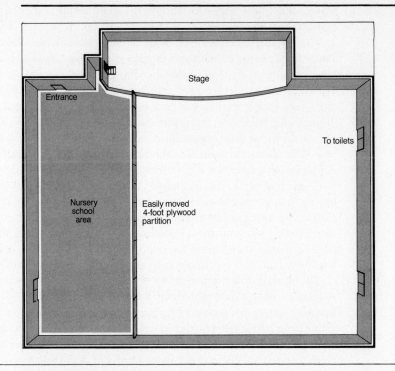

Figure 6.4   **The Auditorium Nursery School**

that the preschool children soon became confused about the standing patterns of behavior for this physical space, for they, too, knew that most adults in the community thought of their nursery school space as something quite different from the way in which they used it.

The staff attempted to adjust to the large size of the area by restricting the preschool space to one end of the auditorium (see Figure 6.4). An impermanent four-foot-high partition had been constructed with plywood which stretched from side to side with one opening near the stage front. Unfortunately, the plywood partitions had to be movable and were easily shifted by the children. The wall often was breached by small groups of children with the effect that the area of the auditorium set apart for the nursery school existed only in the eyes of the staff. The behavior of the children suggested that they considered the whole area, including the stage, to be a part of the nursery school milieu. As if this were not enough, the three, four, and five-year-old children had learned that empty auditoriums and gymnasiums—large open spaces—were places in which running and shouting behavior was legitimate and to be expected.

The preschool area had many of the activities, materials, and learning areas common to most programs for young children. Moreover, the staff were not without ingenuity in presenting ideas which captured the imagination of the children. Children did work with clay, sand, water, and paints; they did play with blocks, listen to stories, and look at children's books. They also "escaped" from the preschool area to the remaining space with considerable regularity and enthusiasm. Their escape was usually accompanied by the shouts and noise fully accepted in recreational areas. As might have been expected, the staff spent too much time capturing and bring back to the "school" those children who had dashed away. This very unfortunate situation came about in large part because it was thought possible to create a nursery school with particular standing patterns of behavior in a gymnasium with a very different and conflicting set of behaviors. There was very little that could be done to salvage the nursery school in this setting. The staff should have searched for facilities in which the standing patterns of behavior of their program would not conflict with the purposes for which the facility was constructed.

The interdependence of behavior settings affects what occurs in the classroom, as suggested by the preschool just described. Special concern must be given to the organization of the environment within the school. In discussing milieu or physical structure Gump's concept of behavior segments was introduced. To review, a segment in any early education setting would be a learning or activity area such as the block area, easels, and circle-time rug, for example. A segment has all of the properties of a behavior setting but in minature. Most important, each segment has standing patterns of behavior and physical structure or milieu; it is a discernibly discrete area within a classroom which, in combination with all other segments, constitutes the early education environment.

The issue of compatibility between segments within an early education behavior setting centers on the question of how to select and locate the learning areas so that the standing pattern of behavior in one will not contaminate that of adjacent areas. This issue will be given special attention in Chapter 8, The Physical Setting and Utilization of Space, so it will not be discussed fully here. By way of example, however, it should be noted that behavior commonly expected in the woodworking area may interfere with that anticipated in the rather quiet children's literature area. To locate these areas next to one another may have the effect of making the literature area all but ineffective. The stronger, more active behavior of the woodworking area may influence the more quiet, reflective behavior commonly expected when children are looking at books. This rather obvious example does illustrate an issue which is not always given as much attention as it should be by program staff.

Four characteristics of behavior settings have been presented. Barker has identified standing patterns of behavior, milieu, the necessary relationship of behavior and milieu, and the relationship of one behavior setting to another as major features of behavior settings. There would seem to be an obvious relationship between Barker's characteristics and Bronfenbrenner's microecological system. The individual behaves within an environmental context and in relation to the features of that context. Perhaps most significant in this discussion is that we all seem to adjust or accommodate to the internal demands of any behavior setting as long as those demands are clearly perceptible.

**Children's
Behavior in
Early
Education
Settings**

Neither Barker nor Bronfenbrenner would suggest that a person has little control over their behavior in any behavior setting. Barker's characteristics of a behavior setting should not be interpreted as a behavioristic account of the dynamic way in which environments shape human behavior. Rather, behavior settings establish the conditions under which person-environment interaction can occur. In the case of the preschool located in the large hall, one of the enduring difficulties for children and staff was that one behavior setting was imposed upon another in such a way that standing patterns of behavior for each setting—the gymnasium-auditorium and nursery school—were in relative conflict. Clearly, the characteristics of a behavior setting were not present in this situation. A consequence was that children only infrequently met the expectations of the early education program established by the teachers.

Barker is very careful in making clear that a behavior setting (in which three characteristics are clearly evident) does not have such coercive power over the inhabitants that a person's will, emotional state, or motives will not affect his/her behavior. Also, variability in human behavior is very much expected and accounted for in Barker's schema. Recall the brief comment on page 104 regarding the reasons why the young lady in the story area might have wanted to engage the group in a discussion rather than listen to the story. It was noted that we can only guess about the reasons for her behavior, but that is unimportant here. The important thing to note is that her particular motive was allowed to influence that setting in a very dynamic way, and yet it remained within the definition of the standing pattern of behaviors for the story area.

It would be unrealistic to establish a nursery school environment and expect that all children who attended would behave just as anticipated. Behavioral setting analysis does not suggest this would occur. Children can manifest very different and individual responses to any situation. Barker is clear in pointing out that there will be variation in the patterns of behavior within any group in all behavior settings. Furthermore, some small degree of deviant behavior, that which is in conflict with the standing pattern of behavior, should also be expected from time to time. It is entirely possible that on some occasions a group of children could behave in a nursery school in ways very different from those commonly observed. They may simply refuse to be coerced by the milieu however carefully organized. Behavioral setting analysis in no way can explain this, nor does it pretend to. Rather, it provides a reason for anticipating that children will respond to the behavioral requirements of a setting when those requirements are clearly understandable and achievable. Most children will try to offer "preschool behavior" at their pre-school if they easily understand what behaviors are required. They will paint at the easel, build with the blocks, attend to the teacher during circle time, and complete puzzles to the degree that the milieu suggests that these be done. Yet within any milieu one must expect a range of appropriate behavior. Not all children will conform to one pattern of painting behavior; there will be great variability in speed, duration of attention to the task, thought and care given to the combination of color and shape, and the degree to which a child seeks comment on the painting from other children or adults.

Children's Influence on Behavior Settings

An ecological explanation of human behavior must account for the ways in which an individual can influence the environment. Barker's behavior setting analysis seems to make clear the strength of milieu on behavioral response but may not be as explicit as is necessary in clarifying the effect of the person's behavior on the setting. The earlier account of the child who influenced the course of the story-reading session is an example of how this can occur. It may be helpful to suggest three ways in which a child could affect any behavior setting.

Modification   One of the most common ways in which a child may affect a segment within a clasroom is by *modification of the intent* of the area or activity. This ocurred in the case of the child in the story-reading example described earlier. The teacher (and the remaining children, it may be assumed) had intended for a story to be read. The behavior of the girl changed all of this but did not destroy that part of the day's program. The children and teacher remained in the area; they followed the lead of the child and engaged one another in a productive conversation.

Another example of a child's modifying a behavior setting was described by his teacher as follows: A housekeeping area—physically bounded space, with appropriate equipment and materials—had been set up in a nursery school. It was occasionally used by children for various episodes of dramatic play, role playing, and so forth. However, one child captured the area with great regularity and transformed it into his restaurant. He became the only child to occupy the bounded area but invited other children to approach the entrance (transformed into a service bar) and to order food from him. He took orders, served the imaginary food, and maintained his restaurant with or without children's participation. This child's modification of the intent of the area, though not conceived by the staff, nonetheless resulted in behaviors which were compatible with those originally planned. His restaurant behavior was very appropriate to and consonant with the role-playing, fantasy, and creative play patterns of behavior for which the area was designed.

Construction   It would be helpful to borrow from Piaget's theory of cognitive development in explaining the ways in which construction can influence any milieu. Piaget believes that a central process in cognitive development is the child's construction of his/her own knowledge and understanding. A child does this by performing actions on objects in his experience from which he/she will derive explanations of cause-and-effect relationships. To be sure, a four-year-old's causal explanation for any phenomenon may be nearer to fiction than reality and may reflect considerable intellectual immaturity. Nonetheless, Piaget maintains that the important and natural process of organizing experience into some understandable cognitive system—construction—is central to intellectual development.

A preschool child will construct knowledge of the relationship of a stack of blocks to their shape by struggling with the impossible task of building a tower from cubes, spheres, and cones. As the child attempts to use all three shapes in building a tower, he/she will discover that cubes can be stacked quite easily and that a cone can rest on top of a cube but that spheres cannot be used at all in a free standing tower. At first, the child's knowledge of the relationship between object shape and tower building will be physical knowledge, that derived from direct experience. Later on it will be possible for the child to construct newer and more accurate systems of knowledge without having to rely on physical action. The child will draw upon his/her memory and ability to envisage the action in the abstract and to derive explanations from logical thought. Whether it is physical action (building with blocks) or abstract action (speculating in his/her mind) the child is constructing knowledge.

Piaget maintains that construction, in all the ways implied in this brief illustration, is a very natural human behavior and necessary to the achievement of full cognitive development. So it should not be surprising if children build upon the intent of any behavior setting. Most preschool teachers will recall an occasion when a child or two dumped all of the inlay puzzle pieces into one large pile on the floor and then proceeded to complete each puzzle, moving from one to another as their selection of each piece from the pile required. When this occurs, the child is constructing a new and more complex task from ones which, quite obviously, are no longer challenging. It can be suggested that from this construction will come new knowledge. Yet, the standing patterns of behavior for puzzle activity will remain intact.

There are many ways in which children's construction can influence a behavior setting. Adding sand to water paint to introduce a new texture in painting is one example. Another would be raising questions about the effect of water and light on plants as they sow bean seeds in a southern window. The children might not be content merely watching the bean sprout and grow, but might prefer to experiment with alterations in the amount of light and moisture, something the teacher had not planned. A key in promoting construction, of course, must be the perception and the sensitivity of teachers to this natural human behavior. Children will want to build on, to change, to alter the task and activity while maintaining the integrity of the original plan.

Nonparticipation   The most carefully designed and supplied learning area will not be functional at all unless children choose to enter. Most, if not all, early education programs rely on children's decisions about what they will do during part of the program day. Frequently children will decide to paint, play with sand or blocks, or listen to records. One of the most potent ways they can influence what teachers have designed is to choose not to enter or to become engaged in an activity or area. In one situation a team of teachers observed their children for some time and decided that they should introduce materials which would provoke thought, involve only one child with the material, and require sequential steps in completing an activity in an attractive setting. They designed a cognitive activities area in a private corner of the room, in which was placed a table, storage shelves, and chairs. They selected games, puzzles, and sensorimotor objects of many types and arranged them in what appeared to be a very attractive way. Unfortunately, for reasons totally inexplicable, the children refused to enter the area. The materials were simply not used.

After a period of agonizing observation, the teachers decided to relocate the materials in areas frequently occupied by the children. They made sure that the behaviors required of the material were consonant with the standing patterns of behavior of the new location. The results were striking: the children began to use the materials as the teachers had intended.

In summary, three ways have been identified by which children can influence any behavior setting. They can modify the intent of the setting, construct new purposes and activities which are consonant with the original intent, and they can refuse to enter the area and to engage in the activity. Each of the alternatives can have a positive and beneficial effect on the early education program and the child's development. Certainly all would recognize that children can influence any behavior setting in at least one more way. They can destroy its intent and structure.

Disruptive Behavior in Behavior Settings

From time to time and for reasons not always understood, children will not meet the expectations of a behavior setting regardless of how carefully and clearly the environment is designed. Instead, they will do all they can to disrupt and destroy any kind of growth-productive behavior which may occur. There doesn't appear to be much that the study of human ecology can contribute to the explanation of the causes and cures for such anomalous behavior. It can and will occur very infrequently in any early education setting and should not be weighed too heavily. There is reason for alarm only if such disruptive behavior is patterned, occurs with significant regularity, and is restricted to the actions of the same child or children. In such cases it would seem necessary to seek the consultation of parents, psychologists, the family physican, and fellow teachers, among others.

The Value of an Ecological Perspective

The value of an ecological perspective becomes obvious if one has read this far in the chapter. Therefore I will not attempt to present an exhaustive accounting of the benefits of the ecological perspective derived from practitioners but restrict my comments to two general statements. First, the nature of the interdependence of environment and behavior becomes clearer as principles of human ecology are applied to early education settings. Second, it, becomes quite apparent that search for the causes of behavior in antecedent conditions needs to be tempered by the realization that the immediate context may be more influential than any other factors. Each conclusion will be discussed separately.

Behavior-Environment Interdependence

The conclusion that the environment influences human behavior and may be subsequently changed as a consequence of that behavior appears to have immediate implications for early education practitioners. The selection of a site for day care or nursery school and the design of classrooms in schools should be carefully considered.

It seems to be especially important to know that the larger physical setting, the building and rooms to be used, will support and be consonant with the goals and purposes of the program. Recall for a moment the example cited earlier of the nursery school located in the auditorium-gymnasium. This is not a minor issue by any means. Recently researchers have begun to study the consequences of large open-space environments on children's scholastic and social behavior (Bennett, 1976; Gump, 1975). The results of these studies suggest that it might have been wiser to explore the outcome of open-space design prior to widespread construction and program design. One effect seems to have been that open instructional space in which 90 to 120 children could be housed with three or four teams of teachers is very soon closed again to accommodate three or four groups of 25-30 children. Teachers often find it necessary to establish barriers and enclose teaching areas in these newly designed schools. We can't say with any assurance what the precise cause of this might be, but without question it is a response to the effects of the open space on the behavior of both the children and the adults.

At a lower, but no less important, level of organization is the application of this generalization to the selection and organization of learning areas within an enclosed program setting. The question of what shall be placed in a classroom or day-care center must also be considered both in terms of the potential impact on the childrens' behavior and how the area will be used by the children. Chapters 8 to 11 will address these issues directly and provide the reader with practical suggestions for applying the knowledge of their interdependent relationship in early education programs.

Attributing Cause

Most of us are naturally inclined to search someone's personal history for causes of their behavior. We are especially apt to consider trauma during development as an etiological explanation for antisocial behavior, symptoms of emotional stress, or psychic dysfunction. The history of our concern for human development with its attendant heavy influence from psychoanalytic theory shows this to be the case. Moreover, sociologists who study persons in groups also have a tendency to ascribe behaviors to individuals primarily on the basis of group affiliation and such demographic factors as sex, socioeconomic status, and age. The fact of a behavior-environment interaction suggests that we could be making serious errors of judgment.

It would seem much more appropriate to begin any search for the cause of a behavior with the context in which it occurs. The presence or absence of task-involvement behavior in a section of a kindergarten classroom may be more a function of the elements of that behavior setting than the personal or social characteristics of the children in attendance. In an example cited earlier, teachers created an elaborate cognitive skills area, only to discover that the children universally avoided it; integrating the materials from this area with those of existing segments led to their being used. It might be appropriate to begin any search for the cause of children's behavior by applying Barker's behavior setting criteria in an examination of the setting.

Summary

It is quite easy for most us to recognize the interdependence of behavior and environment among lower level animals. The example of the titmice is understandable in terms of the relationship between the patterned responses to nesting, reproduction, and the care of the newborn birds. It is quite another matter to suggest that principles of ecology drawn from examples like this might be useful in understanding human behavior. Many of us bristle at the suggestion that we are not always and in every way in control of all of our behavior; that an abstraction like a behavior setting can coerce us to such an extent that we will try to act in ways we believe are appropriate and necessary to the setting. However, there is little doubt that we do act in this way.

It is just as important to understand that features of environments have been identified which help us determine what the behavioral expectations are. Barker has identified four principles of a behavior setting especially important for early childhood educators. They are standing patterns of behavior (the range of acceptable behaviors), the physical structure (the boundaries), the relationship between the physical setting and standing patterns of behavior, and the interdependence of behavior settings (the ways in which they influence one another). It has been suggested that these four principles can be used in designing environments for children which will enhance both the effectiveness of early education and the growth and development of the individual. Ways in which this can be done will be presented in many of the following chapters.

References: Chapter 6

Altman, Irwin. *The environment and social behavior.* Monterey, CA: Brooks/Cole, 1975.

Barker, Roger G. *Ecological psychology.* Palo Alto, CA: Stanford University Press, 1968.

Barker, Roger G., & Wright, Herbert F. *Midwest and its children.* New York: Harper & Row, 1955.

Bennett, Nevile. *Teaching styles and pupil progress.* Cambridge, MA: Harvard University Press, 1976.

Bronfenbrenner, Urie. Toward an experimental ecology of human development. *American Psychologist,* July 1977, *32*, 513–531.

Featherstone, Joseph. How children learn. *The New Republic,* September 2, 1967, *157*, 17–21. (a)

Featherstone, Joseph. Schools for children: What's happening in British classrooms. *The New Republic,* August 19, 1967, *157*, 17–21. (b)

Featherstone, Joseph. Teaching children to think. *The New Republic,* September 9, 1967, *157*,15–19. (c)

Gump, Paul V. Operating environments in schools of open and traditional design. In T. G. David & B. D. Wright (Eds.), *Learning Environments.* Chicago: University of Chicago Press, 1975.

Hess, Robert D. & Shipman, Virginia C. Maternal influences upon early learning: The cognitive environments of urban preschool children. In Robert D. Hess & Roberta M. Bear (Eds.), *Early education*. Chicago: Aldine, 1968.

Kamii, Constance, & DeVries, Rheta. *Physical knowledge in preschool education*. Englewood Cliffs, NJ: Prentice-Hall, 1978.

Lewin, Kurt. *A dynamic theory of personality*. New York: McGraw-Hill, 1935.

Schoggen, P. Ecological psychology and mental retardation. In G. P. Sackett (Ed.), *Observing behaviors: Theory and applications in mental retardation*. Baltimore: University Park Press, 1978.

Weber, Lillian. *The English Infant School and informal education*. Englewood Cliffs, NJ: Prentice-Hall, 1971.

Willems, Edwin P. Behavioral technology and behavioral ecology. *Journal of Applied Behavior Analysis*, 1974, 7, 151–165.

7 Intra-Individual Differences and Program Development

In the two previous chapters issues regarding the nature of development and the interrelationship of environment and behavior have been addressed. There remains one more ecological topic that must be considered in developing early education programs for young children. It is the issue of within-person variability. Up to this point the individual has been discussed primarily in terms of his/her membership in a class or a group regarding the ways all humans are influenced by transactions in their life experience. Within this context, it is not at all difficult to accept the considerable variability between individuals along many behavioral dimensions including cognitive skills, reactions to situations, and likes and dislikes, for example. Our tendency is to refer to such variability in terms of the uniqueness of the person—his/her capacity for learning and personality characteristics. What has not been addressed is the question of individual behavioral variation from situation to situation and from time to time and what such phenomena might imply for the nature of human behavior and the programs we design for the care and education of children.

It is common to assume that most of us have stable reactions to similar phenomena, that our ways of responding to most situations are quite consistent. We speak of the personality of someone in a way which suggests that their behavior in most settings can be predicted. We refer to other individuals as impulsive or reflective, emotional or controlled, as convergent or divergent thinkers, for example, with the implicit assurance that in doing so we have described the nature of the individual *in toto*. For example, we are apt to accept as self-evident that someone described as a "loner" will manifest "loner" characteristics in all settings. Most personality theories and, to a large degree, those of cognitive or intellectual style accept this assumption. Yet theory and research data exist which call into question the very essence of such traditional personality beliefs by suggesting that our behavior may naturally vary from situation to situation even in similar kinds of settings. Furthermore, this alternative view of personality suggests that within-person behavior variability may more accurately reflect well-developing, natural behavior than the stable personality characteristics. I should like to explore these two very different positions paying particular attention to the idea that intra-individual differences may be the more accurate characterization of human behavior. Needless to say, I shall try to develop the implications for the care and education of children from the discussion. The interrelationship of human development theory and principles of human ecology will also be discussed.

Intra-Individual Variability

Observations of children in group care and education settings made over the years have led me to the conclusion that children's behavior quite naturally changes from activity to activity and area to area in ways which may be difficult to predict. Furthermore, these changes in behavior appear to be quite a different sort from the shifts in mood or temperament; they seem to be much more than a manifestation of being energetic one moment and tired later, sad or disappointed now and elated afterward. Though shifts in mood certainly do occur, these are changes in the way in which children address the world, changes in the way in which the world is perceived and acted upon. For example, at one moment a child may be quite involved in completing a jigsaw puzzle and, upon completing it, bolt away, shouting to a peer about an activity they might cooperatively pursue. This same child may just as quickly announce that his cooperative activity has ended, leave his friend, and join a small group of children who are about to listen to a story read by an adult. Patterns of behavior change much like this may occur many times each day and go quite unnoticed by adults, for in each case the child is not demonstrating any antisocial behavior—no shouting, pushing, grabbing of material—nor flighty behavior such as skipping from one task to another without sustained attention or task completion. A child may perform well in each setting, completing the puzzle before leaving, following the cooperative activity to a logical point of departure, and staying with the story until it has been read. Yet the child could be using a very different intellectual process for engaging in the activities in each of these three different settings.

In summary, my experience with children has led me to consider the possibility that they can change the way in which they perceive and act in different situations and that we should consider it natural for them to manifest a wide range of variability in their behavioral repertoire. It seems quite reasonable that children should act with impulse in one situation and with studied reflection in another; that they may be tentative in addressing a task today and very confident at the same task tomorrow. Furthermore, I suggest that such behavioral variability is the result of the convergence of such powerful factors as the demands of the behavior setting, the experience the child brings to the situation, volition (or control from within), and intellect. This shift in *type* of behavior can be illustrated in the following few paragraphs.

A four-year-old was engaged in painting at an easel. He was intensely involved, so much so that he appeared to be oblivious of the activity of other children, including a very noisy episode of creative play taking place in a corner of the room. In fact, he seemed not to notice the painting behavior of a peer engaged on the opposite side of the easel.

As the child worked on his painting, his behavior was calculated and particularly purposeful. His brush strokes were a study in slow motion. He seemed to weigh carefully decisions about what color to use and where. His strokes were measured; he seemed to have a need to get everything right, adding color and texture with care and patience. In fact, the child demonstrated considerable ease in taking his time.

At a moment which can only be judged appropriate by the child, he quickly and with resolve decided that he had finished the painting. His eyes swept over the paper; he replaced the last brush and turned to find an adult, after which he asked her to "hang it up," announcing, "I'm done."

He hung up his smock, surveyed the room, and after a moment raced to join the three very noisy children involved in creative play. The three had begun an imaginary episode of family play in which there were portrayals of mother, father, and child. There was considerable good-natured bickering and negotiating, not to mention shifting of roles. It was during one such negotiation that our subject entered the setting.

Immediately upon entering, he began to assert his presumed leadership by assuming the role of father, assigning tasks to the children (to set the dinner table and pour glasses of milk), and announcing what it was they would all eat for dinner. He very clearly entered the activity with ideas about how the play should proceed and without the slightest hesitation in making his suggestions known. He was impetuous and assertive, even bossy. The three children accepted his entry into the activity but not without a small amount of stormy interchange. The original "father" did not simply agree to the subordinate role of son nor did the "mother" easily defer to the judgment of our subject regarding the composition of the meal. But, accommodations were made, and the group, newly constituted, did remain at the task.

Our subject became increasingly assertive and demonstrative as the activity progressed. He bossed his "children" at the meal and made great demands on his "wife," who was doing her utmost to maintain a strong maternal image. The group was not upset by the child's entry, rather, he seemed to bring a bit of life to a rather commonplace activity.

After some time at creative play our friend announced that dinner was over and he was leaving to watch TV. He got up from his chair and left the group. All of this was done without fanfare but with an apparent attempt on his part to close his participation in the activity. He wandered for a while from area to area without engaging anyone in conversation, asking a question, or making a comment.

In less than two minutes our friend had chosen to enter the quiet-space-book-reading corner located in the most remote and visibly isolated *corner of the room. This was a very small area, in which were placed a crib mattress and two small pillows, a handful of children's books, and a cotton blanket. The space was very much like the reading area described in chapter 6 and was large enough for about three or four children at any time. No other children were in this area when our subject entered.*

His behavior in the quiet corner was very different from that at the easel or in the creative play activity. He did not select a book; in fact, he didn't even handle any. Rather, he lay down on the mattress with his head on a pillow, crossed one leg over the other, and stretched his arms over his head. He didn't close his eyes, feign sleep, wrap himself in the blanket, or present any symptoms of distress. If we may speculate, it appeared that he wanted nothing more than to be alone for a few minutes—a kind of behavior not at all uncommon in preschool settings.

In this account of one child's brief activity, we can identify three very different types of behavior. In the first behavior setting (the easel), the child was very cautious, reflective, and attentive to the detail of his painting. He was painstakingly careful in how he proceeded; his attention seemed to converge on the painting. He said nothing to anyone while he worked at the easel and was not at all distracted by other events in the classroom. He didn't appear to need any social sanction for his work and, in fact, consulted an adult only when it was time to hang up the painting after it had been completed. He seemed to be quite intent on finishing the painting to his own satisfaction and was content to stay with the task until that had been achieved. In this situation, the child was autonomous and quite obviously directed by his own image of what it was he should paint. One can imagine that this child was so resolute in this task and involved with the painting that he could have completed it regardless of the distractions about him. It is important to note that, in asking the teacher to hang up the paper, he announced that the task had been finished; this may have been a statement of confirmation to himself more than to anyone else.

The type of interaction the child had with the painting was abruptly changed when he began his adventure with the children in creative play. The child enthusiastically and with determination forced his way into an active group of children who had selected a theme and assigned roles to one another. He did not reflect on what was taking place, he did not inquire what the theme of their play was, nor did he ask if he might join. On the contrary, he was very assertive in moving into the group and in assuming a leadership role. Without apparent caution or thought beforehand he engaged in a direct confrontation with the three children over role and theme, and he had his way. It seems important to point out, too, that the behavior of the child in this setting was both appropriate and nondestructive; the group coalesced around his presence and moved ahead in their play.

As quickly and as determinedly as our subject entered the dramatic play group, he left. There was no obvious reflection on what had occurred; there wasn't any standing back and asking if the play was over. Rather, he signaled his closing participation by announcing that he was leaving to watch television. Impulsively he entered; impulsively he left.

This child entered each activity with an apparent difference in purpose and in style of behavior. Obviously, this can only by inferred from the observation, but the wide discrepancy in his conduct in each activity, the commitment to completing the task, and his behavior during each activity very strongly suggests a difference in cognitive style and personality. He was reflective, then impulsive; focused on the features of his painting and concerned with shaping the global character of creative play; tediously cautious in selecting color and executing his design and flamboyantly quick in prescribing role and function in "house" play. In the more traditional language of the cognitive psychologist we can say he was first a convergent thinker and then divergent in his style.

Only two of the three behavior settings have been analyzed. How should we describe this child's behavior in the book corner? Should we describe him as reclusive? Could one find reason in his behavior in this setting to suspect childhood depression? Or might we say that he was simply withdrawing from most of the stimuli of the program for a few moments of psychological respite after two quite demanding experiences? Might we also suggest that he chose the book corner as a place where he might think about issues, matters, questions raised in his mind as a consequence of one or both of the previous activities? Whatever the explanation might be (and I would not accept any inference of emotional stress from this behavior), the child in this quiet spot was behaving in a way very different from either of the two previous settings. Here he could be described as contemplative, resting, or engaging in some form of synthesis. The relatively few behavior clues make characterizations of this kind highly speculative unless, of course, we were to ask him what he was doing there and why he chose to lie down when he did.

The point in this rather elaborate description and analysis of the child's behavior is to support the contention that children will *vary the style with which they behave from setting to setting and will almost always demonstrate a style which is congruent with the area and activity*. It should be emphasized that these style changes constitute *shifts in modality* and are not mere variations in trait. Our child in this illustration demonstrated both convergent and divergent thought at different times and in relation to specific activities. The child was perceiving and acting on aspects of his preschool environment in very different ways.

Personality Characteristics and Behavior Settings

The idea that a child's ways of responding to any situation may vary from moment to moment is generally not accepted by personality theorists. It is more common to think of personality as a set of stable characteristics, most frequently referred to as types or traits which direct our responses to all we experience. Personality type is presumed to be so well integrated into our being that it would be impossible not to be directed by its influence. As a consequence, we refer to one another as being introverted or extroverted, pleasant or unpleasant, emotional or rational, for example, as though such labels should serve as a reliable guide for anticipating reactions to every situation. Thus it is, for example, that those thought to be introverts will be expected to control their emotions, to prefer working alone, and to enjoy the challenge of solitary work or activity over that of public performance. We have also come to think of the introvert as the shy person who appears to be uncomfortable with social contact and who would just as soon avoid situations where considerable interaction with others is the norm.

There is a long history of the study and identification of personality types, beginning with the Greek Hippocrates (500 B.C.), who proposed at least two physical types, each of which was suceptible to different kinds of disease. About 700 years later another Greek, Galen, identified four major classes of temperament—sanguine, choleric, phlegmatic, and melancholic—which were assumed to describe both personality and physique. This tradition of typing continues to the present moment and can often be observed being practiced by teachers and child-care providers when, for example, they categorize children as being hyperactive, passive, verbal, and aggressive and act as though such characterizations were a summary of all the child is.

For at least 30 years and very likely much longer, some students of human behavior have taken exception to the practice of assigning one personality type to each person. These researchers have suggested that great variability exists within each of us in the ways in which we respond to situations, even those which are very similar. Rather than describe a person as an introvert or extrovert (one who tends always to be introverted or extroverted), these students claim that it would be more accurate to identify types of behavior in particular situations at precise moments in time. Following this logic, I may be described as introverted at cocktail parties (where I usually feel very uncomfortable) and extroverted in my classes and seminars (where I feel both self-assured and responsible for maintaining the tempo and pace of the activity). Also, I could describe times during this writing when I felt quite unsure of myself and other times when I was quite confident that the task was not beyond my reach. These recollections illustrate this alternative conception of personality. Other more compelling examples can be cited.

Some time ago L. S. Cattrell (1942) asked one of his university classes to listen to the description of child behaviors in two different settings and to characterize and describe the personality of the child in each location. One description was taken in the child's home where he was uncooperative, given to sulking, and quite often a bully. The second description was of a child at school who spent considerable time daydreaming, who was timid and often bullied by his schoolmates. Cattrell's students described the first child as aggressive, hostile, and stubborn. The second child was rated very low on these traits. The students were somewhat chagrined to discover that the observations were of the same child. For reasons about which we may speculate, this child demonstrated two very different personality types, depending on which setting he was in.

Recently, evidence has been presented which, though less spectacular and less conjectural than this, nonetheless brings to our attention the likelihood that a "normal" personality is made up of an array of behavioral modes, each of which will come forth only in relation to particular environmental settings. I should like to review very briefly some of this evidence in relation to two factors: the *naturalness* of varied personality response; and the relationship of *time* to behavior, especially in similar kinds of settings.

Variation in Behavior

As was pointed out earlier, the basis of support for most trait or type personality theories is the presumption of a consistency of behavioral response across all behavior settings but particularly in those which are similar in form and content. For example, if we are introverted at one cocktail party, it is rather assumed that we will be introverted at all cocktail parties and in other social settings. The evidence in support of such an assumption comes from correlational studies in which comparisons are made of individual's behavior in similar settings marked by a lapse in time. To characterize someone as an introvert, we study their behavior in several similar kinds of social settings (at cocktail parties, wedding receptions, and church dinners, for example,) and judge through the use of statistical procedures the degree to which they had responded in the same way to each setting. These types of correlational studies have not produced overwhemingly convincing data (agreement around +.30 average), but the explanation for low correlations has been most frequently attributed to difficulties in the research methodology rather than to the inconsistency in persons' behavior (Bem and Allen, 1974).

Bem and Allen review a number of studies from 1928 on, which demonstrate that traditional personality studies achieve such low correlations not because of a methodological problems but because of true behavior variation. They cite the classical studies of moral character by Hartshorne and May (1982 & 1929), in which they were unable to demonstrate consistency in this characteristic across different situations and thus concluded that such a thing as a moral trait—something which would direct behavior in most situations—may be nothing more than habit. Bem and Allen also drew on Theodore Newcomb's (1929) creative studies of extroversion-introversion in which he found only slight trait consistency from one situation to another.

In yet another study of the punctuality of college students, Bem and Allen cite the 1936 study by Dudycha which revealed that 300 students observed were apt to be very prompt in some situations and not at all reliable in others. Furthermore, it was difficult to determine the kinds of settings in which punctuality would or would not be observed by the students. Their behavior seemed best described as situationally specific.

The frequency with which studies of personality characteristics produce low correlations between similar situations and such valued traits as moral character and conscientiousness seems to suggest that the individual personality is quite naturally variable; it is stable only in the sense that it can and likely will change from situation to similar situation.

Time and Behavior

Teachers of young children and their parents seem to have always known that behavior is affected by time. Obviously, young children become fatigued sooner than older children and adults; furthermore, they very likely will need periods of rest if they are to maintain their attention to an extended nursery or day care program. We rather matter-of-factly accept a time-behavior interaction for children but attribute this primarily to their continuing need for greater amounts of rest and sleep; we don't often act as though time were of equal importance in influencing the behavior of older children and adults. But is this so?

H. L. Raush and his colleagues (Raush, et al., 1959) studied the social behavior of a group of hyperactive boys in a clinical setting and discovered among other things that an individual's relationships with others in the same type of situation might be quite different depending on the time of day. Specifically, they found that the boys treated each other differently at breakfast than at lunch or dinner. Though there was a behavior difference from one day to the next for each of the meals, there was greater variability from meal time to meal time on a single day. Rausch, too, found a relationship between the boy's social behavior and situation, but the greatest variation was observed when time of day was included among the variables.

Alternative Behavior Modes

The argument made in the preceding section regarding the context-related nature of human behavior should not be understood to imply that teachers cannot anticipate the kinds of behavior children might exhibit. It would be difficult in the extreme if humans behaved in such an idiosyncratic way that we could never predict what their reactions to any situation might be. The idea that personality-type and -trait theories are weak means that we should type characterize anyone with considerable caution. To use the example cited earlier, a child may manifest convergent cognitive characteristics in one setting and divergent traits in the very next situation. To label the child as either a convergent or divergent thinker and thus to raise particular expectations about how he/she would perform in every setting would be a mistake. Rather, it seems far better to consider the likelihood that any child may quite naturally demonstrate a rather wide range of behavior modes over the course of a program day, each mode being consonant with the activity in which the child is engaged. The child at the easel in the earlier example was quite reflective and analytic, a very appropriate behavior for that activity; he was just as appropriately impulsive and forceful in the creative play activity. We could also imagine that this same child might behave in a very different way in each of these settings at some time in the future. He might try to incorporate pieces of sponge and cloth or leaves and twigs in his painting in an attempt to create a texture and dimension quite different from the usual two dimensional painting. Were this to occur, it might be more appropriate to characterize his behavior as divergent, moving beyond the normal response in an attempt to reach for something new and different.

It seems quite reasonable to use the language we have created in describing personality types as we discuss the behavior of children in early education settings. The vocabulary of personality and intellect is now so extensive that it seems unlikely that a new lexicon would be an improvement. So we should feel unconstrained in describing behavior as, for example, submissive or dominant, introverted or extroverted, just so long as we remember to restrict the use of such terms to specific times and situations and to be very cautious in using them to characterize the person.

Table 7.1	**Examples of Social and Cognitive Behaviors in Early Education Settings**

Focused (task involved)	Uninvolved (wandering)
Gregarious (verbal)	Reserved (nonverbal)
Curious (questioning)	Uninterested (uninvolved)
Social (engaged with others)	Aloof (rejecting social advances)
Persistent (staying with an activity)	Irresolute (easily discouraged)
Active (interacting with the events)	Passive (allowing events to happen)
Enthusiastic (keenly interested)	Lethargic (indifferent)
Cooperative (allowing others to participate)	Noncooperative (selfishly directive)

On the basis of this discussion it seems reasonable to suggest that children in early education settings can be expected to behave in a variety of ways, some of which may be more highly valued than others. A range of social and cognitive behaviors often seen among young children is presented in Table 7.1.

It is not uncommon to think of behaviors such as those listed in Table 7.1 in terms of absolute categories. That is, we are likely to describe a child as being either focused or uninvolved, as though one were always fully involved or totally uninvolved. There is a tendency to act as though calling someone focused, for example, describes the type of behavior so adequately that we should not also need to characterize them as being active, or aloof. We rarely mix categories of behavior when describing someone, nor do we tend to qualify our description in terms of these characteristics.

Such practice seems quite consonant with traditional personality theory but does not reflect the reality of children's behavior. It is not unusual to observe a child in the block area being *focused* on his/her task, being *persistent* in solving construction problems, being *enthusiastic*, and being *aloof* and *noncooperative* by rejecting other children and by hoarding the blocks. As in the example cited earlier, we might expect that a child could leave block-building to enter another activity and become *cooperative*, *socially* engaged, and very *active* in maintaining the integrity of the group and the activity. It seems not at all unreasonable for teachers and parents to expect that their children will exhibit many of these behaviors in any extended time frame and to do so quite naturally.

Behavior Mode and Behavior Setting

In Chapter 6 the point was made that a behavior setting can effectively coerce the behavior of those in that setting. In fact, much was made of Barker's conception of standing patterns of behavior, a concept which assumes a prescribed set of behaviors for every setting. The relationship of behavior to the post office setting was described in a way suggesting that if a person were to rush ahead of other patrons he/she would be reprimanded by the patrons and the postal clerks. Where, then, do these ideas regarding the demonstration of alternative behaviors and behavior-setting theory intersect, and what might such an intersection imply for teachers of young children?

It would appear that at the very least there are three important ways in which behavior-setting theory and behavior variability are interrelated. First, a behavior setting has coercive power over our behavior in direct proportion to the clarity of the setting. (Recall the four principles of a behavior setting described in Chapter 6.) That is, if the physical arrangement, materials available, and the time in which access is possible are relatively unambiguous, the expectations for our behavior will probably be clearly communicated. Recall, if you will, the example used in Chapter 6 of the nursery school located in the community recreation auditorium and the difficulty the staff had in getting the children to "behave" as the staff had imagined they should. Walter Mischel's (1968) study of personality characteristics revealed that relative stability in behavior from one situation to a similar situation occurs when the stimuli remain very much the same. Mischel found that behavior does vary from situation to situation and that one cannot use traits or styles as valid characterizations of a uniform personality; yet he does say that there is a far greater chance for "style" to remain stable when the milieu and its requirements remain constant. This relationship can be observed quite readily in most early education programs when children are observed looking at books in the book corner, painting at the easel, and engaging in dramatic play in the housekeeping area.

A second way in which behavior setting and variability are interrelated is seen in Barker's comments about standing patterns of behavior. Each behavior setting or activity/area segment should have reasons for being which are often stated in ways which describe children's behavior. For example, a statement of the purpose of a table-games area might include the following: children engaged in solitary task completion; children selecting games, puzzles, or other tasks; children engaged with other children and adults in playing a table game or completing a puzzle. The purposes very often delimit the standing patterns of behavior for each activity/area, as these examples would suggest. And, each area usually provides for alternative standing patterns of behavior. The examples given here allow for individual choice—performing a task alone, being engaged with other children, with adults, or with adults and children. There are choices to be made within any behavior setting although the range of options must be restricted by the nature and purpose of that setting.

For teachers taking into consideration the relationship of intra-individual differences and behavior setting theory, it is most important to design programs in ways which will give each child choices for alternative behaviors. Very simply, a nursery school or first grade should have a range of activities and areas so that children can be actively curious and passively responsive, socially engaged and privately occupied, creatively imaginative and carefully directed. Furthermore, there is an implicit assumption in this discussion that children should have considerable autonomy in choosing their activities. Most programs do offer children a variety of activities. It is very common to find blocks, paints, books, dress-up clothes, science areas, table activities, outdoor recreation areas, and group experiences ranging from teacher-directed instruction to morning meetings and games. This is not to suggest that variety in any ECE program is something new. Rather, I am proposing that each activity and area in the program be carefully selected so that children can find support in the behavior setting for the range of behaviors they will want to express. I should like to illustrate this point with two examples.

Sometime ago a colleague began a Montessori school for preschool-aged children. She received the traditional Montessori teacher training and carefully selected the materials that would be a part of the curriculum. The didactic materials such as the cylinder blocks, the pink tower, the brown stair and the red rods, the sand paper letters, the buckle and button frames were all purchased and arranged very carefully in ways consonant with Montessori's teachings and her philosophy of child development.

When school began, the physical environment was arranged so that the sensorial materials were grouped in one section, the practical life materials were located in a few key areas, and the "academic" materials were placed in the mathematics section and language area. The staff was very careful in making sure that the physical setting and the presentation of material defined the standing patterns of behavior for each activity. Furthermore, they were quite precise in their instructions to the children regarding the ways in which the materials were to be used and cared for. Children were taught to select an activity (material), take it to a table or floor mat, perform the tasks for which the material had been designed, and when finished, return the material to its proper place.

The children were encouraged to work mainly by themselves and occasionally in groups of two or three. They were encouraged to be autonomous, to complete their tasks without instruction or guidance by the teacher. Teachers observed the children's behavior, and commented from time to time; occasionally they would offer assistance to a child who was having considerable difficulty in selecting appropriate materials or in completing a task. By and large, however, the predominant mode for children's behavior was child-material interaction—self-directed, convergent activity to be conducted in a quiet atmosphere where voices and movement were self-controlled.

There is no question that the physical setting, the materials selected and presented to the children, and the teacher's behavior combined to establish particular behavior expectations in that classroom. There was little evident confusion expressed by the children regarding what was expected of them. By the same token, it was obvious to the staff that the "Montessori" type behaviors, though developmentally appropriate, represented an incomplete accounting of the ways in which children could naturally and productively behave. As a consequence, three areas were added, which are not commonly thought to be a part of the Montessori program. First, four single easels were arranged in one section of the school, where paints, brushes, and papers were always available. Children were instructed to paint after having gotten a smock and to clean their hands in the area before leaving for another activity. Beyond these few maintenance activities children were free to follow their creative imaginations as they would.

A second area was located in a room adjacent to that in which the majority of activities occurred. In this room children were instructed in creative movement and modern dance techniques. They were led to discover what they could about expressing themselves in movement and controling their bodies but in a creative, noncoercive way. Children were also allowed to bounce on a miniature trampoline, to engage one another in creative play with unit blocks, and occasionally to enjoy a circle game with other children.

Montessorians are often thought to be rigid disciplinarians who clearly differentiate children's imaginative play from the task of developing intellectual competence. Activities like those described for this special room would not usually be included in Montessori programs. Yet the staff in this school were convinced that it was quite necessary to have these activities for the reasons identified in this chapter: they supported natural behavior—things preschool-aged children choose to do and which seem to be a part of development.

The third area added to this Montessori school was a small climbing area and playground out-of-doors. A wooden structure was built which supported children's climbing, sliding, jumping, creative play, and group activity. This was not an elaborate structure and was used only in ways the children themselves found useful. Yet it too provoked and supported kinds of behavior quite unlike those commonly associated with children in a Montessori program.

The significance of this illustration is that one can carefully and wisely design a Montessori program in which children can easily and readily meet the behavioral expectations of a Montessori curriculum and at the same time include activities and areas which would provoke and support a wide range of natural and growth-producing behavior. The teacher in this school was quite confident that it was necessary to create these three additional areas because each represented a type of behavior not supported or encouraged in the other settings but nonetheless important when one considers child development in the larger context.

The next example is far less dramatic than the one just described but somewhat more precise in its illustration of the third factor, the need for a variety of behavior settings.

A three year old child is observed engaged by herself in an activity involving a doll house and family dolls. She is alone in this area which is partitioned off from the main program area. No other children or teachers are in this isolated section at the time of the observation.

The child observed is quite involved in moving the dolls—mother, father and three child dolls—from place to place in the doll house. The dolls are made of a rubberlike material which allows them to be bent into different shapes. They can stand, sit, bend, and the like. Our friend changes their shapes as she moves them from place to place and in and out of the house. She is very intent on her activity and quite silent; she doesn't utter a sound all the while she is there and does not look up at the observer or even glance in the direction of the activity occurring in the next room.

As the child continues with her task, a teacher announces that she is getting ready to read a story to all who care to listen. Those interested are to finish their work and join her on the rug. Our subject seems not to have heard, though she could have, and proceeds in her solitary play. Meanwhile children begin to move to the rug area and prepare for the story. Once again the teacher announces that the reading is about to begin.

With this last announcement, this child glances quickly toward the rug and proceeds to lay each doll on its back in a separate room in the doll house. She carefully bends all limbs straight and places each doll with its head inward in the house. Once having completed this, she looks in at each doll, moves one very slightly, looks over the whole lot again, stands up, closes the roof, again looks in the house, and then turns away and runs to the rug.

Once on the rug she bounces onto the lap of an adult who is also going to listen to the story. No sooner is she seated than she begins to ask questions about the story: What is the book? Is it a new story? She is one of the last children to become settled down, quiet and ready to listen. She never leaves her friend's lap.

Before long, questions and comments are coming from the group. The child is asking questions and listening to other children. She is very much a contributing, productive member of this group activity, observing, listening, commenting, questioning, and supporting the activity in an animated way. Without question, this child has shifted her behavior mode in a very significant way as she moved from the doll house to the rug.

In each of these two very different early education classrooms there was an obvious effort by the staff to create behavior settings which would provoke and support a range of different kinds of behavior. The staff of the Montessori school was concerned that a standard Montessori curriculum would be insufficient in meeting the developmental demands of the preschool-aged children. They fully accepted Montessori's belief in the importance of intellectual development and supported this through a methodology in which the child worked independently with carefully selected teaching materials. They were also quite sure that the child's social, large muscle, and sensory development, as well as creative expression, needed to be supported and thus established the painting area, the movement room, and the outdoor climber. In the second example the teachers had designed a program which supported both group and solitary activities, which provided children many opportunities for self-directed manipulative/creative engagement and for adult directed/instructional experiences.

It should be obvious that teachers in each of these very different programs shared some assumptions about the nature of children's behavior and the relationship of this behavior to development. Each program staff accepted the belief that children will at times use different strategies for engaging with each other and the materials in their early education environment. At one moment they will consider aspects of their world as they are presented by someone else; they will quite comfortably accept the teacher's instruction, as well as the comments and observations of other children. At another time a child may choose to become engaged in a much more isolated and restricted way, experimenting, testing, observing effects of action in a very private way. The teachers structured their settings to support these different kinds of behaviors. It was apparent, too, that the teachers considered the children's use of alternative interaction strategies as both natural and developmentally appropriate. Finally, it was clear that children were supported in choosing where and how they would like to become engaged. Both programs relied on the children's competence in selecting areas and activities for their involvement. In the second example the responsibility for deciding what to do was left to the children most of the time, even when a story was to be read. Children chose to join the group, but they might not have, and that is a most important point.

Needless to say, the providing of a variety of behavior settings and the freedom for children to decide where they shall become engaged must be limited by the requirements of the program and the purposes of the school. It seems quite unreasonable to expect each primary or preschool to have the same number of activities and areas as every other school. Such important things as philosophy, curricular model, the financial status of the program, and physical setting are only some of the factors which might preclude this from occurring. Furthermore, it is unrealistic to anticipate that first- and second-grade children would have as much time for choosing their activities as would preschoolers or even kindergarten children. The rather universal requirement that six- and seven-year-olds begin the process of becoming literate and mathematically competent means that they would have to complete tasks at the direction of teachers. Yet, though primary school children may have more constraints on their choice of activity than preschool children, there is just as much need to provide for a variety of behaviors. Children who are six and seven will want and need to follow alternative behavior modes as much as young children and may require even more opportunity to be autonomous in deciding what and how they shall become engaged.

Program Support for Behavior Variability

Two major points have been presented thus far in this chapter. First, children's behavior is quite naturally varied from moment to moment and situation to situation, and this variability reflects intellectual and emotional shifts in the ways in which they become engaged in any situation. Second, behavior settings can provoke or constrain behavior; they can encourage engagement or inhibit interaction. Children will choose to enter any setting because of the opportunities it provides for behaving in particular ways. These assertions are quite different from the more commonplace concepts of intellectual and personality characteristics. We are more apt to believe that variability exists between individuals, that some of us are impulsive and others of us reflective; that some of us are emotionally stable and others unstable, that these characteristics remain quite constant across situations and endure over time.

The implications for early childhood education to be drawn from these traditional assumptions regarding human personality are very different. The view that behavior is differentiated but stable from person to person is best reflected in the educational literature in which individualization of instruction is discussed. The advocates of individualized instruction call for the creation of varied instructional programs so that each child may use his/her cognitive style and personality to the fullest advantage. In the recent past, considerable research attention has been given to identifying the aptitudes of students and placing them in instructional settings which make the most of these abilities. For example, we may come to believe that a certain student learns best when given step-by-step instruction by a teacher or through the use of programmed instructional material, i.e., a programmed text or teaching machine. Other students might learn best when instruction is organized around broad themes or concepts and when teachers instruct less directly and engage the students in discussion and analysis.

The teaching strategies developed from such research continue to attract much attention. Individualized instructional procedures are compelling because of the impressive results often found. However, there is at least one difficulty in the work, and that is the assumption that once a child's learning mode has been identified, all instruction in all educational situations should correspond to that behavioral pattern. The idea that alternative learning modes may exist within each person seems not to have been considered as an important probability. It is possible, as suggested by Mischel (1968, p. 20), that cognitive style may appear to be a stable characteristic because the situations in which the investigations are made remain very much the same. One implication of Mischel's conclusion is that if the search for cognitive style were broadened to include a variety of situations, the results of the investigations might suggest that persons have multiple ways of learning.

If, on the other hand, it is assumed that behavior can vary naturally from situation to situation, that we can employ one intellectual strategy now and another quite different later on, the approach to the identification and organization of instructional settings could be quite different, too. Furthermore, if the shifts in behavior were thought to be the result of a psychological process in which each person's experience, will (volition), and the perceived demands of the behavior setting interacted in producing the behavior, then it would seem necessary that teachers consider this relationship when organizing their programs. One way in which this can be accomplished is by having teachers make sure that their classrooms provide for and support alternative interaction patterns. Children should be able to engage one another, their teachers, and the curriculum materials and activities in a variety of different but productive ways without fear of disapproval. I should like to present and discuss three categories of person-environment interaction which, considered together, would probably help implement this principle. The categories are:

1. Social contact: Children will vary in their interaction with others from isolate behavior to participation in total group activity.
2. Type of Direction: At times children will direct their own behavior; at other times they may be engaged in parallel, cooperative, or teacher-directed activity.

3. Modes of Learning: Children will strive to master tasks and acquire particular knowledge. They will also be curious, seek appreciation, or become engaged in solving a problem.

The remainder of this chapter will be devoted to discussion and illustration of these three categories of interaction and their implications for early education practitioners.

Social Contact

Every program must consider the provisions made for various kinds of social contact in the selection and organization of activities and areas. Naturally, the purposes of the early childhood program, the developmental goals and the curriculum model chosen by those directing the program will largely determine the particular kinds of activities and areas. For example, a Montessori classroom is usually recognizable by the selection and organization of the materials, the rather large number of single-person tables, and the careful division of curriculum areas. By the same token, it is just as easy to recognize a primary school program patterned after the English Infant School model: In such a classroom one would probably find an area in which children could manipulate materials used to discover mathematics concepts and principles, another called the reading/literature area, a science corner in which items reflecting a particular theme would be displayed; tables and chairs would be arranged around the areas in a way which would support both individual and cooperative activity. Though the organization of the environment and the selection of materials for these alternative models of early education would reflect differences in goals and beliefs regarding development, both would need to make sure that provisions had been made for the support of alternative social contact modes.

I have identified four social contact modes which support the concept of intra-individual differences and should, therefore, be considered in designing every ECE program. They include *isolated* behavior (a mode without social contact), contact with *one other person*, social interaction with a *small group*, and participation in *total group activities*. Observing children's social interaction in both preschool and primary settings suggests that these are the most common contact arrangements, with isolated behavior and one-person contact being far and away the most predominant modes. From time to time a child may be engaged in an activity with more than six or seven children and less than the whole class, but only rarely does this occur. It does appear that children, given the freedom to choose activities and contact modes, will often choose to become engaged with one or two other children, or to work alone.

Clearly, the frequency of isolated and/or total group activity will be a function of the type of early education program. If we can return to the example cited above, we could expect children in the Montessori program to work largely alone. A major tenet of Montessori philosophy and teaching strategy is that children will learn best through the process of manipulating the specially designed materials *by themselves*, without the assistance of adults or other children. Though the English model stresses engagement with materials as much as does Montessori, there is more emphasis placed on discovery and collaboration. Hence, in an English Infant School one could anticipate observing *much* isolated activity but also a considerable amount of cooperative activity between children and with adults.

Total group interaction might be the most common contact mode in early education settings in which socialization and enculturation goals were stressed. (Recall the discussion of the program implications of human development theory in Chapter 5.) In such programs freedom for children to choose their activities would be sharply reduced and the degree of adult direction of activity would be correspondingly increased. By the same token, the range of intra-individual variation would quite likely be reduced as well. If children are organized for instruction and led from activity to activity, obviously their chances for making decisions about where they will be will be reduced; they may find it difficult to express the full range of social and intellectual behavior. This may or may not present a problem in managing a program. Children may find it difficult to have their behavior so significantly restricted by teachers and the curriculum structure and may act in disruptive ways. On the other hand, they may acquiesce in the demands of the situation and follow the teacher with interest and enthusiasm. Whatever the children's behavior might be, it should be remembered that the organization of the classroom, nursery, or day-care center will affect the predominant type of social contact mode to be found and may, in turn, tend to restrict each child's expression of a wider range of behaviors.

Regardless of the kind of curriculum followed in any ECE program, provision should be made for children to be alone, to be engaged with one other person, a small group, or the total class. To a large extent, the kinds of activities and/or areas included in the program will determine how well such provisions have been made. I should like to illustrate this with two examples (Tables 7.2 and 7.3), one taken from preschool settings and the other reflecting the character of grades one to three. A range of fairly common activities will be presented which reflect both the preschool and primary grades. I will note how well each might support the four social contact modes. It should be pointed out that the activities in each example reflect the kind of program that would be built on an transactionist conception of human development and, more particularly, on the philosophy of John Dewey and the practices of many contemporary early childhood programs in the United States. It should be clear that the activities are not intended in anyway to represent a Montessori classroom nor would many of them be usefully included in a teacher-dominated setting of any kind.[1]

The relationship of activities to social-contact possibilities is represented in the two tables which follow. The first table considers preschool and kindergarten activities. The activities areas were taken from a combined list of areas in nine preschool programs.[2] I have selected the 16 most frequently listed activities or areas and indicated when each

---

[1] I would include programs based on a behaviorist conception of development as well as more traditional educational practices in this group. In both cases, children are much more likely to be given fewer activities and of quite a different kind. See Evans (1975) for a description of both traditional programs and those based on behavioral analysis.

[2] Members of the In-Service, Early Childhood Education, M. Ed. Program at the University of Massachusetts.

supported one or more of the social contact modes. Before discussing Table 7.2 I should like to comment briefly on the process by which the activities were identified and also on the degree to which a child would be assertive or reticent in each contact situation.

It would seem that each child could enter into any of the four social contact modes with more or less enthusiasm, with a desire to be very actively engaged or only moderately so. For example, a child may choose to be alone in the book corner because he/she is intent on studying the pictures in *Make Way For Ducklings*, or the child may be there because he/she wants to avoid any social contact and so picks up the book only as a hedge against being disturbed. The child may look at the pictures but without any real engagement. In another situation, one involving a small group of children, a child may be very assertive and strive to lead the group, as in the example cited earlier when the boy left the easel and joined the creative play activity. It is possible, too, that the child may choose to join the group but be entirely content in following the directions of others. He/she would be much less active in directing the affairs of the activity but contribute just the same to the maintenance of the structure. In brief, the child can be more or less active in any social contact setting and each type of behavior must be considered as appropriate and acceptable. As one might suspect, too, a child may at one time be reticent and later be very active in the same or a different activity. The provision for considering a *more or less active* involvement has been included in the Tables as the A and N columns. Needless to say, such a characterization is not precise, but this is relatively unimportant; the intent, after all, is not to describe two particular types of behavior but rather to bring to the reader's attention that social engagement will be colored by the intentions and needs of each child.

The 16 activities/areas were taken from nine preschool programs, as indicated earlier. Members of the staff of each of the nine programs were asked to list all of the curriculum areas in their program. (A curriculum area was defined as a place where children could become engaged in a significant activity.) It is interesting to note that a total of 30 areas were identified, ranging from a trampoline used in one program with handicapped children to a stage constructed especially to stimulate dramatic play in another. Each of the 16 items selected for use here was included in at least two of the program lists. It might be of interest to note, however, that unit blocks, an art area, book corner, and table games were found in all programs. A housekeeping or creative play area was included in all but one program. The number of areas ranged from a low of 9 to a high of 16 but most had either 9 or 10 activity areas. It can be said that each of these preschools was designed in ways consonant with a transactionist position; the major purpose of each program was to promote and sustain development, and it was assumed that this could best be achieved by encouraging the children to become engaged with materials and one another on their own terms.

If there is a point in all of this it is that the selection of the curricular activities, those events which are supposed to make things happen for the children, can be as varied as the people who staff the programs. For example, it may be less important to have a climbing frame in every program (only two had such an area) than to have considered

Table 7.2   Social Contact In Representative Preschool/Kindergarten Activities/Areas

Social Contact Mode	Isolated		With one other		Small group		Total group	
Activity/Area	A[a]	N	A	N	A	N	A	N
Science	✓	✓	✓	✓	✓	✓	✓	✓
Sand Table	✓		✓					
Water Table	✓		✓					
Cooking			✓	✓	✓			
Table games[b]	✓	✓	✓	✓	✓	✓		
Language Experiences			✓		✓		✓	
Circle/Meeting/Rug					✓		✓	✓
Creative Play[c]	✓		✓		✓	✓		
Climbing Frame	✓		✓		✓			
Snack/Lunch			✓	✓	✓	✓	✓	✓
Art (Easels, tables)	✓		✓		✓		✓	
Unit Blocks	✓		✓		✓			
Book Corner (Reading)	✓	✓	✓	✓	✓	✓		
Woodworking	✓		✓		✓			
Music	✓	✓	✓	✓	✓	✓	✓	✓
Quiet space	✓		✓					

Note. These activities/areas represent the most common among nine preschool programs. Not every program had 16 areas; the norm was closer to 10.

[a] A = active; N = nonactive

[b] The table-games area included manipulative games and other materials, such as puzzles and lotto, which could be completed alone or with someone else.

[c] Creative Play includes the common housekeeping area.

what such equipment would contribute to each child's development and to select from alternative materials those most appropriate for the program. Three brief illustrations should clarify this point. A program director could say that teachers wanted to insure that the four social contact modes were adequately provided for in the program, that it was important for children to choose their activity most of the time, and that special consideration should be given to large muscle development because the children in the program reside in high rise apartment buildings and neither climb stairs nor romp in playgrounds very often. A climber in the classroom might make it possible for teachers in this situation to meet each of these considerations. However, they might be able to avoid using the space in the classroom for a climber if there were a similar structure on the playground and the children were out-of-doors for a considerable period of time *each day.*

A second illustration concerns snack time. Some teachers have a snack time each day in which all of the children eat together. Others have a self-service snack area in which one to four children may help themselves to fruit or vegetables, juice or milk, as they get hungry. Very likely all would agree that it is necessary to provide some nourishment to young children sometime in a three- or four-hour morning program, but there may be wide differences of opinion regarding the use of snack time to promote major program goals. To make the point one last time, it is possible that creative play—role playing, fantasy play, cooperative dramatic play—can be encouraged and sustained just as well without a housekeeping corner as with one. A puppet stage or raised platform with a few carefully selected dress-up hats and jackets might more effectively provide the desired behavior.

Table 7.2 does reflect the ways in which a rather representative assortment of preschool activities might support more or less active social contact modes (alone, with someone else, with a small group, and the total class). As this table is considered, ask if there are a sufficient number of activities for each of the four modes. Only music, art, snack, circle, and language experiences can support a total group mode. Is this sufficient or must more options be made available? Can these activities be modified or altered in a way which provides for different contact possibilities? These questions should be asked with a view to restricting as well as expanding the possibilities for social contact.

Table 7.3 is offered as an illustration of the ways in which activities and curriculum areas of primary grades (one to three) could support each social contact mode. The activities for language development, mathematics, and science are more precisely described here than they were in Table 7.2 (the preschool example) because the kinds of knowledge and skills to be mastered by every child are sharply increased from the moment they enter the first grade. There is an attempt here to reflect this educational reality and at the same time to acknowledge that in most primary settings children are still given many opportunities to choose how they will become engaged in activities. For example, most first graders will begin the process of developing an understanding of at least one arithmetic operation, addition. Often they will be required to complete exercises selected by the teacher and will have little choice about when and how these exercises will be completed. On the other hand, they will still be given considerable opportunity to use the materials in the mathematics area in exploratory ways. For example, one or two children may become engaged in comparing the weight of equal numbers of marbles and washers, of kernels of corn and bean seeds, and a cup of water and a cup of sand. The children may be encouraged to engage in this type of activity in the belief that it will contribute to their understanding of the system of mathematics, their inquiry skills, and their competence in pursuing issues with some autonomy.

It should also be noted that when a child enters the more formal school at first grade, the style of the teachers will very likely change to some degree. As was suggested above, teachers will "teach" or give children particular instruction here more than they would have in kindergarten or nursery school. Direct instruction will, quite obviously, affect the frequency and degree of social contact. However, as the second illustration suggests, there will continue to be time for individuals to make choices about their activities and the kinds of involvement they desire.

Table 7.3   **Social Contact in Representative Primary School Activities/Areas**

Social Contact Mode	Isolated		With one other		Small group		Total group	
Activity/Area	A[a]	N	A	N	A	N	A	N
Language Development								
Literature Corner	✓	✓	✓	✓	✓	✓		
Readers/Reading Instruction	✓		✓		✓	✓	✓	✓
Workbooks	✓		✓		✓		✓	
Writing Exercises	✓		✓		✓		✓	
Mathematics Activity								
Math Area[b]	✓	✓	✓	✓	✓	✓		
Text Materials	✓		✓		✓	✓	✓	✓
Direct Instruction			✓		✓	✓	✓	✓
Tutoring			✓					
Science Activity								
Science Table	✓	✓	✓	✓	✓	✓		
Text Materials	✓		✓		✓	✓	✓	✓
Field Trips			✓	✓	✓	✓	✓	✓
Audio visual Materials	✓	✓	✓	✓	✓	✓	✓	✓
Arts and Crafts								
Painting	✓		✓					
Woodworking	✓		✓		✓			
Other Crafts	✓		✓		✓		✓	
Music								
Listening	✓	✓	✓	✓	✓	✓	✓	✓
Performing	✓	✓	✓	✓	✓	✓	✓	✓

[a] A = active; N = nonactive

[b] The Math Area would include printed and audio visual materials, and manipulative materials such as metric rods, a balance scale, geo-boards, etc.

Type of Direction

The second principle in designing an environment effective in supporting children's behavior preferences states that programs must make provisions for at least four kinds of activity: *self-directed, parallel, cooperative,* and *other-directed*. These four types of activity were derived from observations of children in early education settings, from teacher reports, and from studies of children's play behavior by Parten (1932) and Rubin (1977). I should like to define each as follows: *Self-directed activity* is that in which the child is alone (isolated) and maintains a focus on what he/she is doing without any direction from an adult or other child. A child is engaged in *parallel activity* when he/she is nearby or even in the same activity/area with another child or group of children but not sharing materials or ideas, or exchanging information about the task at hand. Children may be seated at a table sculpting play-dough each with his/her own material and shaping instruments. Each could be respectful of the others' space and material but be working quite independently. *Cooperative activity*, on the other hand, is that in which there is a division of responsibility for maintaining the activity and in which each child contributes to the structure and direction of the activity. *Other-directed* activity is, as the name suggests, that in which the child being observed is directed by an adult or other child. It will be helpful to illustrate each of the four types of activity.

Self-Directed Activity

Self-directed activity can be task related or not, but is always based on the child's decision about what he/she will be doing. We may expect self-directed activity to involve the child's doing something to or with material or playing a solitary game. Certainly these acts constitute the more obvious types of self-directed activity. However, it is just as appropriate to consider a child alone in a private space not doing anything but thinking or dreaming as an example of self-direction. Recall the example given earlier of the child retreating to the book corner for what appeared to be some respite from the other activities of the classroom. The child had purposefully moved to a special place to behave in a very particular way—to be inactive. We should also consider a child's observation of what others are doing without any effort to enter the activity or even to inquire about what the others are doing. There can be at least three ways in which self-directed activity can appear. It can be *task related*, when the child is attempting to complete a task, *isolated* behavior, in which the child removes him/herself from the events of the program for reasons about which we can only speculate, and *observation* behavior, in which the child chooses to watch what others are doing.

Parallel Activity

Parallel activity has been considered a natural behavior among nursery school children at least since Mildred Parten's (1932) study of children's play behavior. She found that 2- to 4½-year-olds spent quite a bit of time working and playing side by side with little contact, either disruptive or cooperative. Her observations indicated that parallel play occupied nearly 50% of the time of 2-year-olds and 30% of that for 4½-year-olds, suggesting that this behavior mode might be linked to social and intellectual development. Rubin (1977) repeated Parten's study with 4- and 5-year-olds. He, too, found parallel play in both groups but less among older and more mature children. In addition, he found a qualitative difference between the older and younger children in their parallel activity. The older children's play seemed to be intellectually more complex and involved a greater amount of construction than did that of the younger children. In his conclusions, Rubin cautioned against assuming that parallel activity disappears as children approach formal school age. Rather, that it would appear to take on newer and more complex meaning (much of it abstract) and to be a very appropriate behavior for children in early education settings.

Both Rubin and Parten found that much of the parallel activity of children involved what Rubin referred to as parallel functional play—the examination of materials, their manipulation, and familiarization with new things. This was rather simple activity but quite necessary because an important part of any transaction must be the process by which children comprehend what they are dealing with. Furthermore, Rubin found that soon after children were involved in this functional (familiarization) period they began to use the materials in creative and fantasy play and for construction.

Observe, too, that parallel activity may be increased by the physical setting itself. C. M. Loo (1973) discovered that groups of six four- and five-year-olds engaged in less interactive play when the physical setting was reduced in size. The groups of six children were first observed playing in an area of 265 square feet or 44 square feet per child (a rather large area for six children; a room 12 × 20 would have 240 square feet, a room 16 × 16 would contain 256 square feet). The area for free play was then reduced to 90 square feet or 15 square feet per child, which substantially altered the children's behavior. There was a significant increase in solitary play in the smaller area and demonstrably less group interaction.

The combined research of Rubin and Parten rather clearly suggests that parallel activity is commonly seen among young children in settings in which they have a choice of behavior. It would seem that children quite naturally, and for important developmental purposes, may decide to be around other children but not always to be engaged with them in any activity. Furthermore, children seem quite capable of playing and working side by side without disrupting each other's activity.

Cooperative Activity

A cooperative activity, is one in which the participants share the responsibility for directing and sustaining action. More frequently than not, a cooperative adventure consists of a group of children engaged in a common activity. At times, however, it may involve adults as well. The composition of the group is not important; the relationship between members is very important. Ideas must be shared, tasks distributed, and the purposes of the activity discussed, with all participants given an opportunity to share in the discussion. Needless to say, cooperative activity among very young children will occur less frequently than among school-aged children primarily because of the intellectual and social maturity necessary to sustain this behavior. Preschool-aged children tend to be more self-centered and have greater difficulty than their older schoolmates in sharing ideas and materials, and accepting compromises regarding the purpose and direction of their behavior. Nonetheless, they can and will engage one another cooperatively if the program, by design and curriculum, indicates that such behavior is valued and expected.

A distinction needs to be made between cooperative activity in which the demands of the task are well prescribed and that which is more open-ended and requires the participants to choose goals, construct a framework for cooperation, and negotiate ways in which participation can be sustained. Some examples of the first type of cooperative activity include games in which children take successive turns and are required to follow rather simple rules for play. Children playing a picture lotto game would be likely to exhibit this type of cooperation. Each child would have a board with nine or twelve pictures on which they would place a replica of each picture as it is presented by a game leader. Children would also cooperate in similar matching games. Participating in a circle game such as "fox-fox-goose", or "London Bridge" could also be an example of a prescribed cooperative activity if the children were not being directed by an adult or other child.

Cooperative activity would also include the creative play which often occurs in the housekeeping area, on the climbing frame, or on the playground. We might imagine three to five children joining together to engage in an imaginary adventure in outer space or a more realistic "family" trip to a restaurant. We might also think of children working together in building with unit blocks or cardboard cartons and large wooden blocks. Another type of rather open-ended cooperative activity might be observed on the playground, when a group of children mount tricycles and play follow the leader.

In cooperative activities like those suggested here, the products of the children's behavior may be more abstract than concrete. The most pronounced activity may be planning, in which they negotiate everything from the characters they will assume to the location of the adventure, the nature and purpose of their activity, and the ways in which it can be sustained over a period of a few days. Recall, if you can, the amount of time you and your friends spent as young children in "organizing" clubs. You might have decided to join together, chosen not to include some other children, "elected" leaders (with everyone having a responsible role), determined where you would meet, and perhaps even decided to collect dues. And then, once the planning had been accomplished, the "club" might have rather quickly expired.

Children will become cooperatively involved with other children and adults if the setting supports such behavior. Though three- and four-year-olds may have great difficulty negotiating with others they nevertheless will join in activities which require them to share responsibility and control some of their demands. By five years of age children not only can negotiate and compromise (some of the time), they will if left alone, create cooperative groups with their peers and sustain such activity over extended periods of time. Therefore, it would seem to be very important that early education settings be organized in a way that would nourish and support both the more directed cooperative activity such as game playing and the open and creative collaboration found in dramatic and creative play and project completion.

Other-Directed Activity

There are three types of other-directed activity appropriate in early education settings. The first involves two persons, one of whom is leading or directing the behavior of the other. In many instances two children may be involved in a task in which one is "instructing" the other. In one such case, a three-year-old taught another child her age how to complete an inlay picture puzzle she had brought to school. Though they were both putting pieces together, the leader showed the other child which pieces needed to be placed in the inlay tray first and explained why. She also told the other child that some pieces needed to be turned so they would fit. It was quite obvious that both children were much involved in the task, but it was just as obvious that one child had absolute control. Teachers, too, will direct children in this same way although they may more likely direct one child as, for example, when they tell the child to return materials, clean up a mess, or to avoid disturbing another child.

A second type of other-directed behavior occurs in a small group of children (more than two but less than ten). A third type occurs in a group also but one with ten or more children. In these situations it is quite usual to have an adult leading and directing the children's behavior. In the small group setting the activity might involve reading a story to four or five children, supervising cookie making by an equal number of children, leading a group on a walk about the neighborhood, or supervising the construction of Halloween masks.

Directing the entire group of children is usually shared by the entire staff in any program. Leading primary school children in an evacuation drill, preparing them for a film, film strip, or a guest are some ways in which the adults could direct all of the children. The common morning exercise seen in both preschool and primary grades is usually a total-group, teacher-led activity; so, too, are some circle games, especially for older children.

It is obvious that directing the behavior of children in early education settings can be productive and is at times both appropriate and necessary. A teacher tutoring a child when it is obvious that such special instruction will help the child leap over an especially difficult hurdle is always appropriate. Leading a small or large group of children in an activity of interest and of potential value to all is just as appropriate. Furthermore, we should be confident that directing any child at a time when it is necessary can be done without damage to the child's sense of self-importance or ability to direct his/her own learning. We should be just as confident that using large group instruction as the major teaching strategy can interfere with the child's development of autonomous social and intellectual skills.

I should like to use the activities listed in Tables 7.2 and 7.3 to illustrate how these important segments of both a preschool and primary grade curriculum might support the four types of behavior just discussed. This material is presented in Tables 7.4 and 7.5. The interpretation of these tables should be guided by two caveats: First, the kinds of activities included in each table may not constitute the basis for a complete and appropriate curriculum. A curriculum should rise from the purposes and goals of the program and not from a list such as is found in these tables. Second, the ways in which each area is considered, i.e., the materials it contains, the access children have to the area, and the importance of the activity in the program will very much influence the degree to which it meets the requirements of the four types of children's behavior. It should be clear, too, that the mere inclusion of an activity area in any early education setting will not insure its full and appropriate use. Special care must be given to the selection, presentation, and organization of the materials. Much more will be said about this issue in Chapters 8, 9 and 10, but an illustration would be appropriate here.

Table 7.4   **Types of Children's Activity in Some Preschool Activities/Areas**

Children's Activity	Self-Directed	Parallel	Cooperative	Other-Directed		
				1 child w/ 1 other	Small group (2–10 people)	Large group (+ 10 people)
Activity/Area						
Science	√	√	√	√	√	√
Water Table	√	√	√	√		
Sand Table	√	√	√	√		
Cooking			√	√	√	
Table games	√	√	√	√	√	
Language Experience			√	√	√	√
Circle/Meeting/Rug			√		√	√
Creative Play	√	√	√	√	√	
Climbing Frame	√	√	√	√		
Snack/Lunch		√			√	√
Art	√	√		√	√	
Unit Blocks	√	√	√	√	√	
Book Corner	√	√		√	√	
Woodworking	√	√	√	√		
Music	√		√		√	√
Quiet Space	√	√				

In Table 7.5 it is suggested that the literature corner could support self-directed, parallel, and one-child, and small-group-directed activity. Directed activities can be managed quite easily in such settings if one identifies an area to be known as the literature corner and then makes sure that a selection of children's books is available *when an adult chooses to take children there.*

Special considerations need to be made in selecting the location and determining the size of any activity area if it is designed to support self-directed and parallel behaviors. The literature corner should be placed where the activities of children nearby would not interfere with the behavior of those studying children's books. For example, it would seem quite obvious that it shouldn't be located next to the woodworking or creative play areas. Behavior appropriate for these two areas could interfere with the quiet, focused behavior common to children who are captured by books. Also, it seems valuable to restrict the size of the literature corner so that no more than six people could use it at any time. It is also quite important to enclose the area

Table 7.5   **Types of Children's Activity in Some Primary Activities/Areas**

Children's Activity	Self-Directed	Parallel	Cooperative	Other-Directed		
				1 child w/ 1 other	Small group (2–10 people)	Large group (+ 10 people)
Activity/Area						
Language Development						
Literature Corner	✓	✓		✓	✓	
Reading Instruction	✓	✓		✓	✓	✓
Workbooks	✓	✓		✓	✓	✓
Writing Exercises	✓	✓		✓	✓	✓
Mathematics Activity						
Math Area	✓	✓	✓	✓	✓	
Text Materials	✓	✓		✓	✓	✓
Direct Instruction				✓	✓	✓
Tutoring				✓		
Science Activity						
Science Table	✓	✓	✓	✓	✓	
Text Materials	✓	✓		✓	✓	✓
Field Trips			✓		✓	✓
Audiovisual Materials	✓	✓		✓	✓	✓
Arts and Crafts						
Painting	✓	✓		✓	✓	
Woodworking	✓	✓		✓	✓	
Other Crafts	✓	✓	✓	✓	✓	✓
Music						
Listening	✓	✓			✓	✓
Performing	✓		✓	✓	✓	✓

with bookcases, partitions or to utilize the corner of a room, as was illustrated on p. 103 of chapter 6. If children's self-directed and parallel book-exploration behavior is important and valued, it seems necessary to locate the activity in a place where children will be less apt to be disturbed; where there is no confusion about the standing patterns of behavior for the setting.

One more comment needs to be made in illustrating the assertion that care must be taken in locating and organizing activity areas. The structure of the literature corner can be drawn upon to illustrate this point, too: Special care must be given to the selection and presentation of the children's literature. The books that will interest and excite three- and four-year-olds' self-directed inquiry may not be the same ones teachers would select for use in reading to the entire group. It may be important to include a collection of books like those written by Eric Carle and Ezra Jack Keats, which combine beautiful art work with compelling stories. Important because it is so easy to overlook is the requirement that the books be accessible, stored on shelves within easy reach of the children. If this would appear to be an obvious suggestion, look for the children's books on your next visit to an early education classroom and note their location. Are they on shelves higher than the children's reach? Are the books stored away in a cabinet? Don't be surprised if you discover that children don't always have books available to them for their use.

Modes of Learning

The way in which we pursue the search for understanding and knowledge can be characterized as a mode of learning. Nowadays this is often considered to be synonymous with *cognitive style* which has been defined by Kogan (1971) as the way in which we perceive, recall, and think about matters under investigation. Kogan identified nine cognitive styles which are commonly used by different individuals. Two examples should illustrate this definition. In one case, a child may approach the problem of a falling block tower by searching for irregularities in the floor or objects under the bottom block which would cause the structure to fall. Another child in the same situation might focus exclusively on the last block placed on the tower before it fell with the implied assumption that the problem lies in the construction and most particularly the placement of this block. Kogan would characterize the mode of inquiry (cognitive style) of the first child as *field independent*: searching for the cause in factors surrounding the tower. The second child would be *field dependent*: so captured by the task itself that he/she cannot consider the possibility that the problem lies somewhere beyond the tower.

Other researchers have described still different ways of inquiring or thinking. Some refer to children as convergent or divergent thinkers, others as inductive or deductive thinkers, or as impulsive or reflective inquirers. There seems to be considerable evidence to suggest that these categories of cognitive style are quite common and may represent the predominant ways in which we address questions of understanding and gaining knowledge. Regarding within-individual variation, much of the study of cognitive style seems to be directed by assumptions similar to those in personality theory. As was mentioned briefly in an early section of this chapter, it appears that those who study and write about cognitive style perceive it as a unidimensional characteristic and believe that each of us tends to use one cognitive style in every setting where inquiry occurs. According to this view the field-independent child in the preceding paragraph would be likely to follow this style whenever he/she is seeking understanding; similarly, the field dependent child would use that mode of inquiry in most settings.

There seems to be considerable support for belief in the stability of cognitive style: that we tend to approach similar types of problems in the same way from time to time and situation to situation. Mischel suggests that the mode of learning that we follow may be one of the most stable personality characteristics (1973). And yet we must be cautious in assuming that a child will use only one style regardless of the nature of the inquiry. Recall the child described in the beginning of the chapter who was observed first at the easel, then in dramatic play, and finally in the quiet space. This child seems to have relied on very different ways of thinking in each of the three situations and may have employed a way of thinking appropriate to each setting. It is entirely possible that a child will not react to every situation in a uniform and predictable way.

Support for the idea that cogitive style may vary from situation to situation can be drawn from studies of aptitude by Tobias (1976). He reported evidence of people shifting their mode of inquiry on a task as they proceeded to complete it. He found evidence that persons may enter a situation following cognitive style A and, as they successfully proceed with the task, the style may shift to B and then C until the task is completed. Tobias also reported on studies which indicated that persons may be inclined to change their mode of inquiry depending upon their perception of the demands of the situation. Someone may at one time be very cautious and consider carefully each step they take and in another similar situation be impulsive and carefree in proceeding.

Whether or not individuals can and do shift their mode of inquiry from time to time and situation to situation, it does seem clear that a range of different cognitive styles would be likely to appear in a group of young children. Some children tend to be reflective some of the time, others impulsive; some may be very creative divergent thinkers, while other children may be captured by a need to focus on the common, known characteristics of any phenomenon. The point is that whether or not we know for certain that intra-individual differences in cognitive style exist, we do know that there are very important differences between persons in the ways in which they perceive, recall, and think about things they experience. Furthermore, programs designed to promote the development of young children must consider the implications of variations in cognitive style in selecting curricula and designing the environment.

There are five kinds of learning behavior which need to be considered in planning early education programs. They are mastery behavior, exploratory/constructive behavior, aesthetic appreciation, curiosity, and problem-solving behavior. Each kind of inquiry can be influenced by a child's resolve to complete the investigation rather immediately or to sustain the inquiry over time. Thus, the influence of short-term or sustained inquiry on the behavior of children should be taken into account in the planning process.

Mastery Behavior

The process of growing and developing competence requires that we gain some considerable measure of skill in doing many things. It seems apparent that achieving mastery is a natural occurrence. For example, the acquisition of language is accomplished by most people in all cultures by age four. Though we cannot yet agree on an explanation of how such competence is achieved, there is a widely accepted belief that it must occur in a social setting in which language is used. Having achieved the ability to understand and communicate in a language by age four does not mean that language learning ceases. Rather, it seems that once the rules of the language are understood, most of us begin the struggle to master the dialect of our social group so that by adolescence we speak in very much the same way as all other adult speakers in our community. Many linguists believe that we all possess an inherent need to master our language once we have been introduced to its use. The point in this discussion is that a natural part of human behavior is the mastery of tasks, knowledge, and situations which are valuable in every culture (language would be an example) and considered necessary in particular societies. It is therefore important to identify and illustrate some of the tasks, knowledge, and situations young children might need to be able to master in early education programs.

Tasks   The number and kind of tasks children will be asked to master in any early education program cannot be listed here. Quite simply there are too many. Yet there are two categories of tasks which seem to be quite commonly included in most programs: gross and fine motor, and cognitive tasks. Some of the more common gross motor tasks include coordination skills such as climbing a ladder, manipulating a paint brush, throwing and catching a ball, hopping, skipping, and standing on one foot. Fine motor skills are often related to readiness for more advanced skill development and include cutting with scissors, printing and drawing with a pencil, dressing oneself, and buttoning and zipping. Cognitive tasks include language acquisition, developing procedures for completing puzzles, playing table games, and learning to decode the alphabet and beginning to read. Many other motor and cognitive tasks which children must master as they proceed through school could be listed.

Knowledge   Children will need to consider such matters as predicting the consequences of their actions: building a tower on an uneven base, mixing red and yellow easel paint, for example. They will also need to acquire very simple but necessary knowledge such as the names of common animals and plants about them, and to begin to comprehend the logic and meaning of the number system.

Students of Piaget believe that the development of knowledge of the physical environment may be the most important purpose of preschool and early education. Kamii and DeVries have written two volumes which illustrate this point. One considers the movement or mechanics of objects and changes that can be made in their location, use, and relationship to all other objects (1978), and the other considers the child's development of an understanding of numbers (1976). Forman and Kuschner's (1978) book considers the larger issue of young children's need to develop understanding by "constructing" theories, explanations, or knowledge of the nature of phenomena and their relationship to other phenomena or actions. The work of these two teams of authors suggests that early educators are becoming increasingly aware of the need to structure educational environments which will foster and support children's apparent need to develop understanding. It seems as though the need to know is innate and very much a part of the developmental process.

Situations   There is a considerable amount of social knowledge that we each must acquire in order to function with any effect at all in society. Children are engaged in this socialization process from the moment of birth and as they move to the school they must learn what Robert Hess has referred to as "the role of learner." This role includes tasks and knowledge suggested in the two prior paragraphs and also the development of competence in using the appropriate social behavior in different settings within the school. Young children will need to learn what is useful behavior at circle and snack times, when sharing materials, listening to the reading of a story, or playing games with other children. They will also need to learn what constraints are placed on their interaction with other children and with adults, and when and under what circumstances the constraints change. From previous discussion we know the importance of knowing what the expectations for our behavior are and the way in which they relate to the setting.

All children in every culture are expected to become members of that culture, a task which requires their mastery of social and intellectual tasks and the acquisition of a growing body of social and cognitive knowledge. Programs designed to support the development of children must provide many opportunities for them to achieve some degree of mastery over those behaviors necessary for their functioning in society.

Exploratory/Constructive Behavior

Exploratory behavior is quite unlike mastery behavior, and yet it is an integral part of growing and developing and naturally an important aspect of inquiry. Exploratory/constructive behavior is defined here as that which children engage in when they would like to try their hand at something new or different. It is an active process, one in which the child becomes engaged in doing something with others or with materials. It is thus a constructive act, the purpose of which is to gain some measure of understanding beyond that already acquired but not necessarily mastery. An example may help describe this behavior.

Very recently we have become acquainted with the adventure playground, an idea brought to us from Europe. It is a play space in which children will find the kinds of materials which can be used in constructing buildings, climbing apparatus, or other structures children find necessary for their play. The play may very well be creative and highly fantastic, as when children play out their version of space travel, or more pedestrian when they assume roles like those seen in their homes and communities. The role playing and construction are very often integrated and supportive in the sense that once the constuction has been completed, the adventure may be complete. Those who have studied adventure playground behavior suggest, too, that construction very often seems to facilitate the exploration of various kinds of social organization such as the club, leaders and followers, authority, and arbitrary control. Adventure playgrounds are used primarily by children aged eight and older.

Younger children can engage in much the same kinds of behavior that older children exhibit on the adventure playground when they engage one another in an adventure with large building blocks or use the climbing structure as a rocket ship. They, too, experiment with roles and behavior. Exploratory/constructive behavior can also involve much less flamboyant activities than those mentioned. Children will add water to sand, throw sand on the floor and slide on it, allow a swing to fall freely in an arc toward another swing to see if they might collide, or try to get equal ends of bar magnets to attract and not repel.

Curiosity

Curiosity is defined as following one's interests, satisfying a need to get some information but not necessarily engaging in an active and sustained quest. Curious children ask adults and other children direct questions and want precise information in return. They can be seen standing by someone else observing his/her activity, but never engaging in the activity or making comments or asking questions; curious children can also observe and ask many questions in a search for explanations about what is occurring.

A curious child will wander away to follow an interest; he/she will become very immersed in studying the pictures of a book or magazine, very taken by events on TV or in a film but may just as quickly move away to another task or activity that has no connection whatsoever with what he/she was curious about. Such behavior in adults and older children may often be defined as dilettantism and considered superficial. In children dilettantism seems quite natural and positive and may become the source of both exploratory/constructive and mastery behavior. In any case, it seems absolutely necessary that provisions be made for it.

Aesthetic Appreciation

It is not uncommon for young children to comment about an event sometime after its occurrence. A child may surprise and puzzle an adult by beginning a conversation with a question or statement about something experienced hours or even days previously. Furthermore, the child's statement may include a judgment about the value or quality of the experience. A kindergartener, for example, was overheard telling another child that lions walked back and forth in their cages because they wanted to find a way out. This occurred several days after a field trip to a zoo. The statement seemed to have no reference with what was taking place but appeared as a conclusion expressed in anticipation of agreement by the other child. The field trip evoked a sensitive, meaningful, and personal response by the child to the caging of the lions. This rather important reaction to experience will be referred to as the expression of aesthetic appreciation and exemplifies still another form of learning.

Elliot W. Eisner (1969) prepared a statement in which he defined and described expressive educational objectives which have many of the characteristics of an aesthetic experience. Eisner said that "an expressive objective describes an educational encounter . . . it does not specify what from that encounter, situation, problem, or task [children] are to learn" (p. 20). The encounter becomes educational to the degree the child reflects on the experience but, as Eisner also said, "meanings become personalized" and the results of the experience are as diverse as the children themselves.

The kinds of activities which might provide aesthetic appreciation would include the following: listening to a recording of the *Sorcerer's Apprentice* or the *Mother Goose Suite*; discussing a spring time visit to a frog pond covered with eggs; experimenting with shades of color, creating different forms, and introducing texture in easel or finger-painting; contemplating one's sculpture made from pieces of glued wood; and exploring the possibilities of body control on a balance team. It is important that the activity be approached from the perspective of the child rather than with direction by the teacher. An expressive experience should rise from whatever meaning children bring to or attach to the experience after the fact. To ask a child to paint a picture using four colors or to see if he/she can balance on one foot on the balance beam might create a reason for the activity likely to inhibit children's reflection.

Perhaps the most salient aspect of an aesthetic experience is its personal quality; we may never know whether or not a child has had such an experience, and when we do learn that it has taken place, it may be after the fact. It does seem clear, however, that it is a rather common and exceedingly important aspect of learning. Such an experience could form the basis for a sense of appreciation and the development of values and thus be a very significant activity.

Problem Solving

It seems very likely that the human organism begins to engage in problem solving behavior at least as soon as it is born. Infants early respond to discomfort and need in ways which suggest that they desire resolution of the "problem." We do know that infants develop very clear nonverbal communication procedures which become useful in getting parents to care for them in ways the child chooses. The early reaction of infants to states of need develops and matures through childhood and adolescence into problem-solving strategies which are likely to continue throughout life. At each stage in development there are conditions or factors which separate problem solving from most other forms of inquiry.

Very simply, problem-solving inquiry begins with a problem which is real and important to the child. A situation is encountered which the child seeks to resolve; in order for any problem solving activity to occur the child must know what the resolution of the problem would be. In other words, the conditions for problem solving behavior require both a problem for the child and the child's perception of what he/she wants to achieve. A very simple example would involve a kindergarten child who needed to have paste to complete his collage only to discover that the paste jar was sitting on top of a shelf far above his/her reach. The problem is that the child cannot easily get that paste; the solution is to have the jar in the child's hand. The conditions for problem solving behavior are established, and so the process can now begin (Smith, 1975, p. 161).

Once the conditions for inquiry of this sort have been met, there are two basic factors in the problem solving process. First, the child needs to be able to generate alternative ways of achieving the solution. In the example of the child with the paste jar, he/she may propose asking the teacher to reach the jar or get a chair to stand on in an attempt

Table 7.6   **The Problem-Solving Process**

The Process	The Situation		
	Needing Paste	**The Pendulum Task**	**Wanting Honey**
Identification of the Problem	Discovering that the paste jar is out of reach	Knocking over a small block with a rubber ball and twine pendulum	The top of the honey jar is stuck closed
Recognition of the Solution	Having the paste in hand	Knocking over the block (Completing the task)	Getting honey for the snack
Alternative Ways of Reaching Solution	Asking an adult for help Standing on a chair and reaching for the jar Pushing the jar off the shelf Having a friend push the jar off the shelf and catching it when it falls	(The pendulum must be swinging when it strikes the block from a marked distance away) Swing in an arc Stand in front and drop the pendulum Swing hard and wait for it to strike the block Swing the pendulum in a circle	Ask an adult for help Place the jar top in warm water Pry the top loose with a knife Tap the top with a knife Ask a friend to hold the bottom while you twist the top
Evaluating the Proposed Alternatives	"The teachers are busy and may have put the jar on the shelf to keep it from being used." "The jar will break if it falls and I don't catch it." "The chair may not be tall enough." "The table is nearby and I can reach the jar, but if I get caught, I'll be scolded."	"I'll try standing in front of the blocks and dropping the pendulum." "If that doesn't work, I'll try another way."	"An adult is asked but tells me to try by myself." "My mother puts stuck things in warm water." "A knife might break the top." "My friend is busy at another table."
Action to Achieve Solution	"I'll stand on the table and take my chances."	Dropping the pendulum. The teacher asks questions about the direction of the arc of the pendulum. Reevaluation and trial again. (A continuous process which may last several days.)	"I put the jar top in warm water and try to open. It doesn't. I try again with no success; I ask the teacher who opens it but tells me the warm water helped."

to reach the jar, he/she may think about climbing up the shelf, using a rod or pole to push the jar off the shelf, having a friend push the jar off the shelf while he/she waits to catch it, and so on. Smith suggests that the ability to develop alternative ways of solving the problem is often referred to as creativity. As important as the art of generating solutions is skill and ability in separating the proposed alternatives into those which are likely to succeed and those which will only lead to failure. Again, Smith suggests that this can be achieved in two ways. A child can think about the consequences of each alternative; he/she may evaluate the choices before acting by careful reasoning. Or, the child may need to test his/her choices by trial and error. Most children will use both procedures in most problem-solving situations. In the end, of course, the child must act; he/she must attempt to resolve the problem.

There are five steps in the problem solving process: recognition that a problem exists, knowledge of the solution, the generation of ways of achieving the solution to the problem, evaluation of the worth of each proposed way of solving the problem, and finally, action to achieve resolution. This process is illustrated in Table 7.6, which begins with the situation of the child in need of paste.

Short-Term and Sustained Inquiry

Provisions must be made in programs for young children for the support of those alternative modes of inquiry discussed in this section. The structure and organization must also provide for variation in the amount of time a child would spend in each type of inquiry. There needs to be an array of materials and activities which support both short-term and sustained inquiry. It would seem that teachers must recognize that the duration of sustained interest in any inquiry will vary from time to time and from situation to situation for every child. At one moment a child will press adults for precise answers to very direct and information-gathering questions; a child will ask to know why paint colors change when mixed with another, why does red and blue produce purple? At another time, the same child will want to know why you can't make more cookies by adding milk to the batter and demand an explanation. Later, this child may be quite interested in testing the effect of various amounts of milk on the cookie batter and the kinds of cookies variations in milk produce.

It is also important to understand that both short-term and sustained inquiry can occur in each of the five inquiry modes presented here. Short-term inquiry need not be restricted to steps in achieving mastery or in observation, and sustained inquiry is not unique to problem solving, or exploratory behavior. Perhaps this can be illustrated by again referring to the situation of the child in need of the paste jar. The child might have immediately decided to stand on a table adjacent to the shelf, remove the jar and proceed with his art work. All of this might have been accomplished in less than one minute, and yet the behavior would have met all of the conditions for problem solving. In another situation, children may spend several days working a jigsaw puzzle, in which their primary task would be the mastery of cognitive strategies necessary for puzzle completion. Time-on-task is a factor that must be considered in designing programs which provide for alternative modes of inquiry for children. Table 7.7 illustrates this by presenting three examples of both short-term and sustained investigation by each type of learning.

Individual Differences Among Children

Two major ideas were presented in the first half of this chapter. The concept of intra-individual variability in behavior was first discussed, followed by the corollary idea that within-person behavior change may reflect a natural shift in cognitive style and mood. The second part of the chapter consisted of a discussion of the three principles that should be considered in designing programs for young children based on

Table 7.7	Short-Term and Sustained Inquiry	
Modes of Inquiry	Short-term Inquiry	Sustained Inquiry
Mastery	Learning to play lotto and other matching games	Practice in identifying the letters of the alphabet, in decoding words, etc.
	Learning to complete puzzles—wooden and paper inlay and more complex jig-saw puzzles	Weaving pot holders on a small frame
	Completing daily work assignments in reading, language arts and mathematics	Playing with attribute blocks in which placement of a piece is based on 1 or 2 attribute changes
Exploratory/ Constructive	Placing an old felt hat on one's head and moving about the room	Creating free form sculpture from pieces of mill-end wood and glue
	Spreading mashed, cooked peas or beans on a celery stalk and sharing it with another Commenting on the task	Testing the effect of various growing conditions on small plants
	Building a wren's house from a paper shoe box	Observing the results of using the shoe box as a bird house
Curiosity	Stopping to watch two children measure the weight of a gerbil	Observing fish behavior in an aquarium
	Asking the custodian why he separates the trash into containers	Stopping by the music room each morning to listen to lessons being given on the piano
	Trying to find the picture of a bird in a field guide having seen it on the playground	Asking the teacher every few days about whether or not the gerbils will have babies. Why? When? How many?
Aesthetic Appreciation	Painting at an easel	Listening to a story being read, a bit each day
	Watching oneself in a mirror while moving about on a balance beam	Making a clay bowl, letting it dry, applying a glaze and firing the bowl. Studying the results of firing on the color, texture and design of the glaze
	Trying to find different ways of describing the colors of green seen in a landscape on a spring day	Spending time regularly engrossed in leafing through old National Geographic magazines
Problem Solving	Finding a way to remove the stuck cover from a jar	Using a pendulum to knock down a verticle pin[a]
	Mixing water colors to get the color pink	Constructing a maze from unit blocks in which guinea pigs can move from pen to food
	Getting a friend to give up an object needed in an activity	Trying to find out why small turtles die soon after they are brought to the classroom

[a] See Kamii and DeVries for an excellent and elaborate explanation of the nature of problems encountered in using and controlling the arc of a pendulum.

the belief in variability in individual behavior. There is one additional issue which should be discussed and that is the relationship of these ideas to a more common concern among American educators, the task of handling individual differences among children.

For quite some time psychologists and educators have been captivated by the obvious fact that each person is unique, that for all our similarities, we are very different one from the other. The acceptance of this belief has led man to search for examples of the ways in which we differ. The study of cognitive style is one of the more prominent examples of such inquiry. As discussed earlier, there seems to be little question that we may find a number of different ways in which a group of children will respond to any learning task. If we expect ten children to learn the history of the first Thanksgiving, for example, we might discover the success of each in this task depends upon ways in which they are instructed. Some children might learn best by having the history told to them in story form; others might be more successful if they were to visit Plymouth Plantation to see the reproduced village and hear about the settlement, the Indians, and the struggle of the colonists to survive.

The identification of individual differences in the ways we learn has been accompanied by homilies about the need for educators to design programs which allow for and support the uniqueness of each student. The call is for the individualizing of instruction. There should be a very natural and sensible relationship between the identification of individual differences in learning style and the structuring of a program which individualizes instruction. Yet in several decades of hard work we have not yet discovered ways in which this seemingly simple match can be made.

In the late 1960s researchers began to study carefully the interaction between teaching procedures and the aptitudes of students. This research has been called *aptitude-treatment interaction* or *trait-treatment interaction analysis*, with *aptitude* and *trait* signifying the variations in learning style and treatment referring to the type of instruction. The researchers have had a difficult time finding stability in the relationship of these two presumably closely related factors. For example, in the research situation it might be discovered that some students learn history best by lecture, others by discussion, and still others by a combination of lecture and discussion. Matching the learning style to instructional mode in subsequent settings may not produce the level of achievement one would predict. It seems that something goes amiss between the research situation where aptitudes are identified and the instructional settings designed to exploit these learning styles.

One possible explanation for the difficulty in finding appropriate matches between aptitude and instruction may lie in the thesis developed earlier in this chapter that cognitive style may change from time to time and across situations, even when the nature of the task remains very much the same. Such a conception of cognition implies that each person can have more than one and perhaps several cognitive styles, which are dependent upon psychological need, the perception of the demands of the situation, and the skills developed in similar past situations. A person may learn one lesson in history best while being lectured because the instructor is introducing the student to the topic, setting a temporal and historical framework, and describing the pattern of relationships between personalities and event. Such a lecture may make it possible for a student to continue his/her subsequent study best through library research and reading with occasional discussions with the instructor. Tobias' studies (1976), cited earlier, lend some research support to this assertion. Recall that he found shifts in cognitive style in response to student's perceptions of what was expected of them and also as a function of their progress in completing a task. This leads me to think that it is quite natural for each of us to develop alternative ways of engaging with experience, of learning, of inquiry, of interacting with one another. Though there may be similarity in our surface behavior day-to-day to allow others some success in predicting how we will behave in certain situations, it may be unwarranted to assume that such important human characteristics as learning style are unimodal.

The struggle to provide the best educational experience for all children is implicit in all that is said about the need to meet individual differences and must continue. The difficulties we have had in designing individualized instructional programs should not deter teachers from helping each child have educational experiences appropriate for his/her aptitude and needs. The material in this chapter does suggest, however, that teachers should carefully consider the ways in which they proceed to meet the individual needs of their students. It may be appropriate to design complex learning environments based on the concepts presented here, in which a wide array of cognitive styles can be followed and in which children have a large measure of freedom in choosing how to proceed in completing tasks. The most efficient way of meeting individual needs may be to provide children with educational settings which are provocative, stimulating, and supportive of alternative modes of social contact, types of direction, and modes of learning. Similarly, allowing children to make choices as to how they shall become involved in the affairs of the program may help serve their individual needs.

Summary

It is commonplace today to urge teachers to do all they can to provide for individual differences between children. Teachers are reminded that students may not share a similar learning style, have common interests and needs, or aspire to the same goals. What I have tried to do in this chapter is to suggest that the variability so often said to exist between individuals may exist in even more important ways within each individual. We all quite naturally vary our behavior from setting to setting and over time in response to different needs and expectations. I have argued that teachers of young children should celebrate intra-individual variability as a natural expression of normal growth-productive behavior.

Early childhood education practitioners can make significant strides in accommodating their teaching to within-person variability and still meet the requirements of the school. Three categories of person-environment interaction were presented and discussed: social contact, type of direction, and mode of learning. Examples of the ways in which preschool teachers and those for children in grades one to three could support each category were offered.

The idea of intra-individual variability is not commonly discussed in education texts, and it challenges much which has been written regarding the need to individualize instruction. Thus the reader is encouraged to consider this thesis carefully, as well as to examine the assertions about children's behavior variations and the need to design educational environments which accommodate the kinds of variability discussed here. If a six-year-old may at one moment be introspective and later be social and in each instance be engaged in activities which are healthy and productive, shouldn't the school offer the child some opportunity for both behavioral expressions? I think that it is essential that the school do so if it wishes to meet the child's needs, however they may be defined. Ways of making such provisions, will be presented in the chapters to follow.

References: Chapter 7

Bem, Daryl J., & Allen, Andrea. On predicting some of the people some of the time: The search for cross-situational consistencies in behavior. *Psychological Review*, 1974, *81*, 506–520.

Cattrell, L. S. The analysis of situational fields in social psychology. *American Sociology Review*, 1942, *7*, 370–382.

Day, David E. & Sheehan, Robert. Elements of a better school. *Young Children*, 1974, *30*(1), 15–23.

Dudycha, G. J. An objective study of punctuality in relation to personality and achievement. *Archives of Psychology*, 1936, *204*, 1–319.

Eisner, Elliot W. Instructional and expressive objectives: Their formulation and use in curriculum instructional objectives. In W. J. Papliarn (Ed.), *American Educational Research Association Monograph #3*. Chicago: Rand McNally, 1969.

Evans, Ellis D. *Contemporary influences in early childhood education* (2nd ed.). New York: Holt, Rinehart and Winston, 1975.

Forman, George E. & Kuschner, David S. *The child's construction of knowledge.* Monterey, CA: Brooks/Cole, 1977.

Hartshorne, H., & May, M. A. *Studies in deceit.* New York: Macmillan, 1928.

Hartshorne, H., & May, M. A. *Studies in service and self-control.* New York: Macmillan, 1929.

Kamii, Constance, & DeVries, Rheta. *Piaget, children, and number.* Washington, DC: National Association for the Education of Young Children, 1976.

Kamii, Constance, & DeVries, Rheta. *Physical knowledge in preschool education.* Englewood Cliffs, NJ: Prentice-Hall, 1978.

Kogan, N. Educational implications of cognitive style. In G. Lesser (Ed.), *Psychology and educational practice.* Glenview, IL: Scott, Foresman, 1971.

Loo, C. M. The effect of spatial density on the social behavior of children. *Journal of Applied Social Psychology*, 1973, *2*, 372–81.

Mischel, Walter. *Personality and assessment.* New York: Wiley, 1968.

Mischel, Walter. Toward a cognitive social learning reconceptualization of personality. *Psychological Review*, 1973, *80*, 252–283.

Newcomb, Theodore M. *Consistency of certain extrovert-introvert behavior patterns in 51 problem boys.* New York: Bureau of Publications, Teachers College, Columbia University, 1929.

Parten, Mildred B. Social participation among pre-school children. *The Journal of Abnormal and Social Psychology,* 1932, *27,* 243–69.

Raush, H. L., Dittmann, A. T., & Taylor, T. J., Person, setting and change in social interaction. *Human Relations,* 1959, *12,* 361–78.

Rubin, Kenneth H. Play behaviors of young children. *Young Children,* 1977, *32,* 16-24.

Sheehan, Robert, & Day, David E. Is open space just empty space? *Day Care and Early Education,* November/December 1975, *3,* 10–13; 47.

Silberman, Charles. *Crisis in the classroom.* New York: Random House, 1970.

Smith, Frank. *Comprehension and learning.* New York: Holt, Rinehart and Winston, 1975.

Tobias, Sigmund. Achievement treatment interactions. *Review of Educational Research,* Winter 1976, *46,* 61–74.

8 The Physical Setting and Utilization of Space

Environmental Factors in Program Development

Sometime ago an observational study of day-care programs in Massachusetts was completed (Day & Sheehan, 1974; Sheehan & Day, 1976). The study began as an inquiry into the state of day care in the Commonwealth but soon became a search for factors which would explain differences in the behavior of children from one program to the next. It was not uncommon to find programs in which the children and the staff were actively engaged in an array of different tasks and projects, where children were enthusiastic and animated but quite comfortable in maintaining a measure of decorum necessary for sustained attention to any task. It was just as likely that children in other day-care settings would be disruptive of each other's activity, less apt to stay at a task for any appreciable period of time, and noisy to the point of distraction.

For some time explanations for such program differences as these had been sought in the differences among the children, in the nature and composition of their families, or in the training and experience of the staff. There seemed to be nearly universal agreement that though factors such as status, race, and culture influence behavior, they cannot fully explain the differences among children. Furthermore, it was found that applying these standard criteria to the programs observed didn't work. Some, but not all, of the high-quality programs enrolled predominantly middle-status children; some quality programs were found in the most depressing urban slums. The same distribution was found when identifying poorer day care programs.

An analysis of the children's behavior resulted in a rather straightforward listing of behaviors which characterized what was observed and served to distinguish the programs by quality. Children's behavior in each classroom seemed, on the whole, to be predominantly *growth productive* or *growth inhibiting*. A judgment regarding the quality of the classroom was made on the basis of this categorization: high-quality programs were those in which growth-productive behavior was commonly observed. The behaviors defining each category are listed below:

GROWTH-PRODUCING BEHAVIOR	GROWTH-INHIBITING BEHAVIOR
1. Children engaged in cooperative activity with adults and other children.	1. Children moving from child to child, activity to activity without much long-lasting contact with adults and other children.
2. Children making choices about what they will do.	2. Children being directed most of the time by adults.
3. Children using the materials and equipment of the program as they were intended to be used.	3. Children using materials and equipment in very aggressive ways, often aimed at other children.
4. Children initiating conversation with other children and with adults regarding ongoing activities.	4. Considerable verbal interchange, often distracting and unrelated to the activities at hand.
5. Children absorbed in the activities, completing games and tasks and attending to what they are doing.	5. Children inattentive, listless, and easily distracted.[1]
6. Children usually considerate of other children and their activities.	6. Children often disrupting the activity of others; heavy reliance upon adult intervention in the maintenance of order and control.
7. Children helping organize activities of the program, assisting staff in arranging equipment, distributing materials, and cleaning up when necessary.	7. Children directed by adults to and from activities. Long periods of random activity or waiting while staff sets up materials and activities for children.

Further analysis of the data revealed that behavior was related to three environmental factors. They are 1) the physical setting and utilization of space; 2) the availability and use of materials; and 3) the amount and type of adult-care interaction. In high-quality classrooms (where growth-productive behavior was commonly observed), it appeared that the staff had given much time and attention to these factors, making sure that each had been considered as the program was designed. It was just as apparent that in classrooms where growth-inhibiting behavior was the norm, little attention seemed to have been given to these environmental variables.

Subsequent use of these factors as organizing elements in program redesign has

---

[1]This necessarily assumes the absence of such factors as malnutrition, psychic distress, and physical or intellectual handicaps among the children. Obviously any ECE program cannot be evaluated by these criteria prior to its addressing the state of physical and mental health of the children.

convinced me of their importance for early education practitioners. In several instances, I have assisted teachers who sought to increase growth-productive behavior by having them analyze their classrooms in terms of the relationship of the children's behavior, the expectations of the teachers regarding activities and areas, and the three factors. In most cases, reorganization of the classroom with consideration of each factor resulted in changes in behavior in the direction sought by the teachers.

In order to produce an ecologically sound program, it seems that teachers must consider the way in which the arrangement of the setting, the selection and presentation of materials, and the role of adults can support children's productive behavior. A detailed discussion of these three factors and their applications in the early education classroom will be presented in this and the two following chapters.

Introduction to the Physical Setting

The physical setting of any day-care center, nursery school, or kindergarten has a profound influence on the behavior of the children. The selection and arrangement of learning or experience areas, the utilization of available space, and whether or not adults use the areas with children are important factors in determining the behavior of the children. The most carefully selected materials, the most aesthetically pleasing setting, and the most ideal child-staff ratio will not alone promote continued development.

The importance of the attractiveness of the setting and the selection of materials in the provision of good early education must also be recognized. There is an urgent need to take children out of the damp, dark, dungeonlike basements of public buildings and churches and give them well-maintained and appropriately designed facilities. Children have for too long been required to spend their preschool days in converted storefronts, worn out houses, and abandoned and crumbling buildings. In one full day, day-care center, which was not atypical, 90 children were required to spend their days indoors because the brick facade of the structure was crumbling and falling into the play yard. A rural day-care and Head Start program was located in an old run-down church parsonage; the church had moved the minister to a new dwelling because the older structure was in such a state of disrepair. The Head Start program was forced to move into this space because it was all that was available in any of the towns served by the funding agency. The building was offered for a very small rental fee but cost the agency over $1,200 per year to heat. In addition, the whole building needed to be rewired before it would meet the requirements of the fire inspector. The cost for this was paid for by the agency.[2]

The realities of group child-care and early education settings need to be made known to everyone. The fact that most young children in early education must be taken to worn-out, reconverted, and totally inappropriate facilities should be intolerable to a

---

[2]The desperate state of housing for preschool programs is described by Keyserling (1972) and Steinfels (1973).

nation that is as wealthy as ours and presumes to be child centered. Our provisions for preschool-aged children should serve as a profound national embarrassment.

Acknowledging the need to improve early education centers does not, however, change the fact that an ecologically sound environment is more than a special building, bright paint, clean floors, colorful fabrics, and modern materials. All of these are needed in addition to love, compassion, and skilled adults. It is imperative that we offer our children every opportunity to experience pleasant surroundings, ample materials for play, exploration and learning, and protection for their physical safety. However, these are only what we should normally expect in any child-care setting. These elements are the prerequisites; they are some of the raw materials from which quality programs are built.

I would like to turn my attention here to matters relating to the organization of child-care and early education settings. It would be ideal if all children were in centers especially designed and constructed for their use, but this is simply not the case. It is necessary, therefore, to consider the ways in which a minimally adequate space can be arranged so that it facilitates children's development. It is also important to consider the ways in which the traditional rectangular classroom can most effectively be structured. Therefore, this chapter will discuss the procedures by which practitioners will be better able to offer their children a developmentally adequate setting. It should be pointed out, however, that settings like the two described in the previous paragraph could never be considered adequate under any circumstance and should not ever be used as child care or early education facilities. Though our provisions for early education facilities are very often less than the best and we will often need to make do with what is available, we demean ourselves as practitioners and persons who recognize the importance of childhood if we accept just any space for a child-care center and make do as best we can. We must learn to say no, to refuse to use space that is intolerably inadequate.

Four crucial issues have been identified that relate to the creation of an effective physical setting. They are 1) the issue of open vs. closed space; 2) the selection and use of learning areas; 3) the organization of learning areas; and 4) the support of children's behavior. Each will be discussed with illustrations of the effective use of space.

Open vs. Closed Space

Over the past decade and a half there has been a gentle but persistent movement among American educators to promote the use of open-space classrooms. Although major attention has been given to elementary education facilities, the movement has had influence in preschools and day-care centers, too. Preschool programs which have for years had to be content with the use of large halls and basements now are told that such open areas can actually promote child development.

The breaking down of elementary school barriers that separate different-aged groups of children is considered valuable in the struggle to achieve individualized instruction, creative interaction among children, and the development of a sense of responsibility for their own growth; it has been suggested that opening up educational facilities could enhance teachers' effectiveness. These justifications will not be examined here. Suffice it to say that the virtue of open space seems more imaginary than real, especially as it relates to the creation of quality early childhood education. But what is open space? What is it that seems to be of such concern?

Open space has several meanings. In some instances, it refers to a child's freedom to move from one activity to another without restraint. Another definition suggests that the essence of open space is that learning areas should transcend the immediate classroom environment: the whole school, nursery, or day-care center including the out-of-doors should become the everyday classroom for all children. In most cases, open space is defined literally as a large, open area, often separated from other large open areas, in which *all* of a child's daily activity takes place. In addition, as used in elementary education, this open area will often accommodate three or four times the number of youngsters commonly found in a classroom. For example, an open-space elementary school may be designed so that each "classroom" (more commonly called a *quad*) will have between 100 and 120 children. The comments here will be addressed to the use of such large open areas. Teachers and child care workers should consider carefully the effects of large, undifferentiated open space on the development of children. It will be suggested that practitioners offer a combination of open and closed space as an alternative to simple open-space areas. Such an arrangement should include large and small areas especially designed to support a variety of different kinds of activity. This recommendation is based on the need to control sound, protect individual and small group activity, and provide for isolation as needed.

Sound

Recall the discussion in Chapters 6 and 7 about the influence of the setting on children's behavior and the assertion that normal behavior covers a rather wide spectrum ranging from the quiet to the noisy. Furthermore, it was suggested that, wherever possible, children should be given opportunity to express the full range of productive behavior. It is within this context that the issue of sound in early education settings is raised. The design of any program should provide for alternative behaviors and attempt to separate the noise and action of one acceptable mode from another behavior which might otherwise be disrupted.

Imagine for a moment a kindergarten program which includes many of the activity areas listed in Table 7.2 on page 141. There would be rather quiet, self-directed, highly focused activities designed, for example, to help a child achieve mastery, e.g., using scissors in cutting a design from a piece of paper. Also included in this kindergarten would be a creative play area, a woodworking area, and a climbing frame, each of which could be expected to produce considerable noise and potential distraction for the child using the scissors. Yet both kinds of activity—quiet and noisy—would be valued, planned for, and anticipated. The task, therefore, is to arrange the environment in a way which would tend to support each type of behavior without the imposition of too many restrictions. One example of the way in which concern for the distraction of sound might be avoided is suggested in the plan in Figure 8.1

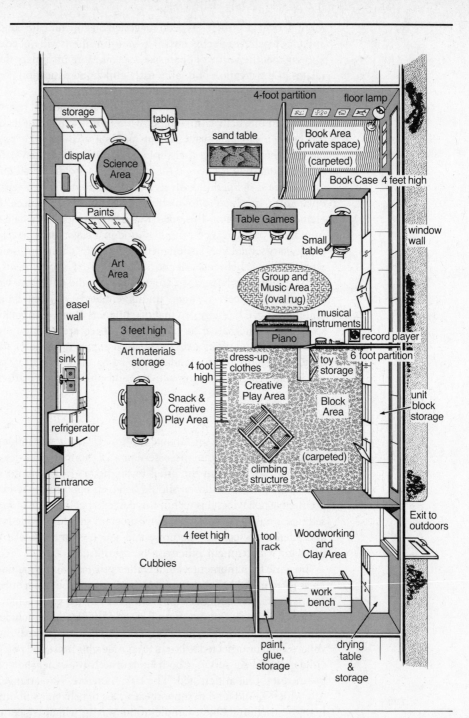

Figure 8.1   **A Designed Environment**

Note that the areas in which the louder, more physically active and collaborative behavior would occur are separated by a six-foot-high partition and an upright piano from those areas where these behaviors would be less apt to appear. Futhermore, the dress-up clothes partition, the climbing structure, and the partition outlining the reading and science areas would tend to moderate the intensity of the sound coming from the woodworking, block, and creative-play areas.

The behavior of any child in a group setting is heavily influenced by that of all other children. The standing patterns of behavior are partially the result of learning what one can do in any setting. If the mode is loud voices, energetic and uninhibited play, and spontaneous movement from one area to another, any child will soon join this behavior. Few children will stay at demanding tasks for any appreciable length of time if the behavior of others suggests this to be atypical. By way of illustration, in a nursery school located in a one-room church basement, children were observed chasing others, riding tricycles, building towers with unit blocks and knocking them down to the hard floor, and yelling to each other across the room. All of this occurred while children singly or with one or two others ate breakfast at a table located in the center of this activity. One child attempted to listen to a recorded story but was unsuccessful even when the volume was turned up high. Within a very short time, the center was a chaotic mass of shouting, scurrying, active children in total control of the program, who never modulated their behavior. Even those children who would have engaged in more restrained activity soon increased the intensity of their behavior to match that of the loudest and most enthusiastic children. This occurred whether children were playing with blocks, painting at an easel, eating their breakfast, or looking at books. Plainly, the physical setting, combined with the reticence of adults to impose sanctions on the children, created a situation in which the behavior of some children interfered with that of others.

In addition to interfering with activities and influencing children's reactive behavior, a high level of sound is simply uncomfortable. There is little question that anyone subjected to a constant, high level of noise from children and their activities will become irritated and tired. It affects all of us—adults and children. Everyone at times needs to move away from children shouting, banging materials, and noisily expressing their satisfaction with what they are doing. An open-space setting almost always prevents a child from getting away from it all. In such a classroom the only alternative a teacher may have is to control the behavior of the children to such an extent that enthusiasm is rare and always cautious. This is as unacceptable as a constant high level of intense sound.

Individual and Small Group Activity

Although it is not commonly acknowledged, children in preschool and primary grades spend much time alone, either actively engaged or passively uninvolved (Berken & Janzen, 1978). In the preschool such behavior is more than likely the child's choice; in the primary grades it may be more a function of the type of instruction in which the teacher leads and directs individual work. In the latter case, a degree of support for self-directed work comes from the restrictions teachers place on children's movement about the room and their freedom to talk with one another. However, supporting the child's choice to work alone or with one or two other people might be accomplished more effectively by designing a classroom which differentiates activity areas by size and function. Some thought should be given to arranging the environment so that children have some assurance that they will not be disturbed by the important activity of others. It is extremely difficult to make these kinds of arrangements in an undifferentiated, large open setting.

We should refer again to Figure 8.1 to illustrate further the need to limit the physical setting. The dimensions of the reading area are approximately 5 by 7½ feet; it is enclosed by a 4-foot partition. The science area has a partition 7½ feet in length separating it from the art area. Mention has already been made of the piano partition. The location of tables and storage cabinets, the use of the rug in the block and creative play areas, and the oval rug in the music and group area contribute much to the differentiation of the segments within the larger behavior setting. Most important, however, the arrangement of dividers, the placement of tables, and the location of the oval rug communicates to the children that support for individual and small group activity has been provided. Children should not have to fight the environment in order to complete a task.

Isolation

Sooner or later every preschool classroom needs to isolate a child or a few children. Occasionally, a child becomes ill but is not able to return home. The staff is required to care for the child until he or she is called for by a parent. More frequently, there is a need to separate children who are sleeping from those who are awake. This is especially true in day-long day-care centers where some three- to five-year-old children take regular naps. It becomes a near impossibility to arrange isolation for the children needing it and a normal program activity for the rest if everything occurs in one large area.

Careful consideration should be given to securing a space in which children may nap without being disturbed by others. Anyone who has had much experience with day care can testify to the fact that getting numbers of children to coordinate their rest and sleep needs is a near impossibility. Some young children rise early and are ready to nap by 11:30 or 12; others will sleep comfortably after lunch; still other children need only a brief rest and quiet period at midday before resuming their normal activity. A separate, somewhat secluded area will provide flexibility in arranging for the different needs of the children without disrupting the program. This is very difficult to achieve when everything occurs in one large, open classroom.

The separated sleeping area can also serve as the isolation room for the sick child. A child with a slightly elevated fever, a headache, or stomach upset needs to be isolated from the on-going activity of the center, but usually need not be placed in total isolation. However, an ill child should be given privacy from the constant attention of other children. Many children who are ill will be taken home, to a physician, or if need be, to a clinic or hospital. There will be times, however, when a parent can't be reached, when the child has no extreme need for special medical care, or when the day is nearly over and the child is soon to be taken home. At times like these, the child needs more than anything else to be away from the other children.

The sleeping-isolation area need not be reserved for these uses only. This area, once separated from other areas in the center, can be used for small group activities and a semiprivate, quiet area for children as they need it and choose to use it. More will be said about learning areas and private space later. Suffice it to say that the separate space necessary to accommodate children who are ill and those who seek a respite from the pell-mell activity of other children should not be overlooked.

Private Space

There is a behavioral phenomenon that occurs rather regularly among many children when the milieu supports it: from time to time, children will leave whatever it is they are doing and retreat to a spot in the room which is visually isolated from everything else. The absence of environmental support for this behavior has the apparent effect of provoking group destructive- and growth-inhibiting behavior. There seems to be a need for children to retreat to a private space from which they emerge after a time fully prepared to join the affairs of the program.

Children aged three to five rather commonly seek out and occupy private space at some time during the program day. This is especially true in programs that last three or more hours each day. Any child may behave very much like the one in the example in Chapter 6, who left his friends in creative play for a rest in the private space of the reading corner. It seems to be very difficult to predict when a child might do this during the program day or whether he/she would do it every day. Furthermore, there doesn't seem to be any relationship between the type of activity and subsequent entry to the private space. The withdrawal occurs without any announcement or fanfare; the child simply walks away from his/her engagement and enters the quiet and isolation of this space.

Children may become so tired from engagement with others or with tasks that they choose to remove themselves from the main activity areas. It is also possible that the children isolate themselves from the major stimuli of the program in order to integrate their experience. Whatever the cause, it seems quite natural for children to remove themselves regularly from activities for short periods of time if and when this option is available.

Not all early education programs have made provisions for private space. It is not uncommon to find nursery schools and day-care programs which are located in one large, open space. Practitioners often find it valuable to be able to see all the activities of both adults and children. What, one might ask, occurs in settings like this where there is no privacy? First of all, there is a growing level of activity and noise in the program as the day progresses. Children demonstrate more exuberance and less introspective and focused behavior in the middle and later periods of the day. In addition, the behavior of adults changes in these settings: they are far less permissive, tend not to participate as much in children's activities later in the day and are much more directive and controlling. Finally, children can be observed trying to create private space. They will crawl under tables placed with one edge against a wall or bookshelf; they can be found in the farthest corner of the cubbies or coat storage area, or even out of sight on the bottom shelf in a materials storage area. In brief, children will create ingenious ways of manifesting this behavior even though the environment is not structured in a way to encourage it.

The child's removal to a private space is not a cause for alarm; on the contrary, it appears to be a natural choice. Children who withdraw when they feel the need will be more likely to support the group or be productive on their own later. They seem to return to the program intellectually energized, ready again to engage in events as they choose.

The private space need not be an elaborate creation although some are ingenious in their design. One program provides an enclosed bunk bed: a plywood structure approximately 3 by 5 feet, enclosed on 3½ sides and top and bottom; it is fitted with a covered foam rubber mattress and an assortment of pillows. The bunk is raised approximately 3 feet off the floor and placed in a remote corner of a large room. Children enter through a small opening along one side.

Another program has a structure shaped like a geodesic dome. A burlap covered a frame which about 6 feet in diameter forms its base. There was one opening at floor level, easy for children to enter but more difficult for adults. This tentlike structure, which contained a small rug and several pillows, was lighted by a lamp hanging over a small opening at the top. It was designed to be used for small group meetings and intimate story-reading; the children added the private-space dimension.

Other private space areas are not nearly so tentlike. A reading or children's literature area can be very effective as a private space. Recall the illustration in Chapter 6 of a 4- by 6-foot area covered with an old but comfortable cotton shag rug. There was a floor lamp, some pillows, and a few carefully selected children's books. The area was separated from the rest of the center by a partition on one side and the abutting walls on two others. A comfortable space behind a partition or a couch in a supply room could also provide the necessary retreat.

It is important to point out that private space is rarely abused. Children learn easily and early that the area is to be used by them for their own needs. About all the staff need do is to make sure that children are aware of the intent of the area and to reinforce its appropriate use. Certainly a key to the creation and maintenance of such an area is its location in the center.

Closing Up Open Space

The most obvious way of securing closed space, the alternative to open space, is to make sure that every early education program is housed in buildings with separate rooms. Unfortunately, this is usually not possible. What, then, is?

Figure 8.2 below is a sketch of the large room which housed a day-care program for 25 three- to five-year-old children. They ate, played, had directed lessons, and slept in this one space. A small office and parent-consultation room was located on another floor. At the height of any day's activity, the noise and movement of the children was distracting. Members of the staff often found themselves shouting above the confusion—simply adding to the turmoil. Observation indicated that the complete

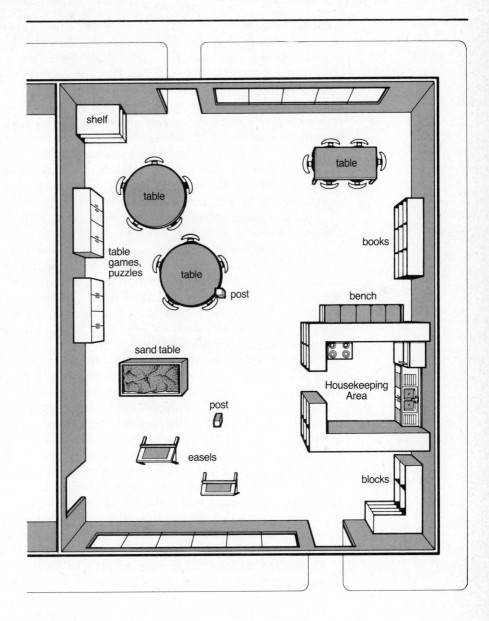

shelf

table

table

table games, puzzles

table

post

sand table

post

easels

table

books

bench

Housekeeping Area

blocks

Figure 8.2   **Open-Space Setting**

openness of the center combined with the natural exuberance of the children created an environment in which loud, aggressive, and undirected behavior prevailed. The movement and the sound from the block area had the effect of raising the level of voices in the adjacent housekeeping area. The activity at the easel became disjointed and unusually frantic. The children's paintings were often incomplete. Their strokes were bold and coarse (not at all alarming by itself), but rarely were there attempts at detail or experimentation with color. Children approached painting as a task to be completed hurriedly, a brief stop in their passage through all the areas in the center.

The children were happy but seemed incapable of differentiating their behavior. They were in high gear most of the time regardless of the task at hand. Furthermore, it was rare and unusual to find a child who would take the time to complete any task. Even those who were engaged in building a tower with unit blocks might break the whole construction down midway to completion and run off to a completely new and different activity.

Several suggestions were made for reorganizing the center in an attempt to add some of the behavioral dimensions discussed in Chapter 7. The staff needed to be reassured that children would differentiate their behavior and attend to activities, complete them and move on to other tasks. The adults wanted an alternative to their behavior; disciplining children, while setting up and arranging for activities that would attract them, was simply not very satisfying. In addition, arranging for any sensible sleeping and rest periods seemed beyond reach.

The reorganization began with a consideration of ways in which the vast openness might be reduced. Figure 8.3 depicts the changes that were made. Careful attention was given to both the selection and arrangement of the areas of the center, but it should also be noted that the room was divided into smaller areas. A floor to ceiling partition was installed (*a* in Figure 8.3). This partition created the illusion of two rooms instead of one large open room. The separation was further extended by attaching a 5-foot-high divider at a right angle to the partition between two permanent posts (*b* in Figure 8.3). The housekeeping area was enclosed creating the impression that it was a separate room. The sink, stove and cabinets (*c*) formed a barrier along one side. A 5-foot-high cork board (*d*) closed one end of the housekeeping area; the children's cubbies (*e*) partitioned the other end. A 4-foot plywood divider (*f*) completed a path running from the entrance to the bathrooms, kitchen, and rear exit. A 3-foot-high bookcase (*g*) and a plywood partition (*h*) were used to set off the reading area.

The results of these few changes were striking. Though the changed behavior of the children and the staff cannot be attributed solely to the changes in the physical arrangements, there is reason to believe that they contributed substantially. The children tended to stay in areas for longer periods of time, and staff were able to concentrate on their relationships with the children. The noise level was reduced, children did not race from one end of the room to another, and the available materials were being used as they were intended to be used.

Finding a suitable arrangement for afternoon naps had also been a problem in this day-care center. Prior to the partitioning and rearrangement, all children slept at the same time on cots spread throughout the room. After the adjustments were made, sleeping and rest were restricted to the arts-and-crafts and adjoining table-games areas. As children

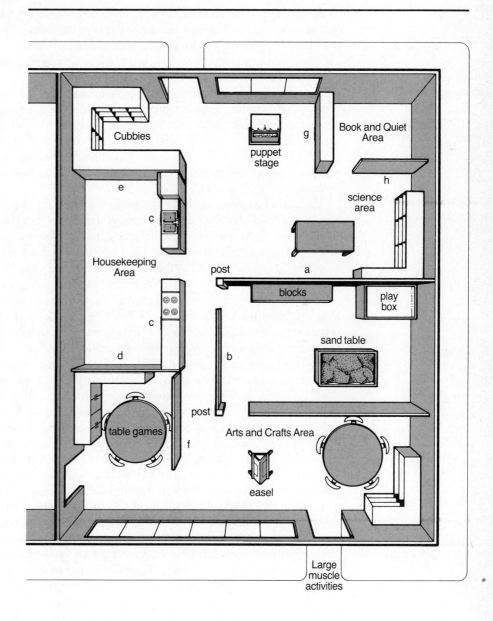

Cubbies

puppet stage

g

Book and Quiet Area

h

science area

e

c

Housekeeping Area

post

a

blocks

play box

c

d

sand table

b

post

Arts and Crafts Area

easel

f

table games

Large muscle activities

Figure 8.3   Closed Space Setting

awakened or got up from their rest, they went directly to the books, puppets, housekeeping, and table-games areas in the far end of the room. The activity of those who were not sleeping was restricted; they were allowed to choose more quiet, reserved activities, interesting and important, but unlikely to wake the sleeping children.

Open space can be closed with advantage to the children and the staff. A facility with separate rooms may be the most advantageous arrangement, but in many programs this simply is not possible. The example described above illustrates one way in which the physical space of a large open classroom can be altered—without prohibitive expense—in ways that will decrease growth-inhibiting behavior and increase growth-productive behavior. I am convinced that subdividing open space into more private, isolated, and separate areas increases the effectiveness and quality of the program.

Many teachers with whom I have talked are reluctant to redesign their physical setting in any way which would reduce the visual control they have over each child in the program. There is a widespread belief that it is necessary for child-care workers and teachers of young children to be able to see everything that is going on in their program all of the time. The reasons for this belief are many and varied but include concerns about the physical safety of children, the need to maintain discipline and an assumption that young children are too immature to care for themselves. I should not like to dismiss these concerns out of hand, but it does seem that they are more imaginary than real. Very young children are capable of making decisions about what they will do. These decisions are not threatening to them or others *if the environment is carefully designed so that potential dangers are eliminated or reduced.* For example, scissors with sharp points should never be left available to children; access to a kitchen should be controlled; electrical appliances which could cause a shock or start a fire should be removed; radiators and heat pipes need to be enclosed; staff should frequently remind the children about the appropriate use of materials and equipment.

Furthermore, we should remember that it is rare today for one adult to manage a preschool program for more than 10 children. Staff can and should move about the school and share the responsibility for checking to see what is taking place. Teachers can, and usually do, develop discriminating hearing. They can often determine by the sound of an activity whether or not there is reason for concern. In short, there are ways for teachers to monitor the behavior of the children in their responsibility without having continuous visual surveillance. The benefits that are derived from a closed environment far outweigh any concerns teachers might have about the potential danger of not being able to see children all of the time.

The Selection of Learning Areas

The composition of any early education program is every bit as important as its organization. The selection of learning areas is one of the chief means by which the curriculum is implemented and thus must be of special concern to all practitioners. There is a degree of similarity in the kinds of areas found in both preschools and the primary grades. Recall the observation made in Chapter 7 that in each of nine preschools there were unit blocks, an art area, book corner, games area, and creative-play or housekeeping area. Yet, there were a total of 30 areas identified among the 9 programs with an average of 10 areas per school. It is not difficult to imagine that the 5 or more areas not common to each program were selected because of emphases and goals chosen especially for the children in attendance.

There is an assumption, too, that a relationship exists between the areas selected and the overriding purposes of the program. Montessorians, for example, rely on the philosophy of child development and the goals developed by Maria Montessori as the rationale for the inclusion of the major curriculum areas and the materials. We should imagine that this should be the case in all educational programs, though the evidence may not be as clear or as compelling as it is in most Montessori programs.

It is important in discussing the organization of the physical setting to consider the selection of the learning areas. I should like to focus on two questions which should help practitioners decide whether or not the areas that they have selected for their programs are appropriate. The questions are as follows: 1) Are the goals of the program supported by the learning areas? 2) On what basis are areas changed, removed, or new ones introduced? Needless to say, much of the data needed to answer these questions must be gathered by observing the behavior of the children in each area.

Support of Program Goals

Deciding what learning areas to include in any program—preschool or primary level—is exceedingly important because, as was said in the preceding section, they may very well determine the content of the curriculum in programs in which children are given considerable latitude in choosing their activities. The selection process should be based on a knowledge of human development theory and a clear sense of the purposes and goals of the program. Teachers should understand the relationship of their beliefs regarding the nature of human development, their role in the classroom, and the kinds of experience provided for the children. As was stated in Chapter 5, the beliefs of the staff will very likely demand the selection of particular kinds of activities and organization.

Problems derived from confusion about the goals of the program, the nature of development, the process of instruction, and the selection of learning areas can be illustrated by recounting observations made in a nursery school for four- and five-year-old children. The children in this preschool were organized into three instructional groups. The morning program was organized so that the children spent 30 minutes in each of three learning areas. A staff member was in charge of each area and stayed with it as the children rotated through all three. The children were given formal and direct instruction in each area each day. They included language development, creative arts (painting, wood sculpture, collage, for example), and group circle games. The group instruction was preceded by a morning exercise for all children consisting of show and tell, a song or two, and a brief story. Group instruction was followed by outdoor play in all but the most inclement weather. The morning program ended with lunch.

Whether or not one would judge this program sound, it is important to note that the learning areas in the main classroom did not reflect the sequence of the program or, for that matter, its apparent intent. There were five permanent learning areas in this room, none of which was related to the curriculum as it was presented by the teachers. There was a table game area around a rectangular table with eight chairs; puzzles, lotto games, dominoes, and assorted small toys were found in cases nearby. The children rarely were allowed to use this area in the way its design suggested. Another area, which was rarely used, housed unit blocks. An attractive science area, with a pair of caged gerbils and a display of natural artifacts including birds nests, wormy wood, and wild flowers was never the center of any teacher-directed activity. The fourth area was comprised of a display of children's literature and a record player. Few children looked at the books and were never allowed to use the record player without the assistance of an adult. The last area contained simply three long, rectangular tables located in the center of the room which were used for breakfast and lunch and an occasional group art exercise.

It is important to note that of the three daily activities serving as the core of the program, only the group circle games were always held in the main room. The language program was conducted in an anteroom, and most of the creative arts took place in an entrance corridor. The permanent learning areas simply did not reflect the thrust of the program, and in many ways they interfered with the teacher-directed activities.

There seemed to be an absence of agreement between the program milieu and the requirements for children's behavior established by the staff. The organization of the five learning areas in the main classroom seemed to suggest one set of behaviors to the children but the teacher's behavior requirements were not at all related to the classroom environment. One result of this arrangement was that the staff had an exceedingly difficult time keeping the children from leaving the tasks and wandering off to the block area, the gerbil cage, or any other area, for that matter. As a consequence, children were carefully controlled in this center, staff were usually tense, and children were not spontaneous but became quite unruly when not supervised carefully. It was difficult, too, to know why the teachers managed the children as they did and why the classroom environment had been structured as it was. Quite obviously, there were more problems in this center than simply the dissonance between program procedure and learning areas. Nevertheless, this example does point up the need to consider carefully the relationship between the selection of learning areas and the goals of the program.

The Modification and Change of Areas

The selection of learning areas includes changing the program component as the behavior of the children indicates the need. The development of children (their progression to increasingly complex stages of social, intellectual and emotional development as they mature physically), necessitates the introduction of new activities and the removal of those which may have been appropriate in the recent past. For children who have not used puzzles, the wooden inlay, simply designed and uncomplicated, can be an exceedingly valuable part of a table-games area. However, too many dust-covered puzzle racks indicate that the children have developed problem-solving skills and memory to the point that this introductory material detracts from, rather than enhances, the table-games area. When this occurs, teachers should move quickly to remove the puzzles, redesign the area, or incorporate the materials with another area. Nothing contributes to the erosion of the quality of a program more than learning areas that neither interest nor challenge the children—that are not developmentally appropriate. The children's use of materials or their avoidance of an area can be most instructive in deciding when a change is necessary.

This point can be illustrated by a situation that occurred in a program for four-year-old children. The director of the program had given careful attention to the selection and organization of learning areas. She had included a housekeeping area with a stove, dishes, refrigerator, small table and two chairs, a mirror, and an assortment of adult clothing. The intent of the area was to foster two kinds of play. First, the director was certain that the children would begin to imitate adult behavior, as Piaget suggests, in an attempt to understand adult roles. In addition, she knew that the children would be likely to engage in creative dramatic play if encouraged and supported by the milieu. It was her belief that young children needed to be encouraged to do this, that it contributed to their creative and cognitive development.

It was with reluctance that the director admitted that very few of the children were using the area. Furthermore, for reasons that may be obvious, girls seemed willing to play the mother's role, but few boys even ventured into the area. It was simply not serving the purposes intended. After careful deliberation, it was decided to remove everything but the dress-up clothing, which was kept on a rack in a corner near the block area. The staff talked to the children about the change and continued to support every child's creative play and adult role playing.

It was not long after that the staff began to notice that play in and about the block area and the climbing apparatus took on a new character. The children were dressing up and building houses with kitchens or camps with campfires. Boys and girls played together, and their creative play dealt with such widely diverse subjects as pioneers, family cookouts, and the Old West. The children had merged the intent of three areas into a fourth. The dramatic play, which the housekeeping area had been designed to promote, became a reality. Furthermore, the children engaged each other and the staff in completing the activities. This occurred in large part because the staff realized that the housekeeping area, as attractive as it seemed to be, was actually inhibiting the children's activity; it was an interference. Removing the housekeeping equipment and relocating the dress-up clothes near two other areas in which considerable cooperative play already took place had the effect of provoking the kinds of integrated dramatic play the director valued.

In summary, the selection of learning areas occurs at two very distinct but important times in the history of every early education program: First at the time the program is begun, prior to the attendance of the children, and then later (during the evaluation of the adventure) whenever it seems appropriate and necessary as determined by the children's behavior.

The Worksheet presented in Table 8.1 is designed to assist practitioners in determining the appropriateness of their learning areas to the child-development goals of the program. It is a rather straightforward worksheet which should be completed for each area as the program is being designed. How it should be used can be illustrated by referring again to the diagram of the nursery/kindergarten classroom in Figure 8.1.

Thirteen areas have been selected for inclusion in this program. They are science, art, reading (and private space), table games, music, meetings area, creative play, blocks, woodworking, snack, cubbies, and the out-of-doors. An activity/area description worksheet would be completed for each of these areas, including a sketch of its location, the maximum number of children expected to use the area at one time, restrictions on when it could be used, the anticipated role of the adults (observing, instructing, cooperating, or being absent), the nature of the child's activity, and its materials and equipment. Most important would be a statement of the purposes of the area written in terms of children's behaviors. For example, the staff may have designed the science area with the intent to promote children's self-directed, problem-solving inquiry, curiosity, and exploratory/constructive behavior with other children and the staff. It might also have been planned as a place in which teachers could work with small groups of children helping them master important observation and recording skills. The staff would need to ask whether the description of the area (those items in the left column of Table 8.1) were consonant with the purposes listed in the right column.

The statement of purposes for each area would be set against a corollary statement of goals for the entire program. If the goals of the program represented in Figure 8.1 included the support and development of children's autonomy in directing their behaviors, the stated purposes for the science area should support this goal. The program goals appropriate to each area would be listed in the bottom segment of the right hand column. Needless to say, this entire evaluation is based on an assumption that the goals of the program would have been considered and presented in a statement by the staff.

The Organization of Learning Areas

The organization of learning areas is as important to the achievement of quality in early childhood education as the selection of these areas. There are two principles that should be followed in arranging any ECE setting. First, learning areas should be arranged so the *reciprocity of activity between areas can occur*. This means that the materials in adjacent areas can be used productively in each area. For example, if a sand table is to be included in the program, staff might consider placing it near the painting area so that the use of sand in painting may occur spontaneously. It also seems to make some sense to consider locating the small, movable floor toys, such as cars, trucks, and airplanes, near the unit blocks so that the children can blend the materials, when, for example, they construct a city. There should be an easy relationship between areas as they are arranged in any classroom. Though each area is selected for particular reasons, staff should give attention to the possible effects of the natural combination of areas on the development of the children and the realization of the objectives of the program.

The second principle in the organization of learning areas relates to the kinds of activities that are likely to occur in each area. Learning areas should be arranged so that activity in one area will not detract from nor interfere with activity in an adjoining area; in other words, adjacent areas should have *compatible standing patterns of behavior*. It

Table 8.1   **ACTIVITY/AREA DESCRIPTION WORKSHEET**

Activity/Area:

Location:	The purpose of the activity/area (or the learning/development goals):
Number of children:	
Adult role(s):	
Child role(s):	
Materials available to the children now:	
Equipment:	Program goals to be addressed in this area:
How the materials are displayed:	
Times when the activity/area may be used:	

simply doesn't make a great deal of sense to locate the woodworking area next to a children's book area. Obviously, the noise and activity of children pounding, sawing, and constructing things would be incompatible within the intense, reflective, quiet behavior of children deeply involved in literature.

The principles suggested for arranging any physical setting and making provisions for the three main types of children's behavior are illustrated in Figure 8.4. This sketch was taken from a program housed in the lower level of a church. All of the rooms were above ground; the main room had windows on two sides. All activity had originally been restricted to the area in the large room, but consideration of the need for semi-isolated areas and the fact that some activities created havoc prompted the teacher to explore the possibility of rearranging the learning areas in the main room, including some new areas, and opening more rooms for use by the children.

The program in this nursery school for 25 children was designed with three major goals in mind. First, it was anticipated that participation in the school would further the children's socialization, especially cooperation among the children. Second, the staff stressed the importance of supporting the development of children's self-concept. Special attention was given to efforts that would tend to promote each child's sense of self-importance without attendant selfishness. The last major goal was to promote the creative expression of each child. The staff sought to promote creative thought, painting and sculpting, dance and movement, not to mention building and creative play. The areas in the nursery school were selected and designed with these goals in mind.

The large room was approximately forty feet square. The storage cabinet and stairway (*a*) and the closed area (*b*) jutted into the room helping subdivide the large open space. The director made an arts area (*c*) by using the wall and a 5-foot-high shelf. The easel was located at the end of the shelf, further identifying the arts area as a separate space. The sand table, located just outside the art area, was used by children in both the block area and art area. The climbing apparatus was anchored to a supporting post in the center of the room; it was situated in such a way that it could be incorporated into the play of the block, dress-up, and floor toys area, as well as with the rocking boat and seesaw. The workbench was isolated from the rest of the activities, placed on the stairway wall. A major criticism of this arrangement would be the location of the table-games area. It was placed as far away from the more active areas as possible, which is good, but it did not appear to be a central part of the program and was not frequently used by the children.

Two storage rooms, *d* and *e*, were cleared and added to the center's space. In addition, one area of the kitchen was used once each day when the children with an adult prepared the mid-morning refreshment at the large table. Room *d*, off of the kitchen was a very small area with no windows, but more than adequate lighting. A carpet was laid on the floor and a chalk board was installed on a wall at floor level. A book case was placed against one wall. In addition, a floor-to-ceiling screen, 4 feet in length, was installed, extending from the entrance on the right side into the room. A foam rubber pallet with a pillow and blanket was placed behind the partition. This served two purposes: children were placed here when they became ill, and at other times it was a private space for use by any child finding the need.

Table 12.2   **Ways of Accommodating to Competing Demands**

Of the Larger Society:

1. Schools—preschool and primary level—will normally provide teachers with a curriculum framework which would, at least, list goals all teachers should strive to meet and, at best, outline the required instructional elements.

2. Practitioners will find handicapped and nonhandicapped children in the group for which they are responsible. They will need to make provisions in the selection of activities and materials and the organization of the setting to accommodate all children.

3. Teachers will organize the classroom environment and arrange a daily schedule in a way which will provide for 40 minutes of reading instruction each day. Materials, records, film strips, charts, posters—will usually be provided by the school. It will be the teacher's responsibility to decide how they will be used. There are numbers of instructional curriculum options from which teachers may select in meeting this demand.

Of Parents and the Local Community:

1. Teachers usually meet the demands of the community for instruction for literacy and other skill development when they meet state requirements. Usually there is no difficulty when children are achieving these competencies. It is only when large numbers of children fail to become literate, for example, that the community raises its voice.

2. Teachers can accommodate parents' concern that self-respect and human relationships be addressed in the curriculum in two ways: First, by arranging activities and areas so that children can develop skill in cooperation, assume some responsibility for maintaining the setting and experiment with ways of establishing and maintaining social relationships. Second, by striving to achieve an integrated population of children, by including materials which address issues of individual worth and present a multicultural perspective, and by reinforcing children's attempts to become self-directed, assertive, and accepting of other children.

Of the Profession:

1. The teacher should carefully examine the instructional program (and the educational milieu) to be assured that the demands of society and the community are being met.[a] He/she can augment the curriculum where it is felt to be deficient, as for example in conducting weekly magic circle activities for small groups of children or in designing a multi-media arts area where children can explore a wide range of materials, textures, and media in painting, construction, and sculpting.

2. Teachers are responsible for selecting activities which meet all school goals. They are also responsible for program design and arrangement and for determining the primary mode of adult-child interaction. Demand for a creative, autonomous curriculum and one which supports the uniqueness of each child can usually be addressed as teachers meet these responsibilities.

[a]It needs to be understood that practitioners need not always accede to the demands of parents or the state. It is the responsibility of the practitioners to examine the demands placed on him/her to ensure that expressions of parents' values or state law do not impinge upon the rights and freedoms of any individual or group in the society. Occasionally one finds adults who would have schools, at every level, indoctrinate children with a belief system in which people are judged more or less worthy, more or less good. We also know that forces are alive in society which would have the schools foster racism, ethnocentrism, and jingoism. Teachers must be vigilant in guarding against this possible use of the schools and refuse to allow groups to subvert the intent of schooling in an open and free society. This is a difficult but essential task.

Curriculum Bibliography

This bibliography is divided into two parts. The first section is comprised of a sample of materials representing alternative curriculum models or edited volumes in which different curricula are described. Included in this list are materials which present the ideas of authors who are behaviorists, exponents of transactionist theory, and those who espouse a more traditional socialization philosophy in early education. Certainly this bibliography is not exhaustive. It reflects the range of alternative early education curricula and materials have been selected for that reason alone.

The second part of the bibliography consists of sources for methods and materials that teachers can consult once they have decided what they should teach. Again, this list represents only a small fraction of the materials available to early educators. Practitioners should find this section helpful as they begin to develop a resource bibliography of their own.

I. Alternative Curriculum Models

Abbott, M. S., Galina, B. M., Granger, R. C., & Klein, D. L. *Alternative approaches to educating young children.* Atlanta: Humanics Ltd., 1976.
An overview of alternative curriculum models organized according to those which stress skill development, cognitive development, or affective development.

Bereiter, C., & Engelmann, S. *Teaching disadvantaged children in the preschool.* Englewood Cliffs, NJ: Prentice-Hall, 1966.
Important from a historical perspective. One of the first modern behaviorist curricula in early education. The basis for much of the curriculum of W. Becker and S. Engelmann.

Biber, B. A developmental-interaction approach: Bank Street College of Education. In M. C. Day & R. K. Parker (Eds.), *The preschool in action: Exploring early childhood programs.* (2nd ed.). Boston: Allyn & Bacon, 1977.
A clear exposition of the Bank Street curriculum by its most articulate exponent. Based on transactionist developmental theory and psychodynamic theory.

Broman, B. *The early years in childhood education.* Chicago: Rand McNally, 1978.
A traditional approach to early education with emphasis on common school subjects.

Copple, C., Sigel, I. E., and Saunders, R. *Educating the young thinker: Classroom strategies for cognitive growth.* New York: D. Van Nostrand, 1979.
A Piagetian curriculum. Based on an experimental preschool directed by Copple.

Day, M. C., & Parker, R. K. *The preschool in action* (2nd ed.). Boston: Allyn & Bacon, 1977.
An important reference. Includes fifteen statements by authors of different curricula for children from infancy to school age. Curricula reflect a wide range of theories of development and education.

Evans, E. D. *Contemporary influences in early childhood education* (2nd ed.) New York: Holt, Rinehart and Winston, 1975.
An essential source book. Five important alternative curricula are described and evaluated, including traditional, Montessori, behavioral analysis, English Infant School, and Piaget.

Forman, G. E., & Kuschner, D. S. *The child's construction of knowledge: Piaget for teaching children.* Monterey, CA: Brooks/Cole, 1977.
As the title would suggest, based on Piagetian developmental theory. This book resulted in large part from two years of an experimental preschool directed by Forman.

Hendrick, J. *Total learning for the whole child.* St. Louis: C. V. Mosby, 1980.
An excellent alternative to traditional subject-matter curricula. The emphasis is on child development. Very useful.

Hess, R. D., & Croft, D. J. *Teachers of young children.* New York: Houghton Mifflin, 1972.
The emphasis in this book is on the role of the teacher in early education and the influence of society and culture on children's development.

Hildebrand, V. *Guiding young children* (2nd ed.). New York: Macmillan, 1980.
A child-guidance approach to early education. Emphasis on psychological development of preschool-aged children.

Hohmann, M., Banet, B., & Weikert, D. P. *Young children in action.* Ypsilanti, MI: The High/Scope Press, 1979.
From the work of Weikert and High/Scope, developed over many years of research and experimentation. Largely Piagetian but clearly influenced by traditional early education practices.

Kamii, C., & DeVries, R. *Physical knowledge in preschool education: Implications of Piaget's theory.* Englewood Cliffs, NJ: Prentice-Hall, 1978.
Drawn from Piagetian developmental theory. Based on research conducted by the authors in an experimental school. Very clear statement of one possible implication for curricula to be drawn from Piaget's theory.

Leeper, S. H., Skipper, D. S., & Witherspoon, R. L. *Good schools for young children* (4th ed.). New York: Macmillan, 1979.
A standard early education text. A comprehensive statement based on traditional subject-matter organization and concern for social and emotional development.

Montessori, M. *The Montessori method.* Cambridge, MA: Robert Bentley, 1964.
The clearest and most comprehensive introduction by Montessori to her psychology of development and teaching, and to the curriculum she devised. An essential Montessori reference.

Parker, R. K. (Ed.). *The preschool in action.* Boston: Allyn & Bacon, 1972.
The first edition of the Day and Parker, 1977, volume described earlier. Authors describe curricula being developed.

Read, K. H. *The nursery school: A human relationships laboratory* (4th Ed.).
Philadelphia: W. B. Saunders, 1971.
A standard preschool reference. Emphasis is on human relationships. Read has carefully revised and rewritten this edition to reflect changes in child developmental knowledge and social need. A useful reference.

Rogers, V. R. *Teaching in the British primary school.* London: Macmillan, 1970.
An edited book with papers by English educators describing aspects of the English Infant School approach to the education of children aged four to seven years.

Spodek, B. (Ed.). *Early childhood education.* Englewood Cliffs, NJ: Prentice-Hall, 1973.
Description of alternative curriculum models by the authors.

Spodek, B. *Teaching in the elementary years* (2nd Ed.). Englewood Cliffs, NJ: Prentice-Hall, 1978.
A clear and useful presentation of the purposes and procedures of organizing curriculum from a traditional subject matter perspective.

Weber, L. *The English Infant School and informal education.* Englewood Cliffs, NJ: Prentice-Hall, 1971.
Describes the English model. A very useful text including a discussion of both theory and practice.

II. *Methods and Materials*
General Sources

Adams, L., & Garlick, B. (Eds.). *Ideas that work with young children* (Vol. 2). Washington, DC: National Association for the Education of Young Children, 1979.

Ashton-Warner, S. *Teacher.* New York: Bantam Books, 1963.

Austin Association for the Education of Young Children. *The idea box: Ideas for creative curriculum.* Washington, DC: National Association for the Education of Young Children, 1979.

Banet, B., McClelland, D., Nederveld, P., Thomas, C., & Silverman, C. *Action in the cognitive preschool model.* Ypsilanti, MI: High/Scope Educational Research Foundation, 1972.

Banet, B., Silverman, C., Allen, M., & Thomson, C. *Levels of representation: The symbol level and the sign level.* Ypsilanti, MI: High/Scope Educational Research Foundation, 1972.

Bauer, C. F. *Handbook for story tellers.* Chicago: American Library Association, 1977.

Croft, D. J., & Hess, R. J. *An activities handbook for teachers of young children* (3rd Ed.). New York: Houghton Mifflin, 1980.
An excellent source book. Strongly recommended for every teacher.

Forman, G. E., & Hill, D. F. *Constructive play: Applying Piaget in the preschool.* Monterey, CA: Brooks-Cole, 1980.

Flemming, B. M., Hamilton, D. S., & Hicks, J. D. *Resources for creative teaching in early childhood education.* New York: Harcourt Brace Jovanovich, 1977.

Hendrick, J. *The whole child* (2nd ed.). St. Louis: C. V. Mosby, 1980.
The chapter bibliographies are excellent. Highly recommended.

Hewes, D. W. (Ed.). *Administration: Making programs work for children and families.* Washington, DC: National Association for the Education of Young Children, 1979.

Hirsch, E. S. (Ed.). *The block book.* Washington, DC: National Association for the Education of Young Children, 1974.

Kamii, C., & DeVries, R. *Group games in early education: Implications of Piaget's theory.* Washington, DC: National Association for the Education of Young Children, 1980.

Lorton, M. B. *Workjobs.* Menlo Park, CA: Addison-Wesley, 1972.

Richardson, L. I., Goodman, K. L., Hartman, N. N., & LePique, H. C. *A mathematics activity curriculum for early childhood and special education.* New York: Macmillan, 1980.

Russell, H. R. *Ten-minute field trips: A teacher's guide using the school grounds for environmental studies.* Chicago: J. G. Ferguson, 1973.

Stone, J. G. *A guide to discipline* (Rev. ed.). Washington, DC: National Association for the Education of Young Children, 1978.
Practical suggestions with discussion for teachers.

Art Activities

Cherry, C. *Creative art for the developing child: A teacher's handbook for early childhood education*. Belmont, CA: Fearon Publishers, 1972.

Graham, A. *Foxtails, ferns and fish scales: A handbook of art and nature projects*. New York: Four Winds Press, 1976.

Haskell, L. *Art in the early childhood years*. Columbus, OH: Merrill, 1979.
Suggestions for the selection and planning of art projects.

Pile, N. F. *Art experiences for young children*. New York: Macmillan, 1973.

Multi-cultural Activities

Griffin, L. *Multi-ethnic books for young children: Annotated bibliography for parents and teachers*. Washington, DC: National Association for the Education of Young Children (no date).

Comer, J. P., & Poussaint, A. F. *Black child care—how to bring up a healthy black child in America: A guide to emotional and psychological development*. New York: Simon & Schuster, 1975.

Schmidt, V. E., & McNeill, E. *Cultural awareness: A resource bibliography*. Washington, DC: National Association for the Education of Young Children, 1978.

Music, Dance, Movement Activities

American Alliance for Health, Physical Education and Recreation. *Annotated bibliography on movement education*. Washington, DC: American Alliance for Health, Physical Education, and Recreation, 1977. (a)

Andross, B. *Music experiences in early childhood*. New York: Holt, Rinehart and Winston, 1980.
Activity resource.

Bayless, K. M., & Ramsey, M. E. *Music: A way of life for the young child*. St. Louis: C. V. Mosby, 1978.

Cherry, C. *Creative movement for the developing child: A nursery school handbook for non-musicians* (Rev. ed.). Belmont, CA: Fearon Publishers, 1971.

Dimondstein, G. *Children dance in the classroom*. New York: Macmillan, 1971.

Glazer, T. *Eye Winker Tom Tinker Chin Chopper: Fifty musical fingerplays.* Garden City, NY: Doubleday, 1973.

McDonald, D. T. *Music in our lives: The early years*. Washington, DC: National Association for the Education of Young Children, 1979.

Physical Development

American Alliance for Health, Physical Education, and Recreation. *Choosing and using phonograph records for physical education, recreation and related activities.* Washington, DC: American Alliance for Health, Physical Education, and Recreation, 1977. (b)

Arnheim, D. D., & Pestolesi, R. A. *Elementary physical education: A developmental approach.* St. Louis: C. V. Mosby, 1978.

Flinchum, B. M. *Motor development in early childhood.* St. Louis: C. V. Mosby, 1975.

Shea, T. M. *Teaching children and youth with behavior disorders.* St. Louis: C. V. Mosby, 1978.

Outdoor Areas

Allen, Lady, of Hurtwood. *Planning for play.* Cambridge, MA: The MIT Press, 1968.

Frost, J. L., & Klein, B. L. *Children's play and playgrounds.* Boston: Allyn & Bacon, Inc., 1979.

Hewes, J. J. *Build your own playground: A sourcebook of play sculptures, designs and concepts from the work of Jay Beckwith.* Boston: Houghton Mifflin, 1974.

Health and Nutrition Activities

Arnstein, H. S. *What to tell your child: About birth, illness, death, divorce and other family crises.* New York: Condor Publishing Co., 1978.

Bernstein, A. C. *Flight of the stork: What children really want to know about sex—and when.* New York: Delacorte Press, 1978.

Head Start Bureau. *Nutrition education for young children.* Washington, DC: Author, Association for Children, Families and Youth, Office of Child Development, HEW, 1976.

Reinisch, E. H., & Minear, R. E. *Health of the preschool child.* New York: John Wiley, 1978.
Good beginning reference for teachers (especially in day care).

Wanamaker, N., Hearn, K., & Richarz, S. *More than graham crackers: Nutrition education and food preparation with young children.* Washington, DC: National Association for the Education of Young Children, 1979.

References: Chapter 12

Barker, R. G., & Gump, P. V. *Big school, small school.* Palo Alto, CA: Stanford University Press, 1964.

Bricker, D. D. A rationale for the integration of handicapped and nonhandicapped preschool children. In M. J. Guralnick, *Early intervention and the integration of handicapped and nonhandicapped children.* Baltimore: University Park Press, 1978.

Duckworth, E. Either we're too early and they can't learn or we're too late and they know it already: The dilemma of applying Piaget. *Harvard Educational Review*, 1979, *49* (3), 297–312.

Katz, Lilian G. Teaching in preschools: Roles and goals. *Children*, 1970, *17*, 42–48.

Kuhn, D. The application of Piaget's theory of cognitive development to education. *Harvard Educational Review*, 1979, *49* (3), 340–360.

Meisels, S. J. *Developmental screening in early childhood: A guide.* Washington, DC: The National Association for the Education of Young Children, 1979.

13 Evaluating Your Program

Gathering information useful in making judgments about the effectiveness of any educational program is an integral part of teaching. For generations, teachers "tested" their students through recitation and by written examination. The students were judged by a measure very often based on accumulated experience; children were able to read and comprehend the second-grade reader or they were not; they could recite the multiplication tables or they could not. Not only were children evaluated by these procedures, but teachers were judged as well. Too many failures could suggest that a teacher was not very effective.

There has been considerable change in program evaluation procedures over the past several years. Though teachers still quiz their children when it is appropriate, the bulk of program evaluation data is gathered by administering standardized tests in which a child's educational progress is either compared to other children his/her age and grade level, or to a standard or criterion score.

The first procedure involves the use of achievement tests. For the past 30 or more years, it has been common practice to have every child in the elementary school complete tests in reading, language arts (spelling and knowledge of grammar), and arithmetic at least once each year. A child's score on an achievement test is usually reported by grade-level and percentile. A grade-level score reflects a student's achievement compared to children of similar age and grade. For example, a child finishing first grade should score at or near one year and nine months or two years, meaning the child has achieved to the ninth or tenth month of the first grade—a successful score on the face of it. However, it is not uncommon for parents, teachers, and administrators to be misinformed by results such as these. Special emphasis is commonly given to the grade-level score; a child who scores above grade level may be judged to have excelled far beyond a classmate whose score falls below grade level. It is entirely possible that they may be quite similar in their skills, each performing quite adequately. Such misconceptions arise from an inadequate understanding of the way in which norms are established. Grade level is not a standard but rather the midpoint or median score for all of the children in the standardization sample. That is, each test is standardized by being administered to a large sample of children for whom the test is designed—in this case children completing first grade. The grade level score is that point at which 50% of the children score higher and 50% lower. It tells us where the middle is but not the range or the relative competence of children who score two or four or even six months apart.

Criterion tests are also becoming widely used in assessing children's progress. In many ways the form and structure of a criterion-referenced test is like that of the achievement test. They can be developed for testing any skill or body of knowledge, but in early education their use is usually restricted to reading, language, and mathematics. The difference between this type of test and the achievement test is that with criterion-referenced tests a standard—a measure of competence—is determined, to which all children are expected to approximate. Quite simply, it may be said that a child completing first grade should be able to correctly complete 10 of 15 one-number addition problems or spell 20 of 25 monosyllabic words. If the child does add correctly 10 or more arithmetic problems and spells 20 words, he/she will be judged to have met the criterion established for children near the end of their first-grade exprience. Criterion tests do not rely on averaging the performance of children as do achievement tests. Rather, educators establish a standard of performance they believe to be a reasonable expectation for all children in a similar circumstance. Quite obviously, criterion-referenced tests will be valid to the degree the test makers establish an appropriate standard or level of mastery.

Without question the results of achievement and criterion tests provide teachers and parents with valuable information about *some* essential aspects of children's development, such as word recognition, comprehension, spelling skill, and performance of basic mathematical operations. Furthermore, comparative analyses of children's achievement can be instructive if the comparisons are based on local and regional norms rather than the national norms provided by the test maker.

The Need for Cautious Interpretation

There are, however, many reasons for treating the results of these test data with caution and reserve. There is absolutely no question that a child's performance on an achievement test will be related to his/her social status, race, sex, and to the location of the school. Poor and minority children generally score less well on their tests than do nonminority and more affluent children. The reasons for this have never been clearly defined, though attempts have been made for more than four decades. What we have learned suggests that the poorer child's performance may be affected by the competence of his/her teacher, the wealth of the school, the relationship which develops between parents and teachers, and the experiences the child brings to school. More than likely we will discover that all of these factors and more interact in a way which influences the child's school performance. The point is, however, that comparing the achievement scores of a group of poor children with those of students with more advantages, when we know the comparison would be flawed by such factors as those listed above, may lead to the belief that the poor child is incapable of reaching even the minimal level of educational achievement. In a word, the observation of the relationship between status and achievement test results may ensure the continuation of that relationship. On one hand, teachers and parents may reduce their expectations for lower-status children based on the annual production of data suggesting these children can't learn very well. On the other hand, they may believe that advantaged children enjoy an elite status in our society merely as an effect of placement on these tests. In either case, the consequences are unfortunate for all children and society.

Reliance on standardized tests as the chief means by which programs are evaluated raises another important issue. By no means are curricula the same in schools across the nation—nor should they be. A teacher of kindergarten or first grade children in Roswell, New Mexico, will find it necessary to create a program quite different from a colleague teaching children in Presque Isle, Maine. The differences in the curriculum would reflect differences in cultures, climate, region, and the economic structure of the area; all of these factors, of course, would influence the developmental needs of the two groups of children in different ways. Each teacher would be likely to emphasize very different objectives in his/her program; they might produce very different educational experiences. Yet the standardized test cannot accommodate curricular variation and, in most instances, will assess only a limited portion of the program planned by the teacher. The tests will provide some information about aspects of children's reading-skill progress, mathematical reasoning and computational skills, knowledge of the rules and structure of formal American English, for example, and, in some cases, even an assessment of children's problem-solving skills. However, a curriculum for young children is always larger, more complex, and more extensive and far-reaching in purpose than those measured by the most comprehensive achievement or criterion testing program. We have seen in the abbreviated history of early education in Part I that the public has always considered the purposes of education to be broader and more comprehensive than the creation of a literate and informed populace. As necessary and valuable as these goals may be, they do not comprise a full school program. Yet there is the danger that the common and widespread use of standard tests across the nation as the chief means by which teaching is judged may eventually influence practitioners in Maine and New Mexico to restrict their concerns only to those areas of the curriculum measured by the tests.

There is a third reason for practitioners to be cautious in their use of a nationally standardized achievement testing program to evaluate school programs. The data are always provided well after teaching has been completed and in a way which makes it difficult to use them for curriculum improvement. Most commonly, tests are administered to the children only days before the close of the school year. In each May and June millions of children across the land complete the tests. These tests are returned to the producer where they are machine scored and analyzed. The results are returned to the schools, copies are provided for the families of the children and for inclusion in the student's academic folder. Teachers no longer find it necessary to spend hours hand-scoring these tests; this, on the surface, is a boon. However, the insights a teacher may gain by scoring the tests can easily be lost because the reports coming from the machine analysis usually arrive well after the close of the school year and may not even be seen by the teachers.

A far more important concern is that these *post facto* data used for program evaluation or in judging any child's progress are attributed to the school curriculum. We know, however, that such attribution is quite impossible without at the same time controlling for such possible influential variables as students' health or changes in the structure of the school (new teachers mid-year, increased student motivation, or personality changes, for example). In brief, a very sophisticated research design in which the curriculum of the school is only one of several factors considered in the search for causes of student achievement is imperative before children's achievement can be attributed with any certainty to a year's program of study. Even if such a research design were used in analyzing achievement test data, teachers would still find it difficult to use the results in curriculum redesign or development. The year's program would be considered in toto; if children performed well, and the analysis showed that it was primarily because of the curriculum, teachers would have reason to take heart; however, they wouldn't know with any assurance what part of the year's work was more or less valuable.

More important, when children do not perform as well as one believes they should and it seems important to know how the curriculum might be improved, *post facto* standardized test score results are practically useless. Teachers can simply not use these data in making any judgment about the relative effect of their reading program, for example, or if the children's literature component was in any way influential. Consequently, teachers who redesign a curriculum solely on the basis of standardized achievement data cannot be at all certain that changes they make are in any way related to the children's performance. There is little practitioners can take from *post facto* analyses of achievement data which would reveal the value, appropriateness, or the effect of timing of the parts of the curriculum on children's behavior.

In short, it is becoming increasingly difficult to use data from achievement or criterion-referenced tests in making *informed* judgments about the quality of children's school experiences. Three reasons have been presented in support of this conclusion.

1. The tests are insensitive to the expression of ability across status or ethnic lines.

2. The tests may be only marginally related to the essential purposes of the program and an inadequate measure of the breadth of the curriculum.

3. Using achievement data for *post facto* evaluation provides practitioners with little help in judging the quality of the components of the curriculum.

There is absolutely no question of the necessity for assessing the quality of the child-development and educational experience offered each child. However, the time has long since passed when practitioners can rely on history, logic, child-development theory or knowledge, or personal preference in making a judgment about the worth of any curriculum. The issue is not whether to evaluate or not, but how.

Ecologically Valid Assessments

Evaluation procedures which are ecologically valid need to be designed; which provide information about the ways in which children influence and are influenced by the activities and experiences of the program day. If we can accept the interactive relationship of behavior and milieu described in Chapters 6 and 7, it is essential that the assessment of any curriculum provide data regarding the congruence between the parts of the curriculum—the segments—and their purposes. For example, we need to know to what degree children are using the table-games area as it was intended to be used. Furthermore, we should have information about the children's behavior which is sufficiently precise to allow us to make a judgment about the progress of their development. Perhaps most important of all is the need to find ways of getting data like these to teachers as the curriculum is unfolding so that they can make adjustments in the program where it seems obvious that such changes are needed to enhance and sustain development.

I should like to describe an evaluation procedure which is ecologically sound and will produce data useful to practitioners in judging the quality of the experiences provided to children and for improving the curriculum.[1] Especially important in this procedure is the fact that the data is to be gathered during the school year and would be immediately available to the staff at a time when they can use it to make adjustments in their program. The assessment provides for an analysis of each essential part of the curriculum—the reading program, the arts activities, blocks, role playing activity, and circle time, for example.

This procedure is based on two important assumptions. First, if one accepts the behavior-environment relationship described in Chapters 6 and 7, it can be assumed that, in the main, children's behavior in the early education setting will be largely a consequence of the interactive relationship of their presence and the milieu of the setting. Second, it is assumed that children's natural behavior is a valid criterion for determining program quality, when natural behavior is defined as that behavior exhibited by children as they complete the day-to-day activities of the program. The description of the evaluation procedure will follow after a discussion of the second assumption. The assertion of a behavior-environment relationship should have been sufficiently covered in earlier chapters. A discussion of evaluation for program improvement (the major purpose of the procedure) will follow, and the chapter will close with a description of the steps in the procedure.

Children's Behavior as the Measure of Effectiveness

Earlier in this text the point was repeatedly made that children's behavior in early childhood programs may be more influenced by what they experience there than by other factors. It has been suggested, for example, that three-year-olds will engage in task involvement behavior to the degree the early education setting communicates the importance of this behavior. More precisely, it seems that the organization of the physical setting, the selection and presentation of materials, and the behavior of adults

---

[1]This section borrows heavily from an earlier description of the evaluation procedure by Day, Perkins, and Weinthaler (1979) published in *Young Children*.

would be critical in sustaining task involvement behavior (see Chapters 8, 9, and 10).

The ecological psychology of Barker (1968) and Gump (1969; 1975), among others, leads to the conclusion that milieu cannot be ignored in any assessment of human behavior. It is quite another matter, however, to select a standard by which observed behavior can be judged to be appropriate or not. Knowing of an environment-behavior interaction tells one only where to search for cause; it says nothing about the quality or the appropriateness of the behavior.

It can generally be conceded that early education programs, regardless of curriculum format, are designed to foster and sustain the development of children, when development includes educational objectives. In addition, it is assumed that social, emotional, and intellectual behavior are included in any definition of development and that any assessment must, as a minimum, gather data on these three aspects of human behavior.

Following the assertion of a behavior-environment interrelationship, it is suggested that children's natural behavior in the early education setting can be an effective measure of the degree to which the program is contributing to development. Children's behavior in the routine of the program day will provide two important kinds of data. First, the children's behavior will reflect social, emotional, and intellectual development. Second, these data will indicate the degree to which the early education setting is supporting these aspects of development. The behavior of a child at an easel, when he or she is engaged with other children in dramatic play, constructing at the sand table, or on the playground can be valid and useful in assessing aspects of development.

This position regarding the validity of natural behavior in assessment of development is based on the belief that children's behavior in any setting is the manifestation of development, as it can be expressed in that setting. Assume for a moment that early educators would agree that four-year-old children should be demonstrating a growing sense of autonomy and that programs should be fostering and supporting this behavior. Practitioners should then record the instances of four-year olds making choices about what they shall do, deciding when to continue a task rather than join a group activity, and resolving some difficulty in getting material; they should use these data as evidence of a child's demonstration of self-directed behavior. These data provide some indication of the degree to which the early education setting was supporting the development of autonomy. For a child to make a choice about what he or she will do, adults must make that choice possible. Also, to resolve a materials problem indicates emotional and intellectual strength but also suggests that materials are readily available and that children are encouraged to use them as they find it necessary. In short, it is assumed that the degree to which any early childhood program is promoting and supporting development—in this case autonomous behavior—may be discerned from observations of the children's natural behavior during the program day.

Though natural behavior may be a valid indicator of competence and achievement, the question of what kinds of behavior practitioners should be observing remains to be answered. I have addressed this issue by building upon the results of the study of day care by Day and Sheehan (1974), reported in Chapter 8. Recall that seven categories of

Table 13.1	Generic Categories of Child Behavior

1. Task Involvement: Children are absorbed in the activities, completing games and tasks, and attending to what they are doing.
2. Cooperation: Children are or seek to be engaged in cooperative activity with adults and other children.
3. Autonomy: Children are making choices about what they shall do.
4. Communication: Children initiate conversation with other children and with adults regarding on-going activities.
5. Materials: Children use the materials and equipment of the program effectively.
6. Management: Children help to organize activities of the program, assisting staff in arranging equipment, distributing materials, and cleaning-up when necessary.
7. Consideration: Children are usually considerate of other children and their activities.

children's behavior were identified which characterized quality day care programs. Those categories have been revised after careful examination by practitioners and used as the basis for an observation instrument, The Behavior Checklist (Day, et al., 1979). The seven generic categories are listed in Table 13.1.

The checklist consists of 34 behaviors subsumed in the revised seven generic categories of behavior (see Table 13.2). These categories reflect aspects of social, intellectual, and emotional behavior commonly expected of three- to eight-year-old children. This observation instrument can be used for recording children's behavior a number of times on successive days, at different times during the program day.

The checklist does not constitute an exhaustive account of children's behavior. Rather it reflects the earlier study, judgments about the developmental behavior of young children, and goals of early education accepted by a diverse group of practitioners. The Behavior Checklist is a fair representation of the intent of some early childhood education programs and an instructive index of child-development behavior. It is used for recording natural behavior in the early education setting.

Alternative Curricula

Though I may have resolved to my own satisfaction the question of what behaviors are important to record in judging a program for young children, there are doubtless many who would believe the seven categories and their parts constitute an inadequate or inappropriate survey of important behaviors. Recall the discussion in Chapter 12 on the use of child development as a primary source for curricula. The aims or purposes of a Piaget-derived curriculum were presented for four teams of scholars: Kamii and DeVries; Copple, Sigel and Saunders; Forman and Kuschner; and Biber. Recall, too, that though they looked to Piaget for direction, each team of authors established a set of objectives quite different from all the others. In effect, each team had established quite different behaviors as the criterion for success for the children. Kamii and DeVries

Table 13.2	The Behavior Checklist

Task Involvement:
Focuses on a task
Resolves a problem
Completes a task
Leaves a task
Is inattentive
Wanders about the room

Cooperation:
Seeks participation with a child or adult
Is involved with a child or adult
Accepts a request to join an activity with a child or adult
Takes turns

Autonomy:
Selects an activity
Asks permission
Works independently
Chooses to join a group activity
Chooses not to join a group activity
Rejects a child's or adult request to join an activity

Verbal Interaction:
Talks with a child or adult
Requests information from a child or adult
Responds to a child or an adult
Speaks to self

Materials Use:
Uses materials in an activity
Combines materials from different areas
Abuses or misuses materials

Maintenance:
Takes responsibility for picking up
Volunteers to assist a child or teacher in a maintenance activity
Helps an adult prepare an area or activity
Waits for a teacher to prepare an activity

Consideration:
Observes the activity of others without disruption
Respects the physical space of others
Shares materials with others
Helps or offers sympathy to a child in distress
Disturbs the activity of others
Threatens or strikes another child

selected two categories of objectives: socioemotional and cognitive. Socioemotional objectives focused on aspects of autonomy, cooperation, and initiative; cognitive behavior included the generation of ideas and the active arrangement of materials and events. Copple and her colleagues identified ten objectives which they felt constituted appropriate intellectual behavior for young children. In some ways the objectives of Kamii and DeVries and Copple et al., are similar to some of the categories found in the Behavior Checklist; yet I feel confident that each of the authors would resist using this list as an appropriate representation of the aims and objectives of their curriculum.

Table 13.3	An Adaptation of the Behavior Checklist: From Copple, Sigel, and Saunders

1. Awareness of objects and events.
   1.1 Children use a variety of materials in an activity.
   1.2 Children listen to suggestions offered by other children.
   1.3 Etc.

2. Use a variety of inquiry methods.
   2.1 Children ask teachers and other children questions about events and materials.
   2.2 Children observe the effect of action on materials.
   2.3 Etc.

In cases like this the procedure need not be abandoned. Rather, one may simply substitute his/her list of essential behaviors for those identified in the Behavior Checklist. For example, Copple, Sigel, and Saunders might use each of their ten objectives as categories of behavior under which could be listed more precise behavior that would define the essence of each objective. This adaptation is illustrated in Table 13.3 above.[2]

Bank Street College of Education has designed an observation procedure similar in many ways to that presented here with a list of behaviors judged to be appropriate and necessary in child-adult interactions. The BRACE system, as it is called, was developed as a partial means of evaluating the Bank Street Follow Through program. Several years ago Kamii (1971) discussed ways in which teachers might be able to gather observational data on aspects of children's socioemotional, physical, and logico-mathematical knowledge, taken directly from Piaget's assertion of the types of knowledge. Though she has changed her position regarding the use of Piaget's stages of development as appropriate educational objectives, her ideas regarding the use of observation of behavior when both behavior and the place it occurred are recorded remains compelling and instructive.

In short, though we have no consensus among early educators about what constitutes the most appropriate goals for any program for young children and though many practitioners would refuse to accept the Behavior Checklist categories of behavior as sufficient, it does seem possible that one could modify this list to reflect particular program goals and values without changing the basic procedure. Practitioners need not agree about child behaviors in order to gather evaluative data in the ways suggested here.[3] However, for purposes of expediency and illustration the discussion here will consider only those behaviors in the Behavior Checklist.

---

[2] Of course, to be valid any statement of appropriate child development behavior must be accepted by a significant number of practitioners and parents and judged to be sufficiently comprehensive by a jury of child development scholars.

[3] Though it cannot be discussed here, the point should be made that preparing a list of behaviors and defining them so that a high degree of reliability among observers can be achieved is absolutely essential if the data produced are to be at all valid. Procedures for such definition of categories and testing for reliability are described in most texts which discuss data gathering and analysis.

Table 13.4   **Behavior by Area Matrix**

Numbers and Percent of behaviors observed by Area	Learning Areas/Activities					
	Free Play (52)[a]	House-keeping (22)	Large Group (194)	Table Games (5)	Blocks (48)	Total[b] (594)
Focuses on task	26 50.0	14 63.6	155 79.9	5 100.0	35 72.9	438 73.7
Inattentive	1 1.9	3 13.6	19 9.8	0	2 4.2	41 6.9
Involved with another child	2 3.8	9 40.9	11 5.7	1 20.0	10 20.8	88 14.8
Involved with an adult	2 3.8	1 4.5	12 6.2	0	6 12.5	38 6.4
Working independently	15 28.8	2 9.1	2 1.0	3 60.0	13 27.1	128 21.5
Talks with another child	26 50.0	16 72.7	15 7.7	2 40.0	11 22.9	187 31.5
Talks with an adult	11 21.2	2 9.1	13 6.7	0	15 31.3	93 15.7
Uses materials	20 38.5	10 45.5	15 7.7	5 100.0	35 72.9	247 41.6
Total Behavior by Area						

[a]Total number of times children were observed in each area.

[b]The total column gives the total number of observations for each behavior over the entire program plus the percentage of times each behavior was observed. These data, of course, do not show all the areas in this program.

Evaluation for Program Improvement

The primary purpose in conducting this naturalistic evaluation is to produce data useful for immediately improving the quality of the experience for children. The evaluative process will provide practitioners with two interrelated sets of data to be used in achieving this goal. First, a valuable index of child development, for the group and individual children, will result from observation of the children's behavior. The observations will provide one with a fair indication of how well children are achieving those developmental competencies represented by each of the seven generic categories. Second, the data will provide insight into the degree to which the program segments—activities and areas—are contributing to each category of behavior. Information regarding each segment will be taken from the Behavior Checklist because each observation will note the activity or area in which the behavior occurs.

The observational data can be graphically presented when using a matrix which includes the behaviors observed, where they occurred, and the relative proportion of area and activity use. Some data have been taken from observations in a preschool for three-to five-year-old children and are presented in Table 13.4. Note that information is given for only eight of 34 behaviors and five of 15 areas in this class. A complete matrix would be difficult to include in this text. Nonetheless, it is possible to get a good idea from this matrix of the kinds of data the observations can produce. Furthermore, the ways in which the information can be used can also be shown.

To begin, note that the number of observations in each area is included in parentheses under each column heading. These data tell us that children were observed engaged in free play 52 times, housekeeping 22, large group 194, table games 5, and blocks 48 times out of a total of 594 observations. This information is valuable for what it reveals about children's use of the entire classroom. Recall that the observations are recorded for children wherever they may be. That is, the children are randomly selected for observation at times over the entire program day. If an observer is to code the behavior of Jamel White at 10:00 AM, he/she must find Jamel and then observe her wherever she is. And, if she moves from the table games to open activity, the observer follows, making sure to record where Jamel is after each observation. Conducting observations in this manner allows us to draw the conclusion that the number of observations recorded in each area represents an accurate record of its use. Looking at the information in Table 13.4, we could say that the table-games area is essentially not used (5 observations out of a total of 594 or .8% of the time). We could also say that children were engaged in open activity, or that occurring in the classroom but not located in any area, substantially more than in housekeeping (22 observations) and as much in the block area (48). Questions could be raised about whether or not children should be engaged in open activity as much as is indicated by these data and whether something is amiss in housekeeping and table games because of their infrequent use.

The matrix will also reveal the kinds of behavior found in each area. Notice that the children were focused on task 79.9% of the time in the large group area, 72.9% in blocks but only 63.6% in housekeeping and 50% in open activity. Though the children engaged in open activity and used the block area about an equal amount of time, there was 23% more on-task behavior in blocks than in open activity, 16% more cooperative involvement with another child, and a 15% greater use of materials.

Casting the observational data on a matrix such as that in Table 13.4 also allows analysis of the time children have to make choices about where they shall be engaged. Each classroom can be analyzed according to those activities which occur at the direction of the teacher and those for which the children have a choice. For example, in the program from which these data were taken all children were required to attend large group activities and snack time, and they all had to go outdoors at the same time. We know there were 194 observations in large group, and in addition there were 113 outdoors and 35 at snack time for a total of 342 observations in activities which offered the child no choice. Fifty-six percent of the time children's choice of activity was directed by the teacher.

It should be clear that observing children as they go about their affairs in any program can provide teachers with many kinds of valuable data. Furthermore, if we accept the assertion that children's behavior in the classroom is to a large extent a function of that environment, these data can be very useful in judging the degree to which the settings have been effectively designed.

Practitioner Participation

Clearly, those people responsible for the education or care of children in a program should be centrally involved in the entire evaluation procedure. Teachers must not forfeit their responsibility for participating in the evaluation process. This procedure begins and ends with the practitioner's involvement. He or she will clarify program goals, gather and analyze data, design and effect program changes which will enhance children's development, and assess the consequences of any program change.

It is just as clear that practitioners may need and want assistance in completing this procedure. A teacher may enlist a colleague, a principal, or a supervisor to assist in the process, especially in conducting the observations. It would seem to make good sense to involve all members of a teaching team in those programs where more than one adult is responsible for a group of children. In any case, whoever participates in the process should do so with the understanding that the data are to be used to help the staff better understand the dynamics of the curriculum and improve the entire program for the children. All members of the team will need to participate in every step of the procedure from beginning to end.

The Evaluation Procedure

There are six steps in the evaluation procedure, each of which will be described. It should become quite obvious as the description proceeds that many parts of each step are considered to be integral to good teaching practice.

Step 1: A Profile of the Children. The evaluation begins with the completion of a profile for each child including five kinds of data:

1. History of socializing experience, e.g., siblings, birth order, playmates at home, and prior preschool experiences.
2. Medical history, e.g., record of illnesses, congenital disorders, allergies, and constraints on activity.
3. Family structure, e.g., one-or two-parent family, foster home, adopted, parents' reasons for enrolling the child in the program.
4. Special needs, e.g., physical or intellectual handicap, recorded or threatened abuse, and emotional stress.
5. Developmental indexes, e.g., results of IQ test, developmental tests, psychologist's assessment.

These data would very likely be kept in a child's school record. However, the chart presented in Table 13.5 is an efficient way for a practitioner to keep abreast of what knowledge he/she has about the development of the children.

There are two reasons why keeping a profile on each child is valuable. First, knowledge of the children is imperative for the creation of an effective early childhood education program. The staff should know at least as much about each child as would

Table 13.5　　　　**Child Profile**

Data	(Children)	
Birth date		
Number of siblings		
Birth order		
Prior school experience		
Number of playmates near home		
Serious illnesses		
Handicaps		
Any activity constraints		
Referred for special needs screening (date)		
Known learning difficulties		
Living with biological father		
biological mother		
adopted (date)		
Why is the child in this program?		
Intelligence tests results		
Developmental tests results		
Psychologial assessment (if any)		
Your assessment: Should the child perform with or without difficulty in this program?		

be required for this profile. Second, the profile constitutes an important criterion in judging the appropriateness of the curriculum. A program requiring a considerable amount of cooperative and autonomous behavior may need to be adjusted for children who are experiencing a large group situation for the first time. Also, to stress arts and crafts in a program in which physically disabled children are enrolled will require special adjustments in the physical setting and presentation of materials.

A word of caution is needed. The profile for each child is a means of determining whether or not the curriculum is appropriate for the children, not an explanation of why children do not achieve the goals set for them. All children, except those suffering from profound physical and/or emotional difficulties, should be able to behave in ways included in the checklist. It is also recognized that sex and ethnicity, perhaps religion, and other factors may influence the pattern or the mode of expressing each category of behavior, but this should be apparent to the staff and not become a criterion by which development is judged. What this means is that this evaluation procedure rests squarely on the behavior-person-environment formula. I believe that children's behavior in any early education setting is more a function of that setting than of their sex, race, ethnicity, or whether they are handicapped. This is not to suggest that these factors are unimportant in a child's behavior; we know they are; rather, it means that if teachers are knowledgeable about the ways in which culture, sex, and handicap can influence or inhibit children's behavior and if they accommodate themselves to this knowledge in the design and execution of a program, then the behaviors observed in the program will be the consequence of the interaction of the child with the environment. In no way does this assertion imply a uniformity of behavior among the children. There is every reason to believe that children's mode of behavior will be quite varied, especially in programs where they are expected to choose their activities for a considerable portion of the day.

Step 2: Program Description. Once the Child Profile has been completed—and it should be early in the year—the evaluation team will describe the program (or curriculum) by completing the Activity/Area (A/A) Description forms shown in Chapter 8 (Table 8.1, p. 181). An activity is defined as an event which occurs regularly and has been planned by the staff. For example, activities could include circle time, morning snack, mid-morning exercise, or story time. An area is defined by its physical boundary and/or its purpose. Common preschool areas would include blocks, the easel, creative play, and table games, for example. A primary grade might have all of these, plus a reading area, math table, science corner, and writing table. At times an area may be clearly defined by its separation from adjacent areas. At other times an area may be defined mainly by the tasks which are performed there, e.g., table-games area. The activities and areas of the classroom would, as a whole, constitute the program.

The A/A form asks for two types of information. Note that the form is divided down the center. The left half asks for data regarding the location, use of the activity or area, and the materials and equipment *now* present. Completing this portion of the form demands that the staff carefully examine each area, their role in relation to the activity, and what it is they expect children to do while engaged there. It would seem that this process alone would be valuable if only because of the attention and consideration staff would of necessity give to each area or activity.

In the discussion of the A/A form in Chapter 8 the point was made that the right-hand half of the form was divided so as to include two statements of purpose, one for the activity or area being described and another for the overall program goals. The first statement would be completed by listing the *behaviors* teachers would expect children to exhibit while engaged in the activity. In Chapter 8 a science area was used to illustrate how this could be completed. It was said that children in the science area should be *self-directed* in *exploring* the materials, should let *curiosity* direct much of what they do with the materials, and yet also engage in *problem solving* activity as they completed teacher-selected assignments and, from time to time, engage in *cooperative* activity with other children. A statement like this makes it quite clear what one should expect to observe of children in this area.

The second statement regarding overall program goals is a bit more abstract but not any less important. Any activity or learning area must contribute to the goals of the program. To complete this section, teachers will list those curriculum goals to be addressed by each activity or area. This would be a straightforward task, assuming, of course, that teachers had prepared a statement of the goals of the program and that the purposes of the areas were directed to achieving those goals. For example, assume that a goal of the program for the science area just described was to *promote children's autonomy*. Can it be said that autonomous behavior (children making choices about what they shall do and about how they shall attack a task) would be among those behaviors teachers would anticipate seeing in the science area? I think so, for they were to be *self-directed* and follow their *curiosity* at least some of the time.

Unfortunately, finding a match between the purposes of any activity or area and the goals of the program is not always as easy as this illustration suggests. Recall the example also given in Chapter 8 of the program in which five permanent learning areas were unrelated to both the goals of the program and its organization. The children were divided into three equal-sized groups, each group being led by a teacher who specialized in one aspect of the curriculum. Recall, also, that the children rotated through three major sets of teacher-directed exercises to complete the curriculum for each day. Areas carefully designed, such as the children's literature area, were seldom used by the children because of the structure of the classroom and because there was little relationship between the goals of the program and the kinds of behavior children would be likely to exhibit in areas like this.

Completing Step 2 will produce information of importance in completing three analyses:

A) The data on each activity sheet will facilitate the logical analysis of program fit and learner profile, described in Step 1. It seems quite unlikely that a team of practitioners would not immediately recognize a situation in which their stated purposes for children's behavior in a science corner, for example, were incompatible with the arrangement of this area and the developmental handicaps of some of the children. By completing the A/A forms they might discover that they had accidentally put a table on which children were expected to perform operations on plant material in a place inaccessible to a child in a wheelchair.

B) The juxtaposition of purposes with the description of learning areas should provoke the question of their relationship. For example, anticipating self-directed exploratory behavior at a sand table that has only a few spoons and some earth movers and in which children are forbidden to use water may precrealization of the goal. Reading the descriptions and asking if the anticipated behaviors are appropriate for the area would be a valuable exercise.

Related to this would be a check to see if the goals of the program (the statement of what the program is designed to accomplish) are being met by the combined purposes of all activities and areas. It is entirely conceivable that each activity or area has been so carefully designed that the purposes are consonant with the setting, materials, and adult roles, and that each meets some of the goals of the program. It is just as conceivable that not all of the program goals would be addressed. That is, there could be a program in which goals of *autonomy, social development, curiosity,* and *problem solving* are fully met by the activities provided, but in which other goals, *mastery of reading and writing*, were entirely neglected in the selection and design of the activities and areas. Comparing the statement of program goals with the A/A forms may be a useful way of checking to see if the entire curriculum is being addressed.

C) These descriptions constitute a baseline against which teachers will judge the observational data of children's behavior. In large measure, the quality of any program will be determined by how well the behaviors of the children in each activity area match those which the staff anticipated. Recall, too, that the entire evaluation procedure is based on the assertion that children's behavior in each area and activity will be a function of the organization of the physical setting, the materials presentation, and the relationship of adults and children *in that setting*. In each case, the A/A description information will be useful in understanding and explaining children's behavior, regardless of what it might be.

Step 3: Observing the Children. The central activity in the evaluation procedure is the observation of the children. Each child should be observed several times during a five-to-ten-consecutive-day observation period.[4] The observers will follow the child and record his or her behavior and where it occurs. The assessment is supposed to provide the staff with a clear picture of what is occurring in the day to day operation of the program.

Once the observations have been completed, the data will then be summarized on a matrix (see Figure 13.4). The evaluation team will summarize the behavior data by each of the items for all of the children and record it by activity or learning area. Data summarized on this matrix can provide a vivid picture of the frequency and location of

---

[4]There are several procedures one can use in conducting the observations. I suggest that each child be observed a total of 25 times, in groups of five observations. Each observation should last for 30 seconds followed by 30 seconds of coding the data sheet. This procedure should be completed five times in succession for each child (taking approximately five minutes time), after which another child would be observed. Any observation period should not last longer than 30 minutes (for five children). And, teachers should probably not expect to complete more than two observation periods in each day. Needless to say, the evaluation team will find it necessary to select the observation schedule for all children randomly and to arrange the observation periods so that the entire program day is represented in the observational data. Again, I would urge practitioners to seek assistance from a local college or university or school system for advice regarding the arrangement of the observation procedure.

each behavior. These data can be very revealing, as for example, when a teacher discovers considerable waiting behavior in adult-directed activities.

Information regarding the activity/area, number of children present, and the role of the staff in the activity are taken during each 30-second observation.[5] This information should be summarized, too. One rather effective way is to add the data for both group size and adult role for each activity or area.

A matrix showing adult role in each area is presented in Table 13.6. Adult role has been defined as absent (not in the area where the observation is taking place); observing (in the area, observing the activity of the child but not engaged in the activity); participating (engaged in the activity in a cooperative way); and directing or leading the activity. The matrix reveals, for example, that 50% of the time children are engaged in free play teachers are absent and that teachers are directing children's activity 92.3% of the time they are in large group activity. Clearly, these data become very useful in interpreting the record of children's behavior by area (Table 13.4) especially when one considers the role of the adult as an essential environmental factor. For example, recall that children were engaged independently in the block area more often with another child (27% to 21%). Imagine, if you will, that the staff would like to increase the percentage of cooperative interaction. The adult role data for the block area may give some hints as to how this might be achieved. By combining the absent and observing data, we note that teachers are not engaged with the children 42% of the time; 31% of the time they are directing children. We may suggest that they increase the amount of child-adult contact in the block area but at the same time reduce the percentage of directing behavior. This can be accomplished by raising the percentage of time adults spend participating in a cooperative activity; if we want to foster more child-child cooperation, the teacher must work to insure that his/her participation involves more than one child at a time. In a word, teachers could consciously attempt to create cooperative activities involving themselves and two or three other children and spend less time observing and directing children's activity in the block area. It should not be difficult to imagine other ways in which these data could be used in evaluating the program and in designing ways to improve it.

Step 4: Data Analysis. The observation data are subjected to alternative analyses.

A) Staff will focus on the summary data over the entire program and by learning area (the Behavior by Area Matrix, Figure 13.4). The purpose will be to identify the kind, frequency, and location of behavior in the program. This inspection will reveal trends that may or may not be anticipated, desired, and/or valued by the staff. For example, in one setting the only incidence of task completion behavior was recorded in adult-directed activity.

B) The second part of the analysis of behavior is the comparison of the data with intended behaviors by each area. It is at this point that the Activity/Area descriptions become central to the analysis. Recall that practitioners were to describe the character

---

[5]The Data Sheet requires that each observation include data about the number of children in the setting with the child being observed and the role of the teacher. Group size is coded as follows: 1-solitary activity; 2-two to five children; 3-more than five but less than the total group; 4-the total class. Adult role is coded as follows: 1-adult absent; 2-adult observing; 3-adult participating; 4-adult directing.

Table 13.6   **Adult Role by Area**

Activity/Area	Adult Role				
	Absent	Observing	Participating	Directing	Total[a]
Open Activity (Observations) (Area percent)	26 50.0%	7 13.5%	8 15.4%	11 21.1%	52 8.8%
Housekeeping	17 77.3%	2 9.1%	1 4.5%	2 9.1%	22 3.7%
Book Area	2 33.3	0	2 33.3	2 33.3	6 1.0
Large Group	5 2.6	3 1.5	7 3.6	179 92.3	194 32.7
Table Games	2 40.0	1 20.0	1 20.0	1 20.0	5 .8
Block Area	5 10.4	15 31.3	13 27.1	15 31.3	48 8.1
Art Activity	26 40.6	16 25.0	13 20.3	9 14.1	64 10.8
Outdoors	65 57.5	33 29.2	13 11.5	2 1.8	113 19.0
Math	16 39.0	8 19.5	12 29.3	5 12.2	41 6.9
Science	2 15.4	4 30.8	5 38.5	2 15.4	13 2.2
Woodworking	0	0	0	1 100.0	1 .2
Snack	10 28.6	10 28.6	12 34.3	3 8.6	35 5.9
TOTAL	176 29.6	99 16.7	87 14.6	232 39.0	594

[a]The total number of observations in each area and the percentage of all observations in the program by area are presented in the TOTAL column. For example, 52 observations of children in Open Activity are translated into 8.8% of all observations in the classroom.

and the purposes for each activity and learning area. They would now examine the matrix to see if children were doing what had been anticipated when the staff established the goals or purposes for each area. For example, if one goal for the block area in the program represented in Table 13.4 had been to foster cooperative interaction among the children, the staff may have reason to believe they only partially succeeded in achieving this goal. The children were involved with another child 21% of the time which is certainly a positive datum, but they were observed working alone 27% of the time. The question, of course, would be whether or not the staff would accept this ratio as appropriate for the children's level of development.

Behaviors should be contrasted with statements of developmental expectations. We should know if three-year-olds in the program under study are engaged in cooperation with other children to the degree three-year-olds should be. This step assumes a knowledge of the range and frequency of each behavior for young children; obviously such a standard does not now exist. What then? It seems possible to assume that an assessment team of early education practitioners would have sufficient experience and expertise to identify behaviors appropriate for children under their care; when they had doubts, they would seek the advice of others whom they believe to be more knowledgeable about child development. In the end, however, practitioners will need to decide for themselves when children's behaviors are sufficient for an assertion that they are or are not performing as was intended. They will need to rely on their ability to make sound and informed judgments.

C) A third part of the analysis involves the identification of behaviors the staff would like to see increased and/or decreased. To borrow from the example used in the previous section, the teachers may decide that the percentage of cooperation behavior in the block area is appropriate, but its near absence in free play activity needs to be remedied. It could be that open activity is valued by the staff because it is presumed to foster cooperative activity among the children. The high percentage of open activity that occurred in this program, coupled with low child-child involvement, suggests that this activity was being used by the children for some purpose other than that imagined by the staff. The teachers must, therefore, decide what it is they expect from the children in open activity or if they want to continue supporting such play. Whatever the decision, the staff will need to devise ways in which the environment can be changed to support the kinds of behaviors they judge to be appropriate and valuable.

Step 5: Program Modification. I must return for a moment to an earlier discussion of the purpose of this evaluation procedure. Recall that it is to be an assessment for program improvement. The data gathered are to be used by teachers and their colleagues as the basis for making judgments about the effectiveness of the program. The data are to be useful to practitioners as they strive to provide children with the best possible learning environment.

Also, it seems important at this juncture in the process to remind ourselves that it is the environment, the behavior setting, which offers or denies the child the opportunity to behave as we have anticipated. Therefore, if we do not find all of the behaviors we had expected in the areas we had designed, we should review the physical setting, materials presentation, and the role of adults as a first step in redesigning the environment. In short, if we are displeased with the results of the observational study, our first step should be to investigate the learning situation carefully with the intent of making changes which would lead to the goals we had earlier established.

Redesigning or changing a learning area or activity of necessity involves careful thought. It should proceed from an examination of purposes and goals. The question needs to be asked, "Are we expecting more than we should?" Clearly, much of this examination will have occurred in part B of Step 4, a comparison of intended and observed behaviors. Teachers will also need to consider the influence of the program organization on children's behavior. It is entirely possible to find a dearth of autonomous behavior because most of the program is organized around teacher-led instructional units. There may be nothing wrong with the presentation of the setting save the control exerted by the staff. It would appear to be useful at this stage of the procedure to consider not only the three significant environmental variables described in Chapters 8, 9, and 10, but also the characteristics of behavior settings from Chapter

6 and the need for providing for intra-individual differences outlined in Chapter 7. In brief, any modification of the education setting should rise from the ecological principles presented earlier in the text.

Step 6: Assessment of Program Change. A period of time should go by—a week or two perhaps—before an assessment of the effect of the modification is begun. At this time, observations should once again be completed and cast on a new matrix. The results can be contrasted with the original behavioral data and measured against the predicted changes. The staff may then consider the effectiveness of the changes they made and consider possible next steps, as indicated by the reassessment data. Obviously, the staff could continue this procedure as the year progressed, examining the whole program or only selected parts.

Summary

Evaluation is an essential part of teaching, and practitioners must not give up this responsibility to others who have little, if any, understanding of the intent of their program. Practitioners, too, need to find ways of conducting evaluations which provide them with data which is reliable and valid and which will be immediately useful to them as they struggle with the task of offering the best early education they can to their children. I have described one way in which these interrelated goals might be achieved—one which is ecologically sound and feasible.

Teachers will continue to find it necessary to administer standardized tests of children's academic or intellectual achievement. It seems unlikely that our society is going to give up this requirement in the near future. Teachers will find it necessary to quiz their students from time to time to see if they are developing skills or acquiring knowledge which is a part of the curriculum. In neither case, however, will these kinds of assessment substitute for the data one can get from the evaluation procedure described here. An ecologically valid assessment provides practitioners with information about children's behavior—their skills and competencies—but also about its relationship to the child development or learning environment. These data are essential.

References: Chapter 13

Barker, R. G. *Ecological psychology: Concepts and methods for studying the environment of human behavior.* Palo Alto, CA: Stanford University Press, 1968.

Berk, L. E. How well do classroom practices reflect teacher goals? *Young Children*, 1976, 32 (1), 64–81.

Bowman, G. W., & Mayer, R. S. *The BRACE System for staff development*, New York: Bank Street College of Education, 1976.

Carini, P. F. *Observation and description: An alternative methodology for the investigation of human phenomena.* Grand Forks, ND: University of North Dakota, 1975. (Monograph)

Day, D. E., Perkins, E., & Weinthaler, J. Naturalistic evaluation for program improvement. *Young Children*, 1979, 34 (4), 12–24.

Day, D. E., & Sheehan, R. Elements of a better school. *Young Children*, 1974, 30 (1), 15–23.

Eisner, E. W. The perceptive eye: Toward the reformation of educational evaluation. Invited address presented at the meeting of the American Educational Research Association (Division B), Washington, D.C., March 1975.

Gump, P. V. Intra-Setting Analysis: The third grade classroom as a special but instructive case. In *E. Willems & H. Raush (Eds.), Naturalistic viewpoints in psychological research.* New York: Holt, Rinehart and Winston, 1969.

Gump, P. V. Ecological psychology and children. In *E. M. Hetherington (Ed.), Review of child development research* (Vol. 5). Chicago: University of Chicago Press, 1975.

Kamii, C. Evaluation of learning in preschool education: Socio-Emotional, perceptual-motor, cognitive development. In B. S. Bloom et al. (Eds.), *Handbook on formative and summative evaluation of student learning,* New York: McGraw-Hill, 1971.

Sheehan, R., & Day, D. E. Is open space just empty space? *Day Care and Early Education*, 1975, 30, 10–13.

Soar, R. C., & Soar, R. M. An empirical analysis of selected follow through programs: An example of a process approach to evaluation. In I. J. Gordon (Ed.), *Early childhood education: The seventy-first yearbook of the National Society for the Study of Education,* Part II. Chicago: University of Chicago Press, 1972.

Stodolsky, S. S. Identifying and evaluating open education. *Kappan*, 1975, 57 (2), 113–117.

Takanishi, R. Evaluation of early childhood education programs: A developmental perspective. Paper presented at the meeting of the American Educational Research Association, Toronto, Canada, March 1978.

Index

Preface

This book presents the reader with a unique insight into the struggles of police forces—from 12 different countries—as they move toward the democratization of their operations and responses.

Although we aimed to compile a list of countries that would represent a minitour around the world, it is still more of a sample rather than an ultimate and perfectly balanced portrayal of the existing situation.

The idea of presenting 12 different countries in a certain rank order representing the "Continuum of Democracy" is rooted in the presumption that policing is a profession that could and should be evaluated based on a number of parameters or qualifiers, regardless of its geographic location. Therefore, the level of adherence to these characteristics could and should be an indicator of the level of its democratic structure and operations.

A police force, being by its true nature an arm of the ruling government, will project not just the level of its democratic development as an institution but first and foremost the state of the democratic union in any given country. It is truly impossible to envision a democratic country with a nondemocratic police force or, vice versa, a democratic police force in a nondemocratic country. Based on this presumption, we created the Continuum of Democracy scale that allows for the differentiation between the levels of development or the current state of the struggle.

While it is always feasible to dream about the perfect Table of Contents, it is rarely possible to translate it into reality. As much as we attempted to reach out to many possible contributors, we were not always successful in securing the chapter contributions we wanted. However, we feel confident that the medley of countries and continents presented in the volume represents a quite balanced approach to comparative policing—balanced enough to allow us to identify the rank order of the countries on the Continuum of Democracy, or in more simple terms, the rank order represents what we feel is the placement of the country on a somewhat artificial scale that spans from the least to the most democratic approach to policing.

The most important function of a book preface is to explain to the readers the concepts and ideas behind the book they are going to peruse. Although the introduction in essence serves as a true explanation of the ideas presented in this volume, there is a very crucial aspect that the chapters do not address, and therefore it needs to be presented here.

We have attempted to explain the criteria that guided us—our decision-making process—in placing a given country at a certain place on the continuum from the least to the most democratic police force. These criteria included the following:

1. History of a democratic form of government

2. Level of corruption within governmental organizations and the oversight mechanisms in place

3. Scope of and response to civil disobedience

4. Organizational structures of police departments

5. Operational responses to terrorism and organized crime

In this introduction we outline the rationale for choosing the above set of criteria and the considerations that guided us in the selection process. However, we would be remiss if we didn't mention that none of our chapter contributors were involved in the decision-making process, and the editors are solely responsible for the placement of the countries on the Continuum of Democracy. It is important to acknowledge that the chapter contributors were provided with the set of criteria around which we would make the placement, and we asked them to provide us with an overview of the respective countries' policing systems, but we did not identify the projected place of the country with respect to its struggle toward democratization.

It might appear as a somewhat arbitrary decision that it was our *a priori* assumption that it would be almost impossible to get a decent contribution from our authors if they were told, ahead of time, that the country they would be writing about would represent, for example, the lowest rank on the Continuum of Democracy. This decision was not based on fear of some resentment that the authors might display but rather on the premise that such an artificial and rather arbitrary placing, prior to the overview of all the countries, would possibly skew the more objective depiction of the conditions.

After the chapters were submitted, similar considerations led us to feel that an open and democratic discussion with all the contributors would not render a consensus about where each country should be placed on the Continuum, as the editors themselves had some doubts about the ultimate place of certain countries on it. Hence, in this less than democratic manner, we decided that the ultimate responsibility for the placement would rest on the shoulders of the editors. Whatever argument the chapter contributors might have with this order will remain in the sphere of a more democratic exchange between the authors and the editors in the privacy of e-mail or verbal communication.

In light of this and similar considerations, the readers of this book, be they students of comparative policing or the academics already involved in the research on democratic transformations, will make their own decisions about the appropriateness of our choices. It is important to note that the criteria chosen to depict the struggles toward democracy are not the only possible parameters one could use to assess the stage of democratic policing in any country. There is no doubt that a host of other variables may possibly reflect and highlight the struggles and errors a country goes through in the transformation process. Nevertheless, it is imperative to identify the contours or baselines of the most potent variables, and we are confident that we managed to identify them.

We wish you, the reader, a pleasant journey through nearby or more remote places, depending where you come from and an intellectual journey that will leave you further pondering about the idea of policing.

—Maria (Maki) Haberfeld

—Ibrahim Cerrah

Acknowledgments

It is always a distinct pleasure to acknowledge people who were the inspiration and the driving force behind the book. We would like to start with one of the original three editors, Dr. Heath Grant, who for personal reasons needed to withdraw from the project.

Heath was one of the authors of the prospectus submitted to Sage outlining this project, and it was his skillful writing and talent that contributed, immensely, to the contract we received and to the product in front of the readers. His ideas, enthusiasm, and drive are unparalleled, and we missed his input and contributions.

The rather long list of peer reviewers was invaluable and helped us shape the contours and thoughts that were loosely dispersed in our academically oriented minds; each editor and author pulled toward a different direction; all were fully convinced that we would arrive at the same destination. Were it not for our insightful colleagues who reviewed the chapters, we would, undoubtedly, still be looking for the alternative detours. Therefore, in no particular order in terms of their contributions, we would like to express our profound gratitude to JoAnn Della-Gustina from Bridgewater State University, Charles L. Dreveskracht from Northeastern State University, Steven Engel from Georgia Southern University, Barry Goetz from Western Michigan University, Hidetoshi Hashimoto from University of Maryland, Otwin Marenin from Washington State University, Eugene McLaughlin from Open University, Steve Owen from Radford University, Peter Puelo from William Rainey Harper College, Phil Reichel from University of Northern Colorado, and Stanley Swart from University of North Florida. This book is the result of a truly peer-reviewed effort, and for this we are indeed very grateful.

Needless to say, all this would have not been possible without the amazing leadership of Jerry Westby, Sage's executive editor, and his assistants Melissa Spor and Vonessa Vondera as well as the editorial team. In addition, we would also like to thank our copy editor, Cate Huisman, who provided us with the most invaluable support, professional insight of the highest quality, and masterful editing that contributed greatly to the chapters' read-ability and comprehensibility. We are indebted to you for all your support and faith in our endeavors.

The last paragraph belongs to our family and friends, who should always realize that they are the real enablers behind our efforts to make a tiny dent in the struggle toward democratization.

1

Introduction

Policing Is Hard on Democracy, or Democracy Is Hard on Policing?

Maria (Maki) Haberfeld and Lior Gideon

Conceptual Framework

Global trends in terrorism and transnational crime have direct effects in both local *and* international contexts. Although the problems of terrorism, organized crime, and corruption are not new phenomena anywhere in the world, governments have shifted the nature of their law enforcement structures, functions, and practices in manners that reflect local internal and external political and socioeconomic forces. In many countries, responses to serious threats have typically resulted in an increasingly centralized and specialized force, even to the extent of merging police and military responsibilities. Such responses in times of threat have occurred in even strongly democratic societies, such as the United Kingdom, even though it has long been taken for granted that the roles of the military and police should be clearly separated in societies built upon the basic tenets of democratic governance (Kraska, 2001).

Issues of national security involving threats from other nations fall clearly within the domain of military responsibility, whereas those surfacing as a result of general criminality or lawlessness are the responsibility of local law enforcement. Where the functions and responsibilities of the military and police have merged, governments are characterized as repressive by those claiming to operate according to the principles of the rule of law. Within a changing global context, the difficulty of balancing due process and public safety needs is a paramount issue that challenges the very legitimacy that is fundamental to the effectiveness of law enforcement. Drawing upon the lessons learned and best practices of comparative policing systems is particularly important in contemporary times.

The extent to which changes in perceptions of the legitimacy of authorities affect the level of compliance with the law in everyday lives is an important question, particularly where we are dealing with countries at different levels of democratization (Cohn & White, 1997). Much of this perceived legitimacy is based on notions of government transparency and citizens' beliefs that they can participate in the establishment of a lawful society both on an individual community level and at the level of national social change.

For example, although democratic rule has returned to many countries in Latin America, "Relations between governments and society, particularly the poor and marginalized members of society, have been characterized by the illegal and arbitrary use of power" (Pinheiro de Souza, 2006, p. 1). While the end of dictatorships brought hopes of human rights and a rule of a lawful society, the reality is that there is a significant disparity in many of these countries "between the letter of the bill of rights, present in many constitutions, and law enforcement application and practice" (Pinheiro de Souza, 2006, p. 1). Access to "justice" in many cases is bought with money, a tool more available to narcotraffickers than the average citizen.

Many countries throughout the world have accepted a semimilitary model of policing in which police administrators see their role as fighting the enemy (crime) regardless of the constraints on arbitrary enforcement meant to be offered by the law and the criminal justice system. Although decreasing, this military ethos has helped to maintain a legal context in which the practices of torture and use of deadly force to suppress social movements has not disappeared. The use of special squads is common throughout Latin America, with many of them becoming the law unto themselves. Specifically this is illustrated in the Brazilian case.

A driving force behind the abuses and citizen perceptions of police impunity in general stems from corruption, beginning with low-level bribes and extending to include protection rackets. Chevigny (1999, p. 62) argues that corruption and police brutality are interrelated because "together they show the power of the police, their independence from the rest of the criminal justice system, and their ability to administer justice as they see fit." Paying bribes is a common practice in countries such as Mexico, not just as a means of bypassing the criminal justice system but also for avoiding a potential beating at the hands of officers for those who refuse to pay.

The above legal context will obviously not go a long way toward socializing citizens as to the value of rules and laws and their enforcement in society. The importance of this cannot be underestimated; legislation is meaningless unless the government is able to "anticipate that the citizenry as a whole will . . . generally observe the body of rules promulgated" (Fuller, 1964, p. 201). Given the fact that laws are created to enforce behavior that many people would often rather avoid, legal authorities are best served by "establish[ing] and maintain[ing] conditions that lead the public generally to accept their decisions and policies" (Tyler, 1990, p. 19). A government that needs to rely on coercion as a means of maintaining compliance with the law will be faced with an insurmountable task, both in terms of resources and practicality.

In a climate of global change, in which traditional boundaries and the presence of a clearly defined enemy are no longer realities, law enforcement has also tried to evolve internationally. For example, from a U.S. perspective, turning points such as the passage of the Patriot Act and the continued reexamination of the Posse Commitatus Act have led to the further blurring of military/police lines that began after the Cold War with the military taking on some drug enforcement responsibilities.

As policing moves away from its traditional responsibilities related to the control of local disorder, it will become increasingly less effective in meeting its objectives. Although it is easy to see how local law enforcement has seen a need to change its practices—viewing itself as the front line and first responder in the war on terror—the danger of further building a military ethos for policing is that it challenges the very legitimacy that makes it effective as noted above. Countries that have battled issues of terrorism for many years, such as Israel, recognize this distinction, seeing law enforcement as a support function to the "takeover" and engagement units responding to terror.

A growing body of useful comparative policing texts introduces the diversity and complexity of policing systems around the world. Important works such as *Policing Change, Changing Police* (Marenin, 1996) provide an overview of selected policing systems, highlighting the relationship between police and the state. Works such as Mathieu Deflem's *Policing World Society* (1998) explore the challenges and issues involved in cross-national cooperation and international policing. Recent efforts such as Das and Lab's *International Perspectives on Community Policing and Crime Prevention* (2002) contrast community policing models in countries as diverse as Canada, Israel, India, and Mexico. Other approaches, such as Ebbe's *Comparative & Criminal Justice Systems* (1996) and Dammer, Fairchild, and Albanese's *Comparative Criminal Justice* (2006) examine police systems within the context of the entire criminal justice system.

These efforts have provided important foundations for the fields of comparative policing and international policing studies, yet the following chapters will offer still new directions. In addition to providing a comprehensive comparative context of policing in the selected countries that will serve as a basic introduction to new students to the field, the material is presented in such a way as to highlight the critical global trends discussed, and thus link the comparative framework with current developments in the fields of democratic governance, legitimacy, human rights, and transnational crime.

The book will also provide some important political, social, and historical contextual information, so that connections between external authorizing environments and police responses can be introduced to the readers.

Topics introduced and discussed through the chapters circle around the following themes:

- Level of democratization
- Police professionalism, including preparation to perform the police function, merit recruitment, formal training, structured career advancement, systematic discipline, full-time service, extent to which police operations are conducted in public, and specialization
- Community oriented policing
- Use of force
- Accountability
- Human rights
- Forces for change and success/failure of these responses
- Responses to terrorism and organized crime, including the effects of such responses on legitimacy of the police force
- The extent of collaboration between the military and local policing

Countries have been selected for inclusion in the volume across a continuum of the democratization of policing practices. The country chapters are presented in a certain order that reflects their position on what the editors defined as the "Continuum of Democracy." By introducing the placement of countries on a continuum, the editors illustrate how no country can operate perfectly within a perfect rule of law. Social forces and the negative actions of human agents can move a country's law enforcement agencies away from democratic governance operating with community consensus and toward more coercive, autocratic practices. Being cognizant of these factors in the context of emerging responses to global terrorism and crime is a necessity and a key ingredient of the current volume.

The Continuum of Democracy: An Innovative Approach

To facilitate cross-fertilization of best practices and lessons learned with respect to policing, a democratization continuum is operationalized, and each country is analyzed along the continuum. Again, each country was selected based on its potential applicability to the continuum and the degree to which best practices and/or lessons learned could be drawn according to the book's themes, as described above.

A country's position on the Continuum of Democracy is therefore operationalized as its overall score based on the following five dimensions: the history of a democratic form of government, the level of corruption within governmental organizations and the oversight mechanisms in place, the scope of and response to civil disobedience, organizational structures of police departments, and operational responses to terrorism and organized crime.

On the scale of 1 to 12 (based on the number of countries represented in this book) the editors assigned a rank order to each country as a representation of the number they scored, measured on the five practical dimensions representing the operationalized definition of the Continuum of Democracy. Therefore, they identified China as the country that scored the lowest on each of the five dimensions, because it has no history of a democratic form of government, a high level of corruption in governmental organizations, and a history of a violent response to civil disobedience, representing a rather archaic structure of policing and a repressive response to problems of terrorism and organized crime. On the other end of the spectrum, representing the highest level on the continuum, they placed the United States, followed closely by or even competing for first place with Canada. Although the history of its democratic government is not as long as the United Kingdom's, the decentralized nature of the U.S. police force, the oversight mechanisms in place to deal with instances of corruption, the accountability required when dealing with civil disobedience, the structure of police organizations, and the modalities of response to the phenomenon of organized crime and terrorism earned the country its first place on the Continuum. It is imperative to note that the five dimensions are measured within the context of policing in the most recent years; therefore, the history of a democratic form of government (the first dimension) provides a context for the other four dimensions.

Additional Dimensions of the Innovative Comparative Approach

It is with the above framework in mind that international scholars have written chapters examining the differing contexts and police practices throughout the world. Although this edited work will allow for the traditional international comparisons common to current collections in the field, it is unique in that it is presented from an analytical context that challenges readers to critically assess global trends in policing. Based upon a review and operationalization of the contents provided throughout the chapter, readers and students of policing can attempt to identify the best universal practices (applicable to any democratic setting) for dealing with newly emerging issues based on the best practices and issues of the discussed countries. However, the need to clearly separate the roles of police and military, and the continued transparency and accountability of local law enforcement, will remain a central focus in international challenges to attain legitimacy. The reader will also be introduced to the basic principles of human rights law and practice in order to frame all of the above discussion.

Another central innovation of this work's conceptual framework is that it highlights how global trends in terrorism and transnational crime affect both local and international policing contexts. For example, departments internationally are rapidly trying to deal with the new threat posed by terrorism on the local level through first response, investigation, and coordination with other local and federal jurisdictions. Coordination with international policing efforts will also be essential. Therefore, rather than treating comparative and international policing as wholly separate fields as found in the rest of the literature, the volume's editors draw these linkages; the final section of the text thus offers an overview of current trends in international policing as a possible, partial, and practical solution to the democratization of the police process across the world.

Countries represented in this volume have been selected based upon both geographical location and underlying issues that can inform the larger analytical context of the work. By taking a brief look at some critical issues and concepts outlined in the following chapters, it is possible to compile a list of fundamental themes that shape and influence the democratization process of policing in each of the depicted countries. The same list however can be easily applied to many other countries struggling to reconcile the notion that democracy is hard on policing and that policing is hard on democracy.

The globalization process exposes many countries that have had marginal exposure to the Western world to rapid and demanding social change and thus new social and governmental challenges. Consequently, law enforcement, as one of the greatest social experiments, is a crucial indicator of the level of democratization.

In very concrete and operational terms, a country's level of democracy can be assessed by examining its law enforcement system(s) and its *modus operandi*. Similarly, the key to the level of developmental and economic success of the Western nations is their adoption of democracy. Within such nations, the police operate under internationally recognized democratic principles to ensure a harmonious society in which political, social, and economic life can flourish (Crawshaw et al., 2006, as cited in Chapter 5).

Cullen and McDonald (2008) argue in Chapter 5 that "democratic civilian policing is an essential component of good governance operating under a range of basic principles" (p. 121). Further argument advances the place of the military as having the primary role in securing the state from external threats, while the civilian police is destined to have "a primary and accountable role in citizen security and serving the law" (p. 121). Extraordinary circumstances, they argue, may require the military personnel to provide assistance to the civilian police in joint public safety operations.

In many countries, responses to serious threats have typically resulted in an increasingly centralized and specialized force, even to the extent of merging police and military responsibilities. When criminal threats, such as those in Israel, Brazil, Mexico, and Sierra Leone, become associated with national threats, the due process model tends to lose its validity, making room for a more centralized rigid police force with special engagement units that respond to terrorist activities.

Law enforcement does not operate in a vacuum. As becomes quite apparent from the pages of this volume, law enforcement reflects the level of democracy in a country, and the democracy of the country is reflected in its organizational structure and operations. Consequently, countries with very long histories of democracy, like the United States, United Kingdom, Canada, and France, will have more democratic policing that cherishes due process over crime control. In fact, as outlined in Chapter 13 on the U.S. police systems, law enforcement in the United States was created on the basis of separating civilian police forces from the central government. Although law enforcement in the United States now is connected to the local government (i.e., the local police) and shares information with other federal agencies, the overall perception is that of democratic policing and the due process model. On the other hand, in countries in transition, like Sierra Leone, Russia, Brazil, and Mexico, it becomes apparent that law enforcement struggles in its attempt to digest and assimilate the concepts of democracy in general, and in particular the ideas embedded in democratic policing, into the standard operating procedures of daily enforcement.

As argued by Gideon and colleagues in Chapter 9 on Israel, law enforcement agencies reflect the priorities, divisions, and social economic conditions of societies in which they exist. Consequently, police forces will demonstrate adaptation to the changing and growing needs of their respective societies. Similarly, Dupont ends Chapter 10 on the French police arguing that "police organizations respond and their reforms are responses to contextual stimuli" (p. 272). Frequently, as argued in the cases of the United Kingdom, United States, France, Turkey, and Russia, such adaptations are also an outcome of a growing concern about threats to homeland security by broadly defined terrorist activities. Such adaptations will shift the pendulum of democratic policing toward a more centralized and thus less democratic police force, departing from due process as can be seen in the Russian Republic, the United States in the days following September 11, Israel, the United Kingdom, Turkey, and France. However, it is not just the threat of assorted terrorist activities that influences and changes the shapes of democratic policing. Countries like Mexico and Brazil that struggle constantly with organized crime, drug cartels, and high violent crime rates experience similar transformations. These are good examples of times where adaptation and customization to an event, a series of events, or a more institutionalized challenge take over the noble cause of protecting civil rights, and the need to maintain public order and safety gains an elevated priority—no matter what the cost.

The primary duty of the police is to maintain social control within the community. What distinguishes the police from the public is their ability to use coercive force to control any given situation. However, such force will be displayed in its most benign version if the public complies with the demanded status quo. In Chapter 5 on the Sierra Leone police, Cullen and McDonald present President Tejan-Kabbah's vision of the role of the public vis-à-vis police work: "In order that . . . police officers can successfully fulfill our expectations, it is essential that all people of Sierra Leone help and support them at all times" (p. 129).

It is important to remember, in this context, that although the primary goal of the police is to maintain social control, the extent and nature of this control is guided by the governing body of any given country. As Haberfeld (2002, p. 15) notes, "Police forces, throughout the history, served and protected the ruler, the king, the politician, and never the public. The safety and security of the public was always secondary to the safety and security of the ruler, king, politician." This is the case in well-established democracies as well, and it can be better understood by examining the origin of the word *police,* which stems from the Greek word *polis,* meaning government center (see Haberfeld, 2002, p. 15). Consequently, while a law enforcement agency may operate in a democratic society, it is by definition not a democratic organization, and its goals are thus not democratic. Yes, it may serve democracy and its goals by maintaining public order, social control, and—more important—the status quo, but it should not be perceived as a democratic institution. Specifically, protecting the status quo suggests that law enforcement serves the government and its purposes. This is essential to understanding the swing of the pendulum of democracy with the challenges it faces: the shift in perception from a civilian police to a more militaristic organization with militaristic goals departing from due process and thus departing at times from the democratic principles.

As portrayed in the following chapters, and also mentioned in the onset of this chapter, responses to serious threats have typically resulted in an increasingly centralized and specialized force, even in the context of merging police and military responsibilities.

In this time and age, the public's demand and expectations of the criminal justice system may seem contradictory. Demands for more control are constantly rising versus demands for less violation of privacy. It is in this context that we raise the question: Is policing hard on democracy, or is democracy hard on policing? One good example of this query is the New York City Police Department's random checks at subway stations after the terror attack on the underground in the United Kingdom in 2005. The overall consensus, at least on the part of the operational police response, seemed to require an aggressive response to secure the subway system, while on the other hand a large segment of the public was infuriated with the police invading their privacy by searching their belongings.

"Democratic Policing"

Democratic policing is "a form of policing in which the police are accountable to the law and the community, respect the rights and guarantee the security of all citizens in a non-discriminatory manner" (de Mesquita Neto, 2001, p. 2). Furthermore, democratic police organizations function within and are accountable to the rule of law. The rule of the law refers to the idea that equality and justice are inseparable and that laws are applied equally to everyone. It is the standard that guides decision making throughout the criminal justice system.

In comparison to any other group in a democratic society, law enforcement personnel are supposed to symbolize tolerance and acceptance of diversity. Teaching officers how to enable their views and beliefs to coexist with the different views and beliefs of other citizens—and other officers— is one of the greatest challenges in law enforcement training. With that in mind and on similar levels, it is argued that teaching officers to preserve democratic principles while displaying firearms is a difficult task that needs to be carefully and constantly balanced. Indeed, Cullen and McDonald argue in Chapter 5 that "unfortunately, democracy is a complicated and often elusive phenomenon" (p. 122). When such balance is not achieved, then corruption may emerge, pushing democracy aside, as demonstrated in Chapters 3–6 on Brazil, Mexico, Sierra Leone, and Russia, respectively.

A police force is a paramilitary organization by nature and is expected to be highly professional. Therefore, an important notation that readers need to keep in mind throughout this volume is that more frequently than not, police forces are a by-product of military regiments, where police officers are recruited directly from the military or have some military training in their background. This is a phenomenon that can be traced to the Roman Empire; it has its roots in the Praetorian Guard created by Augustus Caesar and follows through until the establishment of the first modern police force by Sir Robert Peel. Similar developments can be traced in the case of police forces in Israel, Sierra Leon, Mexico, Brazil, Russia, France, India, and many other countries that are not covered in this volume.

As an outcome of such historical developments, frequently law enforcement agencies are viewed as centralized, paramilitary organizations. As such, their ability to adapt and change this image in the face of changing social and political environments presents a formidable challenge, not just for the organization itself but also for the individual police officer.

Law enforcement officers have evolved into ever-broadened generalists who must instantly answer a wide range of difficult questions and take prompt and correct action, all in the name of social control and public safety. Therefore, the public expects its police to handle almost any problem that surfaces. While police officers must respond to situations within the parameters of the law, they should have the freedom to make a decision based on the circumstances of a particular case. Decisions by police officers are likely to have profound implications for the people with whom they come in contact and for the officers themselves. These decisions often affect people's liberty and personal safety. Often it is precisely during this critical, split-second decision-making process that democracy becomes hard on policing.

On the other hand, police response to society's needs, and more specifically during the times of increased public order and security needs, may hit a brick wall when it faces the challenge of Haberfeld's question: "To enforce or not to enforce, that is the question" (2002, p. 4). Once we agree to the fact that laws should be enforced to maintain public order and safety, a different question needs to be asked: "How to enforce?" Such a question is critical to the discussion of democratic policing and the ways in which law enforcement agencies in different countries interpret the need and magnitude of desired enforcement. It is here that we pose the question: Is policing hard on democracy? Or maybe democracy is hard on policing? As Haberfeld posits, "I don't know the key to success but the key to failure is trying to please everybody" (2002, p. 153).

As previously mentioned, the primary duty of the police is to maintain social control within the community. This rationale has its long roots in the early days of policing, when police officers served the king, the ruler, and the politician. It is within this historical context that the pendulum shifts between crime control and due process or democratic policing, as illustrated in Chapters 2–6 on China, Brazil, Mexico, Sierra Leone, and Russia, respectively. As demonstrated in all the 12 countries whose police forces are presented in this volume, police react to social change. In fact, policing is known to be one of the greatest social experiments ever to exist. Even in countries that can be referred to as strong and established democracies, when the need to maintain public safety and protect against internal and external threats becomes a main priority for its governing bodies, some basic civil rights are being abandoned, and new policing practices emerge to adjust to the new priorities. The emergence of the new deployment techniques and police practices is justified for the sake of maintaining public safety and social order, or at least this is how it is presented to the larger audience on the receiving end.

Within the context of crime globalization, law enforcement agencies around the world became exposed to new challenges that include new forms and scopes of criminal activities, which mandate new methods of crime investigation, collaboration, and intelligence sharing, in particular with regard to terrorism and organized crime. These developments become apparent in countries like China, Russia, Sierra Leone, and Turkey. Additionally and independently, globalization came along with democratization, the ambition to leave behind (in the past) the nondemocratic or less democratic forms of government, and a desire to transition to the principles of democracy. This transition, as depicted in Chapters 3–6 on Brazil, Mexico, Sierra Leone, and Russia and in many ways in Chapter 2 on China (although it is not a democracy), is a long and complex process that frequently causes law enforcement leadership to stray, sometimes unintentionally, from the democratic principles that the country declared in its new hymn, one which usually espouses it ambitions and goals.

The attempt to examine law enforcement organizations by placing them on the Continuum of Democracy is a disputable challenge. As mentioned, a law enforcement force by itself is a nondemocratic organization.

Although on the surface the police aims to serve the public through order maintenance, it is always subjected to the ultimate vision of the current governing body, which is also the body that creates and passes the laws and the rules. This point is best demonstrated by Benoît Dupont in Chapter 10, who argues that France often placed the interests of the state above those of the public. A law enforcement agency begins as a centralized organization that shifts toward decentralization as a result of exposure to globalization and the need for change; however, it rapidly and almost happily regresses to the centralized model to adapt to the newly emerged challenges in the face of increasing crime, terrorism, and threat to the regime/government.

By examining the following chapters, it becomes more apparent how the pendulum of democracy swings back and forth between the historically defined military designation and the present and future idealistic orientation of democratic policing. In the process of transition from totalitarian regimes toward a democratic form of government, all the newly emerged democracies, such as Sierra Leone, Russia, Brazil, and Mexico (and in many ways also China in the era of globalization) are experiencing rising levels of crime due to the vacuum created during the shifting processes. During such transitions, police are perceived as lacking the ability to function, corrupt, and consequently dysfunctional and almost an obstacle to the democratization process.

Frequently, such sentiments cause a reverse reaction. As an adaptation, law enforcement operations shift back into a more centralized model with stricter and more invasive governmental oversight and intervention. This in turn may be viewed as nondemocratic.

To summarize, when reading through the chapters of this volume, readers are asked to consider five dimensions that will assist them to critically evaluate and analyze the countries placed on the Continuum of Democracy. The editors argue that the level of democratic policing can and should be defined by the factors associated with the five dimensions. It is by no means an empirically grounded assertion but rather a testimonial approach to sociopolitical and economic features researched by the volume's contributors. The editors are open to arguments and criticisms related to a given country's place on the democratic scale of policing. It is, however, imperative to look at these five dimensions:

1. History of a democratic form of government

2. Level of corruption within governmental organizations and the oversight mechanisms in place

3. Scope of and response to civil disobedience

4. Organizational structures of police departments

5. Operational responses to terrorism and organized crime

Readers must recognize and acknowledge the relative contribution of these five dimensions to the idea of democratic policing. Rather than imposing on the reader a strict and inflexible ranking order, the authors have opted for a tentative placement of the countries on the Continuum of Democracy, and have opened the floor for an academic discussion that will, undoubtedly, change and be heavily influenced by the current events at any given time and place that will accompany the reading of the chapters.

References

Chevigny, P. (1999). *Defining the role of the police in Latin America: The (un)rule of law.* Notre Dame, IN: University of Notre Dame Press.

Cohn, E. S., & White, S. O. (1997). Legal socialization effects on democratization. *International Social Science Journal, 49,* 151–171.

Dammer, H. R., Fairchild, E., & Albanese, J. S. (2006). *Comparative criminal justice* (3rd ed.). Belmont, CA: Thomson/Wadsworth Publishing.

Das, D. K., & Lab, S. P. (2002) *International perspectives on community policing and crime prevention.* Upper Saddle River, NJ: Prentice-Hall.

Deflem, M. (1998). *Policing world society: Historical foundations of international police cooperation.* New York: Oxford University Press.

Ebbe, O. N. (1996). *Comparative & international criminal justice systems, policing, judiciary and corrections.* Boston: Butterworth-Heinemann.

Fuller, L. (1964). *The morality of law.* New Haven, CT: Yale University Press.

Haberfeld, M. R. (2002). *Critical issues in police training.* Upper Saddle River, NJ: Prentice-Hall.

Kraska, P. B. (Ed.). (2001). *Militarizing the American criminal justice system: The changing roles of the armed forces and the police.* Boston, MA: Northeastern University Press.

Marenin, O. (1996). *Policing change, changing police: International perspectives.* London: Routledge.

de Mesquita Neto, P. (2001, March). *Paths toward democratic policing in Latin America.* Paper presented at the International Workshop on Human Rights and the Police in Transitional Countries, Copenhagen, Denmark.

Pinheiro De Souza, A. (2006). Narcoterrorism in Latin America: A Brazilian perspective. Retrieved May 25, 2007, from http://handle.dtic.mil/100.2/ ADA456509

Tyler, T. (1990). *Why people obey law.* New Haven, CT: Yale University Press.

2

The Chinese Police

Yue Ma

History of the Police

The modern Chinese police did not come into being until the late nineteenth century. Primitive forms of order maintenance, however, can be traced to China's very first dynasty that existed more than 4,000 years ago. The first emperor of the Xia dynasty (2100 to 1600 BCE) named an official known as the *Si Tu* to be responsible for maintaining order in the tribal state. Emperor Shun is reported to have said that if people were not friendly with each other and did not use restraints in their relationship, hatreds would develop and social disturbances would follow. The emperor therefore instructed the Si Tu to maintain order by eliminating hatreds and mediating disputes among tribal members. In addition to the Si Tu, a post of *Shi* was also created. The Shi was given the responsibility of operating jails and investigating crimes committed by tribal members (Yu, 1985b).

The next significant development of law enforcement came in the Qin and Han dynasties. During the Qin dynasty (221–206 BCE), China became a unified country. To strengthen the rule over the newly unified country, the Qin emperors developed various law enforcement mechanisms. The Qin dynasty, however, was a short-lived one. It lasted only 15 years. In contrast to the short life of the Qin dynasty, the Han dynasty (206 BCE–220 CE) lasted for more than 400 years. The Han dynasty was characterized by unprecedented economic prosperity and political stability. The law enforcement mechanisms originated in the Qin dynasty gained significant development in the Han dynasty.

During the Qin dynasty, an official known as *Zhongwei* was given the responsibility for maintaining law and order in the capital. The responsibilities of Zhongwei included patrolling city streets, investigating crimes, and handling emergency situations. Zhongwei was assisted in his duties by subordinate officers (Liu, 1985). By the time of the Han dynasty, the capital city, *Changan*, had developed into a populous city with about 80,800 households and 246,200 inhabitants.[1] It was estimated that Changan's population at its peak reached 500,000 (Gao, 1985a). As the population rose, crime increased. According to historical records, there were numerous criminal gangs in the city. The criminal gangs were engaged in all kinds of crimes, including theft, robbery, burglary, contract killings, and assassinations (Gao, 1985a).

The Han emperors took various measures to strengthen the law enforcement mechanisms in the capital and at the local levels. The chief administrative official in the capital was called *Changanling*. Maintaining law and order was one of the main responsibilities of Changanling. Changanling appointed an official called *Xianwei* to be the chief law enforcement officer of the capital. Under the command of Xianwei, there were officers known as *Xianyu*. Xianyu were responsible for patrolling city streets, maintaining order, investigating crimes, and apprehending offenders. To ensure that Xianyu perform their duties diligently, the Han emperors on several occasions raised the rank and the salaries of Xianyu (Gao, 1985a). In the capital, there were also security agencies in charge of protecting the emperor, the royal family, and the high-ranking government officials.

Outside the capital, it fell upon the administrative official of each prefecture to maintain the peace and order within his jurisdiction. The chief administrative official usually appointed a deputy administrative official to be in charge of maintaining law and order. *Ting*, the basic law enforcement agency, was established in villages, towns, marketplaces, ports, and along post roads. Ting was headed by a Ting chief. The Ting chief was usually selected from among retired army officers. To qualify for the position, the candidate had to be literate, have military knowledge, and know how to operate weapons. The Ting chief had line officers under his command. The responsibilities of Ting included patrolling streets to prevent the breach of peace, apprehending criminals, and producing apprehended criminals before the local court for adjudication (Gao, 1985b).

During the Qin and Han dynasties, the household registration system and the frank pledge system began to develop. The law required that all people be registered with the government. A person must be registered shortly after his birth, and the registration remained in effect until his death. If a person moved away from his original place of registration, he had to report his movement to the government, so that he could be registered in the place to which he moved. The household registration system was developed originally to facilitate the government's efforts to collect taxes and recruit laborers. It later became a social control mechanism. The government took the household registration seriously. Under the law of both Qin and Han dynasties, failure to register under the household registration system was an offense punishable by criminal penalty. In the Han dynasty, the government conducted a census annually to ensure the accuracy of the household registrations.

Under the frank pledge system, every five families were grouped into a unit called *Wu*. Wu was based on the principles of self-help and collective responsibility. Wu members were responsible for policing each other to ensure that no members would commit crime. If any Wu member committed a crime, it was the responsibility of other members to apprehend the offender and present him before the court for punishment. The law imposed a stiff penalty for Wu members' failure to fulfill their obligation. Failure to apprehend the offender would subject Wu members to the same punishment that would have been meted out for the offender. Historical records show that because of the severe penalty stipulated, Wu members were quite diligent in their efforts to report crimes and apprehend offenders. Wu was not only a self-policing but also a self-help system. The law imposed on Wu members the duty to protect each other and assist each other at the time of crime victimization. Wu members were subject to criminal punishment for failure to render assistance to their fellow members at the time of crime victimization (Liu, 1985).

After the Qin and Han dynasties, in the ensuing 1691 years, China was ruled by several different dynasties before the end of the era of imperial dynasties in 1911. The system developed in the Qin and Han dynasties, with some variations, remained the basic law enforcement system in all dynasties (Cao & Qi, 1985; Dutton, 1992; Han & Cao, 1985; McKnight, 1992; Yu, 1985a, 1985b, 1985c). The next significant development in law enforcement did not come until the late nineteenth century, when the concept of modern police was introduced to China.

The Qing dynasty (1644–1911 CE) was the last dynasty in China's history. The law enforcement system of the Qing dynasty bore remarkable resemblance to the system that had been developed nearly 2000 years before in the Qin and Han dynasties. In the capital, various security agencies were established to perform duties ranging from protecting the emperor and high-ranking government officials to maintaining law and order and apprehending criminals. Outside the capital, provincial and county administrative chiefs were given the primary responsibility for maintaining law and order in their localities. The frank pledge and the household registration system remained the main control mechanisms at the local levels. The frank pledge in the Qing dynasty was known as *Bao-Jia*. In the tightly knit Bao-Jia system, every ten households formed a *Pai*, which was headed by a Pai chief. Every ten Pais formed a *Jia*, which was headed by a Jia chief. Every ten Jias formed a *Bao*. The Bao chief was the chief law enforcement officer at the local level.

The traditional law enforcement system remained in force until the end of the nineteenth century. The nineteenth century saw Western powers' invasion of China and China's turning into a semifeudal and semicolonial society. The Western powers, after a series of aggressive wars, forced the defeated Qing government to sign numerous unequal treaties. A notable clause in these treaties was the demand to establish concessions in China. By the end of the nineteenth century, England, France, Germany, and Japan all had established concessions in major Chinese cities and ports. Concessions could not be reached by Chinese law. There the Western powers acquired the authority to exercise the extraterritorial jurisdiction. Under the authority, the Western powers set up their own judicial systems and applied their homeland laws. To maintain law and order within the concessions, the Western countries introduced the modern police system that had emerged not long before in their homelands. The model of modern police thus was introduced to China as a result of imperialist aggression and colonialization.

At the beginning of the twentieth century, the Qing dynasty entered its waning days. To save the disintegrating dynasty, the Qing government was in urgent need of finding new tools to suppress rebellions against the regime. Inspired by the police system established within concessions, the Qing government began to establish its own modern police after the model of Western police. In 1901, the Qing government established the first modern police agency, the Capital Police Bureau. The Capital Police Bureau was placed directly under the command of the emperor. Shortly after the establishment of the Capital Police Bureau, the Qing government ordered that police agencies be established in all provinces and major cities. In 1905, the Ministry of Police, which was given the responsibility of directing the police operation throughout the country, was established.

Though the dynasty was soon to expire, the police system gained quite noticeable development in the remaining days of the dynasty. By 1911, when the Qing dynasty was overthrown, the Capital Police Bureau had developed into a fairly sophisticated force. The bureau boasted of 418 high-ranking officials and 3,843 police officers; it had a number of specialized divisions, including patrol division, detective division, police training division, and police disciplinary division. Notably there was even a police academy established in the capital (Chang, 1985a).

After the demise of the Qing dynasty in 1911 and before the founding of the People's Republic in 1949, China was ruled by the Northern Warlords (1911–1927) and the Guomintang government (1927–1949). The modern police gained further development in this period. A centralized police system emerged. A ministry responsible for police affairs was established in the central government. Police bureaus were established at the provincial and county levels and in major cities. Apart from the regular police force, special police were also established. For instance, under the rule of the Guomintang, there were mine police, railroad police, fishing zone police, highway patrol police, taxation police, and forest police (Chang, 1985a, 1985b; Wakeman, 1995).

The Guomintang government was overthrown in 1949. After the founding of the People's Republic of China, the communist government abolished the old police system and declared that it would establish a police system of its own. The government established the police system by referring to the police model developed by the Communist Party in the revolutionary base areas. Despite the government's claim that it had created a brand new system, the police system established bore resemblance to the police systems that existed before. At the top of the police hierarchy was the Ministry of Public Security. Under the ministry, police bureaus were established at the provincial and county levels. The Ministry of Public Security was responsible for directing and coordinating the police operation throughout the country. In the 1950s and early 1960s, the police did an impressive job in crime control and prevention. The crime rate was low. There was, however, hardly any law governing the police operation. There was neither criminal law nor criminal procedure law. The police operation was governed mainly by party policies and nonpublished internal documents. During this period, the National People's Congress, the Chinese legislature, enacted the Police Regulation of 1957. But the regulation contained only 11 provisions, falling far short of providing necessary guidance to a police force that shouldered the responsibility of policing the world's most populous country.

Police Organization

The current framework of the police organization is laid down in the Police Law of 1995. The Police Law of 1995 is a comprehensive piece of legislation that contains provisions governing almost all aspects of policing, including police organization, police functions, police recruitment, police training, police administration and management, police powers, police disciplinary procedures, and police civil and criminal liability. According to the Police Law, the Chinese police consists of five components or five police forces. The five components are public security police, state security police, prison police, judicial police of the people's courts, and judicial police of people's procuratorates. (The terms *procurator* and *procuratorate*, as used in official translations of Chinese legal documents, refer to a prosecutor and prosecution service respectively.) Each police force performs specific functions prescribed by the law and each has its own organizational hierarchy.

Public Security Police

Public security police are the largest component of the Chinese police. Public security police perform a wide range of ordinary police functions, including investigating crimes, maintaining public order, directing traffic, conducting patrols, administering the household registration system and the citizen identification card system, providing guidance to mass-line crime prevention and security organizations, and providing services to community residents. (The *mass line* refers to a long-standing Chinese policy, especially in Mao's era, that the police must rely on the cooperation of the masses in their work. The so-called mass-line crime prevention organizations are organizations like neighborhood committees and security committees participated in by ordinary citizens.) Public security police are the most visible component of the Chinese police. When people talk about the police they usually think of public security police.

The organizational structure of public security police is set up within the framework of administrative structure of the government (see Figure 2.1). In the current government administrative structure, there are 22 provinces (not including Taiwan), five autonomous regions, and four municipalities directly under the central government.[2] Within each province and autonomous region, there are counties and municipalities directly under the provincial government. Within each municipality directly under the central government, there are counties and districts. The police hierarchy is set within this administrative structure.

At the top of the police hierarchy is the Ministry of Public Security, representing the central control by the national government. The ministry is responsible for directing and coordinating the police operation throughout the country. Under the Ministry of Public Security, in each province, autonomous region, and municipality directly under the central government, there is a provincial-level public security bureau. Under the provincial level public security bureau, in provinces and autonomous regions there are municipal and county public security agencies; in municipalities directly under the central government there are district and county public security agencies. At the bottom of the police hierarchy are numerous police stations that are set up in larger communities across the country.

Each local public security agency is accountable to the immediately higher public security agency and the corresponding local government. For instance, a provincial public security agency is accountable to the Ministry of Public Security and the provincial government, whereas a county public security agency is accountable to the provincial public security agency and the county government. There is no legislation specifically allocating the responsibilities of the central government and local governments in the police administration. In practice, the Ministry of Public Security is responsible for setting professional standards, making rules and regulations, directing and coordinating major criminal investigations, and providing assistance such as crime detection and forensic analyses to local police agencies. Local governments are responsible for determining the size of the police force needed in their localities, providing budgets for the police, and setting local law enforcement priorities. According to Chinese police experts, the dual leadership structure has the advantage of keeping the nation's police under centralized control and meanwhile permitting local governments the autonomy to determine local law enforcement priorities and how to best use law enforcement resources to address the local law and order concerns (Ma & Tian, 1995; Xu, 1995).

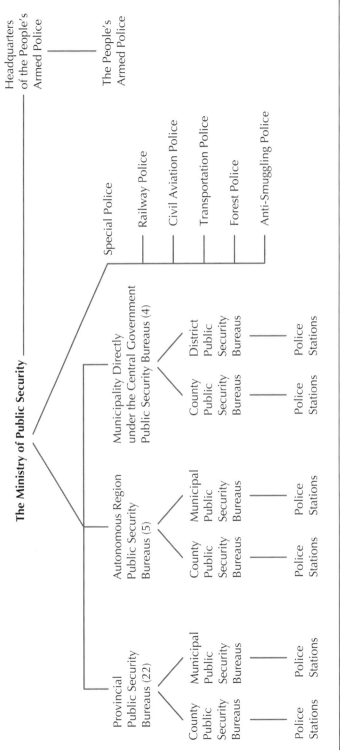

Figure 2.1 Organization of Public Security Police

In addition to regular public security police, there are also five special public security police. The five special police are railway police, transportation police, civil aviation police, forest police, and antismuggling police. The special police bear the responsibility of enforcing the law in their special professional fields. Railway police are responsible for maintaining order on trains and in train stations and investigating crimes committed in relation to railway transportation. Civil aviation police maintain order in airports and provide security for civilian air transportation. Forest police patrol national forests to prevent forest fires, poaching, illegal cutting, and other activities prohibited by the State Forest Law. Transportation police are responsible for providing security in waterway transportation. Antismuggling police are responsible for preventing smuggling.

The joint administrative structure applies to the special police as well. Administratively, the special police are organized within relevant government ministries. Railway police are organized within the Ministry of Railways. Transportation police are organized within the Ministry of Transportation. Civil aviation police are organized within the Bureau of Civil Aviation. Forest police are organized within the Ministry of Forests. The special police receive instructions for their day-to-day operation from respective ministries with which they are affiliated. They are also accountable mainly to their respective ministries. But the special police must follow the regulations and guidelines issued by the Ministry of Public Security and report their work periodically to the Ministry of Public Security. The special police may also seek professional assistance from the Ministry of Public Security. To deal with the increasingly rampant crime of smuggling, a special antismuggling police force was established in 1999. The antismuggling police are under the joint leadership of the Customs Administration and the Ministry of Public Security.

The Police Law contains no specific provisions regarding the organization and functions of the People's Armed Police. The People's Armed Police nonetheless is an important component of public security police. In 1983, the government converted 1 million soldiers from the army to form the People's Armed Police. The Police Law mentions the People's Armed Police very briefly. It states simply that the People's Armed Police perform the tasks given by the state with regard to protecting public safety. In practice, the duties performed by the People's Armed Police include border patrols, maintaining law and order at the border areas, providing security for high-ranking government officials and foreign dignitaries, guarding prisons and reform-through-labor facilities, guarding important government buildings such as radio stations and television stations, and guarding important facilities such as civil airports, bridges, and tunnels. The headquarters of the People's Armed Police are set up in the Ministry of Public Security. The force is under the joint command of the Ministry of Public Security and the Central Military Committee.

State Security Police

The state security police is a relatively new police force. It was established in 1983. The main functions of state security police are protecting national security and preventing and detecting foreign espionage, sabotage, and conspiracies against the state. State security police are under the leadership of the Ministry of State Security. Under the Ministry of State Security, a state security bureau is established in each province, autonomous region, and municipality directly under the central government. Subordinate state security agencies are established in selected municipalities directly under the provincial governments (see Figure 2.2). The lower-level state security agencies are usually set up in municipalities and coastal areas that have frequent contacts with foreign countries (Du & Zhang, 1990; Yuan & Sun, 1986).

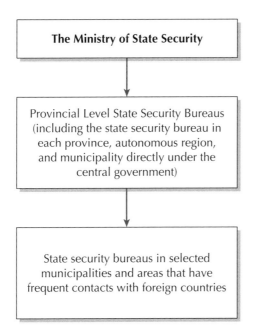

Figure 2.2   Organization of State Security Police

Prison Police

A noticeable feature of the Chinese police is that the police take full responsibility for supervising convicted offenders. The responsibility is divided between public security police and prison police. Public security police are responsible for supervising offenders serving community sentences; whereas prison police are responsible for supervising incarcerated offenders. Prison police are under the leadership of the Ministry of Justice. The Bureau of Prison Management within the Ministry of Justice has the overall responsibility for supervising the administration and operation of the country's prison system. The bureau sets general correctional policies and makes rules and regulations with regard to the prison administration. In each province, autonomous region, and municipality directly under the central government, there is a provincial-level Bureau of Justice (see Figure 2.3). A department of prison management is set up in each provincial-level Bureau of Justice. The department of prison management is directly responsible for the administration of prisons located within its jurisdiction (Xu, 1995).

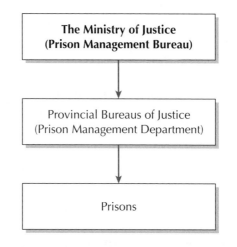

Figure 2.3   Organization of Prison Police

Judicial Police

Judicial police are responsible for providing security for people's courts and people's procuratorates. According to the Organic Law of the People's Court and the Organic Law of the People's Procuratorate, each people's court and people's procuratorate has the authority to establish its own judicial police. The functions of judicial police include providing security for the court and the procuratorate, serving subpoenas, conducting searches ordered by the court or the procuratorate, and executing court orders and judgments. Judicial police affiliated with the people's courts are also responsible for carrying out the death sentences meted out by the courts.

Recruitment and Training

The Police Law sets forth the basic recruitment standards. To become a police officer a candidate must have the following qualifications:

1. Be 18 years old or older

2. Support the constitution

3. Have good moral character

4. Be in good health

5. Have an education level no less than high school graduation

6. Be willing to serve as a police officer

The Police Law prohibits people with criminal records and people who have been expelled from public employment from becoming police officers.

The Police Law specifies only the minimum qualifications. A regulation issued by the Ministry of Public Security sets forth more conditions for police candidates. The regulation enumerates six categories of people that are disqualified from becoming police officers. The six categories are the following:

1. People who have been criminally punished, and people who, either as adults or juveniles, have been sent to camps of reeducation through labor

2. People who are suspected of a crime and for whom the suspicion has not yet been cleared

3. People who have been discharged from public employment

4. People with bad moral character or who have displayed immoral conduct, such as being a hoodlum or a thief

5. People with family members or relatives who have been sentenced to death or are still serving criminal sentences

6. People with family members or relatives who have been, either at home or abroad, engaged in activities aimed at overthrowing the Chinese government

To complement the Police Law's minimum age requirement, the ministry's regulation sets the maximum age limit for police candidates. The regulation states that to become a police officer a candidate cannot be older than 25 years of age. As a preferential treatment for candidates from ethnic minority groups, the regulation extends the maximum age limit to 30 for ethnic minority candidates.

China is a country composed of 56 nationalities. The Han people compose more than 90 percent of the total population, an overwhelming majority. The 55 other nationalities are considered minority nationalities. The population of the minority nationalities makes up about 9 percent of the total population. The central government has long carried out a policy that emphasizes the equality and unity of all nationalities. There is in general a harmonious relationship between the Han nationality and the minority nationalities. There is no problem such as particularly tense relations between police and the minority nationalities. The government encourages members of minority nationalities to join the police force. This is so especially in the five autonomous regions, where there is a relatively large population of minority nationalities. There is a national policy that members of minority nationalities should be given preferential treatment when they seek higher education or employment in government agencies. As required by this policy, police agencies similarly must give preferential consideration to candidates of minority nationalities when recruiting police officers.[3]

Qualified police candidates must take written examinations and go through strength and agility tests. To ensure that new recruits meet the recruitment standards, the Ministry of Public Security requires that the examinations and tests be organized and administered by a provincial police agency. Applicants must take provincewide examinations and tests. In making selection decisions, police agencies consider the scores a candidate receives in the examinations and tests and the information obtained by the police regarding a candidate's past experience and moral character. Once selected, the new recruits are required to go through a one-year probationary period. During the one-year period, the new recruits receive education and training at police academies. Only those who perform satisfactorily and pass the end-of-term examinations will be formally hired as police officers.

The Police Law sets out higher educational requirements for officers holding leadership positions. To be promoted to a leadership position, an officer must be college educated, have the necessary legal knowledge and practical experience in police work, and have administrative talent and skills. The candidate must also complete required in-service training in a police university or academy. The officially stated policy is that no officer can be promoted unless he or she completes the required in-service training.

To raise the level of professionalism among police, in 1992 the Chinese government established the police ranking system. According to the People's Police Ranking Regulation, there are five ranks in the Chinese police:

1. General superintendent (conferred on individuals who hold posts at the level of government minister) and deputy general superintendent (conferred on individuals who hold posts at the level of deputy government minister)

2. Superintendent (first, second, third grade)

3. Inspector (first, second, third grade)

4. Sergeant (first, second, third grade)

5. Officer (first, second grade)

A new recruit usually starts from the lowest rank. After a few years of service, the officer can apply for promotion. To be promoted, the officer must meet the promotional requirements, which include higher educational attainment and completion of required in-service training.

The leadership of the Chinese police has attached great significance to police education and training. Many police education and training facilities are established to accommodate the increasing demand of police education and training. It is estimated that there are now more than 300 police universities, colleges, and academies. The police educational level has improved significantly in recent years. In 1984, police officers with college education made up only 4.3 percent of the total police force. By 1991, this figure had risen to 19.2 percent. The percentage of police officers with a high school education rose as well, from 35 percent in 1984 to 57 percent in 1991 (Luo, 1995; Ma & Tian, 1995). According to figures released by the Ministry of Public Security, in 1999 police officers who had educational attainment of two years of college or higher already made up 44 percent of the total police force (Ministry of Public Security, 1999).

Police Functions

Police Functions in General

In comparison with the police of other countries, the Chinese police perform much broader functions. The Police Law stipulates 14 functions to be performed by the police. The 14 functions are the following:

1. Preventing and investigating crimes

2. Maintaining the public order and preventing activities that endanger the social order

3. Maintaining traffic order and handling traffic accidents

4. Organizing and administering fire prevention work

5. Controlling firearms, ammunition, and knives as well as flammable, explosive, and radioactive materials

6. Supervising the operation of certain types of professions and industries[4]

7. Providing security for high-ranking government officials, foreign dignitaries, and important buildings and facilities

8. Controlling and managing mass rallies, parades, and demonstrations

9. Administering the household registration system and handling affairs of conferring or revoking citizenship, entry into and exit of the country, and foreigners' residence and travel in China

10. Maintaining order and security at border areas

11. Supervising offenders sentenced to control, detention, and deprivation of political rights as well as offenders serving prison sentences outside prison, offenders serving suspended sentences, and offenders on parole

12. Supervising the operation of and providing security for the computer information network

13. Providing guidance to and supervising the work of security units in government offices, social organizations, and enterprises; providing guidance to mass-line security and crime prevention organizations

14. Performing other duties prescribed by laws and regulations

The functions listed in the Police Law are only the tasks of public security police. The Police Law contains no provisions with respect to functions of other police. The functions of other police are specified in other relevant legislation. For instance, the duties and functions of state security police are provided for in the State Security Law; the duties and functions of prison police are contained in the Prison Law; and the duties and functions of judicial police are specified in the Organic Law of the People's Court and the Organic Law of the People's Procuratorate.

Public security police are a highly specialized force. Within the Ministry of Public Security, there are directorates responsible for various types of police work. For instance, there are directorates responsible for ordinary criminal investigation, for investigating economic crimes, for public security, for border control, for exit-and-entry control, for fire-fighting, for traffic control, for drug law enforcement, for guarding high-ranking government officials, for jail administration, for supervision of the public information network, for internal supervision, for officer education, etc. Police specialization exists at lower-level police agencies as well. In lower-level police agencies, there are usually criminal investigation police, public order police, household registration police, traffic police, foreign affairs police, and fire-fighting police. Moreover, China became a member of Interpol in 1984. Within the Ministry of Public Security, the China National Central Bureau of Interpol serves as the liaison agency with Interpol. The Chinese police have ever since actively cooperated with Interpol in exchanging information and apprehending internationally wanted criminals (Ministry of Public Security, 1999).

Antiterrorism Function

Terrorism is not a new phenomenon in China. Over the past several decades, China has had its share of terrorist attacks. How to deal with terrorist attacks has long been a concern of the Chinese police. The September 11 attacks, however, have further alerted the Chinese police about the danger of terrorism. Since the September 11 attacks, the Chinese police have taken a series of measures to strengthen the police ability to deal with and prevent terrorist attacks. The Chinese government has also taken steps to improve its cooperation with the world community in the struggle against terrorism.

In the early 1980s, in response to several incidents of hijacking of civil aircraft, a special antihijacking police force was established within the public security police. In China, the threat of terrorist attacks comes mainly from an Islamic separatist organization operating in Xinjiang Uighur autonomous region located in the northwest part of the country. The separatist group is known as East Tujue (Turk) Islamic Movement. Xinjiang autonomous region has a relatively large Muslim population. The aim of the East Tujue group is to separate the region from China. The group has organized and carried out numerous terrorist attacks, including bombings, kidnappings, assassinations, and arson in the region. The group is connected with international terrorist networks. Members of the group used to train in bin Laden's terrorist camps in Afghanistan. On September 11, 2002, the UN Security Council passed a resolution declaring the East Tujue Islamic Movement a terrorist organization.

After the September 11 attacks, an antiterrorist bureau was established within the Ministry of Public Security. The main functions of the bureau are to conduct research, collect and analyze intelligence, and direct and coordinate antiterrorist work in the country. Following the tradition of mass-line policing, the police leadership emphasizes the importance of combining the work of professional antiterrorist experts and the efforts of mass-line crime prevention organizations. The government calls for waging a people's war against terrorism. Under the direction of the antiterrorist bureau, the antiterrorist police units in Beijing and other cities have worked out anti–terrorist-attack plans and carried out anti–terrorist-attack exercises. For instance, the antiterrorist unit in Beijing carried out exercises to rescue hostages taken by terrorists in seized foreign embassies. Various types of anti–terrorist-attack exercises have also been carried out in other cities.

Since September 11, the Chinese government has significantly stepped up its cooperation with other countries in the global war against terrorism. Soon after September 11, the Chinese police began to share intelligence with the U.S. law enforcement agencies. The Chinese government has reached similar cooperative agreements with a number of other countries as well. Most notably, China, Russia, and four other central Asian countries signed the "Agreement Concerning the Establishment of Regional Antiterrorist Institutions Among Members of the Shanghai Cooperation Organization." The agreement calls for close cooperation of member states in combating and preventing terrorist attacks. It establishes a six-country antiterrorist institution with its headquarters located in the capital city of the Republic of Kyrgyzstan. At the bilateral level, the Chinese army and the army of Kyrgyzstan in 2002 even carried out a joint anti–terrorist-attack military exercise.

Policing Strategies

In the first 30 years of the People's Republic, China adopted a policing strategy that was markedly different from that commonly seen in Western countries. China during this time had little contact with the outside world and was largely a closed society. The government imposed tight restrictions on people's movement. Corresponding to this social condition, the police adopted a strategy suitable for policing a static and stable population. In most Western countries, routine patrols are the mainstay of the police work and are called the backbone of policing. The Chinese police, however, over a time period of more than 30 years conducted no regular patrols. Routine patrols were not essential or necessary to the Chinese police. For the Chinese police, the key to successful policing was not the deterrent effect of routine patrols but their ability to keep a tight control over the subject population through restrictions upon travel and the extensive surveillance system of the mass-line crime prevention organizations.

The household registration system provided the police with the tools of restricting people's travel and monitoring people's movement. The law required that all people be registered under the household registration system. Shortly after a person's birth, parents or guardians of the person had to have the person registered at the local police station. The registration remained in effect until the person's death. Most people remained in the place of their original registration. Relocation due to job transfer was not common. If a person needed to move to another city, he or she had to notify the local police. The police would revoke the person's household registration and give the person a certificate so that he or she could register with the police at his or her new residence. Registration with the police was required not only of permanent residents, it was required of temporary residents as well. If a person came from another city to visit relatives or friends, he or she had to notify the police and register as a temporary resident. The person had to specify with whom he or she was staying and how long he or she would stay there.

The police were assisted in their efforts to monitor the movement of the population by neighborhood committees that were established across the country. Neighborhood committees were the most important mass-line organizations in the urban area. The law required that a neighborhood committee be established for every 100 to 600 households. The neighborhood committee performed a variety of functions related to community's well-being. For instance, the neighborhood committee organized informal patrols around the neighborhood to prevent theft or burglary, organized community residents to clean up the neighborhood, informed residents of crimes that had occurred in or near the neighborhood, reminded residents to take precautions against crime, and mediated disputes among community residents.[5]

The neighborhood committee worked under the guidance of the police. In the urban area, a police station was established in each larger community. A police station was headed by a chief and one or two deputy chiefs.

There were three types of police officers in a police station: household registration officers, public security officers, and internal affairs officers. Internal affairs officers were administrative officers who stayed in the police station to handle all office-related police work. Among the duties of internal affairs officers were processing household registration applications, handling revocation and transfer of household registration, receiving residents who came to the police station with their concerns, and handling citizens' complaints. Public security officers were in charge of maintaining law and order at the locality. Their duties included assisting higher-level police agencies in conducting criminal investigations, apprehending wanted criminals, locating stolen property, detaining people not properly registered under the household registration system, and investigating people engaged in suspicious activities.

Not all police stations were staffed with public security officers. Public security officers were staffed only in police stations located in areas with complicated security situations. In police stations that had no public security officers, the tasks of public security officers were performed by household registration officers.[6] A police station usually divided its jurisdictional area into several subareas, with each subarea consisting of several communities. A household registration officer was assigned to each subarea. The general guideline was that each household registration officer was responsible for 700 households. The household registration officer visited the communities under his or her control frequently and kept close ties with the neighborhood committees in the communities. Due to their frequent contacts with community residents, household registration officers were the most visible police officers in the eye of the public. Because household registration officers played such a key role in policing, it is no exaggeration to say that the work of household registration officers constituted the backbone of policing in that era.

A neighborhood committee in most cases was composed of retired workers or housewives. Members of the neighborhood committee conducted informal patrols in the neighborhood, stood guard against theft and burglary, and reported suspicious people and activity to the police. The neighborhood committee served as the eyes and ears of the police. Under its watchful eye and with its intimate knowledge of the community, any strangers and suspicious activity would be quickly noticed and promptly reported to the police.

Apart from neighborhood committees, internal security units at workplaces formed another link in the extensive network of mass-line crime prevention organizations. Within each work unit, be it factory, department store, hospital, or school, an internal security unit was set up. The internal security unit was responsible for providing security for the work unit and assisting the police in investigating crimes committed at the workplace or by employees of the work unit.

The policing strategy characterized by reliance on mass-line crime prevention organizations worked well for the police in the 1950s and the early

1960s. The crime rate in China was low. According to figures released by the government, the crime rate during this period was about 30 to 40 per 100,000 inhabitants (He, 1992). Apart from the low crime rate, the Chinese police, thanks to the work of household registration officers, in general maintained a close and positive relationship with community residents. The academic study of criminal justice did not exist in China then. It would not be hard, however, to find reports in Chinese newspapers about the harmonious relationship between police and community residents and stories about how police officers provided much needed help to community residents and how community residents helped police solve crimes and catch criminals. Police at this time were called by the Party to carry out a mass line in policing.

The police relied on mass-line policing until the late 1970s; then the situation began to change. Since the implementation of the policy of economic modernization, Chinese economy and society have undergone profound changes. In the past 25 years, China has maintained one of the fastest rates of economic growth. Economic development has brought about prosperity, and in its wake an unprecedented rise in crime. Western criminologists have long observed that modernization is often accompanied by an increase in criminality (Clinard & Abbott, 1973; Rogers, 1989; Shelly, 1981; Wilson & Herrnstein, 1985). China proves to be no exception to the pattern. In 1980 China's crime rate stood at 77.2 per 100,000 inhabitants, which was already much higher than the low crime rate in the 1950s and 1960s. By 1990 the figure had risen sharply to 200.2 per 100,000 inhabitants. There was especially an upward trend in serious and violent crimes. Between 1980 and 1990 the overall crime rate increased 160 percent, whereas the number of serious crimes increased 240 percent.[7] In addition to the sharp increase in the official figures, both government officials and scholars acknowledge that because of inaccuracy of the statistics taken by the police, the actual crime figures could be much higher (see Dutton & Lee, 1993; He, 1989; and Wang, 1989).

Faced with the sharp rise in crime, the police seemed to be at loss in finding effective ways to curb the upsurge in crime. The police found that the old policing strategies were no longer working, and they had yet to find new ones. The introduction of a market economy transformed the Chinese society. The changed socioeconomic conditions in turn resulted in the erosion of the basis of the past effective policing strategies. The opening up of the labor and commodity market created an ever-increasing demand for labor and commodities in urban areas. Tens and thousands of people from the countryside flooded to cities and coastal areas in search of work. These people moved on a temporary basis and usually were not registered in places where they were working. In the 1980s, it was estimated that there were about 80 million migrant workers constituting a floating population in large and coastal cities (Dutton & Lee, 1993).[8]

The presence of the sizable floating population reduced the ability of the police to monitor the urban population. Taking advantage of the weakened police control, criminals, especially criminal gangs, mingled with migrant workers to commit crimes, moving from one place to another. Studies noted a close connection between the increase in crimes and the growth in the floating population. Criminal gangs and the transient criminals committed a large number of ordinary street crimes. They were also responsible for the emergence of a variety of new types of crimes, for instance, drug trafficking, smuggling of cultural relics, the manufacture and sale of illicit arms, and the kidnapping and sale of women and children (He, 1992; Huang, 1991; Li, 1993).

With the erosion of the basis of the past policing strategies, the police were faced with the challenge of developing new strategies to deal with the upsurge in crime. To quickly reverse the upward trend in crime, the Chinese police adopted campaign-style policing. The campaign-style policing was characterized by launching short, sharp assaults upon particular types of crime for a limited period. China for a long time had a relatively low police-to-population ratio. In the early 1990s the police-to-population ratio was estimated to be between 1:745 and 1:1400, which was much lower than that in major Western countries (Dutton & Lee, 1993; Ma & Tian, 1995).[9] The modest police force, relying on the surveillance system of mass-line organizations and the restrictions placed on people's travel, seemed sufficient to police a largely stable and static population. As the basis of the closed system of social control eroded, the police line was suddenly stretched thin. Faced with the unprecedented rise in crime, the police realized that they did not have resources to target all crimes at once. The police thus adopted a strategy of concentrating their forces against particular categories of crimes. It was hoped that striking hard on certain types of the most harmful crimes would result in an overall crime reduction (Dutton & Lee, 1993; Tanner, 2005).

In the 1980s and early 1990s the government launched several "severe-strike" campaigns. The campaign against the "six evils" launched in the late 1980s illustrated this campaign-style policing. Convinced that moral decay was the root cause of the rise in crime, the government launched a campaign against the six evils. The six evils were prostitution; producing, selling, and spreading pornography; kidnapping women and children; planting, gathering, and trafficking in drugs; gambling; and defrauding people by superstitious means. The government claimed that the campaign was a success and achieved its desired goal. It was estimated that in a matter of months the police throughout the country ferreted out 213,000 cases of the six evils that involved 770,000 people. Of the people involved in the six-evil cases, 6,129 were arrested and prosecuted, 5,650 were sent to reeducation-through-labor camps, and 586,000 were punished by the police under public security regulations (Jiang & Dai, 1990).[10]

To maximize the effect of the severe-strike campaign, the National People's Congress substantially increased the penalty for targeted crimes. The legislature also amended the Criminal Procedure Law to make it easier for police to arrest and detain and for prosecutors to prosecute and convict offenders who had committed the targeted crimes. For instance, "The Decision on Severely Punishing Offenders Engaged in Offenses that Greatly Endanger the Public Security," issued by the Standing Committee of the National People's Congress, authorized the courts to punish certain types of offenders more severely than permitted by the Criminal Law. Offenders subjected to the enhanced punishment included those who committed serious violent crimes; those involved in the illicit manufacture, sale, and transportation of firearms and explosives; those involved in smuggling people; and those involved in inducing, permitting, and forcing women to engage in prostitution. According to the Decision, in cases involving the specified crimes, not only could the courts sentence offenders to longer imprisonment terms than were stipulated in the Criminal Law, but also, when there were aggravating circumstances, the courts could even sentence the offenders to death regardless of whether the death penalty was stipulated for the crime in the Criminal Law.[11]

In a companion decision, "The Decision on Expediting the Trial of Cases Involving Crimes that Greatly Endanger the Public Security," the Standing Committee of the National People's Congress relaxed the procedural requirements in cases involving certain serious crimes. The Criminal Law provided that after being sentenced to death, a defendant had 10 days to appeal the death sentence. The Decision of the Standing Committee, however, substantially shortened the appeal period for offenders convicted of certain types of crimes. According to the Decision, in cases involving crimes such as murder, rape, robbery, and sabotage by using explosives, the appeal period was reduced from 10 days to 3.[12] The legislative intent was to maximize the shocking effect of the death penalty. With the relaxed procedural requirement, offenders charged with crimes that fell within the stipulated category could be convicted, sentenced, and executed within days of their arrest. Because of the relaxed procedural protections, curtailed trial procedure, extensive imposition of the death penalty, and fast execution became notable features of severe-strike campaigns.

Despite the fanfare surrounding each severe-strike campaign and the government's claim that the campaigns substantially improved the public security situation, evidence suggests that the campaign-style policing achieved only marginal success. Crime statistics indicate that the overall crime rate dropped precipitously while each campaign was on but shot up once the campaign was over. The fluctuation of the crime rate indicates that the campaigns at best produced only a short-term effect. Commentators, both Western and Chinese, have also noted various side effects of the campaign-style policing. The most serious among them are police recourse to arbitrary and extralegal measures to accomplish the goal of a campaign, for instance, the use of torture to obtain confessions, falsification of crime statistics to exaggerate the effect of the campaign, extensive use of the death penalty, and abusive use of the death penalty, i.e., imposition of the death penalty on offenders who did not commit the targeted crimes (Dutton & Lee, 1993; Tanner, 2005; Zhou, 1999).

To assure objective evaluation of the grounds for searches does not seem to be the concern of the CPL. To the drafters of the CPL, the risk of unreasonable searches appeared to come mainly from street-level officers. Along this line of thinking, the assumption behind the warrant requirement of the CPL is that so long as police officers are required to obtain a search warrant from a high-ranking officer, the risk of unreasonable searches will be reduced. Since the implementation of the amended CPL, no systematic studies have been conducted to evaluate the effectiveness of the self-policing mechanism. Despite some documented cases that high-ranking officers in exercising the warrant authority have prevented low-ranking officers from conducting illegal searches (Liu & Wei, 1999), the overall effect of the self-supervisory system remains unknown. Apart from the potential conflict of interest in the system of permitting police to issue warrants to themselves, the lack of evidentiary criteria necessary to sustain the issuance of a search warrant presents another difficulty. The CPL contains no provision concerning the evidentiary standard necessary to justify the issuance of a search warrant. The practical effect of the lack of evidentiary criteria is that high-ranking officers are more likely for act arbitrarily when deciding whether a search warrant should be issued.

Power to Interrogate

One of the most noticeable revisions in the amended CPL is the grant to suspects the right to counsel at the police investigation stage. The old CPL afforded defendants the right to counsel at the trial stage but contained no provision with respect to legal representation at the police investigation stage. The extension of the right to counsel to the police investigation stage by the amended CPL represents a significant step forward in the development of criminal procedure in China. The effort to extend the right to counsel, however, met with resistance from the police both before and after the promulgation of the amended CPL. At the legislative debate, most legal experts were in favor of extending the right to counsel to the police investigation stage, but the police were against the idea. The Ministry of Public Security submitted a report to the National People's Congress contending that lawyers' involvement would hinder police investigations and undermine the police ability to solve crime.

The final version of the right to counsel contained in the amended CPL is a product of compromise between the two opposing views. The amended CPL grants the right but attaches several restrictions. The restrictions attached, as shown in the course of implementation of the law, seem to have had quite a negative impact on the proper exercise of the right. The statutory restrictions, coupled with police reluctance to faithfully implement the law, have in many cases rendered it impossible for lawyers to provide meaningful service to their clients.

Under the CPL, the police may interrogate a suspect in two circumstances. First, the police may summon a suspect to a police station for interrogation.

This form of interrogation is known as a summons for interrogation. Second, the police may interrogate a suspect after he or she is taken into police custody. The CPL provides for several procedural safeguards for suspects subjected to police interrogation. In a summons for interrogation, the CPL provides that the duration of interrogation cannot exceed 12 hours. The purpose of the provision is to prevent the police from turning a summons for interrogation into a *de facto* detention. To ensure that the police do not proceed from the premise that a suspect is guilty, the CPL requires that prior to interrogation the police must afford the suspect an opportunity to make a statement to profess his or her guilt or innocence. The police may interrogate a suspect only after he or she is given the opportunity to make such a statement. The noble intention of the provision notwithstanding, research studies indicate that police often ignore the procedural requirement and interrogate suspects directly without giving them the opportunity to make a statement. Not only do the police often deprive suspects of the right to make a statement, it is also common for the police to apply psychological pressure on suspects to make them talk. An often-used tactic is for the police to tell the suspect that they have already obtained solid evidence against him or her and that it would be in his or her best interest to confess (Liu, 2001a, 2001b). Tactics of this nature apparently are contrary to the letter and the spirit of the CPL.

Police interference with a suspect's exercise of the right to counsel represents one of the most troubling aspects in the implementation of the amended CPL. The police abuse, however, is at least in part attributable to the legislative regime itself. The CPL states that after completion of the first police interrogation, the suspect has the right to retain a lawyer to represent him or her. The retained lawyer, according to the CPL, has the right to inquire of the police about the crime of which the client is suspected, the right to meet with the client, and the right to ask the suspect about the circumstances of the case. The CPL then sets out several restrictions. It provides that in cases involving state secrets, lawyers must seek approval from the police before meeting with detained suspects. The CPL further provides that the police, when necessary, can be present at meetings between suspects and their lawyers.

The CPL grants suspects the right to counsel, but at the same time it gives police the power to supervise suspects' exercise of the right. The supervisory power given to the police in practice has led to widespread abuse. The police often deny suspects' requests to seek legal advice in the name of protecting state secrets, regardless of whether a case actually involves state secrets. It is also common for police agencies to set time limits on meetings between lawyers and suspects. The time permitted for each meeting is usually from 15 to 45 minutes, and in each case lawyers are permitted to meet with their clients only twice. The restrictions placed on the free communication between lawyers and suspects have greatly hampered lawyers' ability to represent their clients.

The CPL does not mandate the police presence at the meetings between lawyers and suspects. It only gives police the discretion to determine whether a police presence is necessary. Although this is not indicated in the CPL, regulations issued by the Ministry of Public Security make it clear that the police presence is for the purpose of preventing lawyers' wrongdoing, for instance, colluding with suspects to obstruct the police investigation. The intent of the CPL is that the police are not supposed to be present at all meetings between lawyers and suspects. They can be present only when there are reasonable grounds to believe that such a presence is necessary to prevent the possibility of wrongdoing by lawyers. In practice, because there are no guidelines as to under what circumstances the police presence is justified, the police tend in almost all cases to decide that the police presence is necessary.

After the promulgation of the CPL, the Ministry of Public Security issued two regulations concerning the police authority to supervise lawyers' meetings with suspects.[19] The regulations in many aspects further expand the police supervisory authority. The CPL states only that the police may be present at meetings between lawyers and suspects whenever necessary. The regulations provide that the police not only have the right to be present but also the power to suspend the meetings. The regulations state that if the supervising officer believes that a lawyer has violated the law or the rules of the meeting place, the officer is obligated to persuade the lawyer to stop such unlawful conduct. If necessary, the officer may suspend the meeting and report the lawyer's misconduct to relevant lawyers' management agencies. Theoretically, it seems quite incomprehensible to allow police officers, in most cases not legally trained, to judge a lawyer's behavior, including the legality and appropriateness of the advice a lawyer provides for his or her clients. But the real concern is not the theoretical soundness of the regime but the rampant police abuse of the supervisory power.

The Ministry regulations provide that police may suspend meetings between lawyers and suspects on two grounds: One is when lawyers violate the law when providing legal advice; the other is when lawyers violate the rules of the meeting places. Police cannot make the law, but they are in charge of making the rules of the meeting places, which in most cases are jails or other holding facilities. This power to define the rules of the meeting has thus become the main weapon of the police in restricting suspects' exercise of the right to counsel and in suspending lawyers' meeting with their clients. Some police agencies ask lawyers to submit outlines before meetings with suspects and then permit lawyers to ask only the questions contained in the outlines. In the name of ensuring proper conduct of police investigation, some police agencies prohibit lawyers from asking suspects any questions related to the case. Lawyers are permitted only to read statutory provisions or explain the meaning of the law to their clients. When present at the meetings, officers often show little respect for lawyers. They willfully interrupt consultation sessions or simply turn consultation sessions into a police interrogation. Some police agencies install recording devices or video cameras at the meeting place to monitor lawyer's behavior. More outrageously, under the pretense of preventing escape, some police agencies even ask lawyers to prepare handcuffs for their clients. Lawyers are permitted to proceed with the consultation only after they handcuff their own clients (Chen 2000; Chen & Song, 2000).

Despite the offensive nature of these measures, many police agencies seem to feel justified in imposing such restrictions. The police contend that the measures are necessary to prevent lawyers from colluding with suspects to undermine the police investigation. With respect to lawyers, the police seem to hold an us-versus-them mentality. The police regard themselves as crime fighters and guardians of the public interest. They view lawyers as people associated with and speaking for criminals. In their view, what lawyers intend to do is nothing more than attempt to undermine the police efforts to solve crime. With this kind of mentality prevailing in the ranks of the police, it is not surprising that many officers take an uncooperative or hostile attitude toward lawyers. Furthermore, a lawyer's fate in China is far from that of only being distrusted by the police. There is no lack of stories that lawyers are arrested and sentenced to jail for providing legal service for suspects and defendants.

The police distrust of lawyers in part is attributable to the low regard traditionally held by the Chinese for law and lawyers. The origin of the distrust of lawyers can be traced to the very first day when the Western style legal profession was introduced to China. The Western style legal profession appeared in China in the late Qing dynasty. The profession met with official disapproval as soon as it emerged. In an edict issued in 1820, the emperor deplored the trend toward "unbridled litigation" incited by a growing corps of "litigation tricksters." The emperor described these "litigation tricksters" as "rascally fellows" who intended to "entrap people for the sake of profit." The emperor directed that those who made a profession of preparing legal petitions for others be severely punished. The legal annuals of the Qing dynasty reveal numerous cases in which legal draftsmen were punished by penal servitude (Bodde & Morris, 1967). In modern times, the lack of interest in establishing a comprehensive legal system further deepened the disrespect for the legal profession. Because of the deeply entrenched distrust of the legal profession, there probably is a long way to go before lawyers can gain respect and become a truly functional component in China's criminal justice process.

Police use of torture is another serious problem in the current police operation. The CPL prohibits the use of torture as a means to obtain confessions. The statutory prohibition, however, has not prevented torture. Like the low regard for lawyers, there is also a long historical tradition of using torture as a means to extract confessions. Torture was an officially sanctioned method of obtaining confessions in all imperial dynasties. The feudal law gave overwhelming weight to confessions. Regardless of the existence of other evidence, a person's guilt was not certain until the person confessed to the crime. Because of the weight attached to confessions, the feudal law authorized the use of torture as a means to obtain confessions.

The official sanction of the use of torture and its frequent application marked one of the most distinctive features of the centuries-old Chinese feudal legal tradition (Bodde & Morris, 1967; Cohen, 1968; Dutton, 1992; Xiao, 1987; Zeng, 2000).

The remnant influence of the feudal tradition undoubtedly plays a role in the police tendency to resort to torture. But the difficulty in solving the problem is attributable more directly to the permissible and tolerant attitude of some police agencies and officials toward police use of torture. Faced with the demand from the government leadership and the public to bring crime under control, many police officials share the view that forcing suspects to talk offers the most efficient way to solve crimes. It should be noted that torture is not only a prohibited way to obtain evidence, it is also a criminal offense punishable by long-term imprisonment. In serious cases the offense is punishable even by the death penalty. The stiff penalty nevertheless has hardly produced any deterrent effect. This is largely because many police agencies take a hands-off policy toward officers' use of torture. Officers who resort to torture are rarely prosecuted or disciplined. On the contrary, they are praised, rewarded, and promoted for their ability to crack difficult cases (Chen, 2000; Chen & Song, 2000; Zhou, 1999). With the mentality that the end justifies the means prevailing among police officers and officials, it is not surprising that the statutory ban has produced little effect.

Educating police officers, including high-ranking police officials, about the importance of enforcing the law within the bounds of law and cultivating a culture of respect for the law among officers undoubtedly remain key in the effort to overcome the police tendency to use torture. Legal scholars meanwhile also argue that revision of the CPL is necessary to prevent police use of torture. Since the promulgation of the amended CPL, there has been a heated debate in Chinese legal circles as to whether Chinese law has recognized the principle of presumption of innocence. The amended CPL contains no clear language stating that an accused is presumed innocent until proven guilty. The relevant provision of the CPL states that, "Without adjudication by the people's court in accordance with the law, nobody should be determined as guilty of a crime" (Art. 12, CPL). Some scholars are of the view that Chinese law has in effect recognized the principle of presumption of innocence. Others argue that the provision states nothing more than that only the people's court has the authority to determine a person's guilt or innocence (see Lu, 1998; Song & Wu, 1999; Wang, 1996; Yang, 1998; Yue & Chen, 1997b, 1997c).

In contrast to the controversy surrounding the issue of presumption of innocence, scholars seem to agree that Chinese law does not fully recognize the privilege against self-incrimination. Article 93 of the CPL provides that a suspect must answer questions asked by interrogators truthfully. A reasonable interpretation of the provision is that if suspects are innocent, they are certainly entitled to insist on their innocence; but if they are in fact involved in the crime, they are under legal obligation to admit their guilt. To some police officers, the imposition of such obligation provides the justification to resort to torture. Because of the lack of the idea that a person should be presumed innocent until proven guilty, many officers operate on the premise that a suspect is guilty upon arrest. When a suspect refuses to admit guilt, the police naturally feel justified in resorting to torture to make the suspect fulfill the legal obligation to reveal the truth. Concerned that the provision may have contributed to the police tendency to use torture, many legal scholars suggest that the provision be revised. They argue that it is time for Chinese law to formally recognize the principle of presumption of innocence and grant suspects and defendants the full privilege against self-incrimination, including the right to remain silent (Chen, 2000; Chen & Song, 2000; Song & Wu, 1999; Yue & Chen, 1997a). It is not clear, however, whether the Chinese legislature is ready to make such legislative moves.

Police Accountability

The Chinese police in general have a positive image in the eye of the public. However, they are not immune from misconduct. Police misconduct in China, as in other countries, takes different forms. Some often-mentioned forms of police misconduct include corruption, brutality, making wrongful arrests, conducting unreasonable searches and seizures, unjustifiable use of weapons, and illegal use of police vehicles and equipment. Before the adoption of the new economic policy, China was a closed society. Out of concern that discussing police misconduct openly would tarnish the police image, the government dealt with police misconduct internally without public knowledge. Since the implementation of the policy of economic reform, the government has taken a more open view with regard to police misconduct. The government recognizes that police, like other government agencies, should be subject to citizens' and society's supervision. In the past 20 years, the government has made considerable efforts to establish a police accountability system. The basic structure of the police accountability system is provided for in the Police Law of 1995. This law specifies four types of police supervision mechanisms. They are procuratorate supervision, administrative supervision, internal supervision, and citizen supervision.

Procuratorate Supervision

The people's procuratorate has general oversight authority over the police. It has power to review and approve police requests for arrest. If necessary, it may participate in, direct, and provide guidance to police criminal investigations. The people's procuratorate has the duty to assure that all police actions be in compliance with the law. It may receive citizens' complaints against the police and investigate alleged police misconduct. In serious cases of police misconduct, the people's procuratorate has the authority to bring criminal prosecutions against infracting officers.

Administrative Supervision

To ensure that all government agencies abide by the law when performing their duties, the government established an administrative supervisory system in the 1980s. In the administrative supervisory system, all government agencies are subject to the oversight of the Ministry of Supervision. Police, as the government's law enforcement body, are also subject to the administrative supervision. The Ministry of Supervision and its subordinate agencies have the authority to receive citizens' complaints against the police and to send agents to police agencies to inspect their work. Upon receiving citizens' complaints, the supervisory agency has the authority to investigate the alleged police wrongdoing. The law requires that police agencies cooperate with the supervisory agency in its investigation. Upon finding misconduct of a police officer, the supervisory agency may impose sanctions prescribed in the Police Law against the infracting officer or recommend that the police agency take appropriate disciplinary action against the officer.

The disciplinary sanctions prescribed by the Police Law include warning, record of a demerit, record of a major demerit, demotion, dismissal from the post, and expulsion from the police force. The Police Law provides no procedural protections for officers facing disciplinary actions. Certain procedural protections are provided by regulations issued by the Ministry of Public Security. According to the regulations, a hearing is required before disciplinary actions may be imposed on an officer. The officer involved has the right to be notified of the hearing and has the right to defend him- or herself at the hearing. The officer has the right to tell his or her side of the story and produce evidence to aid his or her defense. Once a decision with regard to the disciplinary actions is made, the officer must be notified of the decision in writing. If the officer is not satisfied with the decision, he or she has the right to ask the agency to reconsider the decision or to ask a higher-level agency to review the decision. According to the Administrative Litigation Law, the officer can also request the administrative tribunal of the people's court to review the disciplinary decision rendered against him or her.

Citizens' Supervision

The Police Law provides that in performing their duties, police must voluntarily accept citizens' and society's supervision. The law specifies three ways in which citizens may exercise the right of supervision:

1. The right to make recommendations and suggestions to the police

2. The right to file complaints against the police

3. The right to bring lawsuits against the police

Citizens may file complaints against the police in several ways. They may file complaints with the people's procuratorate, with the Ministry of Supervision or its subordinate agencies, with the police agency involved, or with higher-level police agencies. The law requires that agencies that receive citizens' complaints investigate the alleged police wrongdoing and notify complaining citizens of the result of the investigation and the disposal decisions in a timely fashion.

Citizens have the right to file administrative or civil lawsuits against the police. Cases filed in the administrative tribunals usually involve police imposition of administrative sanctions. Under Chinese law, the police have the authority to impose various forms of administrative sanctions. The police may subject a person to administrative detention or send a person to a camp of reeducation through labor for disorderly conduct that falls short of a crime. These administrative offenses typically include transgressions such as disturbing social order and obstructing public security. For minor administrative offenses, the police may subject offenders to administrative detention for up to 15 days. In serious cases, the police may send offenders to camps of reeducation through labor. The duration of confinement in the camps may run from one to three years.

The police power to impose administrative sanctions has long been surrounded by controversy. Some commentators believe that granting police the power to subject people to administrative detention and to long-term confinement in camps of reeducation without judicial proceedings creates a great potential for abuse (Biddulph, 1993; Fu, 1994). The government nonetheless is not prepared to take away the power from the police. Although the law does not require police to seek judicial approval for imposing administrative sanctions, it does grant citizens the right to ask the administrative tribunal of the people's court to review the legality and appropriateness of the police decisions to impose such sanctions. To a certain extent, the postsanction court review provides some judicial supervision over this broad police power.

Upon reviewing a citizen's complaint, if the administrative tribunal believes that the sanction imposed is inappropriate, it may annul the sanction or order the police to enter into a new decision. Available research indicates that supervision by the administrative tribunal has produced a positive effect on police decision making. To avoid unfavorable court rulings, many police agencies have tightened the internal review of decisions to impose administrative sanctions. Stricter agency reviews have significantly reduced the number of litigations brought against the police in the administrative tribunal and lowered the overall rate of court rejection of police decisions to impose the sanctions (Chen, 2000; Ma & Tian, 1995).

In addition to seeking relief from the administrative tribunal, citizens may sue the police in the civil courts for monetary damages. The State Compensation Law specifies the circumstances under which the police may incur civil liability. According to the law, the police are civilly liable if they unlawfully subject citizens to criminal or administrative detentions, arrest citizens without reasonable grounds, cause citizens to suffer bodily injury or death by beating or instigating others to do so, or cause citizens to suffer bodily injury or death by illegal use of weapons or other police equipment.

Giving citizens the right to sue the police represents a significant development in China's legal reconstruction. In the first three decades of the People's Republic, it was unthinkable that ordinary citizens could bring the police to court. Even after the adoption of the new economic policy, citizens were not given the right to sue the police right away. The State Compensation Law, which was promulgated in 1994, formally gives citizens the right to sue the police. Since the law came into force, many citizens have exercised their rights and brought lawsuits against the police. Imposition of civil liability was not only to assure that citizens be compensated when police violate their rights. More significantly, the system was created to shape police behavior. It is expected that civil liability will increase police awareness of the importance of respecting citizens' rights when performing their duties.

To ensure that citizens receive timely compensation, the State Compensation Law requires the police agency to bear the primary responsibility for satisfying the monetary damages awarded by the court. On the other hand, to make responsible officers learn a lesson from the lawsuit, the law also requires that the police agency order the responsible officers to reimburse wholly or partially the damages paid by the police agency. There is evidence indicating that the civil liability system has produced the effect of making police agencies take more measures to strengthen officers' education and training. Since the law mandates that the infracting officers bear at least partially the cost of the compensation, the system has also created an incentive for individual officers to show more respect for citizens' legal rights (Lang, 1995; Luo, 1995).

Internal Supervision

The Police Law provides that higher-level police agencies must oversee the work of lower-level police agencies. Higher-level police agencies have the authority to inspect the work of lower-level police agencies and correct the wrong or improper decisions made by lower-level agencies. The Police Law further provides that an internal supervisory committee must be established in all county- and municipal-level police agencies. The internal supervisory committee is responsible for receiving and handling citizens' complaints against the police. It has the authority to investigate the alleged police wrongdoing and to discipline infracting officers.

A notable feature of the police internal supervision is that the authority of the supervisory committee goes far beyond handling citizens' complaints. The internal supervisory committee has the obligation to ensure the legality of all police actions and the efficiency and effectiveness of police performance. It has the authority to review all police action decisions, including decisions to arrest, to search, to detain, and to impose administrative sanctions. It is incumbent upon the committee to correct all police irregularities, for instance, wrongful arrests, illegal searches, prolonged detentions, improper imposition of administrative sanctions, etc. The supervisory committee also has the duty to assure overall police efficiency. The committee should inspect police work regularly to ensure that policing plans and strategies are properly implemented. Officers from the supervisory committee conduct routine supervisory patrols. They may follow officers on duty around to provide on-site supervision, or they may pay surprise visits to see whether officers on duty are performing their tasks properly and diligently.

The Chinese police authority does not regularly release police statistics. However, at the fiftieth anniversary of the founding of the People's Republic, the Ministry of Public Security compiled a report to celebrate the accomplishments of the police. The report, published in 1999, offers a glimpse of the work done by the police internal supervisory committees. The report shows that in 1999 the internal supervisory committees in police agencies nationwide corrected more than 300,000 incidents of unlawful or improper police actions and issued more than 20,000 supervision and inspection decisions and recommendations. The supervisory committees took various disciplinary actions against officers found of wrongdoings, including suspending 2,556 officers from active duty and subjecting 1,366 officers to administrative confinement (Ministry of Public Security, 1999).

Most police commentators agree that the establishment of the internal supervision system has played a positive role in maintaining police discipline and raising police professionalism. Some preliminary studies conducted shortly after the implementation of internal police supervision showed the positive effects of the new system. The studies showed that because of the oversight exercised by the internal supervisory committee, there was a significant decline in the rejection rate by the people's procuratorate of police requests for arrest and a noticeable reduction in citizens' complaints against the police (Lang, 1995; Ma & Tian, 1995). Research studies on the subject, however, are in general lacking. Before more empirical studies are conducted and more evidence comes to light, one can only assume that the system is playing a positive role in making the police a more disciplined force.

In comparison with the situation in the first 30 years of the People's Republic, when the concept of police accountability did not even exist, the establishment of the police accountability system marked a significant step forward in China's police development. In the first three decades of the People's Republic, the police were regarded as a tool of the Communist Party to suppress class enemies and to consolidate the dictatorship of the proletariat. Because the police were so intimately related to the exercise of political power, the government not surprisingly would not allow any public criticism of the police, let alone permit lawsuits against the police.

As China enters an era of economic development, there is a change in the perception of the police role. The police are no longer seen as a tool of the

In the police headquarters, there are five major departments: the Department of Operation and Support, the Department of Crime and Security, the Department of Personnel and Training, the Department of Management Service, and the Department of Finance, Administration, and Planning.

The Department of Operation and Support is responsible for police antiterrorist operations and operations of special-duty police units. It conducts regular reviews of tactics used in crowd management and riot control and handles matters such explosives and bomb disposal.

The Department of Personnel and Training is responsible for recruitment of police officers and for their entry-level and in-service training. There is a police training school under the direction of this department.

The Department of Management performs the logistics function. It is responsible for developing and maintaining the police information and communication system, including various computer facilities for the force. It coordinates all matters concerning police administration, for instance, the relationship between departments in the police headquarters and the relationship among different regional formations. It has the duty to ensure the efficiency and quality of police work and service. To accomplish this goal, it regularly reviews and evaluates the work of various police departments and formations. This department conducts research aimed at finding better and more effective policing strategies. It is also responsible for receiving and handling citizens' complaints against the police.

The Department of Finance, Administration, and Planning is responsible for financial management of the force. Its tasks include internal audit and management of civilian employees of the force.

Of the five departments, the one that attracts a lot of attention is the Department of Crime and Security. This department consists of several bureaus. The Commercial Crime Bureau is responsible for investigating commercial crimes, for instance, commercial fraud, computer crime, counterfeiting, forgery, credit card fraud, etc. The Narcotics Bureau is in charge of antidrug operations. In Hong Kong, organized crime, such as crimes committed by triads and secret societies, has long been a concern of the police. To effectively deal with the crimes committed by triads and criminal gangs, there is a bureau in the department in charge specifically of investigating crimes committed by organized crime figures. To enhance the department's ability to solve crime, it has several special bureaus. The Criminal Record Bureau is the repository of all criminal records. The Criminal Intelligence Bureau is responsible for collecting and analyzing crime-related information and intelligence. The Forensic Bureau is responsible for forensic examination of firearms and ammunition used in crimes. The Identification Bureau performs the task of analyzing fingerprints and photographs. Apart from criminal investigation, the department is also responsible for providing security for high-ranking government officials and visiting dignitaries.

The basic requirements for becoming a police officer in Hong Kong are that the candidate must be a permanent resident of Hong Kong and have lived in Hong Kong for at least seven years. The educational requirement for becoming a police constable is that the candidate must have some high school education. To become an inspector, the candidate needs to have an associate degree from a college. To be selected as a police officer, a candidate needs to take a written examination, go through an interview, and pass a physical fitness test, a medication examination, and a psychological screening. It is required that the candidate must be proficient in speaking both Chinese and English. Once selected, the candidate must go to the Police Training School to receive training.

The training requirements are different for police constables and inspectors. An inspector needs to complete 36 weeks of basic training that covers police procedure, law, foot-drill, physical training, and weapon handling. Training for police constables is the same as that of inspectors, except that constables are required to complete only 27 weeks of training. Additionally, since constables are usually the first to be on the scene of crimes, emergencies, or other unexpected situations, they are required to receive first aid training. Both inspectors and constables must pass a professional examination before they can graduate from the Police Training School.

A police constable must complete four years of service before being eligible for promotion to the rank of sergeant. If promoted, the officer must serve in the rank of sergeant for three years before he or she can be promoted to the rank of station sergeant. Apart from the years of service required, to be promoted, an officer must also pass a professional examination and be recommended by the Selection Board. After certain years of service, regardless of his or her rank, be it constable, sergeant, or station sergeant, an officer can apply to be promoted to the rank of inspector. To become an inspector, the candidate must have higher educational attainment, pass a professional examination, and be recommended by the Selection Board. The police ranking system in Hong Kong is similar to that of the British police. The highest rank is superintendent. Below superintendent there are chief inspector, senior inspector, station sergeant, sergeant, and police constable.

Notes

1. *History of Han: Book of Geography.* This is a history book written by Bangu (32–92 CE), a historian of the Han dynasty. See p.1543 of the copy printed by the China Publication Bureau in Beijing in 1962.

2. An autonomous region is the same as a province. It is established in regions with relatively large ethnic minority populations. In theory, an autonomous region has more autonomy and independence in its administration, because it needs to take into consideration the special needs of ethnic minority groups. In reality, the administration of an autonomous region is similar to that of a province. Municipalities

directly under the central government are major municipalities that the central government considers necessary to keep under its direct control. The capital city, Beijing, and China's most important industrial and commercial city, Shanghai, are both municipalities directly under the central government.

3. For China's policy with respect to minority nationalities, see *The White Paper on China's Policy and Practice with Respect to Minority Nationalities* issued by the Press Office of the State Council of the People's Republic of China, 1999.

4. The industries and services that come under regular police supervision include hotels, car rentals, pawn shops, and printing and carving houses. These services are believed to be often used by criminals. Police supervision of these businesses is perceived as necessary to track down criminal offenders' criminal activity.

5. See "Organic Regulation of the Urban Neighborhood Committees," promulgated by the Standing Committee of the National People's Congress, December 31, 1954.

6. The organizational structure of the police station and the functions of the three types of officers were specified in the "Organic Regulation of the Public Security Station" promulgated by the Standing Committee of the People's National Congress, December 31, 1954, and the "Detailed Regulation on the Work of Public Security Station" issued by the Ministry of Public Security in November, 1962.

7. See *Law Yearbook of China, 1981–1991*.

8. Today, it is estimated that the size of the floating population is about 114 million. See Fang (2005).

9. In the same period, the police-to-population ratio was higher in all other major Western nations. For instance, the police-to-population ratio in the United States was 1:377; in Germany it was 1:505; in France it was 1:333; and in Japan it was 1:555 (see Dutton & Lee, 1993; Ma & Tian, 1995).

10. Both authors of the cited article were high-ranking Chinese police officials. Bo Jiang was director of the Department of Legal Affairs of the Ministry of Public Security, and Yisheng Dai was acting director of the Institute of Public Security.

11. See "The Decision on Severely Punishing Offenders Involved in Offenses that Greatly Endanger the Public Security," issued by the Standing Committee of the National People's Congress, September 2, 1983.

12. See "The Decision on Expediting the Trial of Cases Involving Offenders Who Have Committed Offenses That Greatly Endanger the Public Security," issued by the Standing Committee of the National People's Congress, September 2, 1983.

13. See *Law Yearbook of China, 1981–2001*.

14. "Towards Implementing Community Policing in All Large and Medium-Sized Cities by 2004." Speech by Luo Feng, deputy minister of public security, at the national meeting of police stations. Xinhua News Agency, March 20, 2004.

15. "On Strengthening the Community Policing Programs," a directive issued jointly by the Ministry of Public Security and the Ministry of Civil Administration. *Legality Daily*, August 20, 2002.

16. See note 14.

17. "Regulation on Procedures of Handling Criminal Cases by Public Security Agencies" (1996), issued by the Ministry of Public Security.

18. See note 17.

19. The two regulations issued by the Ministry of Public Security are "Regulation on Procedures of Public Security Agencies" (1997) and "Regulation on Lawyers' Participation in Criminal Procedure Activity at the Investigation Stage" (1997).

References

Bakken, B. (2005). Comparative perspectives on crime in China. In B. Bakken (Ed.), *Crime, punishment, and policing in China* (pp. 64–99). Lanham, MD: Rowman & Littlefield.

Biddulph, S. (1993). Review of police powers of administrative detention in the People's Republic of China. *Crime & Delinquency, 39*(3), 337–354.

Bodde, D., & Morris, C. (1967). *Law in imperial China.* Cambridge, MA: Harvard University Press.

Cao, P., & Qi, J. (1985). Security agencies and security system in the Ming dynasty. In China Social Science Research Institute, the Legal History Section (Ed.), *Introduction to China's police system* (pp. 233–247). Beijing: The Masses Publishing House.

Chang, Z. R. (1985a). The police system and its characteristics during the time of Northern Warlords. In China Social Science Research Institute, the Legal History Section (Ed.), *Introduction to China's police system* (pp. 318–336). Beijing: The Masses Publishing House.

Chang, Z. R. (1985b). The police system under the rule of Guomintang. In China Social Science Research Institute, the Legal History Section (Ed.), *Introduction to China's police system* (pp. 337–357). Beijing: The Masses Publishing House.

Chen, G. Z., & Song, Y. H. (2000). *Research on issues in implementation of the Criminal Procedure Law.* Beijing: China Legality Publishing House.

Chen, R. H. (2000). *The frontier issues of criminal procedural law.* Beijing: China People's University Press.

Clinard, M., & Abbott, D. (1973). *Crime in the developing countries.* New York: John Wiley.

Cohen, J. A. (1968). *The criminal process in the People's Republic of China: 1949–1963.* Cambridge, MA: Harvard University Press.

Du, X. C., & Zhang, L. Y. (1990). *China's legal system.* Beijing: New World Press.

Dutton, M. (1992). *Policing and punishment in China.* Cambridge, UK: Cambridge University Press.

Dutton, M. (2005). Toward a government of the contract: Policing in the era of reform. In B. Bakken (Ed.), *Crime, punishment, and policing in China* (pp. 189–233). Lanham, MD: Rowman & Littlefield.

Dutton, M., & Lee, T. (1993). Missing the target: Policing strategies in the period of economic reform. *Crime & Delinquency, 39*(3), 316–336.

Fang, B. (2005). The floating people. *U.S. News & World Report, 138,* 47–48.

Feng, W. G., & Zhang, W. (2003). *A practical course in community policing.* Beijing: People's Procuratorate Publishing House.

Fu, H. L. (1994). A case for abolishing shelter for examination: Judicial review and police powers in China. *Police Studies, 17*(4), 41–60.

Gao, H. (1985a). Social conditions and security management in the capital of the west Han dynasty. In China Social Science Research Institute, the Legal History Section (Ed.), *Introduction to China's police system* (pp. 74–88). Beijing: The Masses Publishing House.

Gao, H. (1985b). *Thing*—the local police agencies during the Qin and Han dynasties. In China Social Science Research Institute, the Legal History Section (Ed.), *Introduction to China's police system* (pp. 98–105). Beijing: The Masses Publishing House.

Han, Y. L., & Cao, P. (1985). Security agencies and security regulations in the Qing dynasty. In China Social Science Research Institute, the Legal History Section (Ed.), *Introduction to China's police system* (pp. 261–280). Beijing: The Masses Publishing House.

He, B. S. (1989). The crime trend, causes and penal policies in our country. *Political Science and Law Forum, 5*, 1–11.

He, B. S. (1992). Crime and control in China. In Heiland, H.-G., Shelly, L. J., & Katoh, H. (Eds.), *Crime and control in comparative perspective* (pp. 241–251). Berlin: Walter de Gruyter.

Huang, W. (1991, July 29–August 4). Crackdown on abduction of women and children. *Beijing Review*, 24–27.

Jiang, B., & Dai, Y. H. (1990). Mobilizing all possible social forces to strengthen public security—A must for crime control. *Police Studies, 13*, 1–9.

Keith, R. C. (1994). *China's struggle for the rule of law*. New York: St. Martin's Press.

Lang, S. (1995). *Questions and answers in regard to the Police Law of the People's Republic of China*. Beijing: China Democracy and Legality Publishing House.

Lawyers Committee for Human Rights. (1996). *Opening to reform? An analysis of China's revised Criminal Procedure Law*. New York: Lawyers Committee for Human Rights.

Lee, T. V. (Ed.). (1997). *Law, the state, and society in China*. New York: Garland.

Li, B. (1993, August 9–15). China cracks down on armed criminals. *Beijing Review*, 16–17.

Liu, G. J., & Wei, Y. N. (1999). *Cases of Criminal Procedure Law*. Beijing: China University of Political Science and Law Press.

Liu, H. N. (1985). The security agencies and the laws and regulations regarding security management during the Qin dynasty. In China Social Science Research Institute, the Legal History Section (Ed.), *Introduction to China's police system* (pp. 59–73). Beijing: The Masses Publishing House.

Liu, J. C. (2001a). *Interpretations of provisions of the new Criminal Procedure Law*. Beijing: People's Court Publishing House.

Liu, J. C. (2001b). *New interpretations and new explanations of the Criminal Procedure Law and relevant regulations*. Beijing: People's Court Publishing House.

Liu, J. G., Li, B. J., & Guo, F. H. (2002). *Community policing and policing norms*. Beijing: Public Security Press.

Lu, Q. Z. (1998). Exploring issues concerning the establishment and implementation of the principle of presumption of innocence in China. *Law Science, 10*, 36–43.

Luo, F. (1995). *Interpretation of the Police Law of the People's Republic of China*. Beijing: The Masses Publishing House.

Ma, Z. Y., & Tian, M. Q. (1995). *Interpretation and explanation of the Police Law of the People's Republic of China*. Beijing: China People's Public Security University Press.

McKnight, B. (1992). *Law and order in Sung China*. Cambridge, UK: Cambridge University Press.

Ministry of Public Security. (1999). *Policing in China*. Beijing: The Ministry of Public Security.

Ni, H. Y. (2003). *Community policing*. Beijing: Public Security University Press.

Rogers, J. (1989). Theories of crime and development: An historical perspective. *Journal of Development. 3*, 315–318.

Shelly, L. (1981). *Crime and modernization.* Carbondale, IL: Southern Illinois University Press.

Siegel, L. J. (2003). *Criminology.* Belmont, CA: Wadsworth/Thomson.

Song, Y. H., & Wu, H. J. (1999). The principle against compulsory self-incrimination and its procedural guarantees. *China Legal Science 1999* (2), 117–128.

Sun, Q. (2000). Some thoughts on perfecting the law of arrest in our country. *China Legal Science 2000* (4), 93–98.

Tanner, M. S. (2005). Campaign-style policing in China and its critics. In B. Bakken (Ed.), *Crime, punishment, and policing in China* (pp. 171–188). Lanham, MD: Rowman & Littlefield.

Turner, K. G., Feinerman, J. V., & Guy, R. K. (Eds.). (2000). *The limits of the rule of law in China.* Seattle: University of Washington Press.

Vold, G. B., & Bernard, T. J. (1986). *Theoretical criminology.* New York: Oxford University Press.

Wakeman, F. (1995). *Policing Shanghai 1927–1937.* Berkeley: University of California Press.

Wang, F. (The Minister of Public Security) (1989). Reform and strengthen the public security work in order to serve the need of establishing a market economy. In *Law Yearbook of China—1989* (pp. 813–816). Beijing: Law Yearbook of China Publishing House.

Wang, J. M. (1996). From "guilt by adjudication" to "presumption of innocence." *Law Science, 5,* 13–15.

Wilson, J., & Herrnstein, R. (1985). *Crime and human nature.* New York: Simon & Schuster.

Xiao, Y. Q. (1987). *A course in Chinese legal history.* Beijing: Law Publishing House.

Xiong, Y. X. (2002). *Community policing in China.* Paper presented at the International Symposium of the Trend and Counter-Measures of Crimes in the 21st Century, Beijing, 2002.

Xu, X. Y. (1995). *On the Police Law of the People's Republic of China.* Beijing: Officers' Education Publishing House.

Yang, M. (1998). On the implementation of and the departure from the principle of presumption of innocence in our country's Criminal Procedure Law. *Law Science, 3,* 21–25.

Yu, L. N. (1985a). The frank pledge system and the security at the local levels in the Song dynasty. In China Social Science Research Institute, the Legal History Section (Ed.), *Introduction to China's police system* (pp. 188–204). Beijing: The Masses Publishing House.

Yu, L. N. (1985b). The origin and development of the ancient Chinese police functions. In China Social Science Research Institute, the Legal History Section (Ed.), *Introduction to China's police system* (pp. 3–4). Beijing: The Masses Publishing House.

Yu, L. N. (1985c). Security agencies and security management in the Tang dynasty. In China Social Science Research Institute, the Legal History Section (Ed.), *Introduction to China's police system* (pp. 145–163). Beijing: The Masses Publishing House.

Yuan, H. B., & Sun, X. N. (1986). *China's judicial system.* Beijing: Beijing University Press.

Yue, L. L., & Chen, R. H. (1997a). International standards on criminal justice and the amended Criminal Procedure Law in our country. *Law Science, 1,* 21–25.

3 Neofeudal Aspects of Brazil's Public Security

Benjamin Nelson Reames

A subtle but perhaps profound shift in the study of Brazilian public security is underway. The dominant scholarly tradition has detailed authoritarian legacies that have shaped public security—e.g., the repertoires of brutal state repression, the state institutions often seen as failing or illegitimate, and the stark spatial segregation of classes. This approach was crucial in calling attention to the institutional holdovers of authoritarianism that (in Brazil and elsewhere) undermine the justice system, weaken citizenship, criminalize the poor, and give rise to repressive styles of policing.

More recent studies of public security tend to portray contemporary urban Brazil as increasingly fractured and stratified by privately secured spaces as well as being webbed together at the political level by networks of corruption and criminality. The notion of "authoritarian atavisms" is becoming less useful, while the idea of neofeudal power structures explains more. Here I use *neofeudal* loosely and generally to refer to various theories that identify growing extra-legal violence, shrinking spaces for public life, the privatization of security, and the absence or illegitimacy of state presence in many areas as alterations in the power relations that determine the Brazilian public security situation.

This shift in focus may lead to a better understanding of how public security and power dynamics have developed in the past 25 years in Brazil. Ultimately, it may also lead to an approach that relies less on the notion of authoritarianism to explain the deficiencies and maladies that plague the developing and modernizing world in an era of prevalent democratization, globalization, and fractured state boundaries. Instead, a more powerful explanation may rely more on relationships among transnational corporations, social networks, private enterprises, and criminal organizations in the context of weakening state control.

Three core problems with the Brazilian police—brutality, corruption, and ineffectiveness—undermine confidence in democracy and degrade the value of it.[1] Analysts have long placed blame for these problems on severe social and economic stratification, the durable legacy of authoritarian regimes (most recently, 1964–1985), the lack of resources and training for the police, a culture of vigilantism and violence, and ingrained racial and class prejudices. All of these factors, which range from the structural to the cultural, surely contribute to police violence, corruption, and poor performance. However, the government and the nature of federalism have much to do with holding these defects in place by inhibiting reform.

Furthermore, there are at least two institutional problems that can easily be overlooked. First, there is the Janus face of Brazil's justice and security system, which projects one reality and recognizes another. Second, the increasingly institutionalized criminal and extra-legal organizations in Brazil have formed networks that embed the entire public security system in connections that weaken its independence and authority. On the first point, one can identify a fundamental institutional paradox that slows progress toward democratic policing. In Brazil, as in many countries, there is the proper way the law is supposed to be enforced on the one hand and the way that justice is commonly meted out on the other. These contradicting realities coexist in Brazil with remarkable resiliency, starkness, and severity—a fact that merits special attention and a term for the phenomenon, "institutional duplicity."[2] On the second point, criminal networks have become so strong, wealthy, embedded in *favelas* (Brazilian slums) and into rich society, not to mention armed to the teeth, that they affect public security institutions by corrupting them and depleting them of legitimacy. One cannot understand the dynamic of crime and public security responses to it without considering the dynamic that I call neofeudalism, in which corrupt groups and organized criminal organizations both reap the benefits of disorder and cripple the ability of the state to maintain order.

Institutional duplicity grows out of dichotomies embedded in the Brazilian justice system: Written rules and regulations do not permit police to achieve the goals and expectations that are placed on them; police mandates outstretch their capacity; the political system is expressly egalitarian but overlays a socioeconomic system that is extremely hierarchical; and multiple agencies share responsibility for law enforcement, often leaving no single agency accountable. Often the prescribed means do not lead to the intended ends, so detours and shortcuts are invented to subvert the system; the shortcuts then stay in place and the two systems—one legitimate, the other illegitimate—operate side by side. The result is a confusing justice system, which serves different people differently, conceals commonplace corruption, and is inefficient and resistant to reform.[3]

However, institutions that are accountable to civilian authorities are precisely what is needed both to improve public security (Agüero, 1997; Frühling, 1998; de Mesquita Neto, 1999) and to consolidate democracy in the region (Dominguez & Lowenthal 1996; Linz & Stepan, 1996; Ungar, 2002). Given the waves of crime and police violence that swept the country with impunity in the 1990s, it would be easier to marshal evidence showing that the arrival of democracy has degraded more than improved policing in Brazil.[4]

So if democracy did not improve public security on its own, the pressing question is the reverse: Can a more transparent, accountable police system be used as leverage to achieve a deeper, consolidated democracy?[5] The evidence for optimism from Brazil is that as civil society groups have gained a more mature and informed understanding of police institutions, they have proposed and implemented practical reforms and improvements. In the last 10 years there have appeared civilian complaint centers (*ouvidorias*), community policing programs, less repressive municipal police services, some functional unification of police forces, witness protection programs, and police stations staffed by and attending to women, to mention a few prominent reforms. These innovations have aimed not only to improve the justice system but also to expand citizenship, and though recent, many reforms have been credited with increasing transparency, responsiveness in government, and the public's sense of participation. The future of policing, crime control, and perhaps democratic consolidation may be chartered by civil society experts and reformers who are engaged and well informed.

This chapter starts with a historical overview and analysis of institutional arrangements of the police, from the meta- to the intrainstitutional features. After defining the Brazilian police, the chapter takes a critical look at the public security apparatus in the context of crime, violence, human rights abuses, organized crime, and the growth of uncivil society. The concluding section uses the thus elaborated institutional framework and context to consider the police reforms that have been implemented or proposed. Throughout this analysis, three outstanding features of the Brazilian public security system are stressed: the nature of federalism, the presence of ingrained institutional duplicity, and the influence of privatized security and criminal organizations that generate a type of neofeudalism.

Brazilian Institutions and Public Security

From the end of the 1970s through the 1980s, Brazil, like most countries of South America, underwent a democratic transition; the transition achieved the basic democratic benchmarks: the legalization of political parties, the popular vote, the end of censorship, and freedom of labor union activity. However, the justice and public security sectors—also essential for democracy—lagged behind.

Part of the reason for Brazil's inability to revamp its police forces is its political structure and size. Brazil contains roughly 180 million people and almost half of the land area of South America and as a federal democracy consists of 26 states and one federal district. The job of policing this vast territory has, for the most part, always been delegated to the states. The 1988 Constitution neither unified police forces nor facilitated further decentralization; instead, it made some of the contradictory or dysfunctional traits of the policing system harder to charge. Brazil exhibits a strong type of "demos-constraining" federalism, which means that reforms at the national level are difficult to pass if a small minority resists them (Stepan, 2000). A number of constitutional amendments have been proposed, typically to unify police forces or make them more accountable to civilian authorities; all have failed due to a strong police lobby or conservative elements in smaller states.[6]

To understand what demos-constraining federalism means at the federal level, one must begin with the fact that Brazil's political parties are nonprogrammatic, inconsistent, and numerous, and they vary over time and from state to state. Thus the policy lobby does not behave like an ordinary interest group, because they are the opposite of political parties. The policy lobby has few ostensive leaders, and it requires little political organization, because its rank and file are already organized, informed of relevant legislation, and reasonably united in their agenda. Police institutions—particularly the rigidly hierarchical military police—are explicit that they oppose unification, infringements on rights and privileges, and civilian trials for police officers (all reforms that are explained below). Further, police threats are not considered empty in Brazil, because police have used their power to disrupt: Police strikes, though illegal, have crippled various states over 60 times since the 1990s and have often resulted in the military being called in to control order. As a result, elected officials rarely admit that the police lobby influences them. Yet reform does not pass. Legislators demonstrate their shades of allegiance or compliance not through discourse or action, but by *not* acting.

Moving to the state level, where the police are organized, managed, and funded, Brazil's federal institutions do not help reform efforts. Governors ostensibly control the police by appointing a Secretary of Public Security (SPS) to manage policing. However, despite a governor's power to appoint and remove officials and control their budgets, the police institutions enjoy a great deal of autonomy because of their constitutional protections (explained below), which they use strategically. Because the police are insulated, armed, and constitutionally protected, and because their cooperation is necessary to achieving core parts of any governor's agenda, they feel emboldened to wait out governors or an SPS that they do not agree with. Police know (and admit) as much (Salles & Lund, 1999). Rather than bend police to their will, governors must strike compromises and develop working relationships with police departments. They do not simply command them. Nor do the Secretaries of Public Security. There is frequent animosity (or at least, institutional competition) between the civil police and the military police. The leadership personnel of the former are trained lawyers, while a militarized hierarchy leads the latter. Thus, an SPS drawn from either corporation has difficulty uniting the two groups. To avoid that bureaucratic loggerhead, the chosen SPS might be a public prosecutor or a retired army official instead. Yet in such an instance the SPS runs the risk of becoming a marginalized figure that knows neither institution well. For all these reasons, it is necessary to take an institutional look at Brazilian public security arrangements.

Primary Police Institutions

Brazil's primary public security institutions are its police, most of which are required by mandate of federal law but organized at the state level. There are two main types—an investigative police force and an ostensive police. Additionally, there are multiple municipal guards (which lack special arrest or investigative powers), two federal forces, and firefighters who also fulfill public safety functions. These forces are presented in Table 3.1, and this chapter analyzes them from a variety of perspectives: constitutional, historical, intra- and interinstitutional.

Each state (including the federal district) has a civil police for judicial investigations and a military police for maintaining order.[7] These organizations are considered "half polices" by some, because the civil police (PC for *polícia civil*) investigate possible crimes and the military police (PM for *polícia militar*) are charged with suppressing and preventing crime, but the activities involved in investigating and controlling crime are not made to coincide. In fact, the Constitution of 1988 requires each state to have these two functionally and organizationally different police forces, but the federal government does not require mechanisms for the PC and PM to share information, resources, planning, or jurisdictions. As a result, the dual police system has created divergent command systems, pay scales, and rules that regulate conduct. Infamous rivalries, competitiveness, and conflicting institutional cultures often further complicate the ability of the PM and PC to work together. This functional duality has exacerbated the problem of institutional duplicity by impeding cooperation and doubling the number of police institutions needed.

Military Police

The 27 corporations of the PM form the largest, most visible type of police force in Brazil with 450,000 officers. The state of São Paulo alone has at least 89,000 military police officers; the states of Rio de Janeiro and Minas Gerais both have over 40,000. The military no longer commands them, but the PM still composes "an auxiliary and reserve force of the Army."[8] This specific responsibility to support the military, though unused, still significantly affects policy, training, and ethos. For instance, the PMs are structured internally according to a military model in which there are

Table 3.1   Police Forces of Brazil

Government Level and Number of Forces	Main Police Forces and Attributes	Personnel (estimate)
Federal (2 forces)		16,000
1	Federal Police (PF)	8,000
	Few in number, highly trained, less corrupt, overextended; responsible for border and immigration control, federal crimes, protection of sensitive areas and important officials.	
1	Polícia Rodoviára (Highway Police)	8,000
State (54 forces)		600,000
27	Military Police (PM)	450,000
	Ostensive, order-maintenance policing; numerous, well-armed; some military training.	
27	Civil Police (PC)	150,000
	Investigative or judicial policing, plain-clothed, have legal training.	
Local (357+ forces)	Municipal Guards	60,000
	Provide security in public parks, schools, and transit; increasingly common in larger cities; generally lack firearms; have few powers, but are the focus of police developments given their proximity to citizens and less violent history.	
Total police forces by jurisdiction: 415+	Total police forces by type: 5	Total police personnel: 676,000

SOURCES: Mariano, 2004; Proença, 2004; de Souza Leal, 2004. Estimates are used, because the actual numbers constantly fluctuate, due to turnover and expanding police forces.

two main hierarchical domains—officers and soldiers (*oficiais* and *praças*) (Lemgruber, Musumeci, & Cano, 2003). As often follows in such bureaucracies, the fundamental values transmitted in regulating conduct are those of hierarchy and discipline.[9] Also, the PM frequently create elite units to deal with specific types of crimes or problem areas, a tendency that has much in common with the military. Further, the PM inherited from the military an excessive number of ranks (12, to be exact) that makes advancement very difficult and creates an elite group of insulated and well-paid brass at the top.[10] In short, the Brazilian approach to policing has created a structural dichotomy within the PM: It performs a civil function with a militarized institution.

Civil Police

The PC are considered judicial police forces, because they carry out investigations of crimes (except those committed by the PMs) under the supervision of the courts and the attorney general (*Ministério Público*). The PC's function is to establish causal connections between the crime, the circumstances, the perpetrators, and the accomplices. The PC also assemble crime reports; perform arrests, seizures, and searches by court order; and manage grossly overcrowded jails and holding cells. In theory, they do not patrol the streets in uniform or do ostensive policing, though this too is an example of institutional duplicity.[11] Much about the PC is dated. For example, most forces were formed during the First Republic (1889–1930); the Penal Process Code (*Codigo de Processo Penal*), which dictates the PC's functioning, has not changed since 1941. A major problem is the paralyzing weight of bureaucratic duties due to the legally mandated *inquérito policial* (formal police inquisition). It has been blamed for contributing to low morale, inefficiency, corruption, and the brutal extraction of confessions (Lemgruber et al., 2003).

The PC constitute the second most important of the police forces, because they are fewer in number and more dependent on other public officials than the PM. Nationally, there are roughly 150,000 members of the PC. Of these, a good estimate is that there are 10,000 *delegados* or high-ranking officials (a *delegado titular* is a chief of a precinct); the rest include investigators, detectives, specialists, and clerks. In many states, all *delegados* have law degrees, which confer a higher status in Brazilian society, but the competitive hiring process with new educational requirements has not yet cleared out a very stagnant body of personnel in other states: Despite the new law, it is estimated that nationwide only 60 percent of delegados have bachelor's degrees in law (Mariano, interview, 2004).

Federal Police

The PF (Polícia Federal) are few in number and overloaded with responsibilities. Most estimate that the federal police personnel numbers 15,000, but the best Brazilian estimate of actual police *agents* is 8,000 (Proença, interview, 2004).[12] The PF are responsible for controlling entry and exit via land, sea, and air frontiers and ports—during a strike in 2004, they managed to slow down all international travelers because of their airport responsibilities. The PF also guards key members of the government, foreign diplomats, and major federal government installations throughout the country. Officials who have received death threats—even from other police forces—are often placed under the protection of the PF. This relatively small force is also charged with finding and destroying hidden airfields, controlling territorial and crime problems with native groups in the Amazon, and investigating sophisticated financial and political crimes. With passport and other bureaucratic duties occupying much of their time, the PF's efforts to control corruption and contraband (arms and drugs) may be pushed onto the back burner, making it easier for organized crime to act with impunity.

Besides protecting Brazil's territorial integrity and public officials, the PF is responsible for managing national security threats. In this capacity, it liaises with international police organizations, including Interpol. The PF provides a central intelligence collection and disseminating service for the various state police forces. In many respects the work of the PF parallels the activities of the Federal Bureau of Investigation (FBI) in the United States. The PF maintains specialized units, such as the Division of Organized Crime Control and Special Investigations (*Divisão de Repressão ao Crime Organizado e Inquéritos Especiais*—DECOIE), which specializes in financial crime; the Tactical Operations Command (*Comando de Operações Táticas*—COT), a SWAT-like force officially formed in March 1990 that has over 50 agents trained in hostage negotiation and rescue, tactical operations such as rapid entry into aircraft and buildings, and of course special weapons training and sniper-shooting; and the Antinarcotics Division (*Divisão de Repressão a Entorpecente*—DRE), which works mainly to intercept illegal drugs sales and drugs in transit. A unique institutional trait of the PF is that the marshals (high-ranking officers of limited number) can form these special units and divisions ad hoc and informally, and very little hierarchical control or approval is needed. The adaptability and the public confidence that the PF enjoys is unique among Brazilian police. Ironically, despite their solid reputations, the size of the PF remains limited due to trepidations about a centralized, federal police amassing too much power, as happened during authoritarian periods.

Municipal Guards

The *Guarda Municipal* is a low-key type of public security force that exists in more than 357 of Brazil's 5,561 municipalities.[13] The characterization of the municipal (or civil) guards as less extreme than the PMs is reflected in their training, weaponry, powers, deployment, activity, and pay. If armed, they typically carry only a nightstick and a radio or more rarely a 38-millimeter revolver. They earn a salary of R$700–800 a month (about US$250–275). On average, training lasts four months. The municipal guards patrol parks and schools and in that sense relieve PMs of some basic order maintenance policing.

Other Forces

On the state level, the departments of *bombeiros* perform functions that include fighting fires, so these services are usually translated as "fire departments"; however this definition leaves out a variety of public safety and civil defense services they provide. For example, in most states bombeiros respond to emergencies such as floods, bomb threats, crowd control for special events, collapsed buildings, rescue operations, and natural disasters—typical police responsibilities in many countries. If there is not a specific suspect to apprehend or a crime underway, the PMs often do not respond to emergency calls, leaving the bombeiros to attend to many public order and safety problems. Many departments of bombeiros are being separated from the PM, into which they had been incorporated; currently, 16 of the 26 states have independent bombeiros.

Other forces at the federal level do policing, but they are either very new or very limited. The National Secretariat of Public Security (SNSP or SENASP—*Secretária Nacional de Segurança Pública*) announced the creation of a National Guard (*Força Nacional*) on August 5, 2004. Luiz Fernando Corrêa, national secretary of public security at the time, announced that 300 officers had been trained and another 1,500 would commence training by the start of 2005. So far, the troops have been recruited from the PM's special operations forces. The National Guard is meant to be deployed when states ask for emergency help, presumably when police strikes or serious crime problems threaten public order. It is almost certain that their first deployment will be in Rio de Janeiro, where the governor has already requested federal help in battling drug traffickers. The forces will be under the command of state authorities. They will wear symbolically important black uniforms like the Tactical Operations Troops of the PF. Two other small, federal, law-enforcement agencies include the federal railway police and a dock police force that guards warehouses and other infrastructure at national ports.

Meta-Institutions: The Current Police System in Federal Law

The police system is needlessly burdened with dualities, some of which are embedded in the Constitution. Besides the bifurcation of police activity into two "half polices," there are three other dualities: First, the PC and PM have national-level protections and mandates, but state-level control, funding, and organization. The Constitution defines policing as a state-level responsibility, while national laws and norms dictate the structure and disciplinary systems of the police. In short, indirect control of the police is centralized, yet direct control is decentralized to the states. This duality of control burdens the police with multiple political masters and impedes reform in the following specific ways: Given that the state-level PM and PC represent about 97 percent of the public security system in terms of personnel,[14] and the states lack the exclusive power to reform and regulate these police forces (and, as mentioned above, the national government has proved crippled in doing so), it seems the nation's main public security forces remain disturbingly insulated from interference by elected representatives.

The second duality is that the 1988 Constitution sustains institutional duplicity by cementing a confusion of policing responsibilities. The responsibility for criminal investigation falls both to the federal and civilian police (Article 144, paragraphs 1 and 4). Order maintenance and crime prevention is the job of the PM (Article 144, paragraph 5), but the armed forces also have the responsibility to guarantee "internal security" and order maintenance (Article 142). As a result, there are conflicts over power and confusion over responsibility among the police forces.

Third, the Constitution preserves an unnecessary link between the civilian-controlled police and the military. Even though the police are subordinate to state governors, the Constitution defines the police as ultimately responsible to the army.[15] The police also won the guarantee of a privileged forum for the trial of police officers. Before 1988, only a few states had military tribunals. With the current Constitution, any state with more than 20,000 active military police officers is authorized to create a State Military Court (Article 125, sections 3 and 4). The upshot is that for an official of the PM to lose his or her job for administrative misconduct or crimes, only military courts and, in effect, commanding officers can order dismissal. As a result, military police officers are—in terms of responsibility to civilians and public officials—the most insulated public servants. The policing system that emerges from the Constitution is confused, insulated, military-minded, and difficult to change.[16]

In sum, when Brazil became a democratic republic again, it adopted a throwback police system that solidified the decentralized structure, functional duality, and complex legal authority in which conditions for corruption and ineffectiveness are fertile. The police have privileges, protections, and overlapping responsibilities in the national ambit yet come under decentralized control at the state level. They are militarized and resistant to change. They are bifurcated into functionally distinct and often redundant and uncooperative police forces whose responsibilities are intertwined without being shared. Paulo Sérgio Pinheiro, not only a noted Brazilian political scientist but an expert on human rights and policing, summarized that the 1988 Constitution reinscribed the repressive apparatuses that were formulated during the dictatorship by reinscribing what the military governments had put into practice, creating a clear continuity in place of a true transition (1994). In other words, though the rules for policing have changed, most of the institutions, mechanisms, and systems for how policing is actually conducted have not changed.

Historical Development of Police Institutions

Most historical analyses of the Brazilian police imply that a sort of ineluctable path-dependency has produced the dire situation of today. Given the enduring patterns of abuse, impunity, and inefficiency, it is easy to see why. Both the ostensive policing that the PM conducts and the PC's investigative practices developed over more than a century and a half. But rather than point to such facts as evidence of cultural continuity or unresolved class conflict, which they may be, I focus on the institutional practices and relationships that became embedded over time.

The PM grew out of a national force that operated in the nineteenth century to protect ruling groups. In the imperial period (1822–1889), Brazil's primary police force was the National Guard (*Guarda Nacional*). Created on August 18, 1831 (reformed significantly in 1841) and composed only of voting citizens (those who earned a minimum income), the National Guard's main function was to repress a majority population of socially and economically excluded people—slaves, former slaves, native people, racially mixed, and other poor groups. The National Guard was organized separately within each province (what would become "states") and used brutal and racist tactics of suppressing disorder. As their size and influence grew, the National Guard forces came to rival the army. So, principally after 1841, the imperial government assigned the army to protect borders, put down revolts, and maintain general stability; the National Guard was left to protect ruling groups and public spaces (Fausto, 1999).

Other inchoate police forces took shape. The Ministry of Justice appointed a chief of police in each provincial capital; parishes and municipalities then had deputies and subdeputies who took on duties as "justices of peace" (Fausto, 1999). These men investigated and, in some cases, tried and sentenced criminal cases. In this sense, they were forerunners of the PC. The imperial government created the Municipal Guards (*Corpo de Guardas Municipais*) in the capital city, Rio de Janeiro, also in 1831, and permitted other provinces to do the same. Many cities followed suit, including São Paulo in that same year. Finally, the provinces developed their own Public Forces (*Forças Públicas*) much in the mold of the National Guard, to protect their own interests and in some cases their sovereignty.

Important traits formed during the imperial period inform the present day policing situation (Mariano, interview, 2004). First, competition between national and provincial powers was a major factor, because the National Guard and state-level Public Forces competed against each other in terms of loyalty and active strength; this state-federal tension persists today. Second, the imperial period inaugurated a "judicial policing" approach in which the chiefs of police, responsible to judges, conducted investigations with an "inquisitorial approach" that easily gave way to torture. Third, order maintenance policing was conducted by armed forces, and therefore ostensive policing became associated with the structure, rules, disciplinary approach, and strategies of military institutions; these police were prepared to confront internal and external "enemies" rather than "citizens." Those same police are not around today, and it is unclear if their ethos is, but their titles, techniques, and divisions still are. Also, following from the second and third points, it is notable that the bifurcation of police activity developed early on and never ceased.

Over the course of the First Republic (1889–1930), the task of ostensive policing remained a state-level activity and, depending on the state, was divided among Public Forces and Municipal or State Civil Guards. The Public Forces grew significantly. For example, in São Paulo the force started with 3,940 officers in 1891 and reached 14,079 in 1924; French advisors were contracted to help train and structure the police in 1906. They developed an infantry, an artillery division, a cavalry, and, by 1926, even a small air force. On the other hand, a State Civil Guard was created in São Paulo on October 22, 1926, to conduct ostensive policing of a nonmilitary variety (Mariano, interview, 2004). By 1964, São Paulo's Civil Guard had 15,000 officers.

Authoritarian regimes left durable legacies on the Brazil's police institutions. During the era of the populist dictator GetúlioVargas (1930–1945), police operations became centralized and militarized, because the police were used to suppress dissent and maintain order. Nonmilitary ostensive policing began to disappear, along with the potential for the state's sovereignty. With the death of Vargas came the ascension of Juscelino Kubitschek, the election of Jânio Quadros, and the brief government of João Goulart. After this mostly democratic reprieve, public security arrangements abruptly changed again under the bureaucratic authoritarian federal government of 1964–1985. It became especially severe after December 13, 1968, when Institutional Act 5 dissolving the Congress was handed down. Civil Guards and Public Forces around the country were merged. Decree 1,072 of December 30, 1969, extinguished Civil Guards in 15 states and annexed them to state military forces.[17] This fusion resulted in the end of the Civil Guards and Municipal Guards (though these were to be reincarnated later) and in the creation the Military Police. The ruling military apparatus then placed the PM under the direction of the Ministry of the Army (Law Decree 667/69, Article 1).

Thereafter, two changes had an enormous impact on policing: The federal government assigned the responsibility of maintaining order to the PM—a responsibility that had been previously shared by a uniformed and active PC (Law Decree 667/69, Article 3; Law Decree 1,072/69). Second, the military exerted greater influence over the PM by creating a special army division to oversee the PM and by appointing military officers to direct the PM and to the state secretariats of public security. As a result, the PM became stronger, singular, and more militarized.

Interinstitutional Problems With Public Security

Taken together, the weaknesses in the justice and public security systems mean that Brazil lacks a coercive state apparatus to protect the rights of the general population (Linz & Stepan, 1996; Stepan, 2000). A state cannot have a coercive apparatus without a law enforcement system, which requires the core institutions of public security to cooperate. As a meta-institutional matter as argued above, the Constitution impedes the ability of the PC and PM to work together. Though that dysfunction manifests itself as an interinstitutional problem, it will not be repeated here; instead this section highlights two other problems: the involvement of the military in policing operations and the difficulty police have in working with the courts.

Relations between the military and the police are a traditional focus of concern in developing democracies. But in that context Brazil is a relatively stable and advanced democracy, and it does not provoke many worries about the military taking over the well-entrenched and sizeable police forces. On the other hand, the armed forces have never been entirely removed from policing operations, because they may be—and have been on numerous occasions—used to preserve internal security and maintain law and order, according to Article 142 of the Constitution. Two main justifications are invoked when using the military in public security: the deployment is either temporary or exceptional (or both). Due to a wave of police strikes starting in the mid-1990s, President Fernando Henrique Cardoso deployed armed forces to control order in a number of states, even though the troops had no arrest powers. Armed forces have also been used in response to "exceptional" crime problems—perhaps most famously in Operation Rio (from November 1994 to May 1995). This joint operation of the armed forces and state government involved controversial invasions into the favelas (or *morros*, the hilly, impoverished areas of Rio) in an attempt to disarm drug traffickers and interrupt organized crime. The media success of Operation Rio and subsequent statements by public officials suggest military incursions into slums and poor neighborhoods to combat arms and drug trafficking will continue. Overall, the federal government employed the military at least 50 times from 1985 to 1997 and numerous times thereafter due to police strikes (de Mesquita Neto, interview, 2004).

A key question that arises is how these cooperative arrangements will be structured. Some experts have called for ongoing arrangements in which the military would support the police in setting up blockades and checkpoints and would have judicial powers in frontier areas to better control criminal activity (Braudel Institute of World Economics, 2003). The trends indicate an interest in and a willingness to blend police and military functions, which if it continues should require legislation and demand careful planning and strict civilian supervision.

The Brazilian justice system is chronically slow and impedes the legal application of justice. The environment of impunity contributes to police brutality and corruption; the frail justice system also contributes to inefficiency, which creates incentives for people to go around the justice system, thus reinforcing the cycle of vigilante justice and institutional duplicity. Consider the fact that the state São Paulo maintains a PC of 36,000 members to investigate crimes, and there were 523,396 officially filed reports of crime in 1999, but only 84,519 police investigations were opened (16 percent of all reported crimes, which usually have a better chance of being solved than the majority that go unreported). Based on these *inquéritos*, the Public

Ministry formally processed 25,300 cases, of which 12,102 began by capturing a suspect in the act, which does not require much investigative activity. In short, only 2.5 percent of all reported crimes reached a judge as the active result of police investigations (Institute of Citizenship, 2002). Ironically, without this filter of investigative ineffectiveness, the court system would be swamped. There is roughly one judge for every 23,000 inhabitants, while the United States has one for every 9,000 (da Silva Filho, 2000).

Questions of control over public security institutions at the state level also exacerbate problems with institutional duplicity. Governors ultimately direct the police, but in most states a Secretary of Public Security (SPS) manages both forces. During the authoritarian regimes, this official would be from the military. Since the country was democratized, the selection of secretaries of public security has been problematic, as both the PC and PM bitterly resent one having "command" over the other. Therefore, an official is often selected who has no experience with either force. Further, the SPS often has little direct control over the two forces; the PM in some states are effectively insulated from the SPS. The SPS's purpose is to harmonize strategies, budgeting, and operations, yet as long as both police maintain separate jurisdictions and operate separate databases and systems of telecommunications, the SPS's capacity to do so is extremely limited, even when welcome. The result is a muddled system of political and operational control.

Intrainstitutional Factors: Internal Problems With the Police

Brazilian police institutions are frequently undermined from within by corruption, impunity, and bureaucratic privileges. These tendencies are often ill-defined and overlapping but clearly contribute to brutality and inefficiency and impede progress toward democratic policing (da Silva Filho & Gall, 1999). Institutional duplicity allows these deficiencies to persist because they are rarely confronted directly, and even reformers who would tackle such problems are often disheartened by their seemingly intractable nature.

Police corruption is a serious problem in Brazil. It not only erodes the rule of law, but police corruption is frequently connected to torture, the excessive use of force, and brutality (Costa, 2004). Petty forms of corruption (or *parasitismo*) that include petty bribes, shirking, and passive corruption (turning a blind eye) are common. More troubling for democracy, however, is serious corruption, which is evident in criminal activities so pervasive that they could not exist without police cooperation or complicity: The rise of drug trafficking; the sale not only of guns, but of heavy artillery like antiaircraft missiles and landmines; theft and robbery of vehicles; the frequent escape of prisoners; and the unstoppable network of *jogo do bicho* (a type of underground gambling) are all testaments, in their own ways, to the involvement of police in organized crime. These problems are examined

code, which most observers consider outmoded and burdensome (Costa, 2004).

In terms of strategy and deployment, the police of Brazil utilize approaches that are almost exclusively reactive and suppressive rather than proactive and preventive. There are signs that this is starting to change as the PM in most states have some type of community policing programs in place. But isolated community policing programs will not necessarily "put more cops on the street" or put them in better touch with society. Further, preventive policing achieves less of its potential impact in Brazil than elsewhere, because resources that might be applied to assign officers to the street are instead applied to maintaining an excessive number of ranks, hiring military cooks and barbers because of the preoccupation with military esthetics, and providing special privileges for public officials. Cutting useless bureaucracies and outsourcing tasks to nonsworn personnel would increase police presence and allow preventive policing to be more effective.

In terms of pay and benefits, there are two outstanding features: disparities and shortfalls. There is remarkable disparity between different ranks, states, and police forces in terms of what police officers earn; also, today police are underpaid, whereas previously they were absurdly underpaid. In recent years, the police have received salary hikes in most states. This followed a wave of police strikes and demonstrations in 1996–1997 and 2002. Strikes by the police, which are constitutionally forbidden, are overt examples of problems that low pay causes. Less tangibly, low pay also makes police officials more susceptible to corruption and bribery, and many are compelled to work second jobs (*bicos*) to support their families. These illegal and dangerous jobs, usually in the clandestine security sector (discussed further below) tire police officers and frequently deplete their ranks: The Ouvidoria of São Paulo found that out of every 10 police officers that were killed (including in traffic accidents), 8 died while off duty, likely working their second or third jobs. The chart in Table 3.2 is based on 2001 data from selected states and lists monthly salaries in the Brazilian currency (the *real*) followed by a U.S. dollar estimate, which includes *gratificações* (or "benefits," such as health insurance and travel allowances).

Context of Public Security Problems: Neofeudalism

An institutionally duplicitous environment, as described above, creates the following paradox: There is a revered legal mechanism to achieve something, and then there is the way it actually gets done (Muniz, interview, 2004; Proença, interview, 2004). The hierarchically rigid fiefdoms of Brazilian bureaucracy are ventilated by shortcuts to or diversions from justice. Police death squads, which persist today, provide a horrifying example of shortcuts to vigilante "justice" (Caldeira, 2000; Huggins, 1998). Investigations that rarely yield enough evidence to prosecute crimes against the poor serve as a more common example of diversions down dead ends; as

Table 3.2 Selected Monthly Police Salaries in 2001

State	Civil Police				Military Police (increasing ranks)							
	Detective/ Investigator		Delegado		Soldier		First Lieutenant		Captain		Colonel	
	real	$	real	$	real	$	real	$	real	$	real	$
Alagoas	550	196	4,000	1,429	464	166	1,063	380	1,612	576	3,657	1,306
Bahia	689	246	1,653	590	764	273	963	344	1,259	450	1,758	628
Federal District	3,009	1,075	6,480	2,314	1,250	446	2,950	1,054	3,500	1,250	NA	NA
Espírito Santo	800	286	2,000	714	300	107	NA	NA	NA	NA	NA	NA
Goiás	905	323	4,204	1,501	650	232	1,384	494	1,822	651	4,980	1,779
Pará	770	275	2,611	933	557	199	1,228	439	1,609	575	2,422	865
Paraná	728	260	6,031	2,154	558	199	2,012	719	3,779	1,350	5,594	1,998
Pernambuco	773	276	3,183	1,137	803	287	2,020	721	2,850	1,018	4,360	1,557
Rio de Janeiro	1,100	393	3,600	1,286	500	179	1,810	646	2,155	770	4,112	1,469
Rio Grande do Sul	644	230	4,800	1,714	524	187	1,259	450	1,674	598	4,172	1,490
São Paulo (city)	894	319	1,750	625	757	270	1,750	625	4,264	1,523	5,962	2,129

NOTE: It is important to keep in mind that because of exchange rate fluctuations, consistent inflation, the ambiguity of what constitutes a "benefit," and pay raises of almost 50 percent in some states, these numbers are not accurate. They are meant to give a general idea of police salaries. Data come from secretaries of public security and police unions and were published in *Folha de São Paulo*, p. C1 (July 22, 2001).

a result, people living in the impoverished favelas often seek justice from local crime bosses rather than from the police. The cumulative result is cynicism and lack of confidence in the police, which only makes their job harder when they try to do it properly.[22] Institutional duplicity, like the old expression, *para inglês ver,* is a tacit situation that can both explain and cause stagnancy.[23] This stagnancy not only slows institutional progress toward a model of democratic policing, it distorts other aspects of public security.

This section briefly explores how policing interacts with the Brazilian context of public insecurity. A major paradox has been that the return to democracy coincided with the increase in violent crime and the spread of criminal organizations (Pinheiro, 1994; Zaluar, 2000). Nor has the fear of crime subsided. In search of ever more security, urban Brazilians have built fortified enclaves for homes and offices that are strewn with barbed wire and surrounded by fences, cameras, and guards; these built structures, as physical reminders of hostility, seem to justify the paranoia that built them (Caldeira, 2000). On average, crime, criminal organizations, the fear of crime, violence, and violent responses from police have all risen over the past 15 years; all of these problems involve the police.

Moreover, there has been stark spatial segregation at the urban level, and increased networking among criminal groups at the transnational level. Feudalism, as an economic and political order, can be characterized by the decentralization of political authority (to lords and barons) in the midst of globalizing forces (such as mercantilists and the Catholic Church) and the use of brutality to extract rents and raise armies. In neofeudalism, mafias, private armies, and barons of international trafficking also collect tributes, administer justice, and muster soldiers from the squalid territories that they control. Private security in Brazil is beginning to outmatch public police forces as the rich contract their own armies of security companies, often illegitimate. If this vicious cycle spins out of control, the legitimacy of the Brazilian state will be compromised, and its ability to establish hegemony, either through coercion or compliance, will be weakened. For these reasons, a dynamic that is justifiably called neofeudalism has the power to bankrupt the public security institutions of Brazil.

Crime and Violence

Crime and violent crime rates rose during the 1990s and remain at very high levels, leaving much of the populace terrorized by fear. According to the Brazilian census, the rate of homicide grew by 130 percent between 1980 and 2000, going from 11.7 for each 100,000 inhabitants to 27. For a span of 10 years after democratization (1991–2000), official data show a steady rise in intentional deaths (not necessarily homicides), going from just over 40,000 per year to just under 60,000. Of these, about 40,000, or about 88 percent of all murders, are homicides committed with guns. Murders outnumber death by diseases such as AIDS. According to one estimate, one of every 20 inhabitants of the city of São Paulo was a victim of armed robbery in 2002; there were 1,704 such incidents daily (Braudel Institute of World Economics, 2003). In 2001, Brazil's homicide rate reached 27.8 per 100,000, based on 47,899 murders; for point of comparison, the United States is a relatively violent country, and its murder rate is usually between 5 and 6 (Lemgruber, 2004).

In favelas and poor communities in the peripheral areas, homicide rates exceed 100 per 100,000 people, among the highest in the world. In general, young, dark-skinned males are the most likely to be killed or suffer violence. In 1999 in the city of Rio de Janeiro, for every 100,000 males between the ages of 15 and 29, 239 were murdered (Institute of Citizenship, 2002). Men are much more likely to be murdered than women, yet nearly one in five Brazilian women has been the victim of violence perpetrated by a man (Global Justice, 2002). Nonetheless, the pattern is for people of African descent as well as the poor, the young, and the male to be the disproportionate victims of intentional death. The disturbing result, often overlooked by considering just demographic data, is a marked concentration of violence in areas of poverty and social exclusion (Cano & Santos, 2001). This concentration of violence, including police violence, and concomitant apathy in wealthy, privately secured enclaves, feeds the dynamic of neofeudalism.

How do police figure into this picture? First and foremost, the ineffectiveness of the police contributes to the public security problem: A May 2003 analysis of homicides in Rio de Janeiro showed that only 2.2 percent of the killers were apprehended at the crime scene, and only 1 percent of all other murders were solved by the police (Braudel Institute of World Economics, 2003). Second, corruption and brutality have allowed some areas of Brazil to develop into zones where drug trafficking, organized crime, and police violence run rampant; the reprisals and friction between police and gangs have produced geographical pockets that resemble war zones.

Police Violence and Human Rights

The history of human rights abuses by Brazilian police is well established and long. Research from the imperial period (Holloway, 1993) through the Cold War (Huggins, 1998) demonstrates a tradition of arbitrary, racist, and brutal police action that informs the present situation. The most extreme abuses are of two types: torture (committed especially by the PC in the investigation of crimes) and summary executions and aggression (more often committed by the PM). After 1990, when the first democratically elected president since the 1960s took office under the new democratic constitution, the trend of police violence rose along with violent crime in general. The numbers of civilians killed by the police in São Paulo and Rio de Janeiro reached 868 and 1195, respectively, in 2003 (Global Justice, 2003). In São Paulo that works out to an average of 2.37 citizens killed by the police each day; in Rio de Janeiro, the average is 3.2.

Widely publicized police killings in the past 14 years have increased conflict and violence between police and society: After Carandiru, the 1992 prison massacre in São Paulo that left 111 dead, prison riots are still commonplace. In Eldorado do Carajás, 19 landless workers in the state of Pará were executed by police; as of late 2003, the case has not been closed, and rural violence continues. Police killings in Corumbiara and Vigário Geral have given way to ongoing drug wars in these peripheral communities; these are marked by periodic police invasions. Many years after the infamous execution of street children in front of a famed church, Candelária, one of the mentally disturbed survivors went on to hijack bus number 174 in Rio de Janeiro, leading to more public fright, international outrage, and an acclaimed documentary ("Onibus 174"). The televised scenes of police brutality and executions in the 1997 cases of Favela Naval in Diadema (outside São Paulo) and of Cidade de Deus in Rio de Janeiro caused international outrage. Rather than foreswearing such tactics, São Paulo's PM formed yet another elite unit that performs raids such as "Operation Castelinho" that killed 12 members of the PCC ("First Command of the Capital") gang in Sorocaba on March 5, 2002.

Organized Crime and Uncivil Society

The power of drug traffickers has become a major problem, especially in Rio de Janeiro and São Paulo. Drug gangs operate with a command hierarchy capable of mobilizing well-armed "soldiers," as they are called, in the winding, hilly streets of Rio's favelas or the suburban satellites of São Paulo. Police estimated Rio drug gangs had an arsenal of 10,000 weapons in 2003. In 2004, they discovered caches that included automatic rifles, landmines, grenades, and shoulder-launched antiaircraft rockets. During the early 2000s, powerful narco-trafficking bosses, such as Paulo César Silva dos Santos ("Linho") or "Fernandinho" Beira-Mar, controlled multiple favelas and armies of more than 500 "soldiers" in their early 20s (in fact, they rarely live into their 30s); sometimes, they carried on this control from jail. Favela residents know corrupt police to be complicit in fomenting unrest when certain criminal bosses escape or are released from jail and then wage war on other gang leaders. Newspaper accounts regularly report on police officials and army officials who have been arrested for selling weapons to drug traffickers, their reputed enemies. The strength of organized crime corrupts the police institutions and escalates the level of violence.

Even uncorrupt police can indiscriminately terrorize favelas. Police violence is often labeled as an authoritarian atavism or the result of sheer savagery, but unfortunately such police officers might be responding to a "rational" desire to shore up their authority.[24] As police feel their power diminish, credible threats and violent shows of force are intended to extend their authority in regions where state hegemony is eroded.

The police seem better able to manage mutual and cooperative existence with lower-key criminal organizations such as the *jogos do bicho* (an illegal numbers game), but this so-called petty crime has led to extreme violence and has funded corruption at high levels.[25] José Carlos Gratz used funds from the *jogo* to finance control of the state government of Espírito Santo. By early 2003, Gratz was president of the State Legislative Assembly, controlled the machinery for electing assemblymen, and had appointed allies as judges and prosecutors (Miranda, 2003).

Networks of criminality, like those cited above, link organized criminal groups and the state by way of corruption. Growing evidence from Brazil, and scholarly work in general, suggests that "uncivil society" can be treated as a conceptually distinct and significant actor.[26] Uncivil society consists of organized groups that are not legitimate economic organizations, but are "rent-seeking" in the sense that they extract duties in exchange for access to the goods, territories, and privileges that they control. They reject the rules of civil society; for example, they use violence to resolve conflicts. They rarely seek to overthrow the state; rather, they seek to co-opt or corrupt it. Research on the robust spread of violent drug and arms traffickers in Brazilian slums demonstrates perhaps the strongest dimension of these networks of criminality (Arias, 2004; Zaluar, 2000). A growing set of examples includes organized criminal organizations, gangs, vigilante groups, illegal security firms, death squads, mafias, and militias.[27]

Death squads perfectly capture the problem with uncivil society and the police: Death squads can be well organized (even registered as philanthropic organizations; see below) and frequently operate extra-legally with the collaboration or complicity of the police. There are two types of death squads: the informal squads (typically off-duty police officers engaged in vigilante killings) and organized groups of on-duty police who hide their actions, not their identities. Two experts trace the modern incarnation of these two types to the mid-1960s under the ruling military regime.[28] Though the activities of torture and death squads slowed after the decline of the repressive regimes of the 1970s, groups such as Amnesty International and Human Rights Watch have testified to their presence today.

The informal type of death squad more clearly involves uncivil society. The case of *Scuderie Detetive Le Coq* (SDLC) and one human rights group that has denounced them, Global Justice (*Justiça Global*) demonstrates the civil/uncivil tension. SDLC was a death squad formed in 1964 during the military dictatorship and named after a legendary detective (Le Coq) from Rio de Janeiro. The group became legally recognized as a "non-profit philanthropic institution engaged in community service" (at least in the state of Espírito Santo, neighboring Rio), and by the 1990s SDLC had 3,800 directly or indirectly involved members (Global Justice, 2002). As street children were found dead on public streets with bullet holes in the backs of their heads, intense public pressure forced Espírito Santo to create a special commission composed of representatives from the PC, PM, and attorney general's office. The commission found police officers affiliated with the SDLC to have been involved in the executions. The commission further found that the SDLC was connected to drug trafficking, arms trafficking, gambling, prostitution, fraud, public embezzlement at all levels of government, and coercion and bribery of public officials. Global Justice, as a civil society actor, has used its international connections (including with the Inter-American Human Rights Court of the Organization of American States) to strongly denounce the SDLC, but the SDLC is not simply a criminal organization. It is an example of a well-organized, officially recognized network of public officials, police officers, and private citizens that cannot be classified as a political party, a gang, or a part of government, and the SDLC rejects the ethics of civil society and the peaceful resolution of conflict. The conflict between Global Justice and SDLC is an instance of a contest between civil society and uncivil society over the nature of public security.[29]

Private security is another realm of activity characterized by duplicity, mixing the criminal with the legal and the private with the public. Private security firms appear as one of the fastest-growing sectors of Brazil's economy. The Federal Police registered some 4,000 private security firms with 540,334 employees in 2000; there were another 811 firms registered to provide their own security ("organic security"). However, most estimates suggest that the number of people working for unlicensed providers is easily double that: 1 million to 1.5 million, not to mention unlicensed organic security firms (Institute of Citizenship, 2002). Teresa Caldeira, a Brazilian anthropologist, traces a number of connections that implicate private security firms with criminality. For example, *justiceiros* (vigilante hitmen) hide behind the façade of private security enterprises; most of these clandestine security services employ police officers or former police officers, and many are involved with gangs and drug dealers. She summarizes: "In fact, although private and public policing may . . . look like opposites, they share a matrix of relationship and structures. In Brazil, the matrix is of unstable relationships between legal and illegal, of abuses and violence" (Caldeira, 2000, p. 206).

Besides overt connections to criminality, private security in Brazil is troubling in two other ways: the demonstrable inability to regulate the industry and the risk of deepening inequality. Most private security goes unregulated. There are approximately 25,000 guards working in Rio de Janeiro's condominiums alone, but there are only 30 authorized entities to work in condominiums (Amora, 2004). Unregistered security services can range from the simply illegitimate to the elaborately clandestine; they can serve as fronts for death squads or the more routine neighborhood vigilante groups.

At the very least, unregistered private security creates a dangerous black market with perverse incentives: Guards are regularly underpaid, undertrained, and drawn from the ranks of off-duty police officers looking for second jobs (*bicos*) to augment their small salaries. Having police officers work second jobs in private security is both illegal and widely recognized: "[Bicos] cause duplicity in functions, physical exhaustion of police troops, besides delegitimizing the nature of public security, since public employees provide services for businesses whose interests come to collide with police functions" (Institute of Citizenship, 2002, p. 28). In addition, poor Brazilians are increasingly likely to suffer double discrimination with the unfettered growth of private security. Because Brazil has one of the largest income gaps between the rich and the poor worldwide, private security in Brazil will continue to create fortified enclaves for the wealthy. Impoverished citizens may continue to suffer disproportionately the cruelty of brutal policing as well as new forms of control and humiliation at the hands of private security.

Civil Society and Prospects for Reform

The institutional problems with the police and the broader context of criminality does damage to Brazilian society. Violent crime, organized crime, and uncivil society—especially when exacerbated by police brutality, corruption, and incompetence—undermine Brazilians' faith in their public security system. A 1999 victimization study in Belo Horizonte (the fourth or third largest and perhaps safest of the major cities) revealed that 66 percent of robbery and assault victims did not report crimes to the police; the lack of confidence was the principal reason (32 percent). Furthermore, when asked to express their opinion of the police, 39 percent of respondents said they did not trust the PM, and 46 percent said the same about the PC (Beato Filho, 2002). Such victimization studies and public opinion surveys regularly reinforce the impression that the Brazilian public has little faith in the police and that this lack of confidence impedes police work by limiting the assistance and information that the PC and PM can count on from society.

Yet organized civil society has not been a passive victim, and it has responded with growing expertise, which can be seen especially in its involvement with public security reforms that may help consolidate democracy by creating a functional justice system and by slowly bridging the disjunctive nature of Brazilian citizenship. Civil society organizations helped dismantle the authoritarian regime in the 1980s, and instead of disappearing under democracy with nothing to resist, these organizations have established "new connections between the autonomous spheres of society and political institutions" (Pinheiro, 2000, p. 134). For instance, the National Movement for Human Rights, formed in 1982, worked to set up research centers on violence in the national universities; in 1987, the University of São Paulo (USP) inaugurated the first Center for the Study of Violence (*Núcleo dos Estudos de Violência*, NEV). Throughout the 1990s, the press, nongovernmental organizations, universities, labor unions, professional associations (like the Brazilian Bar Association), and social movements have worked together to create footholds in government in the form of commissions, congressional inquiries, and ombudsmen. These modest steps allowed civil society organizations (CSOs) to gather more information about police actions and increase the visibility of human rights problems. The National Congress created the Human Rights Commission in 1995, and between 1995 and 1997, 13 states likewise created human rights commissions in their legislative bodies.[30] Today, traditional human rights organizations like the Teotonio Vilela Commission and the *Centro Santos Dias* in São Paulo work with research centers like NEV at USP, the *Instituto Superior de Estudos da Religião*, and the Center for the Study of Security and Citizenship in Rio, and they collaborate with newer organizations like *Movimento Viva Rio* and Global Justice, also both in Rio. In this way, CSOs have been able to accumulate experiences and share knowledge through better networks—some of which, like the Third Sector Information Network, are explicitly designed for that purpose (Pinheiro, 2000).

Civil society organizations have served as a nexus for proposing police reforms, such as community policing programs, civilian oversight, and community councils on public security. Early on, Governor Franco Montoro (1983–1987) created community security councils in São Paulo (by decree 23.455 and by resolution) and women's police stations. In Rio de Janeiro, Governor Leonel Brizola (1983–1987) established a mechanism of civilian oversight called the State Counsel of Justice, Public Safety, and Human Rights, on which CSOs had a seat. Both were left-leaning politicians with significant ties to the democratic resistance. Governor Mário Covas took office in 1995 in São Paulo, was reelected in 1998, and inherited the progressive tradition of working with CSOs. In 1995 Covas created the country's first civilian oversight office of the police (*ouvidoria*) at the request of the archdiocese and staffed it with a trusted activist from the church and civil society, Benedito Domingos Mariano. In 1997, Covas launched the State Program for Human Rights, modeled after the national program inaugurated in 1996 by President Cardoso. Likewise, Brizola returned to office in 1991, restored dismantled projects, established community-oriented policing in Rio de Janeiro, and created working relationships with civil society.

Community Security Councils

Many different forms of the *Conselhos Comunitários de Segurança* (CONSEPs) have appeared throughout the country. A critical assessment is that these local, unpaid citizen groups "tend to be mere meetings to hear complaints from the populace, which always receives the same excuses [from officials]: lack of resources" (da Silva Filho, 2000). Others hold a much more optimistic view. Community forums are a related innovation that allow more input from citizens and have been credited with helping reduce violent crime.[31] Officials in the northern state of Ceará, for example, explain that CONSEPs do a number of things: put police officers in touch with citizens (which is a necessary step in community policing), resolve minor conflicts, defuse tension between groups and between police and citizens, give citizens a sense of empowerment and participation in public affairs in general, and alert police officials to crime trends (Freitas Lopes, interview, 2004). In Minas Gerais, CONSEPs are seen as part of a paradigm shift in policing. As part of the fundamental overhaul, CONSEPs in Minas Gerais broaden the idea of police services, make it possible for community policing programs to function, develop partnerships in the community and with civil society, and allow for decentralization and regionalization of policing (Beato Filho, 2002).

Women's Police Stations

The first police station staffed mostly by women was created, by law, in the state of Santa Catarina in 1985. The state of São Paulo, however, copied the idea and created its own women's station on April 6, 1985, before Santa Catarina's capital city of Florianopolis was able to bring the idea to fruition (Global Justice, 2002). Such stations usually have male officers available, but must have female receptionists and women on staff (officers and psychologists) with whom victims can file complaints and give testimony and from whom victims can receive support. The best stations have day care rooms as well. There are 307 women's police stations in Brazil; this number is growing despite funding cutbacks. Of these, 40 percent are in São Paulo, and 13 percent are in Minas Gerais. They have been successful in raising the number of reported crimes. In 2001, women registered 334,589 cases of violence at São Paulo stations.

Women's police stations, by attending mostly to women and youth, represent an innovation in accessibility. Proponents conceived of these stations as tools to combat domestic violence and sexual assaults, because they would focus on investigating these crimes, be less psychologically and physically intimidating to female victims of sexual violence who wanted to report such crimes, and thus provide greater visibility and reporting accuracy to crimes of sexual, domestic, and gender-specific natures. Reportedly, a substantial number of women have received greater attention, have not had to suffer in silence, and have felt empowered knowing they could denounce such crimes (Global Justice, 2002). However, many activists have withdrawn support from these stations, because they provide such poor services due to lack of funding and resources.[32]

Community Policing

This approach concept calls for regular, nonthreatening contact with the members of a community or neighborhood. Typically police officers leave their vehicle and attempt to build trust with civilians; they treat citizens as partners in preventing crime. This not only reduces fear, it allows police to gain better information about criminal activities. First introduced in Rio de

Janeiro in the 1980s, this concept has now spread to virtually every state PM department and works best when used in conjunction with citizen-based public security councils (Beato Filho, 2002).

Witness Protection Programs

Witness protection programs led and managed by civil society allow police to root out corruption and prosecute organized criminal organizations and drug traffickers. This is a special concern of civil society, because witness protection involves saving the life and ensuring the rights of intimidated and gravely threatened people—often completely innocent bystanders. In Brazil, the provision of this service began with civil society and later received the belated help of government. In 1995, a broad-based human rights movement and other civil society groups formed the PROVITA *(Programa de Proteção a Vítimas e a Testemunhas)* in the northeast. Now part of a national system, PROVITA had protected over 500 witnesses in 17 states as of 2004 (Amnesty International, 2005). (Another version, PROTEGE, started in Rio Grande do Sul, but it does not rely on a civil society to function.)

Ouvidorias

Since 1995, after Brazil's first civilian oversight mechanism for the police was created in São Paulo, the innovation of ouvidorias has spread throughout the most populated and developed states. There are six fully independent and fully functioning ouvidorias and another four inchoate versions. They have created a national forum and have garnered funds from the various foundations and even the European Union to continue their project of diffusing external oversight of the police (see Lemgruber et al., 2003).

Conclusion: In Search of Consolidation

The study of postauthoritarian Brazil has been threaded together by analyses of the cruel legacies of oppressive policing, widespread impunity for state agents, privileges for the rich, and criminalization of the poor. Historians (e.g., José Murillo Carvalho, Thomas Holloway, etc.) and the social scientists mentioned in this chapter have documented these problems and traced their genealogies. The consensus is that the roots of this family tree extend down at least to the colonial period. Though the most recent authoritarian regime (1964–1985) sounded its death knell over 20 years ago, the abuses and social maladies that persist are commonly linked to authoritarian holdovers. These theoretical relationships seem likely to continue evolving.

One Brazilian think tank argues that if problems with crime, violence, and public security institutions are not "addressed constructively, they ultimately will undermine the stability and legitimacy of democratic government" (Braudel Institute of World Economics, 2003, p. 1). Democratic theory is not needed to conjure three reasons why Brazilian democracy may be threatened: First, police forces that act without accountability erode citizenship rights and undermine the rule of law. Second, without effective freedom, the quality of democracy can be eroded. Finally, when the formal institutions of democracy do not function fairly and effectively, the citizenry's faith in democracy fails. But as it happens, common sense coincides with democratic theory.

After the transition (the installation of a democratic government) the consolidation of democracy completes the process of democratization (Valenzuela, 1988). Though less is known about how consolidation happens, one framework provides three dimensions for conceptualizing it: attitudinal, procedural, and behavioral (Linz & Stepan, 1996). Police relate to these three areas as follows: The functioning of the public security and justice systems affects citizen perceptions of the worth of democracy (attitudinal), determines the efficacy of the rule of law (procedural), and influences how police, civil society, and uncivil society decide to resolve conflicts (behavioral). The three core police problems identified at the outset—ineffectiveness, corruption, and brutality—degrade citizenship, weaken the rule of law, and erode trust in democracy. Therefore, progress in police reform is essential to consolidating democracy.

There are institutional reasons for the problems with democratic consolidation in Brazil. The public security system often does not modernize or respond to democratic pressures, because police institutions, which are somewhat insulated from political and civil society everywhere, are especially insulated in the Brazilian case. Further, the ends demanded of the police are incompatible with police capacity and competence, not to mention their handicap of corruption, so there is little incentive for the police to take initiative in tackling internal problems on their own. The result is deadlock. The police may alleviate demands on the system by taking shortcuts or creating dead ends for certain citizens, but this also produces a type of disjunctive democracy—that is, a polity beset by unequal rights and citizenship (Holston & Caldeira, 1998). Institutional duplicity in the police deprives citizens of a fair and useable state, which is the bedrock of a consolidated democracy (Linz & Stepan, 1996). Therefore Brazilian democracy must deal with institutional problems and contradictions to create the effective, accountable police forces necessary for consolidation.

In addition, Brazil is at risk of developing a neofeudal system of citizen security, one that is privatized, spatially segmented, brutal, and subject to the vagaries of warring factions in and outside of the state. In a neofeudal system, nongovernmental organizations and international institutions like the International Monetary Fund consistently make demands of the state, even as the state is fractured and breached by corruption and loses territory to criminal elements. Sérgio Adorno writes: "The criminal justice system continues to prove ineffective in containing violence within a democratic rule of law. Problems related to law and order have affected citizens' belief in the institutions of justice, instigating the not uncommon private solutions to conflict" (author's translation, Adorno, 2002, p. 1). The federal government of Brazil has not yet lost the monopoly on violence to the extent that Colombia's has, but the state's capacity to solve problems and respond to pressures from CSOs, ordinary citizens, human rights groups, and foreign investors is weak.

Democratization has not consistently led to improvements in the police of Brazil, and it seems that improvements in police institutions have yet to consolidate or deepen democracy on their own, though there are positive signs that civil society is engaging these issues with success. A major reason for stagnancy and backsliding is that Brazil, under democracy, has not done away with institutional duplicity and has not dismantled criminal networks that have their tentacles glued to the Brazilian state. The Brazilian state and its justice system go on functioning, but in some sense, informal and illegal activity give it the image of the emperor with no clothes, which the court's observers pretend not to see for the sake of keeping the court in order. Empty legal mandates risk becoming the imaginary threads of democracy with which the emperor cloaks himself. Achieving a more democratic model of policing in Brazil will require honest efforts to consolidate and unify Brazilian police institutions, facilitate cooperation, impose accountability, and bolster the legal mechanisms for achieving justice. It will also require tilting the balance of power in favor of the state and civil society and against the networks of criminality that corrupt and feed off it.

Notes

1. Though the problems with the police are myriad, corruption, brutality, and ineffectiveness stand out as the most severe and distinct. Dozens of prominent experts recently published a national plan for public security, "Projecto Segurança Pública para o Brasil" (from the *Instituto Cidadania* or Institute of Citizenship), which President Lula da Silva endorsed during his 2002 campaign. The report corroborates the above assessment, listing brutality (*práticas violentas*), corruption (*corrupção* and involvement with criminality), and ineffectiveness (actually, inefficiency) among the major problems facing the police, along with lack of public confidence (Institute of Citizenship, 2002).

2. "Institutional duplicity" is my invented term, but the notion is borrowed from Brazilian scholars of the police. Roberto Kant de Lima (1995), Domício Proença, Jr. (interview, 2004), and Jacqueline Muniz (1999; Muniz, interview, 2004), among others, have discussed this problem and are cited throughout this chapter. A crystallization of this phenomenon comes from three other experts, Lemgruber, Musumeci, and Cano (2003), when they observe that the difficulties in controlling the police of Brazil arise from the institutional context in which "on one side, there are laws and rules that formally delimit police action; on the other, there are arrangements and informal cultures that define the collection of practices through

which discretionary power is exercised on a daily basis" (p. 71, author's translation). Proença (2004) says more directly, "There is the way things are supposed to be done, and the way they are actually done."

3. Kant de Lima (1995, p. 1) describes something similar as the "Brazilian legal paradox": "In Brazil, a constitutionally egalitarian order is applied in a hierarchical way through the justice system. Different legal treatments are given for the same infractions, depending on the social or professional situation of the suspect. . . . Consequently, in clear disobedience of the law, the police judge cases and punish criminals."

4. The evidence from the democratizing world—Brazil, South Africa, Russia, Argentina, and Eastern Europe, for example—supports the pessimistic view that democracy does not bring better policing, but it is worth pointing out that these are merely correlations. In-depth studies are the best way to arrive at answers about causality.

5. The term "consolidated" means the establishment of an effective and functioning democracy that citizens have become accustomed to and accept as the "the only game in town"; "deeper" democracy implies effective improvements in rights and liberties, accountability, participation, and equality.

6. By 1998, there were four proposals to reform the police—from Fernando Henrique Cardoso, Mário Covas (former São Paulo governor), Hélio Bicudo, and Zulaie Cobra Ribeiro—all to separate the PM from the military or to change their duties. None of the constitutional amendments were voted on. Rather, in February 1998, the National Congress approved Amendment 18/1998 establishing the PM as "militaries of the states" and reinforcing their military status, making it more difficult to reform the public security system.

7. The customary translation for *polícia militar* is "military police." Hearing the term, many foreigners might mistake the PM for the police of the military (*polícia do exército*) or erroneously conclude that the PM are part of the military. Though the PM were made subordinate to the army during the military dictatorship (1964–1985), and though they remain a "reserve" of the army and maintain barracks and military training, these state police forces are not nationally unified and are functionally and institutionally separate from the military. The PM forces grew out of a separate tradition of state military forces, much in the way the states in the United States had state guards and militias before there was a regular federal army. Thus, a better translation would be the "*militarized* police." However, for the sake of convention, I will also refer to them as the "military police" or more often simply the "PM," which is their common moniker in Portuguese.

8. 1998 Constitution, Article 144, paragraph 6.

9. This observation about military behavior is relevant, because historically, minor disciplinary infractions have been more severely punished than have infractions involving the use of excessive force to detain a suspect. For example, skipping the chain of command in a simple administrative process is a serious offense to authority. As for discipline, appearing with even a too-large mustache would be seen as flippant or negligent and also an offense to immediate supervisors.

10. The ranks are, in order from lowest to highest: soldado; cabo; first, second, and third sargento; subtenente; first and second tenente; capitão; major; tenente-coronel; and coronel.

11. Perhaps out of institutional envy, the PC does maintain a visible fleet of patrol vehicles (*viaturas*), which are painted and bear institutional emblems and

sirens. Some argue that by increasing the number of visible police vehicles, the PC is making citizens feel safer; others argue that it more appropriate for these investigative police officers to use under-cover vehicles, in essence suggesting that the PC is sacrificing effectiveness for pride or public appearances. Whatever the case, this demonstrates that it is not entirely accurate to say that the PC does not do ostensive policing. On paper they are supposed to take investigative action on the orders from the Ministério Público. I have personally taken part in "blitzes" or random traffic stops with the PC and can attest that they were supremely ostensive actions and not investigative.

12. Jane's data most likely included the Federal Highway Police. The number of 8,000 updates the number of 7,000 from da Silva Filho's research (2000) and draws on the best estimates from various other experts (Benedito, interview, 2004; Proença, interview, 2004; de Souza Leal, interview, 2004).

13. The number of municipal guard forces may be as many as 400, according to The Braudel Institute of World Economics (2003). The estimate of 357 comes from Athias (2003).

14. Their numbers—600,000 together—make the state forces the most important law enforcement agencies: The combined federal police number about 16,000 and are extremely overextended in terms of responsibilities and territory. (This percentage calculation, however, does not include municipal guards, public defense forces [bombeiros], or military personnel, to be discussed later.)

15. Article 144, section 6 makes the police subordinate to both the military and state governors: "The Military Police and the *Corpos de Bombeiros Militares* [military firefighters and public defense force], being auxiliary and reserve forces of the Army, are subordinated, along with the Civil Police, to the governors of the states."

16. "The Union [federal government] shall have the exclusive right to legislate on: . . . general norms of organization, troops, military supplies, calling up and mobilizing the PM and Bombeiros [firefighters and rescue squads]" (Article 22, section 21).

17. The states included São Paulo, Rio Grande do Sul, Paraná, Rio de Janeiro, Espírito Santo, Minas Gerais, Bahia, Pernambuco, Paraíba, Rio Grande do Norte, Pará, Amazonas, Ceará, Goiás, and Sergipe (Mariano, interview, 2004).

18. Research conducted in 1987 by the Human Rights Center Santos Dias of the São Paulo archdiocese analyzed 380 cases. They found that officers were absolved in 90 percent of cases in the first category, while officers were punished in 85 percent of cases in the second category.

19. Law Decree 9,299 was passed in 1996 after being proposed by human rights advocates, most notably a federal deputy (congressman) from São Paulo, Hélio Bicudo. Originally the bill called for all crimes against the person to be transferred to the civil court system instead of the military courts (*Tribunal Justiça Militar*) but this definition was limited to ensure passage.

20. Law Decree 9,455, approved by Congress on April 7, 1997, almost 10 years after the country had redemocratized and signed international human rights treaties.

21. For instance, the Ford Foundation helped two universities in Rio de Janeiro develop courses on public security for members of the PM; new recruits and young officers take classes with other students. Federal universities in the states of Minas Gerais and Pernambuco, among others, have also developed coursework along these lines.

22. This analysis is mirrored in the *Projecto* to which President Lula ascribed: "Therefore, the path of the vicious cycle is painfully obvious: lack of investigation, lack of confidence, lack of information" (Institute of Citizenship, 2002, p. 33). It also

cites the "impossibility of applying rational public policies," which in turn leads to "public distrust, generating underreporting of crimes, which contributes to reduced investigative efficiency" (p. 36).

23. *Para inglês ver* translates typically as "for the English to see"; in colloquial terms it is an official mendacity for the sake of appearances, often to seem modern.

24. As Luiz Eduardo Soares, noted anthropologist and former national secretary for public security (SENASP), argued, "Random brutality is the easiest and strongest way for bad cops to impose their own conditions on the [drug] traffickers" (Soares, 2000).

25. See de Araujo Evangelista (2003). Police allow the gambling to persist probably because, as a lottery that is not state-sponsored, it seems like a petty and unstoppable crime, but it can become quite serious for a few reasons: First, police also take a cut of the profits. Interestingly, it is the PC that usually receives the payoffs, and the PM does not. Hence, the illegal betting can generate more friction between the two police forces than between police and criminal organizations. Second, the profits can go to fund political corruption at higher levels. Third, these numbers rackets can grow into larger criminal organizations.

26. Some have called the rise of uncivil society the "dark side" of democratization, because "an inexorable shadow of uncivil society follows the strengthening of civil society" (Pinheiro, 2000, p. 121). Others consider it the result of globalization, reasoning that "organized crimes such as smuggling, drugs, and trafficking in prostitution and children" have fed its growth (Mittelman & Johnston, 1999, p. 119).

27. See also Shelley (1995) and Williams (1994).

28. See Huggins (1998), pp. 136–140. More broadly, Pinheiro writes: "All classes of vigilantes in several Brazilian cities exist, in a certain way, as a continuation of the death squads and other repressive clandestine organizations and practices that prevailed during the dictatorship" (2000, p. 121).

29. This case is very much a conflict. Following a congressional investigation, Brazilian civil society actors, including human rights groups, the very influential Brazilian Bar Association (OAB), and unions, formed a movement to react against organized crime and serious human rights violations. Numerous members of this movement received death threats, and one attorney was killed on April 15, 2002 (Global Justice, 2002).

30. These states include Rio de Janeiro, Rio Grande do Sul, Santa Catarina, São Paulo, Espírito Santo, Bahia, Pernambuco, Rio Grande do Norte, Ceará, Pará, Acre, Maranhão, and the Federal District (de Mesquita Neto, 1999).

31. One research institute claims that a Public Security Forum formed in the São Paulo suburb of Diadema helped reduce the number of homicides by half in that extremely violent periphery (Braudel Institute of World Economics, 2003).

32. For instance, only 61 percent actually have firearms, and 77 percent have phone lines and vehicles, all of which seem essential for police work; in terms of helpful items, only 13 percent have a fax machine, and 12 percent have a copy machine.

References

Adorno, S. (2002). O monopólio estatal da violência na sociedade brasileira contemporânea. In S. Miceli (Ed.), *O que ler na ciência social brasileira 1970–2002* (Vol. IV, pp. 1–32). São Paulo: Editora Bertrand Brasil.

Adorno, S. (2004). O monopólio estatal da violência. *Revista da Oficina de Informações, 5*(52), 50–51.

Agüero, F. (1997). Toward civilian supremacy in South America. In L. Diamond, M. F. Plattner, Y. Chu, & H. Tien (Eds.), *Consolidating the third wave democracies* (pp. 177–207). Baltimore: Johns Hopkins University Press.

Amnesty International. (2005, December 2). *"They come in shooting": Policing socially excluded communities.* Retrieved August 7, 2006, from http://web.amnesty.org/library/Index/ENGAMR190252005.

Amora, D. (2004, August 5). A segurança privada cresce sem regulacao. *O Globo*, p. 16.

de Araujo Evangelista, H. (2003). *Rio de Janeiro: Violência, jogo do bicho e narcotráfico sengundo uma interpretação.* Rio de Janeiro: Editora Revan.

Arias, E. D. (2004). Faith in our neighbors: Networks and social order in three Brazilian favelas. *Latin American Politics & Society, 46*(1), 1–38.

Athias, G. (2003, November 9). Planalto quer fortalecer guarda municipal. *Folha de São Paulo*, p. C1.

Beato Filho, C. C. (2002, January). *Reinventar a polícia: A implementação de um program de policiamento comunitário.* Informative paper of CRISP, Universidade Federal de Minas Gerais, number 2. Belo Horizonte, Brazil: CRISP.

Braudel Institute of World Economics. (2003). *Segurança pública (A plan of action: Public security in Brazil).* Braudel paper number 33. São Paulo: Author.

Caldeira, T. P. R. (2000). *City of walls: Crime, segregation and citizenship in São Paulo* Berkeley: University of California Press.

Cano, I., & Santos, N. (2001). *Violência letal, renda e desigualdade social no Brasil.* Rio de Janeiro: 7 Letras.

Costa, A. T. M. (2004). *Entre a lei e a ordem.* Rio de Janeiro: Fundação Getúlio Vargas.

Dominquez, J. I., & Lowenthal, A. F. (Eds.). (1996). *Constructing democratic governance: Latin America and the Caribbean in the 1990s.* Baltimore: Johns Hopkins University Press.

Fausto, B. (1999). *A concise history of Brazil.* New York: Cambridge University Press.

Frühling, H. (1998). Policía y consolidación democrática en Chile. *Pena y Estado, 3,* 81–116.

Global Justice. (2002). *Human rights in Brazil: 2002.* Rio de Janeiro: Author.

Global Justice. (2003). *Human rights in Brazil: 2003.* Rio de Janeiro: Author.

Holloway, T. H. (1993). *Policing in Rio de Janeiro: Repression and resistance in a 19th century city.* Palo Alto, CA: Stanford University Press.

Holston, J., & Caldeira, T. P. R. (1998). Democracy, law, and violence: Disjunctions of Brazilian citizenship. In F. Aguero & J. Stark (Eds.), *Fault lines of democracy in post-transition Latin America* (pp. 263–297). Miami, FL: North South Center Press.

Huggins, M. K. (1998). *Political policing: The United States and Latin America.* Durham, NC: Duke University Press.

Institute of Citizenship. (2002). *Projecto segurança pública para o Brasil.* São Paulo: Author.

Kant de Lima, R. (1995). *A polícia da cidade do Rio de Janeiro: Seus problemas e paradoxos.* Rio de Janeiro: Editora Forense.

Lemgruber, J. (2004, October). *Violência, omissão e insegurança pública: O pão de nosso cada dia.* Presentation at the Academia Brasileira de Ciências, Rio de Janeiro.

Lemgruber, J., Musumeci, L., & Cano, I. (2003). *Quem vigia os vigias? Um estudo sobre controle externo da polícia no Brasil.* Rio de Janeiro: Editora Record.

Linz, J. J., & Stepan, A. (1996). *Problems of democratic transition and consolidation: Southern Europe, South America and post-communist Europe.* Baltimore: Johns Hopkins University Press.

de Mesquita Neto, P. (1999). Violência policial no Brasil: Abordagens teórics e práticas de controle. In D. Chaves Pandolfi, J. Murilo de Carvalho, L. Piquet Carneiro, & M. Grynszpan (Eds.), *Cidadania, Justiça e Violência* (pp. 129–147). Rio de Janeiro: Editora Fundação Getulio Vargas.

Miranda, R. (2003). *The organized crime in Espírito Santo State.* São Paulo: Braudel Institute of World Economics.

Mittelman, J., & Johnston, R. (1999). The globalization of organized crime. *Global Governance, 5*(1), pp. 103–127.

Muniz, J. (1999). *"Ser policial é, pobretudo, uma razão de ser": Cultura e cotidiano da polícia militar do Estado do Rio de Janeiro.* Rio de Janeiro: Instituto Universitário de Pesquisa do Rio de Janeiro.

Pinheiro, P. S. (1994). The legacy of authoritarianism in democratic Brazil. In S. Nagel (Ed.), *Latin American development and public policy* (pp. 237–253). New York: St. Martin's Press.

Pinheiro, P. S. (2000). Democratic governance, violence, and the (un)rule of law. *Daedalus, 129*(2), 119–143.

Salles, J. M., & Lund, K. (Directors). (1999). *Notícias de uma guerra particular (News from a private war).* Motion picture. Rio de Janeiro: Videofilmes.

Shelley, L. L. (1995). Transnational organized crime: An imminent threat to the nation-state? *Journal of International Affairs, 48*(2), 468–489.

da Silva Filho, J. V. (2000). Reflexões para uma política nacional de segurança pública. In J. P. dos R. Vellos, R. C. de Albuquerque, & A. C. Magalhães (Eds.), *Pobreza, cidadania e segurança* (pp. 234–248). Rio de Janeiro: José Olympio.

da Silva Filho, J. V., & Gall, N. (1999). *A polícia.* Braudel paper number 22. São Paulo: Braudel Institute of World Economics.

Soares, L. E. (2000, October). *Crime, violence and corruption in Latin America.* Paper presented at ILAS Forum on Latin America Policy, Columbia University, New York.

Stepan, A. (2000). Brazil's decentralized federalism: Bringing government closer to the citizens? *Daedalus, 129*(2), 145–169.

Ungar, M. (2002). *Elusive reform: Democracy and the rule of law in Latin America.* Boulder, CO: Lynne Rienner.

Valenzuela, J. (1988). Democratic consolidation in post-transitional settings: Notion, process, and facilitating conditions. In S. Mainwaring, G. O'Donnell, & J. Valenzuela (Eds.), *Issues in democratic consolidation: The new South American democracies in comparative perspective* (pp. 57–104). Notre Dame, IN: University of Notre Dame Press.

Williams, P. (1994). Transnational criminal organisations and international security. *Security, 36*(1), 96–113.

Zaluar, A. (2000). Perverse integration: Drug trafficking and youth in the *favelas* of Rio de Janeiro. *Journal of International Affairs, 53*(2), 654–671.

Interviews

Benedito, M. D. (2004, February). Interview. São Paulo.

Freitas Lopes, F. (2004, August). Interview, Fortaleza, Ceara.

Mariano, B. D. (July, 2004). Interview, São Paulo.

de Mesquita Neto, P. (2004, January). Interview, Núcleo de Estudos da Violência, University of São Paulo.

Muniz, J. (March, 2004). Interview, Secretaria Nacional de Segurança Pública (Senasp) Brasilia.

Proença, D., Jr. (2004, January). Interview, Rio de Janeiro.

de Souza Leal, P. C. (2004, September 13). Interview, Goiánia.

4

Paths to Fairness, Effectiveness, and Democratic Policing in Mexico

Benjamin Nelson Reames

Despite being a functioning democracy, Mexico has not established a strong rule of law. High rates of violent crime and routine police corruption were already serious problems in the early 1990s; then increased drug traffic, more active street gangs, high-profile cases of kidnapping and corruption, unrest in regions like Chiapas, and a string of unsolved murders in Ciudad Juarez added fuel to a fire of public insecurity. Police and justice institutions responded ineffectively in the late 1990s. As a result, Mexico's crisis of public insecurity also manifested itself as a crisis of confidence in democratic leaders. If a democratic government fails to provide a fair and effective justice system that guarantees public security and protects rights, then it risks forfeiting one of its core functions that properly defines it as a consolidated democracy. Thus the real and perceived problems with crime, policing, and justice have left Mexico an embattled democracy. The core question becomes, Will public security institutions in Mexico proceed along the path of democratic policing, or will public security continue to degenerate and weaken the lived experience of democracy?

Public insecurity in Mexico is the result of crime but also of corrupt and poorly functioning police forces, and this has been a primary public concern for many years. The good news is that the heightened sense of urgency has generated increased political will to effect reform. Other factors may also facilitate reform: The federal system has been decentralizing for many years, making it possible for public officials to be more responsive to local needs; the political parties have become competitive, making democracy a functional (albeit messy) reality; also, efforts to stanch public sector corruption and inefficiency are important items on the political agenda. In short, public officials increasingly appear to have motivation and capacity to push for improvements in policing and accountability.

Yet would-be reformers will continue to confront challenges within the prevailing patronage-based political system and the fractured federal governmental system. For instance, when trying to overhaul public security, Mexican institutions at the national level face the predicament of having to further decentralize power and resources to states and municipalities while simultaneously increasing centralized information gathering and oversight. Politically, they are called upon to vet police forces, sever links to organized crime, and reform legal codes. Further, those in government stand a better chance of surmounting these challenges if they leverage the resources and expertise of civil society, but civil society has long been ignored or co-opted. In some sectors, Mexican civil society is active and robust; in others, it lacks technical capacity and public confidence—public-security related nongovernmental organizations (NGOs) usually belong to the latter camp. As a result, reform may hinge once again on personality and political will. To make real progress, political actors will probably need to juggle the politics of federalism and partisanship while managing civil society input and institutional inertia in government.

In short, I argue here that Mexico is at a fork in the path to democratic policing. Various governments around the world have done and do face the same predicament: an erosion of their monopoly on the legitimate use of force becomes coupled with rising crime rates, which requires legitimate state forces to contain. In that context, government officials in Mexico and elsewhere may perceive a choice between providing citizen security and protecting civil rights. However, it is now widely acknowledged that "rights versus security" is a false dichotomy and that the only way to provide both—in fact, the best way to provide either—is through comprehensive public security reform that integrates and invests in both. Furthermore, meeting this challenge at an important crossroads may reap extra rewards. In other words, for a government to reform the police in the face of pressures to further militarize and/or privatize public security could help to reassert the essential role that accountable, rights-respecting public institutions play in maintaining democracy.

Assessing the Mexican Public Security Situation _____

By the end of the century, the idea of *paths to democracy* had gained immense currency among Latin Americanists.[1] The path model suggested that a number of decisive variables could either impede or assist a country in achieving and consolidating democracy. Not surprisingly, at least one analyst noted that democratization of the police can also be modeled in terms of paths (de Mesquita Neto, 2001). To do so requires considering the impact of crime, civil society organizations, and most important, the defining features of the police, legal institutions, and state itself. The present analysis makes clear that the obstacles have so far outweighed the resources and capacity for change. The main obstacles include an ossified bureaucracy that is resistant to change and lacks good information about how to change, a political environment prone to sabotage and deadlock, and the lack of legal authority to make over-arching institutional changes. These features are unlikely to change in the short term. On the other hand, the capacity for reform derives from good information about police reforms and improvements, the concerted effort of civil society to propose practical reforms, and the availability of resources and individuals to actually implement such changes. When the scales tip in favor of capacity over obstacles, Mexico will approximate its promise of providing democratic, effective, and rights-respecting police.

With that framework in mind, this chapter gauges Mexico's progress on the path toward implementing democratic police procedures. In doing so, it is essential to make sense of the various police forces themselves and their mandates and powers through an institutional lens. This chapter begins with a profile of the police. The second part places the police in the context of challenges to public security: private security growth, organized crime, police corruption, and high crime rates. The final part assesses Mexico's prospects for achieving effective and just democratic policing in the context of the obstacles and capacities that the current conditions of Mexican federalism and civil society present, which have gained increased expert scrutiny of late (Cornelius & Shirk, 2007).

Institutional Introduction to the Police of Mexico

First, it is important to understand how Mexico is *not* unique. The legal structure of its police is like that of other large, federal democracies in Latin America—such as Brazil and Argentina—in that there are both federal and relatively autonomous state police forces, bifurcated into judicial (investiga-tive) and ostensive (order-maintenance or militarized) police departments. Mexican police also confront problems common throughout Latin America: low pay, poor training, disorganization, corruption, ineffectiveness, lack of public confidence, and ill-defined or unachievable mandates.

On the other hand, the exceptional features of Mexican institutions and police are instructive. Mexico has been a democracy on paper since 1917, but due to one-party rule, political competition only started to take hold in the late 1980s and was decisively affirmed with the election of President Fox (of the PAN, the National Action Party) in 2000. In short, because Mexico did not fall under military dictatorship in the latter half of the twentieth cen-tury like most countries to the south of it, the principal impediments to police reform in Mexico are *not* those of wresting civilian control over pub-lic security institutions or overcoming entrenched elements of hard-line con-servatives. That said, Mexico does not have the distant, long-standing experience in democracy that some of these same countries have (Argentina,

Brazil, Chile), which is seen as making Mexico's practice of democracy somewhat inchoate (not to mention fragile). For instance, Mexico's federal system has not truly functioned as such due to the seven-decade dominance of the PRI (the Institutional Revolutionary Party) that centralized power; in terms of policing, this has slowed the process of decentralization that might have given more discretion and power to authorities who better understand local crime problems. Finally, Mexico's strategic location between the United States and the rest of Latin America makes it the frequent focus of critical international attention to public security problems, especially issues related to drug trafficking and immigration. The upshot is that the police forces of Mexico are rife with both problems and potential.

Mexico is a large federation of 31 states and one federal district, and it maintains a range of police forces belonging to a variety of jurisdictions and functional separations. Estimates of the force size vary due to inadequate centralized data collection and frequent changes, but it is safe to say there are about 400,000 police officers in the country and about 3,000 different forces at municipal, state, and federal levels.[2] So there is a distinct multiplicity of police forces in Mexico. Other outstanding features include the institutionalized nature of corruption, growing militarization, poor preparation, and ineffectiveness in the face of increasingly severe crime.

With the election of Vicente Fox to the presidency in 2000, Mexico shed one-party rule and raised expectations for public sector reform. Fox experienced increasing pressure—domestically and abroad—to reduce corruption, confront organized crime, and develop modern, effective, rights-respecting police forces. Finally, on March 29, 2004, he presented his first cohesive police reform proposal (*Iniciativa de Reforma en Seguridad Pública y Justicia Penal*). Though fragmented reform efforts had been underway, the proposal was unique in aiming to unify some the nation's police organizations and to give investigatory power to a greater number of police officers. The range of forces means that there is no single police institution that defines Mexican policing. However, some of the more recent reforms, including those in three of the most significant police bodies, nicely demonstrates the kaleidoscopic picture of Mexican policing.

First, the federal attorney general's office (*Procuraduría General de la República*—PGR) established a new police force, the Federal Agency of Investigation (*Agencia Federal de Investigaciones*—AFI) which replaced the notoriously corrupt Federal Judicial Police (*Policía Judicial Federal*—PJF) by the presidential decree of Vicente Fox (2000–2006) on November 1, 2001. The efforts to develop the AFI into a professional, uncorrupted force for the investigation of federal crimes are ongoing.

Second, the Federal Preventive Police (*Policía Federal Preventiva*—PFP) was created in 1999 by the initiative of President Ernesto Zedillo (1994–2000) to prevent and combat crime throughout the country.[3] The PFP comes under the direction of the federal Secretariat of Public Security (*Secretaría de Seguridad Pública*—SSP) and has been assuming its authority in stages over time, as its budget has grown and it has combined and reorganized police departments from major agencies such as those for migration, treasury, and highways.

Third, the Secretariat of Public Security of the Federal District (*Secretaría de Seguridad Pública del Distrito Federal*—SSP-DF), unlike the previous two, does not have national reach, but it does manage a combined force of over 90,000 officers in the Federal District (DF). The SSP is charged with maintaining public order and safety in the center of Mexico City, where public insecurity and crime rates are highest in the nation. As a result, there have been concurrent efforts to increase accountability and improve police effectiveness. Beginning in 1996, authorities began a dramatic restructuring of the SSP-DF, which included replacing major officials with army officers. Recently, the most high-profile effort has been Mexico City Mayor Andres Lopez Obrador's decision in 2002 to contract the consulting firm of Rudolph Giuliani, former mayor of New York City, to advise the SSP-DF on public security policy.

The Mexican police, properly defined, are the public security forces charged with the prevention and investigation of crimes; these forces are therefore meant to support the Public Ministry (*Ministerio Público,* which prosecutes crimes) and the judiciary. Given the changing, complex nature of these police institutions, a clear description of what they actually do is best achieved by using two defining dimensions—function and jurisdiction.[4]

Functional Description of the Police

Mexico's police are divided into a dual set that includes preventive police (the order-controlling *policía preventiva*) and judicial police (the typically plain-clothed and investigative *policía judicial*). The preventive police do what is often called "ostensive policing" and thus maintain order and public security in cities and towns; they do not investigate crimes and assist the Public Ministry in doing so only at its request. They are empowered to act according to police and governmental regulations (Article 21 of the Constitution).

The judicial police are an auxiliary to the Public Ministry and act under its authority and command. The judicial police belong to institutions known as *procuraduría generales,* which are important justice institutions translated usually as attorneys' general offices. There are three key types of police actors in this type of law enforcement: the police officers (*policías judiciales*), investigating agents of the public prosecutor (often simply called *ministerios públicos*), and technical experts (*peritos*). Depending on their jurisdiction, judicial police enforce federal law (*fuero federal*) or local law (*fuero común*).

According to the National Public Security System (*Sistema Nacional de Seguridad Pública*—SNSP), municipal- and state-level police forces employed some 280,000 officers in 1999. The nearly 34,000 preventive police of the federal district and the federal preventive police raised the number to 319,600 preventive police in 1999. Today there are probably over 330,000 preventive police; judicial police officers number over 26,000.

Jurisdictional Description of the Police

There are four types of jurisdictions that affect the nature, activity, and organization of police institutions: the three levels of government—federal, state, and municipal, and the federal district.

Municipal Police

Preventive policing is the shared responsibility of the federal, state, and local authorities, according to the Constitution and reforms passed in 1999. The question is, How much and how well do local authorities manage policing? Mexico has been undergoing a process of decentralization since the 1980s. Police work often gets overlooked in the attention paid to health, education, and fiscal decentralization; however, local law enforcement is likely to increase its order-maintenance (if not investigative) activities for the years to come, and the federal government has not offered much help or guidance.

The *municipio* represents the local level of government and may contain many smaller towns and cities. Like counties in the United States that have sheriffs, a municipio can maintain a police force. Municipios have only preventive police, but not all have them. There are 2,395 municipios; 335 have no police forces. There are 2,000 municipios with fewer than 100 officers, which implies that the police departments are not very developed and probably not very modernized. However, 87 of the largest municipios account for 68.7 percent of preventive police at all levels of government, so some are quite complex.

Policing in the Federal District

The Federal District (DF) covers a territory of 1,500 square kilometers and contains the heart of Mexico City and the seat of federal government. There are 9 million residents in the DF and about 19 million people in the metropolitan region (depending on where one draws the boundaries). The DF has a directly elected mayor who has the power to appoint the heads of the law enforcement forces of the city: the public security secretary of the federal district and the attorney general of the federal district.

Preventive Police—DF: The DF stands out for having the highest crime rates in Mexico as well as a huge preventive police force of approximately 34,000 officers (not to mention 40,000 auxiliary police and 15,000 banking police). These nearly 90,000 officers work for the SSP-DF, which has five major divisions and an annual budget of over 10 billion pesos. [The initial salary for a patrol officer of the SSP-DF was raised to 5,000 pesos per month (about US$500) in 2004.]

Like most police departments of major cities, the DF's preventive police are divided into regional subgroups (a geographically defined police with specific jurisdictions) and into functional divisions with special responsibilities and resources. Slightly less than half of the preventive police are grouped into the geographical distributions of the Sectoral Police (*Policía Sectoral*). Within the Sectoral Police there are six main regions with usually three precincts in each (a total of 16 precincts) and a number of sectors within each precinct (a total of 70 sectors).

The Sectoral Police compose one of the five divisions; the remaining four divisions of the preventive police (over 17,000 of the 34,000) are organized into special divisions rather than geographic groupings. The second division, the Metropolitan Police (*Policía Metropolitana*), consists of six special units: the Public Transit Police, the Tourist Police, the Grenadiers (*Granaderos* protect the historic district), the Mounted Police, the Feminine Police (the *Policía Femenil* work in schools, with juveniles, at public events, and in public parks and gardens), and the Emergency Rescue Squad (ERUM).

The third division is a set of Special Squadrons (*Fuerzas Especiales*) consisting of four main groups: the Helicopter Squadron; the Special Unit, which specializes in motorcycles; the Task Force (*Fuerza de Tareas*), which deals with terrorist and bomb threats; and the Alfa Group, which is a secretive, ad hoc force that works with the Special Unit and fights drug trafficking. The fourth division is Roadway Security (*Seguridad Vial*), which maintains a force of brown-uniformed police that patrol the roads and highways. A chronically understaffed Internal Affairs is the final division.

Though the chain of authority is a source of common confusion, the SSP-DF is not synonymous with the preventive police. There are two other, separate forces—under the charge of the SSP-DF but not part of the preventive police—that compose the Complementary Police: the Auxiliary Police (approximately 40,000 strong), which guards official buildings and other specific locations like the airport, and the Banking Police (about 15,000 officers), which guards businesses, financial institutions, and banks. The complementary forces function in a more ostensive capacity than the police forces that investigate and apprehend suspects; in theory, they should allow for significant decentralization, better use of resources within the preventive police, and for the creation of reserve order maintenance forces when necessary.

Judicial Police–DF: The DF is also unique for maintaining its own force of judicial police, the Judicial Police of the Federal District (*Policía Judicial del Distrito Federal*—PJDF), which are organized under the office of the attorney general of the DF (the *Procuraduría General de Justicia del Distrito Federal*—PGJDF). The PGJDF receives complaints and reports of possible crimes and investigates them. They maintain 16 precincts (delegaciones) with an estimated 3,500 judicial police, 1,100 investigating agents for prosecuting attorneys (*agentes del ministerio público*), and 941 experts or specialists (*peritos*). The PGJDF budget exceeds 3 billion pesos each year. It is clearly a substantial force.

State Police

The 31 states maintain—like the DF, but unlike the cities—both preventive and judicial police. The state-level preventive police are over 90,000 strong. The judicial police, by definition, must enforce the states' local laws (commonly called *fuero común*). By infrequent estimates, there are over 21,000 state-level judicial police officers in the state judicial police forces (*Policía Judicial de los Estados*—PJE) organized under the offices of the attorneys general (*Procuradurías Generales de Justicia*).

Federal Police

PGR and AFI: The federal Public Ministry (*Ministerio Público*) has a separate judicial police force, which operates nationwide under the office of the federal attorney general (PGR), who is appointed by the president. When Attorney General Rafael Marcial Macedo de la Concha was appointed by Vicente Fox, concerns were raised about militarization of the police. The PGR's mandate is to investigate and prosecute federal crimes such as drug trafficking, arms trafficking, kidnapping, and environmental and public health crimes. The PGR under the Fox administration has seen its budget grow from 5.6 billion pesos in 2001 to 7.2 billion pesos in 2004; it employed a staff of 21,838 in 2004.

The PGR reconfigured and renamed the federal judicial police (PJF), which was much maligned for corruption and ineffectiveness. The AFI replaced the PJF and was probably intended to invite comparisons to the FBI of the United States. The AFI had a budget in 2004 of 2,622 million pesos, thus amounting to about a third of the PGR budget. The force consists of more than 5,000 judicial police officers, 1,600 investigators, and 450 specialists.

The rest of the PGR law enforcement activities (besides the delegations for each state) can be broken up into planning departments, internal controls, and more notably, deputy attorney general offices (*subprocuradurías*), which contain special units. Because the federal police are charged with some of Mexico's most vexing crime problems—stanching the flow of illegal drugs, solving kidnappings, and fighting other types of organized crime—it is worth mentioning two subprocuradurías that have evolved over time.

The PGR's first Special Anti–Organized Crime Unit (*Unidad Especial contra la Delicuencia Organizada*—UEDO) appeared as a response to organized crime, which was first defined in Mexico's legal code in February

1994 as "three or more persons organized under rules of discipline and hierarchy in order to commit, in a violent and repeated way or with the purpose of profit, any of the crimes legally defined." The Federal Law against Organized Crime (*Ley Federal contra la Delincuencia Organizada—* LFcDO) was passed in November 1996 to deal with the problem of drug trafficking, though other crimes, such as migrant smuggling, trafficking in arms or infants, and terrorism, were covered and targeted as well.

The Office of the Special Prosecutor for Crimes Against Health (*Fiscalía Especializada de Delitos Contra la Salud—*FEADS) appeared in 1997 after General Gutiérrez Rebollo, head of the National Anti-Drugs Institute (*Instituto Nacional de Combate a las Drogas—*INCD), was arrested on charges stemming from association with leaders of the Juárez cartel. So INCD, which previously dealt with drug trafficking, was dismantled, and FEADS was put under the direction of a civilian, Mariano Herrán, and the UEDO operated out of FEADS headquarters in Mexico City. Two other key units within FEADS were the Border Rapid Response Groups (*Grupos de Respuesta Rápida Fronteriza*) and the Special Anti–Money Laundering Unit (*Unidad Especializada contra el Lavado de Dinero—*UECLD). UECLD was created in January 1998 to implement anti–money laundering legislation, which dates from 1990. The problem of corruption in FEADS was not entirely solved, and agents in Tijuana and Monterrey were arrested for extortion and kidnapping. Both FEADS and UEDO have been reorganized; some examples of their new units are described below.

As it was organized, the Office of the Deputy Attorney General for Special Investigation of Organized Crime (*Subprocuraduría de Investigación Especializada en Delicuencia Organizada—*SIEDO) received 357 million pesos of the 2004 budget. SIEDO contains six special units (with smaller, separate budgets) intended for investigating specific types of crimes: crimes against public health; terrorism and arms trafficking; money laundering and counterfeiting; human trafficking, namely in minors, organs, and undocumented people; kidnappings; and robbery and auto theft. A second example is the Deputy Attorney for Special Investigation of Federal Crimes (*Subprocuraduría de Investigación Especializada en Delitos Federales—*SIEDF), which received about 16 million pesos of the 2006 budget. The four separate units under its direction cover crimes related to intellectual property, financial transactions, environmental damage, and public servants who obstruct justice.

Both examples demonstrate the general rule that Mexican policing institutions try to reorganize themselves in a rational way to respond effectively to specific crime problems. But actually, legislation must first address specific crime problems; most often only then can the police institutions themselves respond to the law. Without specific laws that enable them to act, public institutions in Mexico—police departments included—find it difficult to pursue particular goals, no matter how pressing. Another result of when legislative action is lacking and bureaucratic tinkering is used to address crime-fighting needs is that official reorganizations and departmental shuffles tend to be quite frequent. Ad hoc adjustments and internal regulatory changes in the Mexican type of bureaucracy are uncommon; each department or agency is created with a fixed set of procedures and powers. So when bureaucratic change is deemed necessary, this is often accomplished by renaming, reorganizing, and/or reconstituting a particular organization. An easier but less effective method of bureaucratic reorganization is to move the head of one department to another in an attempt to add a personal imprimatur or change the character of the second institution, though these changes are often largely cosmetic. In short, adjustments are difficult to make quickly and effectively in the Mexican system, making the law enforcement apparatus less nimble than would be desirable.

The SSP and the PFP: Sweeping reforms began to shake up the federal SSP in 2005, as President Fox created the Public Security Cabinet (*Gabinete de Seguridad Pública*) at the federal level with Fox as the nominal head and with the chief of the SSP coordinating activities. The SSP comes under the jurisdiction of the Interior Secretariat (*Secretaría de Gobernación*) and had a budget of 6,462 million pesos for 2004 and a total staff of 22,900, which included members of the police. As a gesture toward integration, the new cabinet will also include the attorney general as a permanent member, in addition to military officials. Fox also transformed an undersecretariat for prevention and citizen participation to work with the newly created Council of Citizen Participation (*Consejo de Participación Ciudadana*—CPC) that is intended to monitor performance, analyze police, and suggest courses of action in the area of public security. Miguel Angel Yunes was appointed to this undersecretary post.

Under President Fox, Alejandro Gertz Manero had been the Secretary of Public Security, which is a cabinet position, though it falls under the Interior Secretariat, which also holds a cabinet position. When Gertz stepped down in 2004, then-Deputy Interior Minister Ramon Martín Huerta replaced him. President Calderon has since made Genaro García Luna the Secretary. The sense of flux in the SSP, the push for reform, and the changing authorities mean that future organization of the SSP is uncertain. As it stands, however, the SSP houses two important public security institutions: the federal preventive police and the National Public Security System (SNSP, discussed further below). The entire SSP had a budget of 6,462 million pesos allocated to it in 2004.

The federal preventive police (*Policía Federal Preventiva*—PFP) is a force that was created in 1999 at the behest of the Zedillo administration (1994–2000) and the prompting of the SNSP to control crime throughout the country. The Mexican Senate passed legislation in December 1998 that called for the creation of a national law enforcement body that would combine the Federal Highway Police (*Policía Federal de Caminos*), the Federal Fiscal Police (*Policía Fiscal Federal*), and the Federal Immigration Police (*Policía Migratoria Federal*). Initially, concerns focused on the fact that the new police force could be politically repressive toward opposition parties, and then attention turned to the military training, service background, and ethic of the new recruits.

The PFP has technical and operative autonomy and is headed by a commissioner named by the president. In 2000, the SSP's PFP had 10,699 officers; 4,899 of these were from the military (3rd Brigade of the Military Police), about 4,000 came from the Federal Highway Police, 1,500 from the Federal Fiscal Police, and 600 from the Interior Secretariat's intelligence agency, the Center for Research and National Security (*Centro de Investigación y Seguridad Nacional*—CISEN). These new members were then trained by the military. In short, rather than creating an entirely new police force, the PFP has cobbled together a force with a decidedly militarized character.

Restructuring of the PFP left it with some notable attributes in 2004. Besides the typical training, development, and planning departments, there are unique coordinating departments (*Coordinaciones*). Reflecting both the military and police background of the incorporated personnel, the Department for Regional Security is organized into four types of deployment: ports and borders, federal highways, other federal zones, and regional commands (34 of them). There is also a Department of Intelligence for Crime Prevention, which is organized internally to mimic closely the PGR units for federal crimes such as trafficking, terrorism, kidnapping, analysis, information, and statistics. Finally, there are federal support forces intended for disasters, special operations, and strategic deployments. The budget of the PFP in 2004 was 3,598 million pesos, which is more than half of the SSP budget.

Security Institutions: It merits explaining at the outset that four bodies have developed over time, often intermingling and evolving in ways that have caused confusion: the National Security Council (*Consejo de Seguridad Nacional*), the National Security Cabinet (*Gabinete de Seguridad Nacional*), the National Public Security Council *(Consejo Nacional de Seguridad Pública*), and the Public Security Cabinet (*Gabinete de Seguridad Pública*).

• President Salinas created the National Security Cabinet (*Gabinete de Seguridad Nacional*) in 1988. Under President Calderon, the Attorney General (or head of the PGR), Eduardo Medina-Mora Icaza, has been made the technical secretary of the cabinet. The cabinet also includes the secretaries of the defense, interior, public security, and the navy.

• The National Security Council was installed by Fox in February 2005, as required by the 2005 National Security Law. Fox tapped Santiago Creel, head of the Interior Secretariat, to be executive secretary of the council. The deliberative body brings together the heads of CISEN, Public Security, and National Defense among of other secretariats and has often been compared to the U.S. National Security Council; however, Mexico's version is especially focused on developing policies to address problems of organized crime and international drug traffickers. Calderon nominated Sigrid Arzt, who is an academic expert also active in civil society, to be the new technical secretary.

- The National Public Security Council (*Consejo Nacional de Seguridad Pública*) was established in 1995 and is currently headed by the Secretary of Public Security, Genaro García Luna. (This is explained further in the SNSP section below).

- The Public Security Cabinet (*Gabinete de Seguridad Pública*) was established in 2004 by the SSP to address public concern with rampant crime problems. (This is described above in the section on the SSP and the PFP.)

The Center for Research and National Security (Centro de Investigación y Seguridad Nacional—CISEN): Created in 1989, this is Mexico's principal civilian intelligence agency. CISEN is an instrument of the executive branch, subordinate to the Interior Secretariat (*Secretaría de Gobernación*). CISEN's primary function is to collect and process intelligence and security-related information.

Because drug trafficking organizations have proved successful in penetrating the security institutions, the anti–drug trafficking part of CISEN's intelligence and operations was transferred in 1992 to the newly created INCD and to its intelligence arm, the Anti-Drugs Center (*Centro de Planeación para el Combate contra las Drogas*—CENDRO). INCD did not solve corruption problems, and FEADS was subsequently created (see PGR, above).

SE-SNSP: Another important addition to the public security apparatus is the Executive Secretary for National Public Security System (*Secretariado Ejecutivo de Sistema Nacional de Seguridad Pública*—SE-SNSP), which began in 1994 with constitutional changes (Articles 21 and 73) that raised public security to the status of a state policy. The expressed idea was to coordinate public security efforts, plans, and data collection as well as to systematically fight crime and address demands for public security.

The Zedillo administration followed in 1995 with legislation formally creating the SNSP. A key decision was to locate the SNSP within the Interior Secretariat (*Secretaría de Gobernación*) rather than the PGR Secretariat. The law also created the National Public Security Council (*Consejo Nacional de Seguridad Pública*) as a coordinating body for the SNSP. The council included the secretary of public security, who presides, as well as the 31 state governors, the attorney general, the mayor of the DF, and the military chiefs. (In 2004, Fox announced that he would dramatically restructure the National Public Security Council, and the final outcome under President Calderon is not clear at this writing.) Also created was a series of coordinating councils at the state and local levels, emphasizing the central government's role in data collection, coordination, and planning, rather than direct control. The SNSP has grown in budgetary terms from 226.6 million pesos in 1996 to 366 million pesos in 2004. By 2000, the resources allocated by federal and state governments reached over 9 billion pesos.

Institutional Problems in Public Security

Ineffectiveness among Mexican police forces has proven durable, partly because the reasons for it are entrenched deep into police institutions. To break the cycle of poor performance and the lack of public trust and resources, police institutions need to develop information collection systems that regularly collect standard and accessible data on police and criminal activities. Most state-level police departments lack the capacity and technology to develop computerized information tracking systems that are necessary to perform large-scale crime-mapping, regularized data collection and sharing, and accountability monitoring, but police institutions of the PGR, PGR-DF, and AFI could develop this capacity and help others adopt it. Also, public resources must be allocated to increase the salaries of police officials if *mordidas* (small bribes) are going to be replaced by legitimate sources of income. Finally, the time and money spent on training and vetting police forces remain insufficient. Such investments are a first step in reforming institutions and chipping away at public distrust and corruption.

Corruption and Public Confidence

It is widely believed that corruption and inefficiency plague the Mexican police. Further, low pay and lack of resources have hindered efforts in improving police performance, battling corruption, and professionalizing the forces. A related lack of public confidence has eroded the ability of the police to respond to crime: Surveys regularly find that around 90 percent of respondents in Mexico City have "little" or "no" trust in the police. Such a lack of public confidence translates into a lack of support—that is, an unwillingness to report crimes or assist in investigations, which is crucial to solving crimes. Fox repeatedly stated, in presenting his reform initiative, that only 25 percent of all crimes are reported in Mexico, which is a high estimate.

Fox made reducing public corruption a key goal of his administration and gained some international recognition for his efforts. Mexico moved up several places to 51st—that is, improved—on the global corruption index published by Transparency International (TI), an advocacy NGO. However, that indication of progress was never sustained. A management consulting firm (A. T. Kearney) reported in 2002 that Mexico's attractiveness to foreign investors had dropped, from fifth to ninth place worldwide, due to concerns with corruption and crime (see the section on crime and public security, below). In 2007, Transparency International reported that 80 percent of Mexican respondents said in 2006 that their law enforcement and police institutions were "corrupt."[5]

Official corruption is prevalent within the police and common to the very practice of policing in Mexico.[6] TI estimated in 2002 that the median Mexican household spends 8 percent of its income on bribes (mordidas). Police officers are the officials frequently extracting these mordidas. Corruption within the

Mexican police force often takes on a pyramidal structure, with those at the bottom receiving low wages, and corrupt officials on the top sometimes taking in huge sums. The average police patrol officer in Mexico City earns an insufficient salary with which to support a family. It is frequently argued that mordidas allow police officials to augment their paltry salaries and avoid processing citizens for minor infractions.[7] However, a large percentage of these bribes flow upward, producing wealthy officers at the top and a wide base of still-impoverished patrol personnel at the bottom of the pyramid.[8]

Human Resources

Training, preparation, and institutional support for the police are generally poor. For the preventive police, academic and professional training are recent additions to policy. Of the 58 police academies, 25 began training operations in the last 23 years; most do not enforce a minimum educational requirement. Basic training lasts an average of four and one-half months; for example, in the DF, basic training lasts for six months. The majority of Mexican police officers have completed only elementary school or less. This situation has accelerated the erosion of institutional standards and postponed the modernization of the police. Police departments often lack: tools to evaluate job performance, guidelines for performance, methods to ferret out corruption, technical support, and understanding of human rights and community relations.

Legal System

Overload is a significant problem in the Mexican criminal justice system. When a complaint is received and a preliminary inquiry (*averiguacion previa*) begun, a criminal case is opened. Alternatively, cases can be initiated when a law officer detains a person caught in the act of committing a crime. The person can be detained for up to 48 hours before being brought before a judge for a preliminary hearing. The judge has up 72 hours to decide on one of three options: The person is jailed subject to trial, freed on bail, or freed due to lack of evidence. If the person is not freed due to lack of evidence, the judge may ask the police to gather more evidence. When the investigation is complete, the judge concludes the trial portion of the process and issues a sentence. Part of the overload problem arises because investigating officers, on average, receive a new complaint for each day of the year. Reported crimes practically doubled from 1991 to 1997, and reported crimes are only a small fraction of actual crimes. When districts (such as the DF) consider policing policies known as "zero tolerance," which require a high number of arrests, this administrative backlog could worsen.

Federalism

Mexico has yet to tap the potential dynamism that federalism offers in terms of innovation, reform, and decentralization. One strategy is to create federal grants that give states incentives to create mechanisms of accountability (such as external oversight), stronger internal affairs departments (which are often nonexistent or nonfunctional), and even experimental reforms (such as crime-mapping, women's police stations, or community policing). A second strategy to utilize federalism in the interest of professional policing is to mandate changes that simplify and streamline police work and information. All police departments might be required to adopt rather simple institutional procedures (such as weapons and evidence registries) and to use uniform crime reporting mechanisms that would make it possible to study crime trends and the effects of state and local police activities. Finally, federalism works best when the central entity disseminates results of research widely—to states, localities, and civil society—so that reforms and successes not only percolate up, but also diffuse throughout the country.

Mexico's main institutional mechanisms in achieving these tasks include INACIPE (*Instituto Nacional de Ciencias Penales*). INACIPE, however, lacks the ability to support local experimentation and study. Furthermore, there are no public entities that are autonomous or external to the police that can audit police performance, investigate misconduct, or impose accountability. Given Mexico's political situation, this movement might have to begin at the federal level.

Paths to Democratic Policing

President Fox presented a coordinated justice and security sector reform proposal on March 29, 2004 (*Iniciativa de Reforma de Seguridad Pública y Justicia Penal*). Though it could not have changed things overnight, citizens were not assuaged. In June 2004, millions of Mexicans marched on the capital wearing white and demanding more security. The president met with many of the groups' leaders on July 1, 2004. In early 2005, President Fox began to revamp the federal public security institutions yet again in response to a rising tide of kidnappings, a massacre in Cancún, and the murders of police officers and prison officials by narco-traffickers. So questions remain as to whether or not Mexico is on the path to democratic policing and what path that would be.

To begin, we should consider what is meant by "democratic policing." Defining democratic policing is a research topic unto itself, but the core idea is a set of public security institutions that increase accountability to the public and a set of police practices that require police to strive to be impartial and rights-respecting.[9] De Mesquita Neto has posited that there are at least five different paths to democratic policing, but none is exhaustive, and they are not mutually exclusive, and therefore they should "open and not conclude a debate" (de Mesquita Neto, 2001, p. 2). Because two of these paths—civil war and foreign invasion—can be safely ruled out for Mexico, only three paths to democratic policing are likely in Mexico's situation: reform led by the government, reform led by civil society, or reform caused by political agreement.

Reform led by government happens when external events and pressure lead political actors within the government to perceive a "significant increase in crime and disorder in the society and/or a significant increase in police corruption and violence" and "initiate a process of police reform" (de Mesquita Neto, 2001, p. 7). Civil society may influence the reform process along this path, but government officials are much more capable of directing and co-opting the process once they initiate it.[10] The overriding influence of elected officials can have a downside, because they often have a shorter horizon for reforms. Elected officials want credit for effective crime control, and they make additional calculations about the police forces they are trying to reform and the institutional structure of government itself. For example, Mexico City's leftist mayor seemed to have embraced "tough on crime" measures, partly because he reasoned he could have an immediate impact on police activity but little impact on the character of police institutions themselves.[11]

The second path is largely hypothetical: An increase in crime and disorder sparks protests and pressures from civil society, which then leads the reform movement. Though police violence and corruption top the agenda, Mexico does not meet all of the criteria of the second path, because one could not say that "civil society is strong and the government is weak" (de Mesquita Neto, 2001, p. 11).

The third path is reform initiated by political agreement, and it might be Mexico's best chance. In this scenario, crime, disorder, and/or police violence and corruption again motivate actors, but in this case government *and* civil society become the actors who have an agreed interest to advance a program of police reform. In such cases, "The nature of police reform depends largely on the strength of the government and the civil society, the position of the police . . . and the degree of public concern" (de Mesquita Neto, 2001, p. 13). Such reform also depends on networks of policy experts to provide some of the ideas that become policy innovations, a governing structure that does not enable hard-line groups to block reform, and an institutional structure of the police that is amenable to change.

In sum, it seems that a system of democratic policing in Mexico achieved by motivated elected officials (the first path) may end up being short-sighted and prone to failure. If reform were achieved through explicit collaboration and partnership between civil society and the government (the second path), it would be more durable and significant. Given that, at least four factors affect how government and civil society respond to the political and institutional environment of public security: crime, organized crime, private security, and civil society.

Common Crime

Crime rates and the perception of public insecurity grew substantially in the 1990s and the first half of this decade. Three major cities, Mexico City, Tijuana, and Ciudad Juarez, stood out with high rates. Kidnapping has gained the most media attention, but the most common crime is theft (*robo*), and it has increased the most since 1993; theft represents nearly 50 percent of reported crimes. Homicide rates also increased in Mexico, though not as severely as in other parts of Latin America. Based on victimization studies, it is clear that crime reporting is low. Surveys reveal that the main reason is lack of confidence in the police. According to official data (*Instituto Nacional de Estadistica, Geografia e Informatica*—INEGI), in 2001 there were 24,742 sentenced criminals and 28,619 people charged (*delincuentes presuntos*) in the federal jurisdiction (*fuero federal*) and 123,071 sentenced criminals and 163,995 people charged in local crimes. Thus, Mexico had a conviction rate of one person for every 10 crimes reported (from a total of about 150,000 convictions for over 1.5 million reported crimes, each of which may involve multiple people) in 2001. As crimes become more personally invasive and the mismatch between victimization and crime reporting continues, one can assume that the public is getting increasingly frustrated and desperate. Hard-line *mano dura* candidates, who neglect civil society, do well in such an environment. Civil society may have to rally the public to earn a place at the reform table.

Organized Crime and Challenges to the State

Another set of forces can bankrupt and sideline civil society, at the same time making the state respond more militantly. Such forces are evident in the growth "in drug trafficking and organized crime, the emergence of armed groups such as the Ejército Zapatista de Liberación Nacional (EZLN, the Zapatista National Liberation Army) and the Ejército Popular Revolucionario (EPR, the People's Revolutionary Army)" which is related to "the increase in public insecurity, and the great crisis in the country's judicial institutions" (Benitez Manaut, 2000, p. 127). Formerly in Mexico, the old National Security Police and the office of the attorney general served as structural intermediaries between traffickers and those in political power (Astorga, 2000, p. 61). When the old power structure began to deteriorate in the 1980s and throughout the 1990s, the political opposition gained ground; thus traffickers showed more autonomy. "Recent changes in the correlation of forces in Mexico have created a context in which democratic forces have not been able to consolidate or to impose the rule of law over the working agreements among power groups, including both established and new bands of traffickers, that do not respect democratic civility" (Astorga, p. 81).

Organized crime is considered a major security threat, because it exacerbates corruption, enables drug trafficking, and brings increasing amounts of violence and high-powered weaponry to Mexico. Criminal organizations began to restructure themselves in 2003, which led to open warfare in some parts of the country. These drug-trafficking gangs are competing to control the *plazas*, which are used as drug corridors into the United States. Seventy-four deaths among rival drug traffickers were registered in the first three months of 2004, with Sinaloa registering the highest number.[12] Though the death tolls and public disturbance are a security problem, should these fragmented drug cartels reunify, the crime problem may worsen.

Popular insurgency can also be considered an internal security threat for the state, though this threat has somewhat subsided since its peak in 2004. In January of that year, the EZLN announced its southern insurgency in an uprising in Chiapas meant to coincide with the implementation of the North American Free Trade Agreement. Though the threat to the state has subsided, reported human rights abuses, assassinations, political turbulence, and concerns about internal security have continued. In addition, other guerilla groups appeared in the south, such as the Insurgent People's Army (ERPI) and the more lethal EPR, which have inflicted casualties on police and army personnel in Guerrero and Oaxaca among several other states. President Fox stated in April 2001 that the guerrilla movements were finished, a claim that rang hollow when, four months later, another armed group called the FARP (*Fuerzas Armadas Revolucionarias del Pueblo*) set off bombs in three Banamex offices in Mexico City to protest its sale to U.S. corporate giant Citicorp. These popular insurgencies and globalization protests, like endemic corruption and the fight against drug trafficking, have led (and threaten to lead) to increased involvement of the military in police work and order maintenance, which troubles many.

Private Security

Mexican security companies have grown significantly in recent years in response to the state's failure to provide security, and this growth further erodes that capacity of the state. Mexico holds third place in the purchase of security equipment worldwide. Between 1998 and 1999, the number of private security companies in Mexico increased some 40 percent. The Mexican government has had serious problems in regulating these companies, most of which are illegitimate, because they lack the necessary legal permits. At least 10,000 private security firms operate in Mexico, yet only 2,000 had some form of official permit in 1999. According to official figures, in December 2000 there were 2,984 private security companies registered with 153,885 employees. The inability to regulate or control these forces creates potential security problems. Because many of these companies are unregulated, some will engage in criminality instead of (or as a means of) protecting their clients, thus exacerbating the problem of insecurity. According to a study by the Mexico City legislative assembly, in 1998 there were more private security guards than police. A substantial number of private security guards were formerly police officers or presently work as security guards while off duty as police officers; these dynamics increase the likelihood of police corruption.

Civil Society

Mexican civil society is becoming involved in public security matters. They have been involved in the creation and management of the *Comisiónes de Derechos Humanos* (Human Rights Commissions or CDHs) as a result of national legislation. Several state-level commissions have been created, but they lack extensive grassroots networks, broad civil society cooperation, and common methods of data collection. Long-term success depends on developing such networks, improving civil society, and allowing organs such as the CDHs to wield more power.

Policing strategies have not yet helped Mexican civil society deal with its deeply embedded crime and corruption problems. Two factors, social stratification and selective policing, everywhere serve to isolate a crime problem for a time, but often later these problems become more intense and spill over into protected areas, creating "national security problems." When national security is invoked as a response to transnational drug trafficking or gangs, all reform bets are off. Police responding to crime as a national security problem may invoke strategies that have actually been linked to "increases in urban gang violence, organized crime, and attacks in wealthy areas," not to mention the curtailing of civil rights (Ungar, 2002, p. 79). Social stratification is also a problem, because it serves as a hothouse for more resilient criminal networks and more violent policing strategies. Enclosed and violent neighborhoods can in turn increase fear and social isolation, limit movement, and curtail the openness of public space, all of which reinforces social stratification and limits the reach of civil society.

Conclusion

The relationship of policing to democracy is manifold in Mexico. As the front end of any judicial system, the police must function effectively and fairly for the legal system to do the same. Mexico's legal system is increasingly important as the country strives to rein in public corruption and grow its legitimate economic sector. Furthermore, Mexico needs accountable and rights-respecting public security forces as the backbone of democracy. Without these protections, Mexico could degrade into a bland, procedural democracy, where elections occur but active participation, due process, and civil rights are not a lived reality for most citizens. Last, where public security forces are incompetent or corrupt, citizens lose faith in public institutions and invest in private security, which sets off a cycle that further erodes the egalitarian nature of citizenship.

Besides the danger of democratic backsliding, there is an upside to consider that makes it possible to frame the challenge in a more positive way: Fair and efficient police earn the confidence of the public and thus serve to bolster the public nature of security, expand citizenship, create responsive public institutions, and legitimize democracy. Because their reach and numbers are so vast, the police institutions of Mexico have the potential to improve the substantive quality of democracy for Mexican citizens if they embrace principles of transparency, efficiency, and democratic policing. The path to doing so may have to be blazed by public officials and government bureaucrats who find a common interest in making the Mexican police fairer and more effective.

Glossary

Attorney General's Office	*Procuraduría General de la República* (PGR)
Attorney General's Office of the Federal District	*Procuraduría General de Justicia del Distrito Federal* (PGJ-DF)
Center for Research and National Security	*Centro de Investigación y Seguridad Nacional* (CISEN)
Experts, technical experts, or specialists	*peritos*
Federal Agency of Investigation	*Agencia Federal de Investigaciones* (AFI)
Federal District	*Distrito Federal* (DF)
Federal Judicial Police	*Policía Judicial Federal* (PJF)
Federal law	*fuero federal*
Federal Preventive Police	*Policía Federal Preventiva* (PFP)
Interior Secretariat	*Secretaría de Gobernación*
Judicial Police of the Federal District	*Policía Judicial del Distrito Federal* (PJDF)
Local law	*fuero común*
Office of the Special Prosecutor for Crimes against Health	*Fiscalía Especializada de Delitos Contra la Salud* (FEADS)
Public Secretariat	*Ministerio Público*
Secretary of Public Security of the D.F.	*Secretaría de Seguridad Pública* (SSP)

Notes

1. A brief tracing of this intellectual development can be seen in the following works: Berins Collier, 1999; Linz and Stepan, 1996; and O'Donnell, Schmitter, and Whitehead, 1986. See also the edited volume that revisited Rustow's 1970 *Comparative Politics* article, "Transitions to Democracy" of eponymous title (Anderson, 1999).

2. These estimates amount to a ratio of about 2.6 police officers per 100 citizens, assuming a population of 104 million and a police population of 400,000. Estimates of the actual number of police came from privately accessed pages from Jane's Information Group (http://www.janes.com) retrieved on October 30, 2004, the CIA fact book (CIA, n.d.), news reports following Fox's announcement of the proposal to reform the justice system (March 29, 2004), Vargas (2003), and data gathered from Mexican government Web sites (see suggested readings).

3. The PFP was created on December 13, 1998; for all intents and purposes, it did not come into existence until 1999.

4. This observation, like many others throughout, is owed to Ernesto López Portillo Vargas (2003).

5. Information can be found at the annual Global Corruption Reports at http://www.transparency.org

6. Police departments are not the only area of the criminal justice system where corruption is found. A recent UN Human Rights Commission special report on the independence of judges and lawyers warned that Mexico's justice system suffered widespread corruption. Based on testimonies, it estimated that 50 to 70 percent of federal judges were involved in acts of corruption and said that in some states, civil matters were not processed without the payment of a bribe.

7. A fascinating response to this reality was the mayor of Ecatepec's decision to abolish all parking and traffic violations so that police officers would have to stop shaking down citizens for bribes (Sullivan, 2003).

8. Since much of this corruption occurs in Mexico City, this practice raises the question of if and how the "zero tolerance" recommendations of the Giuliani consulting group will be effected. If mordidas function to exchange small bribes for not processing civilians through the criminal justice system, and if "broken windows" approaches to policing call for prosecuting minor crimes to prevent more serious ones, there is a necessary conflict.

9. De Mesquita Neto calls it "a form of policing in which the police are accountable to the law and the community, respect the rights and guarantee the security of all citizens in a non-discriminatory manner" (2001, p. 2). David Bayley identifies two main features: *accountability* and *responsiveness* (1997). Otwin Marenin focuses on six principles, two of the most important of which are *accessibility* and *accountability* (for citations and further explanation, see Stone and Ward, 2000). For their part, Stone and Ward concur and add that *accountability* to multiple structures at multiple levels is what makes policing democratic. Also see Charles Call's analysis of the creation of an international "norm" for democratic policing (Call, 2000).

10. Colombia, Chile, and Peru may serve as recent examples.

11. The argument to be made in more detail is that even when reform-minded officials face police institutions whose norms and ethos are notoriously hard to change, they will often adopt zero tolerance policies as a way of reducing crime, because reforming the institutions themselves seems more difficult. The *mano dura*

or *tolerancia cero* policing approaches of Carlos Ruckauf in Buenos Aires and Luis Fleury in Sao Paulo are examples.

12. These figures came from privately accessed pages from Jane's Information Group (http://www.janes.com).

References

Anderson, L. (1999). *Transitions to democracy*. New York: Columbia University Press.

Astorga, L. (2000). Organized crime and organization of crime. In J. Bailey & R. Godson (Eds.), *Organized crime and democratic governability: Mexico and the U.S.–Mexico borderlands* (pp. 58–82). Pittsburgh, PA: University of Pittsburgh Press.

Bailey, J., & Godson, R. (Eds.). (2000). *Organized crime and democratic governability: Mexico and the U.S.–Mexico borderlands*. Pittsburgh, PA: University of Pittsburgh Press.

Benitez Manaut, R. (2000). Containing armed groups, drug trafficking, and organized crime in Mexico: The role of the military. In J. Bailey & R. Godson (Eds.), *Organized crime and democratic governability: Mexico and the U.S.–Mexico borderlands* (pp. 126–158). Pittsburgh, PA: University of Pittsburgh Press.

Berins Collier, R. (1999). *Paths toward democracy: The working class and elites in Western Europe and South America*. New York: Cambridge University Press.

Call, C. (2000, March). *Pinball and punctuated equilibrium: The birth of a "democratic policing" norm?* Paper presented at the annual conference of the International Studies Association, Los Angeles, California.

Central Intelligence Agency (CIA). (n.d.). Mexico. In *CIA—The World Factbook*. Retrieved August 1, 2007, from https://www.cia.gov/library/publications/the-world-factbook/geos/mx.html

Cornelius, W., & Shirk, D. (Eds.). (2007). *Reforming the administration of justice in Mexico*. La Jolla, CA, and Chicago: Center for U.S.-Mexican Studies and University of Notre Dame Press.

Linz, J., & Stepan, A. (1996). *Problems of democratic transition and consolidation: Southern Europe, South America, and post-communist Europe*. Baltimore: Johns Hopkins University Press.

de Mesquita Neto, P. (2001, March). *Paths toward democratic policing in Latin America*. Paper presented at the International Workshop on Human Rights and the Police in Transitional Countries, Copenhagen, Denmark.

O'Donnell, G., Schmitter, P. C., & Whitehead, L. (Eds.). (1986). *Transitions from authoritarian rule: Comparative perspectives*. Baltimore: Johns Hopkins University Press.

Stone, C. E., & Ward, H. (2000). Democratic policing: A framework for action. *Policing and Society, 10*(1), 11–47.

Sullivan, K. (2003, September 8). Mexican town forgoes law for order. *Washington Post*, p. A15.

Ungar, M. (2002). *Elusive reform: Democracy and the rule of law in Latin America*. Boulder, CO: Lynne Rienner.

Interview

Vargas, E. L. P. (2003, May). Interview at the Instituto Nacional de Ciencias Penales, Mexico City.

Further Reading

Alvarado, A., & Arzt, S. (Ed.). (2001). *El desfío democrático de México: seguridady Estado de derecho*. México City: El Colegio de México, Centro de Estudios.

Attorney General's Office (Procuraduría General de la República—PGR). Retrieved August 1, 2007, from http://www.pgr.gob.mx

Bailey, J. & Chabat, J. (Ed.). (2002). *Transnational crime and public security*. San Diego, CA: Center for U.S.–Mexican Studies at the University of California San Diego.

Country briefing (n.d.). *The Economist* [Electronic version]. Retrieved August 1, 2007 from http://www.economist.com/countries/Mexico

Lawyers Committee for Human Rights and Centro de Derechos Humanos Miguel Agustín Pro Juárez. (2001). *Injusticia legalizada*. New York: Author.

Quezada, S. A. (Ed.). (2000). *El almanaque mexicano*. México City: Editorial Grijalbo.

Secretary of Public Security of the D. F. (*Secretaría de Seguridad Pública*—SSP). (n.d.). Pagina principal de la SSP. Retrieved August 1, 2007 from http://www.ssp.df.gob.mx

Smith, J. J. (1992). *Modernizing Mexican politics* (2nd ed.) New York: ISHI Press.

Valenzuela, J. (1992). Democratic consolidation in post-transitional settings: Notion, process, and facilitating conditions. In S. Mainwaring, G. O'Donnell, & J. Valenzuela (Eds.), *Issues in democratic consolidation: The new South American democracies in comparative perspective* (pp. 57–104). Notre Dame, IN: University of Notre Dame Press.

Vargas, E. L. P. (2002). The police in Mexico: Political functions and needed reforms. In J. Bailey & J. Chabat (Eds.), *Transnational crime and public security: Challenges to Mexico and the United States* (pp. 109–135). San Diego, CA: Center for U.S.-Mexican Studies at the University of California San Diego.

5

Postconflict Democratization of the Police

The Sierra Leone Experience

Stuart Cullen and William H. McDonald

Democracies are political systems characterized by popular participation, genuine competition for executive and legislative office, fostering of fundamental human rights, and institutional checks on power. While the actual democratic structure of government may vary, these fundamental concepts remain constant (Siegel, Weinstein, & Halperin, 2004).

The key to the level of developmental and economic success of the Western nations is their adoption of democracy. Within such nations, the police operate under internationally recognized democratic principles to ensure a harmonious society in which political, social, and economic life can flourish (Crawshaw, Cullen, & Williams, 2006).

Democratic civilian policing is an essential component of good governance operating under a range of basic principles. In ensuring that a police organization is civilian rather than military, there must be separate government ministers having control and oversight over the police and military. Similarly, the commander or chief of police and senior police posts should not hold military rank or be associated with the national armed forces. Whereas the military have a primary role in securing the state from external threat, the police should have a primary and accountable role in citizen security and serving the law. Extraordinary circumstances may demand military personnel having to assist the police in joint public safety operations (for example, in protecting the citizenry from terrorists or armed bandits). In these circumstances, it is essential for the police to have primacy in command and control of operations. Legislation or the constitution should prevent the police from being controlled by political parties or the military (Crawshaw et al., 2006).

The police should be accountable to government, for example, through a minister of citizen security or home or internal affairs, and to the citizens through community consultative groups representing all sections of society. The police should be able to respond to community needs and expectations. This can be facilitated by the organization of an independent civilian review board or commission comprising cross-party political appointees and other nonpartisan members. Their role is to oversee and monitor policing functions and senior police appointments and to ensure that matters of public concern are addressed (Crawshaw et al., 2006).

Democratic police organizations function within and are accountable to the rule of law. Their members have a duty to protect human rights. National legislation defines their authority and responsibility, rules of conduct for officers and officials, standards for the legitimate use of force, and similar practices. Torture and extra-judicial tactics are prohibited. Formal mechanisms should exist to investigate allegations of police misconduct and where necessary, to enforce the law (Code of Conduct for Law Enforcement Officers, 1979).

Unfortunately, democracy is a complicated and often elusive phenomenon. The establishment of democracy in postcolonial nations around the world, particularly Africa, has not ensured political, social, or economic development. In many African states, democracy has evaporated or been crushed in the path of intractable and destructive conflicts based on tribalism, race, religious and identity issues, corruption, wealth, and land issues. The sheer impoverishment and ruinous situation of much of Africa, never starker or more revealing, testifies to that reality.

The misappropriation of state and public assets and finances by the ruling or dominant elites have turned many of these democracies into "kleptocracies." The effects of the unattended HIV/AIDS pandemic throughout the continent have further added to political and economic disaster and the decline of civil society. And as citizens react, the unrepresentative and often unelected corrupt ruling cliques characteristically deploy the military and police against ordinary citizens. The resulting spiral of violence frequently leads to civil war.

Background

The political, social, and economic decline of the Republic of Sierra Leone from its independence in 1961 through its 1991 civil war provides a case study at its most brutal and raw. It is a classic example of the importance of the police to democracy. More important, it demonstrates the effects and consequences of the political transformation of a democratic police organization into a repressive and corrupt arm of a despotic government.

The Republic of Sierra Leone occupies 71,740 square kilometers on the west coast of Africa and has an estimated population of 6,017,643 (July 2005 estimate). It remains one of the world's poorest and least developed countries despite vast deposits of diamonds and other natural resources (CIA, n.d.).

Sierra Leone gained independence in 1961 following 150 years as a British protectorate. The nation was established as a constitutional democracy and a member of the British Commonwealth. The legal system and laws of Sierra Leone were based on those of England and Wales and customary tribal practices. The first general election under universal adult franchise took place in May 1962 (Cullen & McDonald, 2005).

The first police force in Sierra Leone, the paramilitary West African Frontier Force, was created in 1900 from the Royal Sierra Leone Regiment and commanded by the British officer corps. Its primary purpose was to protect British colonial interests (Lord, 2005). The Police Act of 1964, part of the national Constitution, established the Sierra Leone Police (SLP) as a national, armed, civil force. The Constitution separated the police from the military and charged them with specific responsibility for citizen security, the prevention of crime, and the detection, apprehension, and prosecution of offenders. The force generally follows the British police model in organization and rank structure (Cullen & McDonald, 2005).

During the five years following independence, the country possessed some critical structural features necessary for the development of a modern democratic state, including an educational system based on the British model, a modern economy, a multiparty political system, a professional civil service, and a Western style constitution. A modern military, police, and judiciary served society with a degree of professionalism and integrity. Despite positive beginnings, Sierra Leone quickly fell into ruinous decline brought about by endemic corruption (Thompson & Potter, 1997).

Political Decline, Corruption, and the Police

In a 1967, a coup d'etat brought Siaka Stevens and his All Peoples' Party (known by its acronym APC in the local language) to power. They quickly moved the nation from a multiparty constitutional democracy to a single-party executive presidency. With them came excesses of systematic corruption in the national government, particularly the police, and in every aspect of daily life (Thompson & Potter, 1997).

Like many African nations, Sierra Leone always experienced some level of government corruption as a by-product of modernization. Under Stevens and the APC, the extent of corruption grew to such proportions that the distinctions between the personal lives and the public roles of government officials and between personal and public finances blurred at every level of the administration (Thompson & Potter, 1997). They openly condoned and encouraged the looting of government funds at levels rarely seen. The adage, "A cow will graze on the land allotted to it for that purpose," often alluded to by Stevens himself, became their operative norm (Thompson &

Potter, 1997, p. 150). Few nations have experienced such a pattern of government corruption (Kpundeh, 1993). Eventually, that culture of corruption allowed economic domination of the entire country by members of the power elite. The entire government structure became a mechanism for profit and personal gain (Kpundeh, 1995).

Once in power, the APC quickly changed the civilian nature of the police and moved to exert complete control over their activities. That control became a critical element in their consolidation of power and the exploitation of society. The inspector general of police and the head of army were made part of the ruling cabinet, and the cabinet operated almost solely for the benefit of the dominant (though not majority) Limba tribe and its allies. Its policy was to divide and rule the nation for the personal gain of its members, and that was only possible through the neutralization of the police (Lengor, interview, April 14/15, 2005).

APC political appointees infiltrated the administrative machinery of the police force and brought with them the widespread corrupt practices of the ruling political party. The police leadership was purged of non-APC personnel (Lord, 2005). Transfers, promotions, and recruitment became APC economic and political opportunities. Promotion depended entirely upon APC membership, political loyalty, and bribes (Lengor, interview, April 14/15, 2005). Political favoritism allowed the recruitment of uneducated and illiterate APC supporters into the police ranks. Officers who failed to support these practices were quickly transferred to undesirable postings or dismissed on trumped up charges (Meek, 2003).

The ruling party soon controlled every aspect of SLP operations, and the police quickly became political agents of the APC (Lengor, interview, April 14/15, 2005). During the 1982 national election, for example, the APC used the police against its political opposition, the Sierra Leone Peoples Party, in a violent conflict known as the Bush Devil War. Its members were licensed to abuse their powers to protect and profit the ruling elite and to seize every opportunity for personal gain through bribes and criminal activity (Lord, 2005). Equally important, any resistance to APC authority from within the police service itself had been neutralized (Thompson, 1996).

Members of the SLP engaged in general policing duties directed by the APC through senior police officers, protected monopolies, collected bribes from sympathetic corrupt businesses, and harassed both the political and financial rivals of the APC. Targeted business people were arrested on fabricated charges, then convicted, imprisoned, or executed and put out of business. "Connected" competitors easily acquired the assets of these closed businesses at ridiculous prices (Lengor, interview, April 14/15, 2005).

Police agents provocateurs were employed to encourage and then reveal "crimes," either real or fictitious, allegedly committed by prominent citizens or political opponents. The accused were then publicly prosecuted, or in lieu of prosecution coerced into state-sponsored delinquency. SLP Special Branch officers, posing as bona fide university and college students, spied on students and professors, reporting back to a paranoid regime that feared subversion from its youth (Lengor, interview, April 14/15, 2005).

In the end, the SLP had been totally politicized. Opposition to the state-sponsored economic corruption that might normally arise from the police had been neutralized. The SLP role in the political, economic, and social fabric of the state had changed. The responsibility for citizen security and the protection of democracy had been replaced by the responsibility to manage and safeguard a national protection racket for the benefit of the ruling clique (Lengor, interview, April 14/15, 2005).

Corruption and an accompanying general systematic neglect of police services by the national government led to the decline of their constitutional role in society. Skills necessary for effective policing were not sought. Officers were untrained and lacked uniforms and even basic equipment. These problems were exacerbated by low wages, illiteracy, the lack of professional standards and ethics, and extremely poor morale. This situation quickly led to a breakdown in the quality of police service, and more important, a breakdown in public confidence in the police (Groenwald & Peak, 2004; Malan, Rakafe, & McIntyre, 2003; Meek, 2003). Restoration of that public trust became one of the critical elements for restoring the police and the society (Groenwald & Peak, 2004).

Widespread societal and political instability followed. By 1991 the country was economically and politically near collapse. Opposition to the APC from the political opponents and the disenfranchised business community reached explosive levels. What followed was one of the most violent and horrific internal conflicts in the history of Africa.

The Civil War

In 1991 a Liberian civil war spread northward into Sierra Leone. Foday Sankoh's Sierra Leone Revolutionary United Front joined with Charles Taylor's National Patriotic Front of Liberia (NPF) to overthrow the government and seize the country's diamond mines. Millions of dollars' worth of diamonds smuggled out of the country financed the rebellion (Lord, 2005). At the same time local militias and delinquent youth gangs such as the West Side Boys, fuelled by the influx of drugs, especially heroin, took control of large sections of the country, adding to the chaos (M. Lengor, interviews, April 14/15, 2005). At the height of the conflict, experts estimate more than 48,000 armed combatants, representing a variety of political and criminal organizations, participated in the civil war (Meek, 2003).

Atrocities committed by all parties to the conflict, but especially by rebel forces, terrorized the population (CIA, n.d.). The limbs of innocent citizens, police officers, and political opponents were systematically amputated. Captives were forced to murder and mutilate their own local political leaders, family members, and tribal officials. Enslavement, forced conscription of child soldiers, and systematic gang rapes of women and children plagued the nation. The Sierra Leone military and SLP proved powerless and lost control of large areas of the country to the various rebellious forces, violent gangs, and criminal thugs. Eventually, elements of the military rebelled, contributing to further chaos and disorder (Lord, 2005).

The Sierra Leone Police and
Restoration of Democratic Rule

In March 1996, after considerable international pressure and military support, and despite continuing violence, free elections established a fledging democratic government under President Ahmed Tejan Kabbah (Lord, 2005). Kabbah's role in the reconstruction of Sierra Leone, and particularly in the rebuilding of the SLP in that process, has proven critical to the nation's reconstruction.

Educated at a private school in Sierra Leone, Kabbah earned his bachelor's and law degrees in Britain. His entire career had been in the public sector. He served as district commissioner in all the regions of Sierra Leone and as deputy chief of the West African Division of the United Nations Development Program in New York. During the 1970s he coordinated United Nations assistance to liberation movements that needed to be assimilated into legitimate governments following the cessation of conflicts in South Africa and Namibia. That experience convinced him of the critical importance a reorganized and democratic SLP would play in the restoration of social order and democracy ("State House," 2005).

Recent international experience in postconflict resolution efforts supported his position. Most experts agreed that, absent restoration and maintenance of the rule of law, all other investments in the peace process would prove meaningless (Malan et al., 2002).

Shortly after assuming office, Kabbah petitioned the government of the United Kingdom for assistance in the restructuring and development of the Sierra Leone Police. The United Kingdom authorized a preliminary project in 1997, but continuing internal conflict forced its early cancellation. A second program, the Commonwealth Police Development Task Force became operational in 1998. Led by a career British detective and former assistant chief constable, Keith Biddle, the task force included a small number of former United Kingdom police officers and police advisers from Canada, Malaysia, Sri Lanka, and Zimbabwe. All had considerable experience in command roles and a wide range of policing skills. Their charge included technical and financial assistance to support community safety through logistical support, the provision of professional expertise, and the delivery of wide-ranging training programs (Biddle, interview, April 13, 2005).

The selection of Biddle to command the project proved instrumental to its success. During his 32 years of service, he had served in a wide variety of ranks and assignments. He had a well-deserved reputation as a direct, tough, no-nonsense police officer with proven qualities of leadership and a sharp intellect (Malan et al., 2002; Meek, 2003).

The task force faced a ruined and demoralized SLP. More than 900 officers had been killed during the various internal conflicts. Many had been tortured, while others suffered amputation by the rebellious forces. Inept and corrupt personnel occupied leadership and other key positions. Much of the senior command staff and many of the middle-level officers were APC appointees. The force lacked even fundamental equipment and training. Most police facilities had been looted or destroyed during the conflict. Various warring factions and criminal elements had commandeered vehicles, communications systems, and weapons. Wages had not been paid in years (Biddle, interview, April 13, 2005; Malan et al., 2002).

Death, torture, and desertion had reduced the force from its prewar size of 9,300 officers to less than 6,600. And the task force faced a psychological crisis within the SLP. Years of war, corruption, and governmental neglect, the loss of public confidence, and the frequent abandonment of officers and police facilities to advancing rebel forces left the SLP a demoralized organization (Malan et al., 2002).

The SLP had little or no presence outside the capital. Remnants of the army and the quasi-official Civil Defence Force (CDF) maintained a semblance of aimless and undirected "security" around the country through a network of road checkpoints. The CDF was a ragtag collection of armed, ill-disciplined, and aggressive youths, often without uniform or identification, known locally as *Kamajors* (brave hunters). They came primarily from local armed militia groups that had earlier colluded with the army and loosely allied themselves with the government. Little more than armed thugs, they terrorized civilians; committed rapes, ritual murders and other violent crimes; and consistently interfered with the military, police, and peacekeeping operations. Their presence disrupted stability and citizen security (Hoffman, 2005).

The military was little better. Basically an armed mob, corrupt and with little organization or purpose, they continued to contribute to the national chaos and mayhem (Malan et al., 2002).

Amazingly, even though the SLP had virtually collapsed, Biddle found that many officers had served bravely under the most difficult of circumstances. Despite the destruction of most police facilities, many police officers still reported for duty and attempted to go through the motions of providing a police presence. Although it was at odds with the SLP's corrupt image and practices, there remained an underlying ethos of loyalty to the state, nation, and organization. As an institution, the SLP had not been involved in atrocities. Many officers had struggled to maintain constitutional order. The majority had remained loyal to the nation (K. Biddle, interviews, April 13, 2005). For example, in May of 1997 they had fought bravely to save the life of the newly elected President Kabbah by holding off attacking army elements bent on a coup (Malan et al., 2002).

The first priority of government and the international community was to restore law and order in a democratic model and to ensure that the SLP had primacy in all matters of citizen security. To do so, the new government had to aggressively address corruption within the force, restore police self-confidence, and most critical, to restore public confidence. That required an entire rebuilding of the SLP, a job made even more difficult by the continuation of the civil war in many parts of the country (Malan et al., 2002).

President Kabbah set the tone for the new SLP in August of 1997 in the official Government Policing Charter.

THE SIERRA LEONE POLICE

Government Policing Charter

Introduction

My Government wants to create a police service which will be a credit to the Nation.

The Role of the Police

The Sierra Leone Police will assist in returning our communities to peace and prosperity by acting in a manner which will:

- eventually remove the need for the deployment of military and para-military forces in our villages, communities and city streets
- ensure the safety and security of all people and their property
- respect the human rights of all individuals
- prevent and detect crime by using the most effective methods which can be made available to them
- take account of local concerns through community consultation
- at all levels be free from corruption

Equal Opportunities

The personnel policies of the Sierra Leone Police will be the same for all members, regardless of sex or ethnic origin. All recruitment, training, postings, promotions and opportunities for development will be based on a published equal opportunities policy.

The Role of My Government

The Government will do all in its power to ensure that the Sierra Leone Police is:

- directed and managed in accordance with The Constitution
- locally managed so as to ensure that community views are always taken into consideration

- adequately resourced and financed
- well equipped to undertake its duties
- professionally trained
- dynamically led and,
- that the terms and conditions of service for members of the Sierra Leone Police reflect the importance of the task they perform.

The Role of the People

In order that our police officers can successfully fulfill our expectations, it is essential that all people of Sierra Leone help and support them at all times.

Conclusion

Our aim is to see a reborn Sierra Leone Police, which will be a force for good in our Nation.

August 1998 His Excellency
The President Alhaji Dr Ahmed Tejan-Kabbah

SOURCE: *From Crisis to Confidence* (1998).

The charter called for a professional service-oriented police organization that would meet the needs and expectations of all citizens by working in partnership with the community. Moreover, it restored the civilian, democratic nature of the national police service. The SLP would become a "force for good"; this slogan became the unofficial motto of the new SLP.

From Crisis to Confidence

Biddle, his task force colleagues, and members of the SLP command staff quickly adopted the theme set by the president. Senior members of the SLP suspected of corruption or of political affiliations with prior regimes were retired or suspended (Malan et al., 2002). Biddle and his team summoned the remaining senior officers to a master planning session in December of 1998. The seminar, entitled "From Crisis to Confidence," was a historic turning point for the SLP and produced a strategic blueprint for it (Biddle, interview, April 13, 2005).

The working group began by identifying the key values and aims of the new police service. From that they formulated a mission statement based on the president's "force for good" concept.

A Force for Good

Our Duty

We will provide a professional and effective service which:

- Protects Life and Property
- Achieves a peaceful society
- Takes primacy in the maintenance of Law and Order

Our Values

We will respect Human Rights and the freedoms of the individual
We will be honest, impartial, caring and free from corruption

Our Priorities

We will respond to local needs
We will value our own people
We will involve all in developing our policing priorities

Our Aim

To win public confidence by offering reliable, caring and accountable police services

SOURCE: *From Crisis to Confidence* (1998).

The master plan identified a wide range of operational and organizational needs. These included human resources and welfare, organizational structure, training, policy making and support, planning, operational management, rules and regulations, ethical standards, recruiting, command and control, and roles and responsibilities. But their main energy focused on restoring the corroded public trust and confidence in the police as quickly as possible. The plan called for the immediate application of community policing principles to the particulars of Sierra Leone's recent history and complex social structure. Organizational changes in support of that objective would start with individual officers and units. The new SLP would then be built up from that foundation (Groenwald & Peak, 2003).

Local Needs Policing

In the months prior to the planning session, the SLP, under the guidance of the task force, had piloted a Sierra Leonean version of community policing in several urban districts and one rural community called local needs policing (LNP). LNP focused on local needs as defined by specific communities. Key issues included victim services, domestic violence, crime prevention, and the needs of those most victimized by the war, especially women and children (Groenwald & Peak, 2003).

These decentralized units delivered police services to meet the expectations of the local community. And with the absence of a meaningful national police service, they became, in effect, independent neighborhood based police forces, addressing immediate local needs in full view of and in close scrutiny by the community. The model allowed for flexibility, enabling local LNPs to develop in different ways to match the pluralist needs of different communities throughout Sierra Leone. Equally important, the model allowed for the restoration of the rule of law and of public confidence in the police at the very foundations of the society (Groenwald & Peak, 2003; Lengor, interview, April 13/14, 2005).

The pilot projects met with considerable success. The idea was adopted as the main mechanism for the restoration and rebuilding of the SLP. Local Needs Policing became the cornerstone of the force strategic plan. LNP would expand as elements of the countryside came under control of the national government. In support of that effort, and in face of the disastrous lack of training, the blueprint called for an aggressive Field Training Officers Program to provide relevant and effective training services (Biddle, interview, April 13, 2005).

Under the LNP initiative, SLP headquarters would continue to be responsible for the strategy and direction of the police force and for managing organizational needs, but police services were decentralized through the LNP units. Neighboring LNP units were clustered into Local Command Units (LCUs) under the direction of a police superintendent. Each LCU worked in collaboration with a Local Policing Partnership Board made up of citizens and local tribal leaders (Moigbe, interview, 2005). Superintendents' authority extended beyond the delivery of routine police services and included the management of local police resources and equipment, training and the development of personnel, job descriptions, and staff assessment (K. Biddle, personnel communication, April 13, 2005).

The LNP concept met another important need of the police force. Because the senior members of the SLP had formulated the program, its success promised to restore self-confidence within the force itself. It was, in effect, their property, their plan, the first organized effort to restore the force and its fundamental role in a democratic society. They had designed it and were accountable for its success or failure (Biddle, interview, April 13, 2005).

By 2002, policing primacy had been established throughout the whole of Sierra Leone. By April 2005, 27 LCUs provided local police services nationwide, each with its own Local Policing Partnership Board (Lengor, interview, 2005).

But a major problem presented itself in the early stages of the plan's implementation: the issue of force leadership. The incumbent acting head of the police, the inspector general of police (IGP), and other senior officers eligible for the position faced both political and practical problems. Politicians and local community leaders threatened to derail the appointment of anyone other than their own political or tribal allies. Considerable infighting between senior police officers over control of the force made matters worse and threatened the potential effectiveness of the reorganization effort (Biddle, interview, April 13, 2005).

President Kabbah addressed the issue immediately. He approached the government of the United Kingdom and asked that Biddle be appointed to head the SLP. The appointment of an outsider had advantages. The candidate would be seen as unsullied by state and institutional corruption and neutral in matters of tribal and kinship allegiances. International donors were more likely to support the nation-building process if the IGP had no connection with previous allegations of corruption or human rights abuses. With permission of the United Kingdom and after approval by the Sierra Leone Parliament, President Kabbah swore Biddle in as inspector general of police on December 1, 1999 (Biddle, interview, April 13, 2005).

Biddle immediately became a member of the Police Council, a statutory body made up of the inspector general of police, the deputy inspector general, the vice president of the republic, the minister of internal affairs, a representative of the Civil Service Commission, a representative of the bar association, and two eminent citizens appointed by the president. The council advised the president on all major matters of policy relating to internal security, including the role of the police, budgeting and finance, administration, and any other matter as dictated by the president (Biddle, interview, April 13, 2005).

United Nations Assistance

At about the time of Biddle's appointment, the promise of United Nations assistance to the SLP arrived. The United Nations Observer Mission in Sierra Leone (UNAMSIL) was to maintain peace and restore a trained, legitimate military and citizen security. Based on the experience of more than 20 such postconflict missions in recent years, the United Nations understood the critical importance of establishing a civilian democratic police service. The UNAMSIL civilian police element, the Commissioner of Civilian Police (CIVPOL), was charged with improving the professional standards of the SLP.

By the year 2004, 9,400 UNAMSIL troops and 119 international civilian police (CIVPOL) were deployed throughout the country; that force was scheduled to be downsized to 3,300 by June of 2005 (Refugees International, 2004). Unfortunately, the initial relationship between the Commonwealth task force and the CIVPOL was somewhat confused and at times difficult (Malan et al., 2002).

A number of problems hampered the relationship. The initial CIVPOL deployment took place 15 months after the British task force was formed and became fully operational only in 2000. By the time CIVPOL arrived, the British contingent had been deeply involved with the SLP for almost three years. A strategic reorganization plan had already been prepared and initiated. At times, however, CIVPOL appeared to ignore or disregard the work that had been done (Biddle, interview, April 13, 2005).

CIVPOL, for example, reported a need for community policing while overlooking the fact that the inspector general and his senior staff had already initiated a progressive model of community policing through the Local Needs Policing program that met the needs and expectations of the communities of Sierra Leone. A community policing command staff had been appointed, and Local Policing Partnership Boards established. And an aggressive Field Training Officers Program in support of the community policing initiative was under way (Biddle, interview, April 13, 2005; Malan et al., 2002). In another incident, CIVPOL's complaints about the British lack of cooperation in providing them accommodations in a rural war-torn district simply failed to recognize that neither the government nor the SLP had the necessary resources to do so (Malan et al., 2002).

CIVPOL demands that the SLP conform to "international best practice" based on the experience of other similar missions around the world, particularly those in the Balkans, complicated matters further. The Balkan experiences were considerably different from those of Sierra Leone (Malan et al., 2002). CIVPOL appeared to have little appreciation that different nations emerging from conflict require different solutions, solutions specific to their circumstances. "Off the shelf" programs were not always appropriate or welcomed by the SLP. Sierra Leone had its own unique history, and the SLP required unique solutions (Biddle, interview, April 13, 2005).

Bureaucratic reporting procedures and CIVPOL accountability to United Nations headquarters in New York made efficient decision making difficult and constrained the provision of promised United Nations funds. Changing and emerging international priorities, especially in the form of international humanitarian disasters, diverted funds initially committed to the SLP, thereby damaging CIVPOL credibility (Biddle, interview, April 13, 2005).

The CIVPOL personnel selection process, directed from United Nations headquarters, caused further difficulties. A number of totally inappropriate officers had been assigned to the project. Many were inexperienced, with less operational practice or knowledge than their SLP counterparts. One had served only 18 months in his home force (Malan et al., 2002). Some came from nations with authoritarian regimes and had little experience of civilian, service oriented policing, modern policing styles and methods, or concepts of institutional reform within the democratic process, while others had gained experience only in countries with questionable human rights records and endemic corruption within government and society (Biddle, interview, April 13, 2005). Many spoke no English and were unable to communicate directly with the English-speaking SLP (Malan et al., 2002).

In time, however, CIVPOL made important contributions to the democratization and rebuilding of the SLP. Among their accomplishments, they played a key role in the reestablishment of the Police Training School, provided a variety of specialized training programs, developed a force evaluation program, conducted important needs studies, designed a human rights manual for SLP officers assigned to election duties and Human Rights issues, provided badly need equipment, and built several new police stations (K. Biddle, interviews, April 13, 2005; Malan et al., 2002).

Combating Corruption

Over the next few years, the SLP and the national government, with the assistance of its international partners, initiated a wide range of programs and changes to move the force and the nation closer to their democratic goals. Donor funding enabled the purchase of equipment, vehicles, training, and a modern radio communications system as well as the building of new police stations and the important refurbishment of the Police Training School (Malan et al., 2002).

The problem of corruption, especially in the midlevel ranks, continues to threaten progress (Malan et al., 2002). To facilitate more rapid and expeditious removal of corrupt officers from the organization, SLP administrative policies have been reformed. Existing practices allowed such officers to remain in the police services until the outcome of the criminal prosecution against them was determined. The new regulations require the SLP to dismiss officers charged with a criminal offense under administrative disciplinary procedures regardless of the outcome of the criminal case. At the same time, effective mechanisms have been introduced to investigate, expose, and prosecute misconduct and to boost public confidence in the organization's ability to deal openly with allegations of misconduct, poor discipline, and inefficiency within the police service (Biddle, interview, April 13, 2005).

In 2000, the government of Sierra Leone passed an anticorruption bill creating the Anti Corruption Commission (ACC). Headed by an independent commissioner and staffed with lawyers, former SLP officers, and Commonwealth task force, the ACC investigates a range of corruption complaints. A toll free anticorruption hotline allows for and encourages anonymous reporting. The 2003–2005 five-year ACC strategic plan contains specific programs for the prevention of corruption, including public education, more effective investigation and prosecution of offenders, and research and intelligence gathering (Biddle, interview, April 13, 2005). A Truth and Reconciliation Committee modeled on that of South Africa has been in operation since 2003 (Dougherty, 2004; Lengor, interview, April 14/15, 2005). In August 2000, at the urging of the Sierra Leone government, the United Nations Security Council established the Special Court for Sierra Leone to try those responsible for the crimes committed during the civil war (Special Court for Sierra Leone, 2005).

The New Sierra Leone Police

The task force, with the help of local journalists, trained police personnel in public and media relations in order to further improve the image of the SLP. A formal press office has been established (Moigbe, interviews, April 14/15, 2005).

The SLP suffered from internal inertia. Because of political corruption and government neglect, all decision making within the organization had become the sole domain of senior officers. Consequently, supervisors and managers abrogated their responsibilities, passing even simple matters to senior management. Political favoritism compounded the problem by creating an illogical and cumbersome rank structure of 21 ranks, many with duplicate roles and responsibilities. The official duties, for example, of constables, corporals, sergeants, sergeant majors, and subinspectors were identical. The organization had become top heavy, a steeply pyramidal and stagnant bureaucracy, where decision-making and organizational communications were impossible. In 2003, the SLP leadership addressed the problem. They reduced the number of ranks to nine and clarified the duties of each. The following year, the SLP collapsed the 15 posts of senior assistant commissioner and assistant commissioner into a single rank of assistant inspector general (AIG).

The current rank structure of the SLP is shown in Table 5.1.

Table 5.1   Current Rank Structure of the Sierra Leone Police

Rank	Number
Deputy Inspector General	1
Assistant Inspector General	15
Chief Superintendent	18
Superintendent	33
Assistant Superintendent	198
Inspector	417
Sergeant	1838
Constable	4251
Total	6771

SOURCE: Moigbe (interview, April 14/15, 2005).

In order to improve the quality of supervision and leadership, a comprehensive promotional system based on merit and performance has been implemented (Biddle, interview, April 13, 2005). SLP officers of the rank of assistant superintendent and above attend the prestigious 10-week International Commanders' Program at the Police Staff College, Bramshill, England. The course, designed specifically to meet the needs of the SLP, provides training in operational planning and command skills, leadership, strategic planning skills, ethical policing, human rights, and the political, social, and economic context of policing. Participants are attached to English police forces, assigned to units specific to their regular SLP duties. On return to Sierra Leone, they design and conduct relevant training programs for middle managers and supervisors based on their Bramshill experiences (Cullen & McDonald, 2005).

Vigorous organizational reforms have moved the police force toward decentralization of resources and greater operational authority for local commanders. The entire organizational structure has been revamped. Under its current structure, the SLP maintains four major operational regions: Western Province Divisions, Northern Province Divisions, Southern Province Divisions, and Eastern Province Divisions. Central headquarters control includes the following key organizational elements (Moigbe, interview, April 14/15, 2005):

- Criminal Investigation Department (CID)
- Complaints, Discipline, and Internal Investigations Department
- Special Branch
- Operations Support Division (Public Order)
- Media and Public Relations Department
- Estates Department
- Marine Department
- Equal Opportunities Department
- Research and Planning
- Police Training School
- Transport
- Communications
- Family Support Unit
- Community Relations Department
- Inspectorate
- Change Management

The force continues to be understaffed, down from its preconflict staffing of more than 9,000, and the problem of illiteracy interferes with progress. To address these issues, the SLP has raised recruiting standards and initiated an aggressive recruiting campaign. Special efforts have been made to bring women and university graduates into the force. Women currently occupy two of the AIG positions, and graduates are joining the force in increasing numbers (Moigbe, interview, April 18, 2005). Current applicants for the SLP must be citizens of Sierra Leone between 18 and 30 years of age, of good health and without criminal convictions. They must possess a minimum of five General Certificates of Education and complete a multifaceted selection process. All applicants, irrespective of education, join at the constable rank. There is no direct entry at officer rank (Cullen & McDonald, 2005).

When Biddle left the SLP in late 2003, the force had clearly achieved measurable and qualitative success in a very short period of time under extremely difficult circumstances (Groenwald & Peak, 2004). His replacement, Deputy Inspector General of Police Brima Acha Kamara, a career Sierra Leone police officer, continues the work begun by Biddle and the Commonwealth task force (Biddle, interview, April 13, 2005).

The SLP and the nation are very much works in progress. Serious problems still exist, and the future remains uncertain. Large numbers of citizens have migrated from rural areas to the major cities. Wide-scale poverty and unemployment, the repatriation of large numbers of refugees and combatants, political and regional instability, the tradition of corruption, and similar issues remain threats to progress. Nonetheless, the country and the SLP continue to move toward democracy. While some increase in robbery and automobile-related crime as well as problems with urban traffic congestion and road safety have been noted, the national crime rate remains low, with an annual national homicide rate of less than 1 per 100,000 (2003). A duly elected democratic government remains in place. Civil war has been avoided.

The successful rebuilding of the SLP to date can be attributed to many factors, but two stand out. First, and perhaps most important, the reform of the Sierra Leone Police was led from the very top of the government and the society. President Kabbah made it a priority for his administration. He personally penned the Government Policing Charter, sought international support, and took the bold step of appointing a well-qualified foreign national to head the force. He endorsed the SLP strategic plan, and his authority made it national policy.

Second, the SLP reorganized itself. Rather than struggling to retrofit tactics and programs developed in other postconflict societies, the force took charge of its own rebuilding by developing Sierra Leonean solutions to its problems. With the help of the British task force and support from the United Nations, the SLP designed its own strategic plan around the specific needs and expectations of the citizens of Sierra Leone and within its existing political system, history, and criminal justice system. And they did so from the bottom up rather than from the top down. The operational success of the SLP is largely a factor of its unique decentralization of police services to the community level in a community-policing framework as the starting point for the force rebuilding process. Only after police returned to the community both physically and philosophically did the formal reorganization begin.

References

Central Intelligence Agency (CIA). (n.d.). Sierra Leone. In *World factbook*. Retrieved April 18, 2005, from http://www.cia.gov/cia/publications/factbook/goes/sl.html

Code of conduct for law enforcement officers. (1979). In *Resolutions adopted by the general assembly during its thirty-fourth session* (Resolution 34/169, pp. 185–187). Retrieved March 18, 2005, from http://www.un.org/documents/ga/res/34/ares34.htm

Crawshaw, R., Cullen, S., & Williams, T. (2006). *Human rights and policing. The Raoul Wallenberg Institute professional guide to human rights.* Boston: Martinus Nijhof.

Cullen, S., & McDonald, W. H. (2005). Sierra Leone. In L. Sullivan (Ed.), *Encyclopedia of Law Enforcement* (pp. 1297–1299). Thousand Oaks, CA: Sage.

Dougherty, B. (2004, Fall). Searching for truth: Sierra Leone's truth and reconciliation commission [Electronic version]. *African Studies Quarterly, 8,* 1–21. Retrieved May 15, 2005, from http://www.africa.ufl.edu/asq/v8/v8ila3.htm

From crisis to confidence. (1998). (Brochure). Freetown, Sierra Leone: Royal Sierra Leone Police.

Groenwald, H., & Peak, G. (2004). *Police reform through community-based Policing: Philosophy and guidelines for implementation.* New York: International Peace Academy.

Hoffman, D. (2005). *The Kamajors of Sierra Leone.* Retrieved 15 Sept 2005 from http://www.ssrc.org/fellowships/gsc/fellowship_and_grant_awardees/individual pages/

Kpundeh, S. (1993). Prospects in contemporary Sierra Leone. *Corruption and Reform, 7,* 237–247.

Kpundeh, S. (1995). *Politics and corruption in Africa: A case study of Sierra Leone.* Washington, DC: University Press of America.

Lord, D. (2005). *Paying the price: The Sierra Leone peace process.* Retrieved April 1, 2006, from http://www.c-r.org/accord/sleona/accord9/intro.shtml

Malan, M., Rakafe, P., & McIntyre, A. (2002). *The restoration of civil authority— Peacekeeping in Sierra Leone—the UNAMSIL hits the home straight.* Retrieved March 29, 2005, from http://www.iss.co.za/Pubs/Monographs/No68/Chap. 8.html

Meek, S. (2003). Policing Sierra Leone. In *Sierra Leone, building the road to recovery.* Retrieved April 21, 2005, from http://www.issafrica.org/Pubs/Monographs/No80/Content.html.

Refugees International. (2004). *Spotlight on Sierra Leone: Continued investments required to sustain peace.* Retrieved August 27, 2007, from http://www.refugeesinternational.org/content/article/detail/3904

Siegel, J. T., Weinstein, M., & Halperin, M. H. (2004). Why democracies excel. *Foreign Affairs, 83*(5), 57–61.

Special court for Sierra Leone. (n.d.). Retrieved April 18, 2005, from http://www.globalpolicy.org/intljustice/sierraindx.htm

State house on line. (2005). Retrieved April 10, 2005 from http://www.statehouse-sl.org

Thompson, B. (1996). *The constitutional history and law of Sierra Leone (1961–1995).* New York: University Press of America.

Thompson, B., & Potter, P. (1997, September). Governmental corruption in Africa: Sierra Leone as a case study. *Crime Law and Social Change, 28,* 137–154.

Interviews

Biddle, K. (2005, April 13). Interview in Cheshire, UK.

Lengor, M. (2005, April 14 & 15). Interview at Police Staff College, Bramshill, UK.

Moigbe, M. (2005, April 14, 15, & 18). Interview at Police Staff College, Bramshill, UK.

6 Policing the Russian Federation

Peter Roudik

Russia belongs to the civil law tradition of continental Europe. Its present legal system is defined by the 1993 Constitution, which provides for a federation of 86 constituent components with a strong executive branch of power. Federal laws and codes constitute the most commonly encountered sources of law in Russia. The difference in name is largely based on how long and how comprehensive the statute is. The president may issue decrees and directives, and the government and federal agencies are authorized to adopt regulations in the areas of their general competency. The current Russian police force is called the *militia*.[1] This name originated during the time when the Soviet people's militia and system of internal affairs were created immediately after the Bolshevik Revolution of 1917. The structural and functional operations of the Soviet police force and the police force during the Russian empire were mainly equivalent. Nevertheless, the Soviet government, due to the extensive politicization of government systems, renamed the police force as the militia. This name was preserved in the course of the democratic reforms that occurred during the last 15 years, because the essence of this institution has not been changed.

Historical and Political Background

In Russia, the police force never was a body responsible for crime control only. It was always a vital component of the state regardless of who was at the top of state bureaucracy. Under all regimes, the police force's main task was to maintain the government's rule over an ethnically diverse population

AUTHOR'S NOTE: Views expressed in this chapter are solely those of the author and do not reflect the position of the U.S. Library of Congress.

spread over large geographical areas. Instead of serving the people, the militia always sought to keep them submissive. Forms and means for implementing this task varied with the times depending on the political atmosphere; however, the basic features of Russian policing are and have been that it is political, arbitrary, and limited in actual effectiveness.

The first regular police institutions were created in the late sixteenth century. For the next 100 years, public order was controlled by local guards and night watches drawn from among the citizenry. Reforms initiated by Peter the Great (1672–1725) introduced the European concept of police in Russia and increased the role of a centralized force fighting crime and supporting public order. The office of the policemaster general was created in St. Petersburg in the early eighteenth century. He subordinated provincial police chancelleries in other large cities. During the reign of Catherine the Great (1729–1796) the authority of central police bodies was continuously expanded beyond the largest cities to the provinces. The creation of a centralized force made up of soldiers transferred for police duty did not obviate the employment of local population in the police force. Following the 1775 administrative reform, police service remained in the jurisdiction of provincial and local authorities until 1802, when the national Ministry of Internal Affairs (MIA) was created by Czar Alexander I. The jurisdiction of the MIA was very broad, because this new institution combined functions of six separate preexisting agencies of state power. The Czar's decree assigned the minister the duty to "take care about the well-being of [the] population, calmness, tranquility, and improvement of the Empire" (Adrianov, 1902, p. 54). The ministry controlled activities of local government offices and managed the police force nationwide. Later, special police departments were created in large military equipment plants, mines, and train stations.

During the nineteenth century, the regular system of police hierarchy was built. In 1837, the central authorities established the appointive office of constable, for the first time extending the state police presence below the district level. In 1862, the district police chief, hitherto elected by the nobility, was converted into a centrally appointed subordinate of the provincial governor. The establishment, in 1879, of a force of sergeants to assist the constables completed the system. In the 1860s, in order to increase police effectiveness, the force was relieved of its tax collecting duties, and its investigative and trial authority was cancelled. At the same time, in addition to regular police functions, the authority of the Ministry of Internal Affairs was extended to control the mass media, postal service, labor and economic data, military draft, and secret service. The extended authority made the police force, which continued to be governed under 1862 guidelines for staff size and pay, extremely overstretched. At the end of the nineteenth century, a total cadre of 47,866 police officers handled a population of nearly 127 million (Weissman, 1985). This made the ratio of police personnel to population in St. Petersburg and Moscow comparable with those of Berlin and Vienna. However, these figures reflected establishment rather than actual strength. They made no allowances for vacancies and included policemen used as clerks, messengers, and servants. Unlike officers in Europe, Russian officers remained most of the time at stations awaiting a public call or a summons by a fellow officer. Also, Russian police were burdened with an unusually wide array of additional duties, from monitoring sanitation to ensuring public respect for the Russian Orthodox Church.

This wide scope of authority was preserved after the fall of the Russian Empire. After the czar's abdication in February 1917, the provisional government supported the development of local self-rule and a democratic people's militia; however, police functions were never transferred to the municipalities, and the police remained a major pillar within the Ministry of Internal Affairs, which exercised strong control over police activities. Government-appointed police inspectors were dispatched to all provinces and administrative districts. They were entitled to make appointments, issue decrees, and intervene in routine police work. This militia was dismantled after the October 1917 Bolshevik Revolution, which marked the beginning of a 64-year Communist regime known as Soviet period. On the third day after the Communists took control of the government, a workers' militia aimed at supporting the revolutionary order was established.

The revolution inspired novel approaches to policing, such as the transfer of police duties to social organizations and the introduction of a mandatory police duty. These proposals were not implemented, and in the mid-1920s, Soviet police structures were finally formed. Newly established police departments were incorporated into the system of internal affairs, which recreated the previously existing multifunctional government agency. In 1922, the functions of the secret police—with jurisdiction over informer networks, concentration camps, internal troops, frontier guards, and crimes against the state and existing political system, including terrorism and serious crimes committed by high-level government officials—were given to the notorious State Security Committee (KGB). The KGB was formally an executive government agency and was subordinate to the Communist party leadership. In theory, the KGB was expected to investigate only a very specific range of criminal offenses, but the politicization of the Soviet state had always ensured its use according to the instructions given by the party leaders focusing on fighting real, potential, and imaginary political threats and destroying the foes of the regime (Gerson, 1976). In early 1990s, the KGB expanded its authority through involvement in combating crime.

Regular Soviet police were simultaneously subordinate to relevant representative bodies, which formed a strong, centralized system of state power, and to higher police departments, which were led by the national Ministry of Internal Affairs. During the Soviet period, the militia moved from being a paramilitary body responsible for suppressing political opposition to a law enforcement body in charge of maintaining social and economic order. Numerous divisions were created within the militia's bureaucracy in order to regulate diverse aspects of people's lives. Even though the degree of centralization varied during different historical periods and the organization of the Ministry of Internal Affairs has been subject to many changes, the police system was always a part of the all-encompassing Soviet regime (Shelley,

1996). Operational changes reflected shifts in policies and power at the highest level and, thereby, the vital role of all police functions in Russia. Until 1990, Russia's regular militia was under the direct supervision of the Ministry of Internal Affairs (MIA) of the Soviet Union. At that time, the Russian Republic established an MIA, which assumed control of the republic's police. The transformation of the Soviet political system in the late 1980s and early 1990s had a low impact on the daily activities of the police, who were neither ready to cope with the crime unleashed by the transition nor prepared to assume their new role as defenders of democracy. Leadership of the Russian police force, which performs a wide range of functions though its accountability to the citizenry remains minimal, continues to view the preservation of the nation's political stability as the most important component of law enforcement activity in all territories of the country (Rushailo, 2001).

The Ministry of Internal Affairs: Status, Structure, Functions

In 1991, Russia obtained its independence from the Soviet Union, endorsed democracy, and implemented principles of the rule of law. However, old Soviet methods have been carried forward by the police, which, unlike other law enforcement agencies, did not undergo extensive reorganization after 1991. After President Yeltsin's unsuccessful attempt, in 1991, to combine all security, intelligence, and police services into a unified system under presidential control (this was outlawed by the Constitutional Court because of the lack of mechanisms to monitor and control such an organization), a separate Ministry of Internal Affairs and the Federal Security Service were created. The Federal Security Service became responsible for the state's internal security; it covers counterespionage and the fight against terrorism, although concerns were raised that it operates like the old KGB, monitoring the telephones of opponents of the regime, spreading misinformation, and intercepting mail. Given that the Federal Security Service was essentially formed from the old KGB, these allegations are not groundless.

The current legal status of the Ministry of Internal Affairs was established by the Presidential Decree of July 18, 1996, which defined the ministry as a federal agency of the executive branch of government charged with "protecting the rights and liberties of the persons and citizens, preserving law and order, and guaranteeing public security" as well as "perfecting the legal basis of its activities." The ministry is subordinate to the president of Russia, and its functions, as defined by legislation, include identifying and forecasting security threats and taking measures for their prevention and neutralization. Within the bounds of its jurisdiction, the MIA manages regular police activities and provides for professional training, legal defense, and social security of MIA personnel.

The ministry operates at both the central and local levels and administers from its main office in Moscow. Its system of internal affairs consists of structural links at various levels within all 98 of the constituent components of the Russian Federation, several administrative districts and municipalities, sections of railway, air, and water transport, so-called regime objects, and regional administrations for fighting organized crime. The ministry also has an investigative committee, supply administrations, a network of educational and training institutions, scientific and research facilities, and special units formed for special tasks. The MIA has its own armed forces to perform designated tasks; these forces are completely separate from the regular army. MIA forces are equipped with heavy weapons and are organized in a way similar to that of military units. After many years of secretiveness, the organizational structure of the ministry is now open and can be viewed on its Web site. The Minister of Internal Affairs and the heads of all regional internal affairs departments are appointed and dismissed by the president of the Russian Federation.

During the last 10 years, in response to an increase in the size of the criminal community and structural changes to it, new services and departments were created within the MIA. These departments are the Main Department for the Fight Against Economic Crimes, the Main Department for the Fight Against Organized Crime, the Committee for Combating Illegal Drug Trafficking, the Main Department for Special Technical Operations, the Federal Migration Service, Special Purpose Detachments, and the National Central Interpol Bureau. These services are integral parts of the MIA system and independently cooperate with foreign partners. In 1993, Russia joined Interpol. The MIA is also involved in regional cooperation between law enforcement authorities of other former Soviet republics. However, it has been reported that, to avoid long and cumbersome bureaucratic procedures associated with reporting operations in territories of the newly independent states to national authorities, Russian police have performed arrests of suspected criminals hiding abroad and transported them to Russia without informing police authorities in the countries where the operations were conducted (Khinstein, 2003). Russian police receive significant foreign assistance, especially from the United States.

Prior to November 1997, the MIA had command over all penal institutions, which were then placed under the Ministry of Justice's authority in response to recommendations from the Council of Europe. Fire protection also was among the MIA's functions before 2002, when this responsibility was transferred to the Ministry for Emergency Situations.

During the last 15 years, the government has attempted to improve training, tighten discipline, and decentralize the administration of the police throughout the Russian Federation so that it might respond better to local needs and deal more effectively with drug trafficking and organized crime. In 1997, President Yeltsin of Russia signed a new Anticrime and Corruption Law presented by the Interior Minister. The law simply poured more money into archaic structures, leaving police as ineffective as before but in greater numbers. The redirection of MIA resources to internal troops during the Chechnya war and to the MIA's new local riot squads, which were often used as a personal military for regional governors, undercut police reform. President Vladimir Putin of Russia recognized in his 2005 State of the Nation address that Russia's system of internal security was "chronically ill and is in need of reforming" (Putin, 2005).

Crime Statistics

After being freed from the control of the Communist party, the overstretched and underresourced police force concentrated on issues of importance to itself, and the effectiveness of police actions diminished while crime rates, which during the Soviet period were lower in Russia than other countries with comparable levels of economic development, skyrocketed. Among the factors contributing to the still growing criminality in Russia are the conflicts that frequently accompany changes of ownership and an increased struggle for power along clan and ethnic lines or between national interests. The lack of an effective system in society for preventing legal infringements, inadequate legal and logistical support for the battle against terrorism, legal nihilism, and the departure of qualified personnel from law enforcement agencies led to the increased criminal threat. After a 33 percent increase in reported crime between 1991 and 1992, the annual crime rate has continued to increase at a much lower rate (5–8 percent annually) during the last 10 years as the economic and political situation in the country has become more stable.

In 2004, 2.9 million crimes were registered in the country of 142 million residents (2,100 crimes per 100,000 population). About 35 percent of them constituted serious and most serious crimes, which are equivalent to first and second degree felonies. About half of all crimes were property related (i.e., stealing, swindling, theft). Every tenth crime was committed by the illegal intrusion into another's residence. About 500,000 reported crimes were business related. During the last five years, the number of registered crimes rose annually by 5 percent. Only one half of all crimes were solved. Among the unsolved crimes are 6,000 killings and attempted killings. In 2004, 1.3 million individuals who had committed crimes were identified. One quarter of all crimes were committed by a previously convicted person. Every fifth crime was committed by a drunkard; every tenth by a minor. The percentage of foreigners among documented criminals is insignificant, and almost all of them are citizens of neighboring former Soviet republics (MIA, 2004).

As the prosecutor general of the Russian Federation reported, while existing criminal statistics do not reflect the real number of crimes committed, these statistics do reflect the erroneous method by which crimes are registered. Presently, reporting crimes is a police function and is often used to adjust statistics. As evaluation of police work is based on the percentage of crimes that police solve, police are interested in registering only crimes that are easily solved (petty crimes and misdemeanors) or that cannot be avoided (most dangerous crimes). Police officers often decide not to initiate criminal proceedings when the case seems difficult to prove. "The pursuit of statistics has given rise to a whole generation of detectives who when they arrive at the scene of crime think about how to conceal a crime rather than how to clear it up" (Thomas, 2000). Their superiors condone and, perhaps, even encourage this practice, because it enhances the department's record by increasing the percentage of successful investigations. Despite the fact that almost all ministers of internal affairs since the mid-1990s have been quoted on many occasions as calling for an end to "deception" in crime statistics, nothing has changed. Perhaps, until crime statistics begin to be received through non-MIA channels, it will be almost impossible to make even an approximate assessment of the scale of crime in Russia.

The police have invented sophisticated techniques to refuse the acceptance of statements from individuals. Unreasonable denials to register crimes are so widespread that in 2000, the Constitutional Court issued a ruling stating that individuals have the right to review police materials substantiating a refusal when a request to initiate police proceedings is rejected. Another reason for the denial of crime registration is the existing system for officer performance evaluations. According to this practice, an officer's number of solved crimes must increase with each year. Even if all the officer's criminals are caught and future crimes are prevented, a police officer's work is unsatisfactory if the officer does not solve at least one more crime each year than he or she solved the previous year. To cope with this practice, policemen have invented so-called paper crimes, where they register and investigate crimes allegedly committed by imaginary people. Another method of inflating a clearance rate is to plant drugs or gun cartridges on innocent people. The consequences of these actions are the concealment of real crimes and the falsification of statistics. However, without the artificial minimization of registered crimes, police workload would increase several fold to a level where they could not handle all cases. According to the prosecutor general, only one-third of crimes committed in Russia are registered and taken into account by police. That statistic means the true number of crimes committed annually in Russia is equal to 9 million (Ustinov, 2005). Independent experts estimate the crime rate at 10–12 million (Galeotti, 2002).

Police Legislation

As soon as Russia became independent from the Soviet Union and started to build a law enforcement system, researchers recommended the adoption of a police code to function as a consolidated legal act that would combine legal norms of police law regarding the protection of public order, public security, and citizen rights and freedoms. The supporters of this idea claimed the application of police related legal norms was complicated, because they were spread over numerous legislative acts. Supporters recommended the code include both procedural and material norms (Belskii, 2004). This idea appears from time to time in Russian legal publications, but it is strongly opposed by police leadership and lacks wide support from legislators.

Presently, Russian police (militia) are governed by the federal Police Law adopted on April 18, 1991. The law was the first to regulate police agencies comprehensively, an event Russian scholars described as part of the democratization process (Peyser & Vitsin, 2005). The law defines the organizational structure of the police force and prescribes its rights and duties. Unfortunately, amendments to the law do not reflect changes in criminal procedure and do not enhance democratic standards in police activities.

Organizational Structure of the Police

The Police Law divides the force into criminal police and public security police. Criminal police prevent and detect crimes and search for persons who have fled from agencies of inquiry, investigation, or a court. Public security, or local, police maintain public order; prevent, suppress, and investigate minor crimes; and assist citizens and legal entities. Public security units run local police stations, temporary detention centers, and the State Traffic Inspectorate. They deal with crimes outside the jurisdiction of the criminal police and are charged with routine maintenance of public order. Local police compose about 60 percent of the total number of police (Butler, 2003).

Even though the Russian police are divided between criminal and public security police, all police are subordinate to the Ministry of Internal Affairs of the Russian Federation. While the criminal police are the centralized federal structure, the public security police are dually subordinate and report to the ministry as well as to the executive authorities of their relevant constituent component of the Russian Federation. The Minister of Internal Affairs oversees the work of the entire police force all over Russia. However, the minister is not a national police chief, as his deputies, the chief of the criminal police and the chief of the public security police, directly head their respective services. Within each constituent component, the police are headed by the chief of the component's internal affairs department, who is appointed and dismissed by the president of the Russian Federation upon joint recommendation of the federal Minister of Internal Affairs and the governor of the relevant constituent component. Police chiefs in towns, districts, and other municipal establishments are heads of their respective internal affairs departments and are appointed by the chiefs of the components' internal affairs departments. All police units have the same government-approved gray uniforms with red piping. Public security police units created by local and municipal governments may have their own insignia.

Criminal Police

The duty of the criminal police is to stop, discover, and prevent crimes that require preliminary investigation, conduct searches for wanted and missing individuals, and assist public security police. The government of the Russian Federation determines the structure of the criminal police. The criminal police force is divided into organizations responsible for combating particular types of crime. For example, the Main Directorate for Organized Crime works with other agencies, such as the MIA's specialized rapid-response detachment offices. In 1995, special units were established at the directorate to deal with contract killings and other violent crimes against individuals. Government Regulation No. 925 of December 7, 2000, states that the criminal police force consists of the following divisions: criminal search, economic crimes, taxation crimes, organized crime, operations and technical activities, internal security, and police detachment for special purposes. The National Central Bureau of Interpol and its territorial branches are included in the criminal police. Chiefs of the criminal police and public security police for the components of the federation are appointed by the Russian Federation Minister of Internal Affairs. The criminal police force is financed from the federal budget.

Public Security Police

The main duty of the public security police force is to secure the personal safety of Russian citizens, maintain public order, and protect property. Public security police prosecute administrative misdemeanors and investigate crimes when preliminary investigation is not required. The public security police manage detention centers and are divided into two parts—federal and local.

The organizational divisions in the public security police extend to its financing. The federal government defines the budget and structure for public security police programs that are financed through the federal budget. Regional and local authorities may create additional detachments or units of public security police. These detachments are financed by local and regional budgets according to the norms established by the federal government. All regional MIA departments have special purpose detachments, commonly known as the Black Berets, which are aimed at combating terrorist and serious criminal activities. They are similar to U.S. SWAT teams and are deeply involved in fighting drug trafficking and tax evasion. Special detachments of police also are created for cities with populations exceeding 300,000 persons.

As part of the trend toward decentralization, some municipalities, including Moscow, have formed their own militias, which cooperate with their MIA counterparts. The Moscow contingent, with reportedly 2000 officers receives support from the mayor's office and the city's internal affairs department as well as from the MIA budget. Municipal police units have the best and most up-to-date weapons and combat equipment available. Furthermore, they enjoy a reputation for courage and effectiveness. Although the law on self-government supports such local law enforcement agencies, the federal government attempted to restrict further moves toward independence by strictly limiting the powers of such formations. For example, municipal police do not carry guns or other weapons except in emergency situations. Public security police include traffic police, area officers, and officers of the street patrol service; they inspect the affairs of minors, and they staff police stations, detention centers, centers for keeping drunkards and vagrants, passport and visa departments, departments on licensing weapons and protection services, and services for escorting criminals.

Internal Troops

The police force also includes military units called Internal Troops who participate in emergency military operations, disperse crowds, and fight public disobedience. Internal Troops are permanently assigned to this duty, as opposed to the regular armed forces, which are also periodically called up for law enforcement duties. The legal status and responsibilities of the force are similar to those of the National Guard in the United States; they are determined by the Law on Internal Troops of the Ministry of Internal Affairs of the Russian Federation of February 6, 1997. Under this law, the MIA maintains armed units whose responsibilities are to assist police in protecting public order, important state objects, and special cargoes; to participate in the territorial defense of the Russian Federation; and to render assistance to the federal Border Service in protecting the state boundary.

Internal Troops have a militaristic structure and appearance and are estimated to number 200,000. They are divided into three mobile groups with five divisions (Jamestown Foundation, 1998). These troops are better equipped and trained than the regular police. The size of the force, which is staffed by both conscripts and volunteers, has grown steadily during the last years, although the troop commander has reported serious shortages of officers. Russia's Internal Troops, by law, are charged with assisting various agencies of Russia's MIA, which, in turn means they are assigned only a support role. These forces are equipped with guns and combat weapons to deal with serious crimes, terrorism, and other extraordinary threats to public order. During the last few years, the crime rate among the troops doubled. A contributing factor to this change was a steep increase in desertions that coincided with service in Chechnya, where Internal Troops are routinely used for street patrol.

Police Rights and Duties

General functions of the police are stipulated by the 1991 Police Law. The law states that the police's duties are to

- Prevent, stop, and discover crimes and administrative misdemeanors
- Assist people suffering from crimes and emergencies
- Receive and register information related to crimes
- Initiate and investigate criminal cases
- Search for wanted and missing people and stolen property
- Secure public order on streets and in public places
- Provide protection services
- Conduct forensic evaluations
- Identify individuals and corpses
- Monitor fulfillment of residence and registration rules by Russian citizens and foreigners
- Administer the passport-visa and other authorization systems
- Enforce rules for the entry, exit, sojourn, and transit of foreign citizens or stateless persons through the territory of the Russian Federation
- Supervise freed detainees and monitor their behavior
- Conduct witness protection programs
- Secure the safety of judges
- Conduct mandatory state fingerprint registration

Police duties also include the issuance of licenses for engaging in private detective or personal security activity and permits for obtaining and possession of weapons. Police departments also are responsible for enforcing rules for traffic safety, registration of motor vehicles, and the issuance of driver's licenses. Police operations and searches are regulated by a specific law and may be conducted by plainclothes officers.

The law does not provide for an exhaustive list of responsibilities assigned to police; this continues the centuries-long tradition of the entity performing a range of functions, some of which have nothing to do with fighting crime. One of the major police responsibilities is patrolling the streets. In addition, the police force, which consists of 0.3 to 2 percent of a town's population, handles applications for driver's licenses, passports, and residential registrations as required by law. Each police district has units that conduct criminal investigations, handle public inquiries, and monitor known criminals residing in the district. As a rule, criminal investigation units focus on several of the city's most problematic crimes. Depending on regional specifics, these can be high-profile killings, residential burglaries, or drug trafficking. Criminal tracking units monitor criminals from the time of their release from prison, when they must register with their local police district. Ex-convicts must report monthly to the local police, although they frequently are visited between those times.

Every police department has a special group of officers assigned to a small geographic area (4,000–6,000 people). In big cities the officers may work in teams of two to three patrol officers, and sometimes these teams may include even an investigative officer. Most area officers police their territory on foot, monitoring sanitation conditions as well as criminal activity out of small offices or apartments in housing complexes. They work with volunteer auxiliary police who assist in patrolling neighborhood streets and developing local intelligence; these volunteers are generally the police's eyes and ears in the community. With the intention of maintaining good relations with local residents, area police officers can cover up minor crimes, chase off predatory criminals from outside the neighborhood, expedite paperwork, and choose to deal with infractions informally. The goal of police administrators is for their officers to be recognizable to people in their patrol area. Toward this end, a recent decree states that it is desirable for officers to reside in the neighborhoods for which they are responsible. The government's obligation to supply area officers with subsidized housing is often a major incentive for police officers to serve.

Area officers undertake efforts to engage citizens in crime prevention. Patrol officers work with local councils on crime prevention projects. Area officers cooperate with other police departments by assisting them to enforce laws in their areas and, according to recent research, by taking responsibility for approximately 140 tasks specified in ministerial instructions.

The law encourages the cooperation of police authorities with other state institutions, bodies of local self-government, and social and labor organizations. Police can encourage individuals to cooperate with other law enforcement authorities. They may issue awards to encourage citizens' assistance and cultivate a system of police informants. It is common for police to hold regular meetings with the public. District police stations usually designate two days each week for individuals to come and discuss neighborhood problems. A "hot-spot" approach to police work is adapted by the Internal Affairs Department in St. Petersburg. In this city, crime complaints are entered into a computer database from local precincts, and crimes are displayed on maps. Proactive steps are taken at locations that appear particularly active (Davis, Ortiz, & Gilinsky, 2004). This method exemplifies an effective approach toward registering crimes and was recommended by the MIA for implementation in other regions.

In their work, the police have the right to demand that citizens and officials stop activities that violate legislation or hinder the work of police or government authorities, check identification documents, search individuals and their belongings (if there is a reason to believe that they may have weapons, munitions, explosives, or narcotic substances), and review the validity of licenses to conduct certain activities. In 1998, the Arbitration Court of the Western Siberian Circuit ruled that it is proper for police to stop trade operations and detain persons involved in trade outside designated spaces or areas. The rights of police extend to summoning individuals and officials in relation to cases under police investigation and bringing them by force when those individuals refuse to answer official summonses. Police detain and keep under arrest suspects and those who avoid the execution of criminal punishment. Police may obtain necessary explanations, information, documents, and references and can conduct criminal procedures prescribed by the Code of Criminal Procedure. In order to secure this right, the law allows police to conduct operations and search activities, to enter residential premises, and to use means of transportation and connections belonging to citizens or organizations, if necessary. The Police Law does not specify limitations on police rights except for a general requirement that these rights be used to fulfill police duties. As the spectrum of police duties is incredibly broad, this provision does not affect daily police activities.

Methods of Operation

As long as police work complies with existing legislation, police are free to select methods of operation depending on the circumstances, the specifics of the crime, and the social status of the criminal. Police must collect evidence through photos and/or through video and audio recordings that signal preparation to commit crime or the conduct of criminal activity. The evidence may serve as a reason to initiate criminal proceedings when the information collected reveals features of a crime. Telephone reports on crimes are not enough to initiate a case, even though they are logged in by an on-duty officer, and the submission of a written personal statement by a person reporting a crime is required. The Code of Criminal Procedure, which entered into force July 1, 2002, obligates the public security police to conduct an inquiry even if they are not prepared to finish the investigation and formulate an accusatory statement. While the number of cases under investigation has tripled since the adoption of the code, the number of cases submitted to courts has decreased by 18.2 percent during the same period (Gavrilov, 2003).

The registration of crimes is performed by an officer on duty at a local internal affairs department, which is a component of the public security police. Written reports on crimes received by mail, fax, courier, or another service are directed to the heads of local police departments, who decide whether to register them after studying these statements. If the police station chief finds signs of a crime, the statement is referred to the officer on duty for registration. Because registration of a statement is based on the presence of criminal facts, the initiation of a criminal case is inevitable. However, the initial review of facts is not required when written statements personally are submitted by the applicant or the applicant's representative to the officer on duty. These claims are registered immediately.

Police officers perform the initial work of gathering evidence of a crime and conduct searches to apprehend culprits. They are granted unimpeded access to private property. According to the federal Police Operations Law, officers may enter homes and businesses to pursue suspects "if facts warrant the assumption that a crime has been committed or is being committed" (Section 14). This law gives officers the right to use vehicles belonging to citizens and private businesses to pursue suspects. The law does not compensate citizens for damage to property or physical harm inflicted during police operations and does not hold police officers responsible.

Procedural police functions can be divided into three groups—main activities, activities aimed at supporting criminal trials, and supplementary procedural activities, as shown in Table 6.1.

Table 6.1   Procedural Police Functions

Main activities	• Review and acceptance of statements on crimes • Conduct of inquiries and necessary operations and searches (inspection of the crime site; performance of searches and seizures; detention and interrogation of suspects, victims, and witnesses) • Compensation for damage inflicted by illegal activities • Undertaking of preventive and prophylactic measures • Direct participation in international legal assistance in criminal matters
Supporting activities	• Regular operational police actions (conduct of discoveries; search for criminals and evidence of crimes) • Completion of a prosecutor's or investigator's assignments • Summons and delivery of participants in trials • Delivery of correspondence between the court and the detainee • Seizures to secure property that is used to guarantee financial obligations of an accused person
Assisting activities	• Guarding, transporting, and escorting suspects and accused persons • Participation of the inspector for the affairs of minors in the interrogations of minors • Securing crime scenes

One of the traditional functions of the Russian police is to conduct investigations. In different times, this was performed by various police components. Even when the position of judicial investigator was created in 1864, police remained involved in investigations. After the 1917 Bolshevik Revolution, investigation in the form of inquiries was included in the police's responsibilities, and later, regardless of changes in legislation, police retained the right to conduct inquiries in a substantial number of cases and to perform preliminary investigations together with other law enforcement agencies, if a crime under investigation had fallen under their jurisdiction. Today, preliminary investigation is required in all cases involving severe crimes and crimes committed by government officials, but it is optional in all other cases. The goal of preliminary investigation is to determine all circumstances subject to proof before the trial. As the gravest crimes—crimes against life, sexual crimes, official crimes, crimes committed by or against judges and law enforcement officials—are included in the jurisdiction of the prosecution service (an office roughly comparable to that of attorney general in the United States), and crimes related to national security fall under the jurisdiction of the Federal Security Service (former KGB), police investigators are dealing with less grave crimes, including crimes against property, crimes affecting public security, crimes committed by minors, etc.

Police investigators are procedurally independent from other agencies. An independent institution with authority to initiate criminal proceedings and conduct investigations does not exist, although numerous proposals have been discussed by the legislature. The MIA Investigative Committee is one of the ministry's structural divisions. It supervises the investigative subdivisions of regional ministry branches and local police departments and oversees preliminary investigations in the most complex criminal cases. The head of the Investigative Committee is a deputy minister. An investigation conducted by a police department concludes with making a decision either for indictment or for terminating the proceedings. Police are entitled to support the state prosecution during the trial of cases where the investigation is included in their jurisdiction. The testimony of a police officer is equal to other evidence brought to the court's attention.

Police personnel and municipal units' officers under specifically issued orders have the right to carry weapons and apply force. The government of Russia regulates the procedure of receiving and carrying weapons. It is the responsibility of police officers to secure their weapons. Off-duty officers wearing their civilian clothes may not openly carry their weapons. Legislation prescribes situations in which the use of force, weapons, and special means is allowed and specifies the procedure for their utilization. Police officers are expected to attend periodical training and pass tests on the usage of force. For example, police are trained and required to issue a warning on the use of force whenever it is possible. Also, the law stipulates that the use of force be proportional to the threat and obligates police personnel to make all efforts to minimize the damage inflicted by the use of force.

The special means used by police include rubber batons, handcuffs, tear gas, paint dispensers, sound-and-light means of distraction, means to destroy barricades, shotguns, armored carriers, water throwing machines, and service dogs. Police in detention centers may use gas weapons in order to prevent escapes and suppress riots. The Law on Handling Prisoners provides an exhaustive list of rules for the use of firearms in prisons and detention centers, and the Police Law has a similar list for police officers, defining what kind of force may be used in a particular situation. However, the law lifts all restrictions in cases where a police officer defends individuals from an attack that threatens their lives or health. Special means and weapons may not be used against women with visible signs of pregnancy, minors, or handicapped people unless they conduct an armed resistance or attack, threatening the health and lives of other individuals. Also, firearms may not be used in crowds when strangers may suffer. Special means may not be used against peaceful assemblies, rallies, and demonstrations, if such assemblies do not disturb the work of Russia's transportation services, communication networks, and organizations. All cases involving the usage of special means or weapons are reported to the prosecutor, who must conduct an investigation and determine whether it was justifiable; however, the existing forms of public protection from indiscriminate use of weapons by police are not sufficient (Lukin, 2005).

Procedural Requirements and Police Abuses

Under the Soviet criminal justice system, criminal suspects and defendants were practically stripped of the rights granted to them in international law and standards. Fair trial standards were systematically violated, as an independent judiciary did not exist, and suspects and defendants were generally considered guilty before trial. Crime policy was based on a state plan, requiring police to solve specific numbers of crimes. The system did not allow for any form of public oversight over prisons or detention centers. The first serious attempts to reform the system were undertaken in the early 1990s. New laws were adopted that established a theoretically independent judiciary and provided due process rights, and crime policies were temporarily changed. However, the reforms came to a premature end several years later as they met great resistance from both the law enforcement institutions and political establishment.

Laws that dictate police behavior have not been brought into full accordance with the Constitution or the international standards to which the government purportedly adheres. The Police Law states that rights and freedoms of citizens are protected regardless of their gender, race, nationality, ethnicity, language, place of residence, religion, ideology, or other circumstances. The police are prohibited from using torture, violence, cruel punishments, and humiliation. Unfortunately, these rules rarely are implemented, because the militia still practices old methods of the Soviet system. Existing police legislation remains vague, and because there is no direct regulation of many procedural situations, it leaves resolution of disputed issues up to the discretion of a police officer. In a poll conducted among police officers in the Far East region of Russia, 44 percent of the respondents acknowledged regular use of illegal and unethical methods of inquiry and investigation, and 4 percent stated that they use these methods from time to time (Kolennikova, 2004).

One disputed issue is the requirement for a police officer to inform detainees of their rights. Russia does not have an equivalent of the U.S. Miranda rule, and the procedure for detention is not formalized. The violation of this procedure does not affect a case's procedural status and the legal rights of a detainee. There is no administrative or criminal procedure law that regulates procedures that occur between the time a person is apprehended by the police and the presentation of accusations by an investigator when the detention officially begins. Police officers are guided by the MIA *Manual on Policing and Patrolling*, which does not have the force of law and leaves a great amount of discretion to policemen.

Another unregulated issue is the legal obligation of police officers to inform a detainee's relatives of the detention upon the detainee's request. The provision stating this requirement is not elaborated. The Code of Criminal Procedural stipulates that information about the arrest shall be released within 12 hours of the detention's initiation, but the law does not specify a way of informing families. There is no obligation for police to inform the detainee's relatives by telephone, and a letter sent by regular mail is recognized as a sufficient method of informing, even though the normal time for mail delivery within a Russian locality is about seven days, and this fact may extend the period of informing substantially. The police officer who conducts the detention selects which relatives are informed. As a rule, these are relatives residing with the detained person; however, if the detained person insists on informing other relatives, his request may be taken into account. If police authorities believe that informing relatives about the arrest may harm further investigation, they may request the prosecutor's permission to withhold this information.

Another area of wide police abuse is a detainee's right to legal defense. The law states that this right starts at the beginning of detention; however, Russian practices exhibit violations of this right. For example, confidential meetings between detainees and their attorneys are often permitted only after the first interrogation (Ryzhakov, 2004).

Other police abuses in the form of brutality, harassment, and corruption constitute another serious problem. The lack of reliable data on the use of reasonable versus excessive force is partially attributable to the absence of a Russian equivalent of the U.S. Violent Crime Control and Law Enforcement Act of 1994. There are no government studies designed to obtain information on the prevalence and nature of citizens' encounters with the police. In 2003, more than 50 percent of residents in St. Petersburg, the second largest Russian city with 4.5 million persons, witnessed the use of excessive physical force and offensive language by police (Davis, Ortiz, & Gilinsky, 2004). Individuals who believe that a police officer's activities or failures to act violated their rights may complain to the officer's supervisors, a prosecutor, or a court; however, people are usually afraid to complain, because they have often heard warnings from victims of police abuse about repercussions should they lodge a complaint. In 2003 (the year from which the latest data are available), only 11 people in St. Petersburg filed appeals alleging police misconduct (Davis, Ortiz, & Gilinsky, 2004).

Police officers may be held responsible for their illegal actions according to existing legislation, and legislation requires that damage inflicted by a police officer shall be compensated. However, legal provisions for compensation for damages to crime victims largely remain a dead letter for victims of police abuse. It appears that there were only two cases of this kind during the last 15 years. Compensation for damages can also be awarded in civil cases; however, civil courts are unlikely to grant compensation for damages to torture victims, unless a criminal court has found the perpetrators guilty of such a crime.

The Internal Security Force, as established within the MIA's structure, inspects compliance of police work with legislation and observance of individuals' legal rights. Federal prosecutors handle cases where a police officer is suspected of having committed a crime or having acted inappropriately. According to MIA, about 100,000 officers were dismissed during the last 10 years. The number of crimes committed by police officers in 2004 increased by 4 percent. According to information reported by the Prosecutor General of the Russian Federation, in 2004, police officers committed 37 murders, 45 rapes, 138 acts of intentional causing of grave harm to health, 130 thefts, 75 plunders, and 41 robberies (Kots & Skoibeda, 2005). Reports of police wearing black ski masks, beating people with rifle butts, and taking victims' money and possessions during regular police raids are often made by the mass media in Moscow and St. Petersburg. In other cities, almost all incidents of police misconduct remain hidden from outsiders.

Sociological surveys demonstrate that age and gender are the strongest predictors of who is stopped by police, with younger male residents being more likely to be stopped than older male and female residents. Ethnic minorities have a higher chance of having involuntary encounters with the police than ethnic Russians. Fifty-two percent of those surveyed believed that the police stop people without a good reason. Human rights organizations have accused the Moscow police of racism in singling out non-Slavic individuals (especially immigrants from Russia's Caucasus republics), physical attacks, unjustified detentions, and other violations (Amnesty International, 2004). From time to time, the MIA leadership conducts a high-profile "Clean Hands Campaign" to purge the force of corrupt elements. In 2004, about 4,500 police officers were disciplined for misconduct, and about 2,000 were arrested for serious crimes.

Police leadership has explained that these abuses result from a low level of officer professionalism, insufficient financing, minimal equipment, and increased labor fluidity within the force. The inadequacy of the force became particularly apparent in the wave of organized crime that began sweeping Russia after the collapse of the Soviet Union. About 1 million qualified individuals have left the police for better paying jobs in the field of private security, which has expanded to meet the demand of companies needing protection from organized crime. Frequent bribe taking among the remaining members of the police has damaged the force's public credibility. Numerous revelations of police information peddling, tolerance of criminal acts, and participation in murders and prostitution rings have created a general public perception that all police are at least taking bribes (Curtis, 1998). According to experts, the main causes of corruption are insufficient funding to train and equip personnel, insufficient funding to pay adequate wages, poor work discipline, lack of accountability, and fear of reprisals from organized criminals (State Duma, 2005).

Policing Terrorism

Terrorism is a relatively new phenomenon in Russia. It is claimed that in post-Soviet Russia there have been over 500 contract murders, and terrorist acts during the 2002–2005 period have taken the lives of almost 2,000 Russians, most of them civilians, with no connection to the actual conflict in Chechnya. Since the first hijacking of an aircraft in the Soviet Union in 1958, there have been more than 110 hijacking attempts, half of which have occurred since the beginning of 1990s. The significance of fighting terrorism became especially important in the 1990s, when increasing Islamic militancy influenced developments in the Caucasus region, where 40,000 terrorists, apparently with considerable al-Quaeda links, formed a well-organized army able to conduct large-scale terrorist operations.

Russian counterterrorism strategy is focused on legal mechanisms to ensure public safety; this strategy views terrorism primarily as a problem of the criminal justice system. The legal framework for the fight against terrorism is defined by general criminal law regulations and a number of special legislative acts. The major role in the fight against terrorism historically belongs to the Federal Security Service, the former KGB. Its Antiterrorism Department was created in 1995, and in 1999, it merged with the reestablished secret police, the Constitutional Defense Department. The Ministry of Internal Affairs (regular police) also is involved actively in antiterrorist activities. In July 2003, management of the counterterrorist operation in the northern Caucasus, including the conduct of military operations in Chechnya, was transferred to police authorities. A federal anti-terrorist "Center T" with subordinated departments in all constituent components of the Russian Federation was created as a supplemental service within the MIA. Officers of this center conducted most of the apprehensions of terrorist suspects. Functions of both services intermingled, and there was no effective coordination between them. Presently, federal legislation determines the duties of the responsible executive agencies as follows:

- *The Russian Federation Federal Security Service* fights terrorism by preventing, uncovering, and stopping terrorist crimes, including crimes pursuing political objectives, and also by preventing, uncovering, and stopping international terrorist activities. The Federal Security Service conducts preliminary investigations of criminal cases relating to such crimes.
- *The Russian Federation Ministry of Internal Affairs* engages in the fight against terrorism by preventing, uncovering, and stopping terrorist crimes in which criminals are pursuing mercenary objectives.

Authorized bodies have a wide range of preventive and repressive measures at their disposal. However, the responsibilities of law enforcement agencies and control mechanisms are not sufficiently specified. The combination of vague proscriptions with the broad powers of executive agencies creates potential threats to fundamental rights because of the lack of appropriate structures and procedures to control the implementation of antiterrorism legislation.

Detention and Interrogation of Suspected Terrorists

The rules and principles governing the criminal investigation and prosecution of terrorism-related offenses are generally the same as for any other "serious" or "especially serious" crime. Apart from the use of specialized investigation bodies of the Federal Security Service, there is, in general, no special procedure in such cases. Because of their classification as first or second degree felonies, most terrorism-related crimes can be investigated and prosecuted by use of early warning measures and urgent procedures, such as use of special means and extension of the maximum duration of pretrial detention up to 18 months. Among other terrorism-related exemptions from existing criminal procedure are the use of pretrial detention of juveniles in regard to terrorism investigations and the right of the police to disregard the mandatory requirement to notify a detainee's relatives or a corresponding consular body in case of an arrest of a foreigner in order to ensure the secrecy of the preventive arrest. However, the minimum standard of judicial guarantees, as set forth in the Constitution, is provided in proceedings against terrorists, i.e., effective judicial protection, a competent court as established by law, the right to legal assistance, and the right to the presumption of innocence.

Surveillance and Intelligence Gathering

Basic investigative measures are the following: searches of private residences, seizure of property, seizure of correspondence, telephone tapping, and interception of communications. Except in exceptional circumstances, there should be a preliminary court order for investigators to take these measures. In urgent cases, investigators can use these measures without a prior judicial order on the condition that within 24 hours the judge is informed and is able to evaluate the legal grounds for the use of such measures. If, according to the judge's assessment, the decision to use special means appears to be unlawful, evidence obtained through these measures would not be admissible in court. The criminal procedural legislation provides for limited judicial oversight and certain derogations in connection with criminal investigations relating to terrorist offenses, including the application of investigative techniques that are not prescribed by the Criminal Procedural Code. These techniques include observation, electronic surveillance, search of buildings and means of transportation, including secret search, and seizure. A court warrant is not required for use of these techniques if the investigation concerns a terrorism-related offense. The same test applies to the control of postal, telegraphic, and electronic correspondence. In addition, under federal legislation, requirements such as the prohibition against conducting investigative actions at night or to cease recording telephone conversations upon expiration of a six-month period do not apply to terrorism-related investigations.

Monitoring of Persons

In 1993 the old Soviet residence permit system, which had been established in 1927 to monitor movements of Russian citizens within the country by means of passport entries made by the police, was replaced by a new residence registration system; however, this did not change the essence of the institution. According to the law, all Russian citizens must be registered at their places of permanent residence. An individual who has changed his or her primary residence must register with local police authorities within seven days after arrival at a new place. Individuals who have arrived at a place of temporary stay for a period longer than ten days must apply for temporary registration within three days after their arrival.

The receipt of obligatory medical insurance, social services, and other benefits depends on the registration, because these services cannot be received outside the territory where an individual is registered. An employer has no obligation to hire only local people; however, an employer is held administratively responsible if an employee does not possess a residence registration. This system is best understood as a control function utilized by police that prevents Russian citizens from exercising their social rights outside of the constituent component of the Russian Federation where they are permanently registered. The existing registration procedure has more restrictions in certain localities, for instance, in the cities of Moscow and St. Petersburg and in some other regional administrative centers. Since March 1997, the application of the registration rules is extended to foreigners if their stay in Russia is longer than three days. Foreigners without registration caught during passport checks conducted by police, who are allowed to search apartments during passport control operations, can be deported from the country immediately.

Based on permanent residence registration, local police departments issue domestic passports, the main identification document for Russian nationals. All Russian citizens must obtain internal passports within three months of reaching the age of 14. Russian passports contain the bearer's photograph, information about his or her name, date and place of birth, marital status, minor children, religion, ethnicity, criminal and military service records, date of issuance, and name of the issuing authority. Passports have no expiration dates; however, when a bearer reaches ages 25 and 45, a new photograph must be placed in the passport. Even though this is not a formal renewal of the passport, passports are not valid without these new photographs. When photographs are replaced, a review of residence registration, military, and criminal records is conducted by the local police.

The Russian police have no restrictions against checking individuals' identification documents and detaining individuals without documents for identification purposes. Ethnic, religious, and racial profiling is often used for selecting people to be subject to random passport checks conducted by police on streets, public transportation, and in places of mass gatherings, and this practice is supported by local administrations and public opinion.

Recruitment, Training, and Employment

Officially, the MIA forces number around 2 million (Sweet, 2002). The Special Purpose Detachment has 50,000 officers, and the Internal Troops have 300,000. These figures are very rough because of high turnover and poor record keeping (Pustyntsev, 2002). MIA estimates require that there is one officer of inquiry for every 165 claims submitted to the police or for approximately every 50 cases brought before the court; yet, the real workload of a criminal investigator is about 200–220 cases per month. According to existing norms, police employ one juvenile delinquency inspector for every 4,000–5,000 persons under 16 years old residing in the territory of a police district and one inspector per every 3,000 vehicles in the automobile inspection unit. Police stations at airports and train stations usually consist of 8 to 12 officers (Thomas, 2000).

The share of women is slightly over 15 percent of the force. In 1994, women constituted 20 percent of the force, but this percentage has decreased, because women are fired first during a reduction in force. As a rule, women are employed in clerical positions, in passport and visa registration sections, and as inspectors for the affairs of the minors. Often, women in the police force work as researchers and forensic experts.

Since 1993, turnover within the force has ranged from 20 to 70 percent. Such a wide range can be explained by the specifics of service in different regions and police units. Some police departments renew their staff every 18 months, and in almost all departments, a complete turnover occurs every five years. This fluidity severely undermines the professionalism of the officers employed. The average understaffing of police units is 20 percent. The biggest shortage of officers is at the Moscow Subway Police Department, where this figure reaches 40 percent. The workload is distributed among the remaining officers, but their salaries remain unchanged. All these conditions make police employment unattractive. Kots and Skoibeda (2005)

was adopted to preserve political neutrality of law enforcement personnel and to increase social awareness that police officials serve only the law and the people. Even though this provision insulates the police from direct use by the dominant political party, the police force remains actively involved in promoting the agenda of the current administration and securing election results favored by governors. Professional organizations of police officers are allowed, but officers may not go on strike to resolve labor disputes.

Another restriction is the prohibition on police involvement in any entrepreneurial activity or supplemental employment, except for teaching or scientific work. MIA salaries generally are lower than those paid in other agencies of the criminal justice system and, as a result, this ban often is violated. It is common for police officers, mostly those of low and middle rank, to work as private guards or provide other security related services. An independent study conducted in 2003 showed that 50 percent of police personnel are involved in illegal economic activity during their spare time, and 18 percent are earning extra money while on duty (Kosals, 2003).

At the end of the 1990s, the MIA reported debts equal to US$717 million, including US$272 million in overdue wages. There were reports of police officers undertaking hunger strikes in order to receive their wages. The situation has improved recently. Since 2000, the budget of the MIA has increased by a factor of 2.5 (MIA, 2004). In 2005, the ministry received US$6 billion, which is 20 percent more than it received in 2004. However, there is no guarantee that all this money will be used for the purposes for which it was appropriated. In 2003, the police received only 87 percent of the amount that had been allocated to them in that year's budget, and a lot of the remaining money was embezzled. For example, the Accounting Chamber (Russia's counterpart to the U.S. General Accounting Office) has investigated the theft of one-third of the budget allocated to the Moscow Regional Internal Affairs Department, and the purchase of Mercedes Benz SUVs for the Ural Regional Police Department when funds were intended for implementation of new technologies (Kots & Skoibeda, 2005).

In addition to federal and regional budget financing, police departments are allowed to draw from nonbudget resources by offering their services in the fields of security, protection services, registration of foreigners, and traffic safety. According to some estimates, nonbudget funds may amount up to US$50 billion annually. There is strong opinion that most of this money is coming from illegal activities and close cooperation with criminal structures. Some Russian researchers conclude that local organized criminal structures are no longer the focus of the police's professional activity, but are really business partners (Kots & Skoibeda, 2005).

Close connections between police and criminals, lack of equipment to solve crimes (computers, weapons, cars), and a history of subjecting persons to sophisticated torture methods (perfected over the Soviet period) all affect the public's perception of the police as a corrupt institution. Russians are fully aware of the futility of working with the police, and it is estimated that 42 percent of crime victims do not approach the police for help (Galeotti, 2002). While it is becoming increasingly popular in the democratic society to think about the police as providing services and to think of the public as consumers of police services, most Russians do not turn to the police when crime or disorder arise. The most common reasons for an individual's contact with the police is to obtain a passport or drivers' license or to register an address.

Russian society has a long history of supplementing or even replacing minimally effective official police activities with self-policing. This tradition started with the prevalence of the mob law of village "self-judging" over often amateurish and overstretched policing in the previous centuries and continues today with people independently taking care of their own security. A willingness to accept the protection of organized crime rather than have no protection at all and the growth of the private security industry, which has expanded dramatically as people and enterprises seek their own "police," exemplify this process. There are about 10,000 private security agencies in Russia, employing more than 1 million people (Ustinov 2005). Largely underregulated, they range from street gangs to private armies of up to 3,000 armed security personnel run by former police and security chieftains.

Conclusion

Significant economic and political changes have had almost no positive effect on policing in Russia. Promises of building a law-governed state have had little effect, and although the new Russian Federation has given the police a wide array of powers and increased the size of the force to go along with the new powers, the daily experience of Russian citizens attests to the police's failure in combating petty and organized crime alike (Galeotti, 1997). The police did not get integrated into the multifunctional national security system, and their ability to be a first responder during an emergency situation is undermined by the ineffectiveness of command, lack of equipment, and lack of professionalism of the staff.

Scattered attempts for police reform have ended in failure. They seldom amounted to more than bringing in new commanders who ceremoniously would pledge to clean up the force and conduct some organizational changes, renaming and resubordinating departments within the MIA. Supporters of reforms have failed to take into consideration the inertia and sometimes even the open resistance of the political establishment and law enforcement bodies, which continue to perform their traditional role of protecting the interests of the elite (Pustyntsev, 2002). Even when crime and police misconduct rose steeply, the government did not introduce fundamental changes to the police force and the laws guiding this body. As a result, Russia's criminal justice system remains a hybrid of half-reformed and purely Soviet institutions and laws.

Public control over police activities is almost nonexistent in Russia today, although it is required under the Police Law. The police are largely controlled by all branches of government within their jurisdiction. The controlling institutions are not allowed to interfere in the procedural work of the police. The Prosecutor General supervises the legality of police activities and the uniform application of Russian laws all over the nation's territory. Recently published books on Russian policing suggest terminating the duality of prosecutorial control and dividing this function between two different institutions, where one would supervise police and the other would control actions of those who are the subjects of police activities. Other proposals recommend canceling the existing system of crime registration and police performance evaluations to stop the falsification of statistics and the hiding of crimes, amending the Criminal Code with harsher punishments for crimes committed by police personnel, and implementing measures of effective public control. Suggestions to produce a bill of rights, to end misleading detentions, and to introduce greater transparency and judicial and public control may lead to the improvement of the force. There is hope that implementing these measures with massive government investments will establish a modern and professional force ready to exhibit the democratic character of policing and to meet the challenges of booming crime, terrorist threats, public demands, and the rule of law.

Note

1. For the purposes of this paper, the term *militia* will be used as a synonym for *police* because of the nature of its operations.

References

Adrianov, S. (1902). *MVD 1802-1902. Istoricheskii ocherk [MVD 1802-1902. Historical survey]*. St. Petersburg: MVD Publishing House.

Amnesty International. (2004). *Concerns for Europe and Central Asia.*. Retrieved June 24, 2006 from http://web.amnesty.org/library/index/ENGEUR010052004

Belskii, K. (2004). *Politseiskoe Pravo [Police Law]*. Moscow: Delo I Servis.

Butler, W. (2003). *Russian law*. Oxford, UK: Oxford University Press.

Curtis, G. (Ed.). (1998). *Russia: A country study*. Washington, DC: Federal Research Division, Library of Congress.

Davis, R., Ortiz, C., & Gilinsky, Y. (2004). A cross-national comparison of citizen perceptions of the police in New York City and St. Petersburg, Russia. *Policing, 27*(1), 37–64.

Galeotti, M. (1997). Cops, spies and private eyes: Changing patterns of Russian policing. *Europe-Asia Studies, 49*(1), 141–157.

Galeotti, M. (2002). *Russian and post-soviet organized crime*. Aldershot, UK; Brookfield, VT: Ashgate.

Gavrilov, B. (2003). Novelly ugolovnogo protsessa [Novelties of the criminal process]. *Rossiiskaia Iustitsiia, (10),* 17–29.

Gerson, L. (1976). *The secret police in Lenin's Russia.* Philadephia: Temple University Press.

Jamestown Foundation. (1998). The interior ministry plans new special units. *Monitor,* 4(194) [Electronic version]. Retrieved August 15, 2007, from http://www .jamestown.org/publications_details.php?volume_id=21&issue_id=1405& article_id=14306

Khinstein, A. (2003, November 16). Vinovaty do suda (Guilty before trial). *Moskovskii Komsomolets,* p. 2.

Kikot, V. (2004). Mesto i rol organov MVD v politike Rossiiskogo gosudarstva (Place and role of the MIA authorities in the politics of the Russian state). *Gosudarstvo i Pravo, (1),* 11–32.

Kolennikova, O. (2004). *Pravoohranitelnye organy Rossiiskoi Federatsii (Law enforcement authorities of the Russian Federation).* Krasnoiarsk: Izdatelstvo KGU.

Kosals, Y. (2003). *Ekonomicheskaia aktivnost militsii v Rossii (Economic activity of police in Russia).* Moscow: Yurizdat.

Kots, A., & Skoibeda, U. (2005, June 7–10). Pochemu menty pytaiut i berut vziatki (Why policemen torture and take bribes). *Komsomolskaia Pravda,* pp. 2–3.

Lukin, V. (2005, April 16, May 27, 30, 31). On activities of the human rights commissioner in the Russian Federation in 2004: Report of the RF human rights commissioner. *Rossiiskaia Gazeta,* p. 3.

Ministry of Internal Affairs (MIA) of the Russian Federation. (2004). *Annual report.* Retrieved May 12, 2005, from http://www.mvdinform.ru/index.pxp?docid=3158

Peyser, M., & Vitsin, S. (2005). Russia. In M . Haberfeld (Ed.), *Encyclopedia of law enforcement* (Vol. 3, pp. 1273–1281). Thousand Oaks, CA: Sage.

Pustyntsev, B. (2002). Police reform in Russia: Obstacles and opportunities. *Policing and Society,* 10(1), pp. 54–72.

Putin, V. (2005, April 26). State of the nation address. *Rossiiskaia Gazeta,* pp. 1–2.

Rushailo, V. (2001). *Militsiia Rossii: Dokumenty I materially (Russia's militia: Documents and materials).* Moscow: Izdatelstvo MVD.

Ryzhakov, A. (2004). *Kommentarii k zakonu Rossiiskoi Federatsii o militsii [Commentaries on the Russian Federation law on militia].* Moscow: Norma.

Shelley, L. (1996). *Policing Soviet society.* New York: Routledge.

State Duma [legislature] of the Russian Federation, Committee on Civil, Criminal, and Procedural Legislation. (2005, March 11). Hearings on police tortures and abuses. *Dumskii Vestnik,* (4), p. 73.

Sweet, K. (2002). Russian law enforcement under President Putin. *Human Rights Review,* 3(4), 20–33.

Thomas, T. (2000). Restructuring and reform in Russia's MVD: Good idea, bad timing? in *Law Intensity Conflict & Law Enforcement,* 9(2), pp. 2–11.

Ustinov, V. (2005). O sostoyanii zakonnosti [State of justice]. Report to the state duma. *Rossiiskaia Iustitsiia,* (4), 3–8.

Weissman, N. (1985). Regular police in tsarist Russia, 1900–1914. *The Russian Review,* 44(1), 45–68.

Further Reading

Baker, P., & Glasser, S. (2005). *Kremlin Rising: Vladimir Putin's Russia and the End of Revolution.* New York: Scribner, 2005. (Examines the failure of democratic changes, including those aimed at reforming of the police.)

Butler, W. (2003). *Russian law.* Oxford, UK: Oxford University Press. (A study of new Russia's legal order, reflecting the demise of the Soviet Union and the transition to market-oriented legal rules and democratic institutions.)

Galeotti, M. (Ed.). (2002). *Russian and post-Soviet organized crime.* Dartmouth, UK: Ashgate. (Essays on the nature of criminality in Russia and specifics of the police response.)

Handelman, S. (1995). *Comrade criminal: Russia's new mafia.* New Haven, CT: Yale University Press. (Author treats the issue of organized crime as a political problem and reviews connections between criminal leaders and law enforcement institutions.)

Human Rights Watch. (1998). *Confessions at any cost.* New York: Author. (A detailed case study that introduces readers to the practice of police abuse in Russia and provides information on police techniques and the status of detainees.)

Knight, A. (1996). *Spies without cloaks: The KGB's successors.* Princeton, NJ: Princeton University Press. (Discusses the KGB role in the breakup of the Soviet Union and the unfolding development of the new Russia; analyzes how Soviet-era institutions have adapted to new conditions and became an integral part of the semidemocratic, semiauthoritarian new Russia.)

Liang, H.-H. (1992). *The rise of the modern police and the European state system from Metternich to the Second World War.* Cambridge, UK: Cambridge University Press. (A cross-cultural comparative study that explores the issue of integrating European police forces into the state structures, looking specifically at France, Prussia/Germany, and Russia/Soviet Union.)

Shelley, L. (1996). *Policing Soviet society.* New York: Routledge. (Examines the history, development, and daily activities of police institutions in the Soviet Union and their impact on the ongoing police reform in contemporary Russia.)

Zuckerman, F. (1996). *The tsarist secret police in Russian society, 1880–1917.* Basingstoke, UK: Macmillan. (Explores the activities of the political police in the wider context of policing and governing late tsarist Russia.)

Web Sites of Interest

http://eng.mvdrf.ru/: Official website of the Russian Ministry of Internal Affairs. Provides information on police legislation, structure, and activities of the law enforcement authorities.

http://www.hrw.org: Reports on police activities provided by Human Rights Watch.

http://www.hro.org/: Commentaries to legislation and analytical materials on law enforcement in Russia.

7 Emergence of Modern Indian Policing

From Mansabdari to Constabulary

Farrukh Hakeem

Policing in India commenced as a military enterprise. It remained a military endeavor during the Aryan and Muslim periods. Early forms of policing were evident only in the big cities of medieval India. Prior to the tenth century CE, forms of policing during the Hindu period were fairly rudimentary (Rao, 1967; Sanghar, 1967). With the advent of the Muslim sultanates of northern India, a clearer structure of the policing apparatus emerged. Policing during this period followed a feudal military model that is referred to as the Mansabdari system. This structure continued to be employed throughout the Muslim period in India (1100 CE to 1700 CE). Even after the advent of the East India Company, this feudal model did not undergo any major changes. During the eighteenth century, the English colonists made a series of efforts to improve the policing apparatus. The initial efforts were feeble attempts to build on the old system of policing and did not lead to any tangible improvement. However, during the course of British rule this model came to be considered ineffective and was gradually replaced with a more civilian model of policing.

Colonial Policing

The reforms initiated by Robert Peel in 1829 in England led to important changes in policing. The directors of the East India Company advised that similar measures should be followed in India. A select committee was

169

appointed in 1832 to look into problems leading to an increase in crime and oppression by the police agencies.

Three reports that were written during the 1830s provide some insight into the state of affairs of the police. These reports were instrumental in establishing the Indian police force. The first of these reports was by Frederick Shore, a seasoned district judge who wrote an insightful note regarding the duties and the problems of the police (*darogas* in Urdu) in 1837. Shore not only outlined the problems but also made some pragmatic suggestions to improve the functioning of the police apparatus. Some of the recommendations were the following:

- Provide respectable salaries for police personnel.
- Give promotions and rewards for good conduct.
- Give additional powers to the police in some petty cases.
- Vest authority in some of the upper-class landholders to persuade them to give their support, which was withheld under the system in place at the time of Shore's report.
- Have the magistrates exercise strict surveillance over all those who were connected to the colonial establishment of the East India Company.

A second report was made in 1838 by Thomas Metcalfe, who set up a committee to examine the problems related to policing. The committee pointed out that the reasons for the inefficiency of the police were as follows:

- The police received inadequate supervision from the magistrates, who were burdened with many other responsibilities.
- The union of the offices of magistrate and collector had a negative impact on the administration of the police force, because police officers had to pay more attention to the collection of revenue than to police duties.
- Due to lax oversight, the subordinate police staff was corrupt and negligent in the performance of their duties.

The committee recommended that the collector should stop exercising control over the police and that a magistrate in each of the districts should perform this task. It further suggested that the districts should be subdivided into subdivisions. In each subdivision, authority over the police would be vested in the deputy magistrate. It also recommended that the village police watch system be revamped.

The third report was by Frederick Halliday, who made some very detailed proposals for establishing a police force. He suggested that the entire police apparatus be placed under a superintendent general of police at headquarters. Under the superintendent general, there were to be 23 superintendents, 32 assistant superintendents, 888 *darogas*, 4,440 *jamadars,* and 66,600 *burkandazes* (see Table 7.1).

This proposal was implemented in part. A superintendent of police was appointed in every district with the superintendent general. A joint magistrate

Table 7.1   Police Structure Proposed by Halliday

Officer	Number
Superintendent General of Police	1
Superintendents of Police	23
Assistant Superintendents of Police	32
Darogas	888
Jamadars	4,440
Burkandazes	66,600

was also appointed in each district to perform the magisterial function. Except for these two changes the police functioned in the same lackadaisical manner that they had before.

The colonial police model originated in Ireland and followed the model of the Royal Irish Constabulary. As opposed to the metropolitan police model, which consisted of unarmed police, the Royal Irish Constabulary was a paramilitary force, a gendarmerie, which had the primary goal of maintaining law and order amongst a populace of which large elements actively or passively opposed the entire system of law that the force sought to uphold. The main purpose was to suppress disorder without the use of the military (Tobias, 1977).

In 1843 Charles Napier annexed the northwest province of Sindh to British India. To maintain order in this new province, Napier decided to implement the recommendations that had been made by Frederick Halliday in order to improve the efficiency of the police. Napier modeled his police on the lines of the Royal Irish Constabulary. This new system was a separate and self-contained police organization under which the officers had to perform only police duties. The system developed by Napier had its basis on two main principles:

1. The police should be completely separated from the military.

2. The police should be an independent body to assist the collectors in matters dealing with law and order, but they should have their own officers.

The main principle here was that the military forces and the civil police should be kept quite separate. This was a novel idea to solve the problem but it gradually came to be followed throughout India in phases.

Upon visiting Sindh in 1847, Sir George Clerk was very impressed by the efficiency of the Sindh police. He decided to organize the Bombay police on the model that Napier implemented. In 1853 a superintendent of police was appointed for each district in Bombay province.

The Indian Penal Code was passed in 1862. It defines basic crimes and punishments and is based mainly on English criminal law. Crimes are divided into nine categories (Hakeem, 1998). The three basic criminal statutes—the Indian Penal Code, the Criminal Procedure Code, and the Evidence Act were passed by the imperial parliament of Britain for its Indian colony during the tumultuous postmutiny era (Ramaswami, 1951).

The Police Commission drafted a police bill in 1860 (Bayley, 1969). The bill was enacted as the Police Act (V) of 1861. The last report of the Police Commission was made in 1862, after which the commission was dissolved (Saha, 1990).

The terms of reference for the commission can be gleaned from a dispatch by Charles Wood, secretary of state for India to the governor general. Some of the main provisions examined were as follows:

- There was to be a special emphasis on the predominance of civil elements for the proposed well-organized police force.
- The entire police force was to be put under the control of an officer who was in direct communication with the local government.
- Adequate measures were to be taken to improve the village watch, and it was to be placed under the control of a magistrate.
- In order to create a good police system, a fair pay scale was to be ensured to all ranks of the police.

The government concurred with the commission that the police organization in India should be placed under the exclusive control, superintendence, and responsibility of English officers only. The recommendations of the commission helped in abolishing the archaic police system and succeeded in ushering in a uniform system of policing under a unified command and established hierarchy throughout British India. The inspector general of police was to have overall control over the police in the provinces. The inspector general was to be assisted by the district superintendent of police in each district. The district superintendent in turn was assisted by a number of assistant district superintendents. These positions were meant for the English officers only, and Indians could not be appointed to these positions. The subordinate police ranks were categorized as inspectors, head constables, and constables. Indians could be appointed only to these subordinate police ranks. With respect to the village police, the commission recommended that they should be continued as an institution.

From an objective perspective, the police in the real sense of the term originated in India from the period when the East India Company got political control of eastern India in 1765 CE. The English authorities carried out a series of experiments over a span of 100 years in order to settle upon the present structure of police. The model of policing that evolved was one that had a definite structure and a robust command and control system.

Postindependence Period

The Police Act of 1861 established the main principles for the organization of the police forces in India. This organization has continued to the present with minor modifications. Though state police forces are separate and show some minor differences in detail, their pattern of organization and operation are very similar.

An inspector general of police who is answerable to the home minister of the state heads police forces in each state. For command and coordination purposes, the domain of an inspector general is divided into police ranges. A deputy inspector general, who in turn is responsible for three to six districts, heads each range. The superintendent of police is in charge of the district police headquarters and constitutes the fulcrum of the state police operations. District superintendents of police have much discretionary authority and are responsible for supervising subordinate police stations along with many specialty elements, which include the criminal investigation detachment, equipment storehouses/armories, and traffic police. The larger districts also have assistant district superintendents. Constables who are assigned to the police stations conduct much of the preventive police work. The number of stations in a district can range from less than 10 to over 50 in some cases. Stations are grouped into subdivisions and circles to facilitate supervision from district headquarters. Major metropolitan cities like New Delhi, Calcutta, Bombay, Madras, and Hyderabad have separate municipal forces that are headed by a commissioner of police (see Figure 7.1).

Within state police forces there is a distinction between armed and unarmed police. Unarmed police staff the police stations and departments of criminal investigation. Though they are uniformed, they are unarmed. They may carry a short bamboo staff called a *lathi*. They constitute the police with whom the public has contact during the normal course of affairs. Some of their typical tasks include searching for lost children, investigating crimes, patrolling streets, regulating traffic, interposing in village quarrels, and generally responding to the needs of the general populace for police assistance.

Armed police reside in cantonments concentrated at a few points across each state. They do not have daily contact with the masses. They do not respond to calls for assistance from individuals but to orders from superior officers. The armed police are recruited and trained separately from the unarmed police. There are two types of armed police: district armed police and special armed police. The district armed police force is composed of armed policemen quartered in each district headquarters under the control of the district superintendent. The special armed police are under the immediate command of the inspector general of police through a deputy inspector general and are concentrated at a couple of points in each state. They may have heavier armor than the district armed police and are often used for special kinds of enforcement actions.

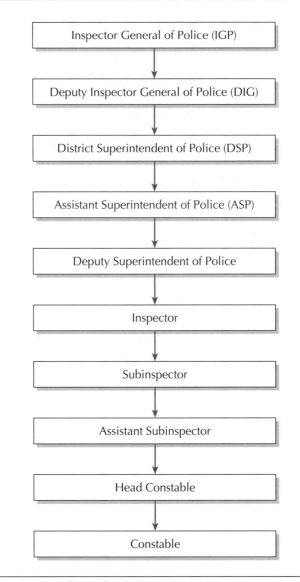

Figure 7.1   Organizational Structure of Indian Police

Structure of the Indian Police Force _____

The Indian police have three main features. The first feature is diversity and
similarity. The police are organized, maintained, and directed by the states
of the Indian Union. The federal government has some police agencies under
its authority, like the Central Bureau of Investigation (CBI). There is diversity of operational control along with remarkable organizational similarity.
India has avoided fragmentation of police under a system of local control
(such as the system in the United States, with its 40,000 separate forces) but
has the rigidity of a national police force controlled by a central government.

The second feature is horizontal stratification. The Indian police are horizontally stratified. They are organized into cadres based upon rank. The principle of horizontal stratification goes beyond the organization of ranks. It accounts for relations between the federal and state governments with respect to police administration and the distribution of police powers among the ranks. The officer cadre, known as the IPS, is recruited, organized, trained, and disciplined according to national legislation. Police power and authority differs with rank. This is different from the system in Great Britain, where a constable has all the authority any policeman can have. Horizontal stratification is reflected in rank structure, relations between levels of government regarding police personnel, and the distribution of legal authority among policemen.

The third feature is vertical division. The police in each state are divided vertically into an armed and an unarmed branch. This is a functional division. Unarmed police staff police stations, go on patrol duties, answer routine complaints, perform traffic duties, and prevent and investigate crime. The armed police perform those duties that require the presence of constituted physical force, such as guarding banks and quelling civil disturbances.

States that have armed police contingents use them as a reserve strike force in emergencies. These units are of two types: mobile-armed police under direct state control and district armed police that are less well equipped. The district armed police are controlled by the district superintendent of police and are normally used for riot control functions.

At all levels, the senior police officers are answerable to the police chain of command along with the general direction and control of designated civilian officials. In the municipal forces, the chain of command runs directly up to the state home minister. The dual hierarchy of accountability to civilian and police authorities has been the source of much confusion and disagreement. Though participation by political authorities can be regarded as a symbol of democracy and a safeguard for police accountability, it can also be considered to be problematic, because police have complained about political interference in police affairs. There are frequent charges that political parties have increasingly tried to influence police activities for their personal or partisan ends (Bayley, 1983; Verma, 1997).

Responsibility for policing is shared by the federal (central) and state government. The federal government elements include the Indian Police Service (IPS), various paramilitary units, and police in the union territories. In the 1970s new paramilitary forces were created under central government control to safeguard borders and provide for industrial security. In 1980 the state police forces were estimated to be about 765,000. These included regular as well as paramilitary forces.

In 1970 the federal government established the Bureau of Police Research and Development. This bureau was set up with the objective of modernizing the police forces. It has research and development divisions. Subsequently other divisions were added, including those for training (1973), forensics (1983), and correctional administration (1995).

Policing Under the Constitution

The responsibility for maintaining law and order rests on the states. Most of the routine policing, such as prevention and detection of crime, apprehension of criminals, and maintenance of public order is carried out by state police forces. The Constitution permits the federal government to participate in police operations and organization by authorizing the maintenance of the IPS. The IPS officers are recruited and trained by the federal government. Most of these recruits are assigned to senior positions in the state police forces, and they are under the operational control of the states.

The Constitution also permits the federal government to have other forces that are necessary to safeguard national security. Such paramilitary forces are legally created to assist the states only upon request of the state governments.

During the 1970s and 1980s, the police came under increasing public scrutiny due to their inability to deal with crime and public disorder. As an institution, the police were considered to be ineffective, corrupt, and unruly. This was a perennial problem with the Indian police. A 1902 report by the Police Commission surmised that the public did not have much confidence in the police. The public also considered the police to be corrupt and oppressive. The position is much the same today, if not worse; the police are considered to be highly corrupt, politicized, and dysfunctional (Dhillon, 2005).

Federal Level Forces

The federal Ministry of Home Affairs is in charge of law enforcement at the national level. It provides assistance and guidance to state governments to perform similar functions. The ministry deals with all matters that address maintenance of public peace and order, staffing and administration of public services, delineation of boundaries, and administration of union territories.

Officers from the IPS occupy most of the senior positions of all state and territorial police services. They are also deputed in national agencies that have responsibility for police and security matters. The Union Public Service Commission, through competitive examinations on a nationwide basis, recruits officers of the IPS. Upon completion of the basic course given to members of all national services, IPS officers attend the National Police Academy, Hyderabad. Upon completion of work at the academy, they are assigned to the state police forces, where they usually remain for the rest of their careers.

Police in the union territories are the responsibility of the Police Division, which also runs the National Police Academy, Hyderabad, and the Institute of Criminology and Forensic Science. The CBI investigates crimes that involve public officials and public undertakings.

The Ministry of Home Affairs also controls the paramilitary forces. These include the Central Reserve Police (CRP), which was established by the

British in 1939 and is one of the largest paramilitary forces. The CRP was established to help the military deal with the independence movement. Since independence, it has had the task of assisting the state police and the army. The CRP is used to quell internal disturbances. This force is called in when disorder escalates beyond the control of the local police. The CRP had a major role in assisting the army in checking insurgency in the Northeast. It is also used to protect the security of the Ministry of Defense and other federal government institutions. Another paramilitary force is the Border Security Force (BSF), which was created in 1965 to release the army from doing all the routine patrol duties on the border with Pakistan. It was organized by consolidating the state border units and had the additional responsibility of controlling smuggling, resisting infiltration, and assisting the army. It is also used for internal policing. The BSF is equipped with more advanced and sophisticated weapons than the other paramilitary forces. It has its own training facilities and has a factory at Tekanpur that produces tear gas and smoke grenades for all the police and paramilitary forces.

Other smaller paramilitary forces that are maintained include the following:

1. The Assam Rifles were established in 1866 as a frontier defense force for the Northeast. It is one of the oldest of the paramilitary forces and has its headquarters in Shillong. After independence, its main task has been to suppress uprisings among tribal people in the Northeast.

2. In 1962 the Indo-Tibetan Border Force was created to provide border security in the mountainous regions of the northern borders. It is mainly a mountaineering force.

3. The Railway Protective Force is assigned to protect and secure the national railroads.

4. The Central Industrial Security Force, which was set up in 1979, provides security for public sector enterprises and some government installations.

5. National Security Guards were established in 1984 as a paramilitary force. Members are used for internal security duties and combating terrorism.

Terrorism and Human Rights

Early instances of terrorism were experienced by the British in India during the nineteenth century. Politics and religious fanaticism combined briefly in the 1890s to create the problem of terrorism in British India. Located in the Sindh region, the Hur Brotherhood specifically resembled the earlier brotherhood of the assassins.

It is customary for Muslims to become followers (*murid*) of a spiritual leader who is known as *Pir*. One of the most important leaders in the nineteenth century was Pir Pagaro of Sindh. His followers were the fanatical sect of Hurs who were blindly devoted to his person. They committed violent crimes and maintained a close secret union within their brotherhood. The Hurs committed dacoities on such a scale that it can only be described as a war on society. This reign of terror could not be suppressed by all the normal methods. A novel method was employed to solve this problem.

The Hurs were proclaimed a criminal tribe, and their villages were constituted as settlements under the Criminal Tribes Act of 1871. The movements of the main inhabitants were restricted, and punitive police were permanently placed to supervise them and take roll call twice daily. There was a three-pronged approach—the incorrigible elders were segregated from the younger members of the tribe; the young were educated, and jobs were provided to the members of the tribe so that they could earn an honest living (Griffiths, 1971). During the 1940s and 1950s, a second Hur uprising occurred in Pakistan (Friedlander, 2004). The Hurs committed more than 200 violent crimes in six months and killed over 200 people in 1942. Martial law was imposed, and even aircraft were used to bring the situation under control. The problem was finally solved when the Hur leader was convicted and executed in 1943.

Current terrorism hotspots can be classified into two broad types: those of an extra-territorial nature and those that are indigenous. The Kashmir problem is one that goes back to the days of partition in 1947. This state was claimed by both India and Pakistan but is now practically occupied by both countries. The present insurgency in Indian-administered Jammu and Kashmir stems from the brutal, high-handed, and shortsighted policies of the Indian government. The other insurgencies are based on popular demands for social and economic justice by indigenous peoples. The federal government is viewed as being exploitative of the rights of local populations in, for example, Punjab, Assam, and Nagaland.

Most of these movements are handled by the federal government by means of special acts. The first in this series of acts was TADA (Terrorists and Disruptive Activities Prevention Act, 1985). When this act lapsed in 1995, it was replaced by POTA (Prevention of Terrorist Activities Act, 2002). There have been serious concerns voiced by human rights activists against these special acts. There are gross violations of human rights by the unfettered use of these acts against vulnerable and marginalized groups such as Sikhs, Muslims, and the Dalits. There have been many instances where the provisions of these acts have been abused by individuals or groups targeting political opponents and religious minorities (Das & Verma, 1998). Recently the state of Gujarat was admonished by the Supreme Court when Muslims were killed in riots all across that state and the provisions of the law were used to harass them (Dhillon, 2005).

_____ **Conclusion**

The problems facing India today are similar to those faced during the early days of policing in the United States (Raghavan, 1999). In fact, India and the United States, in spite of the cultural and religious differences, have very similar problems: India, being a former British colony, is facing the problems faced by the United States during its political era of policing (1840–1930). During this era of the political spoils system, American policing was highly corrupt and politicized, and minorities were segregated and discriminated against. These problems are similar to some of those being faced by the Indian police, though some of the religious issues further complicate the problems. The Indian police are still operating under a legal and administrative apparatus that was designed to maintain order and hold on to the imperial possession that India was in 1850. The system is now being exposed for what it is and has become totally dysfunctional for a modern and democratic society. Local politicians have now replaced the British Raj as users of the police as an instrument for repressive control of the populace and to enrich themselves in all respects.

There have been recent rumblings against the established political elites, and the police apparatus is being mandated by the Supreme Court of India to be accountable to the people and not the politicians. It is also being asked to abide by the rule of law. In the case of _Prakash Singh v. Union of India_ (2007), the court has now stepped into the arena of police reform. The court was highly critical of the police agencies and has begun to move in the direction of mandating certain minimum standards that the police have to meet. It calls for a courageous, fair minded, and farsighted leadership. As with the colonial police enterprise, it calls for solutions that address the core of the problems. Most of the problems facing the police are economic and political in nature. The modern police force of India is still operating under a colonial framework, where there was greater emphasis on order maintenance. A modern police force should be used to prevent and detect crime.

The Indian police were created after the Mutiny of 1857. Their main task was to maintain order and perpetuate the rule of the British over India (Das & Verma, 1998). The legal framework for policing was designed to protect the ruling elites and not to work for the benefit of the community (Dhillon, 2005). Some of the problems that are surfacing now are merely symptoms of a deeper malaise in the system. The goals and mission of the police will need to be reformulated in light of the enormous economic and social changes taking place in India. The reactive order maintenance model of policing needs to be replaced by one that is more proactive and preventive and has much more regard for citizens as customers and the police as service providers who have to treat the public with respect and dignity.

The solution may lie in experimenting with one of the other models that is employed in other parts of the world. India could borrow from one other former British colony—the United States—to solve some of the problems. The Indian system is midway between the political and the professional eras of American policing (Wrobleski & Hess, 2003). The Indian police could benefit from the community policing model so as to reduce the amount of political interference that presently hampers their potential. However, the police may need to move to a professional phase of policing so as to set up the necessary institutional framework and let it mature before a move toward community policing is made. Whether Indian police will move toward the professional or community era of policing is debatable; however it is certain that the present model is unsustainable.

References

Bayley, D. H. (1969). *The police and political development in India.* Princeton, NJ: Princeton University Press.

Bayley, D. H. (1983). The police and political order in India. *Asian Survey, 23*(4), 484–496.

Das, D., & Verma, A. (1998). The armed police in the British colonial tradition: The Indian perspective. *Policing: An International Journal of Police Strategies and Management, 21*(2,) 354–367.

Dhillon, K. S. (2005). *Police and politics in India—Colonial concepts, democratic compulsions: Indian police 1947–2002.* New Delhi: Manohar.

Friedlander, R. (2004). *Terrorism: Volume I. An historical overview.* Retrieved June 15, 2004, from http://web.syr.edu/~efbuitra/law%20school/Counter%20Terrorism/January%2020/historical_overview.pdf

Griffiths, P. (1971). *To guard my people. The history of the Indian police.* London: Ernest Benn.

Hakeem, F. (1998). From Sharia to mens rea: Legal transition to the Raj. *International Journal of Comparative and Applied Criminal Justice, 22*(2), 211–224.

Prakash Singh and others v. Union of India and others. Supreme Court of India. Writ Petition no. 310 of 1996 (Supreme Court of India, January 11, 2007).

Raghavan, R. K. (1999). *Policing a democracy: A comparative study of India and the U.S.* New Delhi: Manohar.

Ramaswami, P. N. (1951). *Magisterial and police guide* (Vol. I). Bombay: Ratanlal Dhirajlal and Thakore.

Rao, S. V. (1967). *Facets of crime in India.* New York: Allied.

Saha, B. P. (1990). *Indian police: Legacy and quest for formative role.* New York: Advent Books.

Sanghar, S. P. (1967). *Crime and punishment in Mughal India.* Delhi: Sterling.

Tobias, J. (1977). The British colonial police: An alternative police style. In P. J. Stead (Ed.), *Pioneers in policing, an anthology* (pp. 241–261). Montclair, NJ: Patterson Smith.

Verma, A. (1997). Maintaining law and order in India: An exercise in police discretion. *International Criminal Justice Review, 7*(1), 65–80.

Wrobleski, H. M., & Hess, K. M. (2003). *Introduction to law enforcement and criminal justice.* Belmont, CA: Wadsworth.

Further Reading

Anand, D. (2005). The violence of security: Hindu nationalism and the politics of representing 'the Muslim' as a danger. *The Round Table, 94*(379), 203–215.

Engineer, A. A. (2006). *Minorities and police in India.* Delhi: Eastern Book.

Mahajan, V. D. (1965). *Muslim rule in India.* Bombay: S. Chand.

Natarajan, M. (1996). Women police units in India: A new direction. *Police Studies: International Review of Police Development, 19*(2), 63–76.

Raghavan, R. K. (1989). *Indian police problems, planning and perspectives.* New Delhi: Manohar.

Raghavan, R. K. (2003). The Indian police: Problems and prospects. *Publius: The Journal of Federalism, 33*(4), 119–134.

Sarkar, J. (1967). *Mughal administration.* Calcutta: Orient.

Sharma, S. R. (1951). *Mughal government and administration.* Bombay: Hind Kitabs.

Thakur, R. (1993). Ayodhya and the politics of India's secularism: A double-standards discourse. *Asian Survey, 33*(7), 645–664.

Verma, A. (1999). Cultural roots of police corruption in India. *Policing: An International Journal of Police Strategies and Management, 22*(3), 264–279.

Verma, A. (2005). *The Indian police: A critical evaluation.* New Delhi: Regency.

Yasin, M. (1958). *A social history of Islamic India.* Lucknow: Upper India Publishing House.

8 Democratization of Policing

The Case of the Turkish Police

Ibrahim Cerrah

Turkey is a unitary state governed by the parliamentary democratic system. The Turkish Republic was founded on October 29, 1923, by Mustafa Kemal Atatürk. Its capital is Ankara. The citizens exercise their sovereignty directly by participating in elections and indirectly by means of authoritative structures. The structures that exercise the sovereignty are the legislative, executive, and judiciary branches of the Turkish government. The principle of separation of powers prevails among these three structures.

Turkey is divided into seven geographic regions. These are the Aegean Region, the Marmara Region, the Black Sea Region, the Eastern Anatolia Region, the Southeastern Anatolia Region, the Mediterranean Region, and Inner Anatolia Region. For administrative purposes, the country is divided into 81 provinces. Each province is also further divided into cities, towns, and municipalities. In the provinces, the central government is represented by a governor appointed by the central government. Each province has a capital city and a number of small towns. Towns are ruled by subgovernors. Subgovernors, who are under the authority of the respective provincial governor, are also appointed by the central government. Governors and subgovernors are all agents of central government and have little, if any, accountability to the local community. Ultimate power over officials belongs to the respective department at the central government. Finally, the respective ministers of these departments have the highest political control and authority over these institutions.

In addition to the officials appointed by the central government, the capital cities of provinces and towns all have elected municipal mayors and a local administration with very limited powers. Responsibility for maintenance of public services is divided between local and central government institutions. Local services, such as road maintenance, water supply, some public health services, and rubbish collection, are provided by local authorities. Other services, such as education, health care, and security are provided by the agents of central government. Unlike mayors who work under the democratic traditions seen in Western countries, elected mayors in Turkey have no formal authority over or participation in policing. Policing and security issues remain a central government task, as they are considered to be too important to be entrusted to local elected representatives.

Turkey's Ministry of Interior (MoI) has the formal mandate to guarantee "in practice" the full enjoyment of rights at the provincial and district levels through the powers and authority it vests in governors and district governors (Goldsmith & Cerrah, 2005). Governors and district governors, as MoI staff, are held responsible for the management and monitoring of the police and the Gendarmerie. Therefore, the police and the Gendarmerie do not fall under the elected mayor's authority. Mayors and other local elected representatives may develop informal relationships and cooperate with appointed police chiefs and the Gendarmerie, but there is no formal hierarchy between them.

Security services are also categorized into two groups: the civilian police for urban policing and the Gendarmerie for rural law enforcement. The civilian police are responsible only for policing urban areas, such as within the municipal boundaries of cities and towns. The Gendarmerie, which is part of the army, is legally responsible only for policing rural areas and villages. However, the Gendarmerie in recent years has maintained its jurisdiction at the expense of violating existing legislation. The Gendarmerie is still serving in some towns and cities, which in the past were small villages, but which have since grown and acquired town status. According to existing laws, these new towns should now fall under police jurisdiction. Furthermore, despite the fact that the Gendarmerie's jurisdiction is by existing law limited to rural areas, it has stations, military posts, military installations, and barracks in cities and towns all over the country. Today, Gendarmerie vehicles with armed soldiers patrol many of Turkey's cities.

Modern Turkey has been ruled by a parliamentary democracy since 1946. It is a multiparty system with a unicameral legislative parliament. However, despite this experience of democracy, Turkey has a highly centralized and authoritarian administration system. The administrative system is overly centralized and lacks essential community participation at a local level. The prominent role of the military in political and public life in Turkey is a well-known phenomenon. Since the establishment of modern Turkey, the military has seized power on three occasions and has exerted influence on the democratic life of the country. Some have described this as a case of "militarized democracy," drawing an analogy to some Latin American states. However, the European Union (EU) has defined a number of political, social, and economic criteria as part of its requirements for Turkey to join the union. In particular, the EU has demanded a number of political reforms from Turkey.

One critical and problematic issue within this context is the role and place of the military in Turkish political, social, and even economic life. As part of this reform process, the structure and functioning of the National Security Council (NSC) has recently been amended (2003), and there have been other legislative and administrative reforms. All of these are expected to have positive impacts on the democratization of the country.

But, the influence of the military is not limited to the NSC, although it exerts power over the day-to-day running of the government and civic life in Turkey. The power legally held—or in some cases de facto assumed—by the Gendarmerie, in terms of providing internal security services, is much more important. Although the current legislation was intended to allow the Gendarmerie to provide security services in rural areas only, it extends its power to urban areas. This is partly due to ambiguities in the law with respect to definitions of the boundaries of rural and urban areas and partly because of the army's deliberate insistence on maintaining a prominent role in the country. Currently, the Gendarmerie is deployed in the centers of cities, which are outside its legally and legitimately defined jurisdiction. This practice is also in contradiction with principles of internal security services of modern countries. The current behavior of the Gendarmerie, which operates under the authority of the military command without any political accountability or community participation, cannot be reconciled with the principles of the rule of law or with those of democratic accountability.

The police and the military (Gendarmerie) are two different and separate professions, and it is difficult for one to perform the other's functions and duties adequately. The entire Gendarmerie personnel are members of the military. However, an overwhelming majority of them are noncommissioned soldiers performing military services with no professionalism. The training and militarized mentality of Gendarmerie personnel is neither sufficient nor suitable for providing internal security services in a democratic society.

Community participation on a local level is a crucial element in democratic policing in Turkey. The central issues with the present policing system and the Gendarmerie should be about bringing accountability and community participation into policing. It is apparent that, with its highly centralized organizational structure, the so-called civilian Turkish police force lacks community participation and is far from being democratic. The Gendarmerie as a military institution will be a major concern regarding the democratization of the policing services in Turkey. Judging from the army's interference with democratically elected governments in Turkey in the form of a military coup and military interventions, the army has historically had problematic relations with politicians. The army sees itself as above the elected government and is not comfortable being controlled by central and local officials. Army officers, who are not at ease with being controlled by the central government, will certainly not be comfortable with being under the control of locally elected officials. Therefore, the Gendarmerie, as an agent of the army, serving as an internal security service, clearly raises more questions about the legitimacy of the regime.

History of Military Intervention in Government _____

Turkey's experience with democracy dates back to 1946. However, since then Turkish democracy has been interrupted by frequent military interventions. Between 1946 and 1997, Turkey experienced several military interventions in different forms, and democratically elected governments were either overthrown or forced to resign from power.

The level and degree of civilian control over the military has turned into an important aspect of the definition of contemporary democracy. Civilian-military relations have been one of the problems of democratic governance in Turkey (Cizre, 2004). The Turkish armed forces have enjoyed wide-ranging political autonomy, especially since the 1960s. "The political autonomy of the military is defined as the ability of the military to go above and beyond the constitutional authority of democratically elected government on matters pertaining to its institutional properties, political goals and influences" (David Pion-Berlin, 1992, cited in Cizre, 2000). The Turkish armed forces with "its self-identified role as the ultimate custodian of the western, secular and modern parameters of the regime and of the unity and integrity of the nation itself" (Cizre, 2000, p. 3) have historically been keen to maintain their above-politics position. As a result, military-civilian relations have always been a subject that raises tensions in the Turkish democracy. Turkey has been struggling with the EU requirements on reducing the political role of the military. The armed forces still retain a de facto and de jure veto power over a wide range of domestic and international issues, which in western democracies would be considered purely political not military issues, but the process of undermining their role in the political realm on issues that should be delegated to constitutionally elected civilian bodies is also making some headway.

The first military coup took place in 1960, 14 years after Turkey's first democratic elections. Following intensive antigovernment student protests, the military overthrew the very popular government from power. The prime minister of that time and two other very popular ministers were put on trial and sentenced to death. The second military intervention took place in 1971. This time, the democratically elected government was forced to resign by the military. Turkey's third experience with military intervention was another military coup in 1980. This time there was a coalition government in power. The prime minister and his deputies were first imprisoned and later released. However, they were banned from politics for some time after this. The last military intervention, the so-called postmodern coup, took place in 1997 when a democratically elected coalition government was again forced to resign by the military.

After the 1960 and 1980 military coups, the army not only overthrew the democratically elected governments but also took power into its hands. The military, who accused governments of violating the constitution, changed the constitution and banned the overthrown political parties from politics. Generals played a key role in the preparation of a new constitution.

They were also very active in establishing the new political parties, and some of them even got involved in politics. However, in the first free elections held after each military coup and intervention, the people chose and indeed brought back to power almost the same people who were overthrown by the army.

For instance, after the execution of the Adnan Menderes, who was prime minister in the years between 1950 and 1960, Süleyman Demirel, who has the same political roots, came to power in 1961 as the successor of Menderes. Demirel was also removed from power twice, first in 1971 by a military intervention and second in 1980 by a military coup. After the 1980 military coup, Demirel and his deputies were banned from politics, but the ban was lifted by a referendum held by the first elected government after the coup. Later Demirel became prime minister and was finally elected by the Turkish Grand National Assembly (TGNA) as the president of Turkey, a position he held for seven years.

The most recent example is the latest military intervention, which took place in 1997 and removed the elected government from power. The second election after this intervention was held in 2002, and it resulted in the overwhelming victory of R. T. Erdoğan, who was also earlier banned from politics and even served a prison sentence for reading a poem. The poem, which was considered to be provocative, was read in a public meeting almost 10 years before his conviction. As a victim of military intervention, Erdoğan, who is presently serving as prime minister of Turkey, and his government have enacted a number of laws and made revolutionary changes in the field of human rights and civil liberties.

_____ Corruption History: Major Scandals and Incidents

Turkey has a very corrupt political past. The credibility of politicians has over the years been damaged by numerous political scandals. This is one of the factors that the army uses as a pretext for their military interventions. Politicians are relentlessly blamed and criticized by the media and each other. Army generals, who enjoy a military immunity, also criticize the politicians in general and the ruling government in particular for corruption. Although the army interferes with a number of nonmilitary services such as education and the economy, it enjoys an integrity based on unquestionable immunity. Politicians have had to be very cautious about their relations with the army. A number of writers and journalists have served prison sentences for criticizing the army. Because of its extensive immunity, the army remains the only "perfect" institution in Turkey. Army members believe that, because they constitute the only uncorrupt institution in Turkey, their job, even their duty, is to put things right when corrupt politicians mess things up.

There was a big rise in corruption and scandals following the economic growth experienced under the Ozal government in the 1980s. Scandals surrounded politicians, businessmen, and high-level bureaucrats. Political scandals have sometimes involved senior police officials in some cities such as Istanbul, Ankara, Izmir, and Bursa. A number of senior police officers were fired from the force for their corrupt practices. Sometimes there have been instances of police officers forming gangs and acting together. In recent years, high-tech surveillance technology has been abused by some intelligence officers working for their own personal benefit. Some politicians' and bureaucrats' telephone conversations were tapped and recorded and later used against them to obtain promotions and economic benefits for the intelligence officers. For instance, a scandal called "tele-ear" (*tele-kulak* in Turkish) took place in Ankara in the late 1990s. The police commissioner of Ankara and a number of police chiefs were interrogated and later removed from their positions.

Crime Trends and Rates

The generally held belief is that crime rates in Turkey have always been low compared to those in Western countries. However, as crime figures are not systematically collected, it is difficult, if not impossible, to identify crime rates and trends in Turkey. Crime statistics are not kept on a national basis, and in some years no systematic data have been collected for comparison with other years. It has also been believed that this lower crime rate was partly due to the influence of religion and Turkish family life on the community. However, this argument seems to be an illusion, as it is not supported by any sound statistics collected in this field.

The Department of Public Order collects statistics about crimes, including those against people and property (see Figure 8.1). In general, there has been a significant increase in almost all crime categories between 1994 and 2004. A noticeable increase recorded after 1995 is believed to have been the result of a domestic migration from the east to the western parts of Turkey, due to the significant economic effects of the First Gulf War. However, it is again difficult to rely on these statistics because of the frequent changes in the ways in which the figures are reported and recorded.

Influence and History of Organized Crime

Since the 1970s, Turkey has experienced an increase in internal immigration from rural areas to big cities. Immigrant communities have had to cope with social and economic hardships and have faced difficulties in urban life. They have tried to overcome these problems and survive by maintaining their close family and community ties. In rural life communal and familial solidarity often required the use of violence against outsiders. This type of solidarity has served as a catalyst for early organized criminal groups. Communal gangs, which were not directly antiestablishment, were at first not seen as a

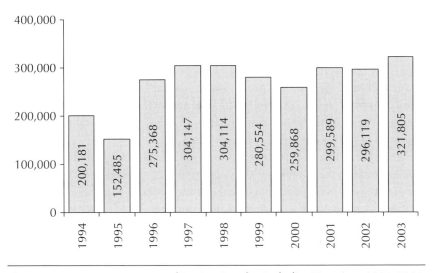

Figure 8.1   Crimes Committed Against People, Excluding Terrorism, 1994–2004

major threat to the establishment. Some of these groups, who had proestablishment political elements, even enjoyed governmental and communal tolerance, if not support, at a time when antiestablishment Marxist terrorist activities were increasing. Some members of these groups, it is argued, were illegally deployed by the state security forces in fighting against subversive terrorist groups such as the Armenian Secret Army for the Liberation of Armenia (ASALA) and Partiya Karkaren Kurdistan (PKK, or Kurdistan Workers Party). (See the section on terrorism at the end of this chapter.)

The dramatic increase in organized crime also has a correlation with the expansion of the free market economy in the 1980s. The free market economy brought a number of legitimate and illegitimate opportunities. Turkey, being a bridge between the East and the Western world, offered illegitimate business opportunities to organized crime gangs, whose activities including human trafficking and trade in illegal weapons and drugs. The tourism sector also experienced rapid growth, and a number of casinos were built. Gambling became a social issue. While the economy was flourishing, some businesses were experiencing financial hardship and difficulties in paying their bills. An illegal sector emerged at the same time as legal businesses. Illegally earned money has to be legalized, so money laundering developed.

On the other hand, as a transit country for illegal smuggling and bidirectional drug trafficking, Turkey has always been subject to massive money laundering schemes. In 1996, when the amount of money laundered in Turkey peaked to 5 percent of the total amount laundered globally, the Turkish parliament enacted an Anti–Money Laundering Law (law number 4208). Although this law was recently written, it has some huge gaps. Instead of generalizing criminal activities, as legislation in Western nations does, this law lists those specific crimes considered to be money-laundering activities. Because of such definitions, many organized criminals simply improved their political connections and acquired political protection and immunity. As a result, traditional organized crime was promoted to the level of white collar crime. Politicians involved in this white collar crime have included prime ministers and a number of cabinet ministers. Connections of very high-level politicians and mafia leaders exposed by the media have eroded public trust in the political structure, and people have begun to talk about a military intervention.

While these major corruption cases were taking place, the Turkish army was involved in the running of the country at an unprecedented level. In fact, the government was even formed at the army's direction after a military intervention. In other words, all these major economic scandals took place at an unprecedented level while the army was involved in running the country. Corruption scandals directly discredited the politicians, while the army, despite its involvement in every aspect of civic life in Turkey, enjoyed an unquestionable immunity. The amount of money involved in white collar crime while the army took a dominant role in government reached tens of billions of dollars and brought the country to the point of bankruptcy. A new term, "bank hosing" was coined to explain the extent of the economic corruption.

For instance, some white collar criminals bought private banks or established new ones and collected money from the people. The capital was then "hosed," or used illegally, and the banks were then declared bankrupt. The money hosed by corrupt private bank owners had to be compensated by the state, as all capital was under state guarantee. Between the years of 1997 and 2002, a number of private and public banks went bankrupt, and the loss had to be covered by the state and the people.

These corruption cases, coupled with a major earthquake in 1999, caused the biggest economic crisis in the history of the Republic of Turkey. An Anti–Organized Crime Law (4422) was enacted in 1999 in order to neutralize such criminal organizations and their threatening links among politicians and government officials. However the strong connections with politicians and the army made the law inefficient and not applicable to white collar criminals. As a result, the public lost trust and confidence in politicians, and the 2002 general election caused a total cleansing of the four traditional political parties (three of which were running the government in a coalition and one of which was the opposition party). In the election, two brand new political parties shared almost 70 percent of all votes, and a new cabinet was established by a single party, the Justice and Development Party, for the first time in 15 years. As soon as this government took power, the U.S.-Iraq war crisis started, and the new government has had to struggle to alleviate the problem for Turkey.

Organized crime in Turkey usually has two major sources: one is the residue of the ideological movements that were involved in the military coup of 1980, and the other is groups with ethnic or communal connections. The first type of organized crime activities can be traced back to the right wing (Ülkücü) and left wing movements. Members of the Ülkücü movement claim that they defended the country against rebellious assaults before the 1980 military coup. A number of them have spent considerable time in prison. After they were released from prison, the majority of them chose to lead decent lives and became businessmen or politicians. However, a large number, who also have criminal records, have been exploited by existing mafia groups, while others have gone on to establish their own organizations and become mafia bosses.

In the second type of organized crime, there are strong ethnic and communal ties. Under this category two different groups can be seen. On the one hand there are mafia groups and families who are called *Laz* or *Karadenizli* (people of the Black Sea region), as they originally come from the part of Turkey near the Black Sea. Members of these groups mainly deal with political and economic corruption. They threaten people and cover checks that might otherwise go unpaid, for a fee. They also deal with real-property crimes, prostitution, gambling, money laundering, and trafficking in drugs and firearms.

On the other hand, there are youth gangs who commit crimes that reflect their community solidarity. In the late 1970s, Turkey experienced a severe economic decline. This gave rise to a black market and created so-called small "father" (*baba*) figures on a local basis. These modern Robin Hoods would deliver social justice by taking from the rich and powerful and giving to the poor and the weak. As the country's economy began flourishing in the 1980s, the babas and their men evolved into big mafia bosses and organized crime on a national level. Youth living in violent inner city areas of Istanbul, such as Kasımpaşa and Karagümrük, formed youth gangs around the local babas.

This type of organized crime was not entirely free from communal and ideological ties. While some babas' organizations had communal and ethnic ingredients, others had right wing or left wing ideological motives. Kurdish mafia groups were an example of the former. The Kurdish community, which has relatively strong communal ties in rural areas, carried these ties with them to big cities. The Kurds migrated to big cities because of economic decline and the PKK terror, and they live mainly in inner city areas where proper housing and job opportunities are minimal. Some of these Kurdish populations engaged in organized crime as a form of maintaining continuity of communal ties. Communal bonds, which can be a source of cooperation and solidarity, sometimes turn out to be a source of cooperation in committing crime.

The Turkish Deep State

Although the issue of organized crime has a very long history in Turkey, a road accident on November 3, 1996, in Susurluk, a small township in northwestern Turkey, revealed very complex mafia relations and sparked a series of fruitless investigations. The car involved in the accident belonged to a member of parliament. Among the passengers were a member of parliament, a young woman model, a well-known police chief, and a fugitive. All the passengers, except the member of parliament, died in the accident. Some automatic rifles were also found in the car. The fugitive in question was involved in right wing student movements before the 1980 military coup. His name was involved in some murder cases. He had been missing for 16 years, since the 1980 military coup. He had a fake identity and a green passport, which is only given to public servants with a very high status.

This accident was instrumental in awakening the public's consciousness to the reality of a criminal triangle of mafia bosses, politicians, and some members of the security forces. This accident played an important role in drawing attention to complex organized crime activities that reached right up to ministers and prime ministers and generals in the army. A joint parliamentary commission was established to investigate the case, but there was no satisfactory result. A number of retired and serving generals, enjoying military immunity, did not even bother to come to the commission's hearings to give testimony. This was only the tip of the iceberg. A number of politicians and state officials were involved in this case. The term "deep state" (*derin devlet*) was coined, referring to an illegal state within the state using state authority and its resources to its own ends. A proper investigation could not be conducted, and the extent of this illegal deep state within the state could not be identified. A number of officials, whose names were linked with this scandal, were later cleared, and some of them even became involved in politics. Police operations carried out against organized crime have proved that all of these groups have some insiders and collaborators within state institutions, mainly political institutions, the army, and the police.

Following the notorious Susurluk accident in 1996, the deep state became the center of debate. A Parliamentary Investigation Committee was established to investigate the issue. The committee contacted certain political figures, civilian and military bureaucrats, who were considered to be knowledgeable about, if not having connections within, the deep state. They were not very cooperative, and nothing important came out of this parliamentary investigation. The deep state remained anonymous and untouched. While some individuals kept writing about the deep state in the mass media, its existence was not officially acknowledged.

Yet, everything suddenly changed after a well-known journalist, Yavuz Donat, conducted a series of interviews with Kenan Evren and Süleyman Demirel, two former presidents, and Bülent Ecevit, a former prime minister (Donat, 2005). All parties acknowledged that a deep state, an unidentified state within the legitimate state structure, was functioning in Turkey. However, interestingly enough, Demirel, in his interview, purposefully stated that the deep state was the military. On the one hand, while his insistence created an impression that he was trying to deflect attention from the real deep state, he was, on the other hand, trying to legitimize an illegal power structure by associating it with the very powerful Turkish armed forces.

The Turkish army neither denied nor confirmed Demirel's claims. It was, however, widely believed that the Gendarmerie, which is a part of the Turkish army, had established, without legislation, an operational unit called the Gendarmerie Intelligence and Antiterrorism (JITEM) to fight against terrorism and other unspecified threats. Confusing and conflicting arguments were made regarding the existence of the JITEM. Some Gendarmerie generals claimed that it was once established at a crucial time but disbanded after completing its mission. Others argued that such an organization never existed ("Varligi tartişilan," 2004; "Veli Küçük," 2004). Some claim that JITEM, as an illegal organ within the army, was used as a subcontractor by the deep state to commit assassinations. A number of unsolved murder cases, including the ones committed by the PKK against its members, were claimed to be the work of the JITEM. Subsequently, JITEM, which allegedly is responsible for many illegal acts, has not been officially endorsed or mandated by the criminal justice system. Finally, the chief public prosecutor for Diyarbakir province, where some unsolved murder cases took place, stated that "JITEM is an illegal organization allegedly operating on behalf of the state" ("İşte JITEM'in," n.d.).

Finally, the so-called deep state is also mentioned in the European parliament's progress report on Turkey. The report states, "In Turkey there are powerful forces at work in the bureaucracy, the army and the judiciary (the 'deep state') which resist reforms and their implementation" (European Parliament, 2003, p. 13).

Public Support for Government and Law Enforcement

Despite its highly centralized and authoritarian administrative system, the Turkish government enjoys an inherited deference from its subjects. However, public support enjoyed by the government in general and security forces in particular seems to be reminiscent of traditionally held deference to the state rather than a benefit that has been earned by the ruling governments. A low level of participation on the part of the people may also be a factor for the people's support of the government. The people have traditionally been used to accepting whatever is offered by the state. For the people, the state always knows what is best for them.

The army and the police are among the most popular institutions in Turkey. Public support for the police also bears the traces of this inherited obedience. Despite the fact that the people do not approve of military interventions, the army is the most respected and popular institution in Turkey. This is partly because the Turkish people, whose religion is overwhelmingly

Muslim, see the army as a holy institution above criticism. The second factor is that, because it is risky to criticize the army explicitly or implicitly, the army is able to maintain credibility.

Use of Force by the Turkish Police

The Turkish police force has, since its inception, been a fully armed paramilitary force (Aydin, 1997). All police officers receive basic firearms training during their preservice training. They also receive refreshment training once or twice a year in order to maintain and develop their shooting skills. Every single police officer, including the ones who are working at desk duties, is issued a personal weapon, usually a handgun. Until the mid-1980s, the Turkish police were armed only with traditional weapons. However, the incidence of coercive policing in Turkey is currently increasing in the form of heavily armed police units. There is also an increase in the number of powerful weapons and armored vehicles available to the police. As a response to an increase in PKK terror campaigns, starting in the mid-1980s, the police have been given more extended powers and weapons. Old handguns have been replaced with new and more powerful ones, and a new, military-style police department, Special Operations, has been set up (Aydin, 2003). The Special Operations department includes Special Operation Teams (SOT), similar to the Special Weapons and Tactics (SWAT) teams in the United States and the Special Air Services (SAS) in the UK. SOTs are equipped with more powerful weapons and armored vehicles than other polices forces, and they also receive very sophisticated antiterrorist training.

The use of force in traditional police tasks is an individual decision left to the discretion of an individual officer in violent crowd events. The officer in charge of the riot police team decides, depending on the circumstances, the level of force to be used. In situations where the use of force is not clearly defined by the law or regulations, the officer on duty has to ask for a decision from the commander in charge and act according to the order given.

Legal Context for Search and Seizure

The police have the power to stop and search any individual in cases where they have reasonable grounds for suspecting that the individual has illegal articles or something made or adapted for use in connection with an offense against the police officer in question or against his vehicle. In addition, the police have the power to enter premises and conduct searches, although a police officer cannot perform a search without written authority from a supervisory body.

The police have the authority to search premises and individuals under different levels of supervision. Under the existing law, searches can be conducted for judicial and administrative purposes. For judicial searches, in principle, the supervising authority is a justice of the peace, and this judge must issue a search warrant. But in cases of great urgency, where there is reason to believe that the evidence or person suspected will disappear during the time application is made to the judge, the authority for a search can be given by a senior police officer or a public prosecutor. For administrative searches and in urgent cases, a judge still has the authority to issue a search warrant, but the police officer may instead go to the head of the police of the province or county to authorize a search. In any case, the written order of the person who authorizes the search must be submitted to a judge within 24 hours after the search. In cases where the search order is not approved by the judge, the search is declared null and void (Eryılmaz, 2003).

Where the police inquiries are being made under the Anti-Terror Act, an application for a warrant has to be made to the State Security Court judge. An application to the judge must indicate how the evidence or person in question is related to the inquiry. An order may be made by a judge, public prosecutor, or senior police officer, but he or she has to be satisfied that there are reasonable grounds for thinking that the items or individuals named in the search warrant will be found at the premises indicated. An order may be given to obtain evidence that is expected to be of substantial value in identifying those responsible or in finding the individuals responsible for the crime committed. Such an order requires the person to whom it was directed to allow the police to look at the items covered by the order. In cases where the person in question refuses to comply with the order, the police have the right to use force to conduct the search.

The order should state (1) the name of the person suspected or the item to be found (2), the nature of the offense to which the evidence is thought to relate, (3) the grounds for suspecting that the evidence is on the premises or on the individual, and (4) the address of the premises. A search must not go beyond what is reasonably required to discover the evidence in question. No general search is permitted. The police have the power to enter and search premises to execute a warrant of arrest in connection with or arising out of criminal proceedings or to recapture someone unlawfully at large that the police are pursuing. Without judicial authority, the police may not search the home of a person taken into custody for evidence connected with the crime for which the person has been arrested. On the other hand, a search of the arrested person's premises is permitted in cases where the arrest is conducted at the premises of the suspect and where there are reasonable grounds for suspicion that relevant evidence might be found there.

The police may seize anything they find that is or that they reasonably believe to be covered by the warrant. The police are also permitted to seize items found incidentally if they provide evidence of any other offense. Persons who have illegal items or evidence on their bodies, in their vehicles, or on their premises may be arrested and detained for interrogation.

Protections for Arrested Persons

The police may arrest anyone without a warrant if the person in question is in the act of committing an offense or anyone about whom they have reasonable grounds to suspect (high degree of probability) of committing an offense. Persons who have been arrested may be searched to find out if there are articles on them that are a danger to themselves or others or that provide evidence of a suspected crime.

Arrested suspects must be informed about their rights as soon as possible. They have the right (1) to learn the grounds for their arrest, (2) to have a relative informed of the arrest and detention without delay, (3) to have the benefit of free advice of a lawyer before and during interrogation, and (4) to remain silent. However, during detention, arrested individuals have no right to demand to have visits, to make phone calls, or to send letters. Arrested individuals must be taken to a police station promptly after their arrest unless their presence is needed elsewhere in the interests of the investigation. Suspects may not be detained for more than 24 hours after they are arrested. In cases where the number of suspects is more than two for the crime under investigation, and the difficulties of the investigation require the collection of further evidence, the public prosecutor may extend the detention to up to 96 hours. The detention may not be authorized for more than 96 hours, after which time the suspect must be brought before a judge for charging.

During detention, fingerprints of suspects may be taken, and they may also be photographed, if photographs and fingerprints will prove or disprove their involvement in a criminal offense and will be necessary to ascertain the identity of the suspect. In any 24-hour period, suspects must have a reasonable period of rest during which they are free from questioning or travel. There is no rule as to the maximum length of an interview, but it is accepted that there must be breaks for meals and refreshments. No one may be subjected to penalty or treatment incompatible with human dignity. The freedom of suspects to determine and exercise their will may not be impaired by ill treatment, fatigue, physical interference or force, the administration of medicines, torture, deception, hypnosis, or different devices. The threat of consequences or the promise of an advantage not permitted or provided by law are prohibited. The prohibitions apply even if the accused person consents to them. Statements that are obtained in violation of these provisions may not be used as evidence, even if the suspect agrees to their use.

Organizational Structure and Issues

Although no single and universally accepted classification of the police has been developed, police organizations can broadly be classified as coercive or consensus. While terms such as *military, para-military,* and *quasi-military* policing are interchangeably used as different versions of coercive policing, democratic policing and its derivative community policing can be seen as the reflection of consensus policing. The Turkish National Police (TNP), as a national force having a highly centralized organizational structure, falls within the category of military policing and the philosophy of policing as force rather than service.

Turkey has a highly centralized administrative system. Institutions are organized nationally and have their headquarters in the capital, Ankara. Every organization, including the police, also has provincial subheadquarters. The head of police in a province is called director of security or police chief and is appointed by the interior minister as the representative of the central government. The police chief is accountable to the interior minister through its local representative, the governor.

The General Directorate of Security

The General Directorate of Security has several departments and subunits that are directly controlled by the general director. These include the following:

- General Directorate
- Inspection Board
- Division of Press, Protocol, and Public Relations
- Police Academy
- Department of Intelligence
- Expert Chiefs of Police for Research, Planning, and Coordination
- Department of Special Operations
- Department of Legal Counsel
- Civil Defense Experts Office

The general director is the only police chief in the country holding a five-star badge. Five deputies who have the second-highest position—four-star police chief—assist the general director with the administration of 24 departments operating within the boundaries of their fields of interest. The departments include the following:

1. Research, Planning, and Coordination

2. Administrative and Financial Affairs

3. Maintenance and Supply

4. Construction and Real Estate

5. Archive and Documentation

6. Communication

 7. Aviation

 8. Counter Smuggling and Organized Crime

 9. Public Order

10. Road Traffic

11. Information Technologies

12. Central Command and Control

13. Foreigners

14. Border and Immigration

15. Training

16. Security

17. Health Services

18. Personnel Affairs

19. Counter Terrorism and Operation

20. Criminal Police Laboratories

21. Interpol

22. Safeguard

23. Foreign Relations

24. Social Services

A four-star police chief also heads each department. They are responsible for administering the services within their department and coordinating the services in the provinces operating in their respective fields.

Provincial Police Forces

Each province has its own provincial police headquarters. However, from the chief to the line officers, all of the appointments are made by the central government. The national headquarters in Ankara determines all issues pertaining to personnel, pay, training, appointments, inspection, and promotion. Local governments have no say or control over policing policies or practices. The mayor of a city or a town does not have any authority or formal involvement with police services. Hence, the highly centralized Turkish administrative system does not allow any formal local participation or involvement in policing.

The provincial forces have copied the departmental structure of the national police headquarters. However, a unit that has the status of a department at the national level is reduced to a branch in the provinces. For instance, the provincial counterpart to the national Department of Personnel is called the Branch of Personnel. Each branch of the provincial police force functions in coordination with its counterpart or corresponding department within the national headquarters.

Civilian Oversight

Presently there are no systematic civilian oversight mechanisms on policing policy and practices in Turkey. The quality of police performance is monitored only by senior police officers at different levels of supervisory positions, and it is they to whom any accusations about the violation of police powers are taken. If the allegations are very serious, inspectors are appointed from the Inspection Board of national police headquarters to conduct an investigation. If the accusations involve senior police officers, some civilian inspectors are appointed from the Ministry of the Interior to conduct an investigation. These oversight and inspection mechanisms are all governmental and do not include any NGO element. There is no NGO type of civilian oversight institution on a local or national level (Goldsmith & Cerrah, 2005). Members of the public are not allowed to visit and monitor police stations and cells as lay visitors. Only the close relatives of the detainees are allowed to visit the people who are detained or are under arrest. Conditions of the police cells and the detainees are not monitored by a lay visitor, a member of the civilian board, or a member of an NGO. The only civilians who are allowed to see the detainees, besides their relatives, are their defense lawyers and the public prosecutor who is in charge of the investigations.

The civilian oversight of the police and Gendarmerie is limited to governors in cities and subgovernors in towns. Yet, the capacity of governors and subgovernors to control the security personnel is limited by institutional capacity shortcomings; they have limited access to decision-making support or the knowledge required for sound decision making. Good governance mechanisms that should underpin this process of decision making in critical security issues are limited as well. The provincial units within and outside each governor's headquarters are not equipped to support the governor and district governor in security sector oversight. Therefore there is a need for Turkey to adopt sector approaches to civilian oversight of the security sector. Turkey's administrative system at the provincial and district levels must also build the appropriate systems of accountability within the context of good governance (Goldsmith & Cerrah, 2005).

The existing administrative system is not at ease with civilian oversight and public scrutiny. The nature of the relationships between the state and members of the public is not based on mutual trust. Despite the so-called democratic system, the highly centralized administrative structure is not transparent enough and open to public scrutiny. Although existing legislation

acknowledges universal principles of the rule of law and innocence until guilt
is proven, there are some common practices that contradict these principles.
For instance, a background check is a standard procedure for every job application in the civil service. However, in addition to the background check carried out by the respective institutions, individuals themselves are also required
to produce a "criminal record paper" as a part of their standard application
documents. Not only ordinary citizens, but even members of the security
forces are sometimes required by law to obtain and produce such a paper as
a standard document when they apply to obtain a driver's license, to enroll at
a university, and so forth. In other words, citizens are required to prove that
they are innocent by submitting a criminal record document. This implies that
all citizens are assumed to be criminals or potential criminals until they prove
their innocence. This can be seen as a direct and total violation of the principle of assumed innocence.

Complaint Procedures

Civil servants enjoy a traditionally high degree of trust by the state, and
hence a de facto exemption when they are challenged or accused by members
of a civilian population. They are always right until they are proven to be
wrong. With this approach it is usually difficult, if not impossible, to prove
that a civil servant is or can be wrong. Again, this discrimination is not based
on any written legislation but rather on de facto practices.

A civilian who is not happy with police practices has a choice of complaint procedures. Technically a complaint can be made to a police station,
to provincial or national police headquarters, or to the offices of provincial
governors or subgovernors, the public prosecutor, or even the minister of
the interior. The most commonly used procedure is to make such complaints to the public prosecutor. A public prosecutor is a civilian lawyer
and a member of the Ministry of Justice, not the Ministry of Interior.
However, he or she is in charge of the police when conducting investigations. Regardless of the agency, any complaints against the police end up
with the public prosecutor where a mindset of civil servant solidarity prevails. The public prosecutor, who is also in charge of the police and to some
extent a working partner, decides whether to start an investigation or to
drop the case. So a public servant is investigated by another public servant
without any public involvement in the complaint and evaluation procedure.

In 2001 the Human Rights Presidency was established within the Prime
Minister's office "to monitor the implementation of regulations related
to human rights," and "to examine and investigate human rights violation
claims" (Prime Ministry, Human Rights Presidency, 2004), mainly those
committed by law enforcement personnel as well as other civil servants. The
human rights presidency has human rights province boards in 81 provinces
and human rights district boards in 850 townships. Provincial governors and
subgovernors, who are also in charge of the law enforcement agencies such

as the police and the Gendarmerie, serve as the chairpersons of the human right boards.

Internal Accountability Mechanisms

Inspectors of the MoI and police inspectors who are members of the Inspection Board investigate criminal and disciplinary cases and handle complaints against police officers. Decisions are made by the provincial or central disciplinary boards, which are composed of police chiefs and some civilian officials. Administrative functions of the police are monitored by the governors and subgovernors, whereas the judicial functions are controlled and monitored by the public prosecutors. Police officials can be dismissed from their organizations owing to disciplinary, corruption, or criminal causes by the decisions of the disciplinary boards. Appeals can be made to the administrative courts.

Turkish police are not usually prepared to acknowledge the existence of systematic police malpractice and abuse of power. Police misconduct and violations are seen only as a personal deviation of officers involved rather than being an organizational responsibility to be dealt with. The lack of a systematic anticorruption policy and mechanisms encourage the corrupt officers to carry on their corrupt practices. In some cases police corruption and malpractices are handled with unofficial disciplinary punishments such as verbal reprimands or the transfer of an officer to a lower and less popular position. If a case of police corruption or abuse of police power is too visible or is covered by the media, a disciplinary and criminal investigation is inevitable, depending on the seriousness of the violation. Police organizations, like many other civil service organizations in Turkey, tend to cover up and overlook minor and less serious police malpractices. The idea that lies behind this state of affairs is that the police already have too many enemies, so "we should shield our own."

Recruitment, Selection, Ranks, and Training of Police Officers

As a highly centralized national police force, the TNP also has a centralized police selection and training system. The selection is made by ad hoc committees formed mainly by police chiefs, a medical doctor, and a physical fitness instructor. Training was revised and major changes were introduced at the end of 2001. Currently, there are four different levels of pre-service police training institutions in Turkey. These include the Police College (of which there is only one in the country), 20 Police Schools at the two-year college level, the Faculty of Security Sciences (a four-year, university-level training program), and the Institute for Security Sciences (at the graduate-school level). There are slightly different application procedures for each institution. However, the basic and common criterion is that police applicants must be Turkish citizens.

All these institutions, with the exception of the Police College, operate under the National Police Academy. (Because the Police College is not a university-level educational institution, it operates under the national head-quarters of the TNP.) The Police Academy is a university operating as an umbrella institution. Either a police chief with at least a master's degree or a civilian faculty professor can be appointed as the president of the academy.

Police Training Institutions

Police College: Training at the High School Level

The Police College is a four-year high school–level training institution. There is only one Police College, located in Ankara. Students of the college are between the ages of 13 and 17 and must pass a national entry exam to gain admittance. The Police College is a boarding school, and the curriculum is delivered by correspondence from other public high schools and does not include any police-oriented instruction. Police-related training is limited to "occupational spirit and marching" training provided by staff officers. Students wear a student uniform and obey strict rules. They are familiarized with the hierarchical structure of policing, as they are required to respect their civilian teachers and senior students. Concurrently the Police High School provides a very early occupational socialization. Students who graduate from this school are directly enrolled in an undergraduate program of the Faculty of Security Science. If they earn a place, they can attend a civilian university with the support of the police, which is in the interest of the police organization.

Police Schools: Two-Year College Level

The second level of police training institutions is Police Schools. Only civilian high school graduates are admitted to the Police Schools. There are 20 Police Schools in Turkey, and they are located on a regional basis. Recruits are admitted based on the grades they receive on a general university entry exam. Once accepted, the cadets receive a two-year, mostly classroom-based, theoretical education in a boarding school environment. This initial education and training period is also an essential part of police occupational socialization and an introduction to police culture. Cadets undertake one month of supervised field experience during the summer. Students who successfully complete their studies at a Police School serve as rank and file officers throughout their careers, unless they pass promotional examinations.

Faculty of Security Sciences: University Level

The third provider of training is the Faculty of Security Sciences, which functions under the umbrella of the Police Academy. There are two different sources for students who attend this training; one is the Police College, and the other is civilian high schools. Students who originate from the Police College are directly admitted, whereas cadets from a civilian high school background need to achieve a very high grade in the general university entry exam to be accepted.

Like the Police College and Police Schools, the Faculty of Security Sciences is a boarding training institution. Cadets from both the Police College and civilian high school background receive a four-year university education. Cadets who complete their studies at the Faculty undertake two months of supervised field experience during the summer. After graduation, they are appointed to the TNP with the rank of sergeant. They have the opportunity of promotion through all the ranks up to police chief.

Institute for Security Sciences: Graduate School Level

The Institute for Security Sciences is a graduate school offering MA and PhD programs in policing and associated fields such as criminology, international policing, police management, comparative policing, and criminal justice administration. The minimum educational requirement for admittance is a four-year university degree from the Faculty of Security Sciences or any other civilian university in Turkey. Civilian applicants who have backgrounds in social sciences such as law, politics, and sociology tend to have a better chance of being admitted than those from other disciplines. Students who receive advanced degrees from this institute are likely to become eminent senior police officers.

Probation Period for New Recruits

Recruits who graduate from the Faculty of Security Science and Police Schools all technically begin their careers as probationary officers. This period varies between one and one-half and two years. However, no specific or special training is given in this period. Probationary officers are not systematically monitored and evaluated by seasoned and tutor police officers. Officers who complete this so-called probationary period without fault automatically become commissioned officers without any formal test or evaluation process. The only further requirement of every probationary officer is to submit a medical report after going through a medical check-up.

Police Ranks

The above mentioned national training institutions offer preservice training for the TNP, while the Department of Training of the national headquarters offers in-service training courses for the whole organization. Some of the departments have their own in-service training centers. For instance, the Department of Counter Smuggling and Organized Crime facilitates the Turkish International Academy against Drugs and Organized Crime

(TADOC), and the Department of Public Order facilitates the Training Centre for Crime Research and Investigation.

The TNP maintains nine operational ranks, which can be categorized as upper management, middle management, and line supervision ranks. The upper management ranks include police chief (police commissioner for metropolitan cities), four-star police chief (commissioner for small cities), and three-star police chief (deputy commissioner). Middle management includes two-star police chief, one-star police chief, and superintendent (major). Line supervision ranks include chief inspector (captain), inspector (lieutenant), sergeant, and police or line officer. Police personnel within each category receive automatic promotion once the rank of sergeant is achieved. Promotional examinations are conducted in the presence of individuals with the rank of superintendent or three-star police chief. The examinations are paper-based written exams and are evaluated and ranked by a computerized system. Individuals who pass the exams then take two-week promotional courses designed by the Institute for Security Sciences.

In-Service Training

The Department of Training, under the Turkish National Police organizes in-service courses for police personnel throughout the country. This department is the only training institution operating outside the umbrella of the Police Academy. Its sole task is to organize and offer in-service courses for the entire force. This department offers a number of basic in-service courses in traditional police tasks. Usually, the Department of Training organizes in-service courses in conjunction with other departments tailored to their specific needs. However departments that need very special training organize their own programs. These departments sometimes receive academic and technical support from outside, such as from the Police Academy and civilian universities.

Some specialist departments such as Intelligence, Counter Smuggling and Organized Crime, and Counter Terrorism and Operation organize their own in-service courses. Once officers are assigned to one of these special departments, they have to go through a number of basic and follow-up courses. Some of these departments, such as TADOC and SASEM (another in-service training organization), even work in collaboration with international police organizations. Their training facilities and the quality of their training have an international reputation and recognition. These training institutions also offer in-service courses, not only to their own staff, but also to officers from neighboring or overseas countries.

The Racial and Ethnic Context of Turkish Policing

Demographic Figures

Turkey is situated between 36 and 42 degrees north latitude and between 26 and 45 degrees east longitude at the intersection of the continents of

Europe and Asia. Its neighbors are Georgia, Armenia, Nakhichevan (Azerbaijan), Iran, Iraq, Syria, Greece, and Bulgaria. Turkey's area is 779,452 square kilometers as projected on a flat map, and the real area as measured on the ground is 814,578 square kilometers. Approximately 97 percent of this area is in the continent of Asia, and 3 percent is in Europe. The population of the country in 2003 was 70.5 million; 40.6 million (65 percent) live in provincial and district centers, and 22.2 million (35 percent) live in rural villages. The largest three cities, in terms of population, are Istanbul with 10 million people, Ankara with 3.6 million, and Izmir with 3.1 million ("Mahalli İdareler," 2003).

Turkey is a predominantly Muslim country. Over 98 percent of the country's population is Muslim. The two main religious minority groups are Christian Armenians and Jews. The relationship between Turks and the religious-ethnic minorities in Turkey has usually been harmonious. Despite an Armenian genocide claim, the Turks and Armenians have peacefully lived together for well over a millennium. The Jews, who were saved from the Spanish Inquisition in 1492 by the Ottoman Turks, were brought to Turkey by Muslim Turks during the Ottoman era and have been living in Turkey peacefully for well over 500 years. Turkey is one of the few countries in the world where Jews have not had atrocities committed against them.

Ethnic Group Breakdown

Turkey has historically been a multiethnic and multicultural land (Ayata, 1997). Because of its geographical location, it has been a stage for many invasions and emigrational waves such as those of the Mongols from the East and the Crusades from the West. It was a meeting place between Asia and Europe, as well as between Islam and Christianity. Cultural, ethnic, and religious heterogeneity was the norm rather than the exception in Turkey. Despite the fact that Anatolia has always been a land of different cultures and ethnic groups, the Islamic-Turkish culture has always been dominant compared to other cultures. For this reason, *mosaic* may not be the best term to describe the ethnic and cultural fabric of Anatolia.

The word *minority* does not have an ethnic connotation but a religious one in Turkey, and only religious groups such as Christians (Armenians and Arabs) and Jews are defined as ethnic minorities. Other groups such as Abkhazians, Albanians, Bosnians, Caucasians, Chechens, Georgians, Kurds, and Laz (people of the Black Sea region) have always been regarded as integral parts of mainstream Turkish identity. The word *Turk* is more of a national umbrella identity rather than a purely ethnic term. What is more, Muslim ethnic groups such as Abkhazians, Albanians, Bosnians, Caucasians, Chechens, Georgians, Kurds, and Laz have preferred to identify themselves as integral parts of Ottoman or modern Turkish society rather than as separate and independent minority groups living under an alien dominant culture. Even the Kurds, who now claim to be an ethnic minority group, chose to be defined as Turks when they had an option during the writing of the

Lausanne Treaty in 1923. One of the most important factors, if not the only one, that made these groups, including the Kurds, identify themselves with dominant Turkish culture and identity is religion, which is Islam.

Languages Spoken

The official and most commonly used language of the country is Turkish. An overwhelming majority of the Turkish vocabulary comes from Arabic, Persian, and some Latin languages. The Latin alphabet was chosen for the written language after the establishment of modern Turkey in 1928. Arabic, Armenian, and Hebrew are also used by very tiny minorities. Other languages—such as different versions of the Kurdish language and dialects, Bosnian, Albanian, and Laz—are also used as spoken languages. However, as these groups are all Muslims, they are not considered to be ethnic minorities just on the basis of language difference.

Trends in Immigration

Turkey has been a country of emigration as well as immigration, and it has been subject to internal migration on a great scale since the postwar period (IOM, 1996). Turkey connects the Asian and European continents like a bridge. Because of its strategic geographic location, Turkey has received a large number of immigrants both as a target and as a transit country. In the early 1960s, Western European countries, mainly Germany, asked for legal immigrant workers from Turkey (Çiçekli, 1998). The number of immigrant workers working and living in Europe today has reached 3.5 million. Over 1 million have now acquired the citizenship of their respective countries. However, the total number of legal and illegal Turkish immigrant workers living in foreign countries today is more than 4.5 million (Ministry of Labor and Social Security, 2002).

Almost in the same time period, Turkey also experienced internal migration from rural areas of the eastern, southeastern, and Black Sea regions to the western, Marmara, Aegean, and Mediterranean regions. A number of cities such as Istanbul, Izmit, Bursa, Izmir, Denizli, Manisa, Antalya, Adana, and Mersin, in their respective regions, were target cities. Ankara has turned into a metropolitan city, while it was only a small town before it became the capital city of Turkey. Economic and social factors played a major role in the internal migration from east to west. However, a dramatic increase in PKK terror in the late 1980s also was an important contributing factor. Many of the occupants of small hamlets in southeastern parts of Turkey were evacuated to the cities, and their houses were razed by government forces to prevent the PKK from using them (Cerrah & Moore, 1997). During the last decade, over 2 million people have moved from rural areas to big cities such as Izmir, Ankara, and Istanbul as well as to regional cities such as Diyarbakir, Adana, and Mersin. However, the PKK has sometimes turned this strategy to its own ends, claiming that Turkish security forces not only razed the houses but also killed the occupants.

Between the years of 1980 and 1990, Turkey had to accommodate an influx of refugees from Iraq, a neighboring country (Kirişçi, 1995). Several times, Kurdish immigrants living in northern Iraq were forced to escape from Saddam Hussein's atrocities and seek refuge in Turkey. Turkey also was a transit country for illegal immigrants from countries such as Iran, Afghanistan, Pakistan, and India (IOM, 2003). Iranian political dissidents used Turkey as a transit and target country. Another external immigration wave came from the Central Asian Turkic republics and other former Soviet bloc countries such as Ukraine, Georgia, and even Russia itself. Turkey again served as a transit and target country for the influx of people coming through the Black Sea region to Turkey. Following the disintegration of the old Soviet bloc, a number of legal and illegal immigrants arrived in Turkey; some were seeking legitimate jobs, while others were involved in illegal activities such as prostitution, drug trafficking, and weapons smuggling. Finally, Turkey is a recipient of immigrants from Europe, mainly from Germany. A large number of retired German citizens have chosen to live in the coastal towns of the Mediterranean region. The number of foreigners migrating to Turkey for work or marriage purposes has also been increasing steadily for the last decade and is estimated to be at around 1 million.

Inter- and Intragroup Conflicts

The disintegration of the Ottoman state and caliphate, which was a binding factor among the Muslim residents, contributed to the rise of Turkish nationalism and the potential for intergroup conflicts. Interesting enough, the frequency of internal conflicts in Turkey has been especially strong since its experience with democracy in the 1950s. All this internal turmoil was followed by a number of military coups or interventions.

In the last three decades, Turkey has had a number of potential intergroup conflicts. Motives for these conflicts were right- and left-wing political ideologies, religious differences such as those between Aleviates and Sunni Muslims, or ethnic concerns such as those between Turkish and Kurdish people, but they have always been coupled with a political affiliation.

In the first period of such conflict, violent student protests began in the late 1950s after Turkey's first experience with democracy began in 1946. The Democratic Party successfully took power and ruled Turkey for 10 years until it was removed from power by a military coup in 1960. The coup took place after the political climate was destabilized by widespread and violent student demonstrations.

In the second period, Marxist-Leninist student protests and early terror activities began in the 1960s after another conservative political party, the Justice Party, came to power after the election that was held two years after the military coup. This party's rule coincided with the student demonstrations all over the world. Again, this government was brought to an end by a military interception in 1971. This period was again marked by violent student demonstrations and Marxist terrorism.

In the third period, armed conflict between left wing and right wing students began in the early 1970s and was brought to an end by another military coup in 1980. Although some sectarian violence occurred between Aleviates and Sunnis in cities such as Çorum and Maraş, this period was principally known for the armed conflicts that took place between right-wing and left-wing students and between unions and workers.

In the fourth period, conflict between government forces and people of ethnic Kurdish origin began in the mid-1980s. The first election that took place after the 1980 military coup yielded the Motherland Party, another conservative party that took power. This party ruled Turkey very successfully for almost 10 years. Following political stabilization, the economy, which was at the point of collapse before the military coup, began flourishing. The PKK, which was established in the late 1970s, began its armed assaults in the 1980s while this government was successfully ruling Turkey.

The final period is known as the 28 Subat Sureci (which translates to 28 February period or process), as the army once again expressed its displeasure and forced the ruling Welfare Party to step down on February 28, 1997. This political party was accused of taking Islamic actions rather than ruling in a secular manner. This political party did not officially identify itself as Islamic, but it was known for its religious sensitivities and priorities. Between the years of 1994 and 2000, religious conflicts were seen to rise between Sunnis and Alleviates. There were some activities that could be seen to be religiously provocative for both sides. Some Sunni villages were attacked and almost completely destroyed.

Some sections of Turkish society, including a number of intellectuals, believe that the above-mentioned religious and ethnic groups and others are manipulated by outsiders. This implies that some neighboring and Western countries have internal collaborators in Turkey. Although this brings to mind often-denied conspiracy theories, the fact that regular and continuous presence of intergroup conflicts started with Turkey's experience of democracy would seem to give some credit to this claim. However, the lack of institutionalized democracy can also be seen as a major factor. Rural parts of Turkey, especially the eastern and southern regions, still maintain traces of feudal social structure. Additionally, the army's self-appointed position as the so-called guardian of democracy has caused frequent military coups and interventions. Turkey's experience with democracy has been limited to the election of deputies to the Grand National Assembly in certain periods. Existing political systems lack local representation and participation and therefore do not represent the diversities of Turkish social structure.

Relationship Between Police and Diverse Populations

The relationship between the police and Turkey's diverse populations is not problematic in the ethnic sense. The two main sections of Turkish society that are officially defined as ethnic minorities are the Armenians and the Jews. The majority of these two religious minority groups live in big cities, mainly in Istanbul, İzmir, Bursa, Adana, and Ankara. They are economically and politically the most powerful groups in Turkey. Because of their prestigious positions and the areas in which they live, they do not very often have adversarial relations with the police.

However, the Kurdish people who immigrated to big cities have tended to have problems with the police. Kurdish immigrants in big cities are mainly concentrated in shantytown areas, and some of these areas are almost seen as "no go" areas for the police. The districts of Armutlu in Istanbul and of Kadifekale in İzmir can be given as two examples. The relationship between the Kurdish people and the police is not a racial discrimination issue; rather it is politically motivated with a hint of ethnic influence.

Representation of Diverse Populations in Government and the Police

All citizens of Turkey are regarded as Turkish, not purely in an ethnic sense but in terms of national identity; therefore no official records are kept about the representation of any ethnic groups in any institution in Turkey. Members of every ethnic group are eligible to join the police through official exams based on merit. Despite this legal position, however, there is a commonly held belief that those who are officially accepted as minorities are excluded from certain positions. However, the issue of discrimination is not limited to ethnic minorities. For example, a number of army officers have been fired from the army because of their religious beliefs.

Secularism is considered to be of utmost importance in Turkey. The Turkish army, as the sole guardian of the regime, puts an extraordinary premium on practices seen to be violations of the secular governing system. As a result of this overemphasis, women are deprived of a number of civil liberties that they could enjoy if they were living in a Western democratic society. For example, women who wear head scarves for religious reasons are not allowed to work in public services. Some in the private sector institutions also, partly for fear of a state reprimand or by their own policy, do not employ women who wear head scarves. For instance, a female who wore a head scarf who was elected to parliament in 1999 was not allowed to take her oath of office by other members of parliament. Wearing a head scarf is considered to be a violation of secularism. What is more, the board of higher education has also strictly imposed a ban on female students wearing head scarves. Female students who wear head scarves are not allowed to attend universities, and thousands of students are prevented by the police from attending. This practice continues even though it is not illegal for women to wear head scarves in Turkey.

There is no evidence to show that there is systematic discrimination on the basis of race, color, or ethnic origin. The Kurdish issue in particular is quite different from the discrimination seen against the blacks for example in the Western world. The Kurdish issue in Turkey is not similar to the racial conflicts that occur in countries such as Germany, the United States, or South Africa. Turkish Kurds are the host, not the guest, in Turkey and enjoy full citizenship. They participate in all aspects of political, economic, and social life. Almost one in three members of the Grand National Assembly is of Kurdish origin. A number of leading officials in Turkey have also been of Kurdish origin. There have been presidents, prime ministers, cabinet ministers, generals in the armed forces, numerous police chiefs, and the general director of the Turkish police among the citizens of Kurdish origin.

Community Policing

Community policing is seen as a dramatic move from traditional policing. It is defined simply as an attempt to reconnect the police with the community they are supposed to be serving. The overall aim is that the police, in an ideal society, should have not only the support of the community but also its consent. Community participation is a vital factor in obtaining the consent of the community. Community policing activities that are not based on community participation will not yield the consent of the community. Such practices are viewed by the critics of community policing as penetration practices into the community.

Factors That Make Community Policing Difficult

Community policing activities can be developed in three stages: policy, program, and structure. Turkish police presently are at the first of these three stages. There are no systematic community policing programs, and the present organizational structure of the police is not conducive to community policing.

Community support, which is a vital element to successful policing, can be achieved by systematic community participation. Yet, the Turkish police lack community participation and institutionalized police-community relations, which are instrumental in creating a climate conducive to community policing. No systematic meetings with members of the local community take place, and there is no community participation in policing on a systematic and regular basis. The majority of senior police officers who are in a position to create a suitable climate are not even conscious of the difference between traditional and community policing styles. Some senior police offi-cials even confuse community policing with public relations. Some efforts toward community policing seen in recent years are not a result of policy change made by the top management. Rather, they are the result of the efforts by some midmanagement police officers who, individually and inde-pendently, strive to develop good relations with their communities.

Factors affecting community policing activities in Turkey can be summa-rized as a resistance stemming from the traditional police culture and police organizational structure. The first major resistance to community policing activities stems from the traditional Turkish police culture. According to this culture, the police force is strong enough to fight against crime. There is no need to involve the community with policing or to ask what their views are in fighting crimes. The police organization, like any other government insti-tution, always knows what is best for the people. Members of the commu-nity should come forward and provide the necessary support. There is no need to develop systematic and regular community involvement with polic-ing issues. Policing is a national security issue. The state and its appointed officials always know what is right and best for the people.

The second major factor affecting community policing is the organiza-tional structure of the TNP. A highly centralized general Turkish adminis-trative system naturally creates an authoritarian state and policing system in the country. Turkish police, as a part of a social structure and establish-ment, persistently maintain the authoritarian government structure. This seems to be more of a "force" than a "service." A highly centralized and authoritarian administrative system is not conducive to systematic and legitimate community participation. Therefore, in Turkey, community policing activities find it hard to flourish.

The Turkish police can be defined as being a highly centralized and mil-itarist force. The policy of the organization can be summarized as being a force rather than a public service, although it is often said in ceremonies and public statements that the Turkish police is there to serve its public. This argument is not supported by systematic community participation and remains only as rhetoric. The present organizational structure is not con-ducive to community policing.

Turkish police practices fall within the category of traditional policing. In other words, community policing activities, as an alternative to tradi-tional policing, have no chance of survival because the present organiza-tional structure is not conducive to community policing (Kavgacı, 1995). Police officers are deliberately removed from day-to-day contact with citi-zens. This is considered a preventive measure against police corruption. Frequent interpersonal contacts with members of the community by police officers are considered to be a source of corrupt relations. Therefore, typi-cal police officers are expected to be out in their cars patrolling, responding to radio calls after a crime has been committed, and dealing more with the criminals and less with the victims. The police spend most of their time and resources responding to calls. They are not expected, on their own initiative, to deal with either the crime problem or the public safety needs of citizens living and working in their unsafe neighborhoods.

Community policing is an aspect of democratic policing and can only be applied to police practices in democratic societies. As long as the Turkish administration system and the police remain highly centralized in nature, community policing efforts are doomed to fail. In other words, resistance to community policing in Turkey is the natural result of a highly centralized organizational structure rather than the result of deliberate resistance to community policing.

In Turkey, policing policies can be determined only by the central government via the general director of the police. Police chiefs in provinces have no room to maneuver. However, some police practices that can be seen as community policing efforts have unconstructive effects, as they are not considered and applied carefully. For example, in the late 1990s, the Istanbul police and some other police departments organized "peace meetings" with people in different parts of the city on a regular basis. However, rather than listening to what the people had to say and taking into consideration the communities' needs and expectations, the police used these meetings to instruct people about what they should do. Police-community relations are usually seen, on the part of the police, as a way of coaxing people to come forward and help with the gathering of information about a particular crime.

Turkish police are not familiar with the idea of involving civilians in policing practices. The community has traditionally accepted whatever the state offers them. The state and its institutions are presumed always to know what is best for its people. This approach summarizes the nature of state-community relations in general. However, senior police officers occasionally make public statements urging people to help the police in fighting crimes. But, community support is perceived as people coming forward with information and helping the police to solve a particular crime. Systematic community involvement in policing policies exercised locally is not an issue that is generally considered. Other types of police-community relations are usually of an adversarial nature, such as people contacting the police when they are victims of a crime or suspects of a crime. The second most common police-community interaction is an individual serving as an informant.

Community policing, as a derivation of democratic policing, is meaningful as long as it is based on civilian participation in policing policies and in practices on both a national and local level. Civil and local participation should be based on systematic communication with regular and planned meetings between the police and the community. Accountability and responsibility are the two key concepts in democratic policing. Police accountability is of pivotal importance, not only to the national government, but also to the local governments and communities. In Turkey, there is a lack of civil involvement in local police practices, and this raises questions of legitimacy in the system in general and in the police in particular.

Systematic civil participation, which is an essential element of participatory democracies, will not only contribute to the legitimacy of the police in Turkey but also to the legitimacy of the police force in general. However, the TNP does not see the concept of legitimacy as an issue to be maintained. Official state perception on legitimacy is that the Turkish state has the inherited consent of its people and there is no need to maintain or encourage this inherited consensus. In other words, consensus of the people and the legitimacy of the TNP are taken for granted. In modern democracies, however, consensus and legitimacy are not static concepts but dynamic ones. Legitimacy of a police force or consent of the society toward a government in general or an institution such as the police may fluctuate up or down depending on its practices and relations with the community.

In short, Turkish police do not have any systematic civil involvement and participation in policing on a local basis. Individually initiated community policing activities, such as police officers visiting schools and meeting students, or a police officer establishing good relations with unofficial community leaders, fall short, because they are not systematic enough to be effective community policing practices. On the other hand, some contacts between civilians and police that have been intended to build good relations between the police and the community have been used by police for nothing more than advising people on what to do at best or instructing people on how to help the police. The peace meetings in Istanbul were an example of this. Instead of seriously trying to involve local people in solving or fighting crime, the police were selling their so-called services or trying to persuade people to help them more. In some of these meetings, the person who was police commissioner for Istanbul at the time had very controversial discussions with the people.

Crime Prevention Programs

In order to implement community policing, a variety of innovative organizational and procedural models and programs need to be initiated. Presently, there are no systematic crime prevention programs such as Neighborhood Watch, nor is any formal community participation embedded into policing. Neither NGOs nor any other civilian institution has any say about policing policy and practices. Crime prevention activities are based mostly on harsh policing methods. Policing policies are designed by senior police officers without consulting civilian boards or NGOs. It is believed that traditional harsh policing practices will deter crime, if not prevent it completely.

Community Outreach

Community outreach, like community policing, is not a familiar concept in Turkish policing. It is assumed that the police, as an agent of the state, are always within reach of all sections of the community. It is true, to some extent, that the police do not have a particular communication problem with society based on ethnic divisions. Police malpractice or corruption is not focused on any ethnic minority or other group. Police malpractice is evenly distributed and there is no discrimination in improper police practices. Members of the two officially acknowledged ethnic minority groups, the Jews and Christians, have economically and socially high standards of living in Turkey and therefore do not have serious adversarial contacts with the police.

However, particularly in big cities, the police frequently have problematic relations with people based on their economic and social status rather than their race or ethnic group. Like many other developed or developing countries, increased urbanization and inner-city deprivation in Turkey has led to societal turbulence. As stated earlier, some inner-city areas are now seen as no go areas for the police, because, within these areas, the police face difficulty in enforcing the law and have little support from the local community. These locations are usually, but not exclusively, populated by people who migrated from rural areas of the country, mainly from eastern Turkey. The police find it hard to reach these locations.

To conclude, police practices that are attuned with the community's needs and expectations will result in improved community and police relations. They will further contribute to the legitimacy of the police force in general. In other words, a lack of systematic and democratic participation in policing will erode legitimacy of the force. Resistance to community policing in Turkey stems partly from the centralized Turkish administration system and the police organizational structure. However, despite the present negative atmosphere for community policing, there is reason to be optimistic about the future. First, an overwhelming majority of current police middle managers and the new generation of police officers are familiar with the ideas of community policing, and they hold positive views about it. So resistance stemming from the traditional police culture seems to be gradually fading away. Second, Turkey is near to joining the European Union, and in recent years a number of legislative changes have been made by the central government to facilitate Turkey's EU membership. These legislative changes will improve the quality of democracy in Turkey and are likely to create a favorable environment for community policing.

Terrorism

Turkey's experience with terrorism began in the late 1960s. Since then, Turkey has suffered from various forms of terrorist activities, including domestic and international terrorism. Having common borders with Syria, Iraq, Iran, and Greece, Turkey has had to fight against a number of terrorist organizations, most of which have had political and logistical support from these neighboring countries. These terrorist organizations could be categorized broadly as either domestic or international terrorist organizations. The following organizations are the most notorious organizations.

Sources of Terrorist Threats

The most infamous international terrorist organization in Turkey is the Armenian Secret Army for the Liberation of Armenia (ASALA), which is of Lebanese origin (Aktan & Köknar, 2002; Cerrah & Peel, 1997). In 1973, in order to achieve autonomy for provinces of northeastern Turkey that had formerly been populated by Armenians, Armenian terrorist groups ran a terror campaign for 13 years that involved the systematic assassination of Turkish diplomats. By 1982, two groups, known as the ASALA and the Justice Commandos of the Armenians, had killed 22 Turkish diplomats, members of their families, and Turkish embassy staff.

Domestic terrorist organizations can be divided into several subcategories, including organizations based on ethnicity, ideology, and religion. Some of the terrorist organizations may well fit into more than one category.

The Partiya Karkaren Kurdistan or PKK

By far the largest and most active ethnically and ideologically motivated terrorist organization operating in Turkey today is the Kurdistan Workers Party (Partiya Karkaren Kurdistan or PKK). The PKK was formed on November 27, 1978, in the province of Diyarbakir. Although they have occasionally ventured outside this area, the PKK generally confines its activities to the mountains of southeastern Turkey.

The PKK is motivated mostly by Kurdish nationalism, but at the same time it is ideologically a Marxist terrorist organization. Seeking independence or at least autonomy for the Kurds, the PKK has been involved in terrorist activities since 1984 and has caused the deaths of over 30,000 people, including Kurdish civilians, members of the security forces, and terrorists (Bal, 1999).

For the first six years of its existence, the PKK was engaged in recruiting people for its organization, building teams, acquiring weapons, and undergoing training. Then it launched a violent terrorist campaign in August 1984, which has now lasted more than 20 years. Initially, its aim was to establish an independent socialist state in southeastern Turkey and then to extend the state into Kurdish areas in Syria, Iraq, and Iran. However, it now has a more limited aim—a degree of autonomy over southeastern Turkey.

Operating in an area that covers tens of thousands of square miles of rugged terrain, the strategy of PKK is first to take over the rural areas and then to move into the cities. In order to achieve this aim, this terrorist organization has attempted to unite workers in the cities with those living in the many small villages dotted all over the area. The poor educational standards in southeastern Turkey have made it easier for the PKK to recruit new members.

Estimates of the number of active members of the PKK vary from 5,000 to 10,000, which includes those based in Syria, Iraq, and Iran, as well as in Turkey. They are organized in teams of between 7 and 11 people. Their tactics are based on those used by the Viet Cong in the Vietnam War—they identify a target, hit it, and run. For some of the larger operations, teams come together to form groups (three teams) and units (six teams). The PKK is in touch with various terrorist groups, and operators have been trained in Syria and in Lebanon.

Unlike other well-known terrorist groups, such as the Irish Republican Army (IRA) in the UK and the Euskadi Ta Askatasuna (ETA or Basque Fatherland and Liberty) group in Spain, who tend to target what they regard as military and economic targets, the PKK is totally indiscriminate when mounting its operations. Bombs are placed in public places with total disregard for who might be affected by the explosions. Men, women, and children have been systematically killed in raids on villages. Because state education is delivered only in Turkish and not Kurdish, the PKK has deliberately targeted teachers and killed at least 90. Despite a claim by the PKK in August 1994 that the organization was committed to Article 3 of the Geneva Convention, which states that people taking no active part in hostilities must be treated humanely and should not be ill-treated or killed, the PKK has continued to kill civilians totally unconnected with the conflict. In late 1994, 19 teachers were abducted and killed in a single raid.

Like the IRA, the PKK acts in a decisive manner to kill its own members in order to maintain discipline and also exercise authority over the Kurds by killing those believed to be traitors or unwilling to cooperate with the organization. Abdullah Öcalan, the so-called general secretary of the PKK, lived in Damascus under the protection of the Syrian government until he was forced to flea the country by the Turkish government in 1998. He went first to Russia and then to Greece seeking protection, and he finally took refuge in Italy. Then the Italian government was forced to surrender Öcalan. He was finally captured by Turkish security forces in Kenya in 1999 and brought back to Turkey, where he was sentenced to life in prison.

Since the terrorist attacks on the World Trade Center in New York in 2001, the international approach to terrorism has dramatically changed, and antiterrorist pressures have reached a peak. As a result, the PKK could not resist the pressure coming from the Western world and decided to transform itself. It changed its name to Kurdistan Freedom and Democracy Congress (Kongreya Azadi-u Demokrasi-a Kurdistan or KADEK) and made a fresh start, aiming both to cover up its violent past and to adapt its infamous reputation into political capital. In 2004, it changed its name again to The People's Congress of Kurdistan (KONGRA-GEL) and claimed to be the legitimate representative of the Kurdish people. However, despite these name changes, it remains known as the PKK, and despite its claim that it is able to solve existing conflicts among the peoples of the Middle East—including the Kurdish issue—by democratic and peaceful means, the residue of armed PKK/KONGRA-GEL terrorists still engage in terrorist activities in northern Iraq. They frequently declare ceasefires and then mount terrorist attacks similar to those that they used to mount.

Politically and Religiously Motivated Terrorist Organizations

Several well-known Marxist terrorist organizations are currently active in Turkey. They usually engage in terrorist activities in urban areas. The Revolutionary People's Liberation Party/Front–Revolutionary Left (DHKP/C–DEVSOL) is a Marxist-Leninist nonethnic terrorist organization. It is principally based in big cities such as Istanbul and Ankara. Originally known as Revolutionary Left, it began its operations in late 1975 and changed its name in 1994. As its name implies, it is a left-wing organization that grew out of the student movements of the late 1960s. DHKP/C operates on a cell structure similar to that of the IRA and ETA. The group tends to target members of the security forces, prosecutors, and politicians.

The Turkish Communist Party/Marxist-Leninist–Turkish Workers and Peasants Liberation Army (TKP/ML-TIKKO) is a Maoist organization with a sectarian element. Although most members of the organization are Alawite, which is an Islamic sect, the second recruiting source is the Kurdish population. The Marxist-Leninist Communist Party/Foundation (MLKP/K) is another Marxist and nonethnic terrorist organization (Aktan & Köknar, 2002).

Terrorist Organizations Motivated Primarily by Religion

Despite the fact that Islamic teachings and tradition have always been against terrorism and the indiscriminate use of violence, some terrorist groups define themselves as Islamic. An overwhelming majority of the Turkish population resent the fact that these organizations are called Islamic. The so-called Islamic terrorist organizations have always been marginal groups and have failed to receive support from the public.

The major religiously motivated terrorist organizations are the Party of God (Hizbullah), Islamic Great Orient Raiders Front (IBDA/C) and Islamic Movement. The most active and the largest in size is the Hizbullah. Although its Lebanese namesake Shieti Hizbullah was a Shiite, the Turkish version of Hizbullah is an exclusively Sunni organization. Despite the fact that Turkish security forces have mounted successful operations against Hizbullah in recent years, the organization still has considerable public support in eastern and southeastern Turkey, where most Kurds live. The other two so-called Islamic terrorist groups, IBDA/C and Islamic Movement, have had to cease their activities as almost all of their members have been captured by the Turkish police.

On November 15–20, 2003, Turkey experienced a wave of terrorist attacks that targeted two synagogues, a British bank, and the British consulate in Istanbul. A total of 61 Turkish citizens lost their lives, as well as

2 British citizens and 6 Turkish Jews. Police identified the suicide attackers within a couple of days. They had ties with a domestic terrorist organization that is seen as a derivation of the al-Quaeda terror organization. However, despite the apparent links with al-Quaeda, some questions have been raised about the real mastermind of these attacks. Because Jews have not been subject to attack in Turkey for many centuries, terrorist attacks apparently targeted against Jewish minorities are believed to reflect some ideology that comes from outside the country. This has raised questions about the true origin behind the attacks. Some commentators have argued that these attacks, which seem to be organized by a so-called Islamic terrorist organization, are manipulated by those who want to destabilize the democratic system of the country and prevent it from becoming a part of the Western world.

It is true that a very small minority of the Turkish population in Turkey does not want the country to be a part of Europe. In addition, there are those in the Western world who argue that Turkey cannot belong to the West and that there will, in the future, be a clash between Christians and Jews on the one side and the Muslim world on the other. Therefore, such terrorist attacks have seemed to serve not only the cause of the so-called Islamic terrorist organizations but also the cause of those who argue that the future will witness a clash between civilizations.

Terrorist organizations acquire funds from a variety of sources. Contributions for the PKK are collected from Kurdish businesses operating in Germany, France, and the United Kingdom in the same way that terrorist groups from Northern Ireland have raised funds for the IRA from Irish Americans living in the United States. One of the other sources of funds for the PKK is smuggling of humans, weapons, and drugs. It has been very involved in trafficking between the Eastern world and Western Europe. In particular, it has smuggled drugs into European countries, which are the source of the majority of its funding.

Counterterrorism Training

Because the PKK terror activities were mainly concentrated in the eastern and southeastern parts of Turkey, which is a very mountainous rural area, traditional urban antiterror methods were not successful. Therefore army units were deployed at the early stages of the PKK terror surge. During these early stages, the Turkish government's military response to terror was handicapped. Despite the continuous presence of terrorism in Turkey since 1984, both the police and the army have lacked the necessary skills and expertise to launch effective counterterrorist operations. On a number of occasions, this has led to armed conflict between security forces and terrorists in which innocent people have been killed. However, while fighting against terrorism, Turkish security forces, both the civilian police and the military, gained a great deal of experience by trial and error.

Later the police established a Special Operations department for counterterror activities. Now both the military and the police have special units that are trained in fighting against terrorism. These units have been very successful using rural guerrilla tactics. However, fighting terrorism with paramilitary methods has always had its disadvantages. The issue has gradually turned into a war between the terrorists and the armed forces. This was a situation the PKK deliberately wanted to create. The PKK has always argued that the eastern and southeastern parts of Turkey were Kurdish lands occupied by the Turks. The Turkish government's use of the army to fight terrorism instead of the civilian police has enhanced the PKK's claims that it was not a domestic security issue but a war between two different and separate peoples.

Weapons of mass destruction (WMDs) have so far not been used by any terrorist group in Turkey, and therefore training against biological attacks and WMDs has not yet been adopted. However, because of its geographic location, Turkey has been used as a transport route for terror related drug trafficking. Following the demolition of the Soviet Union, nuclear materials stolen from former Soviet countries were smuggled into Turkey and were transported between the Eastern and the Western world. The only preparation that the Turkish armed forces have made to counter WMD attacks is the purchase, in 2005, of protective clothing for its personnel that will shield them in nuclear-biological and chemical (NBC) attacks ("Ordu'da nükleer hazırlık," n.d.).

Counterterrorism Policy and Strategy

The Turkish government has adopted a number of strategies in its fight against the PKK. In 1984, it imposed martial law in the nine provinces that were immediately affected by PKK terrorism. By July 1987, this had been replaced by a "state of emergency," which gave the security forces wide-ranging powers. Eastern and southeastern provinces were ruled under this state of emergency from late 1980 until 2002.

Many villages in the region were annihilated by the PKK attacks. A number of villages were encouraged, if not forced, to evacuate because of the inability of the security forces to protect them. The government also encouraged the formation of the civil defense corps of village guards in the mid-1980s. Now numbering about 55,000, village guards mount roadblocks in the affected areas and assist the security forces in mounting operations against the PKK. But the villagers are in a dilemma. Many are reluctant to serve as village guards because they fear being killed by the PKK. But, if they refuse to join, they can be accused by those who have joined the civil defense corps and the security forces of being PKK sympathizers.

To conclude, the Turkish government's strategy to eliminate the PKK has largely been to mount a military offensive. The cost of fighting the PKK with military strength exceeds several billion dollars a year, crippling an economy that might otherwise be blossoming. However a solution that depends solely on a military response has so far showed that it is unlikely to succeed. This is what the British government found in Northern Ireland, the Spanish government experienced in the Basque region, and Israel is currently facing in Palestine. Furthermore, the use of force as the only strategy against the PKK or other terrorist organizations has also raised human rights questions and legitimacy concerns.

Terrorism is a domestic security problem. It has a number of contributing factors such as social, political, economic, and historical influences. Terror as a multidimensional social problem cannot simply be solved by force. The other factors contributing to terror must be taken into consideration and addressed in fighting against terror in general and against the PKK in particular.

References

Aktan, G. S., & Köknar, A. M. (2002). Turkey. In Y. Alexander (Ed.), *Combating terrorism: Strategies of ten countries* (pp. 210–420). Ann Arbor, MI: University of Michigan Press.

Ayata, A. (1997, Fall). The emergency of identity politics in Turkey. *New Perspectives on Turkey, 22,* 59–73.

Aydın, A. H. (1997). *Police organization and legitimacy: Case studies of England, Wales and Turkey.* Aldershot, UK: Avebury.

Aydın, A. H. (2003, October). *Policing system in Turkey: A critical analysis.* Paper presented to the International Police Executive Symposium, 10th Annual Meeting: Policing and Community, Manama, Bahrain.

Bal, I. (1999). *Prevention of terrorism in liberal democracies: A case study of Turkey.* Unpublished doctoral thesis, University of Leicester, UK.

Cerrah , I., & Moore, T. (1997). Public order policing in Turkey: The need for command training. *Turkish Public Administration Annual, 22–23,* 19–22.

Cerrah, I., & Peel, R. (1997). Terrorism in Turkey. *Intersec: The Journal of International Security, 7*(1), 19–22.

Çiçekli, B. (1998). *The legal position of Turkish immigrants in the European Union.* Ankara: Karmap.

Cizre, U. (2000). *Politics and military in Turkey into the 21st century.* Robert Schuman Centre For Advanced Studies, European University Institute, Florence, EUI Working Paper RSC No. 2000/24: Badia Fiesolan, San Domenico.

Cizre, U. (2004). Problems of democratic governance of civil-military relations in Turkey and the European Union enlargement zone. *European Journal of Political Research, 43,* 107–125.

Donat, Y. (2005, April 2). Interviews with Kenan Evren and Süleyman Demirel. *Sabah* [Electronic version]. Retrieved April 2, 2005, from http://www.zaman .com.tr/webapp-tr

Eryılmaz, M. B. (2003). *Türk ve ingiliz hukukuna ve uygulamasında durdurma ve arama.* Ankara: Seçkin.

European Parliament, Committee on Foreign Affairs, Human Rights, Common Security, and Defence Policy. (2003). *Regular report of the commission on Turkey's progress towards accession.* Brussels: Commission of the European Communities.

Goldsmith, A., & Cerrah, I. (2005). *Civilian oversight of the security sector in Turkey.* Unpublished project report. Ankara: United Nations Development Program.

International Organization for Migration (IOM). (1996). *Transit migration in Turkey.* Budapest: IOM Information Programme.

International Organization for Migration (IOM). (2003). *Irregular migration in Turkey.* IOM Migration Research Series, No. 12. Budapest: IOM Information Programme.

İşte JİTEM'in resmi tanımı. (n.d.). *Aktif Haber* [Electronic version]. Retrieved April 17, 2005, from http://www.aktifhaber.com

Kavgacı (Bahar), H. İ. (1995). *The development of police/community relations initiatives in England & Wales post Scarman and their relevance to policing policy in Turkey.* Unpublished doctoral thesis, University of Leicester, UK.

Kirişçi, K. (1995). *Refugee movements and Turkey in the post second world war era.* Research paper, ISS/POLS 95-01, Boğazici University, Istanbul.

Mahalli ıdareler. (2003). Retrieved August 15, 2007, from http://www.mahalli idareler.gov.tr/Home/Home.aspx

Ministry of Labor and Social Security (Çalışma ve Sosyal Güvenlik Bakanlığı). (2002). *2000–2001 Raporu: Yurtdışındaki vatandaşlarmiza ilişkin gelişme ve say?sal veriler.* Publication no. 110, pp. 31–34. Ankara: Author.

Ordu'da nükleer hazırlık. (n.d.). *Aktif Haber* [Electronic version]. Retrieved August 28, 2005, from http://www.aktifhaber.com

Prime Ministry, Human Rights Presidency. (2004). *Document files.* Ankara, Author.

Varlığı tartışılan JİTEM yargıda. (2004, December 11). *Zaman,* p. 3.

Veli küçük: JİTEM yok, devletin verdiği emirleri yaptim. (2004, December 26). *Zaman,* p. 3.

Further Reading

Aydın, A. (1992). *Kürtler, PKK ve A. Öcalan.* Ankara: Kiyap.

Çermeli, A. (2002). *Jandarma genel komutanliği tarihi: Asayiş ve kolluk tarihi içersinde Türk jandarma teşkilatı.* Ankara: Jandarma Genel Komutanlığı Yayınları.

Cerrah, İ. (2002). Ethnic identity versus national identity: An analysis of PKK terror in relation to identity conflict. In J. D. Freilich, G. Newman, S. G. Shoham, & M. Addad (Eds.), *Migration, culture conflict and crime* (pp. 223–232). Aldershot, UK: Ashgate-Dartmouth.

Cerrah, İ. (2003, March). *Teaching ethics to the police: Turkish case.* Paper presented to the Academy of Criminal Justice Sciences 40th Annual Meeting, Boston, MA.

Eryılmaz, M. B. (1999). *Arrest and detention powers in English and Turkish law and practice in the light of the European Convention on Human Rights.* The Hague: Martinus Nijhoff.

Günes-Ayata, A., (1996). *Türkiye'de etnik kimlik ve etnik gruplur.* Toplum ve Göç: II Ulusul Sosyoloji Kongresi, Başbakanlik Devlet Istatistik Enstitüsü, Ankara.

Günes-Ayata, A. (1996). Ethnic identity and ethnic groups in Turkey. *II. National Conference on Society and Migration*. Ankara: Prime Minister's Office.

Haberfeld, M., Cerrah, I., & Grant, H. (2005). *Terrorism, legitimacy, and human rights within a comparative international context*. Unpublished final report of the Fulbright Alumni Initiatives Awards Program, June 1, 2003–June 1, 2005. John Jay College of Criminal Justice, New York.

Türkdogan, O. (1996). *Sosyal siddet ve Türkiye gerçe*g. Istanbul: Timaş.

9 Traditional Policing in an Era of Increasing Homeland Concerns

The Case of the Israeli Police

Lior Gideon, Ruth Geva, and Sergio Herzog

Police studies are very much like field experiments in an ever-changing society, as they correspond to social change and may be seen as an indicator of such change. Being the primary formal social control agency in a democratic society, the police do not operate in a vacuum and thus must be responsive to social change and society needs. Generally, it is argued that law enforcement agencies reflect the priorities, divisions, and social and economic conditions of the societies in which they exist. Therefore, police characteristics and innovations, such as organizational and functional changes, should be viewed from a broader perspective, that is, as an attempt by police forces to adapt to the changing needs and character of the society in which they operate and from which its officers are being recruited (Herzog, 2001).

Such is the case with the Israeli Police (IP), which, since its inception as a national police in 1948 (parallel with the establishment of Israel as an independent state), has been challenged by variety of tasks aimed at order maintenance as well as maintaining the security and quality of life of its citizens. Facing extreme ongoing security threats has demanded that Israeli police officers and the Israeli Border Guard Police (BGP) deal with responsibilities that are somewhat different from the traditional and classical policing duties as manifested in other democratic societies. To a large extent, the IP nowadays is concerned with homeland security and preventing and responding to terrorist threats and attacks as well as preventing and reacting to crime. As such, the IP is usually found in the hub of the most painful conflicts of Israeli society. (For a detailed discussion of such conflicts, see Smooha, 1988, and Smooha & Hanf, 1992.)

The aim of this chapter is to present an overview of the Israeli Police in a fairly young society that is constantly facing new challenges as well as the challenge of mass in-migration and terror attacks.

Israel in a Nutshell

Bordered by Lebanon in the north, Syria in the northeast, Jordan in the east, Egypt in the south, and the Mediterranean Sea on the west, Israel's population at yearend 2005 is about 6.99 million, with approximately 1.37 million Arab Israelis (Israeli Central Bureau of Statistics, 2006). This number does not include about 3 million Arab residents in the recently established Palestinian Authority and in the Administered Territories (i.e., East Jerusalem, the West Bank of the River Jordan, and the Gaza Strip; henceforth *territories*) controlled by the Israeli army since the 1967 Six Day War (Israeli Central Bureau of Statistics, 2006).

Consequent to the widespread immigration from Europe following World War II and the Holocaust, in November of 1947 the United Nations approved a partition of the area that was called "Palestine," then under British Mandate, into two states—Jewish and Arab. As a result Israel declared its independence and statehood on May 14, 1948. Following this, the surrounding Arab countries, which did not agree with this resolution, declared war on Israel (i.e., the War of Independence), but failed to defeat the new state. Since that time Israel has constantly struggled to maintain its independence while experiencing waves of armed conflicts with its Arab neighbors, as well as with Arab residents in the territories.

As noted by Geva, Herzog, and Haberfeld (2005), terrorist activity has been part of daily life in Israel for decades. This activity has been carried out mainly by Palestinian armed groups, escalating during the first *intifada* (the Palestinian uprising against Israel's military control of the territories), between 1988 and 1993, and again in the second intifada, which has been going on continuously since October 2000. This last uprising has resulted in almost constant fighting between the Palestinians in the West Bank and Gaza Strip and the Israeli security forces (including the IP, the BGP, and the Israeli Defense Forces, or IDF), with Palestinian armed groups using terrorist tactics against primarily civilian Israeli targets (Geva, Herzog, & Haberfeld, 2005) killing about 680 Israeli civilians in the years 2000–2004 (Israeli Defense Force, 2004).

Demographic Figures

According to the Israeli Central Bureau of Statistics report of 2004, the Jewish population in Israel is about 5.16 million, and there are about 1.07 million Moslems, 142,400 Christians (Arabs and non-Arabs), and 110,800 Druze.

(In Israel, Druze are granted Israeli citizenship and are distinct from other Arabic-speaking populations; they are expected to serve in the Israeli army.) During the first years of statehood, 1948–1951, massive migration (about 687,624 immigrants) from Asia and Africa as well as from Europe, entered the country as a result of World War II. Such migration waves were observed again during the 1950s and early 1960s, and another huge group of more than 1 million new immigrants arrived during the first half of the 1990s, mostly from the former Soviet Union and Ethiopia (a significant majority was from the Soviet Union). In addition, during the 1990s, and as a result of the escalating terrorist attacks and the drastic reduction in the employment of Palestinian workers by Israeli employers (see Herzog, 2005), Israel opened its gates to foreign workers from Romania and the Far East (especially to Thailand and China). Consequently, the variety of spoken languages in Israel is enormous, with Hebrew being the primary language, although Arabic and Russian are spoken by a large number of the residents as their first language. In such a social climate, conflicts are inevitable, not only due to the difference in language but also due to the differences in culture and values. Such a diversity also demands more police attention in maintaining public order as well as in dealing with new and unfamiliar issues such as alcohol-related problems and human smuggling (in particular female smuggling for prostitution purposes) to name just a few.

In order to reflect this population growth and cultural diversity, the Israeli Police have begun recruiting officers that have a profound knowledge of Arabic, Russian, and Amharic (the Ethiopian language). Also, in areas where there is a high concentration of Arabs, such as in Jerusalem and in the Galilee, Arab Israelis are represented in the force and in particular by members of the Druze community. On another level, in the second half of the 1990s the IP initiated a recruitment project known as "Police 2000." Because of this massive recruitment effort, many university graduates joined the force, thus elevating the educational level of the officers as well as their professionalism and ability to deal with various situations.

Israeli Police: Historical Development and Policing in a Political Context[1]

Since its inception in 1948, the IP has been a national, highly centralized force that has been the responsibility of the Minister of Public Security, formerly called the Ministry of Police (Sebba, Horovitz, & Geva, 2003). However, the first roots of the IP may be observed as early as 1909, when a force called *H'Shomer* (Hebrew for *the guard*) was formed to protect Jewish immigrants to Israel, who faced massive attacks by hostile neighbors. This necessitated the establishment of an organized body to maintain order and protect their lives and property when the Turkish Mandate—which then controlled the Palestine area—failed to do so.

Eight years later, in 1917, after World War I ended, when Palestine was conquered by the British, General Allenby ordered the establishment of police stations within important population concentrations and the formation of a gendarmerie (a military body charged with general police duties) from local police officers. This force was called the Superb Police. Officially it was known by the British as the Palestinian Gendarmerie, and its primary goal was to deal with public order in those concentration areas. Participating in the police force under the British Mandate gave the Jewish population in Israel an opportunity to train and carry firearms, which was later an advantage to the Jewish settlement in Israel, especially during the Arab pogroms of 1936, when the British Mandate government could not protect the life and property of Jewish citizens. Subsequently, a Jewish reactive force was formed that was called the Hebrew Settlement Police; this force later became known as the *Hagana* (Hebrew for *defense*). In its first stages, the Hagana had 1200 men who joined 700 Jewish police officers who already served under the British Mandate. This organization later developed into what is now known as the Israeli Defense Force (IDF).

About six months before the establishment of the Israeli state, strategic plans for the formation of an Israeli police were made under the leadership of Yechezkel Sahar, who later became the first commissioner of police (with the rank of inspector general). The birth of the IP in 1948 was attended by severe wartime conditions (the War of Independence). As a result, traditional police work was very low on the list of priorities of Israel's first government, in contrast to the need for an army, the labor shortage (able-bodied youth had been sent to fight the war), and the very limited budget. Under these difficult conditions, the new police administration chose to adopt the existing militaristic model of the British Mandatory Police, which had operated under the British Mandate in Palestine between 1922 and 1948, for its primary organizational, administrative, and operational structure.

Apart from being the most convenient model to adopt at that time, the choice was also based on the knowledge that British rule had introduced advanced police-work patterns and a professional approach in several areas, including police administration, discipline, and organization. The new IP adopted from the British police its legal basis, conventional policing techniques and tools (uniforms, rank structure, orders, training systems, discipline norms, organizational outlook, buildings, and even their military-style ceremonies), and in particular its centralized administration and structure.

However it should be noted that as a colonial police force, the main role of the Mandatory Police was to assist the British government to rule the colony, with its Jewish and Arab residents, by means of a paramilitary centralized force. Thus, its primary tasks were combat- and security-oriented missions to deal with serious mass disturbances, riots, and terrorism (Herzog, 2001). As a result, training of new officers was done in a military manner. Nevertheless, a sense of mission along with a strong motivation to serve the public characterized the new police officers, who also were engaged in other community services. Taking into consideration a severe shortage of manpower during this era, the IP had to deal with infiltration of terrorists, maintaining public order, dealing with demonstrations, a rising crime rate, preventing black market activity, and even providing social services to new immigrants.

In its second decade of independence, the new state's infrastructure was more established, and other problems began to emerge. Tension from bordering Arab countries increased, and an economic depression resulted in social turmoil. It was during this period that the IP renounced the British Mandatory Police heritage, making room for training in police studies and for the increasing demand for police services. According to Ross (1998), one can argue that the IP chose the liberal reformist approach,[2] as it was constantly trying to improve its ability while increasing its efficiency. Indeed, IP history reveals that between 1958 and 1966, an accelerated process of professionalism and specialization began to emerge in all aspects of police work (IP, 2004).

In 1958, a reorganization of the police separated the role of headquarter units from the operational units. The number of geographical jurisdictions decreased from five to three (i.e., north, south, and Tel-Aviv, which is in the center of Israel). In addition, a police force of full- time officers was formulated, and the Investigation Department was transformed into the proactive Investigations and Crime Fighting Department (the change in name mirrors the change in emphasis—from a merely reactive investigative one to a proactive preventive one). Beat cops were mobilized, and women were integrated into the operational units as well. Juvenile divisions were also established, and in Tel-Aviv all regional investigative units were integrated under one centralized unit. Also during this time, an Academy for Senior Officers was established, and in 1966 the Cadet School for police officers was established in Haifa. Databases were computerized, and forensic labs were improved with an addition of a mobile forensic lab to serve the needs of field investigations.

During the Six Day War (1967), Israel captured territory in the Sinai Peninsula, the Golan Heights, and the territories, expanding the geographical area under its control. Afterward, the Israeli economy came out of an economic depression, though with this recovery, the social cleavage among Israel's diverse residents went deeper, finding its expression in social unrest and the establishment of activist groups that demonstrated and created much civil disorder. Additionally, terrorist activity escalated, reaching new peaks while also targeting Israeli targets abroad. Consequently, the IP reorganized its authority to include the territories, the Sinai Peninsula, and the Golan Heights. In addition there were other organizational adjustments in the structure of the BGP (see below). In the territories new police jurisdictions were formed under the supervision of military governors to address issues of law enforcement and to provide police services to the population. The municipal jurisdictions were turned into regional jurisdictions subordinate to the Jerusalem IP headquarters. More emphasis was directed toward specialization and professionalism; more university graduates and former military officers were hired and received commissioned officers' ranks immediately, and specific activity became more and more dependent on computerized data sets. Research and development were expanded, and information and knowledge were exchanged with countries abroad.

When the Yom Kippur War broke out on October 6, 1973, the IP commissioner declared a mandatory recruitment of all police personnel to military duties. After the war ended, Israeli society was unstable politically until the election of 1977, which later resulted in the peace agreement with Egypt. During the entire period, Arab terrorist activity did not cease, and the northern part of Israel was constantly attacked by terrorist groups infiltrating from Lebanon. As a result, in 1974, following a government decision, additional responsibility for maintaining "internal security" (i.e., providing proactive and reactive functions to fight terrorism within the borders of the country) was transferred from the IDF to the IP (Herzog, 2001; Sebba, Horovitz, & Geva, 2003). Following this, a Civil Guard Department was formed and joined together tens of thousands of civilians that volunteered to guard their neighborhoods. The BGP began securing the air and sea ports, and in 1975 a new department was established—the Operational Department—to coordinate the activities of the various operational units (i.e., patrol, traffic, bomb-disposal, etc.) and increase their efficiency. A special Antiterrorist Unit was formed as well as a Bomb Disposal Division. Additionally, and in order to respond to a steep increase in white collar crime and other sophisticated crimes, the IP revised its ranks. All investigative units, detective work, intelligence, forensic, and juvenile units were united under one special unit—the Investigation and Crime Fighting Department. The 1978 *Shimron Report* (a report prepared by a parliament-appointed investigative committee), dealing with crime in Israel, contributed to this change with its recommendations to formulate guidelines and establish new units to investigate and tackle serious crime. These included the National Serious Crimes Investigation Unit, the National Fraud Unit, the Internal Investigations Unit, the Tel-Aviv District's Central Unit, and others.

After the Lebanon War was over (a period known by its Hebrew term, *Shalom HaGalil*) and throughout the 1980s, the IP faced new challenges. It began this period by drawing up a five-year plan known as the Tirosh Plan. This was the first time in its history that the IP had conducted a formal analysis of its society's need for police services, drawn up forecasts, and laid down clearly drawn policies for each section of its operations. The tasks and objectives for each succeeding year were derived from this long-term plan. In 1981, the IP set up its fourth police district, the Central District. New units were created—among them the Community Relations Unit—as part of the attempt to further prevent crime while providing more support to victims of crime, and the Zvulun Unit for policing the sea and air ports was formed (IP, 2004).

In this regard, it should be added that

> one of the serious challenges that confronted the IP during that time was riotous demonstrations by Ultra-Orthodox Jews [against Sabbath desecration and archeological excavation of Jewish graves], in addition to riots by Arabs, and by a range of political movements. The evacuation of protesting residents from the town of Yamit [part of the Sinai Peninsula returned to Egypt under the Israeli-Egyptian peace agreement] and the new problem of crime motivated by nationalistic ideologies consumed much police time and resources. (IP, 2004)

From the second half of the 1980s up until the first half of the 1990s, the rate of Jewish immigration to Israel began to pick up sharply, especially from the former Soviet Union and Ethiopia, resulting in a demand for new police recruits who could speak the language spoken by these immigrants to be able to communicate with them and serve their needs. Such immigration also brought many new problems that Israel had not witnessed before (e.g., organized crime, higher rates of alcohol consumption, and drunkenness accompanied by violent behavior, to name just a few). At the same time public disorder and disturbances by Palestinian Arabs erupted in the territories and became routine. After a while, this unrest began to spread, although on a smaller scale, into Israeli Arab towns. Arab terrorist attacks became more frequent and took many forms—open attacks in town centers launched for their shock effect, concealed explosive devices placed in markets and on the streets, arson, attacks on individual soldiers and civilians, infiltration attempts from the sea, and the like.

As a result of the economic depression and the 1985 economic emergency plan that was put into place at that time, recruitment to the IP was frozen, and because the demand for policing kept increasing, prioritizing had to be done. The first three priorities were dealing with drug abuse while tackling drug trafficking, combating the high accident rate on the roads, and increasing public order in Jerusalem. During this period the IP continued to search for useful technological and scientific advances to be introduced to its daily activities, while promoting the professionalism and specialization of its personnel (especially in the area of forensics, bomb disposal, and intelligence), who could benefit greatly from use of new advances in technology. The IP also decided to invest in education for values and professional ethics within the service itself. The aim was to instill into every officer that any lapse of integrity and improper behavior would not be tolerated. Because of pressure from the public regarding the need for transparency in the investigation of complaints submitted against police officers, the IP's Internal Investigations Unit (called *Yahash*—the Hebrew acronym for the unit) was transferred to the Ministry of Justice, and in 1992 Israel's new civilian board for the investigation of suspect police officers was established. (For a review of this topic, see Herzog, 2000.) In addition, in 1997,

> the IP's new Code of Ethics was officially introduced. The aim of the Code was to make precisely clear to every serving officer the standards

of professionalism and integrity and public service he or she was required to attain and maintain. (IP, 2004)

The second half of the 1980s was also characterized by the first intifada, in which daily violent rioting became reality. Arab terrorism rose to new levels. Once more the IP priorities had to be changed. The police forces in Jerusalem and other areas of disturbance (i.e., in the north—the Galilee and Northern Valleys—and in parts of the Central and Southern Districts) were heavily reinforced with police officers to maintain order. Such rearrangements resulted in mobilization of officers from all other areas of traditional policing responsibilities, which inevitably suffered more and more from this change in the order of priorities. Such was the case at the beginning of the 1990s, when the intifada intensified, and terrorist attacks also became more frequent. Again the IP had to reallocate its resources, transferring officers from its conventional anticrime policing functions to the maintenance of internal public order and public security. Some effort was made to compensate by using the BGP and the Civil Guard volunteers for regular police work in addition to their internal security duties. Restoring law and order demanded a militaristic approach and in many cases use of force, which sometimes was deemed excessive and also resulted many times in the escalation of the conflict.

Along with the gradual development of an Israeli civil society at the macro level, the demand for more police services had raised the emphasis on the police officer as a public servant who needs to provide the public with efficient and reliable service . (For a review of such social changes, see Herzog, 2001). Accordingly, attention was given to increasing collaboration between the public and the police, resulted in the implementation of the community policing philosophy, which began in 1995. The idea was to make police work more responsive to the needs of the ordinary citizen and to integrate the resources and goals of the police with those of local government authorities and community agencies (Herzog, 2001; Weisburd, Shalev, & Amir, 2002).

Another important organizational modification during this period was the creation of two new departments—the Traffic Department and the Intelligence Department (which was taken out of the Investigation Department and set up as a separate entity). The purpose of the change was to coordinate widespread operations and to upgrade the methods and technologies employed—the one in the battle against the heavy toll of road accidents and the other in the battle against crime.

Additional resources were also allocated to deal with serious crimes, while the war on drugs was reinforced by creating an Anti-Drugs Unit in the Southern District. This kind of unit had been operating successfully for some years on the northern Lebanese border. This unit was designed specifically to prevent drug trafficking across the Egyptian border.

It was also during the second half of the 1990s that the IP made good on its long-term intention to improve officers' working conditions, wages, and welfare. It further upgraded and refined its in-service training system. Recruitment efforts were expanded with the specific purpose of raising the quality of candidates for police work. Within the context of bringing the IP to up-to-date levels of organization and logistics, the computerization of the service was extended, particularly into the Manpower Division, and a massive equipment procurement drive was set in motion. Sophisticated, high-performance antiterrorist and anticrime equipment and technologies were bought, and relevant officers were carefully and thoroughly trained in their use (IP, 2004).

From this review, it may be seen that the development of the IP is intertwined with the historical development of the Israeli society and state of Israel. From its inception, the IP has adapted continually to serve the constantly changing needs of its citizens. Thus, as argued before, the IP can be reviewed as an organization that adopted the liberal reformist approach to policing; that is, the IP regularly adapted its operation and organizational structure to the changing needs of its society. From its inception in 1948 and up until today, the IP strives to enforce the law in the spirit of the basic values of a democratic state, while aiming to ensure the security of both individuals and society as a whole and enhancing the quality of life of its citizens. Especially when taking into account the complexity of combining two major tasks—the traditional enforcement and crime prevention role of police with the task of preventing terrorist activity—this has not always been easily accomplished.

Organizational Structure and Issues[3]

Structure and Organization

The IP is commanded and directed, operationally and organizationally, by its commissioner, who is appointed by the government on the recommendation of the minister of public security and who is responsible for the police and prison services. Seven departments constitute the IP's national headquarters located in Jerusalem, Israel's capital: Investigations and Crime Fighting (incorporating the intelligence function, which for the past few years was a separate department), Patrol and Security, Traffic, Logistics, Personnel, Planning, and the Community and Civil Guard Department.

In 2003, the IP employed 25,700 policemen and women, including soldiers doing their mandatory military service in the IP, a ratio of one for every 293 citizens. Twenty percent of police officers are women. Nearly all staff are sworn members of the force. Since 1999 the IP has employed civilians, primarily in secretarial and logistical support jobs.

As of 1994, the IP was organized into six district commands. The district commanders report directly to the police commissioner; they and the department heads at police headquarters all hold the rank of major general and compose the senior command staff of the force. The commander of the BGP also reports directly to the commissioner. These districts are divided again into subdistricts, each of which is under the direction of a police commander. The subdistricts are, in turn, divided into large regional police stations or smaller police stations and police substations. The commanding officers in each of these police units are all selected by national and regional headquarters.

In 2003 there were 10 large regional stations (mostly in the metropolitan centers), 53 stations, and about 100 substations. In addition, there were approximately 350 community policing centers—usually these are one-person police centers in neighborhoods or rural villages, but sometimes a mobile or temporary center is set up in a specific area to deal with specific problems— and about 400 neighborhood Civil Guard bases, some of them within or attached to the community policing center.

Each district and subdistrict is managed by an administrative and operational headquarters that parallels the organization of the central IP headquarters in Jerusalem. Since 1997, reorganization has attempted to flatten out the organizational structure and do away with the middle management (subdistrict) levels, and there has been some success.

Personnel: Selection, Training, and Promotion

Between 1995 and 2000, an average of more than 1,000 men and women were recruited to the IP each year, the majority for core duties such as patrol work, investigations, intelligence, traffic control, bomb disposal, and service in the Community and Civil Guard Department. Some were recruited to the BGP or other branches of the police as part of their compulsory military training after completing their high-school studies at the age of 18. (Mandatory service has a duration of three years for males and two years for females.) However, it is possible that some of these will later pursue careers as regular police officers in the BGP or in other units within the police. Other than that, the minimum age for regular police recruitment in Israel is 21 years, and the minimum educational requirement is a high school diploma.

Candidates are examined for general suitability and for suitability to a particular area of activity of the IP. They must pass a security clearance and assessments of their psychological and physical health as well as educational and intelligence testing. Although candidates are obligated to have at least completed high school (which requires 12 years of schooling) and taken their matriculation exams, many times the Israeli police will seek to recruit candidates with more then just a high school diploma, as they did during the second half of the 1990s when recruitment targeted former military officers and people with an associate's, bachelor's, and in some case higher academic degrees.

A new police officer, once recruited, participates in a basic 25-week training course. New officers become eligible for promotion after three years, subject to performance on a proficiency test in their area of work. After another year on the job, they can be recommended by their commanders to go to the advanced police officers' course, which consists of four to six weeks of specialized training in a particular field of work. Also, during their fifth year in the service, officers are eligible to attend a five- to ten-week senior police officers' training for those who will become noncommissioned commanders. Only after this second training course can a police officer become eligible to be recommended for promotion to commissioned officer status.

The commissioned officer course lasts 30 weeks, and during this training, the officers also take part in academic studies for one semester at Haifa University (for those who do not have academic degrees). Commanders then receive further specialized training.

Promotion from rank to rank is achieved by seniority, completion of training courses, and individual evaluation by both commanders and peers. The IP has the following ranks:

1. For noncommissioned officers: constable, lance corporal, sergeant, sergeant major, staff sergeant major, advanced staff sergeant major, senior staff sergeant major.

2. For commissioned officers: subinspector, inspector, chief inspector, superintendent, chief superintendent, commander, brigadier general, major general, and the commissioner's rank—inspector general.

Today, unlike in the 1970s and 1980s, potential police officers holding academic degrees are also recruited to the lowest noncommissioned rank, but they can advance to commissioned officer after approximately one year of service if they pass the assessment exams and complete the commissioned officer's training course.

The Border Guard Police

Rooted in the early days of the Israeli state, the purpose for the formation of the BGP was to deal with security and guard tasks in areas that are located outside the main cities and on the borders of the country. This paramilitary gendarmerie within the IP was established at first by recruiting senior Jewish officers of the British Mandate Police. It was determined that this force would remain small and highly professional. The force was also designed to protect and assist the regular police in maintaining order and as an "iron fist" force for suppressing civil disorders. With its own independent organization and structure, it was determined that this unit would act under the direction of the district commands. The BGP has separate bases and training centers from those of the districts' regular police personnel, and accordingly those who serve in it are called "soldiers." The BGP has existed in its current form, as known today, since April 1953. Since its establishment, it has had a crucial role in protecting the country's borders against infiltration while also protecting the life and property of its citizens in rural areas.

In 2003 there were some 8,000 soldiers serving in the BGP. Its tasks are to deal with security and antiterrorist activities, to guard and patrol the Israel-Palestinian Autonomous[4] Area border, to deal with disruptions to public order, and to prevent agricultural theft. In addition, the BGP serves as a highly mobile, rapid response and reinforcement force—both in criminal and civil order matters—and is available to the IP districts as well as to the IDF upon request. From the time of the Oslo accords in 1993 until October 2000, when the second intifada broke out, the BGP's police officers conducted joint patrols with the newly established Palestinian Police Force in areas where there was joint Israeli-Palestinian responsibility.

Major Functions of the Israeli Police

Criminal Investigations

There are approximately 2,500 investigators and police prosecutors in the IP. Police prosecutors present misdemeanors and some felonies to the magistrate courts.[5] The Investigations and Crime Fighting Department also is responsible for dealing with juveniles—both as suspects and as victims—from age 12 (the lowest age of criminal responsibility) to age 18 in coordination with the agencies responsible for child and youth welfare, juvenile delinquency, and juvenile parole as well as with other organizations assisting in victim support. A Victim Support Unit (VSU) provides professional input on all policy and its implementation regarding the support given to victims of crime—especially regarding special groups of victims, such as those of domestic abuse, sexual abuse, "helpless" victims (such as the mentally retarded), or the aged. Special domestic violence investigators have been trained and deployed since 2001 to deal with and investigate both the victims and the perpetrators of domestic violence.

The Division of Identification and Forensic Sciences, also in the Investigations and Crime Fighting Department, analyzes evidence with an entire range of tests (DNA, fingerprints, drugs, explosives and flammable materials, ballistics, etc.) in specialized laboratories at IP headquarters in Jerusalem. Each regional subdivision has its own crime-scene technicians who gather evidence from crime scenes and send it to the IP's centralized laboratories, or if possible, make initial tests *in situ* or at the regional station. An automatic fingerprint identification system (AFIS) helps compare latent fingerprints found at the scenes of crimes with a centralized database of known criminals and is used to authenticate identification of suspects with the help of their fingerprints. A mobile crime lab from the headquarters is often mobilized to gather evidence in complex crime scenes or those involving murder or terrorist activities.

There are two national investigation units: one for serious and international crimes, (such as the operation of car theft rings, money laundering, and drug trafficking) and the second for dealing with white collar crime, fraud, and computer crime. All these units are considered understaffed and are constantly inundated with cases. A system of prioritization of investigation cases, using standardized guidelines, has recently been established in order to assist officers in dealing with their caseload.

Intelligence

The Intelligence Division coordinates and directs the intelligence and undercover work undertaken throughout the country at all levels. Efforts are concentrated upon serious target criminals in accordance with an evaluation that is made at the various levels of the police hierarchy. In addition to the above functions, the division is responsible for all drug-related enforcement work, as well as for international cooperation with foreign police forces. At the district level, there are some centralized intelligence units whose tasks are to gather evidence and perform undercover work.

Since 1949, Israel has been a member of the INTERPOL, and extensive operational cooperation takes place on a regular basis via this organization. Several police representatives are stationed abroad (e.g., in the United States, Germany, France, the Netherlands, Russia, Ukraine, and Thailand) in order to facilitate international investigations.

Patrol and Operations

The IP's central and largest force is the patrol unit, whose main responsibility is responding to public calls for assistance, usually received by the Emergency Calls Center. (A "100" telephone number allows the caller quick connection to these centers.) The patrol officer is also the first line of response to an emergency, whether road accident, natural disaster, or terrorist attack. In events and gatherings requiring a massive police presence (e.g., mass-attendance events, events of particular political and public significance, protest marches, big sporting events), patrol units maintain public order and safety.

Special patrol units have been established to give the IP a highly skilled and rapid response capacity for incidents of particular severity or danger. Together with the BGP's special units (such as its Anti-Terrorist Special Combat Unit), they are the first to respond to any life-endangering security incident or mass-casualty disaster. They are routinely deployed against particularly dangerous criminal targets or where there are geographical concentrations of criminal activity. Any unit within the IP can request the assistance of such a unit for immediate reinforcement, and backup.

In the context of its direct responsibility for antiterrorist activity, the government placed responsibility for school perimeter security on the IP in 1995 and for public transport security in 1997. For these assignments, the IP allocated a fleet of motorized patrol units that were briefed to patrol the perimeters and vicinity of schools and other educational institutions and of bus, train, and taxi stations to detect and prevent terrorist or criminal activity.

As one of the methods to assist in proactive crime prevention, the Patrol and Security Department is also responsible for providing input regarding the security standards needed to enable the local licensing of high-risk businesses. [6] Other units under the direct supervision of the Patrol and Security Department include the Helicopter Unit, the National Vehicle Theft Prevention Unit, and a National Negotiation Team, which is used when hostage situations arise.

The Civil Guard Department[7] and Community Policing

In order to prevent terrorist and criminal activity in residential areas, the Civil Guard maintains a network of neighborhood Civil Guard bases (some 400 in 2004). The Civil Guard recruits volunteer citizens for armed mobile and foot patrols. It also runs training programs and organizes rapid response teams for emergency duty.

In 2004, Civil Guard volunteers, ages 17 to 90, numbered approximately 50,000. While on duty—guard members have four hours of compulsory duty per month—Civil Guard volunteers have police authority (i.e., they may search cars and suspects, detain suspects, ask for identification papers, etc.) and are usually armed with police rifles and provided with portable radio transmitters and identification vests. The regular volunteers patrol in groups of two to three on foot or by car (using private or police vehicles) in their own neighborhood, providing for a crime and terrorist prevention patrolling function. The Civil Guard also includes special units that provide volunteer aid to regular police units in a range of activities: traffic control and enforcement of traffic regulations, patrol functions, emergency rescue units, and agricultural theft prevention (mainly as volunteers with the BGP), to name a few. These uniformed volunteer auxiliaries undergo specialized training and usually volunteer for many more hours than the compulsory minimum—about four to six hours per week.

In 1994 the IP command adopted a community policing strategy and began to implement its ideas on a large scale in January of 1995. The essence of this approach is that local police forces should work in partnership with the Civil Guard, local government (municipalities and local authorities), and community agencies, all pooling their resources to minimize crime, social problems that lead to crime, and incivilities that decrease the quality of life (Geva, 2003; Herzog, 2001). The implementation process was initially led by the Community Policing Unit, which was directly responsible to the commissioner. Since 1999 the unit has been merged with the Civil Guard Department, thus joining the two functions of mobilizing volunteers and working with the community on crime prevention and enforcement activities. This department has since been called the Community and Civil Guard Department.

In 1999 a system to make the police commanders more accountable to their communities and for achieving their measurable objectives was implemented based on the COMPSTAT (COMPuter STATistics or COMParative STATistics) method used by the New York City Police Department. The IP commissioner holds biweekly meetings with each area commander and uses statistical information to pinpoint areas and patterns of crime that need to be addressed. The computerization of most policing activities and the linking of the stations to the central computer at head-quarters via an intranet allows local commanders as well as management to keep track of changing crime and traffic accident patterns and to provide appropriate responses—both proactive and reactive.[8]

When community policing was conceived and planned in Israel, it was seen as part of a total reformation of the Israeli police in structure, philosophy, and action (Geva, 2003). However Weisburd, Shalev, and Amir (2002) suggest that "this broad idea of community policing was not implemented in Israel, and indeed the program of community policing was found to lose ground. . . . While community policing did have specific impacts on the Israeli police, it did not fundamentally change the perspectives and activities of street level police officers" (p. 102). According to Weisburd and his colleagues (2002; see also Herzog, 2001), one of the possible explanations for the failure of implementation is due to "the resistance of traditional military style organizational culture within the Israeli police to the demands of community policing models" (p. 80). However, they argue that "such barriers to successful community policing are not unique to the Israel case, and are indeed likely to be encountered in the development of community policing in many other countries" (p. 105).

In recent years, although it has been pushed aside by security matters, there has been a renewed increase in the formation of community policing centers around the country and especially in the Arab towns and villages in the northern part of the country. Community policing officers have been trained to implement interagency models of crime prevention in dealing with various common crime problems. Implementation of this model is initiated mainly by the police officer. However, these officers rarely use "problem-oriented policing" strategies to analyze problems and encourage communities to form their own original crime prevention strategies, as was suggested by the original community policing strategy. (For a review of the difficulties with implementation, see Herzog, 2002.) Furthermore, these police officers are usually taken off their beats to participate in security-related activities together with the other officers in their area, thus affecting their ability to respond to their assigned communities.

Other Departments

Traffic: The IP's Traffic Department enforces road traffic laws, keeps traffic moving smoothly, investigates road accidents, brings offenders to justice, provides for research and development in the traffic enforcement areas, and educates and informs the public in road discipline.

Management and Logistics Departments: Other departments include the Logistics Department, charged with the management and care of the IP's material supplies and equipment, and the Planning Department, which manages all IP resources and its budget, staff, and computerized databanks as well as research and development of technology within the force.

Personnel/Human Resources Department: Israeli Police human resources (HR) management is designed to develop the organization's human resources by providing each officer with high-quality services and support. The department constantly develops its training track and programs according to changes and needs within the organization and in its changing environment. While doing so, the department looks after the personal welfare and work conditions of employees, and it organizes in-service training courses and study days. The department constantly encourages its officers to continue their education. Recruitment and promotion decisions are done on objective and professional grounds, with equal opportunity given to both genders and all ethnic groups.

Accountability

Complaints against police officers about the unlawful use of force or about criminal matters punishable by over one year of imprisonment are dealt with by the recently established external civilian Unit for Investigation of Police Officers (known in Hebrew as *Machash*), which is headed by an attorney and is under the supervision of the Ministry of Justice. According to Herzog (2001), about 1,000 police officers are investigated each year, which is less then 4 percent of all uniformed police officers. The main innovations of the newly established civilian board include the following (Herzog, 2000):

1. *The investigation of suspicions against police officers:* All the investigators are former police officers; the board's criteria for membership include experience in police investigations, knowledge of police work in the field, and a high level of professional discretion. As noted, the function of the investigators is to investigate police officers suspected of committing offenses (on or off duty) involving the illegal use of force as well as criminal offenses punishable by over one year of imprisonment. Less serious cases that do not meet these criteria continue to be dealt with by the (police) department's internal investigations unit.

2. *The recommendation to continue treatment of a complaint:* This specific recommendation, made after the external investigation, is made by the board's attorneys, headed by a district prosecutor. Recommendations range from a disciplinary trial (in a one-official trial or a disciplinary court) to trial in a

criminal court to the closing of the case. In offenses involving the use of force (as opposed to other criminal offenses, in which the board can only make a suggestion), this recommendation becomes a formal decision for the police force.

According to Machash's internal regulations, complaints against police officers may be submitted to Machash in person, in writing, or by fax, in different languages, at any police installation, including police stations and Machash's offices, in any part of the country. If the complaint is submitted at a police installation, the duty officer is required to receive it immediately, and there is a strict prohibition against advising a complainant otherwise. After receipt of the complaint, an investigative file is opened if, on the one hand, it is suspected that a criminal or a use of force offense has been committed, and if on the other, there is public interest in the investigation as defined by the head of the unit.

Files are distributed among the board's investigators according to the geographic location of the offense. Upon completion of the investigation, the file together with the recommendations of both the investigator and the head of the team (who has the authority to demand further investigation) is scrutinized by the head of Machash. Only the head of Machash and its attorneys are entitled to decide on continued treatment of a file. At the end of the process, notification has to be sent to the complainant, the suspect police officer(s), and relevant police bodies (personnel department, direct commander, etc.). If the case is sustained, it is transferred to the state prosecutor (for criminal cases) or to the police attorney (for disciplinary cases) (Herzog, 2000).

However, less serious cases (disciplinary in essence) continue to be dealt with by the internal investigations unit within the IP, usually following a complaint from the public brought to the public complaints officer at the district or headquarters level, or to the Ministry of Public Security's ombudsman or complaints' unit. At each district, a public complaints officer receives these less serious complaints from the public and investigates them. Alternatively, the public can send such complaints either to the police headquarters ombudsperson or to the Ministry of Public Security ombudsperson. The Discipline Division draws up indictments for the IP's disciplinary court, where hearings are heard before the police judge, two additional officers who act as judges, and usually a public representative, who is a lawyer from another agency. There is also an appellate court. This internal unit also decides on whether a complaint is sustained or not. If it is, then a disciplinary board hears the case and provides judgment. All verdicts are subject to appeal and are then passed on to the disciplinary appeals board for further decision.

Terrorism[9]

As noted above, the early seeds of the IP can be found in the establishment of the *H'Shomer* organization in 1909 that declared itself as the first Hebrew police and a Hebrew gendarmerie in the land of Israel. Its purpose was to guard and protect Jewish settlers from Arab attacks. Israel has suffered repeatedly from infiltrations and terrorist attacks on civilian targets since it became a state in May 1948, and as stated in 1974 the IP was given the additional responsibility of maintaining internal security. It is under these historical and developmental conditions that Israel has one national centralized police force that is geared toward mobilization of its forces from crime fighting to homeland security upon demand.

Following the 1974 decision, two special units were established: The Civil Guard and the Bomb Disposal Division.

The Civil Guard

The Civil Guard has already been described above as a department of the IP. But the establishment of this department was a result of the escalating infiltration and terror attacks on Israeli citizens, mainly in the northern part of the country, in Jerusalem, and in the surrounding area. At first it was decided that the Civil Guard would operate as an auxiliary to the IP and not as a unit within it. This voluntary organization's preliminary aims were to assist the BGP and a military Civil Defense Unit (known as HAGA, a Hebrew acronym for *civilian protection,* this is different from the previously mentioned Hagana). Six months after its establishment, the Civil Guard had about 60,000 volunteers, of which a tenth were senior high school students, trained to patrol their neighborhoods with police cars and to use police weapons—all with the intention of detecting and preventing terrorist activity. During 1975, and as a result of the steep increase in terror attacks in Jerusalem and other parts of the country, the number of volunteers reached 110,000. In its first years of operation, the activities of the Civil Guard focused mainly on patrolling the streets during the night. In many ways it can be seen as a paramilitary organization with former military commanders acting as commanders of the local Civil Guard stations and operations. Also, in its first stages, this organization received its support from the IDF, the BGP, and HAGA.

It is only a decade later that the Civil Guard was incorporated into the police and began to provide auxiliary policing services as well, as discussed briefly above.

Bomb Disposal

Established in 1975, the Bomb Disposal Division (under the Patrol and Security Department) operates in the realm of both criminal and terrorist sabotage activities. The division's teams, at the local level, handle about 100,000 calls per year to check suspicious objects, parcels, and cars, and lately also to check persons suspected of carrying on their person bombs in the form of bomb belts or vests. On average, less than 1 percent of these calls actually involve incendiary or explosive devices.

An important aspect of the Bomb Disposal Unit's work is its prevention program, which includes surveillance of crowded public areas and facilities and educational programs in the schools. Police headquarters has its own research and development unit to develop specialized equipment and techniques to address bomb threats as well as a separate laboratory to provide analysis of explosive devices and modes of operating. The Israel Bomb Disposal Information Center gathers, analyzes, and disseminates information to police sappers and to other security organizations in the country and worldwide.

In addition to the above, the IP's Anti-Terrorist Special Combat Unit (which organizationally belongs to the BGP) deals with terrorist activities within the borders of the country, operates in hostage-taking situations—both terrorist and criminal in nature—and sometimes assists in the handling of serious public disturbances. To comply with these emerging problems, specialized equipment and techniques—some of which are developed in-house—allow for quick deployment throughout the country.

Although they are geared toward fighting terrorism, these organizational entities are not the sole players in the IP war on terrorism. Each of the other departments may at any given time allocate resources to such activity.

Between September 2000 and the end of July 2004, there were 22,406 terror attacks on Israeli targets both in the territories (against Jewish settlers living in the vicinity or driving through) and inside Israeli borders, resulting in the death of 677 Israeli civilians and about 300 members of the security forces (Israeli Defense Force, 2004). As a result all the IP units work in close collaboration with the IDF and with the National General Security Service (indicated by the Hebrew acronym SHABAK), placing the war on terrorism and the security of the Israeli citizens as their top priority.

Figure 9.1 shows the never-ending challenge of this struggle. Starting in the beginning of 2002 there has been a steep escalation in the number of terror attacks, both successful and unsuccessful. The successful prevention of planned attacks is due mainly to thorough intelligence work as well as to collaboration among the above mentioned bodies. One can also see that from February 2002 until the end of November 2004, a higher percentage of attacks were successfully prevented. This goal could not have been achieved if Israeli forces had used the model known as "due process"[10] by many Americans and had operated with local and municipal police forces, because the challenges of terror attacks threaten public safety rather then civil rights. In other words, operating under the assumptions of due process while using municipal police forces will limit the ability of law enforcement agencies and the other organizations they collaborate with, and this may result in the loss of critical reaction time that is highly important to the prevention of terror attacks.

For this reason, a national centralized police force has merits, as it can work more efficiently under such constant emergency and stressful

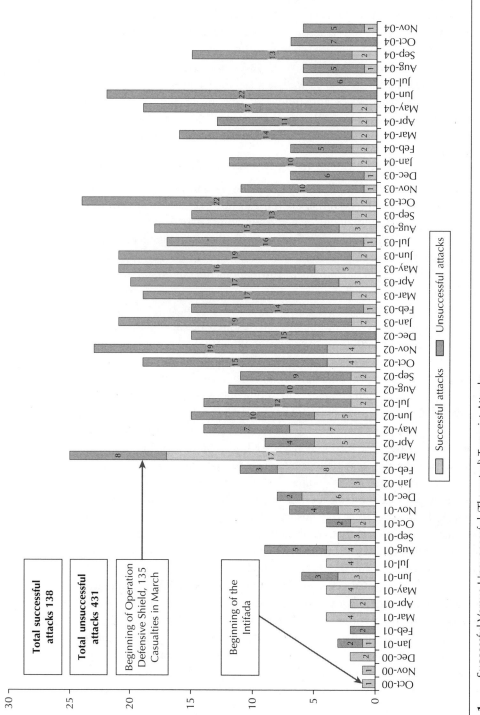

Figure 9.1 Successful Versus Unsuccessful (Thwarted) Terrorist Attacks

SOURCE: IDF official Web site (http://www1.idf.il/dover/site/mainpage.asp?sl=EN&id=22&docid=16703).

conditions than a local police force, which is decentralized in authority and mobilization potential and has fewer resources as its command. A centralized national police force can provide massive and quick deployment of emergency forces where needed, throughout the country. Furthermore, a national agency allows for centralized intelligence gathering and investigating processes, as well as for analyzing complex national data. This makes easier the task of detecting, identifying, deterring, and preventing potential terror attacks.

Summary

The Israel Police (IP) is trying to deal simultaneously with maintaining public order, preventing crime, and performing classical and traditional law enforcement duties while also providing a public service and security to the public it serves. Taking into account the dearth of resources available to the force, the IP is constantly trying to adapt to the changing social environment as well as to the macro-level needs of homeland security. These last needs often demand the IP's almost exclusive attention, causing it to reallocate, reorganize, and reassign its crime-fighting, traffic, and other operational units according to immediate, midrange, and long-range needs.

As a result many times harsh public criticism is directed toward the IP way of doing its job and regarding its competence to prevent crime. Gideon and Mesch (2003), describe the image of the police in Israel and the Israeli police officer in particular as "not especially good; nor is the image of the level of service given by the police. . . . Usually they [Israeli police officers are] perceived as slow, violent . . . and impolite" (p. 115). One must keep in mind that the police are under high pressure as a result of constantly feeling as though they are taking part in a combat situation, as is the case when they are dealing with high-risk terror attacks, and this causes police officers to burn out (Herzog, 2001). On the other hand, about 13 percent of Israeli citizens who have been victimized and did not report their victimization to the police rationalized their failure to report by saying they "did not want to bother the police" (Gideon & Mesch, 2003, p. 110). This suggests that the public is somewhat aware of the national priorities and makes a rational decision in regard to the damage done by their victimization and their expectations for service. Nevertheless, fighting terrorism also brings other outcomes—some positive—as described by Herzog (2003), who found that motor vehicles stolen from Israel and smuggled into Palestinian Authority areas decreased when counterterror activities of the police and security forces brought about a strict closure of the borders or increased surveillance of traffic crossing roadblocks.

Being under constant terror threats, both external and internal to the state, the IP is challenged to maintain public safety. In such a milieu, it is often hard to follow a due process model and to maintain civil rights and liberty—in particular those aspects of this model that pertain to search and seizure. For this reason, a policing style that is other than national will not be suitable. Using a militaristic organizational culture and approach under such conditions corresponds well to current national security needs, allowing the IP to operate countrywide while responding to the rising demands of the public. It is for this reason, we believe, that community policing in Israel did not manage to become entrenched as an all-embracing operational philosophy in its first years of implementation and up to the present, as described by Weisburd and his colleagues (2002). This is also the reason why the idea of municipal or local policing—as it is practiced in the United States and in most European countries—will encounter difficulties in Israel, where police are seeking to respond to growing national demands (Weisburd, Shoham, & Gideon, 2001).

Notes

1. The majority of the material presented in this section is taken from IP (2004).

2. According to the liberal reformist approach, police activity is constantly being evaluated in order to improve its efficacy and efficiency. Advocates of this approach propose recruitment of higher-quality personnel while improving and prolonging training and introducing more women to the police force as well as recruiting members of minority groups to serve as police officers. In addition, they argue for academic studies as a supplement to police training. Usually, advocates of this approach are academic scholars, policy makers, and other police executives that emphasize the need to modernize police work to meet the needs of today's changing environment.

3. The majority of the material in this section is taken from Geva, Herzog, and Haberfeld (2005) with permission from the authors and the editor.

4. These are territories that were transferred to Palestinian authority after the Oslo agreement signed by Israel and PLO in early September 1993. The agreement involved autonomy for parts of the Gaza Strip and the West Bank with Jericho as the first territory to achieve autonomy.

5. Other categories of offenses are presented to the court by civilian prosecutors.

6. For an in-depth survey of the development of the crime prevention function and community policing implementation within the Israeli Police, see Geva, 1998 and 2003.

7. Further discussion of the Civil Guard in regard to homeland security is presented in the section on terrorism.

8. The setting of measurable objectives by each police unit in their yearly plans started in 1998, and in January 2005 it was put on hold while new proposals for setting objectives and measuring success at achieving them were being considered.

9. See Geva, 1995.

10. Unlike the United States, Israel does not have a constitution; therefore "due process" as known by U.S. criminal justice practitioners is not a valid concept.

References

Geva, R. (1995, April-May). Effective national and international action against terrorism: The Israeli Experience. In R. Geva (Ed.), *The prevention of crime and the treatment of offenders in Israel*. Paper presented at the Ninth UN Congress on the Prevention of Crime and the Treatment of Offenders, Cairo, Egypt.

Geva, R. (1998). Crime prevention strategies: Twenty-year summary. *Innovation Exchange*, 7, 228–237. Jerusalem: Ministry of Public Security.

Geva, R. (2003). Crime prevention: A community policing approach. In S. P. Lab & D. K. Das (Eds.), *International perspectives on community policing and crime prevention* (pp. 95–112). Upper Saddle River, NJ: Prentice-Hall.

Geva, R., Herzog, S., & Haberfeld, M. (2005). Israel (State of Israel): The Israeli Police. In L. E. Sullivan & M. Haberfeld (Eds.), *Encyclopedia of law enforcement: international* (Vol. 3, pp. 1130–1134). Thousand Oaks, CA: Sage.

Gideon, L., & Mesch, G. (2003). Reporting property victimization to the police in Israel. *Police Practice and Research*, 4(2), 105–117.

Herzog, S. (2000). Treatment of illegal-use-of-force complaints against police officers in Israel: The beleaguered path to civilian involvement. *Police Quarterly*, 2(4), 477–501.

Herzog, S. (2001a). Militarization and demilitarization processes in the Israeli and American police forces: Organizational and social aspects. *Policing and Society*, 11(2), 181–208.

Herzog, S. (2001b). Suspect *police* officers investigated by former *police* officers: Good idea, bad idea? *Law and Policy*, 23(4), 441–467.

Herzog, S. (2002). Does proactive policing make a difference in crime? An implementation of problem-solving policing in Israel. *International Journal of Comparative and Applied Criminal Justice, 26*(1), 29–52.

Herzog, S. (2003). Border closures as a reliable method for the measurement of Palestinian involvement in crime in Israel: A quasi-experimental analysis. *International Journal of Comparative Criminology, 3*(1), 18–41.

Herzog, S. (2005). The relationship between economic hardship and crime: The case of Israel and the Palestinians. *Sociological Perspectives, 48*(1), 77–104.

Israeli Central Bureau of Statistics. (2006). *Selected demographic data from the annual statistic report*. Publication Number 57. Retrieved August 6, 2007, from http://www1.cbs.gov.il/reader/newhodaot/hodaa_template.html?hodaa=200601204.

Israeli Defense Force. (2004). *Successful vs. unsuccessful terrorist attacks*. Retrieved December 27, 2004, from http://www1.idf.il/dover/site/mainpage.asp?sl=EN&id=22&docid=16703

Israeli Police (IP). (2004). *Welcome to the Israel police website!* Retrieved December 27, 2004, from http://www.police.gov.il/english/default.asp

Ross, J. I. (1998). Radical and critical criminology's treatment of municipal policing. In J. I. Ross (Ed.), *Cutting the edge: Current perspectives in radical/critical criminology and criminal justice* (pp. 95–106). Westport, CT: Praeger.

Sebba, L., Horovitz, M., & Geva, R. (2003). Israel: *Criminal justice system in Europe and North America* (pp. 14–19). Helsinki, Finland: The European Institute for Crime Prevention and Control, affiliated with the United Nations (HEUNI).

Smooha, S. (1988). Internal divisions in Israel at forty. *Middle East Review*, *20*(4), 26–36.

Smooha, S., & Hanf, T. (1992). The diverse modes of conflict-resolution in deeply divided societies. *International Journal of Comparative Sociology*, *33*(1–2), 26–47.

Sullivan, L. E., & Haberfeld, M. (Eds.). (2005). Israel (State of Israel). *Encyclopedia of law enforcement* (Vol. 3). Thousand Oaks, CA: Sage.

Weisburd, D., Shalev, O., & Amir M. (2002). Community policing in Israel: Resistance and change. *Policing: An International Journal of Police Strategies and Management*, *25*(1), 80–109.

Weisburd, D., Shoham, E., & Gideon, L. (2001). Municipal policing in Israel—Problems of efficiency, community, equality and integrity [in Hebrew]. *Police and Society*, *5*, 5–25.

10 The French Police System

Caught Between a Rock and a Hard Place—The Tension of Serving Both the State and the Public

Benoît Dupont

The French model of policing is often presented in English-language histories of policing as an exact opposite of the Anglo-Saxon model. This symmetrical and elegant antagonism has more than theoretical or academic implications. It also conveys a rhetorical and normative message, which asserts the democratic superiority of one system over the other. This posture dates back to the parliamentary debates that led to the creation of the London Metropolitan Police in 1829, where the idea of a new structure modeled on the French centralized and professional system was strongly opposed, the terms "odious" and "repulsive" being used by some politicians to describe it (Critchley, 1967; Emsley, 1996). On the issue of effectiveness, it also seems that Anglo-Saxon popular culture has assigned to the French police an image associated with pompous, ridiculous, and inadequate practices, fuelled in part by the fictional character of Inspector Clouseau, brilliantly interpreted by Peter Sellers in the *Pink Panther* movies. If those representations are of little consequences beyond their immediate purposes—political reform and entertainment—they must nonetheless be gently pushed aside in the context of a more rigorous comparative policing approach.

These opening comments are particularly important in the case of the French policing system because of the scarcity of texts available in English on this topic. This situation can partly be attributed to the anemia of French criminology and police studies, the language barrier, and the lack of linkages between the Anglo-Saxon and French academic communities (Ferret, 2004). For those reasons, most accounts of French policing written in English so far tend to be the work of outsiders (Mawby, 1990), an arrangement whose potential for omissions and misinterpretations has been highlighted by Bayley (1999). Furthermore, most of those texts are outdated and are more interesting for their historical value than for their contemporary accuracy. Hence, a majority of the references used in this chapter will be taken from the expanding French literature. Until the early 1980s, very little research had been done on policing, which was considered a "dirty research object" by academics (Brodeur & Monjardet, 2003), essentially for ideological reasons. The creation of a research committee by the Ministry of the Interior in 1982, followed in 1989 by the foundation of a National Institute for the Study of Homeland Security (IHESI) and the availability of research funding facilitated the development of a scientific knowledge on the work of the police and its organization (Loubet del Bayle, 1999a).

The aim of this chapter is to offer a contemporary overview of the organization and latest policing reforms in France. In line with the approach taken in this book, I will follow a structure that will facilitate implicit cross-country comparisons. First, I will examine the history of the French police and its current political context. In the second section, immigration trends and their impact on the delivery of policing services will be described, with a particular emphasis on the problems faced by poor North African families in public housing neighborhoods. The third section will delineate the dual organizational structure of the police system and assess some of the recent efforts made to rationalize it and make it more accountable. The fourth section will be dedicated to the implementation of community policing strategies and their impact. Finally, the last section will briefly examine the various forms of terrorism experienced in France over the past 20 years and the antiterrorist capabilities developed by the French police. Whereas it would be an insurmountable task to provide a comprehensive outline of a policing system that comprises so many bureaucratic and cultural layers sedimented over centuries, in the following pages the writer hopes to provide the reader with a window on the evolution of democratic policing in a country that has often placed the interests of the state above those of the public.

The Police of the Republic:
A Monarchical Creation

The history of policing in France can be characterized by the predominance of political influences, from the first edicts passed by monarchs in the seventeenth century to the early dualism of its structure and the constant tension between national and local political authorities. The far-reaching legal powers conferred to police officers derive from this role of instruments of the state.

Early Police Structures

If the birth of the English model of policing coincides with the creation of the London Metropolitan Police in 1829 by Sir Robert Peel, the French model is generally said to have appeared in 1667, with the proclamation of a royal edict that created the office of general lieutenant of the police for the city of Paris. In 1699, this arrangement was extended to the rest of the country. A fragmented night watch system had nevertheless existed since the year 580, and criminal investigation officers had been appointed for the first time in 1306 by King Philippe le Bel, but the reform implemented between 1667 and 1699 asserted the authority of the king over policing and was accompanied by a centralization of other public services such as the administration of justice and revenue collection (Gleizal, Gatti-Domenach, & Journès, 1993). A number of years before the establishment of permanent professional police officers in urban centers, a constabulary force or Gendarmerie had also been established to patrol the roads and protect isolated settlements from looters and mercenaries. This force was geographically reorganized in 1720, when five-man stations (or *brigades*) were built at strategic locations all across the kingdom.

The Revolution of 1789 caused the fall of the monarchy, and most of its symbols, such as the centralized police, were abolished. Policing became for a short period of time a municipal responsibility: Elected mayors took over from general lieutenants and appointed national guards—armed citizens—to patrol the streets and other public places. However, this local form of policing soon became too impractical to administer for the various undemocratic regimes that seized power after the Revolution. Most of the nineteenth century and the first half of the twentieth century can then be characterized by the efforts of central governments to reassert control over the police while legally maintaining the fiction of some form of local responsibility. This was accomplished by defining police powers as "delegated" by the state to municipal governments, and by regulating the appointment of police chiefs and constables, while letting local authorities pay for their salaries.

This strategy encountered strong resistance from local politicians, who argued in favor of more democratic and direct arrangements (Gleizal et al., 1993). As a result, reforms were implemented gradually—and sometimes temporarily halted or withdrawn—to avoid open conflict, particularly in large cities. This less-than-linear process remained nevertheless a high priority for successive central governments, mainly because of the rapid industrialization and urbanization of the country, leading to social and political unrest that municipal police forces could not handle adequately. The centralization and unification of the French police were finally completed in 1941 by the Vichy régime, under German occupation. All police forces in municipalities with more than 10,000 people were brought under state control to form one single entity, the Sûreté. Only Paris kept a separate force until 1966, when the Paris police and the Sûreté were amalgamated to become the modern National Police.

The history of the Gendarmerie, a rural police force operating under military command, has not been affected to the same extent by the debate on centralization and unification. It was originally known as the *Maréchaussée*; its current name was adopted in 1791, during the Revolution, in order to sever the ties of the organization with its royal origins. The law of 1798 and the reign of Napoleon gave the Gendarmerie its modern structure and its military character. The institution's subsequent evolution and multiple reforms never altered the founding features of the Gendarmerie. This dual civil-military police system, which was "exported" to other European countries and African colonies, is the result of a tension among the social and political agitation that threatened governments, the limited capacities of local police forces in the field of public order maintenance, and the reluctance of the state to use the military to suppress revolts. The creation and maintenance of the Gendarmerie, a police force made up of soldiers, which is also primarily responsible for civil police duties in rural areas and can conduct criminal investigations on its own initiative, must be understood as a compromise between democratic values and the fear of political disorders. To borrow the words of Emsley (1999, p. 2.), the Gendarmerie was "providing the first line of defense against insurrection in [the] capital" and was regarded "as a valuable prophylactic against economic and social disorder." This historical dualism and the duplication of resources associated with it are nevertheless questioned in the face of increasing crime rates.

The Crime "Inflation"

The past 30 years have seen a sharp increase in criminal activity, particularly in the areas of property crime and assaults. However, the data available to us are not as detailed or complete as we would expect, since crime statistics are collected in France by the two main police organizations and by the justice ministry. As a result, they mainly reflect police activity, which can vary with the adoption of new practices or strategies. Furthermore, in the absence of independent and transparent protocols for their collection and presentation, they are not subject to the same amount of scrutiny found in other countries and must be analyzed with caution (Mucchielli, 2001). Of course, annual victimization surveys have been conducted by the National Statistics Institute since 1996, but they are merely an add-on to the more general household survey (Aubusson, Lalam, Padieu, & Zamora, 2002).

The data available from the 1970s show that property offenses represent two-thirds of all crimes recorded in France. Among them, breaking-and-entry and car thefts are especially problematic. If official statistics show a decrease for those crimes since the beginning of the 1990s, victimization surveys indicate that they are now underdeclared by their victims, despite the incentive to obtain a police report for insurance purposes (Robert & Pottier, 2002), and that they are evenly distributed across urban and rural areas, while they were previously mainly experienced in large cities (Mucchielli, 2001). The levels of interpersonal violence have also increased significantly over the past 25 years. If murders and homicides are stable (1.6 per 100,000 population in 2003), assaults have multiplied by a factor of three since 1972 to reach 220 per 100,000 population in 2003, generating strong feelings of insecurity among the public.

Other interesting categories include drug-related crimes and destruction and damage to property, which accounted respectively for 3 percent and 13.6 percent of all recorded crimes in 2003. The later category of crimes, which has seen a 10-fold increase since the early 1970s, has constituted a sore point for governments and police forces for many years, signaling to the public the slow decay of the social fabric. It includes the vandalism and arson of public buildings such as schools, police stations, and community centers; the frequent plunder of popular clothing and music stores during public protests; and more routine acts such as the burning of public transport buses, phone booths, and private cars. This category of crimes is usually concentrated in or around public housing neighborhoods, where a majority of the tenants are poor first- or second-generation immigrants. This has led some observers to conclude that this phenomenon, which very often directly targets the police or any symbol of authority, reflects the despair and anger of an entire generation of young people of foreign origin who have little or no prospect of social and economic integration (Duprez & Hedli, 1992; Mucchielli, 2001).

An Evolving Legal Context

The legal system distinguishes two main police functions: administrative policing and judicial policing. This distinction is linked to the dissociation of public and private law and to the historical development of the idea of policing. Prior to the Revolution, the notion of policing encompassed all areas of government intervention (Napoli, 2003), and it is only in more recent times that it acquired its contemporary meaning, which is defined by the detection and control of crime (L'Heuillet, 2001). Hence, administrative policing refers to the remnants of this earlier era, designating all ancillary tasks and regulatory activities conducive to the maintenance of public order in its most general definition. By contrast, judicial policing is confined to the detection and repression of specific offenses that administrative policing is unable to prevent. This dual legal framework does not mean that different units or forces are exclusively responsible for one form of policing or the other, but instead helps determine which judges and courts (administrative or judicial) should oversee particular policing activities. Administrative jurisdictions are hence more concerned with the defense of civil rights on a general level, while judicial courts deal with the integrity of criminal procedures.

The inquisitorial nature of the French criminal justice system creates a particular set of constraints on the work of police investigators. A judge is involved from the early stages in the collection and preparation of evidence by the police, directing the investigation. It also entails a secret, written, and noncontradictory procedure in the discovery of truth, where the judge acts on behalf of all parties. When a crime or a grave offense is detected, the district attorney opens a file and assigns the investigation to a specialized magistrate: the investigating judge. Investigating judges exercise their authority over criminal investigators, and the criminal procedure code specifically states that they can choose to assign a case either to the National Police or the Gendarmerie investigative units. This entails a constant monitoring of the effectiveness and professionalism of investigators by magistrates. If they are dissatisfied with the performance of one agency, they are at liberty to transfer the case to the other. A result of this prerogative is the development of a fierce competition between the National Police and the Gendarmerie to secure and retain the most prestigious investigations and a certain reluctance to cooperate and exchange information. The term *police war* is frequently used when this competition reaches extremes.

Investigators from the National Police and the Gendarmerie are divided in two groups with different legal powers. Judicial police officers (OPJs) are granted full investigative powers after having passed a legal exam, while judicial police agents (APJs) include all rank and file police officers, who may undertake only basic investigative activities. Both judicial police officers and judicial police agents need a delegation of power from the judge to undertake tasks such as detaining and interrogating suspects, entering and searching premises, seizing assets, or intercepting telecommunications. It must be noted that police officers may detain suspects for up to 24 hours, the limit being extended to 96 hours in cases of terrorism and drug trafficking. However, certain tasks, such as interrogating suspects and confronting them with witnesses, are often carried out by the judges in person.

The Code of Criminal Procedure also states that all police officers have the power to check the identity and address of individuals in public places who are suspected of having committed a crime, suspected of preparing to commit a crime, able to assist the police in its investigations, or wanted by the police. Such a "control of identity" may also be carried out in order to prevent a breach of public order, particularly when the safety of persons or goods is threatened. This very vague wording allows police officers to check people's identity at the officer's discretion, and numerous cases have been reported of officers using this power to harass young people of North African origin (Garcia, 2002).

These traditional powers have been extended in the wake of the terrorist attacks of September 11 by the socialist government through the Daily Security Act of 2001. Violently opposed by civil rights organizations, the act grants more extensive stop-and-search powers to police officers and private security guards, extends the surveillance of Internet communications, and criminalizes meetings held in the corridors of public housing residences. This last measure seeks to forbid loud gatherings of young people, mainly of North African origin, but it has been ridiculed, the link between the fight against terrorism and this mild form of incivility appearing tenuous at best (Monjardet, 2003). More recently, the Chirac administration, elected on a law and order platform, pushed through parliament another law, the Homeland Security Act of 2003, which effectively removed the sunset clause of the Daily Security Act of 2001 and made most of the new police powers permanent. It also created new offenses such as aggressive begging or "passive solicitation for prostitution" in public places and made it easier to incriminate suspects in cases of assaults or threats against police officers and their families. These new measures have certainly increased the legal arsenal of the police, but they have also strained police relations with ethnic minorities, and these relations were already of poor quality.

Racial and Ethnic Context

Immigration Trends

According to the latest census data, France has a population of 59 million people. The number of immigrants was estimated at 4,310,000 in 1999, or 7.4 percent of the mainland population. They originated mainly from other European countries (45 percent) and from Africa (40 percent), with a minority coming from Asia (9 percent) (Boëldieu & Borrel, 2000). Other data, from the Ministry of the Interior, placed the number of legal immigrants at 4.5 million in 1990. The main countries of origin are immediate European neighbors such as Portugal (17 percent), Italy (6.2 percent), and Spain (5 percent). The majority of immigrants from Africa come from former North African colonies such as Algeria (18 percent), Morocco (16.2 percent), and Tunisia (6.5 percent). Officially, permanent work visas have not been issued since 1974, except to European Union nationals, but family reunion programs and regularization initiatives account for a yearly intake of 60,000 people.

In 1990, the Ministry of the Interior believed that there were a million illegal immigrants in France, but recent estimates are more conservative and oscillate between 300,000 and 500,000 people. The impact of illegal immigration on crime and delinquency has been used as a recurring political theme by the far-right National Front Party since its inception. However, the geographical features of the country and its involvement in the construction of the European Union make border control very difficult. In 2002, for example, approximately 40,000 illegal immigrants were ordered by the courts to leave the country, and 7,500 of them were effectively deported. Simultaneously, 68,000 asylum seekers who had entered the country were refused permanent residency, making them de facto illegal immigrants (Sarkozy, 2003).

The cultural and ethnic diversity of a country is also reflected by citizens of foreign origins. According to statistics compiled by the National Institute for Demographic Studies, immigrants and citizens of foreign origins (either through naturalization[1] or by right of birth) account for approximately 20 percent of the overall population. There is very little information available on spoken languages, but a 1992 survey by the National Institute for Statistics and Economic Studies showed that 68 percent of French children (all origins included) spoke French at home with their parents. The second most spoken language in the survey was Arabic, with 11.5 percent, and the third Portuguese (6 percent).

An Exhausted Model of Integration

The statistics enumerated above describe a diversified racial and ethnic fabric, but mean very little in terms of social integration. The French sociopolitical system is based on a secular and universalistic idea of citizenship, which is encapsulated by the "Liberty, Equality, Fraternity" motto. As a consequence, immigrants of various ethnic and religious backgrounds are denied any minority status and are summoned to embrace a Frenchness that acts as the cement of the Republic. Unfortunately, this republican model of integration is not working as well as it ought to or has been, particularly in the case of immigrants from former North African colonies, a majority of whom are Muslims who suffer from discrimination and poverty, and as a result, violently question the legitimacy of the republican principles. Disproportionate numbers of young people from this background are experiencing learning difficulties in school, leave school without any diploma or formal qualifications, and are unemployed or underemployed (HCI, 2004). These social challenges are compounded by a phenomenon of spatial segregation: A large majority of North African families live in high-rise public housing neighborhoods that lack basic public services, are remote from economic and cultural hubs, and are poorly served by public transportation. The disintegration of parental supervision mechanisms and the development of illegal underground markets are two additional problems that afflict poor immigrant communities and strengthen their disaffection, despite attempts by central and local governments to design and implement mitigating policies.

It is therefore hardly surprising to find that public housing neighborhoods, whose number is estimated to be close to 1,500 (HCI, 2004), experience higher levels of crime and insecurity (Peyrat, 2001) than the rest of the country. More surprising maybe is the fact that they have been consistently blamed by a number of politicians and social commentators for being responsible for the general increase in crime and disorder over the past 20 years (Mucchielli, 2001, 2003), segregating their inhabitants even more.

This convergence of factors has led to systematic conflictual relations between young unemployed immigrants, who spend most of their days congregating in public places,[2] and the police, who are perceived as a force of occupation in those spaces. So entrenched is the level of antagonism between the two groups that the National Police has developed over the years an "urban violence scale" that contains eight degrees, the most extreme representing "urban riots and massive destructions for more than three nights by more than 50 youths" (Bui Trong, 1998). As we have noted above, this violence is randomly directed against all public services and symbols representing the authority of the state, and in 2003, more than 44,000 incidents of destruction and vandalism against public property were recorded (Ministry of the Interior, 2004). Social and health workers as well as firefighters are not spared and are also frequently attacked (Peyrat, 2001).

The tensions between immigrants of African origin and the police culminated in November 2005 following the accidental death in a Paris suburb of two teenagers who were fleeing a police patrol. Urban riots quickly erupted and spread from the capital to the rest of the country. For more than 21 nights, young people attacked public buildings and burned 10,000 cars in hundreds of cities in defiance of a state that had abandoned them. The unprecedented levels of violence and the poor police response overwhelmed the government, which proclaimed a state of emergency on November 8. The police arrested more than 4,700 rioters, and considering the number of belligerents on each side, very few casualties were recorded (Cazelles, Morel, & Roché, 2007). It is nevertheless telling than a couple of years after these critical events, no public inquiry has been held, and very little empirical research has been published on the subject, as if ignoring the symptoms could magically cure the disease.

Organizational Structure and Issues

The history of the French police has produced two national forces with discrete geographical responsibilities: the National Police in urban areas (towns and cities with more than 10,000 people) and the Gendarmerie in rural areas. Both enforce the same laws with the same legal powers, over different geographical jurisdictions, but while the former is a civilian organization located within the interior ministry, the latter is a military force placed under the authority of the defense ministry. This dual structure has led to criticism related to the lack of coordination and the episodic emergence of turf wars in sensitive domains, such as counterterrorism or international police cooperation. As we will show in a subsequent paragraph, attempts have been made in recent years to better integrate the operational activities of the two forces.

A third group of small municipal forces must also be mentioned. There were 3,143 of them in 2001, serving municipalities ranging from small resort towns on the Riviera to large cities such as Paris, Marseille, and

Toulouse. Despite these statistics, only a minority of the 36,000 municipalities maintains municipal forces, and most of them employ fewer than 10 officers. The number of municipal forces expanded significantly between the 1980s and the 1990s in response to the rise of the fear of crime, with a geographical concentration in the south and around the capital. Sixty-two percent of municipal police officers carry firearms, but they do not have any powers of arrest or investigation and do not compete with the law enforcement and order maintenance activities of the two major police forces. The main responsibility of municipal police officers is to provide a visible uniformed presence in the streets, enforce local bylaws, and deal with quality of life issues. They represent a second tier of policing, and they have little training, low pay, and reduced prestige. Table 10.1 represents the size of these police as well as the National Police and National Gendarmerie.

Table 10.1   Police Strength

Police Division	2002
National Police	132,000
National Gendarmerie	98,000
Municipal Police	15,400
Total	245,400

National Police

The French system is probably one of the most centralized administrative systems in the world, particularly in terms of policing (Bayley, 1985; Brodeur, 2003). In the case of the National Police, for example, a director general answers directly to the minister of the interior. The director general supervises and coordinates the work of the various directorates, which reflect the high degree of specialization of the institution. Each directorate is subdivided into central and local services, the latter being characterized by important variations in terms of geographical jurisdiction. The annual budget of the National Police was US$5.7 billion in 2002.

The Administration Directorate of the National Police (DAPN) is in charge of human resources, logistics, general administration, and finances, as well as procurements. The Training Directorate (DFPN) manages 33 police academies and training centers all over the country. The Central Directorate of the Judicial Police (DCPJ) handles most criminal investigations. It deals mainly with murders, drug trafficking, organized crime, white collar crime, human trafficking, terrorism, and art theft. Other units of the National Police can be called to investigate in less serious cases. This directorate also houses forensic units and the National Central Bureau of the International Criminal Police Organization (ICPO)—Interpol—which dispatches all requests for information and assistance, including those emanating from the Gendarmerie.

The Central Directorate of Public Security (DCSP) is in charge of maintaining public order in urban areas. It staffs and coordinates the work of police stations all over the country. Its tasks include patrols; answering calls for assistance from the public (17 is the French equivalent of 911); crime prevention and detection; road safety and traffic management; organizing the security of large political, cultural, and sports events; and supporting the judicial process. The Central Directorate manages local directorates at the department level, which are themselves subdivided into public security districts. A security district is usually covered by a large police station. There are 463 of them in 1,606 municipalities, providing security to 30 million people. It must be noted that separate arrangements exist for Paris, where the police prefecture brings together the judicial and public security functions. The Paris prefect is directly responsible to the minister and manages a structure that parallels that of the national organization. It constitutes more than a quarter of the National Police's strength.

The General Intelligence Directorate (DCRG) collects political, economic, and social intelligence in order to inform the government's decision-making process. It is also responsible for monitoring casinos and racetracks. The surveillance of political parties' internal activities was discontinued in 1995 following a number of scandals. This directorate now focuses its activities on terrorist organizations, sects, extremist religious and political groups, organized crime, and urban violence phenomena.

The Central Directorate for Border Policing (DCPAF) protects the integrity of French borders and combats illegal immigration in close cooperation with its European counterparts. It also assists French consular offices all over the world. The International Technical Police Cooperation Service (SCTIP) is placed under the direct authority of the director general. It arranges bilateral and multilateral cooperation initiatives, manages the careers of police attachés and liaison officers posted in 52 permanent delegations and 40 hosting police organizations abroad, and participates in the work of European and United Nations institutions in the field of security. Other units directly attached to the director general include an antiterrorist and hostage-rescue unit (RAID), an antidrug coordination unit (MILAD), a counterterrorism coordination unit (UCLAT) and an antimafia coordination unit (UCRAM).

The Central Service of the Companies for Republican Security (SCCRS) constitutes the permanent mobile reserve of the National Police. The 61 companies for republican security were created at the end of World War II and can be dispatched nationally on short notice for antiriot and emergency situations.

National Gendarmerie

Just like its police counterpart, the Gendarmerie is centralized to the extreme. A director general heads the Gendarmerie. He must be a civilian, but he answers to the minister of defense. For administrative policing functions (53 percent of its activities), the Gendarmerie obeys to the highest-ranking public servant in each department, the prefect. For judicial policing functions (35 percent of its activities), it is placed under the authority of the district attorney and/or investigating judges. Moreover, the Gendarmerie institutes proceedings in a number of cases on behalf of the Ministry of the Economy and Finance and other ministries and administrations. The Gendarmerie is geographically divided into seven regions that match the army defense zones, a legacy of its military origins and current missions. The Gendarmerie consists of two major forces that reflect the division of labor within the organization and an array of miscellaneous specialist units. The annual budget of the Gendarmerie was US$4.5 billion in 2002.

The Departmental Gendarmerie is the generalist component of the Gendarmerie, with more than 63,500 officers in its ranks (2002). It operates 3,600 police stations in rural and suburban areas and is in charge of public security, highway policing, police investigations, mountain rescue, criminal intelligence, river patrol, and youth crime prevention. It also runs air wings in each region. The Mobile Gendarmerie, which employs 17,000 officers, is a force dedicated to policing public protests and dealing with riots. The GIGN (National Gendarmerie Intervention Group), a unit specialized in antiterrorist and hostage rescue operations, and the GSPR (Security Group of the Republic's Presidency), a team assigned to the protection of the president, are also attached to the Mobile Gendarmerie.

The most famous of the specialized units is the Republican Guard, a mounted corps of 3,000 that provides security and honor guards to state institutions and during foreign dignitaries' visits. There are other arms of the Gendarmerie dedicated to air transport safety and to the protection of air force and navy bases. The Gendarmerie's Institute of Criminal Research develops new scientific and forensic capabilities to support the work of investigators. As a result of its military status, the Gendarmerie also assumes responsibility for certain aspects of national security, such as the recall of the reserves or the protection of military nuclear capabilities. Furthermore, it regularly sends officers to civilian police operations coordinated by the United Nations or NATO in Lebanon, Albania, Haiti, Kosovo, East Timor, etc.

Toward the End of Dualism?

In 2002, the newly elected government placed the coordination and redeployment of the two police forces at the top of its reform agenda. In order to minimize the duplication of resources and efforts, a presidential decree (Number 2002-889) transferred operational control of the Gendarmerie from the minister of defense to the minister of the interior. This new authority allowed the president to end the long-standing rivalry between the two forces and facilitated the implementation of the Homeland Security

(Orientation and Programming) Act, promulgated in August 2002. This special appropriation act, among many other measures, provided a financial and administrative framework for the reshuffle of National Police and Gendarmerie resources in order to better reflect the demographic makeup of the country and the spatial distribution of crime. Also, the planning and implementation of policies is now made by a single ministry, offering more homogeneity in service delivery.

In addition, Regional Intervention Groups (GIR) have been formed to investigate the underground economy's hidden financial transactions and bring down the criminal networks that operate in public housing neighborhoods. These 29 permanent task forces bring together investigators from various National Police directorates, the Gendarmerie, customs and revenue agencies, and labor and fraud inspectors as well as prosecutors. It is still too early to determine whether they will have a lasting impact on crime levels, but one of their major achievements has been the cultural change they have brought about, replacing an entrenched animosity between competing agencies with a culture of cooperation and information sharing (Le Fur, 2003).

Weak External Oversight and Opaque Internal Accountability Mechanisms

The recent changes in homeland security policies have not been exclusively concerned with effectiveness but have also addressed the issues of accountability and oversight. Up until the implementation of the National Security Ethics Commission Act of 2000, the internal affairs departments of various police units provided the only means of monitoring the accountability of the police, creating a situation where the independence of oversight mechanisms could not be guaranteed. The new law created an independent administrative authority, the National Security Ethics Commission,[3] that is responsible for investigating ethical misconduct by both public and private security providers such as the police, corrections and customs officers, and private security guards. It is perhaps the most original aspect of this law that it confers on a single organization oversight powers over the fragmented world of security producers. Unfortunately, the commission faces many challenges and does not seem at the moment to be able to realize this ambitious mandate.

There are several reasons for this inability. First, it does not have any regulatory, injunction, or disciplinary powers, and its sole means of pressure is the yearly public report outlining the cases addressed and the actions taken by the organizations implicated (Le Roux, 2001). Second, the procedure for complaining to the commission is cumbersome: Citizens must lodge their complaint through a member of parliament (either a representative—*député*—or a senator) or through the prime minister, who then decides whether it falls within the jurisdiction of the commission. This procedure creates a political filter between the commission and the citizens and makes it difficult, if not impossible, for people from minority or hard-to-reach groups to signal unethical conducts. This is particularly true when law and order politics dominate the agenda and politicians do not wish to be seen as weakening the authority of the police. The low number of complaints reported by the commission confirms this: Nineteen were recorded and investigated the first year (CNDS, 2002), while 33 were lodged the second year (CNDS, 2003), none of them related to the private security industry.

Such low numbers of complaints, considering that the public and private security sectors employ altogether more than 340,000 people (Simula, 1999), can also be attributed to the inadequate infrastructure of the commission, which employs only three full time clerical staff and received in 2001 a budget of US$510,000. The eight members of the commission are appointed for six years on a nonrenewable basis, but their main professional activities do not allow them to investigate the complaints they have to examine.[4] Under those constraints, it is not surprising that many consider the commission to be a paper tiger and that the public makes very little use of it to call public or private security organizations to account. Furthermore, the commission does not maintain any ties with existing internal accountability mechanisms, which also receive complaints from the public (Labrousse, 2001).

As a result, police deviance remains essentially investigated and dealt with internally by two units: the IGPN (General Inspectorate of the National Police) for all officers posted outside Paris and the IGS (General Inspectorate of Services) for the Paris region. The latter was formed in 1854, while the former appeared in 1884. Statistics are not released every year, but in 2000, the IGPN investigated 300 cases of police violence, misconduct, and corruption[5] (Razafindranaly, 2001). The same year, the IGS opened 932 new files, either at the request of investigating judges or because of complaints lodged by members of the public or police officers (Labrousse, 2001). The police's use-of-force policies have proved contentious, particularly in cases of shootings involving young fleeing suspects—often of North African origin—which have led to urban riots through the 1980s and 1990s. However, the fragmentary data available show a low frequency in the area of firearms discharge by French police officers, with an average of 0.3 annual firings per 1,000 officers between 1990 and 1996 (Jobard, 2002).[6] There appears to be no overrepresentation of one group of victims over another. Other forms of police violence are not measured, and it should certainly be a future priority of police researchers to fill this void. In line with the inquisitorial model, internal affair units are placed under the authority and control of the judiciary when criminal investigations are launched against police officers, which might explain the more aggressive stance taken by investigators and the relative underdevelopment of external oversight mechanisms.

Lateral Entry Recruitment and Training

The recruitment and training of French police officers is based on a lateral entry model that mirrors the human resources practices found in the military and in most other public services and in the private sector: Recruits join the police at a rank commensurate with their level of education, their skills, and their career aspirations. Of course, a promotion system based on merit and seniority also allows officers to climb the hierarchical ladder, ensuring the diffusion of frontline experience among administrators and managers. The recruitment and training system is centralized, with the exception of the system for municipal police officers, whose recruitment and training is left to the mayors.

In the National Police, applicants can join at the level of constable, lieutenant, or commissioner. There is no diploma required to take the constable entry exam, but a high school diploma is the norm. At the middle management level, two years of college are required. For applicants who want to take the commissioned officers' exam, a minimum of four years in university with higher-than-average marks is essential. These tests are very competitive and attract a lot of candidates vying for permanent positions. However, their emphasis on legal knowledge and rote learning is being questioned, in favor of more modern assessment techniques based on cognitive and leadership skills. Depending on the level of entry, an additional period of training ranging from 12 months (for constables) to 24 months (for commissioners) is undertaken. In 2001, the makeup of the National Police was 20 percent women and 80 percent men.

The Gendarmerie's lateral entry program operates under a two-tiered system. Noncommissioned officers must hold French citizenship, be at least 18 years of age, and pass a number of physical and written exams. The usual education level of recruits is at least a high school diploma. Commissioned officers must either have completed an officer's course in one of the three military academies or have successfully completed four years of university education. They must also pass physical and written exams. The length of training for commissioned officers is 24 months; for noncommissioned officers it is 9 months.

Like all other military personnel, Gendarmes are denied the right to unionize, but nevertheless they voice their demands for better working conditions through retired Gendarmes' associations and spouses' associations. It must be noted that the obligation of the Gendarmes to live in barracks with their families was at the origin of some tensions during the 1990s (Mouhanna, 2001).

National Police officers won the right to unionize in 1946, but they are barred from going on strike. More than three-quarters of officers, all ranks included, are members of a police association. Police unions are fragmented and represent narrow interests, such as those of uniformed or plainclothes police officers, constables, middle managers, or commissioners. Political and ideological divergences are also at the origin of a multiplication of police associations (Loubet del Bayle, 1999b). The main police unions are the SNOP, Synergie, Alliance, UNSA, and the SCHFPN (commissioners).

Community Policing

In the early 1990s, it became obvious to the population, the media, and politicians that the police no longer provided a level of service that could be called satisfactory. As the author has shown, property crime has grown exponentially over the past 30 years, and this has been accompanied by a symmetrical collapse of the clearance rates—down from 36.8 percent to 26.8 percent in 2000 (Courtois, 2001). Violent crime has also increased sharply, and the fear of crime is prevalent in France; 40 percent of the total population fears victimization in the very near future (ENA, 2000). Over this same period, one of the main criticisms voiced against the French police has focused on its isolation, its incapacity to listen to the public's demands, and its failure to deal with the types of crimes that affect citizens most. If the expertise of the French police in the fields of order maintenance and other specialist areas such as criminal investigations and intelligence is widely recognized, uniformed street-level policing has never enjoyed the same level of attention or resources. However, the pressure of spiraling crime rates and frequent public outcries over the impunity of young delinquents has become unbearable for the government and the police organization. The result has been community policing reform, inspired by American and British programs.

In line with its centralized tradition, in 1995 the French government passed the Orientation and Programming Security Act (LOPS). This law articulated officially the new concept of "security coproduction," in which the centralized state shares its responsibility for security provision with local and private actors. The outcomes of this law remained mostly a rhetorical statement until June 1999, when the government and the Ministry of the Interior finally implemented police reform under the label of *police de proximité*, or "proximity policing." It is important here to explain why this term was preferred to the more traditional *community policing:* This very deliberate choice was made to emphasize the universal aspiration of the French integration model and its refusal to see various communities treated differently or receive special benefits from state agencies. As a result, proximity policing does not entail outreach or liaison programs directed at specific minorities, such as can be found in other countries. This new strategy was implemented gradually: It was initially implemented in five pilot sites, then was extended to 62 districts, and was finally rolled out to all police districts in three waves between 2000 and 2002.

This community policing program is designed around five major operational principles (Ocqueteau, 2003):

1. A new territorial organization that increases the visibility of police patrols at the local level and that lets police stations decide how to allocate their personnel in order to meet local needs

2. Individual officers at all levels given more responsibility

3. Recruitment and training of police officers for multiple skills; they must be able to undertake a broad range of patrol, preventive, and investigative tasks

4. Frequent interactions with local stakeholders in order to build strong partnerships

5. A "privileged relationship with the population," implying better service to the public (especially victims of crime), better identification of its needs, and better information about the outcomes achieved

The reform was not limited to a redefinition of the roles and tasks of police officers. A significant budgetary effort was made initially to accompany the change, with a net increase of 5.7 percent in the National Police budget in 2000. However, this effort was not sustained in 2001 and 2002.

Most of the new resources were allocated to the recruitment of new police officers and special constables. These special constables, or more precisely police auxiliaries, are young people, recruited under five-year contracts, whose tasks put them in direct contact with the public. The training they receive is considerably shorter than that given to their full-fledged colleagues (2 months instead of 12). They wear a police uniform adorned with distinctive features, but they are not granted any of the legal powers required to conduct investigations or even make an arrest. Some cynical commentators compare them to "bodies in uniform" that free well-paid and better-qualified police officers from their most mundane tasks. If such harsh criticisms are somewhat warranted, these new jobs have nevertheless allowed young people from ethnic minorities to gain employment with the police, making the institution more diverse and bridging the gap between the police and a group in the community characterized by its confrontational relationship with the police. These police auxiliaries numbered 28,000 at the end of 2002,[7] representing a significant addition to the 233,000 police officers and Gendarmes already active.

However, this centrally planned reform has faced a number of challenges. Some of these challenges are intrinsic to the resistance experienced during any change process undergone by large bureaucracies. Others are more specific to the centralized character of the French police, and it is this particular group on which I want to focus here.

Concerted Action and External Partnerships:
The Local Security Contracts

The external challenges are probably the first that come to mind in a centralized police environment such as the one outlined in this chapter. By "external challenges," I mean the reluctance of other institutional actors to support the police. It is one of the central tenets of community policing that police organizations must rely on institutional and civil society partners in order to resolve the complex social problems that produce or at least have an effect on crime. However, when all the potential partners share the same high level of centralization, they derive from it the strength to resist any form of partnership that they do not see as useful or at least beneficial to their own institutional interests. In short, the larger and the more complex an organization, the more inertia it develops to resist external stimuli that do not threaten its existence or offer immediate rewards. By definition, the kind of partnerships involved in community policing strategies do not fit either of these two conditions.

In order to overcome this inertia and to integrate the diverse dimensions of community policing and crime prevention, a new administrative framework was implemented at the end of 1997 at the initiative of the central government. Its aim was to facilitate the development of interinstitutional partnerships that would also be able to integrate major civil-society stakeholders. This new tool follows contractual principles, which explains the name it was given: Local Security Contract or *Contrat Locaux de Sécurité* (CLS). The aims of the CLS are to encourage the coproduction of security by offering to a range of state and nonstate actors a common platform to identify, discuss, and negotiate a joint response to the problems of all kinds that negatively affect communities and the quality of life in their immediate environment.

One of the strengths of the CLS is that it acknowledges for the first time the fact that crime problems and incivilities[8] cannot be systematically delimited along administrative boundaries, whether these are geographical or functional. The centralized state is attempting an exercise in partial devolution, encouraging its crime control agents to organize themselves at the local level and collaborate with local political, business, and social actors in order to create a collective intelligence in the response to crime problems (Tiévant, 2002). To this day, more than 637 CLSes have been signed. They involve the police and their rural counterparts, the Gendarmes, but also judges and prosecutors, corrections officials, educators, health and social services managers, mayors and town councilors, community groups, housing authorities, public transport operators, etc.

Once a territory and the parties to the contract have been identified by the representative of the state (the prefect), a local security audit (or diagnosis) is commissioned. It must be noted that the territory in question varies from one district to another and can consist of a town or an entire county or can be limited to a transport network. Sometimes, it can even be a number of adjacent neighborhoods, if the problems they experience are specific. The diagnosis provides an overview of the situation prior to the implementation of the contract, addressing issues such as crime rates, incivilities, school attendance levels, urban decay, and fear of crime. The effectiveness and efficiency of existing strategies are assessed in order to detect opportunities for improvement and to determine priorities. At this stage, the local actors that should be involved in the CLS are identified and consulted in order to secure their participation early on. At the end of the diagnosis, all the actors meet and negotiate together a set of objectives, strategies, and deadlines that are best suited to the local environment. The contract represents this mutually agreed-upon action plan and the formal engagement of each participating institution to channel its resources and pool them with others toward its completion. Tools that will allow the evaluation of each institution's and the collaborative strategy's performances are also designed at this stage of the contract, so that all parties can monitor the progress made.

The link between the CLS and proximity policing is not obvious, and in centralized states, two such policies can easily be implemented at the same time without any sort of coordination, if they happen to be placed under the responsibility of two different ministries. In France, for example, such a situation occurred in the 1980s, when the National Police attempted to reform its operational philosophy within the portfolio of the Minister of the Interior, while a national crime prevention strategy inspired by the Bonnemaison report was established under the umbrella of the Minister for Urban Development (Dieu, 1999). These two efforts to provide better security to the French people were less than successful, partly because their fragmented administrative approach exacerbated differences between the two bureaucracies and duplicated services that had to be paid for with the same sparse resources instead of encouraging the emergence of a synergy. Hence, in order to avoid a repeat of this policy failure of the 1980s, the government decided to provide a financial incentive to the districts that had demonstrated a firm commitment to the CLS, facilitating the early move to community policing and allowing the recruitment of police auxiliaries. However, this was not sufficient to avoid some of the pitfalls that can be attributed to a long established tradition of centralization. Even though the policy placed the emphasis on partnership, some partners remained more equal than others.

Unsurprisingly, institutional heavyweights such as the local police authority and the justice ministries are overbearing and have a tendency to talk more than they listen, ensuring that their interests take precedence over their partners' interests. Episodically, there is also a blur between the primary objective of the CLS, which is to target local crime priorities and to bring the police closer to the community, and the tendency of all participants to see this process as a political game that could negatively impact their organization's standing and future resources if not played well, placing the interests of the institutional structure to which they belong ahead of the needs of the citizens (Ocqueteau, 2004). When this is the case, the CLS and the notion of partnership become an empty shell with few practical implications for the public. For example, the community policing reform was at the origin of some misunderstandings between the centralized police hierarchy and the centralized judicial hierarchy, which was not kept informed of all the details of the reform and its implications for the workload of prosecutors and other judicial officers, and which therefore undermined the implementation of the reform (Mouhanna, 2002).

The implications for each institution in terms of reputation and image are high, and none of them wants to be seen failing in the eyes of the public. For example, research shows that this reform generated high expectations among the public. However, the reforms were rarely followed by any visible effect, leading the population to feel even more frustrated and dissatisfied. The outcomes were contrary to the ones desired, and the public came to trust the police even less (Ferret, 2001). Additionally, some partners had a lot of difficulty entering into collaborative arrangements with the police, mostly for ideological reasons: Social workers or teachers, for example, tend to perceive responses to crime problems through a black-and-white repression/prevention dichotomy. For some of them, who see the police as the oppressor of young people and ethnic minorities, entering into a partnership with law enforcement representatives would be unethical. Prejudices also run high among police officers, who sometimes see social workers more as enemies than as potential partners.

However, when formal institutional partnerships were complemented by informal interpersonal relationships, evaluations showed that the CLSes achieved their objectives and that the partnerships became productive and sustainable (Tiévant, 2002). The consequences of a positive individual experience also created a transfer-and-diffusion effect, whereby public servants who had participated in a successful partnership at the functional and personal level were eager to promote the model when transferred to a new district.

Promoting Community Policing Competencies and Police Training

The transition to community policing has been accompanied by a huge effort in terms of recruitment and training in order to equip police officers with the toolbox required to translate the community policing philosophy into reality. Redesigned training curricula were offered to new recruits and to experienced police officers in order to make them more aware of the diversity of the population they serve. In this regard, recruitment strategies have an important role to play in shaping police organizations that reflect more accurately the ethnic composition of the French society. However, the number of young officers recruited from ethnic minorities and delinquent-prone neighborhoods remains very small because of these young people's academic scores, which are low compared to those of their middle-class counterparts who join with university diplomas. As we have seen above, many have been recruited as police auxiliaries, but their salaries are close to the minimum wage, and their career prospects are limited by the short duration of their contracts, making them second-rate police officers. This also results in very low retention rates. Special preparatory classes have been established in a few high schools located in socially disadvantaged neighborhoods, and the constable exam has been simplified in order to increase the number of young recruits from ethnic minorities who join the National Police,[9] but it is still too early to assess the outcomes of these measures. This lack of minority representation is amplified by the national and centralized nature of the recruitment and promotion systems, which make local adjustments almost impossible.

In the area of police training, courses in communication, conflict resolution, sociology of delinquency, and ethics have gradually been added to drilling exercises, weapons training, and the traditional courses covering criminal law and procedure. External consultants and community members are also invited on a more regular basis to share a different perspective with the students on a range of issues. More than 10 percent of National Police instructors must for example come from other organizations, but finding and keeping them is not always easy. Changing and updating training programs almost overnight has also been problematic for an organization that trains thousands of recruits each year. Trainers who have taught the same police doctrine for many years must learn, understand, and teach new procedures and practices.

Moreover, the training challenge is not limited to new recruits, as all operational officers must also be exposed to the new ways of policing. The continuing education program that supports community policing reform is costly, both financially and in terms of human resources taken off the streets to attend training. Too often, it has been apparent that training is not regarded as a high priority, leaving it to those on the street to work out on a case-by-case basis how to improve their skills, if they wish to do so (Mouhanna, 2002).

At the organizational level, the engagement of middle management officers or the lack thereof proved to be a crucial element. For example, the French police included some middle managers who were true believers or missionaries that had advocated closer relationships with the community for years and who acted accordingly, almost in a clandestine manner (Ferret, 2001). When these police officers took the lead and showed their reluctant colleagues how they could benefit from the reform, a favorable environment was created, facilitating the implementation of the new strategies more than any central directive could have. By contrast, when no positive role model was available in their midst, police officers proved a lot more hesitant to adopt the new strategies and often ended up discarding them as a fad that would eventually go away, when the central bureaucracy would come up with a new reform.

In retrospect, this strategy reflected a detailed understanding of the cyclical nature of police reform, and the 2002 presidential election announced a shift in the policing strategies promoted by the Ministry of the Interior. Without formally abandoning proximity policing, a new emphasis was placed on aggressive crime reduction, performance indicators, a more intensive use of criminal intelligence, and the creation of regional integrated task forces. What will remain of community policing in a few years is relatively hard to predict.

Terrorism

Over the past 30 years, four different types of groups have been at the origin of terrorist acts against the French government or French citizens. Regional independence movements (also called separatists), secret organizations, revolutionary organizations, and transnational terrorist organizations have been active and at times successful in reaching their targets. This section will provide a brief overview of the four categories, followed by an examination of the antiterrorist structures that have been put in place to respond to these threats.

Resistance to the centralist form of government found in France has led to the creation of the most active terrorist organizations and the most resilient to police intervention, mainly because of the strong support they enjoy among some segments of the population. Their form of political violence is concentrated in two regions: Corsica and the Basque country. A third region, Brittany, was the scene of marginal terrorist activity between the 1960s and the 1980s, but the levels of violence never reached the heights seen in Corsica or the Basque country (Crettiez, 1993). The reasons for the development of this particular form of terrorism are complex and interrelated, but the existence of a common local language and culture, the successes of the wars of independence and the ensuing decolonization process in Africa (especially in Algeria), and the popularity of leftist ideals are important factors.

In Corsica, terrorism appeared in 1975 with the creation of the FLNC or National Front for the Liberation of Corsica. The FLNC is responsible for a large number of small-scale bombings against government buildings and similar state symbols, but it has always voluntarily limited its casualties (Crettiez, 1993, 1998). In 1990, ideological disagreements within the FLNC led to a split and the creation of three entities: *FLNC–canal historique*, *FLNC–canal habituel*, and *Resistenza* (resistance). The old tradition of interpersonal violence rooted in the honor code or vendetta created an environment that explains the widespread support enjoyed by the FLNC and its offshoots. The only detailed study of Corsican terrorism depicts a core of 100 operational terrorists trained in combat and sabotage techniques, a second circle of 200 people in charge of logistics, and a third group of 1,000 active sympathizers. This three-tiered structure committed an average of 500 bombings a year on the island in the 1980s and early 1990s (Crettiez, 1998). At the end of the 1990s, the violence in Corsica reached a peak with the assassination of the highest representative of the central government on the island, Prefect Erignac (in 1998), but it now seems that this action was carried out by a rogue cell loosely operating at the periphery of the main terrorist organizations.

Terrorist violence emerged in the Basque country in 1959 with the creation in Spain of ETA (*Euskadi Ta Azkatasuna* or *Basque Country and Freedom*) by a group of students opposed to the Franco dictatorship and asking for the independence of the Basque provinces on both sides of the border. This organization is one of the most violent in Europe: Since 1968, ETA has been responsible for the death of more than 800 people.[10] Its military and support structures are complex and very compartmentalized and are often compared to the ones developed by the IRA. ETA maintains many links with terrorist and guerilla organizations all around the world.[11] For many years, with the tacit knowledge of the French government, it used France as a logistical base, establishing infrastructures such as weapons caches, bomb factories, safe houses for operational members, etc. The fact that it restricted its attacks to Spanish targets might explain the lack of interest of the French government at the time. The fight for the independence of the Basque country crossed the Pyrénées in 1973 with the creation of Iparretarak ("those from the North"), the sister organization of ETA (Crettiez, 1993). However, Iparretarak never reached the levels of violence of ETA and ceased to operate after the arrest of its leader, Philippe Bidart, in 1988.

It was the activity of a new antiterrorist terrorist organization, the GAL, in 1983 that precipitated the involvement of French police authorities alongside the Spanish government to fight ETA. For five years, the GAL, or Antiterrorist Liberation Group, killed Basque refugees (suspected ETA members living in France) each time ETA struck, forcing the French government to acknowledge the role of sanctuary played by France and to take action. Recent judicial developments have implicated the highest spheres of the Spanish government in the creation and financing of GAL (Amnesty International, 2000, 2001). The GAL represents the perfect example of a secret or front terrorist organization acting on behalf of hidden interests.

Besides separatist groups and secret or front organizations, a revolutionary movement inspired by the German Red Army Faction and Italian Red Brigades emerged under the name of *Action Directe*. Grounded in radical leftist ideals and believing in the need to destabilize capitalist governments, this group was active during the first half of the 1980s and carried out a number of assassinations against high-ranking public servants and CEOs before being dismantled by the police.

Islamic terrorism is certainly the most prominent form of transnational terrorism to have targeted the French government. Over the past 20 years, it has caused the death of 900 people, 300 of them on French soil (Conrad,

2002). In the early 1980s, the Lebanese conflict fuelled a number of attacks, such as the bombing of a French military compound in Beirut in 1983, which killed 54 paratroopers who had been sent on a peacekeeping mission.[12] Thirteen French hostages were also detained by Iranian-backed Hizbullah during the conflict. Between December 1985 and September 1986, a terrorist cell closely connected to Hizbullah and calling itself the CSPPA (Support Committee for Arab Political Prisoners) planted 15 bombs in various Paris department stores, killing 13 and wounding 325 (Conrad, 2002). Iran's motivation in supporting this terrorist violence was to put pressure on France in order to obtain the delivery of enriched uranium under an agreement signed with the shah's regime and to halt the support provided to Saddam Hussein's armed forces.

In the 1990s, the main "exporter" of Islamic terrorism to France proved to be Algeria, where the cancellation of elections won by Islamic parties led to the installation of a military dictatorship and a bloody civil war between the two forces. As Algeria's former colonial power and its main creditor, France is considered to be the main supporter of the military regime. As a result, the GIA (Armed Islamic Group), known for its gruesome civilian massacres in Algeria, became very active in France between 1993 and 1996.[13] It committed a number of assassinations and bombings, the most spectacular being the hijacking of an Air France plane on December 24, 1994, which ended with a successful assault by the National Police's antiterrorist unit. It is assumed that the hijackers intended to crash the plane over Paris, in an ominous sign of things to come (Wilkinson, 2002). In stark contrast with the terrorist wave of the 1980s sponsored by countries such as Iran, Syria, and Libya, the GIA depended heavily on local cells implanted in Muslim disaffected neighborhoods, enrolling young second-generation immigrants and even native-born French converted to a radical brand of Islamism.

This new phenomenon raised concerns about the emergence of direct links between low-level delinquency, drug trafficking, and terrorist activities in "difficult" neighborhoods and about the development of a new form of homegrown terrorism, directly linked to the al-Quaeda terror network. However, it appears that young Muslims have not embraced political violence, contrary to what some pessimist politicians predicted, and according to recent data released by the Minister of the Interior, no more than 200 young people from Muslim backgrounds have traveled to Al Qaeda's training camps (Sarkozy, 2004).

Counterterrorist Capabilities

A number of police units are engaged in the fight against terrorism and enforce the provisions of section 15 of the Code of Criminal Procedure, which defines the objective and subjective elements of terrorist acts. This section was added by the Fight Against Terrorism Act of 1986, which deals specifically with terrorism and grants specialized investigating judges with exceptional powers, such as extended periods of detention. Pursuant to this law, a pool of four investigating judges was created within the Paris district attorney's office and granted national jurisdiction over terrorist activities. The magistrates work closely with the various police units in charge of terrorism and have accumulated over the years an impressive expertise in this field, but some hasty decisions and procedures have also annoyed their own hierarchy and colleagues, and human rights organizations have called for greater accountability on their part (Courtois & Garrec, 1999).

Most specialized police units have been assigned leadership over specific forms of terrorism. The General Intelligence Directorate (*Renseignements Généraux* or DCRG) of the National Police is in charge of internal terrorist groups such as ETA or FLNC. This unit mobilizes more than 750 agents in counterterrorism related activities. Since general intelligence officers do not have powers of arrest, they must work closely with their criminal investigation colleagues to initiate an arrest. They must deal with the National Antiterrorist Division (DNAT), a specialist section of the Judicial Police Directorate, which can mobilize more than 150 agents. The DST, or Directorate for the Surveillance of the Territory, is in charge of international and transnational terrorism. This responsibility derives from the broader counterespionage mandate given to this arm of the National Police, and its expertise is in the area of foreign intelligence. A little less than half of all DST's agents are assigned to antiterrorism tasks (Sarkozy, 2004). The Gendarmerie also collects intelligence related to terrorist activity, particularly in rural areas, which have been used extensively by members of the ETA and FLNC to evade surveillance. In the field of intervention, both the National Police and the Gendarmerie have formed their own tactical and hostage rescue teams (RAID for the police and GIGN for the Gendarmerie). In times of crisis or heightened alert, the *Vigipirate* plan allows the prime minister to mobilize the army in a support capacity to protect government buildings and critical infrastructure such as airports, public transport systems, nuclear power plants, etc. Since 1978, it has been activated four times.

The diversified terrorist threat and the allocation of responsibilities to various units on an *ad hoc* basis has impeded coordination of the counterterrorism effort. The work of the antiterrorist magistrates somehow compensated for this trend, but significant overlaps persisted between services that maintained their own set of practices, informants, and databases and were engaged in an unproductive competition in order to benefit from the prestige associated with successful operations. Sources were also seen as an asset to protect at all costs, including protecting them from other agencies that might need their information. In order to remedy this situation, UCLAT, the Antiterrorism Coordination Unit, was created in 1984. UCLAT is staffed by liaison officers detached from the various antiterrorist units and intelligence services. Its mandate is to "improve processes related to the allocation of responsibilities, the assessment of threats and to advise, manage and permit a more effective information and intelligence sharing between services."[14] It is however important to note that UCLAT does not have any power over those services and that it must rely on persuasion rather than coercion.

Conclusion

Most texts on French policing available in English emphasize the differences between the French system and the more familiar North American or British systems. This approach allows their authors to rely on the assumed knowledge of the readers. I have voluntarily refused to follow this path in order to provide a more neutral view of the elements and forces at work in this complex assemblage. Instead, I have highlighted the dualist structure of the French police, inherited from the royal era, and the adaptations required in the face of exploding crime statistics, public demands, and the pressures of globalization. In contrast to the bipolar situation depicted in certain academic texts, this chapter and the other contributions in this book have confirmed the relevance of a conceptual framework based on the idea of a continuum that can accommodate local variations and evolutions.

We are witnessing for example an interest among French police managers and politicians in strategies developed in the U.S. or the UK: the national proximity policing reform, largely inspired by the community policing philosophy; the temptation of zero-tolerance and "get-tough" policies; and the new culture of performance indicators all attest to the intensity of policy transfers at work (Jones & Newburn, 2002). Similarly, the acknowledgment by foreign observers of the French police's expertise in combating terrorism (Shapiro & Suzan, 2003) and running a large centralized and professionalized system must be highlighted. In this regard, the concept of *policy convergence* seems much more appropriate to describe the relationship between French and Anglo-Saxon policing. Obviously, police organizations respond and their reforms are responses to contextual stimuli, and it is highly unlikely that the French system will ever resemble its American or British counterparts. However, as ideas, practices, technologies, and officers travel from one system to another with increased frequency, exaggerated statements such as the ones cited in the first paragraph of this chapter are likely to fade away and be replaced by more objective assessments.

Notes

1. In 1999, 4 percent of the population was naturalized.
2. As noted previously, a section in the Daily Security Act of 2001 criminalized meetings in social housing stairwells.
3. This organization has a Web site: http://www.cnds.fr.

4. Current members include a senator, a congressman, an administrative judge, a high court judge, a general accounting office counselor, a professor of forensic medicine, and a writer.

5. Excessive use of force by the police represents 40 percent of the cases, and more minor forms of police misconduct represent 30 percent.

6. Interestingly, the rate in the Paris area is double (0.6 per 1,000 officers) the national average.

7. Auxiliaries numbered 14,200 in the National Police and 13,800 in the Gendarmerie.

8. I will define *incivilities* as behaviors and incidents that are not strictly unlawful but that are disturbing enough to elicit among those who experience them a feeling of insecurity.

9. This lowering of exam requirements has occurred to the dismay of police associations, which feel that this will result in lower standards and affect the professional image of the police.

10. Most victims have been police officers and military personnel.

11. These included links to individuals and organizations in Cuba, Algeria, San Salvador, Peru, Nicaragua, and Yemen in the past, and more recently, in Colombia.

12. The same day, 241 U.S. Marines were killed in the same fashion by a car bomb.

13. For a more detailed chronology of those events, as well as the wave of bombings in 1986, see Shapiro and Suzan (2003).

14. This is the mandate according to a high-ranking antiterrorism official quoted in Crettiez (1993, p. 46).

References

Amnesty International. (2000). *Annual report 2000*. London: Author.

Amnesty International. (2001). *Annual report 2001*. London: Author.

Aubusson, B., Lalam, N., Padieu, R., & Zamora, P. (2002). Les statistiques de la délinquance. In *France: Portrait social 2002-2003* (pp. 141–158). Paris: National Institute for Statistics and Economic Studies.

Bayley, D. H. (1985). *Patterns of policing: a comparative international analysis*. New Brunswick, NJ: Rutgers University Press.

Bayley, D. H. (1999). Policing: the world stage. In R. I. Mawby (Ed.), *Policing across the world: Issues for the twenty-first century* (pp. 3–12). London: University College London Press.

Boëldieu, J., & Borrel, C. (2000). Recensement de la population 1999: La proportion d'immigrés est stable depuis 25 ans. *INSEE Première*, (748), 4.

Brodeur, J.-P. (2003). *Les visages de la police*. Montréal: Presses de l'Université de Montréal.

Brodeur, J.-P. & Monjardet, D. (2003). En guise de conclusion. In J.-P. Brodeur & D. Monjardet (Eds.), *Connaître la police* (pp. 417–425). Paris: La Documentation Française.

Bui Trong, L. (1998). Les violences urbaines à l'échelle des renseignements généraux: un état des lieux pour 1998. *Les Cahiers de la Sécurité Intérieure, 33*, 215–224.

Cazelles, C., Morel, B., & Roché, S. (2007). *Les violences urbaines de l'automne 2005, événements, acteur: Dynamiques et interactions*. Paris: Centre d'Analyse Stratégique.

Commission Nationale de Déontologie de la Sécurité (CNDS). (2002). *Annual report for 2001*. Paris: Author.

Commission Nationale de Déontologie de la Sécurité (CNDS). (2003). *Annual report for 2002*. Paris: Author.

Conrad, J.-P. (2002). Origines et réalités de l'islamisme activiste. In G. Chaliand (Ed.), *Les stratégies du terrorisme* (pp. 19–71). Paris: Desclée de Brouwer.

Courtois, J.-P. (2001). *Projet de loi de finances pour 2002—Tome II—Intérieur: Police et sécurité*. Paris: Assemblée Nationale.

Courtois, J.-P., & Garrec, R. (1999). *Rapport de la commission d'enquête sur la conduite de la politique de sécurité mené par l'État en Corse*. Paris: Sénat.

Crettiez, X. (1993). *Terrorisme indépendantiste et anti-terrorisme en France*, Paris: National Institute for the Study of Homeland Security.

Crettiez, X. (1998). Lire la violence politique en Corse. *Les Cahiers de la Sécurité Intérieure, 33*, 195–214.

Critchley, T. A. (1967). *A history of the police in England and Wales 900–1966*. London: Constable.

Dieu, F. (1999). *Politiques publiques de sécurité*. Paris: L'Harmattan.

Duprez, D., & Hedli, M. (1992). *Le mal des banlieues? Sentiment d'insécurité et crise identitaire*. Paris: L'Harmattan.

École Nationale d'Administration (ENA). (2000). *La police de proximité: Une révolution culturelle?* Paris: Author.

Emsley, C. (1996). *The English police: a political and social history* (2nd ed.). London: Longman.

Emsley, C. (1999). *Gendarmes and the State in Nineteenth-Century Europe*. Oxford, UK: Oxford University Press.

Ferret, J. (2001). Police de proximité en France: Une expérience de recherche institutionnelle à l'IHESI (1998–2001). *Les Cahiers de la Sécurité Intérieure, 46*, 97–117.

Ferret, J. (2004). The state, policing and "old continental Europe": Managing the local/national tension. *Policing & Society, 14*(1), 49–65.

Garcia, A. (2002, April 20). Les contrôles d'identité abusifs aggravent les tensions dans les cités. *Le Monde*, p. 11.

Gleizal, J.-J., Gatti-Domenach, J., & Journès, C. (1993). *La police: Le cas des démocraties occidentales*. Paris: Presses Universitaires de France.

Haut Conseil de l'Intégration (HCI). (2004). *Le contrat et l'intégration: Annual report 2003*. Paris: HCI.

Jobard, F. (2002). *Bavures policières? La force publique et ses usages*. Paris: La Découverte.

Jones, T., & Newburn, T. (2002). Learning from Uncle Sam? Exploring U.S. influences on British crime control policies. *Governance: An International Journal of Policy, Administration, and Institutions, 15*(1), 97–119.

L'Heuillet, H. (2001). *Basse politique, haute police*. Paris: Fayard.

Labrousse, F. (2001). L'inspection générale des services, la légitimité d'un service de contrôle interne et judiciaire. *Les Cahiers de la Sécurité Intérieure, 44*, 171–188.

Le Fur, M. (2003). *Rapport d'information sur les Groupes d'Intervention Régionaux*. Paris: National Assembly Committee on Finance, the General Economy and the Plan.

Le Roux, B. (2001). Sécurité et déontologie, la création d'une autorité administrative indépendante. *Les Cahiers de la Sécurité Intérieure*, *44*, 143–151.

Loubet del Bayle, J.-L. (1999a). Jalons pour une histoire de la recherche française sur les institutions et les pratiques policières. *Les Cahiers de la Sécurité Intérieure*, *37*, 55–71.

Loubet del Bayle, J.-L. (1999b). L'état du syndicalisme policier. *Revue Française d'Administration Publique*, *91*, 435–445.

Mawby, R. (1990). *Comparative policing issues: The British and American experience in international perspective*. London: Unwin Hyman.

Ministry of the Interior. (2004, January 14). *Annual press release on homeland security*. Paris: Author.

Monjardet, D. (2003, February). *International terrorism and the stairwell*. Paper delivered at the International Conference on Policing and Security, Montreal, Quebec.

Mouhanna, C. (2001). Faire le gendarme: De la souplesse informelle à la rigueur bureaucratique. *Revue Française de Sociologie*, *42*(1), 31–55.

Mouhanna, C. (2002). Une police de proximité judiciarisée. *Déviance et Société*, *26*(2), 163–182.

Mucchielli, L. (2001). *Violences et insécurité*. Paris: La Découverte.

Mucchielli, L. (2003). Délinquance et immigration en France: Un regard sociologique. *Criminologie*, *36*(2), 27–55.

Napoli, P. (2003). *Naissance de la police moderne: Pouvoirs, normes, société*. Paris: La Découverte.

Ocqueteau, F. (2003). Comment évaluer l'impact du travail des policiers de proximité. *Criminologie*, *36*(1), 121–141.

Ocqueteau, F. (2004). Public security as "everyone's concern"? Beginnings and developments of a useful misunderstanding. *Policing & Society*, *14*(1), 66–75.

Peyrat, P. (2001). *Habiter et cohabiter: La sécurité dans le logement social*. Paris: Secrétariat d'État au Logement.

Razafindranaly, J. R. V. (2001). L'inspection générale de la Police Nationale (IGPN): Entre discipline et prévention. *Les Cahiers de la Sécurité Intérieure*, *44*, 153–170.

Robert, P., & M.-L. Pottier (2002). Les grandes tendances de l'évolution des délinquances. In L. Mucchielli & P. Robert (Eds.), *Crime et sécurité: L'état des savoirs* (pp. 13–24). Paris: La Découverte.

Sarkozy, N. (Minister of the Interior). (2003, July 3). *Introductory comments on a bill dealing with immigration controls and the stay of foreigners in France*. Address to the National Assembly, Paris.

Sarkozy, N. (Minister of the Interior). (2004, February 11). *The results of international cooperation in the fight against terrorism*. Presentation to a hearing of the National Assembly Foreign Affairs Committee, Paris.

Shapiro, J., & Suzan, B. (2003). The French experience of counter-terrorism. *Survival*, *41*(1), 67–98.

Simula, P. (1999). Offre de sécurité et forces publiques régaliennes. *Les Cahiers de la Sécurité Intérieure*, *37*, 135–159.

Tiévant, S. (2002). Partenariat et police de proximité: Dilution ou consolidation des spécificités professionnelles? *Les Cahiers de la Sécurité Intérieure*, *48*, 149–170.

Wilkinson, P. (2002). Comment répondre à la menace terroriste. In G. Chaliand (Ed.), *Les stratégies du terrorisme* (pp. 195–218). Paris: Desclée de Brouwer.

Further Reading

Body-Gendrot, S. (2004). Police race relations in England and in France: Policy and practices. In G. Mesko, M. Pagon, & B. Dobovsek (Eds.), *Policing in central and eastern Europe: Dilemmas of contemporary criminal justice* (pp. 134–145). Maribor, Slovenia: Faculty of Criminal Justice, University of Maribor.

Filleule, O., & Jobard, F. (1998). The policing of protest in France: Toward a model of protest policing. In D. Della Porta & H. Reiter (Eds.), *Policing protest, the control of mass demonstrations in Western democracies* (pp. 70–90). Minneapolis: University of Minnesota Press.

Hodgson, J. (2001). Police, the prosecutor and the juge d'instruction: Judicial supervision in France, theory and practice. *British Journal of Criminology, 41*(2), 342–361.

Horton, C. (1995). *Policing policy in France.* London: Policy Studies Institute.

Liang, H.-H. (1992). *The rise of modern police and the European state system from Metternich to the Second World War.* Cambridge, UK: Cambridge University Press.

Monjardet, D. (1995). The French model of policing. In J.-P. Brodeur (Ed.), *Comparisons on policing: an international perspective* (pp 49–68). Aldershot, UK: Avebury.

Monjardet, D. (2000). Police and the public. *European Journal of Criminal Policy and Research, 8*(3), 353–378.

Roché, S. (2002). Towards a new governance of crime and insecurity in France. In A. Crawford (Ed.), *Crime and insecurity: The governance of safety in Europe* (pp. 213–233). Cullompton, UK: Willan.

Stead, P. J. (1983). *The police of France.* New York: Macmillan.

Williams, A. (1979). *The police of Paris: 1718-1789.* Baton Rouge: Louisiana State University Press.

Zauberman, R., & Levy, R. (2003). Police, minorities and the French republican ideal. *Criminology, 41*(4), 1065–1100.

11

United Kingdom

Democratic Policing— Global Change From a Comparative Perspective

Matt Long and Stuart Cullen

I n historical terms, although the United Kingdom is one of the world's oldest democracies, policing is a comparatively modern phenomenon. Following the founding of the London Metropolitan Police by Sir Robert Peel in 1829, the formation of other police forces throughout the country was an incremental process, with each newly created local police force operating according to the needs of the individual communities they served. Hence, policing was part of the democratic process insofar as it was intended to reflect the needs of the people. This chapter will provide an overview of the history of modern policing in the United Kingdom, examining events that either threatened or helped to reinforce the principles of policing within a liberal democratic society. Further, an examination will be made of how, both operationally and organizationally, policing in the United Kingdom has been able to prepare to respond to the effects and consequences of globalization that threaten the security of the state and its citizens.

History and Political Context of Policing

During the eighteenth century, civil power was insufficient to deal with dire emergencies of public disorder. Local constables were unable to deal effectively with major outbreaks of disorder, and the government deployed the military in a public order role. For example, during the Gordon Riots of 1780, the government deployed the military, which used disproportionate force by firing on and killing hundreds of anti-Catholic rioters (Stead, 1985).

Despite there being a constitutional power allowing the police to call upon the military, there is in practice nowadays a distinct separation of powers between the military and the police. In Britain, according to Wright, "There had never been a strong military influence on policing" (2002, p. 62). As policing became more systematic and bureaucratized, government felt that civil disorder could be dealt with without having to call on the military. The relationship between the police and government is however more intertwined and complicated.

Henry and John Fielding were progressive thinkers who advocated reform, and in many ways their London-based Bow Street Runners were a precursor to Sir Robert Peel's Metropolitan Police. Peel was an advocate of preventive policing, and that is precisely why members of the force wore visible and readily identifiable uniforms. Officers were both unarmed and equipped with minimal powers in order to reinforce the philosophy that policing should be with the people in terms of gaining their consent, rather than a force against the people to be used in a coercive way. It was intended that the Metropolitan force serve as a model for other county-based forces throughout the country. Following attempts to encourage local areas to establish their own forces throughout the 1830s, police forces were made compulsory through legislation in 1856 (the County and Borough Police Act), which ensured that forces would be at least partly funded by the Home Office (see Rawlings, 2002).

What is referred to as the tripartite system of policing was established by the Police Act of 1964. This is basically a power-sharing relationship between the following three bodies: (1) central government (via the home secretary), (2) chief constables of individual forces, and (3) police authorities. The exercise of powers through government circulars and regulations was something that the home secretary could effect under the 1964 act. Such regulations, for example, related to pay and conditions of service, the approval of certain equipment for police use, and the endorsement of chief officers selected by their local police authorities. In financial terms, the 1964 act meant that policing was funded by both central and local government (51 percent central versus 49 percent local).

The number of police forces rapidly expanded throughout the late nineteenth century due to the existence of both county-based forces and more locally based, smaller borough forces. Forty-three individual county-based police forces currently exist in England and Wales, and this more localized structure is distinct from other European countries such as France and Finland, which are characterized by far more centralized policing systems. Although there is no national force, there are in existence mutual aid procedures that allow for a more centrally coordinated response to crisis situations that require assistance above and beyond that available through the county-based policing arrangements (see Long, 2005).

Following the 1964 Police Act, each police force in England and Wales had a police authority. These authorities consisted of two-thirds members who were elected councilors and one-third appointed magistrates.[1] The defining purpose of these police authorities was and still is to secure the maintenance of an adequate and efficient police force for its local area. Police authorities had the specific duty of appointing senior officers and receiving an annual written report with regard to force performance from the chief constable. The act made chief constables responsible for the "direction and control" of forces in operational terms. This latter point has come to be referred to as the "doctrine of constabulary independence" in that theoretically, the home secretary should not get too heavily involved in operational matters, because it would be deemed to be detrimental to the professional judgment and impartiality of chief officers (see Reiner, 2000).

The National Policing Plan 2005–2008 outlines five key priorities that the police should focus on. These are the following (Home Office, 2005):

1. Reducing overall crime (including violent and drug-related offenses)

2. Being citizen focused and responsive to local communities, in order to inspire confidence especially amongst minority ethnic communities

3. Taking action along with partner agencies to target prolific or repeat offenders

4. Reducing community concerns and fears about crime and antisocial behavior

5. Combating more serious and organized crime

Serving police officers themselves are either uniformed or nonuniformed. While uniformed officers tend to conduct routine patrol work, nonuniformed officers are ordinarily associated with the criminal investigation department (CID) within particular forces. After serving a number of years in uniform, many officers attempt to develop their careers either by gaining promotion to the supervisory or managerial ranks or through lateral career development. Specialist departments may include child protection, fraud investigation, firearms, public order, media relations, and corporate development.

Upon completion of their two-year probationary period, officers are allowed to undertake an examination that qualifies them for the rank of sergeant, which is a first-level supervisor. Further promotion to the middle management ranks of inspector and chief inspector is then a future option. Ranks from constable to chief inspector are referred to as the federated ranks. These ranks are represented by a staff association (rather than a union, because police officers are not allowed to strike) known as the Police Federation. Above these ranks, the Superintendents Association represents the interests of both superintendents and chief superintendents, who are responsible for policing in local divisions (now called basic command units) within force areas. The ranks of assistant chief and chief are found above the superintending ranks, and these officers lead the force and work with the Home Office and its police authorities in order to formulate policy and strategy. These most senior officers are represented by the Association of Chief Police Officers (ACPO).

Corruption History: Major Scandals and Incidents

The United Kingdom ranks as the eleventh-least corrupt nation on the planet (Transparency International, 2006). In light of this finding, it would be safe to suggest that the UK police are not institutionally or routinely corrupt. However, periodically, a minority negative subculture emerges within any police organization when a small element of police officials becomes involved in crime, dishonesty, corruption, or other malpractices (see Zander, 1994).

The term *police corruption* most commonly tends to refer to violence and brutality, bribery, and the fabrication and destruction of evidence. Whilst we have argued that in comparative terms the UK police should not be seen as institutionally corrupt, nevertheless corruption was something that seems to have been present prior to the birth of modern public policing in the mid-nineteenth century. According to Reiner (2000, p. 17), "Those members of the old constabulary who were not ineffective were represented as corrupt, milking their offices for rewards and fees. Thief-takers became thief makers." Periodically, corruption scandals have dogged the "modern" police in Britain as well. As early as 1902, a Metropolitan Police constable was sentenced to five years in prison for planting a hammer on a man and then arresting him. After the wrongful arrest of a woman charged with street prostitution, a Royal Commission upon the Duties of the Metropolitan Police in Relation to Cases of Drunkenness, Disorder, and Solicitation in the Streets was established in 1906. Despite this, allegations against and convictions of serving police officers continued. In 1928, for instance, the head of the vice squad at Vine Street, in London's West End, was exposed as having taken bribes from nightclub owners for whom he had a policing responsibility (see Rawlings, 2002).

More recently, in the 1960s, Detective Sergeant Harry Challenor's squad of detectives appeared in court charged with corruption, including the brutalization of prisoners to gain confessions. Throughout the 1960s and 1970s, detectives from the Metropolitan Police were found to be involved with fabrication and destruction of evidence. According to Cox, Shirley, and Short (1977), the spotlight focused heavily on both the force's Drugs Squad and its Obscene Publications Squad. Corruption was not confined to London, however, as there was also concern over the illegal activities of the West Midlands Serious Crimes Squad in England's second city of Birmingham. In 1972, Sir Robert Mark was appointed Metropolitan Police commissioner. Having set up a department to proactively investigate complaints and corruption, he pressed on to further reform that force's criminal investigation department by introducing greater interchange between the CID and uniformed ranks (Mark, 1979).

In 1981, a Royal Commission on Criminal Procedure was established to investigate, inter alia, what is commonly referred to as noble cause corruption. This is where the police basically claim that the end justifies the means in terms of the manner in which suspects are detained and interrogated. The overwhelming majority of cases were in the context of Irish Republican terrorism. Throughout the 1980s and 1990s, high-profile miscarriages of justice saw the release of the so-called Guildford Four, Birmingham Six, Tottenham Three, and the Maguires. The Royal Commission made recommendations for significant reform of police powers in order to attempt to prevent further abuse of human rights (see the section below on the legal context for police powers).

It would be fair to say that despite legal and procedural reforms, however, allegations of corruption still occur. Indeed, Reiner spoke of "a repeated cycle of scandal and reform" (2000, p. 62). The inquiry into the murder of the young black teenager Stephen Lawrence as recently as 1999 brought criticism of the Metropolitan Police, who were found to have failed to properly investigate the murder of an innocent minority ethnic young man by white racists (MacPherson, 1999). The lack of an efficient investigation by police was attributed to institutional racism within the force. This issue is discussed further below in the section on the racial context in which policing occurs in the United Kingdom.

Despite these events, and particularly since the Stephen Lawrence inquiry, the British police service has attempted to make progress to ensure that ethical standards are met through more effective leadership, more stringent management and supervision procedures, increasing levels of accountability, and the delivery of training for awareness of diversity and community and race relations issues to all ranks (see Marlow & Loveday, 2000).

Crime Trends

Since 1995, when a total of almost 19 million crimes were estimated to have been committed, recorded crime has been falling ("Crime Statistics," 2007). According to British Crime Survey data, it is estimated that just over 11 million crimes were committed in the 12 months between December 2005 and December 2006. On average, one in four people is likely to be the victim of a crime within this 12-month period (Lovbakke, Taylor, & Budd, 2007). As well as focusing on crimes such as burglary, robbery, and theft, the police and various partner agencies have in recent years been keenly encouraged by the government to focus on tackling antisocial behavior. This may include such social problems as noisy neighbors, teenagers hanging around on street corners, and littering (Squires & Stephen, 2005).

According to official statistics, the United Kingdom is one of the least violent societies in the world. Compared to a world average of 8.8 homicides per 100,000 citizens (World Health Organization, 2002) the homicide rates for England and Wales are 1.3 per 100,000 citizens (Home Office, 2007) and 1.8 per 100,000 citizens in Scotland ("Homicide in Scotland," 2006).

It is because of the most stringent firearms laws that historically gun crime, including homicides, has been rare. However, the effects of leakages of firearms from Balkan conflicts and the trafficking of firearms by organized crime groups has led to their increased availability and use by criminals in some of the major cities—notably London, Manchester, and Nottingham. The carrying and use of firearms and knives by young members of street gangs and their readiness to use extreme violence in the course of street robberies has become a worrying crime trend in some cities. In an unpublished 2007 Metropolitan Police report, 169 separate gangs were identified throughout London, with more than a quarter involved in murders ("Police Identify 169," 2007). The gangs are based largely on ethnicity, with Afro-Caribbean youths constituting almost half of them. Disturbingly, there was empirical evidence that the most violent of young gang members—those who were likely to commit multiple homicides or other acts of violence—were from immigrant groups seeking refuge from countries engaged in violence and armed conflict, including the committing of atrocities by armed groups (for example, Somalia).

Black on black homicides, primarily shootings over drug-selling territories and gang rivalries, have resulted in the Metropolitan Police forming Operation Trident. Over 300 police officers are dedicated to Trident and operate closely with London's black communities in targeting known criminals, preventing and investigating gun crime, arresting and prosecuting anyone involved in shootings within the black community, supporting witnesses and victims of crime, and reducing the fear of crime in London's black communities (Metropolitan Police Authority, n.d.).

The emergence of street gang cultures in the United Kingdom is beginning to present special problems requiring a multipronged strategy from government, education, police, and other agencies. Most challenging will be resolving how alienated youth, particularly from increasing numbers of immigrant groups, can be encouraged to share a sense of national identity and be provided with opportunities to become equal and valued members of mainstream society.

History and Influence of Organized Crime

According to Levi,

"Organized crime" used to be a phenomenon that was central only to American and Italian crime discourses about "the Mafia," but— stimulated by the growth of international drugs and people migration trades and by the freeing up of borders since the collapse of the USSR— the debate about it and specific national and transnational powers to deal with "it" has extended to Britain and other parts of Europe and beyond in the course of the 1990's. (2003)

The debate about international organized crime has also spread because specific crimes that pose a "new" threat, such as human trafficking and identity theft, are on the increase. It is impossible to examine organized crime without appreciating the truly international context in which it has to be policed. Mechanisms are in place to facilitate exchanges of intelligence between nation-states. At the national level in the United Kingdom, specialist force squads have been established to concentrate on specific crimes. Commonly these may include vice squads, fraud squads, and drug squads. In 1996, The Phillips Report (see Levi, 2003) was authorized by the Association of Chief Police officers in order to look at how police effectiveness in dealing with cross-border criminality could be improved. The report found that almost half of "serious" crime crossed traditional police borders.

In 2006, UK national law enforcement agencies and the National Criminal Intelligence Service were amalgamated to form the Serious Organized Crime Agency (SOCA). SOCA describes itself as "an intelligence-led agency with law enforcement powers and harm reduction responsibilities. Harm in this context is the damage caused to people and communities by serious organized crime" (SOCA, 2006). A major strategic target of SOCA is organized immigration crime. The United Kingdom is a destination nation for the smuggling of Eastern Europeans and Chinese into the agriculture and fisheries sectors and the human trafficking of females from Eastern Europe, the Balkans, and the Far East for exploitation in prostitution and the sex industry ("The Scale and," 2006).

Postconflict societies are especially vulnerable to the activities of organized criminal groups who seek to exploit the misery of those attempting to escape economic deprivation. Globalization is likely to increase the scale of these crimes. It is estimated that worldwide trafficking in persons (essentially a modern form of slavery) and migrant smuggling is generating income of US$30–35 billion per year to organized criminal groups. Yet currently, these crimes remain a low priority for the majority of most law-enforcement agencies around the world, certainly much lower than drug trafficking.

Additionally, SOCA seeks to enhance intelligence through covert methods and to target identified organized crime activities including drug trafficking, individual and private-sector fraud, money laundering, and other organized crime (SOCA, 2006).

Public Support for Government and Law Enforcement

It would appear to be the case that white people are more likely than those from minority ethnic backgrounds to publicly support the police. The British Crime Survey conducted in 2000 found that 38 percent of blacks had been "really annoyed" by police actions, compared to 23 percent of Asians and only 19 percent of white respondents. The same survey found that more than half (54 percent) of white respondents thought the police were doing a good job, compared to only 42 percent of Asian respondents and 40 percent of black respondents (Bowling & Phillips, 2003). This may well be due to the fact that historically, the police have tended to recruit white males into the organization. Due to the requirements of positive action, more black people, women, and members of other minority groups are being targeted for recruitment (see Chan, 1997). As the police force itself becomes more and more diverse in terms of its composition, so one may expect the police institution to be perceived to be more legitimate by minority groups who have traditionally been underrepresented (see Walklate, 2000).

History of the Use of Force

The modern UK police force is unarmed and is underpinned by what is often referred to as the doctrine of minimal force. It was believed by Sir Robert Peel that to have routinely armed the police would have compromised the notion of policing by consent. Since the creation of modern policing in 1845, the UK police have tried to present themselves as mere citizens in uniform, using no more power than is absolutely necessary in order to carry out their duties. For police use of force to be legitimate, it is expected to be used as a last resort and that no more force is used than is needed in order to prevent anticipated harm. According to Mawby, "Recent years have seen considerable pressure from within the ranks to issue firearms on a routine basis" (2003, p. 18). This is mainly due to the fact that some perceive that it is almost impossible to police an increasingly violent world without recourse to arms.

Every single force in the UK has trained officers who are qualified to use firearms, and armed response teams can be deployed where it is deemed necessary. These response teams tend to be deployed alongside police issued with riot gear in public order situations. Police officers routinely carry truncheons and also in recent years have become more likely to be armed with counter-strike sprays in order to temporarily incapacitate citizens who may be becoming increasingly violent or who are resisting arrest vigorously.

Legal Context for Search and Seizure, Detention, and Interview

Historically, it would be fair to say that the police have had considerable powers to stop and search people whom they suspect of criminal activity. Throughout the 1970s, for example, what became known as the "sus" (*suspected* person) laws allowed the police to arrest people who were deemed to be loitering with intent to commit a crime in a public place, by recourse to the Vagrancy Act of 1824. In the late twentieth century, the Police and Criminals Evidence Act of 1984 (PACE) and its five accompanying Codes of Practice introduced greater legal controls over police powers, which had previously been the subject of common law only. Under this key legislation, in order to carry out most arrest and stop-and-search powers, the police need to have "reasonable suspicion" or "reasonable grounds" to believe a crime has been or is about to be committed. These suspicions or grounds must have some objective basis and cannot rely purely on the subjectivity and discretion of the individual officer. Despite this introduction of bureaucracy designed to prevent corruption and abuse of power, in reality, officers still have to exercise their discretion in making decisions as to whether to stop and search (Sanders & Young, 2003). One of the positive requirements of PACE was its introduction of the requirement that police officers make written records of each search, in order to prevent misuse of power.

Suspects may be detained and questioned under PACE and are taken directly to a police station upon their arrest for these processes to occur. It is the decision of the custody sergeant (first-level supervisor) as to whether a suspect is to be detained or not. Under PACE, free legal advice can be given to suspects who request this, although civil libertarians often point out that in practice many do not do so, because they are persuaded it could be counterproductive. Suspects may be detained in order to be charged or held while extra evidence is collected. The normal period of detention lasts 24 hours, but in serious cases the police may apply to the courts for a 36-hour extension, which can be ultimately further extended up to 96 hours.

Over half of suspects who are detained at police stations under PACE are interviewed (Bucke & Brown, 1997). Basic standards for interviews, in terms of access to legal advice and comfort breaks, are provided by the 1995 PACE Code of Practice for the Detention, Treatment and Questioning of Persons by Police Officers. Interviews, which were previously written up by police officers, now have to be tape-recorded to safeguard the rights of the suspect, and over the last few years many custody suits have been covered by the use of CCTV. This is designed both to protect suspects from maltreatment and to protect police officers against malicious allegations. Under section 76 of PACE, confessions can be excluded as constituting legitimate evidence if it is determined that they were obtained by the police through oppressive means, be they physical or psychological. In addition to the relatively long-standing PACE legislation, the more recent Human Rights Act of 1998 has had an even greater impact on the attempt to safeguard the rights of suspects and to prevent inhuman and degrading treatment. This has had a big impact in terms of ensuring that the police treat suspects as citizens who have rights.

In the context of search and seizure, police most commonly use powers granted to them under section 18 of PACE, which allows them to search the homes of arrested persons. According to Sanders and Young, "Over the last 20 years or so the police have been given increasingly extensive powers of entry, search and seizure, consistent with the growing crime control orientation of the system" (2003, p. 244). Currently, due to the West's war on terror, many of the provisions to search and seize under PACE can be used together with provisions from antiterrorist legislation such as the Regulation of Investigatory Powers Act of 2000 and the Anti-terrorism, Crime and Security Act of 2001 (see Matassa & Newburn, 2003).

Racial and Ethnic Context of Policing

The United Kingdom has a population of 60 million. Its capital city, London, is considered to be one of the three main financial capitals of the world, alongside New York in the United States and Tokyo in Japan. The United Kingdom's inhabitants are predominantly of European ethnic origin (90 percent). Significant minority ethnic groups are Afro-Caribbeans and Africans, Indians, Pakistanis, Bangladeshis, and Chinese. The United Kingdom is predominantly Christian in religious terms, with large communities of Muslims, Hindus, Jews, and Sikhs also being in existence. English is the main language spoken throughout the United Kingdom. Many Welsh people can speak English as well as their native Welsh. Urdu is the language spoken by members of the Pakistani community.

Trends in Immigration

After World War II, in the late 1950s and 1960s, immigration from the Commonwealth countries increased. Black Afro-Caribbean people were invited to come to Britain by the government, which was keen for them to fill available jobs and to boost the growing economy at that time. In terms of monitoring immigration, a decade or so later, the Immigration Act of 1971 gave police increased powers to detain and question persons suspected of violating the law by entering the country illegally or overstaying their terms of entry (Gordon, 1984). Since the September 11 attacks on New York and Washington, immigration cannot be separated from issues of national security, terrorism, and civil liberties (see section on terrorism later in this chapter). Some commentators have questioned whether more recent legislation such as the Immigration and Asylum Act of 1999 and the Antiterrorism Act of 2001 may be discriminatory against minority ethnic groups (see, for example, Bourne, 2001, and Fenwick, 2002).

Inter/Intragroup Conflicts

Race was an important factor in accounting for much of the urban, inner-city unrest and rioting that occurred in the early and mid-1980s. A police tactic known as *Operation Swamp*, whereby large numbers of young black males were stopped and searched on suspicion of possessing illegal drugs, was perceived by many blacks to be overly aggressive and an infringement on their civil liberties. In his report on one of these riots, Lord

Scarman (1981) found that this tactic was a contributory factor in leading to the riots in Brixton. Similar riots occurred in Toxteth in Liverpool and Handsworth in Birmingham in the 1980s, and relations between police and minority ethnic communities reached a low point in 1985 following the brutal murder of Police Constable Keith Blakelock on the Broadwater Farm estate in London.

In the summer of 2001, similar outbreaks of disorder occurred in several cities and towns in the north of England, most notably Bradford, Burnley, and Oldham (Ousley, 2001; Ritchie, 2001). Waddington notes however that "this time they were more closely associated with Asian youth rather than Afro-Caribbeans and appeared to have been sparked by opposition to far-right political activity in conditions of increased racial tension" (2003, p. 397). More recently interracial conflict occurred in 2005 in Britain's second city, Birmingham. This followed an apparently false rumor that a young black girl had been raped by a group of Pakistani youths. While there was no evidence brought forward to suggest rape and apparently no victim, two people lost their lives as a result of the riots (Vulliamy, 2005).

Relationship Between the Police and Diverse Populations

At the time of the urban unrest in the early 1980s, the Scarman report (Scarman, 1981) recognized the often strained relationship between the police and minority ethnic communities and made a number of recommendations in order to attempt to improve this relationship. Such recommendations included attempting to recruit more ethnic minority police officers, making racially prejudiced language and practices a sackable offense for police officers, requiring police units to consult more with communities, and introducing lay visitors to scrutinize police detention facilities.

Despite these recommendations and the appearance of a genuine commitment to reform by the police, allegations concerning excessive force and police violence and brutality against members of minority ethnic groups persisted (Inquest, 1996). Additionally, in the context of stop and search, Bowling and Phillips point to the continued "extremely heavy use of these powers against people from ethnic minority communities, particularly young black people" (2003, p. 534). Statistics have showed that black people are eight times more likely to be stopped and searched by the police than whites, while Asians are three times more likely (Bowling & Phillips, 2003). According to the Home Office (2003), in 2001–2002, blacks were five times more likely to be arrested than whites, while Asians were twice as likely as their white counterparts to be arrested.

Representation of Diverse Populations in the Department

Despite recent attempts at recruitment, minority ethnic individuals continue to be underrepresented in police forces relative to their representation in the wider population. There is good news, however, in that the proportion of serving police officers from minority ethnic backgrounds has risen from less than 1 percent in 1986 to 3 percent in 2001–2002 (Home Office, 2003). Retention rates are also lower amongst minority ethnic officers than white officers, with minority ethnic recruits leaving the job for a variety of reasons more often than their white colleagues (Bowling & Phillips, 2003). Empirical evidence also demonstrates how minority ethnic officers have been less likely to be promoted than white colleagues (Home Office, 2003). In order to attempt to counter this, local and national targets for the increased recruitment, retention, and promotion of police officers were set by the home secretary in the late 1990s (Home Office, 1999). This process, referred to as *positive action,* also includes initiatives like attempting to persuade so-called hard-to-reach groups to consider joining the police.

The stimulus for much of this kind of change came from the murder of Stephen Lawrence back in 1993. Lawrence was murdered in an unprovoked attack by five white youths. The flawed police investigation into this murder led the subsequent MacPherson report to cite professional incompetence, institutional racism, and a failure of police leadership (MacPherson, 1999) as reasons for the failure of this police investigation. In all, the report made some 70 recommendations for police reform, including improvements in the monitoring and investigation of racist incidents, police training on issues of diversity, and the regulation of stop-and-search powers. In addition to the MacPherson report, the Race Relations (Amendment) Act of 2000 made both direct and indirect or unconscious discrimination on the part of the police unlawful.

Organizational Structure and Issues

As was mentioned earlier, there is no national police force in the United Kingdom. The delivery of policing in England and Wales continues to be divided among 43 semiautonomous individual county and metropolitan area forces,[2] all of which operate under the same national laws and legal standards. Some specific policing functions are provided nationally; an example is the National Policing and Improvement Agency described later in this chapter.

Centralization and Decentralization: Overview of Organizational Structure

Periodically, a debate arises as to whether the police forces of England and Wales should be centralized into a national police force or larger regional units. During 2006, the home secretary proposed such mergers, deeming them necessary to make policing more effective against the threat of organized and transnational crime and terrorism. The proposals were shelved after concerted opposition by local and national politicians, who typically claimed they were excessively expensive to implement. There was an additional sensitivity to their potential to erode the local accountability of police (*Police Amalgamations*, 2006).

There is no national force in Scotland, but rather eight forces were created by the (Scottish) Government Act of 1973. Scotland has a tripartite system of policing not unlike that of England and Wales, with responsibility for policing delivery being shared among respective force chief officers, joint police boards, and the justice department of the Scottish Executive (Donnelly & Scott, 2002a). As in England and Wales, chief officers are expected to be nonpolitical in terms of their independent management of police operations. Resource and budgeting issues are made by locally elected councilors who sit on joint police boards. Overall policing policy is directed by ministers who sit in the Scottish Executive. Since the Scotland Act of 1998 and the creation of a devolved Scottish Parliament and Scottish Executive, more control over policing has been exerted from within Scotland rather than from the English Parliament in Westminster (Donnelly & Scott, 2002b).

The Province of Northern Ireland is served by a single police organization, the Police Service of Northern Ireland (PSNI). The majority of Protestants in Northern Ireland are Unionists in that they see themselves as British rather than Irish, hence their reference to maintaining "the Union." The majority of Catholics on the other hand are Nationalists or Republicans. Some believe that Britain colonized Ireland without their consent, and they have long wished for the North to unite with Southern Ireland, Eire. After much violence in the twentieth century (particularly between the 1970s and 1990) and prolonged negotiations, the signing of a multiparty peace agreement between the UK and Irish governments took place on April 10, 1998. This fundamental part of the peace process has become known as The Good Friday Agreement (Mulcahy, 2000). The creation of a power-sharing executive to include all major political parties was made possible through conditions allowing for the release of paramilitary prisoners plus a commitment to the decommissioning of weapons.

As a product of the Good Friday Agreement, an independent commission on policing was established with the intention of attracting support from both Catholics and Protestants within the community. The Royal Ulster Constabulary has existed since 1922 and was composed of mainly Protestant and Unionist officers, and it thus became associated with English colonial rule according to some Catholics. Precisely because of the underrepresentation of Catholics in the force, the commission felt that reform was necessary in order to achieve policing by consent. The commission was chaired by the Right Honourable Christopher Patten (formerly governor of Hong Kong), and by late 1999 it had produced 175 recommendations for reform. Better representation of both Protestant and Catholic sections of the community was to be achieved through the creation of a new policing board.

Positive discrimination measures were put in place for recruitment, in that equal numbers of Protestants and Catholics were to be selected and drafted into the force. (A target was set of reaching 30 percent Catholic representation in the force over the next 10 years.) The Policing (Northern Ireland) Bill of 2000 ensured that the Royal Ulster Constabulary was renamed the Police Service of Northern Ireland (PSNI) with new badges and symbols designed to avoid overt association with either Britain or Ireland (Independent Commission on Policing in Northern Ireland, 1999).

Civilianization

Since the 1980s, police forces have recruited civilian staff into specialist posts. This occurred for two reasons. First, there was a conviction that there were some specialist skills that police officers did not normally possess and that needed to be filled by outsiders to the organization. Second, there was a drive in the 1980s toward cost cutting, and civilians tend to be cheaper to employ than police officers. Civilians are typically employed in posts such as crime and forensic analysis, training, and performance management. Since the 1990s, civilian staff have been recruited into equivalent chief officer rankings alongside their uniformed colleagues, and it is an ongoing debate as to whether we are likely to witness a chief constable who is a civilian rather than a uniformed officer in the near future. At the other end of the spectrum, The Police Reform Act of 2002 was a precursor to the creation of community support officers, whose work is designed to complement that of uniformed patrol officers. In addition to this, the Police Act of 1964 established what is known as the Special Constabulary. These are volunteer officers who work a number of hours every week supporting the regular work of full-time officers.

The current government has been keen to endorse what could be referred to as a mixed-economy approach. In the south of England, Surrey Police have led the way on this issue by means of the introduction of mixed-economy teams as part of their Wider Workforce Modernisation Programme. Under this scheme, relatively well-skilled and well-rewarded constables have been made responsible for the management of teams consisting of both trained police staff and civilian administrative assistants (Loveday, 2006).

Complaints Procedures

Great care needs to be taken in interpreting figures of complaints against the police. If any police complaints system is easily accessible, coherent, and transparent, then, paradoxically, citizens seeking redress are more likely to complain because they have confidence in the system. Hence, complaints may rise and will be higher than in societies where citizens fear the police and complaints are ignored or discouraged.

Citizens in the UK can make a formal complaint about police misconduct through the Independent Police Complaints Commission, which was established by the Home Office in 2000. Despite the existence of this relatively new body, there are still occasional allegations of policing cover-ups and what is often referred to as the "blue wall of silence" (Bowling & Phillips, 2003). Increasingly however, official complaints procedures are being overlooked in favor of attempting redress through civil litigation. We live in a society of ever-increasing litigiousness, and to demonstrate this, the Metropolitan Police had to pay out £3.9 million in damage payments between 1999 and 2000, compared to just over £1 million five years earlier (Metropolitan Police, 2001).

Internal Accountability Mechanisms: Policies and Procedures

Police forces in the United Kingdom are made up of a headquarters and a varying number of basic command units (BCUs), depending on force size. There are some 318 BCUs in England and Wales (Mawby & Wright, 2003). Strategy and policy are set by force headquarters. Headquarters also has the job of controlling the overall budget set by the police authority and allocating resources accordingly (Audit Commission, 2001). The pressure to devolve more and more resources and decision-making power to local BCUs has greatly increased in recent years, and since 2001, the Police Standards Unit (an inspectorate body along with Her Majesty's Inspectorate of Constabulary and the Audit Commission) has focused heavily on BCU performance rather than force performance (Home Office, 2001). Since the late 1990s, as well as demonstrating transparency in the way in which they perform, forces have had a legal obligation, under the Crime and Disorder Act of 1998, to work in partnership with other agencies in other to deliver better social outcomes. These are referred to as Crime and Disorder Reduction Partnerships.

Recruitment and Selection: Strategies and Standards

Eighteen and a half years is the minimum age for a constable, there no longer being an upper age limit for applying to join the service.[3] As with age, due to equal opportunities legislation, there is no longer a minimum height requirement to join the service, although good eyesight is normally a precondition for entry. In theory, recruitment is not formally dependent upon achieving specified educational levels, but due to the nature of a postindustrial economy, more and more graduates are entering the service. While applicants are recruited by specific forces that do retain the right to set their own standards and conditions of entry, in practice there is little variation in recruitment and selection procedures across the United Kingdom.

The first stage of recruitment typically involves all applicants being required to pass two written tests, which are designed to make sure potential recruits have a sound grasp of the English language. These written tests alongside a numeracy test and an examination of observational skills together form what is collectively referred to as the Police Initial Recruitment Test. The second stage in the process involves a fitness-related physical test in a gymnasium. The third stage typically involves an assessment center where candidates face a number of role-playing scenarios designed to test their suitability for a public service role. The fourth and final stage involves interview by a panel consisting both of senior police officers and equivalent civilian personnel officers. At this stage, acceptance into the police is still conditional and is dependent upon a positive outcome being obtained from criminal conviction checks and national security clearance.

Policy and Discretion

Each force may determine its own policy after consultation with its local police authority. Policies are however not simply determined from the bottom up and based on local needs, concerns, and expectations. Rather, each force's annual policing plan has to take account of the centrally driven objectives and targets set out by the home secretary. This is often why police managers feel a tension between the pursuit of central targets on the one hand and the attempt to take into consideration local perceptions of what constitutes crime or social problems on the other.

Recruit and In-Service Training

New recruits have to undertake an extensive period of training as probationer constables. In Scotland and Northern Ireland, core policing skills are developed during a residential phase of training at the Scottish Police College and Northern Ireland Police College respectively. In England and Wales, training of probationer constables is now localized and delivered at in-force facilities according to a common curriculum and agreed-upon national standards of competence. Probationer training also involves spending time with an experienced tutor constable so the new recruit can gain invaluable practical operational experience to equip him or her for the demands of policing the streets. It is intended that this combination of classroom-based learning with on-the-street policing will enable the probationary constable to develop sufficient confidence to be able to perform patrol duties independently.

Strategic Training and Change

To be successful, any organization has to be in a constant state of change. Change is especially problematic for police leaders. Elected governments and police organizations are accountable to society. Only governments have the mandate to change or introduce laws. The mandate does not extend to the police, who are the servants of both government and people. The police must operate only within the law and enforce it with fairness and discretion (Crawshaw, Cullen, & Williamson, 2007).

The police should also be tolerant of diverse radical and alternative causes and lifestyles that challenge the values of the majority of mainstream society. As society and its values and laws change, the police must respond accordingly. In management terms, this puts the police at a disadvantage: They are not directing society but responding to it. They are always a step behind. As a consequence, it is difficult to keep pace with training needs to meet the ever-changing demands of society. Additionally, training is expensive, and resources are finite. Therefore, critical choices have to be made in the prioritization of training content and delivery. As a general principle, police training in the United Kingdom is utilitarian: It is delivered only to specific personnel identified as requiring the training at a specific time on an absolute training needs basis in accordance with operational and organizational demands. Significant emphasis is placed on training in response to quality of service issues and matters that are of greatest concern to citizens. Such matters are often raised at meetings with community forums and in other interactions with the citizenry and their representatives. Thus, the people have a democratic voice in training.

Since the early 1990s, there has been a succession of training change and reform programs in England and Wales in an endeavor to match training and development with local, regional, and national priorities and to enhance professional competence. In April 2007, the National Policing Improvement Act (NPIA) was launched. In addition to providing national training and development programs for police officers of all ranks, the body will also be responsible for national information systems such as the Police National Computer (PNC), the DNA database, and the national fingerprint and palm print system. Additionally, the NPIA provides round-the-clock specialist operational policing advice to police forces for murder investigations, public order events, major incidents, and searches. (For further information, see the National Police Improvement Agency Web site at http://www.npia.police.uk.)

Higher-level training for those officers in managerial ranks continues to take place at the former Police College at Bramshill in the south of England. Rank-based courses have traditionally equipped police officers from the inspecting ranks and above with the skills to perform as middle managers in the organization. The Strategic Commanders Programme, for example, must be negotiated by middle managers who wish to progress to membership in the Association of Chief Police Officers and become assistant chiefs and perhaps chief constables eventually. The High Potential Development Scheme (formerly the "special" course) has been in existence since the 1960s and aims to take those recruits with the most ability and develop them into the police leaders of tomorrow.

There has been a restructuring of leadership and management training at Bramshill over the past few years due to the belief that leadership should increasingly be a role-based rather than a rank-based activity. It was noted, for instance, that many chief inspectors had to assume more of the roles and responsibilities of superintendents, who were their superior officers, due to the pressures of increased workload (Long, 2003). Recent years have seen the rise of facilitative learning taking the place of traditional didactic or "front-loaded" learning. Learning is now expected to be experiential and tends to be based on case-study exercises or simulations.

Training of international officers through the international leadership programs and other customized courses is also delivered at the International Faculty, Bramshill, to senior and middle ranking officers from around the world identified as likely to become the most senior leaders of their nations' police organizations. These courses are designed to equip them with the strategic awareness, knowledge, skills, and attitude necessary to operate effectively in the ever-changing global policing environment and to encourage adherence to the principles of progressive service.

Community Policing

It has become a maxim that community policing is democratic policing. Moreover, if their practices are to be truly defined as community policing, police leaders should have a high degree of public accountability for effective operational performance and use of policing resources.

Police and community collaboration, particularly with respect to relations between police minority ethnic communities, has traditionally been poor, as evidenced in an earlier section of this chapter. That section mentioned how the Scarman report (Scarman, 1981) on the riots in Brixton at the start of the 1980s focused attention on the need for the police to develop closer engagements with members of the communities that they served. This was because the police had lost the confidence of large sections of the community, particularly young, black males in this case. This led to a feeling that the police were detached from the community and that therefore they lacked the legitimacy required to police by consent. Indeed Bennett describes community policing at its simplest as "a greater working partnership between the police and the public" (1994, p. 224). A key advocate of community policing in the United Kingdom, back in the late 1970s and 1980s, was the former chief constable of Devon and Cornwall police, John Alderson. Alderson (1979) stressed the need to police with and for the community rather than to police against the community in a more authoritarian manner.

For community policing to take place there needs to be a significant degree of decentralization to local policing areas, which is only now being encouraged (see section above describing this process). Authority has to be devolved from the center in order for local responsiveness and two-way dialogue between police and community to occur. According to Tilley (2003), community policing involves the following:

- Defining what constitutes problems or policing needs
- Shaping forms of local policing by the police service
- Involving the community in taking responsibility and working along-side the police service in identifying local problems
- Determining responses to identified issues
- Implementing responses to issues as participants in community policing
- Working with the community to address community-defined problems
- Informing or supplementing the operational work of police officers

It would seem to be the case that community policing works best in more affluent and middle-class areas where police-community relations are already relatively good. The evidence suggests that alternatively, the poorest and most deprived areas, where there is distrust of the police, tend to be the very areas that are resistant to the implementation of community policing schemes (Hancock, 2001). Sustainability of community policing schemes also appears to be a problem.

Crime Prevention Programs

We have seen that modern policing has existed since the nineteenth century, yet it was not until the latter part of the twentieth century that crime prevention was accorded specific attention in the United Kingdom. The Cornish Committee on the Prevention and Detection of Crime (Home Office, 1965) was a precursor to some forces establishing crime prevention sections within their preexisting criminal investigation departments. It was recommended that each force have a designated crime prevention officer and that this job should be carried out by a police middle manager. The work of the Cornish committee was complemented two years later with the establishment of the Home Office Standing Committee on Crime Prevention in 1967, which recommended the creation of crime prevention panels in all towns and cities in the United Kingdom (Byrne & Pease, 2003).

In 1995, the Crime Prevention College in Easingwold in the north of England was established. What became known as the Morgan Report (Standing Conference on Crime Prevention, 1991) made recommendations that were given statutory backing via the Crime and Disorder Act of 1998. The act required the police and local authorities to work together in partnership rather than independently of each other. After consulting local citizens and designing local strategies, partnerships have to satisfy central government by producing crime audits every three years. Critically, section 17 of the act makes it essential that local authorities give due consideration to issues of crime in all of their decision-making processes. Despite the establishment of a crime prevention college and the more recent legislation, according to Byrne and Pease, "crime prevention has never fully permeated police thinking and practise" (2003, p. 287). According to the Audit Commission (1999) crime prevention is not something that the overwhelming majority of police officers are concerned with in their day-to-day duties. This is probably due to the fact that police performance continues to be judged around indicators of detection, such as burglary, car crime, and theft. It is in fact notoriously difficult to establish indicators of performance around crime prevention. Byrne and Pease (2003) further note that the Home Office seems to be keen to allocate much of its funding to closed circuit TV monitoring systems, which is only one small aspect of what should be a much bigger picture in crime prevention terms.

On a more positive note, the police are now more aware of criminal hotspots and the phenomenon of repeat victimization than they ever were before, and future attempts at taking crime prevention seriously will be assisted by rapid developments in crime analysis and mapping (Byrne & Pease, 2003).

Community Outreach

Examples of specific community crime prevention programs in the United Kingdom include such things as conducting crime prevention seminars and creating neighborhood watch programs (Laycock & Tilley, 1995). Additionally, drug education projects became very popular from the mid-1980s onward (Collison, 1995).

Terrorism

Until the peace settlement was signed in Northern Ireland at the end of the last century, the policing of terrorism in the United Kingdom had been dominated by the "troubles" in Northern Ireland, which began in 1969 (Ellison & Smyth, 2000). The dispute over the issue of a united Ireland meant that the policing of Republican paramilitary groups such as the provisional Irish Republican Army (IRA) and Loyalist paramilitary groups such as the Ulster Volunteer Force took precedence over other issues. From the point of view of the British government and policing, it was the IRA bombing campaigns throughout the 1970s, 1980s, and 1990s, targeted at pubs, hotels and shops predominantly in Northern Ireland's capital Belfast and London in England, which were perceived to present the most dangerous threat (O'Leary & McGarry, 1993). Since the troubles ended with the ceasefire by Republican and Loyalist paramilitaries, the decommission of terrorist weapons, and the final power-sharing agreement by all political groups to work together in the devolved Northern Ireland Assembly, police attention has tended to

withdraw from Irish terrorism and focused on the more potent and dangerous threat of the global terrorism of Islamist extremists.

Counterterrorism

Until al-Quaeda's September 11 attacks were made, it would be fair to
say that counterterrorism training was not a policing priority. It has traditionally been seen as something that is undertaken by specialist departments
and individuals and something that is divorced from the realities of day-to-
day operational policing. This attitude has had to change fast. On March 11,
2004, Islamist terrorists carried out the Madrid train bombings that killed
191 people. On July 7, 2005, British Islamist suicide bombers caused explosions on the London transport system resulting in the deaths of 52 people
and the injury of 700. On September 1, 2005, al-Quaeda officially claimed
responsibility for the London bombings on the Al Jazeera news network.

The need to fund additional resources for counterterrorism, intelligence
gathering, and associated training has been given added impetus by the perception, since the bombings occurred, that Britain is an inevitable target due
to her foreign policy and political alignment with the United States over the
Iraq war and the military presence in Afghanistan. All forces are now taking
the training of designated officers very seriously with regard to preparing for
the possibility of chemical, biological, radioactive, and nuclear attacks. (For
more information on this subject, see the Web site of the National Counter
Terrorism Security Office, http://www.nactso.gov.uk/index.php.)

Counterterrorism Policy and Strategy

The Metropolitan Bomb Squad was formed in 1971 largely as a response
to the sectarian killings that were associated with the struggle over the
future of Northern Ireland. This bomb squad became known as the Anti-
Terrorist Branch from 1976 onwards. The police were given the statutory
backing of the Prevention of Terrorism (Temporary Provisions) Act of 1974
in order to arrest, search, and detain without warrant those suspected of
terrorist activities. London's Metropolitan Police are also supported by
agencies like Special Branch, the Diplomatic Protection Group, and the
Royalty Protection Group (Matassa & Newburn, 2003). Special Branch
has departments within every force in the United Kingdom. The metropolitan force's antiterrorist squad is expected to work closely with Special
Branch and the Security Services (M15 and MI6), whose role it is to protect
national security.

Due to the changing nature of globalization, in recent years the UK
police have had to work in greater cooperation with Europol, which was
established via the Maastricht Treaty in 1992. When terrorist activities go

beyond European boundaries, then the UK police will work in collaboration with Interpol (Matassa & Newburn, 2003).

Section 1 of the Terrorism Act of 2000 defines terrorism as an actual or threatened act of violence against people or property effected to try to influence the course of government for political, religious, or ideological reasons. This act, along with the Regulation of Investigatory Powers Act of 2000 and the Anti-terrorism, Crime and Security Act of 2001, has greatly extended police powers with regard to those people and organizations suspected of terrorist activity. This legislation cannot be divorced from the outrage at the September 11 attacks in New York and Washington launched by al-Quaeda. In an attempt to counter the argument that the policing activities of the Security Services are largely unaccountable, the Regulation of Investigatory Powers Act of 2000 attempts to police the police by establishing a tribunal, founded on human rights principles, which can deal with complaints.

Terrorism and Its Threat to Democracy

During 2007, a number of young British Muslim male citizens of Pakistani descent have been convicted of conspiring to plant bombs in public places with the intent of causing maximum fatalities of innocent citizens. Other such young British Muslim Asians residing in various cities in the United Kingdom are awaiting trial for similar alleged crimes. All are alleged to be connected to the al-Quaeda network or similar organizations. Disturbingly, many are alleged to have received training at terror camps in Pakistan and Afghanistan. It is of the gravest concern to British society, government, security services, and police that a minority of young Muslims who have been born, brought up, and educated in Britain feel so alienated from British society that they feel compelled to vent their frustrations through extreme radical violence. The situation begs questions about allegiance to citizenship in a democratic society and about how society can respond to prevent such young people from falling prey to the inflammatory and extreme rhetoric of resident radical mullahs and other Islamist exhortations to attack the West. The police will have an important part to play, not only in enforcing laws but also in fostering harmonious community relations. They will need to be seen to be operating equitably, not as operating a witch hunt and marginalizing the great majority of the 1.6 million UK citizens who are law-abiding Muslims ("Religion in Britain," 2003).

Looking to the future, the threat of terrorism from extreme Islamist groups is a long-term potential threat to democracy and freedom. Terrorists seek to provoke governments and law enforcement agencies into disproportionate responses to their acts. They seek to undermine democracy. Thus, the terrorist can claim the moral high ground (Marighella, 1969). Following the London suicide bombings, government, police, and security services sought additional powers to detain terrorist suspects for up to 60 days without trial in order to complete effective investigations. A public and political debate ensued: Sixty days was considered by many to be an excessive period, and there was concern that allowing such a lengthy detention period would set a precedent that undermined fundamental principles of the freedom of the individual and the detention of suspects without charge. In November 2006, Parliament rejected the period of 60 days and reduced the legal period of detention of terrorist suspects without charge to 28 days ("Terrorism Bill," 2006).

The above exemplifies a special challenge to lawmakers and law enforcement officials: namely, the question of how to effectively deal with acts of terror while maintaining freedom and harmony between communities within the democratic framework of the United Kingdom. It seems likely that this challenge will remain for many years to come.

Notes

1. This was with the exception of London's Metropolitan force, which had a police committee rather than a police authority.

2. This number does not include forces with a special jurisdiction throughout the United Kingdom, such as the Ministry of Defense Police and the British Transport Police.

3. Ordinarily retirement is at age 55 years however.

References

Alderson, J. (1979). *Policing freedom.* Plymouth, UK: Macdonald and Evans.

Audit Commission. (1999). *Safety in numbers—Promoting community safety.* London: Author.

Audit Commission. (2001). *Best foot forward: Headquarters' support for police basic command units.* London: Her Majesty's Stationery Office.

Bennett, T. (1994). Community policing on the ground: Developments in Britain. In D. Rosenbaum (Ed.), *The challenge of community policing* (pp. 224–246). Thousand Oaks, CA: Sage.

Bourne, J. (2001). The life and times of institutional racism. *Race and Class, 43*(2), 7–22.

Bowling, B., & Phillips, C. (2003). Policing ethnic minority communities. In T. Newburn (Ed.), *Handbook of policing* (pp. 528–555). Devon, UK: Willan.

Bucke, T., & Brown, D. (1997). *In police custody: Police powers and suspects. Rights under the revised PACE Codes of Practise,* Home Office Research Study 174. London: Home Office.

Byrne, S., & Pease, K. (2003). Crime reduction and community safety. In T. Newburn (Ed.), *Handbook of policing* (pp. 286–310). Devon, UK: Willan.

Chan, J. (1997). *Changing police culture: Policing in a multicultural society.* Cambridge, UK: Cambridge University Press.

Collison, M. (1995). *Police, drugs and community.* London: Free Association Books.

Cox, B., Shirley, J., & Short, M. (1977). *The fall of Scotland Yard.* Harmondsworth, UK: Penguin.

Crawshaw, R., Cullen, S., & Williamson, T. (2007). *Human rights and policing: The Raoul Wallenberg Institute professional guide to human rights.* Leiden, the Netherlands: Martinus Nijhoff.

Crime statistics for England and Wales. (2007). British Crime Survey data. Retrieved June 8, 2007, from http://www.crimestatistics.org.uk/output/page54.asp

Donnelly, D., & Scott, K. (2002a). Police accountability in Scotland: (1) The "new" tripartite system. *The Police Journal, 75,* 3–14.

Donnelly, D., & Scott, K. (2002b). Police accountability in Scotland: (2) "New" accountabilities. *The Police Journal, 75,* 56–66.

Ellison, G., & Smyth, J. (2000). *The crowned harp: Policing Northern Ireland.* London: Pluto Press.

Fenwick, H. (2002). The Anti-terrorism, Crime and Security Act 2001: A proportionate response to 11 September? *Modern Law Review, 65*(5), 724–762.

Gordon, P. (1984). *White law.* London. Pluto Press.

Hancock, L. (2001). *Community, crime and disorder: Safety and regeneration in urban neighbourhoods.* Basingstoke, UK: Palgrave.

Home Office. (1965). *Report of the Committee on the Prevention and Detection of Crime* (Cornish Committee). London: Author.

Home Office. (1999). *Staff targets for the Home Office, the prison, the police, the fire and the probation services.* London: Author.

Home Office. (2001). *Policing a new century: A blueprint for reform.* (Cm 5326). London: Author.

Home Office. (2003). *Statistics on race and the criminal justice system 2002: A Home Office publication under Section 95 of the Criminal Justice Act 1991.* London: Author.

Home Office. (2005). *National policing plan. 2005–2008. Safer, stronger communities.* London: Author.

Home Office. (2007). *Criminal statistics. 2007.* Retrieved May 14, 2007, from http://www.homeoffice.gov.uk/rds/

Homicide in Scotland, 2005/06—Statistics Published. (2006). Retrieved May 14, 2007, from http://www.scotland.gov.uk/Publications/2006/11/17112458/1

Independent Commission on Policing in Northern Ireland. (1999). *A new beginning: Policing in Northern Ireland—the Report of the Independent Commission on Policing in Northern Ireland.* (Patten Report). Belfast, UK: Independent Commission on Policing in Northern Ireland.

Inquest. (1996). *Lobbying from below: INQUEST in defence of civil liberties.* London: University College London Press.

Laycock, G., & Tilley, N. (1995). *Policing and neighbourhood watch: Strategic issues.* Crime Detection and Prevention Series Paper 60. London: Home Office.

Levi, M. (2003). Organized and financial crime. In T. Newburn (Ed.), *Handbook of policing* (pp. 444–466). Devon, UK: Willan.

Long, M. (2003). "Leadership and performance management," in T. Newburn (Ed.), *Handbook of policing* (pp. 628–654). Devon, UK: Willan.

Long, M. (2005). United Kingdom. In L. E. Sullivan & M. R. Haberfeld (Eds.), *Encyclopedia of law enforcement* (pp. 1358–1364). London: Sage.

Lovbakke, J., Taylor, P., & Budd, S. (2007). *Crime in England and Wales: Quarterly update to December 2006.* London: Home Office.

Loveday, B. (2006). Workforce modernisation: Implications for the police service in England and Wales. [Special issue: Evaluating HMIC, 2004 Thematic: Modernising the Police Service]. *The Police Journal, 79,* 105–124.

MacPherson, W. (1999.) *The Stephen Lawrence inquiry.* Report of an Inquiry by Sir William MacPherson of Cluny. Advised by Tom Cook, The Right Reverend Dr. John Sentamu, and Dr. Richard Stone (Cm 4262-1). London: Her Majesty's Stationery Office.

Marighella, C. (1969). *Minimanual of the urban guerrilla.* Retrieved May 17, 2007, from www.marxists.org/archive/marighella-carlos/1969/06/minimanual-urban-guerrilla

Mark, R. (1979). *In the office of constable.* London: Fontana.

Marlow, A., & Loveday, B. (Eds.). (2000). *After MacPherson: Policing after the Stephen Lawrence inquiry.* Lyme Regis, UK: Russell House.

Matassa, M., & Newburn, T. (2003). Policing and terrorism. In T. Newburn (Ed.), *Handbook of policing* (pp. 467–500). Devon, UK: Willan.

Mawby, R. (2003). Models of policing. In T. Newburn (Ed.), *Handbook of policing* (pp. 15–40). Devon, UK: Willan.

Mawby, R., & Wright, A. (2003). The police organisation. In T. Newburn (Ed.), *Handbook of policing* (pp. 169–195). Devon, UK: Willan

Metropolitan Police Service. (2001). *Annual report.* London: Author.

Metropolitan Police Authority. (n.d.). *What is Trident?* Retrieved May 16, 2007, from http://www.stoptheguns.org/whatistrident/index.php

Mulcahy, A. (2000). Policing history: The official discourse and organisational memory of the Royal Ulster Constabulary. *British Journal of Criminology, 40*(1), 68–87.

NaCTSO: National Counter Terrorism Security Office. (2007). Home page. Retrieved October 25, 2007, from http://www.nactso.gov.uk/index.php

O'Leary, B., & McGarry, J. (1993). *The politics of antagonism: Understanding Northern Ireland.* London: Athlone Press.

Ousley, H. (2001). *Community pride not prejudice: Making diversity work in Bradford.* Bradford, UK: Bradford Vision 2001.

Police amalgamations forced through. (2006). Retrieved May 16, 2007, from http://conservatives.com/popups/print/cfm?obj_id=127690&t

Police identify 169 London gangs. (2007). Retrieved on May 19 from http://news.bbc.co.uk/2/hi/uk_news/england/london/6383933.stm

Rawlings, P. (2002). *Policing. A short history.* Devon, UK: Willan.

Reiner, R. (2000). *The politics of the police* (3rd ed.). Oxford, UK: Oxford University Press.

Religion in Britain. (2003). UK National Statistics Online. Retrieved June 15, 2007, from http://www.statistics.gov.uk/cci/nugget.asp?id=293

Ritchie, D. (2001). *Panel Report, 11th December 2001: One Oldham, One Future.* Manchester, UK: Government Office for the North West.

Sanders, A., & Young, R. (2003). Police powers. In T. Newburn (Ed.), *Handbook of policing* (pp. 228–258). Devon, UK: Willan.

The scale and nature of human trafficking in the UK. (2006). Retrieved May 14, 2007, from http://www.publications.parliament.uk/pa/jt200506/jtselect/jtrights/245/24507.htm

Scarman, L. (1981). *The Brixton disorders 10-12 April 1981: Report of an inquiry by the Rt. Hon. The Lord Scarman, O.B.E.* London: Her Majesty's Stationery Office.

Serious Organized Crime Agency (SOCA). (2006). *About us.* Retrieved May 14, 2007, from http://www.soca.gov.uk/aboutUs/index.html

Squires, P., & Stephen, D. (2005). *Rougher justice: Anti-social behaviour and young people*. Cullompton, UK: Willan.

Standing Conference on Crime Prevention. (1991). *Safer communities: The local delivery of crime prevention through the partnership approach* (Morgan Report). London: Home Office.

Stead, J. P. (1985). *The police of Britain*. London: Macmillan.

Terrorism Bill—Extension Of Period Of Detention to 60 Days—25 Jan 2006 at 18:38—Lords Division No. 2. (2006). Retrieved May 14, 2007, from http://www.publicwhip.org.uk/division.php?date=2006-01-25&number=2&house=lords

Tilley, N. (2003). *Community policing, problem-oriented policing and intelligence-led policing*. In T. Newburn (Ed.), *Handbook of policing* (pp. 311–339). Devon, UK: Willan.

Transparency International. (2006). *Corruption perceptions index*. Retrieved May 16, 2007, from http://www.transparency.org/policy_research/surveys_indices/global/cpi

Vulliamy, E. (2005, November 29). Rumours of a riot. *The Guardian* [Electronic version]. Retrieved August 17, 2007, from http://www.guardian.co.uk/race/story/0,11374,1653120,00.html

Waddington, P. A. J. (2003). Policing public order and political contention. In T. Newburn (Ed.), *Handbook of policing* (pp. 394–421). Devon, UK: Willan.

Walklate, S. (2000). Equal opportunities and the future of policing. In F. Leishman et al. (Eds.), *Core issues in policing* (2nd ed., pp. 232–248). Harlow, UK: Longman Pearson Education.

World Health Organization. (2002). *World report on health and violence*. Geneva: Author.

Wright, A. (2002). *Policing: An introduction to concepts and practise*. Devon, UK: Willan.

Zander, M. (1994). Ethics and crime investigation. *Policing, 10*(1), 39–48.

12 Democratic Policing

The Canadian Experience

Curtis Clarke

As occurs in many jurisdictions, the perspectives of Canadian policy makers and police leaders have and will continue to shift over time. In the context of Canadian policing, policy analysts currently emphasize the need to reorganize police administration and operational strategies so that they may reflect practices and language drawn from private-sector management. Pat O'Malley states that policing has begun to reflect "the ascendance of neo-liberal political rationalities and related social technology of new managerialism" (1996, p. 10). Others suggest that the previously insular culture of Canadian policing "is being increasingly colonized by business concepts, values and terminology. In this context police services are encouraged to see themselves in the 'business' of supplying policing services to clients, customers and consumers" (Murphy, 1998).

And yet, this recent critique offers us a limited analysis of the contemporary reality of Canadian policing, a pursuit that has been shaped by a range of political, economic, and social factors. Notable among these are the 1982 enactment of the Canadian Charter of Rights and Freedoms, federal and provincial government fiscal policies, extensive budget reductions, specific commissions of Inquiry, transnational policing responsibilities, and growing competition from the private security sector. These elements, while consistent across the country, have not always been addressed in a similar fashion, and as such have created an interesting array of policy and operational responses. In order to illustrate both the diversity and similarity of these responses, it will be necessary to place these outcomes into a contextual framework that captures the political and historical reality of Canadian policing.

Historical and Political Context

Prior to Canada's confederation in 1867, it would have been difficult to characterize Canadian policing as a blend of any two models. The nature of preconfederation policing may be best captured in comparing it to the diverse Canadian geography. The early expansion of settlements and increased commerce presented particular pressures for the Atlantic region of Canada, Lower Canada (now the province of Quebec) and Upper Canada (now the province of Ontario) to adequately provide law and order. It was not until the mid 1800s that communities began to replace the night watch system with full-time police forces. Between 1835 and 1847, the cities of Toronto, Hamilton, Ottawa, Quebec, and Montreal all instituted systems whereby chief constables were appointed and a varied number of full-time and special constables were employed. In 1858, the government of Upper Canada enacted the Municipal Institutions of Upper Canada Act, enabling communities to form police forces and institute boards of commissioners to oversee the governance of these newly formed police agencies. One of the first organized police forces was created by an order in council in 1864 for the Upper Canada county of Essex. The goal of this service was to serve as a frontier police force, a trend that was to be repeated in numerous regions throughout Canada.

While the Constitution Act of 1867 delegated to the provinces the responsibility for enforcing the criminal law and authority to make laws in relation to the administration of justice, it also ensured that upon entry into confederation the provinces would create provincial police services. The creation of provincial police services began with Manitoba and Quebec in 1870; they were followed by British Columbia (1871), Ontario (1909), New Brunswick (1927), Nova Scotia (1928), Prince Edward Island (1930), and Newfoundland (1935). The provinces of Alberta and Saskatchewan broke from this trend by contracting with the federal government to police their regions using the Royal North West Mounted Police (RNWMP). This negotiated agreement was in effect until 1916, at which time both Alberta and Saskatchewan withdrew from the federal/provincial agreement in order to create their own provincial police forces.

While a number of these provincial forces would evolve into viable and current police organizations, others would eventually be disbanded. For reasons including fiscal concerns, lack of qualified personnel, and inappropriate facilities, many provincial police services could no longer offer the required levels of policing. The first service to disband was the Saskatchewan Provincial Police (SPP) in 1928; the services of Alberta, New Brunswick, Nova Scotia, and Prince Edward Island would follow in 1932 and British Columbia's in 1950. The policing void left by their dissolution would be filled by the Royal Canadian Mounted Police (RCMP). Currently, there are three remaining provincial police services: the Ontario Provincial

Police, the Sûreté du Quebec, and the Royal Newfoundland Constabulary.

As various forms of municipal and provincial policing were taking shape, so too was federal policing developing in its unique way. The concept of a federal police service had evolved, in part, from the Canadian government's need to assert its sovereignty in the face of American frontier expansion. In 1873, by way of an act of Parliament, the North West Mounted Police (NWMP) was founded and modeled after the Royal Irish Constabulary. In its early incarnation, the NWMP was tasked with the imposition of civil law in Canada's western territories. It was a role that would contrast with the violent and anarchistic nature of the American frontier. The NWMP presence in the western territories ensured the orderly settlement of the region and guarded against the American annexation of the Canadian west.

In 1904 the North West Mounted Police (NWMP) would undergo a name change and become the Royal North West Mounted Police (RNWMP). In parallel to the evolution of the RNWMP, another federal police service was created by the enactment of the Police of Canada Act of 1868. This newly formed Dominion Police Force was responsible for protecting the parliament buildings and enforcing a range of federal and criminal laws. The force's region of operation was predominantly within the Atlantic provinces and Ontario. These two federal police services would exist separately until 1920, when the Royal North West Mounted Police Amendment Act would create the Royal Canadian Mounted Police (RCMP) by amalgamating the RNWMP and the Dominion Police Force.

Equal Protection, Accountability, and Reform Mechanisms

The above historical review indicates that over the past two centuries Canadian policing has been shaped by both regional and political factors. Yet a more detailed historical analysis offers us the opportunity to examine how Canadian police services can stray from their legal and political function, how these actions undermine Canadian citizens' trust in the justice system, and how these concerns are also remedied. While officer misconduct and disreputable actions have profound implications for police credibility, it is perhaps the process by which such officers are held accountable that is most interesting for this analysis. It is these mechanisms of accountability that both assist in recapturing a community's faith in their police service and bring about procedural and operational change.

One prominent mechanism for change and redress has been the use of commissions of inquiry. Depending upon the severity of police misconduct and the need for public accountability, various levels of government have through orders in council mandated commissions of inquiry to investigate the conduct of police services and individuals and to make recommendations for change intended to prevent further miscarriages of justice. Notable examples of these commissions are the following:

- McDonald Commission (Royal Commission of Inquiry into Certain Activities of the RCMP, 1977)
- Keable Report (Quebec, 1981)
- Royal Commission on the Donald Marshall Jr. Prosecution (Nova Scotia, 1989),
- Ontario Race Relations and Policing Task Force (1992)
- Report of the Saskatchewan Indian Justice Review Committee (1992)
- Policing in British Columbia Commission of Inquiry (1994)
- Commission on Proceedings Involving Guy Paul Morin (Ontario, 1998)

Commissions of inquiry traditionally focus their attention upon the "behaviour of an organization, taken as a whole" (Brodeur & Viau, 1994, p. 246), and thus the resulting recommendations are tailored to address problematic organizational practices. This is not to suggest that the activities of individual or groups of officers are not scrutinized, but they are critiqued in terms of how organizational culture, structure, and practices may support disreputable conduct, etc. One might argue that at this level of inquiry proceedings are guided by the questions: What proportion of an organization facilitates or supports elements of wrongdoing, and how might these organizational/operational characteristics be remedied? Commissions of inquiry have throughout Canadian history been valued mechanisms of accountability and procedural change. And yet they are but one mechanism for accountability and change.

The Charter of Rights and Freedoms (1982), as many would argue, has had the most profound influence upon police powers and practices. Sections 7 through 14 of the charter set out the guiding principles whereby police activity and authority are framed and ultimately governed. Section 7 articulates the broad provisions of legal rights by stating, "Everyone has the right to life liberty and security of the person and the right not to be deprived thereof except in accordance with the principles of fundamental justice." More directly, sections 8 to 10 reference the principles of fundamental justice applied in the context of police powers:

- Everyone has the right to be secure against unreasonable search or seizure (§ 8)
- Everyone has the right not to be arbitrarily detained or imprisoned (§ 9)
- Everyone has certain rights on arrest or detention including the right to retain and instruct counsel without delay (§ 10)

Furthermore, under section 24 anyone whose rights and freedoms have been infringed upon or denied may apply for a remedy to a court of competent jurisdiction. It is in the context of these remedies, more specifically Supreme Court decisions, that police powers and practices have been challenged and reformed.

The following are selected examples of Supreme Court of Canada decisions corresponding to challenges under sections 8, 9, and 10 of the charter. What is most important about these examples is the manner in which they have set clear parameters for future police actions and distinct boundaries of police powers.

Court Decisions Affecting Police

In *Hunter* (1984), the Supreme Court decided that section 8 required that unjustified searches be prevented. The court asserted three constitutional standards. It first established basic requirements for a search warrant and then declared charter standards for such warrants:

1. Where feasible, prior authorization is a precondition for a valid search and seizure.
2. The person authorizing the breach of privacy must assess the need for the breach in an entirely neutral and impartial manner.
3. There have to be reasonable and probable grounds, established upon oath, to believe that an offence has been committed or that evidence will be found at the place of the search.

In *Collins* (1987), the Supreme Court outlined the following dictum:

A search will be reasonable if it is authorized by law, if the law itself is reasonable and if the manner in which the search was carried out is reasonable.

In *Simpson* (1993), the Ontario Court of Appeals held "that, where an individual is detained by the police in the course of efforts to determine whether that individual is involved in criminal activity, detention can be justified under common law ancillary powers doctrine if the detaining officer has some articulable cause for detention" (Stuart, 1996, p. 246). In this case, "articulable cause" was clearly contrasted to the broad understanding of a "hunch," which is based on intuition and subjective assessments.

With respect to the right to retain and instruct counsel, in *Bartle* (1994), the Supreme Court held that

the purpose of the right to counsel guaranteed by section 10 (b) of the Charter is to provide detainees with an opportunity to be informed of their rights and obligations under the law and, most importantly, to attain advice on how to exercise those rights and fulfill those obligations. This opportunity is made available because, when an individual is detained by state authorities, he or she is put in a position of disadvantage relative to the state. Not only has this person suffered of a deprivation of liberty, but also this person may be at risk of incriminating him or herself . . . Under section 10 (b), the detainee is entitled as a right to seek such legal advice without delay and upon request.

Here, the court sought to ensure that detained individuals were not merely read a statement but had to be afforded the opportunity to retain and instruct counsel without delay. This placed an onus on police officers to not treat the process as merely a programmatic statement without any requirement to implement.

While these are specific examples, they do emphasize the direction and role of the courts. Moreover, they are a representation of how police services have been held accountable for actions and policy as they pertain to the preservation of rights and freedoms. As these cases suggest, the Charter of Rights and Freedoms has and will continue to guide Canadian policing, but more important, the Charter will continue to offer a remedy for miscarriages of justice attributed to police activity. The ongoing importance of this redress mechanism cannot be underscored enough, particularly within the current context of antiterrorism initiatives and legislative guidance set out by the federal government's Bill C-36 (the Anti-Terrorism Act). Bill C-36 gives new investigative tools to law enforcement agencies to ensure "that the prosecution of terrorist offences can be undertaken efficiently and effectively" (Department of Justice, 2001, p. 3). Some of the measures referred to here are powers that make it easier to utilize electronic surveillance against terrorist organizations. A more contentious component is the creation of the "preventive arrest" power that will allow a "peace officer to arrest and bring a person before a judge to impose reasonable supervisory conditions if there are reasonable grounds to suspect that the person is about to commit a terrorism activity" (Department of Justice, 2001, p. 3). The premise supporting these and other powers is the need to protect Canadian citizens with respect to the new reality of risk, and yet, there remains the need to be vigilant in terms of potential abuses. As the current realm of antiterrorism activity is uncharted, it will be necessary for Canadian policing to be held accountable to the principles of justice, and therefore the role of the courts will continue to shape the future of policing.

Further Layers of Accountability and Governance

As indicated previously the constitutional responsibility for policing is shared between the federal and provincial/territorial governments. The Constitution Act of 1867 confers authority on the federal government to legislate in relation to criminal law and procedure as well as the power to legislate in respect to peace, order, and good government. The act empowers the provincial governments to make laws in relation to the administration of justice, of which policing is one facet (Ministry of Human Resources Development, 2000). The result of this is that police services are accountable to a range of governing bodies inclusive of local and regional oversight bodies, provincial authorities, and with respect to the RCMP, the federal solicitor general. In most instances the responsibility for policing falls to the attorney general or solicitor general in each province. The exceptions to this are Quebec, where this responsibility is held by the director of public security, and Ontario, where this responsibility is in fact shared between the attorney general and the solicitor general. The governance of municipal police services is generally set out by provincial legislation, which outlines the requirements of local authorities, such as municipal councils and municipal boards of commissioners as well as provincial police commissions.

Municipal oversight plays a critical role in the assurance of police accountability. These oversight bodies undertake the task of ensuring fiscal and legal accountability as well as providing policy direction. Municipal oversight bodies also have the important task of representing citizen concerns and priorities in relation to pertinent public security issues. There are two models of municipal oversight used in Canada. Within the provinces of Quebec and Manitoba, the responsibility for police oversight is assumed by the municipal council. With respect to the remaining provinces, police oversight is the responsibility of either a police board or commission. These particular oversight bodies are made up of civilians appointed either by the province or by the municipal council. In most instances there is representation from the municipal council. In 1989, the Canadian Association of Police Boards was founded with the goal of providing support and direction to municipal boards and communities in order to ensure they achieve effective representation for their police oversight bodies. There are also provincial associations mandated with similar support functions.

While municipal oversight bodies are a key component in the governance of policing, it is also important to ensure that a healthy regulatory environment is maintained. In order to accomplish this task, provincial and federal governments have established legislation and policy that regulate standards and policing authority. Most provinces have set (or are in the process of defining) formal police standards throughout their jurisdiction. The common objectives are as follows (Ministry of Human Resources Development, 2000):

- Promote consistent service delivery.
- Establish clear expectations for procedures and operations.
- Guide human resource practices and ensure particular standards of administration.

A specific example of these standards can be found in Ontario's Police Services Act Regulation 3/99, "Adequacy and Effectiveness of Police Services." The objective of these adequacy standards is to articulate and ensure the delivery of the six core policing functions prescribed by the Police Services Act. Moreover, these core functions are understood as the foundation of adequate and effective police services. The six core functions are crime prevention, law enforcement, victims' assistance, public order maintenance, emergency response services, and administration and infrastructure. To ensure police services could achieve these core functions, the Ontario Policing Standards Manual was revamped to contain guidelines and sample board policies designed to assist police services in understanding and implementing the Police Services Act and its regulations, including the *Adequacy Standards Regulation*. The Manual, to-date, has included 70 separate guidelines, establishing a framework to provide consistent police service delivery in the province of Ontario. All police services were to be compliant with the *Adequacy Standards Regulation* by January 1, 2001. (Blandford, 2003, p. 1)

The assurance of governance and accountability is aided by the establishment of provincial police commissions. To assist these agencies in holding police services accountable, most commissions have the authority to conduct inquiries into police activity and practices. This authority of inquiry can include the review of municipal police boards and internal police discipline decisions. A complementary layer of accountability is achieved through the establishment of formal complaint bodies such as public complaint boards, law enforcement review boards, etc. The task of these oversight bodies is to field and investigate civilian complaints about individual officers or police services. In many jurisdictions the concept of a civilian oversight and complaints process has been viewed with some disdain by police services. And yet, the option of allowing only the police to investigate themselves is considered problematic by many citizens. In response to these concerns and the perceived bias of internal police oversight, there are provisions for investigation and review established by provincial police acts and, in the case of the RCMP, under the RCMP Act.

Essential to the success of these oversight mechanisms is the requirement of civilian review and the assurance that the process is open and transparent. For example, in Manitoba all complaints against police are investigated by the Law Enforcement Review Agency. In British Columbia, public complaints proceedings are chaired by an independent commissioner, and in Ontario the special investigations unit, "which operates under the jurisdiction of the Attorney General, investigates all cases involving serious injury or death" (Griffiths, Whitelaw, & Parent, 1999, p. 438). The following are further examples of provincial police conduct review agencies:

- Ontario Civilian Commission on Police Services
- Alberta Law Enforcement Review Board
- Quebec Police Ethics Commissioner
- British Columbia Office of the Complaints Commissioner
- Commission for Public Complaints Against the RCMP

While these various agencies have been tasked with oversight authority, they have tended to respond to a traditional understanding of police core functions. In a post–September 11 environment, there is little argument that these functions are changing. This is particularly true with respect to the RCMP and its renewed national security responsibilities. The concern over whether or not appropriate oversight exists was thrust to the foreground with a complaint filed on October 23, 2003, by the Chair of the Commission for Public Complaints Against the RCMP, Ms. Shirley Heafey, This complaint centered upon RCMP conduct in relation to the deportation and detention of Mr. Maher Arar. The thrust of this complaint

> requires the RCMP to report on whether members of the RCMP improperly encouraged U.S. authorities to deport a Canadian citizen, Mr. Maher Arar, from U.S. territory to Syria. Similarly, it requires the RCMP to report on the allegation that members of the RCMP failed to discourage U.S. authorities from deporting a Canadian citizen, Mr. Maher Arar, from U.S. territory to Syria. The RCMP must also report on whether members of the RCMP improperly divulged information and/or conveyed inaccurate or incomplete information about Mr. Maher Arar to U.S. and/or Syrian authorities. Finally, the RCMP must report on allegations that members of the RCMP improperly impeded the efforts of the Canadian government and others to secure the release of Mr. Maher Arar. (Commission for Public Complaints Against the RCMP, 2003)

Under the new antiterrorism legislation (Bill C-36), the RCMP has been granted new powers that will enable it to combat terrorism. And yet, an underlying concern of the commission chair is that the "new security legislation did not provide the Commission for Public Complaints Against the RCMP with similar new oversight powers to review the RCMP's antiterrorism activities" (Commission for Public Complaints Against the RCMP, 2004). The tone of recent commission statements suggests a profound concern for the lack of effective civilian oversight with respect to the national security activities being performed by the RCMP (Commission for Public Complaints Against the RCMP, 2004).

In summary, Canadian police services are held accountable through a range of mechanisms. These fall into five categories (Law Commission of Canada, 2006, p. 88):

1. Political accountability to governing authorities and beyond, through normal political processes

2. Legal accountability or accountability to the law through the courts and judiciary

3. Accountability to administrative agencies such as complaints commissions, human rights commissions and tribunals, government departments, provincial police commissions, treasury boards, auditors general, or ombudsmen

4. Direct public accountability through such mechanisms as freedom of information legislation

5. Special ad hoc accountability mechanisms such as royal commissions and other public inquiries

Racial and Ethnic Context

Philip Stenning (2003) aptly captures the challenges of policing Canada's increasingly culturally, racially, and ethnically diverse society by suggesting it is a task of policing a cultural kaleidoscope. Over the past four decades the cultural and racial composition of Canada has undergone dramatic shifts. In 1961, 97 percent of the Canadian population were identified as being of European extraction, with the largest percentage having British ancestry. Between 1961 and 2001, 5.5 million immigrants entered Canada. The greatest number of these arrived from Asia, with Europe as the second prominent geographic region of origin. The 2001 national census indicates that visible minorities represent 13.4 percent of the Canadian population; this represents an increase of 24.6 percent since the 1996 census. Not included in the above percentages are aboriginal peoples, who make up 3.3 percent of the Canadian population. The growing trend of immigration will continue to shape the cultural landscape, as it is estimated that in order to meet projected labor market needs Canada must accept a minimum of 250,000 immigrants per year.

The importance of diversity and support of a multicultural society was given legislative direction when the Canadian Parliament enacted the Canadian Multiculturalism Act of 1988. The thrust of this act was to proclaim that the policy of the Canadian government was to ensure "that all individuals receive equal treatment and equal protection under law, while respecting and valuing their diversity" (paragraph 3.1.e); moreover; it would ensure that all federal government institutions would operate in a manner consistent with these objectives. Thus the RCMP and other federal law enforcement agencies must operate in accordance to these objectives. Legislative support for a multicultural society is further supported by section 15 of the Charter of Rights and Freedoms, which includes the following: "Every individual is equal before and under the law and has the right to equal protection and equal benefit of the law without discrimination based on race, national or ethnic origin, colour, religion, sex, age or mental or physical disability."

Although these legislative guidelines are in place, this does not necessarily suggest that the adoption of these principles has been an easy process for Canadian policing. One hurdle that police services have needed to confront is that of equal representation within police services. In a report entitled *Strategic Human Resources Analysis of Public Policing in Canada* (Ministry of Human Resources Development, 2000), 1996 statistics highlight the status in the labor force of various designated groups, comparing minority representation in policing to that in other sectors. For example, aboriginals make up 3.1 percent of all police officers, and other visible minorities represent 2.9 percent. This is compared to all Canadian industries, which aboriginals make up 1.7 percent of the labor force and visible minorities make up 9.9 percent of it. As one can tell by these statistics, police services do not accurately reflect the multicultural makeup of Canadian society.

Yet, this does not suggest that police services have not actively engaged in attempts to recruit members of visible minorities. In fact, as Stenning (2003) notes,

> Despite genuine and often quite vigorous attempts by many police leaders to change the faces of their organizations to better reflect the cultural makeup of the communities they policed, and despite some formal statutory employment equity requirements introduced in the 1990s, the ethnic and cultural composition of police services in Canada has remained stubbornly out of alignment with that of many of the communities they police. (p. 19)

The policing needs of Canada's multicultural communities cannot be dealt with by simply attempting to meet employment equity criteria. In fact, police services have required wholesale reviews of their internal cultures in an effort to encourage an understanding between police officers and members of the diverse cultural communities they interact with. The premise for this assertion is influenced by the belief that if police services are to effectively offer equitable service to ever-changing communities, then officers must both understand and recognize the diverse values, beliefs, and customs of those communities. In an effort to address existing shortcomings of cross-cultural understanding, police services and training academies have been tasked with the development and delivery of cultural diversity programs. And while this level of program development had received legislative support, there has been little ongoing research into the effectiveness of these programs in altering the attitudes and practices of police officers.

Unfortunately, recent cases of police officer misconduct, such as the September 1995 shooting of aboriginal protestor Dudley George by the Ontario Provincial Police and the 2002 conviction of two Saskatoon Police officers for apprehending and abandoning an aboriginal male in subzero temperatures, have undermined the various police services' relationships with aboriginal communities.[1] More important, these incidents have refocused the debate on whether or not existing cultural programming is indeed effective. And while these events have brought increased attention to the need for greater cultural sensitivity, they do not represent any systemic rot within policing (Barry Leighton, cited in Quigley, 2004). Moreover, a British Columbia provincial poll undertaken in the fall of 2003 and cited in the same article indicates that "89 percent of respondents" agreed that the police were doing a good job (Quigley, 2004).

Other efforts to bridge cultural divides have manifested themselves in the efforts of police service liaison committees. Stenning (2003) suggests that while these committees had proven successful in facilitating dialogue between community and police, they were fraught with problems. These concerns have evolved from legitimate queries as to whether or not the liaison committees were truly representative of the community to whether or not they were effective forums for community consultation. RCMP findings suggest that the failure of these committees was due to "lack of genuine consultation, lack of response by police and dissipating interest" (Topp, 2003). In review of both legislative and operational initiatives, one can readily argue that efforts have been undertaken with the purpose of addressing the ever-shifting cultural mosaic of Canada. And yet, from a policing perspective little has been done to capture the effectiveness of these initiatives or examine best practices. As several scholars have suggested, if we are to ensure that policing effectively protects and embraces the principles of diversity, we must at some level engage in proactive analysis of police initiatives (Jain, 1995; Stenning, 2003; Topp, 2003). We cannot merely wait for incidents of conflict and misconduct to be the gauge of success or failure.

Organizational Structure and Issues

Like many postmodern organizations, Canadian police forces are adapting to an increasingly multicultural society, economic constraints, changing international/domestic crime patterns, and shifting governance paradigms. Response to this changing environment is made more difficult by the fact that Canadian policing is carried out at three levels (municipal, provincial, and federal). In this context consistent and coordinated adaptation is further complicated by the existence of differing provincial and federal police acts, criss-crossing jurisdictional boundaries, and a history of disparate national and provincial standards. From a statistical point of reference, contemporary Canadian police forces consist of 62,458 police officers (Canadian Centre for Justice Statistics, 2007) providing for a national citizen per officer ratio of 520/1, an annual expenditure on policing of $8.8 billion (Canadian Centre for Justice Statistics, 2007), 579 municipal police services, 3 provincial police services, and one federal police agency. (All dollar amounts in this chapter are in Canadian dollars.)

And yet, to understand Canadian policing one must move beyond the thumbnail sketch that these broad statistical snapshots offer. A more thorough statistical analysis indicates the existence of disparate levels of policing from province to province. Some of these differences are aptly noted in a comparison of provincial population per police ratios. In 2002 the range varied from 237.5/1 in the Yukon Territory to 682.4/1 in the province of Newfoundland and Labrador, with Canada's most populous provinces of Ontario (533.4/1) and Quebec (516.7/1) representing the mean. These differences are further articulated when one examines the differential in per capita spending on municipal and provincial policing by province. Once more the range varied from $97 per capita in Prince Edward Island to $179 in the province of Quebec, with the province of Alberta representing the median of $132 (Canadian Centre for Justice Statistics, 2007).

A further understanding of Canada's policing arena can be accomplished by examining the different jurisdictional responsibilities, mandates, and organizational structures inherent to municipal, provincial, contract, and federal policing.

Municipal Policing

Communities with a population of 10,000 or more are required under legislation to have a police service operated by the municipality or under contract to either the RCMP or a provincial police service. There are no requirements placed upon municipalities under this population threshold. Conversely, there are no restrictions preventing these smaller communities from developing their own police service. Municipalities in all regions have the option of providing their own service as long as they meet relevant legislative guidelines and standards. This legislated framework and a community's desire for public safety and law enforcement has created a national patchwork of police services ranging in size from one or two officers to those with over 7,000 officers (e.g., in Toronto and Montreal).

With respect to enforcement responsibilities, municipal officers are tasked with the enforcement of municipal and provincial statutes, the criminal code, and specific federal statutes, e.g. the Controlled Drugs and Substances Act. The authority of municipal police officers is limited by the jurisdictional boundary of the municipality they are employed by. (There are exceptions to this restriction when, for example, RCMP or Ontario Provincial Police officers are policing communities under contract. This exception is due to the broader enforcement mandates and authority these officers are granted via provincial and federal legislation.)

Municipal policing is an integral component of Canadian policing, and any change in the structure or practices of municipal policing has a direct impact on the nature of Canadian policing. For example, recent provincial requirements for increased regionalization of municipalities and the resulting amalgamation of existing police services has had a direct impact on the governance, size, and enforcement tasks of municipal police services. Furthermore, these initiatives reflect an increased desire by provincial governments to assert greater control and impose particular legislative guidelines upon police services.

Contract Policing

Contract policing is an interesting feature of Canadian policing, a practice that traces its history to frontier policing undertaken by the NWMP. Today it accurately refers to cost-sharing agreements that exist between large police services and provinces or municipalities to undertake policing operations. In Canada there are two police services that are characteristically associated with contract policing, the Ontario Provincial Police (OPP) and the RCMP. The OPP is limited to the provincial jurisdictional boundary of Ontario, and as they are in fact Ontario's provincial police service, the extent of contract policing is limited to municipalities that, for a range of reasons, have not developed their own municipal service. The RCMP on the other hand is involved in contract policing nationwide and undertakes provincial and municipal policing in all but two Canadian provinces (Ontario and Quebec). The RCMP commits 57 percent of its budget and 47 percent of its members to contract policing. Current contract agreements are governed by a cost-sharing formula wherein the province pays 70 percent and the RCMP (federal government) covers the remaining 30 percent. This contract formula changes when the RCMP polices municipalities with a population greater than 15,000; here the municipality is responsible for 90 percent of the cost and the RCMP the remaining 10 percent. These agreements incorporate a review mechanism whereby the cost-sharing formula can be renegotiated every five years. (As of the winter of 2007, the RCMP and provincial governments have begun preliminary negotiations regarding the upcoming 2012 contracts.)

Provincial Policing

The Constitution Act of 1867 granted the provincial and territorial governments responsibility for the administration of justice and with it the responsibility for overseeing the operation and development of policing within their jurisdictional boundaries. Provincial police services are charged with enforcing the criminal code and provincial statutes in areas not policed by municipal police services, usually rural areas and small communities. These police services are traditionally under the purview of the provincial attorney general or solicitor general. As noted previously there are three independent provincial police services in Canada: the OPP, the Sûreté du Quebec (SQ), and the Royal Newfoundland Constabulary (NRC). The NRC is unique in that it does not police rural areas of the province but is limited to the municipalities of Corner Brook, Churchill Falls, Labrador City, and St. John's. (The RCMP polices the remaining sections of the province.) While both the OPP and NRC police municipalities, there is no provision under Quebec law for the Sûreté du Quebec to provide municipal policing.

Aboriginal Policing

In 1991 the federal government introduced the First Nations Policing Policy, which set out the foundation for future developments in aboriginal policing. At the core of this initiative was the need to negotiate the development of cost-sharing agreements between the First Nations communities, provincial governments, and the federal government. But more important, this policy enabled First Nations communities to articulate the type of policing best suited for the needs of their reserve communities. Within the context of this policy, communities could continue to utilize the services of the RCMP or OPP under the realm of contract policing, or they could develop their own autonomous police services. Examples of these autonomous police services are the Six Nations Tribal Police in Ontario, the Amerindian Police in Quebec, and the Blood Tribal Police in Alberta. The number of First Nations communities that are adopting autonomous police services continues to increase, as communities are now embracing the need for self-governance and the desire to articulate policing appropriate for their community. In the past many aboriginal police services were subject to the authority of a senior police service, such as the RCMP, OPP, or Sûreté du Quebec, and were limited to by-law or band law enforcement. Currently, aboriginal police officers generally have full powers of arrest and enforce the criminal code, federal and provincial statutes, and band by-laws within the jurisdiction of reserve lands.

Federal Policing

The concept of federal policing more accurately refers to the broad tasks that the RCMP undertakes as a branch of the federal solicitor general's office. Unlike other police officers, RCMP officers have jurisdiction in all provinces and territories; they enforce federal statutes in all regions, police federal property as required, and have the powers of both peace officers and customs and excise officers. And while the RCMP has national jurisdiction, it does not enforce provincial or municipal statutes in the provinces of Ontario and Quebec.

The RCMP is tasked with a range of policing responsibilities that include the operation of a number of specialized directorates serving the needs of police services nationally. For example: The RCMP's L Directorate operates crime detection labs across the country, offering identification services such as DNA analysis, fingerprinting, criminal history files, etc. Its V Directorate operates the Canadian Police Information Centre (CPIC), the computerized information system that provides police services with instant criminal records, vehicle information, stolen property data, missing persons information, etc. The P Directorate serves as the international liaison with Interpol and foreign services. The RCMP is also the lead organization in the national partnership with the Canadian Association of Chiefs of Police and the National Research Council in the development of the Canadian Police Research Centre. This centre is responsible for the development and evaluation of high-technology products for police services. This array of common services provides continuity throughout Canada's law enforcement community.

Training and Education

Training and education is regulated by a combination of federal and provincial legislation. These regulations, acts, and by-laws set out the provisions for police training facilities, funding, and basic training requirements and

relating to money laundering, counterfeit currency, payment cards, and intellectual property. The sub-directorate seeks to provide National Central Bureaus with expertise in specialized areas and enhance partnerships with relevant organizations, develop and coordinate best practices, and increase the flow and exchange of information related to these forms of crime (retrieved May 5, 2004, from http://www.interpol.int/Public/FinancialCrime/Money Laundering/default.asp).

Counterfeiting

The internationally waged battle against counterfeiting is led by the Counterfeit and Security Documents Branch (CSDB) of Interpol's General Secretariat. This body has fostered relationships with such entities as the U.S. Secret Service (USSS) and Europol as well as the European Anti-Fraud Office (OLAF), the European Central Bank (ECB), the Central Bank Counterfeit Deterrence Group (CBCDG), leading law enforcement and banking agencies, and innovative leaders in private industry. Interpol activities in this field encompass, among others things, exchange of information using the I-24/7 global police communication system, training classes, dedicated publications (for example, a regularly updated *List of Currencies* of all 186 member countries), working group meetings, and global and regional conferences (for instance, an International Conference on Protection of the Euro against Counterfeiting, which Interpol organized in cooperation with Europol and the European Central Bank; Interpol, 2007a, 2007b).

Payment Cards

Interpol assumed responsibility for counterfeit currency as a result of an international treaty, the 1929 International Convention for the Suppression of Counterfeiting Currency (known as the 1929 Geneva Convention), but there are no similar arrangements for counterfeit payment cards, and it is unlikely that there will be such arrangements in the near future. Payment cards are increasingly being used as a substitute for cash. With the growth of debit card activity and the emergence of electronic applications, the trend is likely to increase rather than diminish. Although it is difficult to be specific about the quantity of counterfeit currency in circulation, which varies considerably from country to country, its monetary value is thought to be far less than the millions of dollars in losses a year as a result of payment card counterfeiting (retrieved May 5, 2004, from http://www.interpol.int/Public/CreditCards/Default.asp).

In the year 2000, Interpol created a central database to allow for the classification of altered or counterfeit cards submitted by certified law enforcement and industry experts through forensic analysis. The database is currently accessible to member countries and has proved to be a useful tool for the law enforcement community (retrieved May 9, 2007, from http://www.interpol.int/Public/CreditCards/Default.asp).

Money Laundering

The international police community is aware that there is a need to achieve major results in the struggle against the financial criminal activities related to organized criminal groups. During the past 20 years, Interpol's General Assembly has passed a number of resolutions that have called on member countries to concentrate their investigative resources on identifying, tracing, and seizing the assets of criminal enterprises.

These resolutions have also called on member countries to increase the exchange of information in this field and have encouraged governments to adopt laws and regulations that would allow police access to the financial records of criminal organizations and would also allow the confiscation of proceeds gained by criminal activity. A concise working definition of money laundering was adopted by Interpol's General Assembly in 1995: It is defined as any act or attempted act to conceal or disguise the identity of illegally obtained proceeds so that they appear to have originated from legitimate sources.

Another important innovation in combating money laundering is the IMOLIN (International Money Laundering Information). This is an Internet-based information network that serves as a clearinghouse for money-laundering information for the benefit of all national and international anti–money laundering agencies. The IMOLIN database is administered by the Global Program against Money Laundering of the United Nations Office on Drugs and Crime for the United Nations and other international organizations, including Interpol (retrieved May 9, 2007, from http://www.interpol.int./Public/FinancialCrime/MoneyLaundering/default.asp).

Intellectual Property Crime

This particular area of crime covers an array of offenses from trademark and patent right infringements to software piracy, and it affects a vast range of products— from medicines to aircraft and vehicle spare parts, from clothing to music CDs and computer software. The total losses caused by this form of crime add up to hundred of billions of U.S. dollars globally every year. Interpol has recognized the extensive involvement of organized crime and terrorist groups in intellectual property crime. In 2000, the Interpol General Assembly mandated the Interpol General Secretariat to take action not only to raise awareness of the problem but also to provide a strategic plan in close cooperation with private industry (retrieved May 5, 2004, from http://www.interpol.int/Public/FinancialCrime/Intellectual Property/Default.asp).

Interpol's first international conference on intellectual property crime (Lyon, France, November 15–16, 2001) led to the establishment of a Group of Experts on Intellectual Property Crime, bringing together representatives of all the key stakeholders, including customs authorities, international agencies, and the private sector. The Group of Experts functions as a forum for the exchange of information and facilitates investigations into intellectual property offenses. It will also offer support through tailored training programs. This is a multiagency group, drawing its membership from public and private sectors (retrieved August 21, 2007, from http://www.interpol.int/Public/FinancialCrime/IntellectualProperty/Default.asp). The first meeting of the Group of Experts took place on July 23, 2002, and the group adopted the name *Interpol Intellectual Property Crime Action Group* (IIPCAG) (retrieved May 9, 2007, from http://www.interpol.int./Public/FinancialCrime/IntellectualProperty).

Corruption

Interpol's International Group of Experts on Corruption (IGEC) was established in 1998. Its membership consists of law enforcement representatives from eight countries (including the United States), a representative of Interpol's General Secretariat, and seven other persons representing a variety of international organizations, the international financial services community, and academia. This group was mandated to develop and implement an anticorruption strategy with the objectives of not only raising awareness of the major issues but also, and in particular, improving the capacity and effectiveness of law enforcement in the fight against corruption (retrieved May 5, 2004, from http://www.interpol.int/Public/Corruption/IGEC/Default.asp).

Among its activities, the IGEC prepared a code of ethics and a code of conduct (subsequently adopted by Interpol's General Assembly in 1999), a survey of police integrity in its 186 member countries, and global standards to combat corruption in police forces and services (adopted by Interpol's General Assembly in 2002). These global standards consist of several principles and numerous measures designed to improve the integrity of police forces and services, to improve their efficacy in combating corruption, and to represent an ideal toward which the Interpol member countries should strive. These standards have been well received by the international law enforcement community and mark the beginning of a proactive approach for law enforcement in combating corruption (retrieved May 5, 2004, from http://www.interpol.int/Public/Corruption/IGEC/Default.asp).

Among the many initiatives of the IGEC, the most important seem to be the following two: the Global Standards to Combat Corruption in Police Forces/Services, institutionalized by the Interpol General Assembly held in Cameroon in October 2002; and the Library of Best Practice, published in

2003, which is designed to aid individuals investigating corruption cases (retrieved May 9, 2007, from http://www.interpol.int./Public/Corruption/IGEC/Default.asp).

Publications

Interpol's primary publications include the *International Criminal Police Review* and *International Crime Statistics*. The *International Criminal Police Review*, which was published between 1946 and 2001, is not currently in production as Interpol reassesses the publication's role. Interpol has published *International Crime Statistics* every two years since 1950 and every year since 1993. Since 2000, the publication has been available electronically on a country-by-country basis.

The data are provided by the National Central Bureaus, and Interpol publishes them as submitted, without any attempt to process them. Due primarily to the legal and procedural differences in the different countries and the differences in statistical methods, the statistics cannot be used for comparative purposes. Police statistics reflect only reported crimes, which represent only a fraction of the real level of crime. Furthermore, the volume of crime reported to the police depends, to a certain extent, on the action of police and can vary with time, as well as from country to country. Consequently, the data (available to authorized users only) published in the current set of statistics should be interpreted with caution (retrieved September 27, 2004, from http://www.interpol.int/Public/Statistics/ICS/default.asp).

In addition, a sample of very valuable Interpol publications include the following titles:

Interpol: An Overview	*Crime Against Children*
Notices	*Interpol and Drug Trafficking*
Connecting Police	*DNA Gateway*
Databases	*Disaster Victim*
Terrorism	*Identification*
Bioterrorism	*Intellectual Property Crime*
People Smuggling	*Money Laundering*
Trafficking In Human Beings	*Project Geiger*

All of the above fact sheets (available on the Internet in portable document format [pdf]) are published in four languages: Arabic, English, French, and Spanish, which are Interpol's official languages. Interpol's *Annual Report* is also published in these languages; at the time this book was published; the most recent report had been issued in May 2007 and covered the year 2005. Interpol also issues the following guides and manuals:

Bio-terrorism Incident Pre-Planning Guide—2006

DNA Handbook

As well as the following posters:

Most Wanted Works of art

Most Wanted

And the following leaflets and brochures:

For a Safer World

Mind/Find

There is also a work on CD/DVD: *Stolen Works of Art.* All of these publications are available through Interpol's Web site (retrieved May 6, 2007, from http://www.interpol.int/Public/Icpo/Publications/default.asp).

Regional Activities

In 2001, the Interpol General Secretariat set up the Directorate for Regional and National Police Services. It is comprised of five sub-directorates: one each for Africa, the Americas, Asia and the South Pacific, Europe, and the Middle East and North Africa; there is also a subregional coordination bureau. The directorate design recognizes that practical law enforcement needs in each region vary to some extent. By promoting a network of regional institutions and developing effective strategic alliances with other institutions, Interpol seeks to provide better-tailored assistance through its National Central Bureaus (retrieved May 5, 2004, from http://www.interpol.int/Public/Region/Americas/Default.asp).

All Interpol National Central Bureaus in the Americas are connected to the I-24/7 communication system (retrieved May 9, 2007, from http://www .interpol.int.Public/Region/Americas/Default.asp).

Europol

The European Union was originally established largely to promote the economic integration of its member states. Economic integration, however, brought with it new opportunities for offenders, above all the ease with which they could transcend national borders. Because crime was being organized increasingly at a European level rather than on a national or local level, politicians agreed that an organization was needed that could coordinate the law enforcement resources of member states to effectively tackle crime on a pan-European level (a level that as of May 1, 2004, encompassed

25 countries).[1] As of August 2007, the number of member states had increased to 27. In 1992, the Maastricht Treaty established Europol's predecessor, the European Drugs Unit. It formally began operations on January 3, 1994. The European Drugs Unit had a rather limited mandate; it was focused on supporting each member state's fight against illicit drugs and the associated money laundering.

The Convention on the Establishment of a European Police Office (the Europol Convention) was adopted on July 26, 1995, and by 1998 had been ratified by all the member states. On July 1, 1999, Europol formally took over the work of the European Drugs Unit. It is based in The Hague, in the Netherlands. Its responsibilities have grown from drug policing to include areas of serious crime as diverse as terrorism, drug trafficking, human trafficking, illegal immigration, trafficking in radioactive and nuclear substances, trafficking in stolen motor vehicles, counterfeiting, and money laundering associated with international criminal activities (British Broadcasting Corporation, 2003; see also http://www.europol.eu.int/index .asp?page=facts&language=en, retrieved May 3, 2004).

Mission

As is the case with Interpol, Europol is (at least at present) not an operational entity, in that Europol staff members do not have police powers in the individual member states. Thus, they do not, for example, investigate offenses or question suspects. Instead, Europol seeks to support the law enforcement agencies of all its member states primarily by gathering and analyzing information and intelligence specifically about people who are members or possible members of international criminal organizations. This information is received from a variety of sources, such as national police forces as well as other international crime-fighting organizations (such as Interpol), and is entered into computers for processing and analysis. When Europol identifies information that requires action by national law enforcement agencies, such as connections identified between criminal offenses, it notifies the appropriate authorities without delay.

Europol is also charged with the task of developing expertise in certain fields of crime and making this expertise available to the member states when needed (retrieved May 3, 2004, from http://www.europol.eu.int/ index.asp?page=facts&language=en and from http://www.europol.eu.int/ index.asp?page=faq&language=en). Europol thus serves as a link between the law enforcement agencies of the member states of the European Union. On October 16, 1999, a unit called Eurojust, which may be said in broad terms to be parallel to Europol, was created to serve the same function among the prosecution authorities of the member states. To foster closer cooperation between Eurojust and Europol—necessary in particular because of the key role that prosecutors have in many member states in guiding the course of police investigations—Eurojust also has its headquarters in The Hague, in the Netherlands (Eurojust, n.d.).

Organizational Structure, Management, and Control

Europol is above all a body for the coordination of international law enforcement. The police officers working at Europol fall into two categories: regular staff members and liaison officers. The regular staff members (some 590 as of May 2007) take care of the joint activities, such as planning and analysis. The liaison officers (some 90 as of May 2007) represent a variety of national law enforcement agencies: the police, customs, gendarmerie, immigration services, and so on. Their function is largely to work together on individual cases that affect their national law enforcement interests. For example, if an analysis of data shows that a case may have connections with Germany and Spain, the German and Spanish liaison officers will meet to discuss how to deal with the case. They will then liaise with the competent national or local law enforcement authorities to ensure follow-through (retrieved May 10, 2007, from http://www.europol.europa.eu/index.asp?page=facts).

Europol is accountable to the European Union Council of Ministers for Justice and Home Affairs (retrieved May 3, 2004, from http://www.europol.eu.int/index.asp?page=mgmtcontrol&language=en). The council is responsible for the main control and guidance function of Europol. It appoints the director and deputy directors and adopts the budget. It also adopts regulations related to Europol's work. Each year, the council forwards a special report to the European Parliament on the work of Europol. The European Parliament is also consulted if the Europol Convention or other Europol regulations are amended.

Europol's management board is composed of one representative of each member state. Each member has one vote. Members of the European Commission (the executive branch of the EU government) are also invited to attend the meetings of the management board with nonvoting status.

The management board meets at least twice a year to discuss a wide range of Europol issues that relate to its current activities and its future developments. It adopts a general report on Europol's activities during the previous year, as well as a report on Europol's future activities, taking into account the operational requirements of member states as well as the budgetary and staffing implications for Europol. These reports are submitted to Europol's Council of Ministers of Justice and Home Affairs for approval (retrieved May 3, 2004, from http://www.europol.eu.int/index.asp?page=mgmtcontrol&language=en).

Europol is headed by a director appointed by the council acting unanimously, after obtaining the opinion of the management board, for a five-year period. The director's mandate may be renewed once for a further period of four years. The director is responsible for the day-to-day administration of Europol, the performance of its tasks, personnel management, and other tasks assigned to him or her by the Europol Convention or by the management board. The director is assisted by deputy directors, also appointed by the council for a four-year period, renewable once.

After the events of September 11, Europol was partially restructured. The three departments—Investigation Support, Intelligence Analysis, and Organized Crime—were combined into one single department called Serious Crime, thus combining information exchange, analysis, and expertise.

Cooperation With Third Countries and International Organizations

Europol has improved its international law enforcement cooperation by signing bilateral agreements with the following non-EU countries and international organizations: Iceland, Norway, the United States, the European Central Bank, the European Monitoring Centre on Drug and Drug Addiction, Interpol, and the World Customs Organization. In the sprit of cooperation, Europol has opened a liaison office in Washington D.C. (retrieved May 3, 2004, from http://www.europol.eu.int/index.asp?page=facts&language=en).

The Europol Computer System (TECS)

The Europol Convention calls on Europol to establish and maintain a computerized system to allow input of, access to, and analysis of data. The convention lays down a strict framework for human rights and data protection, control, supervision, and security. The Europol Computer System (TECS) has three principal components: an information system, an analysis system, and an index system (retrieved August 18, 2007, from http://www .europol.europe/eu/index.asp?page=facts).

Strict data protection legislation in many member states of the European Union prompted the Europol Convention to set up a special body to ensure compliance with such legislation: the Joint Supervisory Body. This body is composed of two representatives from each of the national supervisory bodies, each appointed for five years by each member state. Each delegation has one vote. Its task is to review the activities of Europol to ensure that the rights of the individual are not violated by the storage, processing, and use of the data held by Europol. It also monitors the permissibility of the transmission of data originating from Europol. Every European citizen has the right to request a review by the Joint Supervisory Body to ensure that the manner in which his or her personal data have been collected, stored, processed, and used by Europol is lawful and accurate (retrieved May 3, 2004, from http://www.europol.eu.int/index.asp?page=mgmtcontrol&language=en).

Financing

Europol is funded by contributions from the member states, calculated on the basis of their gross national products. The budget for 2007 was

€67.9 million ("Budget for Europol," 2006), which is approximately US $91.7 million. The annual accounts of Europol are subject to an audit, which is carried out by the Joint Audit Committee (retrieved August 18, 2007 from http://www.europol.europa.eu/index.asp?page=mgmtcontrol)

Activities

Europol is deeply involved in combating all kinds of major crimes taking place in the member states. The results of its activities are published in detail in the *Europol Annual Reports*. The following is a presentation of selected Europol activities based on its annual reports for 2001 and 2002 (retrieved August 20, 2007, from http://www.europol.eu.int/index .asp?page=publar2001 and from http://www.europol.eu.int/index.asp? page=publar2002).

Combating Terrorism

Following the events of September 11 and the subsequent decisions taken by the EU Council of Justice and Home Affairs Ministers on September 20, 2001, Europol together with the member states set up a Counter-Terrorism Task Force (CTTF) to implement a comprehensive set of measures. The CTTF consists of experts and liaison officers from the police forces and services of member states as well as their intelligence services in an unprecedented exercise of cooperation and collaboration.

In addition to creating the CTTF, Europol has provided several products and services related to counterterrorism. The exchange of counterterrorist information between member states by way of the Europol liaison officers and the network of national units has expanded. A special conference on terrorism was held in Madrid (January 29–February 2, 2002). Several directives were updated—for example, on the counterterrorism responsibilities at the national level within each member state, counterterrorism legislation in member states, and counterterrorism competencies/centers of excellence in the member states.

The *Open Source Digest* on terrorism-related activity is disseminated to the member states on a weekly basis. Also provided is the *Glossary of Terrorist Groups,* containing basic details about these groups' origins, ideologies, objectives, leadership, and activities.

Periodical trends and situation reports are provided on topics related to terrorism, based on open sources of information that are reported by member states to Europol. The first report, *EU Terrorism Situation and Trend Report TE-SAT 2007,* was presented at the European Parliament in Brussels by Europol director Max-Peter Ratzel (TE-SAT, 2007).

This document provided an analytic overview of the phenomenon of terrorism in the EU. The report for the first time collated detailed statistical data on terrorist attacks and plots in the eleven member states, covering all the 498 attacks in 2006. Among the several annexes, one describes implementations of the Framework Decision on Combating Terrorism in Member States, an agreement that provided Eurojust with information on court convictions of terrorists. *TE-SAT 2007,* being a public document, allows EU citizens to get acquainted with major Europol activities that normally are not publicized due to their confidentiality (retrieved May 10, 2007, from http://www.europol.europa.eu/index.asp?page=news&news=pr070410.htm).

Financial Crimes and Other Crimes Against Property and Public Goods, Including Fraud

In the area of financial and property crime, Europol's activities currently focus on providing strategic support while preparing for more operational activities in the immediate future. In the field of money laundering, Europol has begun to systematically collect information on suspicious transactions that have been identified by law enforcement and judicial authorities of the member states. Further strategic support includes the issuing of information bulletins on specific matters related to financial investigations and assistance in an initiative to create a *European Manual on Money Laundering.* An EU "situation report" is updated periodically in the area of combating credit card fraud. The result of this work is used to define a common EU strategy to fight this phenomenon.

The Financial Crime Information Centre was further developed with a view to providing member states with secure access to Europol's Web site. This Web site includes a library of information related to financial matters and various technical subjects related to financial investigations.

In 2001 Europol was involved in three operations concerning trafficking in stolen motor vehicles in Europe. Europol supported these operations by providing analytical support, coordinating international cooperation, and coordinating the information exchange. Europol also initiated several bilateral investigations among third countries and member states.

In cooperation with German and Austrian authorities, Europol developed the international European Vehicle Identification Database. This database was developed and translated by Europol and is now available in German, English, and French. Europol also developed the Blanco Documents Database containing stolen blank vehicle registration documents of various countries.

Vehicle theft is still one of the most common crimes in Europe. The scope of this problem can be illustrated by the fact that in the EU countries alone, 771,745 vehicles were stolen in 2004 (retrieved May 11, 2007, from http://www.europol.europa.eu.publications/SeriousCrimeOverviews/2005/overview).

Combating Drug-Related Criminality

Europol took over the tasks of the Europol Drugs Unit on July 1, 1999. It is responsible for combating drug trafficking within the European Union and works to improve police and customs cooperation between member states ("Action Plan," 2005).

Europol has supported operational projects against, for example, Turkish, Latin American, and indigenous criminal groups. There has been an improvement in both the quality and quantity of information supplied to Europol. This has led to the identification of criminals, new common targets, and links between investigations, as well as improvement in cooperation among the member states based on intelligence and analysis supplied by Europol.

During 2001, Europol assisted law enforcement teams in three member states in the dismantling of nine illicit laboratories and the collection of evidence. Europol's efforts contributed to seizures of synthetic drugs and laid the groundwork for the arrests of several suspects. Currently, there are two expert systems related to drugs in place at Europol: the Ecstasy Logo System and the Cocaine Logo System. These systems improve law enforcement cooperation in member states by identifying links between all seizures of ecstasy tablets and all seizures of cocaine, primarily based on certain particularities of the seized drugs.

Following a ban on opium poppy cultivation in Afghanistan and the events of September 11, Europol drafted a report on the status of opium production in that country, the world's largest producer of opium. Within the framework of its Joint Action on New Synthetic Drugs, Europol, together with the European Monitoring Centre for Drugs and Drug Addiction (EMCDDA), drafted joint progress reports on GHB (gamma-hydroxybutyrate, a "rape drug"), ketamine, and PMMA (polymethyl-methacrylate). As a direct result of the EU Action Plan on Drugs 2000–2004, a Collection Model for drug seizure statistics was drafted by Europol in close cooperation with experts from member states and the EMCDDA. A Model of Parameters for the Assessment of the European Drugs Strategy, drafted by Europol in cooperation with experts from member states and the EMCDDA, was adopted by the Horizontal Working Party on Drugs and was implemented in 2002.

During 2001, under the Synthetic Drug Assistance Program within PHARE (Poland and Hungary Assistance for Economic Restructuring), Europol organized and gave training courses to law enforcement officers, forensic scientists, and public prosecutors from several East European countries on the dismantling of illicit laboratories. In addition, training was provided to specialist teams in the Netherlands. Europol also assisted French authorities in a joint training program on synthetic drugs and their precursors for law enforcement staff from Latin American countries.

Fulfilling its mission of combating drug trafficking and other drug-related crimes, Europol is the main cooperation partner EMCDDA. This institution, established in 1993 and based in Lisbon, is one of the European Union's decentralized agencies. EMCDDA's Annual Report 2006, is available in 23 languages (EMCDDA, 2006).

According to Max-Peter Ratzel, director of Europol, a special focus has been given to the preparation of Europol's first Organized Crime Threat

Assessment (OCTA) report. The goal is to identify crime trends and to give decision makers a better basis for prioritization (retrieved August 21, 2007, from http://www.interpol.int/Public/ICPO/InterpolAtWork/iaw2005.pdf).

Further developments in the area of operational agreements and strategic relationship with key partners were made in 2005. Both the U.S. Secret Service and the Federal Bureau of Investigation (FBI) stationed liaison officers within Europol. Following the signing of an operational agreement with Canada, the Royal Canadian Mounted Police (RCMP) included their representatives.

The progress in cooperation between Europol and various countries can be illustrated by the fact that during only two months, from January 16 through March 15, 2007, four bilateral agreements on strategic cooperation were signed. The agreements were signed between Europol and Australia, Moldova, Albania, and Macedonia, and a multilateral agreement on witness protection was signed as well (retrieved May 10, 2007, from http://www.europol.europa.eu/index.asp?page=news&language).

Peacekeeping Operations: The Police Component _____

From 1948 up to the present, more than 65 international peacekeeping missions or operations have been established worldwide,[2] primarily, but not exclusively, under the flag of the United Nations. All these operations have included the contribution of law enforcement agencies, which so far have come from a total of 89 countries. Nonetheless, the main components of these peacekeeping forces have been military units, and the police components usually played only a minor part.

A few examples illustrate the role of the police in peacekeeping operations. The UN peacekeeping operation in the territory of the former Yugoslavia (the UN Protection Force), which lasted from 1992 to 1995, involved 37,795 military personnel and only 803 police officers.[3] The UN peacekeeping operation in Cyprus, which began in 1964 and continues at the time of publication, has involved 1,373 military personnel and only 35 police officers.

This ratio of police to military was more weighted toward the police component in the peacekeeping operation in Namibia from April 1989 through March 1990. The operation involved 4,493 military personnel and 1,500 police officers.[3] The more recent UN peacekeeping operation in East Timor, which began on May 20, 2002, is being carried out by a contingent of 5,000 troops and 1,250 police officers from 33 countries.[3]

In the sections that follow, peacekeeping operations that have involved a sizable police force component are examined more closely, in chronological order.

The UN International Police Task Force in Bosnia and Herzegovina

The first peacekeeping operation involving a sizable police force component followed the work of the UN Protection Force mentioned above. This was the UN Mission in Bosnia and Herzegovina (UNMIBH), which included the UN International Police Task Force (IPTF). UNMIBH began in January 1995 and continued until the European Union took over the responsibility from the United Nations in January 2003 (in the form of the EU Police Mission in Bosnia and Herzegovina).

Since IPTF was an organic component of UNMIBH, understanding the place and role of the IPTF requires a description of the organizational structure, the scope of the mission, and the other components of UNMIBH.[4]

Background

In 1946, the Socialist Republic of Bosnia and Herzegovina (BiH) became part of the Federal People's Republic of Yugoslavia. The population of the republic (almost 4 million) was and remains ethnically diverse. According to the 1991 census, 44 percent of the population were Muslims, 31 percent were Serbs, and 17 percent were Croats. For many years, a seemingly endless conflict had been carried out among these ethnic groups in the fields of religious, economic, cultural, and political life. As long as Yugoslavia was under communist rule under the leadership of Marshall Tito, these conflicts were hidden. The post-Tito regime in Yugoslavia was not able to deal with these and other, no less important, conflicts, which beset all six federal republics that made up Yugoslavia (Bosnia, Serbia, Slovenia, Croatia, Herzegovina, Kosovo). As a result of growing tensions in Bosnia and Herzegovina, on April 7, 1992, a civil war broke out. Serb paramilitary forces started firing on Sarajevo, and the bombardment of the city by heavy artillery began soon thereafter.

During this war, which spread to all the parts of the territory of BiH (about 20,000 square miles) and lasted until November 1995, approximately 200,000 people died and more than 2 million were driven from their homes.

The member states of the United Nations were unable to agree on military intervention, although the United Nations did send troops to facilitate the delivery of humanitarian aid. This mandate was later extended to the protection of a number of territories declared by the United Nations as safe areas. A ceasefire negotiated in December 1994 generally held until mid-March 1995.

In May 1995, North Atlantic Treaty Organization (NATO) forces launched air strikes on Serb targets (70 percent of the territory of BiH was then under Serb control), after the Serb military refused to comply with a UN ultimatum to remove all heavy weapons from a 12-mile exclusion zone around Sarajevo. Further NATO air strikes against Serb targets and a new offensive by the BiH and Croatian military helped to bring about U.S.-sponsored peace talks in Dayton, Ohio, in November 1995. Formalized in Paris in December of the same year, the subsequent agreement called for a federalized BiH in which 51 percent of the land would constitute the Croat-Bosnian federation, and 49 percent would constitute the Serb Republic (Republika Srbska).[5] The Dayton-Paris Agreement,[6] which contained 15 detailed articles and 11 annexes, covered a broad range of issues, from the military aspects of the peace settlement and the delineation of a boundary between the Federation of Bosnia and Herzegovina and the Republika Srbska to the holding of democratic elections, the protection of human rights, and assistance to refugees. Part of the Dayton-Paris Agreement called for the withdrawal of the UN Protection Force and the deployment of the NATO-led multinational Implementation Force (IFOR), and in this connection also the establishment of the IPTF.

On December 20, 1995, IFOR replaced the UN Protection Force. On the next day, December 21, the UN Security Council set up the IPTF and the UN Civil Affairs office, brought together as the UNMIBH, originally for a period of one year. The Security Council renewed the UNMIBH mandate on several occasions, the last one extending the mandate to December 31, 2002, at which time UNMIBH was terminated (UN Peace and Security Section, 2003a).

UNMIBH's mandate was to contribute to the establishment of the rule of law in Bosnia and Herzegovina, to assist in reforming and restructuring the local police, to monitor and audit the performance of the police and others involved in the maintenance of law and order, and to monitor and investigate police compliance with human rights (UN Peace and Security Section, 2003b).

Components

The main components of the UNMIBH were the IPTF, the Civil Affairs unit, and the Division of Administration, which included the work of the UN Trust Fund (three separate trust funds were established by the UN secretary-general: a fund for the restoration of essential public services in Sarajevo in March 1994, a fund for a police assistance program in December 1995, and a fund for emergency assistance trust projects outside Sarajevo in 2001). UNMIBH had a nationwide presence with regional headquarters in Banja Luca, Bihac, Doboj, Mostar, and Tuzla and a district headquarters in Brcko (UN Peace and Security Section, 2003a).

Personnel

The IPTF had an authorized strength of 2,057 police officers representing 43 countries, approximately 336 international civilian staff members from around 48 countries, and 1,575 locally recruited staff members. As of October 10, 2002, the largest contingents in the IPTF came from the United States (200 police officers) and Jordan (147). Other countries that contributed large numbers of police officers included Bulgaria (34), Egypt (47), France (93), Ghana (97), India (94), Ireland (28), the Netherlands (54), Pakistan (89), Poland (48), Portugal (30), the Russian Federation (32), Sweden (27), Turkey (30), Ukraine (28), and the United Kingdom (70). During the seven years that the IPTF was in existence, due to the rotation of police officers, more than 8,000 police officers from these 43 countries took part (UN Security Council, 2002).

Mandate Implementation Plan (MIP) 2000–2002

The Mandate Implementation Plan (MIP) was a consolidated strategic and operational framework for the completion of UNMIBH's core mandate in Bosnia and Herzegovina. On the basis of the relevant Security Council resolutions, the MIP identified the objectives of the mission and the programs and modalities used to achieve those objectives. With the support of international partners and the full cooperation of other international organizations,[7] UNMIBH established the following goals (UN Peace and Security Section, 2003b):

That all law enforcement personnel must meet internationally determined standards of professional competence and personal integrity

That all civilian law enforcement agencies must meet internationally determined standards of organizational capability and institutional integrity while progressively meeting the bench marks for multiethnic representation

That the institutional, legislative, and operational requirements for effective civilian police and judicial cooperation in law enforcement must be in place

That the State Border Service (SBS) must be fully established and that there is effective cooperation between law enforcement institutions at interentity, state, and international levels

That the public and the police must know their respective rights and duties and how to exercise them

That BiH must be supported in playing a full role as a member state of the United Nations

The Police Component (IPTF)

The IPTF monitored and advised local police with the objective of changing the primary focus of the police from the security of the state to that of protection of the individual. In so doing, IPTF helped to restructure and reform the local police to create democratic and professional police forces that were multiethnic, effective, transparent, impartial, accountable, and representative of the society they serve and that facilitated the return of refugees and displaced persons.

IPTF aimed to create a professional police force that met international standards and accurately reflected the ethnic composition of the population according to the 1991 census in the federation and the 1997 election results in the Republika Srbska and by encouraging female recruitment. IPTF registered some 25,278 local police personnel.

Special Trafficking Operations Program (STOP)

This program was established in June 2001 to address the issue of the trafficking of women and girls for prostitution in Bosnia and Herzegovina. STOP teams (IPTF staff together with the local police) throughout the country actively coordinated their efforts with the relevant entity and cantonal authorities to ensure that all establishments determined to be involved in using trafficked women and girls for prostitution were closed and that traffickers and brothel owners were brought to justice (Human Rights Watch, 2002).

The End of the Mandate

On December 31, 2002, the mandate of the UNMIBH, including its police component (the IPTF), was successfully completed. This mission and the IPTF made up the most extensive police reform and restructuring mission ever undertaken by the United Nations.

On a global scale, when we take into consideration the approximately 8,000 police officers from 43 different countries who served in the IPTF during the seven years of its existence, the task force was unprecedented. The service of so many police officers in the BiH was quite fruitful. The UNMIBH and its main component, the IPTF, left behind a legacy of democratic law enforcement, ensuring a secure environment for returning refugees. Independent local police structures were established in the country, with approximately 16,000 law enforcement officers certified after a comprehensive verification process. All local police officers were trained in basic standards of democratic policing. Progress was made on minority recruitment and gender balance through the two police academies established by the UNMIBH and the IPTF.

It is highly symbolic that the police forces from various countries that served in the UN Integrated Mission in Timor-Leste (UNMIT) included a team of police officers from Bosnia and Herzegovina, who developed under the help and supervision of the IPTF in that country. As of March 31, 2007, the UNMIT is composed of 10,027 military troops from 70 countries and a contingent of 651 police officers from 43 countries ("August 2007 Timor-Leste," 2007).

The UN Liaison Office in Sarajevo

The UN Liaison Office in Sarajevo was established in January 2003. Its main task was to ensure a seamless transition from the UNMIBH and its IPTF, which completed their mandate on December 31, 2002, to the European Union Police Mission (EUPM).

The UN Liaison Office assists the EUPM in the implementation of its mandate. The aim is to preserve and build on the achievements of the UNMIBH in police reform and restructuring. The Liaison Office provides the institutional memory of the UNMIBH mission to EUPM to ensure continuity in the democratization process of law enforcement agencies.

Another task of the Liaison Office is to maintain close contact and continue the political dialogue with the authorities of Bosnia and Herzegovina on the state and entity levels. In addition, the office continues communication and close liaison with the Office of the High Representative, the Organization for Security Cooperation in Europe, the Office of United Nations High Commissioner for Refugees, and other international organizations.

The UN Trust Fund, after the successful implementation of its projects to equip the local police, continues with the implementation of a number of projects in Bosnia-Herzegovina aimed at the rehabilitation of the devastated infrastructure and the restoration of essential public services. The Liaison Office has assumed the role of observing the implementation of UN Trust Fund projects and organizes media coverage when projects are completed (UN Liaison Office Sarajevo, 2002).

The European Union Police Mission (EUPM) in Bosnia and Herzegovina

The establishment of the European Union Police Mission was endorsed by both the Peace Implementation Council Steering Board (an international board established to observe and streamline the agreement between Bosnia and Herzegovina) and by the United Nations Security Council (Resolution 1396). The mission was established for a period of three years. Its annual budget was €38 million, of which €20 million came from the EU budget.

The EUPM began operations on January 1, 2003, following the departure of the IPTF. The mission was part of a broad approach followed by the EU and other actors that included activities to address the whole range of rule-of-law issues.

The refocused EUPM follow-up mission will have a duration of two years (from January 1, 2006 until the end of 2007). It supports the national police reform process and continues to develop and consolidate local capacity and regional cooperation in the fight against major and organized crime. The number of EUPM personnel in the follow-up mission is substantially reduced in comparison to 2003. As of May 4, 2007, the force was composed of 157 police officers and 29 civilian specialists from 32 countries, including 25 from the European Union (European Union Police Mission in Bosnia and Herzegovina, n.d.)

The Multinational Police Specialized Unit of the Kosovo Force (KFOR)

Kosovo lies in southern Serbia and has a mixed population, of whom the majority are ethnic Albanians. Until 1989, the region enjoyed a high degree of autonomy within the former Yugoslavia. In 1989, the Serbian leader Slobodan Milosevic altered the status of the region, removing autonomy and bringing the region under the direct control of Belgrade, the Serbian capital. The Kosovar Albanians strenuously opposed the move.

Military and paramilitary forces from the Federal Republic of Yugoslavia and the Kosovo Liberation Army were fighting day and night. Ethnic tensions were high and claimed the lives of many. More than 1,500 Kosovar Albanians were killed. Nearly 1 million people fled Kosovo to seek refuge.

Under the UN Security Council mandate (Resolution 1244 of June 10, 1999) the peace-enforcing Kosovo Force (KFOR) was set up. The objectives of KFOR were to establish and maintain a secure environment in Kosovo, including maintaining public safety and order; monitoring, verifying, and when necessary, enforcing compliance with the agreements that ended the conflict; and providing assistance to the UN Mission in Kosovo (NATO, 2003, 2004).

KFOR has two main components: a military component, consisting of five multinational brigades, and a police component, the Multinational Specialized Unit (MSU). In total, the KFOR troops come from 30 NATO and non-NATO nations. As of May 2007, NATO has approximately 16,000 troops deployed in Kosovo (NATO, n.d.b).

The MSU is a police force with a military status and an overall police capability. It consists of a regiment of the Italian Carabinieri (police), a contingent of the French Gendarmerie (militarized police), and a platoon of the Estonian Army (NATO, n.d.a).

The MSU has substantial experience in combating organized crime and terrorism. It possesses the human resources and dedicated investigative tools needed to analyze the structure of subversive and criminal organizations. It also provides prevention and repression resources to be used as KFOR assets.

The MSU conducts general patrolling operations to maintain a regular presence within KFOR. Such operations are in support of KFOR routine patrol activity and allow the MSU to interact with the local community while deepening their overall knowledge of evolving criminal and security threats in each area. Each detachment in KFOR has a different strength depending on the public order and security situation of the area.

The primary tasks of the MSU are to maintain a secure environment and establish a presence through patrolling, attend to law enforcement in close cooperation with the UN Mission in Kosovo, gather information, police civil disturbances, gather and analyze criminal intelligence on organized crime, conduct antiterrorism and VIP escort operations as well as special police operations, and investigate crimes related to military security (Bureau for International Narcotics and Law Enforcement Affairs, 2003; NATO, 2003; n.d.a).

The Next Steps

The deployment of the police in peacekeeping missions originally occurred, exclusively, under the auspices of the United Nations and the European Union, which continue to recognize the primacy of the UN Security Council for the maintenance of internal security. Increasingly, however, the United Nations calls on regional organizations to take responsibility for civilian crisis management in trouble spots closest to them. In June 2000, at a meeting of the European Council at Santa Maria da Feira, the member states of the European Union agreed that by 2003 they should be able to provide up to 5,000 police officers for international missions across the range of crisis prevention and crisis management operations. Within this goal, member states also took upon themselves the task of identifying and deploying, when the needs arises, up to 1,000 police officers within 30 days as part of a so-called European Union Rapid Reaction Police Force (Lindborg, 2001).

The unexpected mass looting in Baghdad, Basra, and other Iraqi towns in April 2003 placed a new and very urgent task on the agenda of the police forces: preparing and setting up new well-armed and specialized antilooting police detachments. According to the Geneva Convention, in wartime the armed forces are responsible for the safety and security of hospitals, museums, banks, and the like in operational areas. The lessons from the recent war in Iraq are that the army alone is not capable of effectively preventing and combating mass looting. It should be supported with well-trained and highly specialized antilooting police units acting, where possible, in cooperation with the local police forces. Until now, police force detachments that participated in war operations were not brought into action until some time had passed since the liberation of towns. However, in Baghdad, organized gangs of looters broke into several museums including the National Archaeological Museum. Libraries, banks, and even some hospitals were looted almost simultaneously with the arrival of U.S. tanks and troops. Thus in the future, police antilooting detachments should be prepared for action and positioned with forward combat detachments. For example, the Italian Police (Carabinieri) have already started forming such antilooting detachments (Gruner, 2006).

Future Trends

The future of international police cooperation can and should be evaluated from the perspective of the assessment of the two supranational law enforcement organizations, Interpol and Europol. Despite their quite impressive geographical mandate, these organizations remain nonoperational and serve more as clearinghouses for the exchange of information rather than as fully operational entities. To fully assess the potential of those two organizations, we must also look at the hybrid creations: international police task forces, which currently are the only actively operational solution to global law enforcement–related problems.

To target, effectively and efficiently, increasing transnational criminal activity, we need to identify operational responses. Even though Interpol and Europol are not operational in the traditional sense, they can serve as a very important backup system for operational agencies around the world. The key word, however, is *can*.

Recently the authors have seen an increased number of opinions and proposals for the establishment of international operational joint military-police combat units, with a rapid reaction status. For example, Canadian newspaper columnist Olivia Ward proposed that the United Nations establish a 15,000-strong force as quickly as possible. It should be composed of military, police, and civilian international staff, including medics and conflict transformation experts, who would be based at designated UN sites and ready to deploy with 48 hours notice (Ward, 2006).

It is rather obvious that a number of problems emerge as an outcome of such multinational cooperation. First, to borrow from the terminology used in literature dealing with terrorism, "One person's terrorist is another's freedom fighter." The membership, especially of Interpol, is open to virtually all countries, give or take a few. Among those members, one can find many countries that do not have friendly relations with one another about a variety of issues. Sharing information about potential terrorist threats with a country that harbors terrorism might prove to be quite challenging. Sharing information with the police force of a country that is well known to be infiltrated by organized crime doesn't seem prudent, either. Finally, making sense of statistical data that are grouped and defined in a somewhat archaic manner won't contribute an efficient response to the particular crime. For example, for statistical purposes, Interpol still groups murder and attempted murder in the same category.

Finally, here are a few recommendations for the future of international police cooperation. First, the need for an efficient and effective operational force, such as an international police task force, is a priority, especially given the recent developments in Iraq and Afghanistan. Such a task force needs a well-developed support system in the form of valid intelligence, and this could and has to be supplied by organizations such as Interpol or Europol. However, the composition of such a task force has to be very carefully defined, and it remains to be seen who could be put in charge of such decision-making processes. Second, the existence of numerous international law enforcement academies, not discussed in this chapter, will further some informal cooperation among law enforcement agencies, and such friendly cooperation is frequently more valuable than a reliance on formal entities. Finally, the exchange of police representatives among allied countries similar to what was established by the

New York Police Department after the September 11 attack will continue to facilitate formal and informal cooperation.

What we now need is a clearly defined policy for international police cooperation, information exchange, and operational assistance. The answer to the question of who will be in charge of this remains open for now.

Notes

1. At the time of the establishment of Europol, in 1999, the European Union consisted of 15 countries: Austria, Belgium, Denmark, Finland, France, Germany, Greece, Ireland, Italy, Luxembourg, the Netherlands, Portugal, Spain, Sweden, and the United Kingdom. Additional states that had joined as of August 2007 included Bulgaria, Cyprus, the Czech Republic, Estonia, Hungary, Latvia, Lithuania, Malta, Poland, Romania, Slovakia, and Slovenia. Already in advance of the accession of these new member states to the European Union, agreements were drafted on cooperation to form Europol. The first such agreement was signed on March 21, 2001, with Poland. As of August 2007, The European Union comprised 27 states, including recently joined Romania and Bulgaria, while Europol, as of May 2007, had 34 member states.

2. See, for example, the *European Foreign and Security Policy Newsletter*, Issue 9, April 2002, page 9, which lists 20 UN peacekeeping missions in which the Irish Garda (the Irish police force) has participated. For a full list of UN peacekeeping missions from 1945 until the present, see http://en.wikipedia.org/wiki/List_of_UN_peacekeeping_missions.

3. Regarding all the UN peacekeeping missions in East Timor, including UNMIT (United Nations Integrated Mission in Timor-Leste), UNMISET (United Nations Mission in East Timor), UNTAET (United Nations Transitional Administration in East Timor), UNAMET (United Nations Mission in East Timor), and all other related topics see the following sources:

- August 2007 Timor-Leste (2007). Retrieved August 20, 2007, from http://www.securitycouncilreport.org/site/c.glKWLeMTIsG/b.3041225/k.275/August_2007BRTimorLeste.htm.
- UN Security Council 5516th Meeting (AM). (2006, August 25). Retrieved August 21, 2007 from http://www.unmiset.org/UNMISETWebSite.nsf/60325cf 12626b2a3.
- The very essential (many useful links) Wikipedia source retrieved August 21, 2007 from http://en.wikipedia.org/wiki/List_of_UN_peacekeeping-missions

4. All information about the UNMIBH and the IPTF, unless specified otherwise, is taken from the UNMIBH official Web site at http://www.un.org/Depts/dpko/missions/unmibh/mandate.html, retrieved August 21, 2007.

5. This Serb Republic in the territory of Bosnia and Herzegovina should not be confused with the Serb (Belgrad) and Montenegro Republic, which recently officially replaced the former Socialist Federal Republic of Yugoslavia.

6. The full text of the Dayton-Paris Peace Agreement is available at http://www.oscebih.org/essentials/gfap/eng, retrieved August 21, 2007.

7. See OSCE (n.d.).

References

Action Plan to Combat Drugs (2000–2004). (2005). Retrieved August 20, 2007, from http://europa.eu/scadplus/leg/en/lvb/l33092.htm

August 2007 Timor-Leste. (2007). Retrieved August 20, 2007, from http://www.securitycouncilreport.org/site/c.glKWLeMTIsG/b.3041225/k.275/August_2007 BRTimorLeste.htm

Bittner, E (1970). *The function of the police in modern society.* Washington, DC: U.S. Government Printing Office.

British Broadcasting Corporation. (2003, December 2). *Crime fighters: Policing— Europol.* Retrieved May 3, 2004, from http://www.bbc.co.uk/crime/fighters/europol.shtml

Budget for Europol for 2007. (2006, August 2). *Official Journal of the European Union, C180, 49,* 1–9 [Electronic version]. Retrieved August 20, 2007, from http://eur-ex.europa.eu/JOIndex.do?year=2006&serie=C&textfield2=180& Submit=Search.

Bureau for International Narcotics and Law Enforcement Affairs. (2003, January 10). *United States participation in international police (CIVPOL) missions.* Retrieved April 18, 2003, from http://www.state.gov/g/inl/rls/fs/16554.htm

Cameron-Waller, S. (2001, December 17). *Interpol statement: Second world conference on commercial exploitation of children.* Retrieved March 21, 2003, from http://www.interpol.int/Public/Icpo/speeches/20011219.asp

Deridder, W. (2001, October). *16th annual Interpol symposium on terrorism.* Retrieved May 5, 2004, from http://www.interpol.int/public/ICPO/speeches/20011022b.asp

Eurojust. (n.d.). *Welcome to Eurojust's website.* Retrieved May 3, 2004, from http://www.eurojust.eu.int/index.htm

European Monitoring Centre for Drugs and Drug Addiction (EMCDDA). (2006). *Annual report 2006: The state of the drugs problem in Europe* [Electronic version]. Retrieved August 20, 2007, from http://ar2006.emcdda.europa.eu/en/home-en.html

European Union Police Mission in Bosnia and Herzegovina. (n.d.). *Overview.* Retrieved May 12, 2007, from http://www.eupm.org/Overview.aspx

Glazer, A. (2007, May 8). *LAPD brass reassigned after May 1 clash.* Retrieved August 19, 2007, from http://abcnews.go.com/US/wireStory?id=3149965

Gruner, S. (2006). Italy's special Carabinieri unit fights art looting. *WSJ.com opinion journal from the Wall Street journal opinion page* [Electronic version]. Retrieved August 20, 2007, from http://www.opinionjournal.com/la/?id=110008219

Haberfeld, M. R. (2002). *Critical issues in police training.* Upper Saddle River, NJ: Prentice-Hall.

Human Rights Watch. (2002). Hopes betrayed: Trafficking of women and girls to post-conflict Bosnia and Herzegovina for forced prostitution. *Bosnia and Herzegovina, 14(9[D])* [Electronic version]. Retrieved August 21, 2007 from http://www.hrw.org/reports/2002/bosnia/

Interpol. (2007a). Counterfeit currency. Retrieved October 26, 2007, from http://www.interpol.int/Public/FinancialCrime/CounterfeitCurrency/

Interpol. (2007b). Financial and high-tech crimes. Retrieved October 26, 2007, from http://www.interpol.int/Public/FinancialCrime/Default.asp

Lindborg, C. (2001). *The EU rapid reaction force: Europe takes on a new security challenge.* Basic paper no. 37. Retrieved August 21, 2007, from http://www.basicint.org/pubs/Papers/BP37.htm

North Atlantic Treaty Organization (NATO). (2003). *KFOR information.* Retrieved August 19, 2007, from http://www.nato.int/issues/kosovo/index.html

North Atlantic Treaty Organization (NATO). (2004). *Kosovo force.* Retrieved August 19, 2007, from http://www.nato.int/kfor/structur/units/msu.html

North Atlantic Treaty Organization (NATO). (n.d.a). *Multinational specialized unit.* Retrieved August 18, 2007, from http://www.nato.int/kfor/structur/*unOOits*/msu.html

North Atlantic Treaty Organization (NATO). (n.d.b). *NATO in Kosovo.* Retrieved May 12, 2007, from http://www.nato.int/issues/kosovo/index.html

Organization for Security and Co-operation in Europe (OSCE). (n.d.). *Mission to Bosnia and Herzegovina.* Retrieved August 18, 2007, from http://www.oscebih.org/security_cooperation/?d=4

TE-SAT: European terrorism situation and trend report. (2007). [Electronic version]. Retrieved August 20, 2007, from http://www.europol.eu.int/index.asp?page=publar2001

UN Liaison Office Sarajevo. (2002, December 31). *About us.* Retrieved August 19, 2007 from: http://www.un.org/Depts/dpko/missons/unmibh.pdf

UN Peace and Security Section. (2003a). *Bosnia and Herzegovina: UNMIBH—Background.* Retrieved May 7, 2004, from http://www.un.org/Depts/dpko/missions/unmibh/background.html

UN Peace and Security Section. (2003b). *Bosnia and Herzegovina: UNMIBH—Mandate.* Retrieved May 7, 2004, from http://www.un.org/Depts/dpko/missions/unmibh/mandate.html

UN Security Council. (2002). *Report of the Secretary-General on the United Nations Mission in Bosnia and Herzegovina.* Retrieved May 18, 2004, from http://216.239.51.104/search?q=cache:ZjDRIz7mTTcJ:www.womenwarpeace.org/bosnia/docs/sgreptosc5jun02.pdf+iptf+ghana&hl=en

Ward, O. (2006, June 15). United Nations "army" proposed. *Toronto Star* [Electronic version]. Retrieved August 20, 2007, from http://www.globalpolicy.org/security/peacekpg/reform/2006/0615army.htm

Further Reading

European Union Police Mission. (2003). *European Union police mission in Bosnia and Herzegovina.* Retrieved May 7, 2004, from http://www.eupm.org/index.html

Interpol. (1999, February 17). *Drug control.* Retrieved May 5, 2004 from http://www.interpol.int/Public/drugs/Default.asp

Interpol. (2003, March). *Interpol's international notices system.* Retrieved May 5, 2004, from http://www.interpol.int/Public/Wanted/Fugitives/Default.asp

Interpol. (n.d.). *Brief history of Interpol.* Retrieved May 3, 2004, from http://www.interpol.int/public/ICPO/history.asp

Appendix A

Atlas of Regional Maps

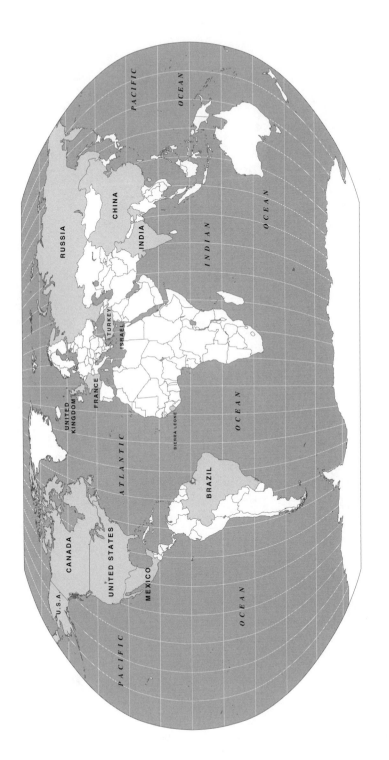

Map 1   The World. See Chapters 1 and 14.

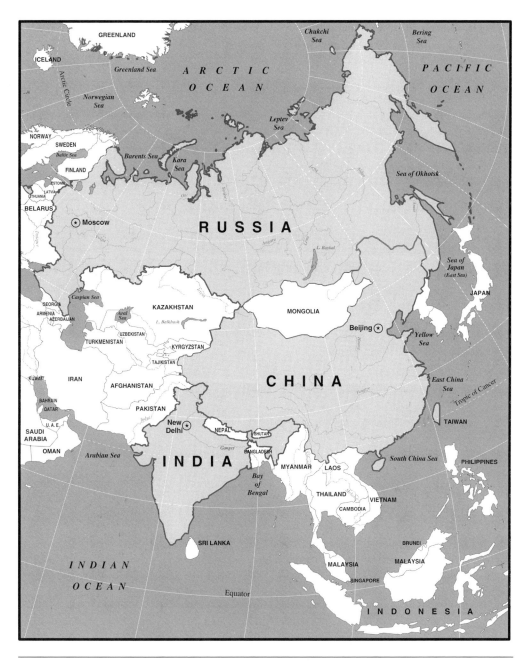

Map 2   Asia. See Chapters 2, 6, and 7.

Map 3   South America. See Chapter 3.

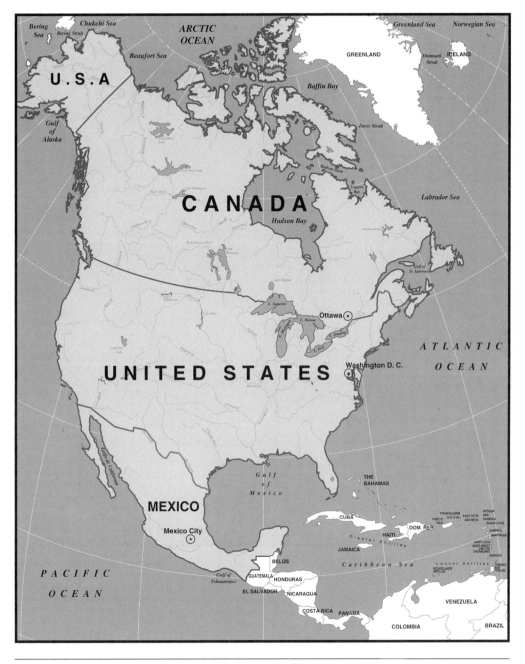

Map 4   North America. See Chapters 4, 12, and 13.

About the Editors

Maria (Maki) Haberfeld is a professor of police science and chair of the Department of Law, Police Science, and Criminal Justice Administration at John Jay College of Criminal Justice, City University of New York. She was born in Poland and immigrated to Israel as a teenager. Prior to coming to John Jay, she served in the Israeli Defense Forces and left the army at the rank of a sergeant; she then joined the Israel National Police and left the force at the rank of lieutenant. She also worked for the U.S. Drug Enforcement Administration in its New York field office as a special consultant. She holds two bachelor of arts degrees, two master's degrees, and a PhD in criminal justice.

Her recent publications include a book that she wrote on police training entitled *Critical Issues in Police Training* (2002), two books that she coedited—*Contours of Police Integrity* (2004) and *Encyclopedia of Law Enforcement, the International Volume* (2005), another book that she authored, *Police Leadership* (2005), and a book she coauthored, *Enhancing Police Integrity* (2006).

For the last six years (2001–2007), Dr. Haberfeld has been involved in developing, coordinating, and teaching in a special training program for the New York City Police Department. Currently she is also an academic coordinator of the Law Enforcement Executive Police Institute for the state of New York, where she oversees the delivery of the training modules and teaches leadership courses. She is involved in two major research studies, one on the use of force by the police in 10 different countries and the other on training police in counterterrorism response post–September 11, which also involves comparative studies of a number of countries around the world.

Ibrahim Cerrah graduated from the Turkish National Police Academy and was appointed as a police sergeant to Ankara Police College in 1986. He worked there until he was transferred to a civilian/academic position at the Turkish National Police Academy in 1989.

Between 1990 and 1995, he completed his MA and PhD studies at the Scarman Center for the Study of Public Order, University of Leicester, UK.

Since then he has been teaching as a member of the full time faculty of the Turkish National Police Academy.

During 2001–2002, 2004, and 2007, he visited the John Jay College of Criminal Justice, City University of New York as a Fulbright fellow and taught several courses such as Introduction to Law Enforcement, Police Administration, Comparative Police Systems, Police Ethics, and Terrorism.

His study and teaching interests/areas include police ethics, police subculture, police education, democratization of policing, and issues involving domestic security. He has authored and edited a number of books and other publications, both in Turkish and in English. He is the founding editor-in-chief of a bilingual journal, *Turkish Journal of Police Studies*. Since 2001, he has been working as the director of the Institute for Security Science in Ankara, Turkey. He became a full professor in 2006. He is married and has three children.

About the Contributors

Curtis Clarke is an associate professor and coordinator of the criminal justice program at Athabasca University. He has carried out empirical studies on the implementation of community-based policing, on police organizational and managerial change, on intelligence-led policing, and on the shifting boundaries between private and public policing. Professor Clarke has completed research for the Canadian Association of Chiefs of Police, the Federal Solicitor General, Health Canada, the Edmonton Police Service, the Metropolitan Toronto Police Service, the Alberta Association of Chiefs of Police, and the Law Commission of Canada. Dr. Clarke currently chairs a research subcommittee for the human resources department of the Alberta Association of Chiefs of Police, and he is treasurer for the Canadian Association of Police Educators. At present Dr. Clarke is seconded to the Alberta Solicitor General and Public Security Ministry, where he is overseeing the development and coordination of the provincial police and peace officer training strategy.

Stuart Cullen completed a 32-year police career in 1995, having attained the rank of superintendent. For the past 15 years he has been an associate tutor to major international command and leadership programs at the International Faculty, Leadership Academy for Policing, Bramshill, England. He has also been extensively involved in international police training and reform programs in Africa, Eastern Europe, Latin America, and the Caribbean. His clients have included the United Kingdom Foreign and Commonwealth Office, Department for International Development and the European Union. He has special experience working on reform programs in postconflict societies and societies in transition. Stuart Cullen is author or coauthor of a number of chapters and books on comparative international policing, human rights, and democratization and policing.

Benoît Dupont is professor of criminology at the Université de Montréal and deputy director of the International Centre for Comparative Criminology there. He is also the holder of the Canada Research Chair in Security, Identity, and Technology. His areas of interest include the governance of security (especially the functioning of security networks), the impact of new technologies on policing, and the impact of mass surveillance on privacy. He recently coedited a book with Jennifer Wood entitled *Democracy, Society and the Governance of Security* (Cambridge University Press, 2006).

Ruth Geva, a freelance organizational consultant, specializes in community policing, crime prevention, and emergency management. For almost 30 years, she was employed by the Israel Police and by Israel's Ministry of Public Security in various operational and management positions, retiring in 2001 with the rank of chief superintendent. Ms. Geva initiated and set up the National Crime Prevention Council in Israel, was the Israeli delegate to the UN Crime Prevention Division, coordinated the international relations of the ministry, and was part of the team that implemented community policing in Israel. A graduate of the University of Toronto (BSc) and the Hebrew University in Jerusalem (MA in criminology), she is also a graduate of the Home Office Crime Prevention Centre in the UK and has a diploma in organizational management. Ruth Geva is the author of over 70 professional publications and 2 textbooks on crime prevention. For the last four years, Ms. Geva has acted as coordinator of a project to set up Community Emergency Centers in all Jerusalem neighborhoods.

Lior Gideon, currently a full time professor at the Department of Law, Police Science, and Criminal Justice Administration at John Jay College of Criminal Justice, City University of New York, earned his PhD from the Faculty of Law, Institute of Criminology at the Hebrew University of Jerusalem. He received a postdoctoral fellowship at the University of Maryland at College Park. His main research interests are comparative criminal justice and rehabilitation, reintegration, and reentry issues for criminal offenders, in particular examining offenders' perceptions of their needs. Additionally, he specializes in correction-based program evaluation.

Farrukh Hakeem is an associate professor of criminal justice in the Department of Social Sciences, Shaw University, and teaches criminal justice courses. He has also taught at John Jay College of Criminal Justice, City University of New York and at The College of New Jersey. He teaches courses in the areas of law enforcement, corrections, comparative laws, and computer applications. After completing his graduate work in sociology and law at Bombay University, he was admitted to the Indian bar in 1979. While practicing law at Bombay High Court, he attended evening classes and completed an LLM in property law and matrimonial law at the University Department of Law, Bombay University. He obtained a fellowship to complete an MA in sociology at the University of Arizona. He then earned a PhD from the Graduate School and University Center of the City University of New York. His dissertation focused on the socioeconomic determinants of punishment. His current research interests are in the area of comparative law, international policing, disparities in punishment, and health. He has published articles in the *International Journal of Comparative and Applied Criminal Justice, The Encyclopedia of Law Enforcement,* and *Public Health Reports.*

Sergio Herzog is a senior lecturer at the Faculty of Law, Institute of Criminology at the Hebrew University of Jerusalem. He received his bachelor's degree in psychology and his PhD in criminology (direct track) from the Hebrew University of Jerusalem. His research interests lie in the areas of criminology, criminal justice systems, and social psychology. He conducted empirical research on the serious phenomenon of police violence in Israel; he collected and analyzed data on use-of-force complaints against police officers, their historical trends, the functioning of the civilian board in Israel that has handled these complaints, and the personal attitudes of suspected police officers, complainants, and civilian investigators concerning the roots, situations, and treatment of police violence. He has published six articles that have added both to the theoretical understanding of the phenomenon and to the specific treatment of public complaints against police officers by both internal (police) and external (civilian) complaints boards.

Matt Long is senior lecturer in criminology at Nottingham Trent University. He has previously worked at Sheffield Hallam, Manchester, and East London Universities. Between 1998 and 2004, he lectured at the national police training college at Bramshill. In 2002 he was appointed visiting professor in law and police science at John Jay College of Criminal Justice, City University of New York. He continues to act as a police trainer in a consultant capacity.

Yue Ma is a faculty member in the Department of Law and Police Science at John Jay College of Criminal Justice, City University of New York. He received his PhD from Rutgers University. Dr. Ma also holds a JD from Rutgers University Law School and an LLM from University of Minnesota Law School. Dr. Ma is interested in the comparative study of legal and criminal justice issues. He has published articles exploring a wide range of legal and criminal justice issues in the cross-nation context. Among the topics covered by his research and articles are the development of criminal justice standards in Europe under the European Convention on Human Rights, comparative analysis of exclusionary rules, comparative analysis of prosecutorial discretion and plea bargaining, comparison of lay participation in criminal trials, comparative study of the law of interrogation, and the judicial role in supervising the exercise of prosecutorial discretion. Dr. Ma has also published articles and book chapters on China's criminal justice system.

William H. McDonald is the founder and dean of the School of Criminal Justice at Monroe College, Bronx, New York. He holds a PhD in criminal justice and a master's in philosophy from the City University of New York, a master of science degree in public safety administration from Central Connecticut University, a graduate certificate in criminal justice education from the University of Virginia, and a bachelor of science degree in criminal justice from American University. He is a Neiderhoffer Fellow, a graduate of the FBI National Academy, and a former visiting professor at Bramshill, the police college for England and Wales. In addition to having taught for years, he was the director of public safety for Connecticut State University, a special agent with the U.S. Treasury Department, and a senior homicide detective with the Metropolitan Police Department of Washington, D.C. He has served as a technical consultant to a number of domestic and foreign criminal justice agencies.

Benjamin Nelson Reames holds a PhD in political science from Columbia University and a master of public policy from the University of Michigan, where he also earned his BA in social sciences. He is currently working for the U.S. Department of State in Asia. (He wrote his chapters for this book independently, prior to his employment with the State Department, and none of his views reflect U.S. policy or opinions on any matters, in any way). Previously he has been an anticorruption specialist at Partners of the Americas, a Fulbright-Hays fellow researching police reform in Brazil, a senior associate working with the Lawyers Committee for Human Rights (now Human Rights First) on their Mexico Policing Project, and a consultant to the UN Development Programme's country office in Guatemala on police reform. He was also a senior research associate for the Civilian Complaint Review Board of New York City, which investigates complaints against the police department.

Peter Roudik is a senior legal specialist at the Law Library of Congress, where he is responsible for doing research on laws of the former Soviet states. He joined the Law Library in 1996 after 10 years of academic experience, during which he wrote and lectured extensively on constitutional law issues. He authored a volume on Russia and the Commonwealth of Independent States for the *World Legal Systems Cyclopedia*. He has testified frequently before the U.S. Congress, and his legal commentaries have been broadcast by the Voice of America, Radio Liberty, and C-SPAN. Before coming to the United States, he worked as a legal advisor to the Russian government where he was involved in drafting legislation.

Agostino von Hassell spent his formative years in the United States, studying European history at Columbia University and graduating with a BA in 1974. He then attended Columbia University Graduate School of Journalism and graduated with awards in 1975. He is the president of The Repton Group LLC, a business consulting firm. von Hassell has extensive expertise in national security matters, high-level investigations around the globe, terrorism and military issues, and global trade problems. He has published numerous books on military history, including *Alliances of Enemies* about the U.S. Office of Strategic Services and Germany's Abwehr in World War II. That book was published by St. Martin's Press in November 2006.

Anders Walker, who is currently an assistant professor at the Saint Louis University School of Law, is interested in the relationship between democracy and law, particularly the manner in which popular politics can influence legal doctrine. A graduate of Duke University School of Law, Walker first became interested in clashes between popular politics and law while pursuing a JD/MA in history at Duke. He pursued this interest as a PhD candidate in African American Studies and History at Yale, focusing on the manner in which African American history, read as the story of a disenfranchised electoral minority, actually casts into stark relief a much larger story of the excesses of populist rule in democratic societies, a force that law is often unable to influence.

was probably not surprising that we came to feel happier with our father at a safe distance, even dreading the times when he came home.

We could not understand the punishing schedule through which he was pushing himself. Nor could we appreciate that, for much of the time, he was not in the best of health. We would hardly see him for days on end and when we did he was almost inevitably in poor humour through lack of proper sleep. Family life could certainly have been smoother.

It must be remembered that we were by no means a rich family. Although Father was in work, doing a responsible and reasonably rewarded job, we had few luxuries. Most of my clothes were hand-me-downs from my brother, there was no car in the family, and we did not have a television until my father spent some savings on one in order that we could all see the Coronation. Even after that, we were not encouraged to watch it, and were officially banned from watching ITV simply because Father was employed by the opposition. This did not stop us, of course, but as soon as we heard Father's key turn in the door, we had to rush to switch channels.

The strictness of the regime extended to food. We were expected to eat everything put before us on the often-repeated principle that there were many starving youngsters who would have given a great deal for a meal. This might explain the vast appetite I developed in later years, but I don't think it did me any harm.

Although pocket-money was severely rationed, our parents were not mean. Whenever any of us had to go out on a school outing or anything else, Father would always ensure that we had more than enough cash to cover all conceivable emergencies. 'Folding money' he used to call it, pressing a ten-shilling or one-pound note into our hands before we set off.

Short of luxuries though we may have been, we did not consider ourselves deprived. I had a bike by the age of ten, considerably earlier than some of my contemporaries, and it was responsible for a hairy accident very close to home when a pedal came off the machine, ejecting me spectacularly over the handlebars. Landing chin-first on a concrete surface, I needed stitches in hospital, bravely refusing to cry when they were inserted without anaesthetic. The scar can still be seen now.

In all things to do with my future, my parents were tremendously supportive, which I think one always appreciates far more in retrospect than at the time. They wanted me to have a good education and to be brought up with all the right opportunities in life.

I think they achieved these objectives, though whether I used the opportunities in the way they would have wished is open to doubt.

Cricket had begun to consume me by the age of ten. Although still at junior school – and, moreover, at a school which did not play competitive cricket – I used to play the game non-stop in the playground. Mostly it was a version of the game which would not find favour with the MCC coaching manuals but which fitted snugly into the confines of the school's facilities and was even presided over by one of our more enthusiastic teachers. He would bowl underarm at a batsman standing in front of a half-moon shaped litter bin masquerading as the stumps; the batsman, if he hit the ball, would run to square-leg and back. If he had not made good his ground next to the litter bin by the time the ball had been returned by way of eager hands in the field to the teacher/bowler, he was out and the next boy took his place. It was a pleasingly rumbustious way to pass break times and it certainly helped teach some of the fundamentals of the game, even if good running between the wickets was not one of them.

By now, however, I was spreading my cricketing wings way outside the boundaries of the school. I had developed an interest in Test cricket and, during the school holidays and weekends, I would sit silently all day, listening intently to the radio Test match commentaries and scoring faithfully in my personal scorebook. My brother and I took this one stage further by erecting a blackboard outside our house and updating the Test scores at the end of each over. This began as a game for us, but as our house was so near to the railway station, it turned into a genuinely popular service for cricket-lovers among the home-going commuters.

It was a natural progression for me to become involved with local club cricket and, like many young boys, first did so through scoring. Father used to walk down to the recreation ground to watch Stoke d'Abernon play if he was off work at weekends, and I would always take the chance to go with him, sitting next to the club scorer and keeping my own book. The village's players were like Gods to me and I would hang avidly on every word as I stood, pint-sized and silent, on the brink of conversations in which the myths and legends which belong to every local club were expounded for the thousandth time to dutifully attentive visiting players. Stoke d'Abernon had seen players who could hit the ball high over the trees onto the railway line at one end of the ground, or into the gardens at the other end. I never actually saw it happen, but I drank in every anecdote.

LESSONS FOR THE FUTURE

Most of the village players turned out every Saturday and Sunday, some bringing along wives and girlfriends, others seeming to do nothing but play, drink beer and play again. Many of them had old, crumpled cream flannels which looked as if they only ever left the bags on match days, but the team was improved by a young marine who came to play during his holidays, immaculately turned out in sparkling whites, and who I thought was the best fielder I would ever see in my life.

I began to score regularly for the Second XI on an official basis, travelling away with them and proudly keeping their book as correct and tidy as I could. This experience introduced me for the first time to the social side of cricket and it was not very long before I was bought my first half-pint of bitter by one of the players. I got through it with great difficulty, trying hard to disguise the fact that I found the taste indescribably foul, and wondered how on earth these men could enjoy standing around hour after hour drinking what seemed like gallons of the stuff. I hastily went back to drinking weak shandies and it was some years before my taste-buds had developed sufficiently to appreciate good ale. I then made up for lost time.

Like most boys of that age, I did a paper-round to raise some extra spending-money. Like all too many, I did very little schoolwork, so it was a great surprise to me, if not to anyone else, when I was the only one out of 90 pupils in my year to pass the 11-plus exam at the first attempt. I had always considered myself useless at the type of mental arithmetic problem which dominates this exam and I simply could not understand how I had sailed through it – especially as my brother David, far more intelligent and industrious, had failed.

David had done well enough to gain an interview for a joint-stream school in Leatherhead, subsequently to be accepted into their grammar-school stream to study for GCEs. My own reward for this unexpected success was selection for a place at the Royal Grammar School, Guildford. My parents, quite properly, saw this as an honour and were delighted for me, but it involved them in a great deal of expense as everything from uniform to sports' equipment to books and stationery needed to be new before I started my first term.

That first day was an ordeal I still clearly remember. We new boys arrived on a September afternoon in our short, grey trousers, feeling lost in the jumble of old and new buildings which is the RGS. I, for one, was absolutely terrified of what lay in store and would gladly have gone home never to turn up again. Early events did little to bring me peace of mind as it quickly became plain that the first-formers faced a painful initiation ceremony carried out by boys one year their seniors. Somewhere in the school grounds lay an enormous patch of stinging nettles, and into this area – known colloquially as 'The Pit', virtually all the newcomers were thrown in turn by excitedly malicious second-years. Only first-formers were obliged to wear short trousers and tradition had it that they would pay for being so young and silly by suffering a vast and bumpy array of nettle stings on their unprotected legs. Not yet being as unusually tall or forbidding as I was soon to become, I had no good grounds for missing out on this delight, but despite getting the full treatment, I was grateful to escape with surprisingly few stings.

The first year was divided by age into three forms. Form I was for the youngest of the entry and it was into this group that I was cast. We sat alphabetically, leaving me in a front seat on the extreme right of our room in an extremely old building, where a huge solid fuel stove dominated the middle of the room and the frightening appearance of our first form master, Arthur Pheby, dominated most of us. We were soon to discover that his temper by no means matched his looks, and life settled down into a relatively agreeable pattern.

All the masters wore gowns and one, a Mr Maas who taught us Latin, was a real card. There was an iron beam across the middle of our form room and his routine was to tie himself to this with the cord of his gown, lean backwards and get someone in the form to recite a passage. Those who did so without error were rewarded by a liver pill from a tin he carried everywhere with him, plus the sight of this eccentric but engaging gentleman disengaging himself from the beam.

The cane was both used and feared at the RGS and, although I managed to survive my school career without feeling the whack of wood on my backside, there was one occasion when I was bracing myself for it in some horror. The worst of it was, I thought I was about to be caned for something which had not been my doing. It arose from the strictures of a certain master on the subject of talking during dinner. Most masters allowed a measure of conversation when their turn came to preside over the midday meal, but Mr Blackwood would not permit the uttering of a single word. I can hear him now, standing to address us as we shuffled into our places behind the long tables, thundering: 'There will be silence throughout the meal.' We were divided into tables of eight or ten and on this particular day I was unlucky enough to be on a table at which someone was unwise enough to speak within earshot of Mr Blackwood. Instantly, he sentenced not only the offender but the entire table to detention.

This in itself would have been bad enough, most of us fearing additional reprimands from aggrieved parents whenever we incurred a detention, but to make matters worse the headmaster, Mr Hallowes, came into the detention room after school that day and glanced through the book in which the various misdemeanours were logged. 'Talking at dinner', he said. 'That is a caning offence' . . . and I found myself quaking at the back of the room. Our saviour, to everyone's great surprise, was none other than Mr Blackwood himself who, having turned up to supervise our punishment, now successfully persuaded the headmaster that we had suffered enough for our foolishness.

The playtime football and cricket sessions, depending on the season, were simply carried forward from junior to senior school, growing in vigour, intensity and perhaps in ability as we grew older. Only looking back is it possible to wince at the inevitable residue of sweat and grime on clothes which must have been the bane of many a mother's life. Personally, I was allowed two white nylon school shirts each week, one of which had to be worn for three days before being washed, and the other for two. Our lunchtime ritual involved bolting our food down as rapidly as possible before dashing out onto the playground to organise the day's game. Almost an hour's frenetic activity tended to involve a good deal of perspiration and, although boys tend never to notice it at the time, the nauseous smell of stale sweat which pervades most classrooms is the first thing that always strikes me when I vist a school now. I honestly wonder how teachers can tolerate it. It is probably just the same in prison.

None of these thoughts concerned us at the ages of 11, 12 and 13, however, and playground games were our only opportunity of competitive sport until we qualified for the Under-13 level, when we could begin the serious business of playing against rival schools. This coincided with my second year at the RGS, but when our housemaster, Mr Bishop, saw me practising cricket one day, he recruited me and one other second-year boy for his Under-15 side, two years before our time.

This form of sporting promotion was unheard of within the school and created a good deal of jealousy. Not only my contemporaries resented it, but our rugby master, a Welshman named Dawkes, seemed to take it as a personal affront and wasted no time in venting his feelings on me. Still weak and under-developed, I found myself at a severe disadvantage against the heftier specimens when it came to playing rugby. I played in the scrum, hating every minute of it, the entire game presenting itself before me as nothing more appetising than being trampled on and kicked in one part of the ground, then being obliged to pick myself up and hobble painfully to another part of the field for similar treatment. I seemed constantly to be bruised and uncomfortable finding no pleasure in the exercise at all. Perhaps Mr Dawkes sensed that the game upon which he doted was not up my street; certainly he taunted me habitually, and at least once found cause to hit me because, he said, my white shorts were not pressed properly. As if that was my fault!

At the age of 14 I was five feet six inches tall. Two years later I was six feet four. It was a quite incredible process and, looking at myself at the mirror in a state of some bewilderment, I swear I could see myself growing day by day. One effect of this was that my trousers rapidly became several inches too short; another was that I was encouraged to bowl fast. I was considered an all-rounder at school, opening the bowling and – odd though it may now seem – batting at number three. I still maintain that I could have developed into a respectable batsman if anyone had ever been able or willing to coach me properly, but as the years went by I became regarded exclusively as a bowler, the rest of the game being pushed into the background.

However, it meant a good deal to me to be playing in a higher age-group of cricket and I was quite prepared to put up with the petty jealousies in order to do so. This was the start of a syndrome which was to have considerable effect on the rest of my schooldays because, from then on, I found I was never content in the company of boys my own age, always seeking the competition and conversation of my elders. This was not because I was especially advanced, simply that I first got used to it through school cricket and then through being asked to play both soccer and cricket for the Old Guildfordians, which meant mixing not only with older boys but with adults two and three times my age. I played for the club Second XI at both sports, goalkeeping at football and bowling my rough-edged brand of inswingers at cricket. It was a step on the sporting ladder, a minor one maybe, but to a 14-year-old this seemed like the big time.

David and I had the sort of relationship most brothers of similar age probably have. We fought a lot, both verbally and physically, but most of our free time was spent playing together, the majority of it peacefully and some of it to quite pleasing effect. I am thinking now of the staged matches we put on, both in the recreation ground and the back garden, organised in quite intricate and sophisticated detail.

We were very often in trouble for being late back from the recreation ground. Tea would be getting cold on the table when my father came to march us back, his face set in a portrait of anger. But it was when we played on his immaculately kept back lawn that we most extended our imaginations, and most tempted his wrath. Knowing we would be asking for punishment if we caused any damage, we devised an improvised and very effective set-up. Mats were laid down at each end of the pitch to protect the lawn – one for the batter and one for the bowler. The stumps were put in a plant pot so that they did not deface the lawn, which was an altogether better arrangement anyway because they would fly spectacularly out of the pot when hit. Chairs were carefully placed in the area behind the batsmen to act as slip fielders – anything touching one of these counted as a dismissal – and the French windows of the house were opened at such an angle that it was impossible for us to break them. The greenhouse at the top of the garden was our pavilion and whichever one of us was batting would formally emerge from the door to walk down the rockery (the pavilion steps) in full gloves-and-pads regalia.

In the winter, when our thoughts turned to football, we would make a passable net out of chicken wire and old carpets. Our inventive minds did not stop at the accessories – we wanted the actual games to be as exciting and grand as possible, so each of us would select our team. David, being the elder, would usually insist on first choice, so that if we were playing football he would select Manchester City and if the game was cricket he would invariably be England. We then had to nominate our players and the game began to the sound of a non-stop commentary, which we shared between us.

Cricket could sometimes be complicated, as I discovered when I nominated an Australian side which included Neil Harvey and Bill Lawry in the top order. This meant that my limited batting skills were still further minimised by having to bat left-handed when these players were 'at the wicket'. Runs and wickets were faithfully recorded and the bowlers were rotated in authentic fashion, although I don't recall going so far as to bowl left-handed.

One of the major hazards was the neighbours. The man on one side of our semi-detached home was perfectly pleasant and did not seem to mind how many times we turned up on his doorstep to retrieve carelessly lost balls. On the other side was someone we thought rather intolerant. One interruption he would stand, but the second time he would be most unwelcoming, at which point David and I would invariably argue over which of us was going to go round. The games tended to disintegrate at this stage and we eventually introduced a rule whereby you were out as soon as you hit the ball over the fence.

This sort of game continued throughout the day during our holidays, until the time when David began to keep wicket. He was given a pair of gloves as a birthday-present – Arthur McIntyre autograph brand, and very proud of them he was too – so we had to devise a game which involved wicketkeeping. This we managed by turning upside down a table with steel tubular legs. I acted as bowler, or rather pitcher, throwing a hard rubber ball at the table while David kept wicket. If the ball clipped the legs and David caught it, we would both leap skywards, letting out raucous appeals which, I am quite sure, made us still more unpopular with the neighbour. We played it for hour after hour, never tiring, and as I mixed up the bowling between speed and spin I am sure our childish imagination helped David become a very proficient club wicketkeeper.

As cricket became more and more of a passion for me, school became less and less of a pleasure. I also began to behave like a spoiled brat, even at home. If things did not go my way in a park game of cricket with my brother, I would often run home with either the bat or the ball, simply bad-tempered and unpleasant. So it was at school, where I did progressively less work and, not surprisingly, made a dreadful mess of my O-levels. I managed to score four per cent in my mock physics O-level and fared little better at biology or chemistry. The papers were always returned to their owners in descending order of merit, so when mine did not appear until last I knew I could hardly expect a pat on the back from our physics master. All he said as he handed it to me, stony-faced, was 'Burn it'.

Latin left me similarly cold, but for most of the time I was able to fall into a system which alleviated the need for doing any work at this subject. Our master, who had a terrible stutter, usually tested the strength of our homework by making us recite the translation a section at a time, in alphabetical order. This routine seemed so unchanging that we were able to get one accurate translation done by a single bright boy and then pass the crib around the room, surreptitiously under the desk, as poor Mr Atkinson stuttered his way from one name to the next. This worked very well until, after two terms of satisfactory cheating, a boy named Holdstock loudly broke wind just as he was starting to read his piece of the translation.

Mr Atkinson quelled the ensuing uproarious laughter and furiously sent Holdstock out of the room. Then, plainly flustered by what he considered a gross impertinence, he forgot who had been translating and stammered: 'Carry on, W-W-W-Willis! Having done not a stitch of work on my Latin for the best part of a year, and being uncertain what point we had reached in the text-book, I was ill equipped to oblige, and managed to match Mr Atkinson stutter for stutter until the crib came flying across the room at emergency speed.

Failing the exams was an inevitable consequence of my general idleness and I was forced to stay back a year. While those who had passed a reasonable number of exams progressed to the informality and responsibility of the sixth form, I had to remain in the fifth, with a set of boys who were not only strange to me, but a year younger. This was almost too much to bear and I found myself grating my teeth with impatience as they excitedly prattled about their first cigarette, their first pint of beer or night in a pub – things which I had done three years earlier. If I had found it difficult to relate to my own contemporaries after spending so much time with adults, this was absolutely intolerable.

It had to be done, though. Somehow I had to force a degree of my attention away from cricket in order to concentrate on my studies enough to pass the exams and escape. For that was how I felt. The sooner I could leave school, the sooner I would be free to pursue the life I wanted to lead in cricket.

I became a bit of a rebel, wearing my hair long and refusing to wear the school cap which all but the sixth form were obliged to wear. So stroppy did I become on this issue that I accepted detention after detention, still holding out on the misguided principle. Having grown so much that it was impossible to find a pair of regulation school shoes to fit me, I wore hush puppies, and got into hot water for that, too. I began my infatuation with the music of Bob Dylan, even going to the extreme of adding Dylan to my given names. I became a loner and have no doubt, in retrospect, that I was a thoroughly disagreeable young man.

13

Only on a cricket pitch did I feel I was expressing myself adequately. I had been in the First XI for two seasons now, playing a good standard of schools cricket, which involved travel to such 'faraway' places at Portsmouth, Southampton and Winchester. I started bowling faster, initially fired by the thought of getting back in practice at some of the lumbering dummies who had gleefully flattened me so often on the rugby field. Then I began to get a real kick out of bowling fast, realising that, at this level, I was something a little different. I was actually regarded with some suspicion by the master in charge of cricket at the RGS, who thought I was bowling so fast that my action was perhaps illegal.

I was chosen for the Surrey Schools side, which was supervised by a man named Watcyn Evans, a master at Byfleet. Watcyn played for a good club side called Avorians, based in Cobham, and when I began to do well for the schools side, he asked me to join his club. Avorians played all-day games around the county and this really seemed like a different world to me. My social life improved so that often I would not be home before midnight after a game.

Six of the RGS side were chosen to go to The Oval for a trial. I was the only one of the six not to be given a game for Surrey Colts, and at the time it hurt. It seemed the ultimate rejection, but my chance to make amends came much sooner than I could have expected when a match was arranged between Surrey Schools and Surrey Colts, on the Test ground at The Oval. I bowled well, took wickets and found myself being asked to play for the Surrey Young Cricketers on a week-long tour of the West Country, based at a hotel near Wincanton and playing our cricket in the Dorset, Somerset and Wiltshire area. Now, I felt, I was really making progress.

Having at last passed some O-levels and progressed to the sixth form, I found my wishes to do English, French and German at A-level thwarted by our new headmaster, who insisted that I should do geography instead of French. I hated the subject, and received my first-ever Saturday detention – serious sentence indeed – for refusing to do a geography essay. I was out in time to join the First XI for their afternoon match and have the statutory few pints of bitter at 1s 8d a pint in our local, The Elm Tree, but it did not improve my affections for geography and there was never a chance of my passing the exam.

I had decided I wanted to go to university. David, having done well at a supposedly inferior school, was already installed at York and one visit to his campus had convinced me that this seemed a good way to spend the next three years. But it was not to be. English I passed easily enough; German I made a nonsense of, and with only one A-level no polytechnic would accept me, let alone a university. Suddenly I had to look for a job.

2

MAKING THE GRADE

I might have been a typewriter salesman, an insurance agent, or even a journalist. But I fancy that every would-be employer of R. Willis gathered the distinct impression that he would have half my attention at best.

There were two main problems preventing my launch into the world of commerce. The first was that I held a strong resentment about not going to university. I felt the world had done me a bad turn and, despite my father's justifiable insistence that, 'I had ideas above my station', I could not accept that the fault lay firmly at my own door. The second problem, of course, was the obsession with cricket which showed no sign of abating. Some boys have merely a passing flirtation, a schoolboy crush on one sport or another. But not me. I felt I belonged on a cricket ground, and during that summer of 1968 I crammed as many games as possible into the weeks remaining of the season after I had left school.

I had done well enough for Surrey Young Cricketers to earn a couple of games with the county Second XI towards the end of that season. Again it involved a week away, and when we gathered at The Oval on the Saturday of the Test match against Australia, Ken Barrington, taking me under his wing, shepherded me into lunch in the players' dining room where I probably sat goggle-eyed and silent, such was my innocent awe at being in the company of such legends.

That afternoon we set off for Evesham. This little market town between Stratford-upon-Avon and Worcester was not, perhaps, the most glamorous of places at which to make any sort of county début, but I was in no mood to worry about that. In his normal fashion, my father had made certain I would not go short of cash and pressed a £5 note into my hand before I left home. As all our meals and accomodation for the week were taken care of by the county, this seemed more than enough to cover all eventualities.

However, my first night away with the side was an eye-opening experience.

After dinner in the hotel we moved into the bar and, pretty soon, some of the more experienced hands began 'spoofing' (a game involving guessing the total number of coins held in all the participants' outstretched hands). As usual, the penance for the last man out was to buy the next round and, not wishing to be thought either unsociable or unversed in the bar-room arts, I accepted their offer to join in. It goes without saying that I lost, discovering that the game involved more than mere luck, and to my horror the round I was obliged to buy amounted to £1 17s 6d. More than a third of my emergency money gone, and we had not even started the week's cricket!

Somehow I survived the week solvent and greatly enjoyed the matches against Worcestershire and Glamorgan. My figures were not startling, but neither had I disgraced myself, and I went home more convinced than ever that my future lay in cricket.

It came as a shock when September arrived bringing the end of the season and a need for gainful employment. With a sinking heart I scanned the 'situations vacant' columns and fired off some letters, being granted a number of interviews at companies which included Olivetti, Lever Brothers and Sun Life Assurance. It was the latter who hit the nail on the head. In their letter to me following the interview they said: 'We feel your heart is in playing cricket and that you should pursue this ambition.' They were good enough to add that, if I failed in the game, I should feel free to reapply, but to all intents and purposes it was just another rejection.

The story was similar when I went to London to do a week-long journalism course run by the NUJ. I made no great impression because my interest was mostly in sport, and all but a few journalists have to start life on the weddings, funerals, flower shows and general news columns of local papers, a prospect I found not remotely appealing.

I began to think I would have to go on the dole. It was a worrying time in my life and I was buoyed up only by weekend soccer matches for the Old Boys, who continued to be a sociable bunch. Indeed, after one game for them – followed by the usual long session in the bar – I got on the train at Guildford slightly past my best. It was only a four-stop ride to Cobham, but the train had reached its destination at Waterloo before I woke up, faced with changing platforms and making a tiresome and slightly embarrassing journey back again.

Temporary salvation came in two guises: a tour to Pakistan with a side made up of Surrey and Middlesex Young Cricketers, and a job as a petrol-pump attendant. Neither would appear at this distance to have had much glamour attached, but to a 19-year-old in my position this was all I could have asked for. I worked long hours on the pumps from eight in the morning until six at night, leading a solitary existence. The garage was a five-mile cycle ride from Stoke d'Abernon, on the Effingham crossroads, and for two months I made that journey five days a week, spending every lunchtime in the nearby pub on a diet of one sausage sandwich and one pint of bitter, which was all I could afford.

Boredom was the enemy but, knowing I would not be making a career of serving petrol, I found it a fairly painless experience, seeking constant consolation from the thought that I would very soon be playing cricket again. The tour left England in December for a month, and although I knew little about Pakistan, the fact that we were all directed to visit a hospital for a number of vaccinations told me something about the type of place to expect. I was fortunately not anticipating luxury.

California it certainly was not, but teenage cricketers being healthy of body and mind, uncluttered by the cynicism which tends to afflict all of us after a few years in the game, we managed to have a lot of fun in sometimes quite adverse conditions.

Pakistan practised what I was later to know as a typical ploy by billing us as 'England Young Cricketers', which meant they could put out their national side against us (including a number of blatantly over-age players) and call the three-day games Test matches. We were quite simply stitched up. The opposition was in a different league, and despite very good individual performances from some of our lads, the result of the series was never in the slightest doubt.

We played the major games in Lahore (on the University Ground), Karachi (on the Gymkhana Ground) and Rawalpindi, other mystical-sounding places we visited including Bahawalpur, Sahiwal and Peshawar. Almost without exception, they were hot, dusty and, to westerners, rather inhospitable, but despite arduous train journeys, the spartan accomodation and the illnesses which afflicted most of us at some stage, I remember the laughs more than the moans.

Our team included several others who were later to go on to county cricket – including the Hampshire pair, John Rice and Andy Murtagh – and one, in Graham Barlow, who was to be an

England team-mate in India eight years later. We were a friendly crew and, if some were homesick over Christmas, we managed to drown our sorrows in the master-in-charge's scotch.

My memories are of sitting round log fires in the army camp which comprised our 'hotel' in Peshawar, of wearing cricket socks in bed to counter the quite unexpected cold there, and of suffering severe blisters on the hard wickets which forced me to bowl in plimsolls in one of the 'Tests'. It was a test of character as much as anything, the whole month-long trip bringing one unknown hazard after another, but I can honestly say that despite visiting Pakistan twice more, and staying in far better accomodation, I have never enjoyed it as much again.

Winter nets with Surrey brought me down to earth with a thump. There is always something strangely unreal about indoor nets while the ground outside is covered with snow or ice, and although the county practised only once a week, it was not something to which I especially looked forward. For one thing, the journey from my home to Crystal Palace was such an ordeal. I had wheels by this time, having passed my driving test in Weybridge at the first attempt, and borrowed my brother's rather smart Saab while he was at university. Yet if I tried to do the trip by road I would invariably end up getting lost in Croydon. On the other hand, the journey by public transport involved two changes on the train followed by a long walk from the station to the sports centre, frequently in biting cold.

Arthur McIntyre, the Surrey coach, did not share my vain view that I had the perfect bowling action and tried hard to make me bowl with a higher arm. His adjustments were plainly designed to turn me into another Alec Bedser, sacrificing pace for control with the left arm up high and the left leg braced at the point of delivery. All very laudable, I'm sure, but every time I tried to bowl like that, the ball would end up in the side of the net as if it had a mind of its own. Mike Edwards, who was one of the most approachable of the Surrey seniors at the time, came to my rescue by confiding his view that I should ignore all the technical advice and simply run up and let the ball go as fast as I could.

Whether or not this made any difference to the end result I am not sure, but towards the spring I was taken aside by Arthur Mac and offered a season's trial with the county. My pay was to be £12 10s a week for the summer but I felt like a millionaire. I took less than five seconds to accept and went home walking on air, to break the news to my folks.

It did not bring the whoops of delight I would have liked. Stony silence would be nearer the mark. My father, I think, accepted it reluctantly but philosophically, unwilling to stand in the way of what I plainly wanted to do but regretful that I had not chosen a steadier, more secure way of life. My mother, however, was just appalled and made no secret of her feelings. She would spend ages staring at the jobs adverts in the local papers, apparently hoping to persuade me into a change of heart. It was to be a very long time before the lady I had affectionately nicknamed 'Grummidge' would mellow towards the idea; indeed, for two or even three years, I think she convinced herself that it was purely a temporary interruption in my life and that before long normal service would be resumed in the shape of 'a proper job'.

They could not be blamed for their attitude. One way and another, they had invested a good deal of money in my education, and to see me first make a mess of it and now choose a sporting career which was still poorly paid and boasted an exceptionally high failure rate cannot have been easy to bear. But, although disappointed by their absence of enthusiasm, I was not about to change my mind. Far from it. I presented myself at The Oval in April 1969 for pre-season training, confidently expecting the whole vista of the professional cricketer's life to open up invitingly and enthrallingly before me. Nothing, I thought, could stop me now. How wrong can you be?

The days were long and tiring. I left home to catch the train at nine each morning, changing onto the tube at Waterloo to arrive at The Oval by ten. For the first week, under the watchful gaze of Arthur Mac, we trained right through to 5.30, and trained hard. Even the regular games of football, which I would have expected to provide a light-hearted variation, were taken so seriously as to be completely exhausting. Generally, we split into two teams – the capped players against the uncapped – and, as the senior side included a number of accomplished footballers all of whom seemed keen to show off their skills and strength, it always turned into an endurance test.

When at last the time arrived to get out onto the field and play cricket I thought things would begin to improve. The weeks of training had taken their toll and had not been at all what I had expected, but now surely I would make progress. I didn't. In fact, I appeared to be going backwards. Of course, I did not expect to walk straight into the first team squad, but I had hoped I would prove good enough to be an automatic selection for the Second

XI. Instead, I was humiliatingly packed off to score for the Seconds, or to play for the Colts team. As my confidence began to suffer, I had the growing suspicion that I had made a horrible mistake and that my parents had been right all along.

I have never considered myself a quitter. In later years, indeed, I pride myself in the belief that I became a true fighter and would seldom accept any defeat, no matter how inevitable it may have seemed. But in the misery of that 1969 spring I came close to giving up on Surrey, giving up on cricket, and going back with my tail between my legs – maybe to take up the half-hearted offer of the Sun Life Assurance Society and spend the rest of my working days behind a desk. It almost seemed preferable.

All this culminated in the tearful night I have already described, the stern but not unkind words of my father, and the realisation that I could succeed, if only I went about the job with a proper sense of commitment. I knew my father still didn't like the idea of my playing cricket for a living and he would often come out with the adage, 'Many are called, but few are chosen'. At times it seemed a very apposite summary of my own situation, but now, fired with a new determination to be one of those lucky few, I at last began to show better results.

Some days still seemed interminably long and unproductive. When the first team were playing at The Oval, the rest of us had to bowl at them in the nets on the outfield between 10 and 11.15 a.m. The likes of me never had a chance to bat – I even remember watching journalists, Chris Martin-Jenkins and John Thicknesse, being invited to put on the pads before we were – and I could never come to terms with the logic of this. But at the time, mine was not to reason why . . .

After the net session, if there was no active cricket for us, we second-teamers had to stay and watch the whole day's cricket. We did not sit in the same room as the senior side, but upstairs in our own changing area, and I was struck immediately by the ferocity with which a lot of the second XI players picked holes in their alleged superiors. I suppose it is a fact of life in every job, but although I certainly found myself being dragged into it, I do feel it was an indication of a slightly unhealthy atmosphere prevalent at The Oval in those days. Surrey had gained a reputation for having rather too many unsociable moaners in their side and over the next 18 months or so I was to discover the truth of the rumour.

The Second XI was an odd mixture. There were public-school types such as Mike Hooper and Dudley Owen-Thomas, both hailed as tremendous cricketing prospects but now struggling to justify the fanfare; there was Lonsdale Skinner, a black boy from Balham; there were middle-class, middle-of-the-road types like Chris Waller and myself. And there was Roy Lewis.

Lewis was something else. He was really no more than a good club cricketer, never likely to make a great name at first-class level, but to listen to him you would have thought he was being kept out of the England team only by some scandalous personal prejudice. He could be engaging company, never short of something to say, but his know-all approach could also be infuriating, and I often wondered how he got away with some of his remarks. He was quite prepared to make his criticisms and views to their recipients face to face. I remember once when Peter May came into our dressing-room – P. B. H. May, one of the men who had featured so heavily in those back-garden matches with my brother and still virtually a God to me. But Roy had a different attitude altogether. He brazenly walked up to the retired England captain and candidly inferred that he had never been much good against leg-spin. I am not sure whether P.B.H. took this as an outright accusation or a query designed to settle an argument, but he took it with a far better grace than some might have done.

By July, I had advanced enough to be given the chance of making by first-class début. It was not the sort of match to merit big headlines or pack in the crowds, the visit of Scotland to The Oval probably passing unnoticed by all except the most ardent devotees of *Daily Telegraph* cricket reporting. But it was a start and I was grateful for it, taking a few wickets before retreating back into the second team, more determined than ever to make the grade.

My big breakthrough was the result of a conspiracy of circumstances which cost Surrey a number of established players at one time. John Edrich and Geoff Arnold were involved in a Test, Jim Cumbes had gone back to Tranmere Rovers for the start of the soccer season and two others were injured. David Gibson, who might have been the first choice to fill the bowling vacancy, was about to retire from the game and so I was called up to play in two away Championship matches, at Scarborough and Trent Bridge.

I travelled to Scarborough in no style at all. This was probably the longest journey Surrey had to undertake during the course of that season, and I spent it uncomfortably cramped in the back of Younis Ahmed's Hillman Imp. Younis having elected to take along his girlfriend, I, as junior professional, had no choice but to squeeze myself into the inadequate back seat for the five-hour drive. To make matters worse, Younis was an adventurous driver and, although I was bubbling with excitement about the match ahead, I have seldom been more relieved to reach a journey's end.

We stayed at the Grand Hotel, overlooking the sea, and to me it seemed like a palace. Yorkshire, like Surrey, were depleted by Test calls, but for all that the game was as competitive and entertaining as any in the tradition of great games between these two counties. I still have a clear recollection of a big crowd, of the arena resembling a bullring and of an atmosphere that previously I had done no more than dream about. Yorkshire v Surrey has always been considered a big game, perhaps particularly in the north, and to play in such a showpiece match for my championship début was quite something. I took the new ball with Robin Jackman, my first Championship wicket coming when I bowled Barrie Leadbeater. My first Championship 'duck' followed soon afterwards – bowled by Richard Hutton!

Surrey won a tense, low-scoring contest by about 30 runs and we drove down to Nottingham in good heart. Although this game began in good weather on an August Saturday, the sparse crowd and comparatively non-existent atmosphere might have seemed an anti-climax to the new boy if I had not created a bit of a stir on the first evening of the game.

We had made a good score of just over 300, and by the end of that first day Notts stood shakily at 26 for four, Willis having taken all four wickets at a cost of 11. If only the Sunday papers did not suffer from such prohibitively early deadlines I might have been the recipient of my first flattering headlines the next morning; as it was, I floated through the Sunday with heady hopes of taking all ten wickets in only my second game.

A man named Sobers put the young upstart back in his place. Stalking in at his favourite number six, he smashed his first ball from me straight back over my head. It bounced five yards inside the boundary fence and was the prelude to the kind of Sobers onslaught I had witnessed many a time on television without imagining I might one day be on the receiving end. Trent Bridge had proudly pioneered the first electronic scoreboard around that time and I watched increasingly forlornly as my proud figures were destroyed by this extraordinary cricketer who remains to this day the greatest I have ever seen. I finished up with five for 78 which seemed a let-down at the time but in other circumstances would have been cause for celebration.

This game had the dual benefits of encouraging me into thinking I was capable of succeeding and reminding me of the gulf which still separated me from the best players. I had done enough, though to earn a few more Championship games during August and September, ending the season deliriously happy compared with the dejection I had felt only a few months earlier. There were to be no more tormented thoughts of giving up the game. I could hardly wait for the next season to start.

First, however, I had the problem of winter employment, at the time a serious dilemma for many county cricketers. It remains a problem to this day, but the number of cricketers forced onto the dole or into thoroughly unsuitable jobs has been greatly decreased by the volume of coaching work now available overseas, particularly in South Africa and Australia. At the tail-end of the sixties, only Test players and a favoured few others were able to venture abroad to escape the clutches of winter; most ended up as I did, scouring adverts for part-time jobs.

Much to my surprise, I landed a job at Harrods. Not being accustomed to shopping there, I had never considered the possibility of a chap like me finding employment within its affluent walls, but I answered an advert for a vacancy in the sanctions department and was duly appointed. The job, in truth, sounds a little grander than it deserves to. The department existed because very few Harrods regulars pay in cash, the system being that credit customers would sign the bills, which were then shot up to our floor through a series of air pipes, whereupon we would check off the signature against our records, issue the authority for release of the goods and return the customer's copy of the bill down the pipes to the shop floor. We sanctioners were split into different areas of the alphabet and it was my duty to deal with customers whose surnames fell into the L to S category.

I was a boring, mechanical job but the people were friendly, the money steady, and I had no cause for complaint. For the first time I had to commute regularly, joining the bowler-hat brigade on the early-morning train from Cobham to Waterloo, taking the Bakerloo line to Piccadilly Circus and then the Piccadilly line to Knightsbridge. If nothing else, I think it instilled some discipline in to me, which was no bad thing at such an impressionable age.

By now my musical tastes had broadened. Although I was still a firm fan of Bob Dylan, and had gone to his Isle of Wight concert that August in the middle of a Championship game, I was becoming more and more attracted to classical music and had begun to attend concerts at the Festival Hall. At Harrods, staff received a discount on goods of up to 33 per cent, so I would spend the majority of my lunchtimes raiding the record department and handing over a high proportion of my spare cash.

I still played football every Saturday and had now attained the dizzy heights of a regular place in the Guildford City Reserves side in the Hampshire League. Guildford's manager had recently joined the Surrey promotions staff, which was how I came to join the club, but there was never much chance of my breaking into the first team, who were a considerable force in the Southern League. I was once selected for a match against Bedford Town when the regular goalkeeper fell victim to a flu epidemic . . . when five more players were struck down the game was postponed.

Playing in the reserves entailed a lot of travelling and little cameraderie, the side being a mix of professionals and part-timers, of fringe first-teamers who felt they were demeaning themselves and of eager youngsters trying to make an impression. We didn't lose much and were paid reasonable 'expenses' for the privilege, but for someone like me, to whom the Saturday soccer was chiefly for fun and relaxation, it was not an ideal set-up.

I had my mates at Surrey of whom I saw a fair bit in the winter. There was Chris Waller, whose trusty Triumph Herald had carried the pair of us many miles together, and Geoff Howarth, who had joined the staff in 1969 and was now lodging with me at my parents' house. He was a constant source of bewilderment to my mother, not being the tidiest of men and having a strange penchant for cheese and strawberry jam sandwiches, but we grew closer during the course of that winter and spent many an evening in the local, The Plough at Stoke d'Abernon, our respective financial plights determining which of us paid for the night's beer. We have remained close buddies ever since, and it seemed almost too good to be true when we ended up in opposition as the captains of England and New Zealand.

That, though, was still in the realms of distant and improbable dreams when we reported back at The Oval prior to the 1970 season, my own position having been stabilised by a one-year contract earning me the relative fortune of £425. I suppose I began the season with high hopes of holding down a regular first-team place, but in that I was to be frustrated. The problem was that Surrey now had six bowlers for five places. Stewart Storey, the all-rounder, was an automatic choice, and as both of the spinners, Pat Pocock and Intikhab Alam, were current internationals, the club seemed to feel they must play. This left two places between the three main seamers – Geoff Arnold, Jackman and myself – and each of us had to suffer occasional disappointments.

Arnold was a better bowler by far than either 'Jackers' or myself and could be quite unplayable when given a greenish wicket on which to operate. Unfortunately for him, The Oval pitches were rarely even remotely green, which was a constant source of irritation to the man commonly known as 'Horse'. Great bowler though he could be, Geoff was also inclined to do his share of moaning, never missing an opportunity to vent his feelings about the wickets on which he had to bowl.

I could certainly sympathise with him. Matches at The Oval generally became tediously predictable by the second day, captains being unwilling to make adventurous declarations in the quest for victory, so that more often than not our home games would drift quietly to stalemate, the batsmen polishing up their averages while the bowlers toiled fruitlessly and hopelessly. Surrey tended to win more matches away, where the pitches might be less good, and I think this contributed to the fact that Micky Stewart constantly felt himself to be living in the shadow of the more successful sides of the fifties. Though it is true that the Surrey side of my time could not compare with the title-winning side under Surridge, we would have been a good deal closer to their record but for the infamous negative pitches.

As a fairly consistent member of the senior squad, though still naturally uncapped, I came face to face with the gripe which other counties often voiced about Surrey, both then and later. We were accused of being a dour, unfriendly side – and to a large degree it was an accusation with which we could not argue. I reckon there were only three really sociable guys in the side that year – Jackers, Mike Edwards and me when I played. Neither Howarth nor Waller played much first-team cricket and out of 'office hours' I saw hardly anything of the other blokes. This could sometimes be embarrassing. If we were playing a three-day game at The Oval, it seemed natural for me to wander into the Surrey Tavern afterwards for a pint, normally accompanied by Jackers, often to be confronted by the all-too-familiar sight of ten of the opposition outnumbering three of the home team.

This went on long into the seventies. When I went back to The Oval as an opponent, I would still have a drink with Jackers afterwards, and still there would be only two or three other Surrey players present. The moaning went on for years, too, coming to a head when the rest of the team apparently united against John Edrich's captaincy, Jackers being the brave man who stood up to say he thought him unsuitable for the job. In a sense, the lack of togetherness tore the team apart and made way for a new and friendlier regime – with R. D. Jackman, at least until recently, still ever-present but no longer so lonely in the evenings.

Edrich might sometimes have been accused of playing for his England place during my time with Surrey, although it was not difficult to confuse this with his regular, unhurried style of playing. I never had reason to dislike him as a man; in fact he seemed to go out of his way to encourage and promote me. I bowled well at him in the nets, which plainly impressed him and, I have no doubt, caused him to press my case for the England team. Whenever we were out together during an away game he would say, 'Make sure you get some steaks inside you', and then take practical steps to ensure that I did. In those days, teams invariably ate their evening meal in a convenient Berni Inn and if John and I were at the same table he would order an extra steak for me.

One thing which came home to me during the 1970 season was the lack of any decent relationship between the players and the majority of the committee. It was a standing joke that some of the committee did not even know the players by sight, an allegation borne out at an end-of-season party when one of their number approached Younis Ahmed and asked: 'Who are you?'

So all in all it was an unsettling summer. I ended it in the second team and, while there had been no return of the disillusionment which had afflicted me the previous year, I did feel a shade disappointed at what I considered a stall in my career. A few months later everything changed.

On the final day of the season, a man turned up at The Oval announcing himself as the manager of Corinthian Casuals FC, an Isthmian League side for whom a good friend of mine, Martin Tyler, played. When asked if I was available to play for them on the following Saturday I naturally assumed he meant the third team or at best the reserves; but when he said, 'FA Cup first qualifying round – Hornchurch away', I realized he meant the first team.

I had already decided to stop playing for Guildford, and never had reason to regret it, even if my début for Casuals was a fraught affair. I played in brand new toe-pinching boots on a very wet day, and from leading 2–0 with ten minutes left we somehow managed to lose 3–2. It would have been 4–2 if I hadn't saved a penalty during that frantic period which prematurely ended our march to

Wembley. I was to play 13 times for Casuals before we recorded our first victory – against Clapton on the Spotted Dog Ground in East London – but the spirit and friendship among the lads was so good that it hardly seemed to matter.

I had left home during the autumn, setting up in a flat on Streatham Hill with Martin Tyler after giving my old blue serge suit one of its rare outings when the landlady interviewed us. There was only one bedroom containing two single beds – not an ideal arrangement for two healthy young bachelors – so we shifted one of the beds into the living room and tossed up for choice of sleeping accommodation. I won and selected the bedroom, which became known as 'the fridge' owing to the lack of heating.

There was a comedy on TV at the time called *The Odd Couple* and it seemed very apt. Martin was obsessed with football, later to work in television reporting the game, and has also compiled some soccer encyclopaedias, although his infatuation at that time extended to the active side, his dirty football gear often being mixed up with a week's dirty dishes, while I, surprisingly enough, took on the role of the straight tidy person, gathering up debris after him and even doing most of the cooking. Sainsbury's steak and kidney pies and macaroni cheese became our staple diet.

My days were occupied coaching kids at Crystal Palace and it was in mid-November, when I was interrupted from a routine session by a call to the office telephone, that the world seemed to stand still.

3

TESTS AND TRAUMAS

It hardly seemed possible. Here I was, a raw, lanky 21-year-old with only a handful of first-class games under my belt, being summoned to join the England team in Australia. I simply gave up the unequal struggle to take it all in.

The message to take a phone call had not prompted any such fanciful thoughts. I suppose I expected it to be a social call from a mate, or possibly someone from Surrey with a coaching query. True, there had been some mutterings in the papers when the tour party had been announced, and Keith Miller for one had accused the selectors of blundering by not taking me as a 17th player to gain experience. But I hardly took such flattery seriously. After all, I had not even finished the previous season in the Surrey side, much less in England contention, and fine bowlers like Geoff Arnold and David Brown who had been left out of the tour party would surely be ahead of me in the queue. I never gave the matter another thought but carried on with my coaching, played my football for the Casuals and looked forward to the return of summer and a new cricket season.

Even when the caller announced himself as Billy Griffith, secretary of MCC, the purpose of his call did not immediately dawn on me. I simply wasn't on the same wavelength. He said: 'We would like you to go to Australia. Alan Ward is coming home injured and you have been chosen as his replacement.' I can't recall my words in reply; they probably didn't make a great deal of sense, but it was certainly the most amazing moment of my life.

Unlike the players originally selected, who had a leisurely six or seven weeks to prepare themselves mentally and physically, I had precisely 36 hours to get ready. There seemed to be a hundred and one things to cram into that short period but the most pressing was to make certain I was properly kitted out and, remembering my father's words, would at least look the part of an England player.

I had to buy my own cricket case from Lord's – a long brown trunk which I kept for 14 years, long after its useful life had ended, before passing it on to a club cricketer friend. The signwriter at The Oval put my name on this, and also on a brand new personal suitcase, bought for me by my father.

The England team traditionally wore suits for all functions in those days, so I selected a lightweight outfit from Simpsons in Piccadilly, which set me back £52. It seemed like a ransom, the equivalent of about three weeks' wages, but there was no way I was going to begrudge it at a time like this.

A smallpox jab completed my travelling requirements and, still slightly bemused but undeniably excited, I turned up on time at Heathrow airport to board a Qantas 707 bound for Brisbane.

I can't recall where the plane put down, only that it seemed to stop six or seven times on the way and that the journey appeared to take a week. Squeezing my legs uncomfortably into the cramped space between seats, totally inadequate for a man approaching six feet six inches, I survived the flight rather than enjoying it, arriving at Brisbane in the early morning sunlight to be met by the tour manager, David Clark, and physiotherapist, Bernard Thomas, neither of whom I had ever set eyes on before.

My first base was the Park Royal Motor Inn, where I was given a double room on my own so that I should not interrupt the other, still-sleeping players. First, however, I ate some breakfast and tasted my first paw-paw. I was not instantly impressed, failing to understand why the Australians should consider a delicacy something which reminded me strongly of coal-tar soap.

I slept most of the day, meeting the players when they returned from the Gabba ground, where they were engaged in a match against Queensland state. It was an odd experience joining a group of players most of whom were completely unknown to me outside the pages of the newspapers. A few I knew reasonably well, of course – none better than John Edrich, who quickly made much of the fact that I had long been his protégé back at Surrey – but men such as John Snow and Colin Cowdrey were schoolboy heroes turned team-mates. I had not been abroad a great deal, much less mixed in this kind of exalted company, and I confess to feeling extremely nervous.

Among the players I had never met before was Geoffrey Boycott, but I was soon to be educated. The next day I spent at the ground, watching day two of the Queensland match, the feature of which was a century by Boycott. This was all to the good, proving him to be in excellent form prior to the start of the more serious business, but the priority thereafter was for as many as possible of the other batsmen to take some much-needed practice as well. Boycott was unwilling to co-operate. Most players, having completed a hundred against a state attack, would feel that their job was done and get themselves out to make way for someone else. Not Geoffrey. He categorically refused to give away his wicket, coming into conflict with his old Yorkshire colleague, captain Ray Illingworth. Eventually, when he had advanced to 124 not out, Illy managed to persuade Boycott to retire hurt with some invented injury. It was an acceptable compromise, allowing Boycott to keep his 'not out' entry which seemed to mean a lot to him, and someone else got some practice. It was also a revealing episode for the newcomer to the party.

Snow was the other controversial member of the side and it was not long before I became aware of the common moans about his attitude. No-one could question his effort or effectiveness when the Test matches came round, but his dilatory approach both to nets and to the interim matches annoyed some players, outraged others. The accusation was that he didn't try his hardest and made little or no effort to correct run-up faults which brought a stream of no-balls. I was soon to find myself drawn towards Snowy, however, adding friendship to admiration. He explained to me that he used nets, and to some extent state matches, to 'bowl for rhythm and rhythm only', and although this was a new one on me, I could see the sense behind it. I was impressed by his careful preparations before taking the field, notably the time he put aside to strap a big heel pad inside his left boot to avoid unnecessary wear and tear on a very susceptible joint. Snowy, I decided, was all right, even if everyone did continually get on at him.

There were other, more serious and more deeply rooted disputes within the side, of which I knew little or nothing when I played my first match for MCC – an up-country one-day game at a place called Redlands Bay. I was told to take it easy rather than rushing in and trying to impress everyone, and the advice was good, because the first thing that struck me was the unbelievable heat. It was sticky, humid and roasting hot and I am quite sure I could not have bowled a spell of more than three or four overs even if I had been asked to. I took one wicket and was grateful.

I quickly lost my individual double room and joined the regular pattern of touring teams in sharing a twin-bedded room. My first room-mate was Bob Taylor, who was also on his first official

England trip at the age of nearly 30. He was very much second-string wicketkeeper, with no real hope of ousting Alan Knott barring injury, so his first question should perhaps not have taken me by surprise.

'Do you go to parties?' asked Bob, and I was soon to find out how he earned his nickname 'Chat'. About one third of our squad did not socialise at all, and although there was a healthy proportion of players happy to go out and share a drink and a chat with the locals, at Test match time that number dwindled dramatically, with the gregarious non-players, like Bob, left to fly the flag at the bevy of functions. I was happy to go along with him, and plainly recall my first collision with Aussie beer, which tasted insipid to me after the strong English bitter. Expressing loud scepticism as to its strength – no doubt to the silent amusement of the assembled company – I launched into the 'tinnies' as Australians call their canned lager, with gay abandon, only to find my legs suddenly feeling wobbly and my head apparently engulfed in a swirling fog. Despite having been completely plastered, I woke the next morning with barely a hint of a hangover and sweated out the effects in the nets. A lesson had been learned, though.

Having only just arrived, I was not considered for the first Test in Brisbane. That would have taken the fairy tale too far into the realms of fantasy. I sat on the sidelines and watched a high-scoring draw, both sides topping 400 and the stocky Australian opener Keith Stackpole making a double-hundred after being palpably run out while still in single figures.

We flew across the continent to Perth for our next match, which turned out to be my first-class début for MCC, against Western Australia. I also played in the country districts game, a bus-ride away at a place called Narrogin, and if I had thought Redlands Bay was the hottest spot I was likely to play in, this very soon put me right. Narrogin was an oven, so hot that any form of physical activity would, under other circumstances, have been considered foolhardy. My clearest memory of the place is that we have lunch in a shed-like pavilion with, of all things, a corrugated iron roof – just to keep the warmth in, of course. We sat there, chomping through our salad and watching the ice-cream, which had been handed out for dessert, rapidly melting before our eyes.

On the way back to Perth our coach broke down and, while we waited for essential repairs to be carried out, the crates of beer we had with us were raided and a singsong initiated – probably by John Hampshire and Don Wilson. Fortified by a can or two, I proceeded to give my risqué rendition of 'Barnacle Bill the Sailor', a performance which, I imagine, branded me as something of a rogue in the eyes of the accompanying press party.

The Perth Test was drawn, too, the deadlock as complete as it had been at Brisbane. Snowy ensured that the crowd did not drop off to sleep by digging in a series of short-pitched balls. He was warned for bowling too many bouncers and, just to illustrate his own view of a real bouncer, immediately dropped one so short that it flew over the batsman's head by a distance, requiring Alan Knott to leap to take it. This was the Snow the crowd loved to hate, demonstrating the aggressive streak that was to make him a brilliant fast-bowling weapon as well as a cricketing rebel.

At the end of this second stalemate, our manager, David Clark, made a statement which even I, the tour rookie, considered unfair and which graphically painted for me a picture of the relationship between our manager and captain. It is customary, and has been for years now, to hold a press conference at the end of each Test, chiefly for the purpose of media men questioning the respective captains on critical factors in the game, the effect of the result and the immediate future. In Perth, David Clark, whose attendant role as manager was usually a silent one, issued some plainly rehearsed remarks on the state of the series, including the priceless line that he would prefer to lose the rubber 3–0 than have any more draws like the first two.

At best this was a tactless put-down of players who had been sweating buckets for their country. At worst, it could have been thought an incitement to further conflict between Clark and Illingworth who, it now became plain to me, might as well have come from different planets.

None of the players was exactly pleased by the manager's comments but Ray was fuming. Just as angry was John Snow, who had also been the target for some of the manager's barbed remarks on the number of bouncers bowled. In his subsequent book, *Cricket Rebel*, Snow recalls: 'Let me say at once that nobody wanted the parting of the ways between management and ourselves but it was inevitable as a result of the manager's attitude. Perhaps, as a result, a greater effort is being made to ensure that tour managers and players are more of a like mind in future. At the time, Ray and I sat with the manager in the stands at Adelaide trying to put our point of view about his statement but, after an hour, we were no nearer a mutual understanding and just gave up.'

Although Snow and Clark were to come into violent verbal

contact later in the tour, during which they never once saw eye to eye, the relationship between Clark and Illingworth was by some distance the worst I have ever known between a captain and manager, with the result that the spirit among the team was never entirely harmonious.

Little better, probably, was the relationship between Illingworth and Boycott, although in stark contrast to their out-and-out war of later years, they did spend a lot of time together. It was understandable that Illy, as captain, could not be wholeheartedly behind Boycott when stories were reaching him from his players in the style of the now well-known one from the Perth Test. Geoff was batting with Basil D'Oliveira and Johnny Gleeson, the mystery spinner who was baffling many of our batsmen at the time, was bowling. 'Dolly' eventually began to play him with more comfort and between overs he walked down the wicket to tell Boycott: 'I've got it now. You just play him as you would play an off-spinner.' Boycott is alleged to have replied: 'Yes, I know . . . but don't tell the others, will you?'

Dolly became my room-mate for a spell in Adelaide and he really was an education to a young tourist. I was not exactly a shrinking violet myself when it came to having a sociable beer or two in the bar, but I would almost always be in bed by 11.00. Bas, invariably wearing his check crimplene suit, would lurch back into the room some time between 2.00 and 3.00 a.m., shake me awake, roar something like 'I told them, Bob, I told them', and collapse fully clothed on his bed. I would dutifully get up to remove his shoes and at some stage in his foreshortened night he would rouse himself enough to get undressed and under the covers. Each morning he would look wretched, sipping black coffee while I tucked into a four-course breakfast, and catching the team bus with seconds to spare.

Bas was a one-off. For all his excesses, his cheerfully admitted drinking sessions, he would often go out to bat all day and score 150, showing no ill effects at all. He was a quite extraordinary cricketer and I would not have wanted him any other way . . . despite the disturbed nights.

We spent Christmas in Tasmania, staying at the famous Wrest Point Hotel which houses one of the most successful casinos in Australasia. Then it was on to Melbourne and what was due to be the third Test, over the New Year period, although three days' continuous rain ensured that the game would never even start.

Unknown to the players, and even to our captain, a meeting took

34

place between manager Clark, MCC officials Sir Cyril Hawker and 'Gubby' Allen, both of whom had flown out to see the match, and Sir Donald Bradman, with the upshot that an extra Test match was slotted into the schedule to replace the one lost to rain. The first we knew of this was when Bradman came into our dressing-room to say how good it was of us to agree to another match. Illingworth was once again angry – and rightly so. How on earth such a decision could have been reached without any reference to the captain is, frankly, beyond me and Illy swiftly called a team meeting to discuss our position.

The fee for those chosen for the entire tour was £900 (I received rather less, having missed the first three weeks). Illingworth proposed that we should decline to play this extra game unless our fee was proportionately increased, whereupon the issue was put to a vote, everyone supporting the captain except Derek Underwood, who maintained he would be happy to represent England without pay. There was also one silent dissenter as Colin Cowdrey had not turned up for the meeting, underlining his allegiance to his Kentish colleague and friend, Clark, in what was becoming open warfare against Illingworth.

It was not long before the Australian Board announced their intention to pay their players extra for the newly arranged game; very much longer before our management relented sufficiently to offer us an additional £100 per man, which was accepted without question. If only there had been some consultation at the outset, all the unpleasantness could surely have been averted.

Much of this was still passing me by as I did not expect to play in any of the Tests. Until one memorable day up-country in New South Wales. We flew to a small town called Parkes in a DC3, piloted by a captain of daredevil ilk who proudly announced he would 'show us the cricket ground' from the air before cheerfully ushering us off the plane only just the right side of air-sickness. Still feeling green we went straight into the field, where Ken Shuttleworth, the Lancashire pace bowler, broke down with a strained groin muscle, during his new-ball spell giving me my opening into Test cricket.

Having been told the night before the game that I would be playing, I think I could be excused for barely sleeping a wink. What I did not know at the time was that insomnia was to plague me throughout my Test career, being eased only some years later following a chance meeting with a doctor of hypnotherapy on a return visit to Sydney.

Sydney was all I had heard it would be. I could hardly have picked a more atmospheric ground on which to make my Test début and, England having won the toss and chosen to bat, I sat looking out from the dressing-room all through the opening day in a state of high anxiety. We were eight wickets down at stumps, which meant I was padded up ready for my first England innings at number 11. I went in on a hat-trick early next morning and felt myself shaking with nerves until I walked through the white pavilion gate and onto the famous ground. Quite suddenly, I felt composed if not entirely in control. I lunged forward, characteristically, at my first delivery, which missed the off stump by a whisker but, having thus narrowly avoided the most ignominious of all possible starts, I surprised myself and everyone else by sharing a last-wicket stand of 41 with Peter Lever.

After we had piled up a forbidding second-innings total, the top began to crumble and the pitch became a batsman's nightmare, although I took only one wicket – Ashley Mallet caught down the leg-side by Alan Knott off a gloved hook. Snow was lethal, making the ball leap wickedly from a good length and once striking Graham McKenzie full in the mouth with a delivery that could never have been termed short. He finished with seven for 40, looking quite unplayable, and we won the game easily to take a 1–0 lead in the series.

It was a dream start and the fairy tale was to continue as I kept my place for the three remaining games. Melbourne's rearranged match, now the fifth Test of seven, was a dull draw I recall only for the ferocity of the sun and the fact that I could not bowl in spells of more than three overs. Turning at the end of my run-up was like walking through an open oven door. Adelaide was also drawn, but there were those who believed we threw away a good chance of victory when Ray Illingworth decided not to enforce the follow-on with Australia 200-plus behind on first innings. His explanation was that the seam bowlers had done the majority of the work and it was not fair to them, nor to the benefit of the side, to ask for another all-out assault immediately. Right or wrong, the move backfired, as Australia responded to our setting of an impossible target by scoring 328 for three.

This match was also notable for the début of a wild, woolly Australian fast bowler named Dennis Lillee, already quick and aggressive enough to create a big impression, and for another Boycott incident. This time the man created a storm by throwing down his bat when he was adjudged run out. It was a petty affair, but just another in the saga as far as he is concerned. Another black mark, too, in a tour which might so easily have been one of uninterrupted glory for Boycott, whose magnificent 142 not out set up the opportunity for Snow's destruction of the Aussies at Sydney.

Australia have a habit of over-reacting when faced by defeat and now, one down with one to play, they did just that. Bill Lawry, the dour, rather negative man who had led them throughout the series, was dropped and Ian Chappell took over for what was to be the start of a long and momentous spell in charge. Here, however, he had an unfamiliar crew under him, McKenzie, Gleeson and 'Froggy' Thomson having joined Lawry on the scrapheap. We could scarcely believe some of the selections made in their places and certainly did not consider the changes had harmed our hopes of hanging onto our advantage and clinching the Ashes. In the event we did rather better, but only after a series of traumas and a nerve-wrenching Test which left me feeling quite drained.

Our last game but one before the Test was a one-day match against the Australian limited-overs champions, Western Australia, and 'Garth' McKenzie, whom I always rated a charming man and a superb bowler, was plainly out to prove that it had been a great mistake to axe him. During the course of a fiery spell, he made one delivery rise sharply enough to strike Boycott on the forearm, breaking his arm and depriving us of our best batsman for the Test.

We had already suffered an epidemic of injuries, stretching our squad to its limits, so that when Chappell won the toss and put us in on a damp pitch it was easy to fear the worst. We were dismissed for 184, but had reason to be thankful we did not have to face McKenzie, for whom the conditions would have been ideal. By the end of the opening day Australia had lost two cheap wickets and the game was evenly balanced again.

My own contribution to the second day was not great, other than taking a spectacular catch – Rod Marsh off Lever – but it was an explosive day, on which John Snow and umpire Lou Rowan came into violent conflict and the Sydney crowd bayed for the blood of our greatest fast bowler.

Australia had inched ahead, thanks largely to a resolute innings from Greg Chappell, but batsmen likely to lend him any support were becoming thin on the ground by the time Ray took the new ball and naturally threw it to Snowy. Chappell's partner was the leg-spinner Terry Jenner, and what happened next is best described by Snow himself: 'I decided to bowl him (Jenner) a shortish delivery just to remind him he could not go safely on to the front foot. It was not a bouncer and would not have got above rib high if Jenner had not ducked into it, the ball catching him on the head. Down he went. When he returned from hospital, he admitted it was his fault entirely.'

Between Jenner's departure from the field and his admission of responsibility a great deal happened. Umpire Rowan, who had not exactly been Snowy's favourite personality throughout the series, issued a warning for intimidatory bowling. Snow protested, as did Ray Illingworth, and the crowd, already angered by Jenner's mishap, now grew so unpleasant that when Snowy returned, seething, to his fielding position at long-leg he was greeted by a hail of beer-cans.

Illingworth tried to calm the situation by calling John back into the middle and holding up the game while the cans were cleared away. He resumed his position, greeted by an odd mixture of boos and cheers, and had turned his back on the crowd when some large Australian, probably boozed-up to the point of belligerence, reached over the fence, grabbed Snowy by the shirt-sleeve and tried to pull him off the field. By the time he had freed himself, with the help of some more sober spectators, the beer cans had started raining down again and I was cantering across to lend my mate a hand.

It was probably a fatuous gesture on my part. As Bill O'Reilly, the former Australian Test player, wrote in the *Sydney Morning Herald* next day: 'What did Willis think he could do to help – he looks like a two-iron with ears!' I was, however, able to pass on to Snowy the valuable information that Illingworth had decided the thing had gone too far and intended to take us off the field while the spectators sorted themselves out. I believe Illy was right, but David Clark disagreed and the two of them had another stand-up argument on the matter.

When we did resume in relative peace and order, the game continued its tense path. Australia's lead was narrow, and although we fared slightly better in our second innings, they still required only 223 to square the series and retain the Ashes. On the fourth afternoon, at a psychologically disastrous time for us, Snow was put out of the game when he collided with the boundary fence, breaking the little finger on his left hand. First Boycott, now Snow. Our two key figures out of action. Were the Ashes about to slip away?

They were not. Peter Lever and I bowled steadily and well to the end of that penultimate day, leaving Australia to begin the final day of the series needing another 100 runs with five wickets standing. It was then that Illingworth made his bravest and best decision of the entire series.

Lever and I, expecting to bowl, were both loosening up when Ray came over to say that he and Derek Underwood would be opening. Ray was often criticised for not bowling himself enough when captain, but now at the most critical time of all, with the success or failure of the tour resting on it, he took the matter into his own hands. The move succeeded. Greg Chappell was stumped early on and the rest folded tamely to give us a victory none of us was likely to forget. It may not have been the smoothest or happiest of tours off the field, but this was undoubtedly a memorable triumph, and for me, an incredible manner in which to set out on the long road with England.

Back in the dressing-room, Doug Walters and Rod Marsh were, as ever, quick and sporting in joining us for a drink, while Boycott and Snow sat side by side with their arms in slings. And there was my father, pouring a glass of champagne for me . . .

4

TIME TO MOVE ON

Throughout my career, things seldom worked out quite the way I expected. Just as I had had no inkling that I might be summoned to Australia, so I could never have envisaged the upheavals I would undergo within months of my return. I came back as an England bowler. All too soon, I was a county Second XI player again, and before the end of the year I had left The Oval for good.

Disenchantment with the situation at Surrey had, I suppose, been a gradual process, but it came to a head on the strength of more than one issue during the summer of 1971, convincing me that my future would be rosier and happier elsewhere.

The first matter arose even before the season had started. I had returned from the tour to some trumpeting publicity, the new season not far distant, as from Australia we had flown on to play two Tests in New Zealand. The anticlimax had begun in New Zealand, who were still at that time regarded as a second-rate Test nation and unlikely to give us a serious contest. For this reason, several of our fringe players were included in the first Test at Christchurch, Bob Taylor being chosen ahead of Alan Knott, who was rooming with me at the time and seemed distinctly unimpressed by the gesture. I was also rested, but brought back for the second match in Auckland, so that having begun the winter with a coaching job back home in London, I finished it with five totally unexpected Test caps.

Fast bowlers are news. They always have been and always will be. They are the equivalent of the goalscorers in soccer or the heavyweights in boxing, possibly no better at the job than many of their colleagues and rivals, but their roles attract glamour and publicity. For this reason, the newspapers made quite a fuss of me when the team arrived back in England, more than one writer posing an apocryphal question regarding the Surrey hierarchy, asking why someone had not met me at the airport with my county cap.

To be honest, I had hardly given that possibility a thought. It seemed enough, for the time being, that I had made the giant advance into Test cricket and I blithely assumed that any niceties of my domestic cricket employment would now take care of themselves. I was very wrong. Surrey made what I considered an insulting offer of £750 for the season and, fired by righteous indignation, I asked Stuart Surridge for an appointment to put my case.

The interview was not especially amicable. In fact, the chairman at one point banged his fist on the table and told me in no uncertain terms that I was expected to earn my wages at Surrey. However, I did not back down and, amid a degree of bad feeling, I was eventually given an increase.

I can appreciate the view of those involved in running the Surrey side. My achievements for the county had been strictly limited, I was still unable to command a regular place and they considered me worthy neither of a cap, nor of capped players' wages. A Test player I might be, but I had yet to prove my long-term worth at county level.

My own opinion being naturally at variance with this, the type of unhealthy climate developed that I have seen on many occasions since, in which a young player's international progress arouses domestic jealousies and backbiting. Perhaps I did not help the situation myself, coming back with inflated ideas of my own importance, puffed up by the media praise and campaigns for my cap. But I still maintain that Surrey did not do all they might have done to make me feel I was wanted at The Oval.

A few weeks into the season, however, they were probably relieved to have had acted the way they did. Physically still exhausted from the tour, and mentally not mature enough to come to terms with the more mundane routine of county cricket, I bowled abysmally. I felt tired all the time and just could not summon up the energy or the enthusiasm to bowl with any real hostility. Micky Stewart was plainly concerned, to the extent of visiting the flat to ask Martin if I was looking after myself properly and eating the right things, but my problem was simply a belated reaction to the exertions and emotional outputs of the tour.

England's selectors showed some faith in my ability, and none in current form, by making me 12th man for the first Test against Pakistan at Edgbaston, where I seemed to spend most of the match in the field after Alan Ward, whose injury in Australia had granted me my international opening, ironically broke down again. Pakistan made 608 for seven, their highest total in a Test against

England, forcing us to follow on before honour was salvaged in a draw.

I returned to The Oval and virtual oblivion, languishing for two months in the Second team, apparently a million miles from the elations I had experienced so recently in Sydney. I suspect there was a lot of smug satisfaction in certain quarters of the Surrey dressing-room that the young pretender was in such a mess. It was a thoroughly unpleasant time, and although my strength and appetite for bowling returned, I grew more convinced that I was wasting my time at The Oval.

On one occasion when I was feeling particularly low, I voiced my intention to leave at the end of the season to Roy Lewis, with whom I was sitting in the dressing-room of Hornsey Cricket Club during a match with Middlesex Seconds. He was sure I would change my mind, but on this occasion I knew for certain he was wrong.

That evening when, as usual, we returned to The Oval for a drink in the Tavern, I took Robin Jackman aside. With anyone else, the situation might have been delicate or even unfriendly, for after all Jackers was the man who was keeping me out of the side and he had been capped the previous year whereas I was still waiting. Yet there was never a trace of animosity between us. 'The way things are,' I said to him, 'one of us is going to have to leave Surrey to get on in this game. You've won your cap and you're in the side, so it should be me. I'm off as soon as the season ends.'

I told the relevant club officials of my decision in the weeks which followed, although by that time I had won back my place in the first team and I imagine they felt confident I would change my mind. I kept my place for the last six weeks of the season and joined in the celebrations as we brought the Championship back to The Oval for the first time since 1958. Three successive away wins had brought the title into sight and we began our final match against Hampshire needing only two bonus points to ward off the challenge of Warwickshire. We wasted little time in taking the four wickets which, in those days, were enough for two points. Micky's wife, Sheila, immediately rushed onto the field, flinging her arms around our relieved skipper, while Jackers, now relegated to the role of 12th man, further delayed the game by striding out to the middle with champagne for us all. We didn't take another point from that game, but we had done enough.

It probably came as a surprise to Surrey that I stood by my decision to leave, despite the change of fortune. I saw the president,

Maurice Allom, lunched with Micky, who told me my best chance of Test selection was to play at The Oval, and had a visit at my flat from Ken Barrington bearing a similar message. But I was not to be diverted from the course I knew in my own mind to be right and once again found myself in the headlines.

Although I had not played a Test match that summer, my stated intention to move created a great deal of publicity – possibly because it was even more unusual at that time that it is now. Players did not move from one county to another unless they were sacked or released, so I knew I had to handle my situation very carefully. It was a big step, cutting myself adrift from Surrey with no other job to go to – not even a part-time winter job. I signed on the dole and tried to rebuild my career.

In all, I had letters from nine counties expressing interest. Some of the proposals were more attractive than others, of course, but by far the most inventive was Glamorgan's offer of a winter contract with Swansea Town Football Club to run concurrent with my cricket commitments.

With regard to football I was now more of a spectator than an active player – and there were more important considerations that my new county had to offer, playing potential in particular. I narrowed my options to a short-list of three: Leicestershire, with their impressive secretary-captain team of Mike Turner and Ray Illingworth; Lancashire, who offered me the security of a winter job at Hawker Siddeley in Manchester; and Warwickshire.

Lancashire's attraction owed as much to sentiment as anything else. Having spent my formative years in Manchester, and watched my first Test match day at Old Trafford, it seemed fitting to play county cricket there. I went up to Manchester for an interview, and also travelled to Leicester to talk to Mike Turner, but Warwickshire scored by coming to me.

Edmund King, their chairman, and Alan 'A.C.' Smith, their captain, drove down to London, where their approach made an immediately favourable impression. For the first time since going into cricket, I was dealing with county administrators who treated me like an adult yet made me feel that I was hot property. Perhaps they deliberately appealed to my vanity, but I have a feeling this was the natural business sense of two very shrewd men who took an interest in my personal life, speaking intelligently and openly about their club and its ambitious plans. Despite putting me under no overt pressure, they left me in little doubt that I would be passing up something special if I opted to go anywhere else.

So I didn't. Giving my regrets to Leicestershire and Lancashire, I went up to sign on the dotted line in Birmingham, my first impression of which was of an ugly concrete jungle set beneath a muddle of motorway flyovers. My old Surrey mate, Jim Cumbes, who was then with Worcestershire, invited me to visit him at his winter 'office', the West Bromwich Albion training ground. Set directly alongside the M5, it gave me a frightening introduction to the city that was to become my home, although I thankfully discovered it was not typical of the whole place. This visit also had its benefits, Jim taking me to a cafe near the ground where I met a man named David Billings, a good friend of Jim, great supporter of Albion and energetic city solicitor. David, it transpired, had a room to spare in his house, and it was arranged there and then that I would move in with him.

Although my future was now resolved, I was still officially out of work. There being no England tour that winter, and in the absence of any alternative cricket overseas, I would take the train every Friday morning from Birmingham to London, then the tube to Brixton, where I had to sign on for my dole money.

As the 1972 season approached, my registration went before the sub-committee of the Test and County Cricket Board set up to deal with such rare occurences as players changing counties. I had first met officials of the Cricketers' Association, which represents the players rather like a trade union, to put my case for being allowed to move, and then on went the blue serge suit again for my appearance before the registrations committee.

My high hopes of being permitted to play for Warwickshire immediately were dashed, there being talk of a complaint that I had been unethically hawking myself around the counties. I found this an unjustified objection and have no idea whether it was taken into consideration, but the conclusion of the committee was that I should not be allowed to appear in first class matches for my new county until 1 July. Left to my own devices, I might have been tempted to appeal against the delay, but Alan Smith advised me firmly to say nothing and accept the decision with good grace. I soon came to know why.

Until going to Birmingham I had seen A.C. only as a rather eccentric figure, an amateur who wore a white cravat and floppy pads on the field, a wicketkeeper of dubious pedigree whose strange walk and flapping hands were ridiculed around the counties. I dismissed him as a successful oddball, thinking no more about it until, coming under his wing, I began to realize the depths and

44

strengths of the man. A.C. and Edmund King were very powerful men at Warwickshire, anything to do with the team being decided by A.C. and all other policy decisions being mutually agreed. Alan Smith was not only a fine batsman but also a forceful and ambitious captain, who had by 1972 gathered around him an array of international stars with the sole aim of avenging that narrow failure of the previous summer and prising the title away from Surrey.

Unlike others of similar ambition, Alan refused to deviate from the rule-book. An establishment man with designs on an establishment job once he gave up playing, he was not prepared to do anything which might cast a slur either on the club or on his own reputation. The very hint that Warwickshire might have poached someone else's player was anathema to him, and it was for this reason that he placated me in my disappointment over the two-month delay, telling me there was to be no question of challenging the verdict. I respected him for it, once I had the time to assimilate all the facts, and in the years to follow we grew closer until I could call him a very good friend.

A.C. had certainly done an outstanding job with his team-building. The rule stipulated that no county should have more than two overseas players but then, as now, there were loopholes to be exploited. Deryck Murray qualified for us through his Cambridge education and Alvin Kallicharran, having seen out the required period of residence, was considered to be 'English'. Lance Gibbs and Rohan Kanhai made up our West Indian quartet, and a formidable contingent they were, too.

Although such policies may not be in the long-term interests of the club, or of the game, Warwickshire were breaking no rules by doing it – they had simply been clever and very few cricketers around the country were in any doubt as to the likely winners of the 1972 Championship.

It was frustrating for me to spend half the season in the Second team, feeling fit, aggressive and eager to bowl – an altogether different story from my weariness of a year earlier. Yet I enjoyed the comradeship of my time in the Seconds, the feeling of being welcomed in a friendly but competitive atmosphere, and being well looked after in every way with some good and amusing times.

Financially, I was far better off than I had ever been, Warwickshire paying me approximately twice as much as Surrey had. Even during my spell in the Seconds I was made to feel as if I was one of the squad, with a place in the first-team dressing-room at Edgbaston between Billy Blenkiron and David Brown. I remember where everyone else changed as if it was yesterday. All through my time with Warwickshire, I kept the same place in the dressing-room, and although never thinking of it as a superstitition, I would have been far from pleased had anyone taken it away from me.

My social life, too, had improved. Having Jim Cumbes nearby was a great bonus, as we shared the same hobbies and the same sense of humour. Our local pub was The Sportsman in Harborne, close enough to the Queen Elizabeth Hospital to attract a healthy parade of nurses. Every Thursday night I would join Jim and some of the other Albion players on their week's big evening, drinking at a club called the Binton Barn, going for a curry and generally ending up less than sober, supping a little more scotch at his house.

I was relieved when the stated day in July arrived giving me a chance to justify some of Warwickshire's outlay and, most dear to my heart, set about trying to retrieve a Test career which had come and gone all too quickly for my liking. Warwickshire being already well on the way to the Championship by the time I was able to start playing, I can claim no special credit for the fact that they won it with plenty in hand. They were, by some distance, the most powerful team in the land and it would have been much more of a surprise had they failed. Yet it gave me the unusual honour of winning the Championship in successive seasons with two different counties.

I didn't play any Test matches in 1972 but was chosen as 12th man for the final match against Australia, at The Oval. The England side contained a lot of very experienced players, quite a few of whom had decided they would not be available for the winter tour to India and Pakistan. Even Ray Illingworth had opted out, Tony Lewis becoming captain, and, encouraged by many remarks passed by other members of the Test side, I began to believe that my selection for the tour was nothing more than a formality.

Because my surname begins with W, I have always had an agonisingly long wait for the verdict when listening to Test teams and tour squads read out on the radio. When Brian Johnston ran down the list of names that year, I had an even longer wait . . . I had not been chosen.

At the time, it was a big disappointment. Having built myself up to thinking I was virtually certain to tour, I was suddenly left with another empty winter. The vacuum was very soon filled by an offer to coach in South Africa, where I was to be based in Northern Transvaal, coaching schoolboys most afternoons during the week and playing club cricket at weekends. I was accompanied

46

by the much-travelled seam bowler, Allan Jones, both being put up by very hospitable families. Disaster threatened when, shortly after our arrival, the secretary of the local cricket Union vanished, taking with him their funds and paperwork. Not only were we now in the dark as to whom and where we were supposed to be coaching; there was also no money with which to pay us.

Once this hurdle had been cleared the winter passed enjoyably – so much so that I took little persuasion to return for three months at the end of 1973, although by then I had at last broken back into Test cricket. Having missed out on the first five matches of the split summer against New Zealand and the West Indies, I finally won back my place in the Lord's Test.

For English cricket, it could not be called a monumental success, West Indies scoring 652 to beat us easily. A bomb scare brought the unthinkable to life with the Lord's ground being evacuated on a Saturday afternoon; and Ray Illingworth was sacked as captain. But for me it was a real breakthrough. Despite the circumstances of the match I took four wickets, and I was described in the pages of *Wisden* as 'the young fast bowler who performed with great heart and enthusiasm'. The selectors cannot totally have disagreed because just after the New Year I found myself on a plane bound for the Caribbean, under the new captaincy of Mike Denness.

5

YEARS OF DESTINY

The mid-seventies were years of destiny for Test cricket, in which the game changed to a quite dramatic degree. It has never been the same since.

There is no doubt in my mind that the catalysts in the revolution were three Australians named Chappell, Lillee and Thomson and that, for a time, their country was the chief beneficiary. Using tactics which relied hugely on intimidating fast bowling, Australia beat England 4–1 in 1974–75 and West Indies by an even more demoralising 5–1 a year later. But the worm was about to turn. West Indies equipped themselves for the new type of warfare and, where the Australians only ever used two main weapons, they were to employ four. The battle of the bouncers was escalating and life for the Test batsmen was turning into a fight for survival.

I saw the first evidence of the impending change during MCC's tour of the West Indies in 1973–74. His name was Andy Roberts and he was fast, hostile and young, the outrider for the regiment of aggressors who were soon to march into the side under the direction of Clive Lloyd.

Roberts's part in that tour was confined to that of a walk-on actor. There were still political overtones to many selections for the West Indies side and Roberts was given his début in Barbados because he was a Leeward Islands player and Barbados was part of that group. In the previous Test, his place had gone to a Jamaican spinner because the match was played at Kingston, and in the first of the series, in Port-of-Spain, a Trinidadian spinner was chosen. This had always been the way of things in the Caribbean and although, under Lloyd and with their recent enormous success, their side has been much more settled and chosen entirely on merit, the local jealousies persist, England's visit to Trinidad in 1981 being marred by demonstrations over the omission of local hero Deryck Murray from the side.

48

Rohan Kanhai, my Warwickshire team-mate, retained the captaincy of West Indies for our visit, and it would be fair to say that their strengths were more in batting than bowling. The winds of change had not yet reached the Caribbean and, with a batting line-up which read Fredericks, Rowe, Kanhai, Kallicharran, Lloyd and Sobers, they were justified in believing they could bat most sides out of the game.

Nor were they entirely devoid of aggression in the bowling department. Keith Boyce was at his peak as an athletic and belligerent quickie; Vanburn Holder was a clever bowler, and much sharper than most gave him credit for; and there was the left-arm swing of Bernard Julien with that man Sobers to follow up. It might not compare with the full-frontal assault of Marshall, Holding, Roberts and Garner, but it was far from being a negligible force.

This had been proved in England the previous summer when a 2–0 defeat in a three-match series against Kanhai's side cost Ray Illingworth his job as captain. His refusal to tour India and Pakistan the previous winter had probably been held against him when the decision was taken, but there was no getting away from the fact that we were beaten hollow in the final Test of the summer at Lord's, a match memorable for a number of things but also personally notable for being my first in England, and my first anywhere since Auckland in March 1971.

Having proved myself with Warwickshire, I won a recall to the side and could hardly have asked for more than dismissing the top four West Indian batsmen. But if this was encouraging, and certainly assured me of a winter overseas, the team's performance was deplorable. West Indies declared with the little matter of 652 for eight, three batsmen having made hundreds, and we were beaten by an innings despite two fine and brave knocks by 'The Gnome', Keith Fletcher. Our first innings was nearing its undistinguished close when the Saturday crowd was evacuated from Lord's by that bomb scare and there were those who joked that the crank who made the call must have been an ardent England supporter unable to bear the sight of such a drubbing.

My recall had been prompted by consistency for Warwickshire and a purple patch in mid-season when I took two hat-tricks within a week – one in a John Player League game against Yorkshire and the second for D. H. Robins' XI against Cambridge University. Warwickshire, shorn of their four West Indians and of Dennis Amiss for all six of the summer's Tests, could do no better than seventh in the Championship, but I had enjoyed the season. In fact, I was very much enjoying life in Birmingham, and when the season ended on such a high personal note with my England place reclaimed after what seemed a very long gap, I went happily off, full of confidence about the future, to complete a coaching stint in South Africa before the New Year tour departure.

Once again I came heavily down to earth. Any thoughts of a harvest of wickets in the Caribbean were rapidly dispelled and, in a series which we eventually and remarkably managed to draw after being outplayed virtually from start to finish, I picked up a meagre five victims. It was not a good series for most of the English bowlers but, although I doubtless discovered plenty of excuses at the time, I can now put the record straight and admit that I bowled badly. I was still hot-headed and immature, reluctant to train properly and simply naïve regarding the type of physical and mental preparations necessary to succeed at Test level.

The angry young man in my character emerged most forcefully in what was possibly the least important game of the entire trip. We stopped off in Bermuda on the way home to play a match against a national side, hardly of decent club standard by English comparisons. After suffering many a disappointment in the preceding months and determined to redeem myself one way or another, I could not have been accused of lacking effort in the morning session. Having had one of their young batsmen out twice in three balls, both palpable dismissals adjudged not out by the umpire, I lost control of the flag-waving spirit of diplomacy and fired in two or three very aggressive bouncers.

When we trooped off the field for lunch, Donald Carr – the tour manager – met me at the dressing-room door, his expression telling a story, demanding to know what on earth I meant by bowling in that way in what was intended as a friendly challenge match. I told him, in no uncertain manner, what I meant and the ensuing argument was loud and heated enough to have been heard by the spectators outside.

We had been fighting against the odds all through the tour, which was by no means the most enjoyable I have ever experienced. There were bound to be problems following Mike Denness's appointment as captain because, whatever his credentials for the job – and these were certainly disputed by some – at least one member of the team felt that the position should have been filled by Geoffrey Boycott. That, of course, was Geoffrey himself.

Mike had two pretenders to his position in Tony Greig and

Boycott, who found it almost unbearable to have been passed over for the vice-captaincy, too. The situation made for some unpleasant incidents which dampened any team spirit, and through it all I felt Denness suffered for his own personality. A shy man, unwilling to impose himself and sometimes apparently unable to communicate, he was the type of reclusive captain who could not help us in our predicament.

My own view is that our lack of team spirit stemmed from poor liaison between management and players. On tour, and a long way from home, there is a real need for players to feel they are being kept aware of what is happening within their group, yet I remember one occasion in particular when Mike Hendrick learned he had been left out of the Test side to play in Barbados from Crawford White of the *Daily Express*. This had quite an effect on me and I vowed at the time that if I ever reached a position of power (something which must then have appeared a very remote prospect) I would make it my business to ensure that players knew of team selection before anyone else.

It should never be difficult on a tour to put this into practice. The entire group of players is a captive audience and the one inconvenience you put them to is holding them in readiness to hear the team through what would otherwise be an afternoon off. It seems a small price to pay for peace of mind. In England the business of telling the players their fate is more complicated. The team is usually chosen on a Friday night but not announced until the Sunday lunchtime, a system which can never preclude leaks during the hours of county play on a Saturday as one player receives a TCCB selection letter and tells his friend, who happens to let it slip to a hovering journalist. The only safe way is for the captain to make contact with as many of his players as possible on Saturday morning, the difficulties of which can be well imagined. If you happen to miss someone at his home or, if he is playing an away match his hotel, you have to phone him at the ground where, invariably, he will be in the nets on the far side of the playing area. When I became England captain I considered this to be such an important issue that I did not lightly give up. But Denness, as I have said, fell down as a communicator, and the party suffered for his failings.

This was also a tour on which team meetings tended to be stormy and sometimes divisive. One especially stands out in my memory. We had been quite comprehensively beaten in the opening Test in Trinidad, and when we gathered on the eve of the second match in Jamaica there was much discussion about where our bowlers had gone wrong in their line to particular batsmen. I listened dutifully, appreciating certain of the points, but eventually could hold back no longer, asking: 'What about the batting?'

I was referring to the sorry slide in Trinidad which had seen us collapse from 328 for 2, losing our last eight wickets for 54 and with them all chance of saving the game; but my question provoked a pregnant silence followed by one or two indignant comments clearly aimed at telling me the batsmen could look after themselves. This attitude has angered me throughout my career with England. It is easy to dissect bowlers, who may be operating for a long time under the close gaze of all their team-mates, each of whom have a point of view about how to get the current batsman out. But batsmen, I have found, are very prickly at the highest level, resenting criticism or advice, hating reminders of a single indiscretion which might have brought their downfall, and generally believing that they should not be distracted from pursuing the technique which won them Test selection.

England batsmen of my experience will, with very few exceptions, delay asking for advice until their form has irretrievably broken down. It is taking personal pride to an almost suicidal extent, but I have seen it happen time after time. To cite just one case, Derek Randall lost his way completely during our tour of Australia in 1979–80 and his problems clearly encompassed technique, confidence and just about every other batting requirement. On the sidelines, wincing at the sight and eager to help out, was one of the greatest post-war English batsmen in Kenny Barrington who, as assistant manager, was charged with some responsibility for coaching, but could not overrule the captain. With Mike Brearley unwilling to involve him in Derek's troubles, and Derek himself never allowing Kenny near enough to help, the problems multiplied until it was all too late. Nothing quite like this happened in the West Indies under Denness but, if the circumstances had been similar, I am inclined to think it would have done.

For a tour which might well have been an outright disaster, honour was salvaged in quite extraordinary fashion. After Trinidad, I think most of us silently feared we were to be annihilated. Everything had gone wrong in that match; we had been bowled out cheaply on a damp pitch, West Indies had made an enormous score and then had come our second-innings collapse just when it seemed we were making a fight of it.

To make matters worse, there was an ugly incident involving

Greig and Kallicharran. The last ball of the day had been bowled and Alvin, well on the way to a big hundred, had set off for the pavilion when Greig fielded the ball and, seeing him out of his ground, threw the stumps down and appealed for a run-out. Umpire Douglas Sang Hue had no real option but to give him out.

I have never seen Alvin quite so furious. He stalked off the field at great pace smashing his bat on the concrete steps leading up to the pavilion. As one or two small fires broke out in the crowd to register displeasure, I was thankful firstly that some of the spectators seemed uncertain of what had happened and secondly that the incident had not occurred in the more volatile atmosphere of Guyana or Jamaica.

Greig, I felt, got a slightly rough deal. He had learned his cricket in South Africa, where they play in just such an uncompromising fashion, as do most Australians, giving nothing, asking for nothing in return. It would have been almost unthinkable for an English-born cricketer to have run out a batsman as he left the field, but for all his commitment to the side, Greigy was no more English than Allan Lamb, Chris Smith or Basil D'Oliveira.

Overnight negotiations between the management of the two sides concluded that Greig and Kallicharran should shake hands and that the game should continue as if the run-out had never happened, which was probably the only sensible solution even if it did contravene the rule-book.

Greigy was involved in another upset during the next match in Jamaica. We were once again doing more than our share of leather-chasing and, with Clive Lloyd in full flow, Tony decided he would bowl seamers to him with an entirely defensive seven-two field. It was a tactic that did absolutely nothing for the entertainment value, but in the position in which we found ourselves seemed defensible. It quite possibly played its part in saving the game, although that did not stop Greigy from coming in for some criticism from our management.

Our saviour there was Dennis Amiss, who played a quite incredible innings against the odds, finishing unbeaten with 262. Even when I went in at number 11 to join him the game was not entirely safe, and had I been out first ball West Indies would have been chasing something like 90 in 20 overs, which for them would have been easy. In the event I managed to hang around long enough to ensure that his marvellous marathon was not in vain.

In Barbados Greig and Fletcher shared the rearguard action as once more we wriggled off the hook, my own contribution again being sketchy, although I did dismiss the great Sobers for nought with the help of a magnificent catch by Greig at second slip. In Guyana it was rain which held the West Indies at bay, although here their firepower had already been disturbed by the government's refusal to allow Sobers into the country. He had recently been on a coaching trip to Rhodesia, then still mentioned in the same political breath as South Africa, and the president, Forbes Burnham, took as firm a stand with one of his own West Indian heroes as he was later to take with England's Robin Jackman.

Somehow we arrived back in Port-of-Spain for the fifth and final Test still only 1–0 down. I suspect most of us were feeling rather pleased about this, and in truth if we had escaped from the series with such a narrow margin of defeat, it would not have been a bad performance considering the quite evident gulf between the teams. In Trinidad, though, everything changed. Boycott batted like a master, Greig took 13 wickets with off-breaks and we levelled the series. It was ironic that Denness was thus kept in his job by the two men who were rivals as next in line. Boycott probably dwelt on that, although I doubt Greig gave it another thought. That was the difference between them.

Another irony was that it was in this game, I would wager, that Greig's later, misguided reference to the West Indians 'grovelling' was planted in his mind. They had batted well throughout the series, but there had seldom, if ever, been any great pressure on them. Now, for the first time, the tables were turned as England employed four spinners, crowded the batsmen with close fielders and exerted heavy pressure, hour after hour. To coin a colloquialism, West Indies' 'bottle went'. The ball turned, but not excessively as they were psyched out rather than bowled out, intimidated by the sight of their kingpins falling (especially Kallicharran who made 0 and 0 after an extremely prolific series) and generally panicking, if not grovelling.

Much as I delighted in this remarkable turn of fortunes, my celebrations were tempered by my omission from the side after the third Test. It was a bad blow, but I could not argue with the reasoning, having bowled poorly. I had lost my rhythm and hostility after reverting to a long run from the 12-yard approach with which I had been experimenting late in the 1973 season and in the early stages of the tour. I had not known enough about bowling, or about its athletic demands, even to try to put things right, so I ended the trip in a muddle, with much to be done to sustain my hopes of a long-term England future.

I had not found the West Indies the paradise place to tour that some people seem to imagine. Sure, the sun shines most days, the beaches are long and golden and the barbecues attractive, but while an atmosphere like that can be a treat for a fortnight, it can be an aggravation over a three-month period, surrounded as one is by holidaymakers yet quite unable to behave like them.

The good thing about West Indian tours is that they do not begin until January, giving the players the rare pleasure of spending Christmas at home. The bad thing is that they continue until mid-April, which inevitably means plunging directly into the hurly-burly of the new county season without so much as a week's break.

In 1974, India and Pakistan were the visitors for twin tours and the selectors arranged for a Test trial to be held at Worcester during May. In principle, I am in favour of this idea, although in practice I am not sure it works. The difficulty lies in making the matches competitive. Individuals are naturally going to be competing with each other for the eye of the selectors, but cricket is a team game and there is limited value in any game unless both sides want to win, thus putting their players into pressure situations. I hate to say it, but if trials are ever revived, the only way of curing this might be to put up a cash incentive for the winning team.

That particular trial was not without its controversy. It was virtually monopolised by Geoff Boycott, who scored a century in each innings and batted for nearly two of the three days, so that with John Edrich also making a big score there was precious little opportunity for anyone else to shine. There was little the selectors did not already know about Boycott – certainly no doubt at all that he would be in the side for the opening Test of the summer – and had he been less of a single-minded cricketer, he would have volunteered to drop down the order in the second innings, or even given away his wicket at 50 or 60 in both. John Snow showed his disdain by bowling leg-breaks at Boycott.

The sequel was even more dramatic. Boycott did, indeed, play in the first Test against India at Old Trafford in a match marred by filthy weather. A rule operated then by which an hour's loss of play in a day meant that the close was put back to 7.30 p.m., and on one such evening, Geoffrey was dismissed at 7.28, caught behind by Farokh Engineer off the apparently innocuous left-arm seamers of Eknath Solkar. This was Boycott's swan-song. At the end of the game, without reasonable explanation, he announced that he was no longer available for England and began his three-year exile from Test cricket.

55

His run-making ability was to be sorely missed; his company less so. For, although one must accept that in a team game like cricket not every member will fit the ideal personality pattern and that there will be eccentrics and recluses, Boycott had upset enough people during his time in the game for the mourning to be muted when he withdrew to his south Yorkshire eyrie for a period of silent meditation.

Having played in the first Test with him, I picked up an injury which kept me out of the next match at Lord's, so was unable to assess the instant reaction of the England players to this strange retreat by the country's best batsman. It certainly made no difference to the result there, India erecting minimal resistance to the seam attack of Arnold and Chris Old and being bowled out for 42. England won the third Test easily, too, and Ajit Wadekar's players were so concerned at the inevitable fury of their cricket-crazy countrymen that they separated and took a variety of routes home to India in order to avoid publicity. Having suffered one or two pastings overseas myself, I know how they must have felt.

I was fully fit again by this time, but as the team had won overwhelmingly without me, I had to content myself with county cricket for most of the season, finally winning back my England place for the third and last Test against Pakistan. We went into the game 1–0 up with little likelihood of the score changing. The wicket was of the variety which earned The Oval a bad name – flat to the point of negating all chance of a result. Having spent more than two days in the field at a stretch I arrived at Chelmsford the next day for a county game almost too tired to run up to the wicket.

This, of course, was the crux of my problem. Not fit enough for the rigours of Test cricket, I could not avoid the niggling injuries in the stomach, side and hamstring which kept recurring to frustrate my progress. The irritating syndrome of making it into the England side only to drop out again all too quickly was to come to a head in Australia the following winter.

Denness, having led England to victories over both India and Pakistan, naturally kept the job for a tour which we began full of confidence and ended in a state of shock. With Dennis Lillee evidently struggling to recover from a serious back injury, we optimistically expected Australia to be short of fire-power. We all underestimated Lillee's tremendous commitment and will to recover . . . and none of us had ever heard of Jeff Thomson. Together they formed a new-ball attack nothing short of frightening, to which we had no adequate answer.

We played well enough in the warm-up matches at the start of the tour; most of the squad found form, and the spirit was good, Denness having improved dramatically as a communicator, paradoxically helped by a kidney illness he suffered early in the trip. He got closer to the guys because they were forever popping in to ask how he was, and the shyness which had been such a barrier in the West Indies a year earlier was now broken down. We looked forward to a happier tour, feeling we had every chance of retaining the Ashes.

'Thommo', who had by now been brought to our attention by the Australian press, had distinguished himself by some dubious comments printed in a magazine article about how he enjoyed hurting batsmen. When he played against us for Queensland, prior to the first Test, he was not especially impressive and, although by this stage we also knew that Lillee, having made a marvellous recovery, was likely to line up against us, no-one could be sure whether he would be the potent force of old after such a serious setback.

It took only a few days of the first Test at Brisbane to teach us that we were in for an extremely rough ride. It was not even a fair contest, the match being played on a joke pitch prepared by the Mayor of Brisbane, Clem Jones. Despite various attempts to assist, Mr Jones was unshakably intent on doing the thing his way, and made a dangerous mess of the job. His pitch began the game green, damp and bouncy and although I enjoyed bowling on it when Australia batted first, we all knew what was in store for us.

Australia made 309. Then Lillee and Thomson got to work. The first thing to become crystal clear was that Lillee was as good as ever, if not better, and the second was that Australia had sprung a decisive wild-card on us with Thomson, whose slinging thunderbolts were close to being lethal. Peter Lever and I had both employed the short ball to some effect, Ian Chappell and Walters both getting out to the hook against bouncers from me. But when Lillee and Thommo got stuck in it was obvious our efforts were not in the same league.

The comment which reached us from England was that our batsmen looked to be offering slip catching practice. Maybe they did, but they were in the unenviable position of facing the most venomous bowling that any of them had ever encountered. Only Tony Greig found an antidote, his century being among the most audaciously brilliant innings I have seen. If the ball was up to him he would give it everything, booming straight drives back past the bowler. If it was short, as it usually was, he would play it flat-batted over the heads of the slip cordon – a shot not found in any textbook, but mightily effective when played well against bowling of this sort. In addition, Greig deliberately baited Lillee, which may not have been wise in the long term but certainly had the effect of adding a ragged edge to his bowling.

Greig had asked for trouble by dismissing Lillee with a bouncer of his own at the end of the Australian innings, and as he recalled in his autobiography, *My Story*:

'There are those who still insist that it was that single delivery from me that sparked off the bouncer war to follow. I reject the theory totally and refuse to accept that it made the slightest bit of difference. What it had done though, was to rile Lillee, and as he passed me on his stalking path back to the pavilion he uttered enough words to let me know that my turn had come.'

'. . . We were in real trouble when I went out to bat and the sight of Lillee pawing the ground at the end of an enormous run was enough to send the crowd into a frenzy of anticipation. Lillee had not forgotten his threats and he proceeded to try and kill me. . . . I continued to play up to him and, the more upset he became, the worse he bowled, for Brisbane was a sporty wicket on which the ball of fuller length was the danger delivery.'

Despite Greigy's 110 we still trailed on first innings, and an Australian declaration required us to bat all through the last day for safety, which never looked likely. Worse still, both Edrich and Amiss received hand injuries from balls which reared from not much short of a length and we ended the game in disarray. Suddenly Australia were in complete command, and Test cricket had set out on its new, and some would say sinister direction. From then on, the fast, short balls were to be employed more and more frequently as the killer punches on wickets that had any semblance of life.

Old-timers will still insist that the fast bowlers of their day were just as swift as most of today's tearaways. Maybe they were, but it is the length of the fast delivery which has changed, ever since that Brisbane Test ten years ago. More recently, of course, it has been West Indies who have thrived on this aspect of the game, producing a steady stream of bowlers with the ammunition to intimidate. I think the game has gone seriously wrong in not checking the trend.

The umpires are at fault. They will claim that they have only the law of intimidation to guide them and that this law stipulates they register a bouncer only as a ball which passes above shoulder height. The law is an ass, and even at this late stage it needs changing, for many a vicious delivery has been bowled, even to me, without passing anywhere near as high as my shoulder. The law should be altered to give the umpire complete responsibility to decide when a bowler is deliberately trying to intimidate, and the umpires should then be strong enough to interpret the law and act firmly. In 1984 'Dicky' Bird stepped in to warn Malcolm Marshall during a particularly aggressive spell in the Edgbaston Test against England, whereupon some of the West Indians, including Clive Lloyd, challenged Dicky on his interpretation of the flabby law, although he tells me others in the team later praised him for his actions.

Surely nobody involved in the game wants to see it degenerate into a bloodthirsty battle in which the pace bowler holds complete control? It happened to an extent in 1974-75 when the umpires never moved a muscle to restrain the use of the short ball. Because the fast men were dominant they tended to bowl most of the time, causing the over-rate to drop to about 12 an hour. Of those 72 balls, approximately half were short-pitched, so that if two batsmen stayed together for an hour they might each receive 18 balls of reasonable length. Of those, two in each over (total 12) would probably demand a defensive stroke, leaving each batsman with six deliveries in the hour off which to score!

The bowlers eventually brought about an impasse. They knew that the bouncer was at worst a 'dot ball', at best a wicket, and that it just might hit the batsman or pass close enough to frighten him. As no English batsman out there played the hook shot, only the improvisations of Greig, and later of Alan Knott, could gather any runs at all from the mountain of short balls.

Brisbane had been bad enough, but at least the sub-standard wicket had provided some excuse for the carnage. At Perth, in the second Test, we were pulverised by nine wickets on a blameless pitch so that any hopes we may have harboured that the tide would turn were painfully dashed.

Thomson took seven wickets in the match for a running aggregate of 16 in two, grievously extending our injury list, by hitting Luckhurst on the hand and David Lloyd, excruciatingly, in the groin. His reputation was now virtually complete – the beach bum turned pom-basher – and the Aussies loved him. There was a suspicion of a vindictive streak in his bowling, for which the Aussies liked him more rather than less, but I always considered it to be a false image. Although he tried desperately hard and could be an awesome prospect, I never thought he bowled with the intention of maiming. I liked the guy and even came to find his rough, anti-pom manner engaging.

Lillee was different. I admired him for his matchless fast bowling and the way in which he had battled to overcome serious injury, but he thrived on the macho image, playing up to it with endless histrionics, gestures and verbal performances, which to my mind did nothing for the game at all. 'Sledging' – the verbal abuse and rubbishing of batsmen by bowlers and close fielders – was a prominent and unsavoury feature of this tour, and if Ian Chappell was the orchestrator, Dennis Lillee was a willing player.

There is no doubt in my mind that fear was a factor in this series, batsmen emerging shaken and bewildered as if they had just come out of the trenches after some particularly violent crossfire. It is amazing that the possibility of wearing helmets was never mentioned. Other, less sophisticated types of protection were brought into play, notably by Colin Cowdrey, who had received the call to join our injury-stricken team shortly before his 42nd birthday. Denness and Greig had both considered 'Kipper' to be the man most likely to blunt the Australian attack, even at this advanced stage of his career, and he arrived in Perth to step directly into the fray. Colin wore a forearm protector when he went in at number three, and was immediately struck on it by Thomson. When he came off at lunch, there was a wry smile on the veteran's face as he said: 'That could have been the shortest tour of all time.' But if the years had dulled his reactions and confined his repertoire of strokes, they had done nothing to impair his technique, and he coped as well as anyone during this humbling defeat.

Things temporarily improved in Melbourne, where a tense third Test was drawn with Australia eight runs short, two wickets standing. The game was watched by more than 250,000 people, stretching over a hot Christmas holiday, and although we survived and stayed afloat in the series, the battle had now taken its toll of our captain. After scoring only 65 runs in six Test innings, Mike Denness dropped himself from the next game in Sydney leaving John Edrich to take over the reins.

Maybe Mike knew something. The Sydney pitch was fast and green and might almost have been made to measure for Lillee and his mate. This was the game in which Fletcher was hit flush on his cap-badge virtually before he had moved, and when I – sitting 100 yards away – felt fear for poor Geoff Arnold, an adequately equipped tail-ender in most circumstances, but horribly exposed as a ball from Lillee seared past his temple. He appeared to be a fraction of an inch from death, and would have been able to do absolutely nothing to get out of the way.

We lost heavily again – and again in Adelaide, despite the fact that Thomson sprained his shoulder playing tennis, of all things, on the rest day and was put out of the remainder of that game, as well as the final Test back in Melbourne. We went into that last game trailing 4–0 and it said much for the spirit and fortitude of the blokes that they could come back to win by an innings to gain some consolation. There were reasons, of course. Not only was Thomson absent; Lillee bruised his foot early in our innings and took no further part with the ball. As *Wisden* was to comment, 'Never was the value of two men more obvious than in their absence, for without Lillee and Thomson to worry about England's next three wickets added 149, 192 and 148 . . . compared to a lone three-figure stand in the previous ten innings of the series!'

I was not even present to see our one victory, let alone take part in it. Although by some distance the quickest bowler on England's side, I had once again been exposed as physically ill-prepared for the job. Lillee and Thomson against myself and either Peter Lever or Geoff Arnold was a no contest and I simply was not an accomplished enough bowler to give back the sort of treatment they were meting out to our blokes. By the time we reached Sydney and the fourth Test, I had begun to feel discomfort from my knees; by Adelaide I was hobbling badly, stiffening up so much that I had to pull myself up the hotel staircases by way of the bannisters. It was clear that I was not going to get through the tour, and sure enough a decision was taken to dispatch me back to England for treatment. I flew out on the fourth day of the final Test, missing the victory celebrations and the subsequent 1–0 win in a two-Test mini-series against New Zealand. By then, I was far away in Birmingham, trying to strengthen the knees with daily exercises at Bernard Thomas's gymnasium, pushing myself through 1200 straight-knee raises when each one was more uncomfortable than the last. The surgeon did not want to operate, but I think I knew in my heart that one day he might have to.

Ian Chappell had probably summed up my value and my limitations. He was quoted during the tour as saying that I was a force to be reckoned with before lunch, but was there for the taking after tea. No doubt I bridled indignantly at this slur when I read it, being still at the immature stage of finding excuses whenever I bowled badly, but the plain fact of the matter is that I was not resilient enough for the job I was trying to do.

It had been a strange tour in many ways, not least in that the lads were somehow brought closer together by defeat, the attritional spirit of wartime saving us all from going slowly mad at the hopelessness of it all. I have always been one to take defeat very hard, and was dejected when we slumped to 2–0 down at Perth. Thereafter it was so obvious we would lose the series heavily that I made a conscious decision to enjoy the rest of the tour, come what may.

This did not mean I intended getting drunk every night, more that I was determined not to explore the other extreme, sitting in my lonely hotel room brooding over the situation each night until homesickness set in. I detached myself from the cricket blues whenever possible, met new friends and came to like Australia a lot.

One aspect of the tour which did stir me into my outspoken vein, however, was the appearance of a multitude of wives and children. They came for Christmas and many stayed up to a month, with some players forced to economise to the extent that a whole family was sharing a room which can hardly have helped mental preparation for a Test match.

It was hard to criticise players for bringing out their wives on such a long tour and, mothers invariably finding it hard to leave their children for any length of time, the family came too. While in recent years I have mellowed on the subject of bringing wives on tour, I remain very much against the distracting company of children and was not prepared to make any secret of my feelings that winter, because it divided the party just when we needed to stick together. Our manager, Alec Bedser, had great problems adjusting to the family nature of the tour, nor was the situation improved when he was caricatured in newspaper cartoons carrying a teddy-bear onto the team bus. I came home convinced that the rules should be changed, but then I was biased. I had no plans to marry and not the remotest thought of being a father.

6

SURVIVING SURGERY

While the breakdown in Australia and the subsequent return home punctuated my career with a comma, 26 April 1975 might well have added a full stop. It was certainly the end of a chapter, and there was to be a considerable pause before the next one began – almost four months to be precise, during which I endured the lengthy rehabilitation process from the surgery which had proved to be inevitable.

Five or six weeks of exercises and treatment had convinced me I was fit to start the 1975 season. I felt well, and any who saw the match will confirm that I ran in with life and vigour during Warwickshire's opening fixture, a Benson and Hedges Cup qualifier at Worcester. But although I finished my quota of 11 overs with respectable figures during a comfortable win, I had broken down again, and knew in my heart that this time it would need more than straight-knee lifts to put me right.

I stayed that night in the Worcester home of David Brown, who by now had taken over as Warwickshire captain. With my father who, having travelled up to see the game stayed too, he watched my feeble attempts to scale the tight, winding staircase. I had to admit defeat. I just could not raise my knees enough to climb, and finished up sitting at the bottom, sliding backwards up the stairs to bed.

Within four days I had been admitted to the Woodlands Hospital in Birmingham for repairs to both knees. The surgeon found that the trouble emanated from the disintegration of the pad of fat behind each kneecap, owing both to the wear and tear caused by bowling on hard ground and by the lack of tone in my thighs. He scraped and cleaned the mess, rather as a mechanic would give a car its 50,000-mile service, as well as removing the cartilage from my right knee.

Having both knees operated upon simultaneously left me completely immobilised. For nine days after the surgery I was confined to bed, and for the first three of them found it completely impossible to lift either leg even a fraction of an inch. The removal of the bandages revealed the horrifying sight of two great, swollen knees with legs like twigs either side, where the muscles had wasted. Had I ever been in doubt, I knew then that a lot of hard work and probably discomfort lay ahead before I would be able to play cricket again. Yet I never considered the possibility that my career could be over, coming to terms with the fact that it would take a long time, but never once despairing.

My worst moment came with some drama on the evening of my first day out of bed. Having spent much of the day hobbling around on crutches, I was quite relieved to sink back onto the bed when my friend, David Billings, came to visit me. As we drank a glass of gin and chatted I became acutely aware of a pain in my arm, imagining at first that it had something to do with the unusual pressure of the crutches. When my eyes began to water with the pain though, David, studying my face, asked if I felt all right. I admitted I didn't, whereupon he summoned the nurse and things began to happen very fast.

The nurse plainly recognised the cause of the trouble immediately and rapidly hustled David out of the room before hurrying to find the specialist. He prodded me for some moments before pronouncing that I had suffered a 'pulmonary embolism'. In laymen's language, he explained, a blood clot had developed – in my case starting in the right calf – and moved around my body, directly through my heart. The danger now over, he was prepared to tell me that had it passed less swiftly through the heart, I would have been dead.

The doctors and nurses were clearly surprised that this should have happened, especially to a physically fit sportsman. I was put on a course of Warfarin, a type of rat poison, with the aim of thinning my blood and preventing any repetition, but the remainder of my three-week stay passed without further drama.

Alan Smith drove me back to the flat in Harborne which was now my base. It took me fully five minutes to climb the single flight of stairs on crutches that day, but within a week I was getting around with the aid of a walking stick and, surprisingly quickly, I was back in the gym trying to strengthen my muscles. At the end of July I tentatively returned to action with a few gentle club and social matches, and by late August was ready to play county cricket again, my comeback match, ironically, also being against Worcestershire, this time in the John Player League. Before the season ended there was time for only three Championship games, in the second of which I took nine wickets against Notts at Trent Bridge, doing wonders for my confidence. Although the operation appeared to have been a complete success, I was determined not to make the mistake of pretending it had never happened, turning down the offer of a winter job playing and coaching in South Africa, where the ground would have given my knees a battering they did not need.

In the absence of any good alternative, I signed on the dole . . . and that was how it stayed all winter. I cannot pretend to have suffered the sorry humiliation that surely afflicts the long-term unemployed, nor that I underwent any great hardships for being out of work. The effect it did have was to bring out the lazier aspects of my character until I virtually wallowed in the idleness, not especially having fun, but simply allowing myself to slip into a routine based on talking, drinking and eating. I certainly failed to make the best of the time on my hands, and know now that such lengthy periods of inactivity cannot be good for anyone's brain, particularly that of a professional sportsman who is used to an entirely opposite existence.

Most afternoons I drove to the home of a very good but sad friend in Sutton Coldfield, known as 'The General', who was a schoolteacher with a good brain and a kind heart; but he was also an alcoholic, and in the years to come I was to feel totally helpless, unable to help as he destroyed himself with drink.

Two men with strong opinions who had been brought together by The General's staunch efforts for David Brown's benefit three years earlier, we would put the world to rights each evening when he finished teaching. Now he was on the slippery slope, drinking increasingly heavily and becoming ever more maudlin. Alcoholism, I firmly believe, is not something the average man can slip into by increasing his nightly intake in the pub from three pints to five, then five to eight. It is usually brought about by a weakness of character exploited by a bad experience, which in Roy's case was a broken relationship diverting him from his chosen course of life.

Roy's wretched state was, strangely, my inspiration. We set off together during his Christmas holidays to a mid-Wales school-house in Betws-y-Coed. The weather was foul, with gale-force winds ripping across the road, bringing down bushes and trees. At some point on the A5, The General pulled into the side of the road, saying he felt too rough to go on driving. I took over the controls, but the visit was socially a disaster, poor Roy being too ill to go out at all on New Year's Eve. Watching him helplessly as he lay writhing in obvious pain, I decided on my New Year resolution.

At that unhappy moment I realized I had been wasting away the weeks and months when I could have been doing something to benefit my career, and sparked into action by the sight of a very good friend slowly killing himself, I vowed to start training the very next day. Although not the most momentous point of my roller-coaster career, it was undoubtedly a junction where I chose the right path. I kept my promise. The next morning, in weather scarcely better than the storms which had ushered us into Wales, I went running around the pretty roads of the remote village.

By Easter I felt a good deal fitter and, with permission from Warwickshire to miss the first few days of pre-season practice, I accepted an invitation to spend a month on the west coast of America, fulfilling a most unusual coaching engagement. The offer came from a good friend of Alan Knott, an eccentric herbal doctor known to us as Doc Severn. A cricket nut intent on establishing the game in Hollywood, Doc had created the initial interest there before asking me to coach the locals and play a few games.

It was a month well spent, fascinating but strange. I stayed with various members of Doc's family who were fanatically, but not uniformly, religious, two of his sons being evangelists and two Mormons. Shuffled between them as I was, I found it hard to come to terms with some of their customs, particularly the Mormon rule which prohibits the drinking of tea or coffee, let alone anything stronger!

Back in Birmingham, refreshed by the break and invigorated by my training programme, I set about the new season with enthusiasm, determined to regain my England place, although I was well aware I had a fight on my hands. John Snow, overlooked for two recent tours he ought to have been on, had come back into the England fold against Australia the previous summer. Snowy, having played in the inaugural World Cup, something I had been very sorry to miss, then bowled well in all four Tests for the Ashes, especially when England staged a stirring revival under his county captain, Tony Greig.

Greig was destined to have a considerable bearing on my future, both in terms of attitude and direction, although when he looks back on what was certainly a very influential career in English cricket, I would guess he might describe the summer of 1976 as his darkest days.

His problems stemmed from a statement which I still maintain was misunderstood and taken largely out of context. The West Indians had arrived in England, stung by the hostile tactics which had brought about their 5–1 embarrassment in Australia and intent on putting them into practice themselves. Having studied the Australian series, Greigy was convinced it had exposed the suspect temperament of the West Indians and proceeded to play on this angle as a battle-cry to the cricket-watching population. His choice of words was unfortunate, but when he said he hoped to make the visitors 'grovel' I am convinced there was no racial connotation, nor inference that the blacks should be servile. It was just Greig being Greig, and overdoing the relish.

Whatever his premeditated intentions, they all went sadly wrong. The reaction of Clive Lloyd's men to what they took as a gross insult was to bowl faster and hit harder than virtually any of their predecessors or successors in the West Indian success story. No-one, I think, took the 'grovel' quote to heart more than Vivian Richards, who was transformed from his diffidence in Australia just a few months previously to a cool destroyer with the bat, quite plainly one of the finest prospects to emerge for many a year.

Poor Greig; everything went wrong for him. In the first Test at Trent Bridge he decided that the way to counter and frustrate the West Indians' strokeplaying batsmen was to resist all-out attack against them, to try to pin them down and provoke reckless shots. So, even with the new ball at his disposal, he set a largely defensive six-three field with just two slips and a deep gully close to the wicket. The press criticized him mercilessly for this, but I think the idea was sound enough. All too often in recent years, England have attacked far too enthusiastically when their slender bowling resources didn't justify it. This was the only occasion on which I can recall a policy of clever, cat-and-mouse containment being tried for any length of time until it was abandoned in some disarray for the simple reason that the fielders were in entirely the wrong place for Richards, who proceeded to club everything through mid-wicket, racing to 232. At that early stage of his dominating career, no-one, including Greig, was sure where Richards's strengths lay, and this was a painful method of finding out.

We escaped with a draw at Trent Bridge and drew again at Lord's. But on a corrugated pitch at Old Trafford the new menace of West Indian fast bowling was revealed as veteran openers Brian Close and John Edrich were hounded by bouncers in a thoroughly tasteless Saturday evening session. England were hammered, and in the shake-up before the Headingley Test I was at last recalled to the side.

It was not exactly a gentle way to begin a comeback. West Indies, batting first, were 147 without loss at lunch, 330 for two at tea and 437 for nine at the close of a quite astonishing first day, having scored at more than five runs an over all day. It was greatly to the credit of our batsmen that we came back into the game well, Greig and Knott each scoring hundreds before a memorable, breathless game ended in relatively narrow defeat.

That, however, was game, set and series to the West Indies, and when Michael Holding's 14 wickets on a low, slow pitch at The Oval made it 3–0, Greig – who had twice been yorked by the ferociously fast Jamaican – crawled off the field in a symbolic and very human gesture to the thousands of West Indian fans on the popular side of the ground.

English cricket was then perched on a precipice. One more shove and it could have tumbled over the edge. Having been beaten twice by Australia and then, heavily, by West Indies in successive years, we could no longer claim to be pre-eminent on the Test circuit, nor could we make a reasonable case for being thought second best. If things went wrong on the winter tour of India, the mumblings of public and press unrest would become very loud condemnation.

Fortunately that did not happen, but I would suggest it was no thanks to the way in which the tour party was chosen. In those days, the one-day internationals were scheduled to follow the final Test at the end of the season and this, combined with the timing of the Gillette Cup (later the NatWest Bank Trophy) final, has been the prime cause of some crazy selections for England tours.

It had long been a matter of concern to me that the tour party is not picked when it should be, immediately following the last Test of the summer. If the selectors don't know their own minds about who should be included by then, they are not doing their job, because all that remains of the season is a maximum of three Championship rounds, a couple of Sunday games and the 60-overs cup final. To draw any major conclusions from that little lot is dangerous and probably doomed. Invariably one joker has been sprung on the unsuspecting public in each tour party, and almost without exception in recent years, success in a one-day match has swayed the selectors.

Geoff Cook, Roland Butcher and Chris Cowdrey have all, I suggest, won places on overseas tours by doing well in a one-off, one-day showpiece final at Lord's bearing no resemblance at all to the kind of cricket which will be demanded of them for most of their time abroad. I am not saying that all three are not useful and worthy cricketers, although I do happen to think they were bad selections for particular trips. In 1976 the selectors followed their usual trusted tradition of waiting until the dregs of the season had gone, basing at least two of their choices on performances in the two one-day internationals against the West Indies. Derek Randall and Graham Barlow were included in the 16-strong party to go to India, yet neither was then a great player of spin, and each had a wretched tour. Still the pattern remains unchanged. In my time as captain I tried unsuccessfully to bring the date of selection forward, remaining convinced that the current system encourages the short memory and the easy option of picking someone whose heroics before a big one-day crowd still linger fresh in the mind, rather than delving further back in search of the quality and resources needed for the prevailing conditions.

Despite all that, the Indian tour was among the most enjoyable and successful I experienced, long, taxing and variable though it was. I fell ill, as I have always seemed to do when in hot climates for any length of time, but having shaken off whatever virus was ailing me in time for the first Test, I stayed in good health and physical fitness to play my part in what was a satisfying 3–1 success.

We had won the series after three Tests, and won it in a way many people would have thought impossible, taking on the fêted Indian spinners with an attack which relied largely on seamers. Such was our dominance of those first three Tests that the spinner as a Test match weapon took two more steps backwards towards oblivion. That in itself was not something I celebrated. The demise of the spinner is a bad thing for cricket because, as we all agreed, the series out there was all the more interesting for being virtually free of bouncers. We seldom bowled any, and they had no-one quick enough to try; but if Bedi, Chandrasekhar, Prasanna and Venkat, bowling on their own wickets with Indian umpires and a partisan Indian crowd, could not prevent a 3–0 deficit, what hope was left for the spin bowler?

Pitches and their preparation could be held responsible for the demise of the spinner. Groundsmen nowadays seem to be terrified of their wickets breaking up and turning sharply on the later days, so they over-compensate by leaving them too damp at the start. This immediately puts the quicker bowlers in command and, if the groundsman's dubious tactics succeed in holding his pitch together, the spinners will never get to bowl in suitable conditions.

My own view is that the standard of groundsmanship in this country has sunk to a new low in recent years, but in this life you only get what you pay for. I was horrified to discover the pittance our groundsmen were paid for their year's labours, and it struck me that if players were also paid so scandalously poorly, their standards would inevitably tumble, too. Why should a chap with a simple job looking after a couple of putting greens and a tennis court for the local council want to improve himself, accepting the responsibility and attendant hassles of being a county groundsman when, in all probability, he would have to take a pay cut? If our cricket is to improve, our groundsmen must be more competent, and for the game to attract the best men far more money must be made available to them.

The spinner has also been poorly served by the law-makers, virtually every law-change in the course of my career having conspired against slow bowlers. I think especially of the front-foot no-ball law, which has meant there is far less rough for the spinners to exploit. Similarly the end of uncovered pitches, on balance a good thing for cricket, knocked another nail in the spinner's coffin.

Attitudes of captains and umpires have also changed. Until the mid-1970s it was virtually unheard of to put the opposition in to bat. You aimed to bat first, establish an unassailable position and try to bowl the opposition out twice. The one thing you did not want to do was bat last because the ball would surely turn, but now, with the changed rules and the altered proportions of pace to spin, it is commonplace to insert on winning the toss. Umpires have added to the evidence for the death-warrant by consistently reporting pitches which turned excessively to produce an early finish, yet taking no such action against wickets which produced a similar result by seam or bounce.

It is a complex subject which I have often debated, but one thing that cannot be disputed is that 1976–77 in India was virtually the last occasion on which any Test-playing country attempted to win a series entirely through the skills of their slow bowlers. It backfired on them to a disastrous extent, for not until the fourth Test at Bangalore, where red sand had been spread on the pitch, did they finally hit on the formula for making the conditions their spinners needed. At Delhi the ball had swung, John Lever marking his Test début with ten wickets, while at Calcutta the ball turned slowly, the game being won by a quite magnificent hundred from Greig while suffering from a fever. Madras, though, was the game

I enjoyed most of all, chiefly because it was played on the quickest Test pitch I have ever experienced.

Victory in Bangalore cut the margin to 3–1 and the ball also turned at Bombay, where Keith Fletcher batted for an age to save the game. It had been a thoroughly entertaining series and a triumph for Greig, who had engendered a healthy team spirit, commanding the support and loyalty of everyone by leading from the front. But when that last Test in Bombay finished we had already been abroad for three months and I for one was tired and ready for home. The thought of 17 days in Sri Lanka and a similar period in Australia was not appealing.

Sri Lanka was as horribly hot as I had feared. Because of the climate I hardly trained at all despite being given a lot of time off, and by the time we arrived in Australia, I was in no great shape for another Test match, let alone one which was to be as physically demanding and emotionally draining as the Centenary Test. Having misguidedly assumed that we were simply going to be decoration for the celebrations and that the match would be treated no more seriously than an exhibition, we had a shock in store.

It was the first time sponsorship had infiltrated cricket to any great extent, and we were caught up in the commercial razzamatazz of the occasion as soon as we landed in Melbourne. Everywhere were the familiar faces of legendary ex-players reunited after absences of many years, most of them determined not to waste a minute of a day, moving from one function to another and one bar to the next in a nostalgic haze.

Frustrated at missing out on the festivities, we had the feeling that this was a splendid occasion for all but the 22 unfortunates who had to get out on the field and play. Off field, we were constantly signing autographs, wading through the mountains of bats, programmes and menus which were deposited in our dressing-room every other minute by the flushed former players. But on the field the fun swiftly stopped. It was a deadly serious game.

I had distinguished myself even before the start, telling Greig and Brearley that I thought it would be 'lunacy' to put Australia in. My reasons were unworthy – I really didn't fancy bowling first – and I was proved monumentally wrong when we exploited what turned out to be very damp conditions to dismiss Australia for just over 100. They, in turn, put us out for just under 100 before making a big score. We fought back in a gripping game, entirely fitting for the 100 years of Tests, and the individual battle between

Randall and Dennis Lillee was as fine a spectacle as anyone could have wished to see.

One of Australia's heroes was Rick McCosker, their opening batsman. I broke his jaw with a bouncer on the opening day, yet he came out to bat in the second innings, cutting a hideous picture with the injury wired and bandaged. Personally, I do not think he should have been allowed to bat in that state, but what happened next said a great deal about the difference between Australians and Englishmen.

The first thing to be said is that McCosker scored a brave 25 and put on 54 runs with the century-maker Rod Marsh which proved to be decisive in Australia's 45-run victory. It was a display of guts and courage which was typically Australian, and I have to say I do not believe many of the modern generation of English batsmen would have gone out to bat in similar circumstances. I remember other Australians playing with a black eye or bruised hands, having been hit in the nets the day before a Test; English players will not even venture into a net if they consider the surface to be remotely suspect. This, perhaps, is the key to the missing grit in our batting. Australians and West Indians will always practice, no matter what the net is like, and I have a vivid memory of watching Colin Croft charging in off his full run-up during the 1980 tour, bowling flat-out on a poor net pitch to batsmen striving for a Test place. In this respect, we consistently prove ourselves to be over-cautious at best, soft at worst.

The other aspect of McCosker's performance is that we pitched the ball up to him throughout his second innings. If the situation had been reversed and an English batsman had gone out with such an injury, he would almost certainly have been ducking a bouncer first ball.

I have no criticism of this English attitude, probably because it is exactly the way I was brought up, being taught from childhood to play fair and having never been any good at all at gamesmanship in its many forms. I have even taken this very English attitude a stage further, feeling genuine compassion whenever we have been in the process of thrashing an inferior team. It has not, I hope, detracted from my will to succeed, but I have always felt sorry for any side clearly out of their depth being beaten hollow. Looking back on my recent England career the only pity is that I have not had more opportunities to feel sympathetic.

7

THE BIGGEST DECISIONS
OF MY LIFE

Tony Greig achieved two things with a clinical verbal dissection of my failings as a fast bowler, provoking a response which was to change entirely the course of my career, and giving a plain hint about the greatest revolution in world cricket. Greig and I argued in the idyllic surroundings of a terrace barbecue staged for us by a man named Arthur Jackson, whose significant part in my life was only just beginning. Arthur is a doctor of hypnotherapy, in which I was later to place a great deal of faith. Having met during the 1974–75 tour, also at one of his barbecues, we became firm friends when our paths crossed again two years later. I went to his house after the Centenary Test and, at a party also attended by Mike Brearley and Graham Barlow, Greigy came along with the former Essex and Australian opener Bruce Francis.

To say we argued is probably stretching a point. Greigy told me exactly where I was going wrong while I tried to wriggle out of the accusations with some feeble excuses. I knew all along that he was right. Tony said his piece in reply to some admiring remarks I had passed on the subject of Dennis Lillee's performance in Melbourne. 'You should be able to bowl like that too', he snapped at me. 'But you're always knackered after five overs.' I retaliated, saying it had been a long tour, I had done my stuff in India and that I was justifiably exhausted by the time we reached Australia. Greigy pointed out that I had been given time off in Sri Lanka and should have recharged my batteries.

He then said something which at the time sounded stupid but was later revealed as a meaningful message. 'You should get fitter', he concluded. 'It could mean the difference between earning peanuts and 70,000 dollars a year.' Having heard Greigy talk like this before Brearley and I exchanged raised-eyebrow glances, clearly agreeing that our ebullient captain had taken leave of reality again. This time, though, he had not. He was referring to the plan by media magnate Kerry Packer to hijack international cricket, and while neither Brearley nor I knew anything of the subterfuge at the time, Greig obviously did.

I was to think no more about that parting shot for some weeks, although I did spend a lot of time weighing up Greig's more general criticisms. Despite my dissenting pleas, I had no real illusions about where the truth of the argument lay, and instead of sulking at the insults I tried to do something about it – belatedly perhaps, but at least I was doing something. I have been thankful ever since that I reacted the right way to the abuse, especially when I see modern young players being unnecessarily sensitive about constructive criticism, taking up childish stances rather than heeding the advice and trying to improve themselves.

It was Arthur Jackson who put me on the road to the remedy. Talking long and hard about my weaknesses after that barbecue, he recommended two main courses of action, the first being long-distance running to build up my lacking stamina, and the second being hypnotherapy to improve my mental approach.

I will not pretend that I jumped at the chance to be hypnotised, having the customary layman's suspicions and reservations about it, with a fear of the unknown and an unreasonable dread of what really happens while one is 'under'. But I had come to like and respect Arthur and, not wanting to throw his suggestion back in his face when he was clearly anxious to help, I went to his home, along with Graham Barlow, for a session of hypnosis.

The careworn, tension-filled Willis who lay down on the couch that March morning in 1977 was a different, refreshed and more vital man when he got up an hour later. I found it hard to believe quite how good it made me feel, and needed no further convincing that I should pursue the treatment. Arthur made me a half-hour cassette of his own voice with which I was to learn to hypnotise myself at home, and has occasionally sent me updated tapes in recent years, while I continued to use the process until I gave up the game in 1984.

I am quite aware that there are those who considered me a crank for resorting to such unconventional methods. Until I experienced it myself I would have been just as uncharitable about anyone else doing so, but for me, at least, the process works, not just in releasing tension, but in its secondary function of instilling a positive, confident approach. I am even convinced that I would not have achieved the same degree of success in cricket had I not allowed myself to come under Arthur Jackson's wing. Insomnia remained a problem throughout my playing years, but with the tape close at hand I could always control the situation, and when things were going badly wrong – as they often did during my latter years with England – I could prevent myself literally getting ill with worry. It is not a method which would work for everybody for you have to want it to work and have to learn not to fight its effect. Some people are not made that way, many others have no need of the remedy anyway, but if I had nothing else to thank Arthur for – and there is much – I would always be in his debt for introducing me to his own form of therapy.

As soon as I returned home from Sydney, I began a physical training programme. It was not something I felt immediately enthusiastic about, there still being plenty of laziness in my character, which was not attracted to the prospect of running around the roads of Birmingham soon after dawn each day. But Greigy's words stung and I was determined he would never again have reason to criticise me in that way.

As my fitness bible, I used a book by Ernst van Aaken, who labelled his theory LSD – nothing to do with drugs, but standing for long, slow, distance running as a means of building up resources of stamina. I set myself targets, running for only five minutes on the first day, ten on the second and 15 on the third. It was that third morning which nearly put me off the idea, for having survived the first run well, increasing to ten minutes without problems, I felt quite pleased with my progress. But on the third day I was so painfully stiff that merely getting one leg in front of the other was agony.

The crisis passed and I was able to press on to greater distances, never making myself physically sick – I slowed down if I began to feel ill – but learning to cope with stitches and to overcome the desire to rest for a few minutes. Fast bowling being all about rhythm, it was important that my running also had a rhythm to it, so I went out early to avoid the rush-hours in which I would inevitably have lost momentum by having to dodge mothers and schoolkids. I chose a route on which I knew I would be able to keep going, because had I halted while waiting for the lights to change at a crossroads, standing on the street corner might quickly have seemed more comfortable than running. It was a psychological game with my own worst weaknesses and, by trial and error, I won through, soon feeling the benefits of the programme as I came to enjoy it, seeing it as a new challenge although I never ran at any great pace.

Apart from my early-morning run, I often trained alone during the day. After four months away on tour, I was not expected to devote as much time to net practice as the rest of the Warwickshire squad, so while the lads went into the indoor school, or began a practice game in the middle of Edgbaston, I would usually lap the ground for 40 minutes.

The evidence that this training, coupled with hypnotherapy, made me a more resilient cricketer, if not a better one, is chronicled plainly in the pages of *Wisden*. I did not miss a Test match until the summer of 1979 and then, after one minor injury, enjoyed another long, uninterrupted run in the team. I was able to bowl longer spells, thinking more clearly about my own game and about cricket itself, becoming a better ambassador for the sport with an altogether more mature outlook. Part of this, of course, can easily be put down to growing up, but the great proportion, I am convinced, is due to the two great changes in my routine. At the turning point of my career, I had chosen the right road.

Not everyone agreed with this thinking. One man with strong reservations about the value of both running for fitness and hypnotherapy was Bernard Thomas, the England and Warwickshire physiotherapist. We did not fall out about it at the time: Bernard simply put his view that I was attaching too much importance to the mental side of my game, and that long, slow distance running was not the ideal method of training because it did not take my leg muscles, and in particular my thighs, to their limit. We agreed to differ and I carried on doing what I thought was right.

It was in later years that I began to question the amount of influence Bernard was having over the England team's preparation, although in this I found myself delicately placed for Bernard, a friend for years, had worked thoroughly and hard on my benefit committee. He had been an efficient physio, travelling with England on every tour since the 1968–69 trip to Pakistan and, since 1977, being on hand at all England's home matches, too. This continuity was the idea of Mike Brearley and in many ways it was a laudable scheme, for Alan Knott, and others like him, were glad to have Bernard around to reassure them about niggles which would otherwise have been a worry. His value in this direction could not be over-estimated.

What I doubted was the wisdom of giving him authority in cricketing matters, because by his own admission Bernard knows nothing at all about the game. His positive contributions were made in fitness and treatment, yet as far back as the 1970–71

Australian tour he took on the job of assistant manager and, by definition, this gave him a say in areas of cricket policy-making, being present at selection meetings. He has been privy to all such meetings on tour and, although ostensibly this has been only for the purpose of informing the selectors about the fitness, or lack of it, of doubtful players, he has sat through the discussions.

In his defence, Bernard spends long hours at the cricket, which he must sometimes find boring through having no real knowledge of the play, and until the day when he is no longer around, none of us will fully appreciate his worth. His main problem in such a close association with us was a complete inability to come to terms with the changing attitudes of young players. There are, it would seem to me, three stages in this disenchantment. I admit I have found it increasingly hard to deal with the approach of the new generation; Bob Taylor, in his England days, found it even more difficult; Bernard Thomas finds it virtually impossible.

Bernard, having once been an outstanding gymnast accustomed to an army style of discipline and training, expects others to fall into line with this, unable to accept that the square-bashing mentality simply does not suit the majority of modern cricketers. Young people's attitudes to training have changed so that it is no longer possible to snap one's fingers and expect them to jump into line, day after day. Their interest and enthusiasm has to be stimulated and maintained by constant injection of something different. If my views seem hard, they may well be influenced by Bernard's efforts to turn me away from hypnotherapy, to which I credit 50 per cent of the transformation in my career.

England might never have seen the best of me, however, for soon after I had taken these momentous decisions, the birth of World Series Cricket was announced, and cricket split in two, leaving me very torn about which camp to join.

This did not happen at once. When the Packer coup broke in mid-May 1977, I knew only what I read. The England players to sign were Greig, of course, Derek Underwood, Alan Knott and John Snow, who were joined by most of the best Australians and almost all the best West Indians, along with a smattering of South Africans and Pakistanis. It was an impressive array of talent, following months of background recruiting, and as soon as I heard the news, my mind flashed back to that throwaway remark made by Greigy at Arthur Jackson's barbecue. It was natural to wonder whether they would approach me, and what my answer would be if they did.

I had all summer to wait. We were at The Oval for the last of the five Tests against a demoralised and hopelessly divided Australian side when Greigy told me I was among the additional players wanted by the WSC roadshow. He also asked Bob Woolmer, who to the best of my knowledge accepted readily, and Derek Randall who, like me, preferred to weigh the thing up slowly and methodically. One evening during that Test, Derek and I went to see Richie Benaud, who was closely involved with the Packer operation and might have been expected to give us a hard sales talk to match those that I had already heard from Greig. Instead, he put both sides of the argument, venturing some thoughtful views as to the direction in which the game of cricket was now inevitably heading, particularly in Australia. He thought that if the WSC players were prepared to work hard for their money, they would break certain unhealthy strangleholds within the game, that agents would assuredly take a more prominent role in cricket and that players would cease to be poorly paid servants, becoming commercial properties. He also believed, for a time at least, that the two sides of what had already become a war within cricket would take up entrenched positions, everyone concerned adopting an attitude of 'us and them'. It was an impressive piece of reasoning, and every one of his predictions came true. Although I did not leave him that night convinced that I should join the stampede away from traditional cricket, I certainly came away with food for thought.

As soon as possible I spoke with two main advisors – David Brown, not only my county captain but a very good mate, and the man who was as much a friend as a solicitor. Brownie said that on cricketing grounds he very much hoped I would reject the offer, but that on financial grounds he could not possibly recommend me to turn down such security. My solicitor, wanting quite properly to question various clauses in the contract, set up a meeting in Birmingham with Packer's solicitor, at which the terms being offered were slightly altered and improved.

It was a very good offer. I make no bones about how strongly I was tempted to go. At the end of the negotiations between solicitors, I had a contract which would have tied me to WSC for five years, earning me a minimum of £75,000 – that is before any win bonuses and advertising contracts. It was more money than I had ever dreamed I could earn from cricket, but I was still far from sure it was the right thing to do. They gave me until the end of September to make up my mind, a luxury not accorded to some of their other recruits, and I got away from the phone, away from prying pressmen's questions and away from all other distractions for a while in order to be certain of making the right decision.

The fact that I had done some hard bargaining and had a favourable contract in my hand did not necessarily indicate a desire to sign, although many people have since construed it that way. Whenever I have been faced with a decision of real significance, I have taken both options as far down the road as possible, consulting as many trusted advisors I can before committing myself.

I had grave reservations about the cricket I would be required to play. At a meeting in the Strand Palace Hotel, I had asked Greigy for whom I would be playing if I signed up to join 'the circus'. On hearing it would be a World XI, led by himself, I foresaw problems in motivating myself to play for such a loosely grouped international team. Greigy's response was: 'Isn't £15,000 a year enough motivation for you?' It might have been enough for him, but it was not enough for me, and there lay the fundamental difference between us.

I also had doubts as to where my natural loyalties lay. Until then, I had never considered myself to be very establishment minded, and there were certainly areas of the game's hierarchy which I thought would benefit from a challenge such as this, but I did feel some loyalty to Warwickshire, who had treated me so well since I joined them in 1972. The crux of the problem was that I believed I would be sacrificing not only my England career but also my county career, should I sign for WSC. I did not think the moves afoot to ban all the Packer players from the domestic game outrageous; I simply had to decide if I could cope with that fate.

My father was predictably very much against the whole idea, and by now my own doubts had grown until I was pretty sure I did not want to give everything up, even for a small fortune. I went to see Alan Smith, now the secretary of Warwickshire, and told him of my dilemma. It was quite obvious that the county could not raise the financial incentives to match Packer and make me stay even if they had wanted to, but I asked Alan if there was anything they were able to do for me if I rejected the offer. After consulting the club's senior officers, he informed me that, Warwickshire were prepared, for the first time, to underwrite a new three-year contract. In other words, I was to be paid the full amount for the three seasons, even if I broke my leg in my first match and never played again. The money, of course, was not remotely comparable to the WSC offer (from memory it was around £3,500 per year) but this improved security, and the clear show of good faith from the county finally tilted the balance. I made contact with Packer's solicitor and told him I would not be joining up.

Within two months of my decision, a High Court action brought by Greig, Snow and Mike Procter succeeded in tying the hands of the cricket establishment. Not only were they prevented from banning the Packer players from domestic cricket, they were also warned it would be a restraint of trade if they refused to select any of them for Test matches simply because they had joined WSC.

I am not sure if my decision would have been any different had I been able to foresee the outcome of this case; some time or another, security must guide us all. But of course things were not as pleasantly uncomplicated as that. I was stung and took up a very establishment stance, believing that WSC was bound to create such disruption in world cricket that there should be no place in the traditional game for any of its employees. After the court case, there was no grey area left; you were on one side or the other, and I lined up with the harassed men of Lord's.

People apparently thought it odd, even hypocritical, that I was suddenly so anti-Packer, having by my own admission come very close to joining them. I can understand their bewilderment, but my thinking was quite straightforward. I had always considered the WSC offer in the light that I would certainly end my career with Warwickshire and England by signing. WSC had refused to alter their scheduled dates in Australia to avoid a clash with the official Test matches, so there had been no doubt they were hellbent on a collision course. My moral thoughts about this are hardly relevant, but I did feel that everyone who joined should automatically have sacrificed his right to play in what was now a rival form of cricket. After all, if Packer's project was taken to its logical extreme, it could have put Test cricket out of business – and without Test cricket there would be no county cricket.

I won't pretend that, having chosen my course and pledged my loyalties, there were not moments when I privately considered I might be insane. Just a few months later in Pakistan, for instance, while feeling violently ill in a country to which I have never been attracted, I remembered that I could be in Australia, which I like, playing cricket for a relative king's ransom. There was the odd moment of regret, too, when I saw people who had taken the Packer money stroll back into the England dressing-room as if nothing had happened. But on balance, I know I did the right thing.

One of the assertions of those close to WSC is that their project raised the wages of Test and county cricketers. Both are contentious arguments but, to deal with Test cricket first, I do happen to know that the subject was under discussion and that players were about to receive a 100 per cent increase. The arrival on the scene of first businessman David Evans, and second Cornhill Insurance as official Test match sponsors, meant that this figure was subsequently redoubled to £1,000 per man per Test – a situation which, I agree, owes something to the influence and impact of WSC.

While it probably helped to improve the lot of the Test player, I have never been convinced that professionals – average, middle-of-the-road county cricketers – have benefited at all from this stormy period in the game's history. The Cricketers' Association had been fighting a long and determined battle aimed at raising the bottom level of county players' wages, so that there was not such a glaring disparity between the salaries of the uncapped player and the capped. I refuse to believe WSC had anything to do with their winning the battle.

One thing they undoubtedly achieved was the unhealthy division within most of the counties employing WSC players; we felt it keenly at Warwickshire, where the anti-Packer sentiment was as strong as anywhere. There was only one Packer player on our staff, as I had turned it down and Alvin Kallicharran had backed out after signing. Dennis Amiss, however, was utterly committed to the scheme, and consequently alienated himself within his own dressing-room.

It was a messy business, Warwickshire wanting to sack him, but aware that it would be legally unwise. They said he would not be re-engaged when his existing contract expired at the end of 1978, on which there was no legal comeback, although it provoked a strong reaction from his supporters among the Warwickshire membership, a number of whom threatened to resign over the issue. It split the club, but could hardly be said to have split the dressing-room, where it was simply Dennis against the rest of us.

He would turn up, play his cricket and go home again, frequently not speaking to anyone all day because nobody spoke to him. He still scored heavily but the side was so poor in bowling that we were never in a position to win anything, and I had the strong impression he felt he was batting for himself rather than for the team. The dressing-room seemed to regard him as an outcast and the atmosphere throughout the period of conflict – which, in this instance stretched through to the end of the 1978 season – was strange and unpleasant.

Some counties were not set against the WSC ideal at all, and talked about the ensuing improvements in public image, handling of sponsors etc. I admit WSC hastened the commercial advances of the game, bringing more money in the pocket for top players and, for those who cherished it, more star projection. Yet I seemed to me that those who blindly went along with what Packer had done and talked of, in terms of the benefit to cricket as a whole, had simply been brainwashed by the clever public relations machine which churned out WSC propaganda by the ton.

Brownie and I might have been regarded by some as simple, dumb fast bowlers, and it is true that as long as we had enough money for beer and grub, we were happy with our existence. We thought of Dennis Amiss as a mercenary and the friendship we had both enjoyed with him was certainly damaged. In fact, it was probably our very disregard for financial stability which set Brownie and me into such a hard line about Packer, and although the cracks within the game were eventually papered over, neither of us has altered his opinions.

Back in the summer of 1977, though, even before any advance had been made to me, England won back the Ashes by trouncing an Australian side which, for the first time in my experience, lacked the 'smash the poms' obsession which usually made them such fearsome opponents. They were taking stick from all sides – from their own Board at home, from the accompanying press and from the tour management, and the minority faction within the side which had not signed up with WSC wore a permanent look of bewilderment. For them, it must have seemed a very long tour.

For England, however, it was a memorable summer, despite the constant rumblings of background battle. It was particularly notable for a comeback, a takeover, and an introduction. It was the summer of Brearley, Boycott and Botham.

8

BREARLEY, BOYCOTT
AND BOTHAM . . .

Mike Brearley was hastened into the hot-seat as England captain
following the inevitable decision to relieve Tony Greig of the job.
I suspect the cricket-watching nation hardly rejoiced at the change.
Greig, after all, was a larger-than-life character, a storm-trooper
with whom the punters in the stand could associate – outspoken
but plainly committed. Brearley, by comparison, remained a
publicly distant and slightly cold figure, a batsman who struggled
to justify his place in the England side and a captain who had
achieved honours for Middlesex but was completely unproven at
Test level.

Outside the inner sanctum of cricket, where fury over Packer
knew no bounds, I am sure there were plenty who sympathised
with Greig, feeling he had done cricket a service. Many were
certain to mourn his passing as England captain just when he had
created a winning team with a plainly happy spirit. In most
respects, the players were also sorry to see him go, but we accepted
the inevitable. There could have been nothing more absurd than
allowing a man to captain England when he was an admitted ring-
leader in an operation which was effectively holding the established
game to ransom.

To Greig's great credit, he put aside his obvious dismay at
losing the job, pigeon-holed his efforts to justify WSC and fend off
the tirades of abuse, and channelled his entire enthusiasm into
beating Australia. In fact, he did rather more. By his attitude, he
ensured that every one of the Packer men who remained in the
England side still played as if they were fighting for their country
rather than, as some people had inevitably feared, merely marking
time before the first of the pay-cheques arrived from Sydney.

Brearley, of course, deserves his share of the accolades, for it
was no small achievement to hold an England side together and in
good spirit, on and off the field, during such a torrid time. The

Australians, admittedly in an even more difficult situation through being away from home, certainly didn't manage it. I believe Brearley helped himself by refusing to take an extremist stance on either side of the battle. Unlikely ever to have joined the Packer circus himself, he was not willing to condemn it out of hand. His conciliatory approach extended to his dining with Greig and Packer at the Dragonara Hotel in Leeds during the 1977 series where, knowing Mike, I'm sure he listened very carefully to the motives of the Australian mogul.

Mike had changed appreciably from the time when he came into the game during the 1960s as an amateur. A strange selection for the MCC tour to South Africa in 1964–65, he may well have been considered something of an oddball during those years, having no apparent interest in money, but by the time Packer came on the scene – and, more specifically, in the few years which followed – Mike had developed quite a keen interest in the subject. Realising that his time in cricket was limited, both by age and by choice, he was anxious to make the best use of the years available to him and I remember sharing a frank discussion with him during a rainy Test match day when he confessed to having become quite mean about money.

Mean he may have been, but selfish he was not. Brearley went out of his way to find the fairest route when it came to financial matters, and when David Evans – whom Mike knew better than anyone else in the team – offered to pay the eight non-Packer men in the England team £1,000 each for staying loyal to Lord's, Mike considered the offer carefully and then told David, in confidence, that he did not think it right to exclude the three WSC players. So, with Mr Evans's approval, the £8,000 was handed over and split 11 ways, Messrs Greig, Underwood and Knott taking their share.

Brearley went into psychoanalysis when he retired from cricket in 1982, and his greatest qualities were all concerned with offshoots of this subject – in other words, with assessment of human strengths and frailties within both his own team and the opposition. A master at applying pressure in the field, he was also very good at man-management in the dressing-room. Yet, while his years as England captain were undeniably successful and, in some instances, euphorically triumphant, he would readily admit he was not always right.

I like to think that in the series, both at home and abroad, which followed his accession during that stormy summer of 1977, 'Brears' and I had a good relationship, usually as captain and vice-captain but always as friends. Sometimes we argued about cricket, as two opinionated sportsmen would, while at other times we argued about matters which had nothing to do with cricket at all. Although our politics were far from similar and our social likes and dislikes only occasionally coincided, we always remained on good terms.

He was a fine captain, one of the best I ever played under, but he did have at his command an extremely capable bowling attack, with which more recent England captains, including myself, have seldom been blessed. Mike had Botham and Willis at their peak, as well as Underwood and Emburey to bowl spin and a back-up queue of seamers which included Hendrick, Old and Lever, all very talented men usually jostling for one place. A captain, in my view, is only as good as the bowlers at his disposal, and in this regard many captains have had a far rougher ride than Mike.

Because he was never quite of true Test calibre as an opening bat, Brearley's England sides usually carried the extra batsman. This would often leave only four front-line bowlers in the side, with the danger that they would be overbowled. In the case of Ian Botham, I believe this happened to a damaging degree and that Mike was to some extent responsible for finishing Ian off as a truly potent bowler. Ian himself always denies that his bad back affected his bowling and he would defend Mike's tactics by saying that he likes to bowl all the time. There were occasions when Ian bowled 40 overs into the wind – willingly, certainly, and usually to some effect – but although his body was capable of rising to such excessive demands at the time, the damage manifested itself over a longer period.

In the 1981 home series against Australia, when Brearley brought us back from a match down under Botham to win the Ashes 3–1, I also suffered from overbowling, and it told, as eventually it had to, in the final innings of the rubber at The Oval, where I bowled only ten overs before being forced off with a stomach injury. Mike Hendrick was also handicapped by a side strain and Botham by a pinched nerve in his backside, unsurprisingly as, with only four bowlers playing, we three seamers had bowled an aggregate of 109 overs in the Australian first innings.

I must balance this criticism with my own tribute, as there were times when he was quite brilliant – especially when the game was tightly balanced. During our 1978–79 series in Australia, we were so much the better side that we should have won 5–0 or even 6–0 instead of 5–1. But we batted so timidly throughout the tour that every Test seemed to find us in a corner, scrambling for survival, and it was here that Mike's tactical acumen shone through. Surely no other side has ever won a series by so wide a margin after batting so deplorably.

Brearley's greatest moments probably came in 1981 and particularly at Edgbaston where the 'impossible' happened for the second time in a fortnight and threatened to become commonplace. There are myths existing about this extraordinary win, the first being that Mike decided Ian should come on, just as Australia looked to be winning the game on the Sunday afternoon, and persuaded him to bowl against his will.

What actually happened was slightly different. We had virtually given the game up, so hopeless did the scoreboard look, when I suggested to Mike that he might as well give the golden boy a try. Ian was at first unwilling, but there were ways and means of talking him into it. I often used to tell him that my grandmother could bowl faster than he was doing, galvanising him to rush in with indignant aggression. On this occasion he took five wickets for one run, almost all with ordinary deliveries, and was a hero again.

Where Mike had contributed a significant and underplayed part in the victory was earlier on that memorable Sunday when, with John Emburey bowling, he had the close fielders in the right positions and manipulated the game to put maximum pressure on the batsmen. Supervising and masterminding the defence of a low score or an unhopeful position he was unrivalled.

Back in 1977 Brearley did not waste the talents of the raw young Botham, but I wonder, looking back, just what the educated and publicly reserved Brearley thought of his rumbustious newcomer.

Botham had first played for England in the one-day internationals against West Indies at the tail-end of the previous season, making no great impression on me at the time. I next came across him during the Centenary Test in Melbourne, he and Graham Stevenson of Yorkshire – playing club cricket in Victoria – having come along to help out in the dressing-room. 'Stevo', acting like the model junior pro, was very subdued, but Ian clearly considered himself to be one of the lads, behaving without the slightest sign of inhibitions. His main topic of conversation – more of a monologue, actually – began: 'When I'm playing for England next season . . .' I admit I did not take to him at all, wondering who on earth he thought he was, for even among the many legendary cricketing figures who were scattered around Melbourne during that frenzied week, Botham showed no shyness or humility. He would mingle with the likes of Percy Fender and Eddie Paynter, boasting about how he intended to take more wickets than Jeff Thomson and score more runs than Greg Chappell. I hate to imagine what the old-timers thought of him, but the wonder of the whole thing was, first, that he believed every word he was saying, and, second, that he was very soon proving they had not been idle words.

I knew nothing of his personality when I met him in Melbourne, nor of the eccentricities and the excesses which were to mark him out both as an unusual person and an unusual cricketer. He has not significantly changed from that day to this – he remains just as combative, just as indomitably self-confident and just as happily outrageous in company.

Ian enjoyed a lucky Test début. He would probably describe it differently himself, but I maintain it was lucky. He was dropped twice on nought before attracting some favourable attention by blasting a rapid 20 or 30, and when he bowled he dismissed Chappell with a bad ball which he chopped into his stumps. This was the way, we were to learn, that Botham played his cricket – hit or miss, the cheerful cavalier approach which was complete anathema to the likes of Boycott and myself.

I don't suppose either Geoffrey or I has ever gone out on the field to play the percentages game in which Ian revels. We never thought: 'If it's my day, great, if not, it's not the end of the world'. We took it all too solemnly for such outward flippancy. The differ-ence is that Geoff and I had only very limited natural talent. We both found it very demanding to maintain our standards in Test cricket, and probably expended 60 per cent of our energies actually reaching that standard in the first place. Ian, with unlimited natural ability to fall back upon, could express himself on the field without worrying too much about technical details.

Whatever people may have accused him of in more recent years – and one could add up all the allegations to make him seem a spoiled, lazy, overweight mischief-maker – Ian has never been less than totally committed to England, often disregarding his personal comfort for the sake of the team. It was the same in 1977. Towards the end of the series he was injured, but kept it to himself, taking five wickets in the next Test before it was discovered that he had a broken bone in his foot. Only much later that winter, in Pakistan, did Kenny Barrington and I convince him that his bowling action was such that he landed on the ball of his foot, both rendering him prone to injury and accounting for the crop of no-balls he was bowling. It took us weeks to make him accept this – but, that is Ian. If he said black was white, he would believe it unhesitatingly.

While Botham's name was creeping up on the public during 1977, Boycott's was throwing itself back into the headlines. He returned to Test cricket when Brearley took on the captaincy, making an emotional comeback at Trent Bridge which he marred by running out the local hero Derek Randall.

Boycott was never the most popular man among fellow cricketers, but there were few who did not – I should say do not – value him as a player. His famous quote: 'They don't want me but they want my runs' is, rather sadly, accurate. When he came back into the England fold he was immediately accepted on a cricketing level; everyone knew he could contribute a great deal on tactics, the way to practice and how to approach various aspects of a five-day game. But we soon knew he had not altered as a person when he decided he would change by himself in the little annexe to the home dressing-room at Trent Bridge.

To be fair, his motives here were not solely those of the unsociable recluse. Geoff liked time by himself to prepare mentally for his batting and considered this was best achieved by changing somewhere quiet, although he did rather carry the idea to extremes. In Hyderabad the following winter, for instance, he was so distraught at the layout of the dressing-room that he went to change in the toilet.

Boycott displayed suitable remorse, both on the field and back in the pavilion, when he ran out Randall, the Nottingham crowd's hero. It was not, of course, the first controversial run-out in which Geoffrey had been involved, but on this occasion he shouldered all the blame and admitted it, although he was not always so humble. I have already listed some of the qualities he can offer to a side, but all too often during my career his quest for personal success would override these values and cause incidents within the side.

His great ability to play long innings could, of course, make a major difference to any team. I always felt, and am sure the Yorkshire lads have felt the same for years, that we had lost three wickets when he got out, so important was his role as the backbone of the batting. Geoff often talked a great deal of good sense about cricket. He always said that when you were batting you should mentally add two more wickets to the scoreboard to avoid any feeling of complacency. While 210 for two might seem a very comfortable position, 210 for four gives cause for concern and concentration. This, I thought, was sound advice.

He seemed forever to be taking notes and must have chronicled every moment of his life. Whereas at some team meetings he would be expansive and helpful, at others he would lie silently on the floor, simply scribbling on his note pad. He could be a difficult customer in a team situation and although I had very few outright rows with him, I can also remember very few occasions when we had a long, friendly conversation about anything other than cricket.

Despite the fact that most of his character and make-up is as far removed from mine as it is possible to be, I have an unstinting admiration for his application and determination to make things happen for himself. This quality was never better emphasised than in the second match of his comeback, when, having scored 107 and 80 not out at Trent Bridge, he was in front of his own adoring Headingley public, with 99 hundreds to his name. On an idyllic summer's day, with a perfectly flat wicket and the crowd, large and partisan, willing him to succeed, it was the nearest thing to predestined fate I have ever known in the game of cricket.

'If I get to lunchtime, I'll make it', he confided to me with that characteristic, grim half-smile of his, when he came back to the dressing-room from pre-match nets. Despite losing captain Brearley for nought, he did just that. I recall the now famous shot down the ground, past mid-on to the football stand boundary, followed by hordes of Yorkshiremen invading the pitch and Boycott, who had complained of a near-sleepless night, pumping both arms in the air, not even seeing his partner, Graham Roope's, outstretched hand of congratulation. He was quite visibly lost in the emotion of the moment and, on that of all days, one could not begrudge him anything, but simply admire the tenacity with which he had carried it through despite being under such tremendous local pressure.

That innings established Boycott as a super-hero in Yorkshire. To the majority of cricket-watchers in the county, and probably to everyone on the stands to see the innings, he had truly joined the ranks of the immortals. How ironic that this growing hero-worship should eventually backfire so explosively within Yorkshire, causing the type of split no county has ever previously suffered. The wounds of the battle between pro-Boycott and anti-Boycott factions are sad to see. It is not for me to judge the rights and wrongs, but I will make the observation that if Boycott had failed to carry out his starring role to such perfection on that almost stage-managed day in 1977, it may never have happened.

Meanwhile, Boycott was now back in the England fold and plainly revelling in it. He was named vice-captain for the winter tour to Pakistan and New Zealand a decision with which I found no reason to argue, although I found plenty to dispute in the remainder of the team selections.

I was driving home on the M1 soon after the season's end, when the party was announced on the radio. So astonished was I at some of the names that I almost had to stop the car. At least four times, while the list was being read out, I winced fiercely wondering, 'How on earth could they have chosen him for this tour?' Most surprising of all were such selections as Roope, Rose, Gatting and Downton for a tour that was guaranteed to suit none of them. Considering the conditions under which we were to play, and the sketchy make-up of the itinerary, it was the strangest tour party I have ever seen.

Knowing Pakistan of old, I did not set off starry-eyed on this trip, so was not disappointed. It was the most boring tour I've ever experienced, partly because there is so little to occupy the mind in Pakistan but also because the weather was so variable and the itinerary so poor that we simply did not seem to play much cricket. Places like Pakistan are much more easily tolerated if you can stay active; when you have to spend day after day in hotels, any glamour which might initially have been attached to the voyage very soon wears off. We had to spend an unbroken stretch of something like three weeks in Lahore, and although the Intercontinental there was one of the better hotels we patronised on the tour, it was in the throes of being refurbished, giving the impression that we were living our lives on a construction site. In addition, the building work had taken its toll on the restaurant facilities, leaving a drastically shrunken menu which never seemed to contain more than three choices. One of the perpetual starters was a thick bean soup, of which I consumed gallons in the course of our stay.

Those who have never been to Pakistan might consider such complaints to be mere whining, but the plain fact is that although social facilities have improved markedly in the Pakistani cities since I first visited there as a schoolboy, there are still precious few restaurants outside the major hotels where I would willingly sit down for dinner.

Even with its rebuilding, Lahore was heaven compared to Hyderabad, where I shared a room with John Lever in an obscure establishment called the Sangees Hotel. We knew things were bad as soon as we were shown to our rooms; the 'plumbing' consisted

Not the most elegant of actions but one that served me, with a few modifications, for more than 48,000 first-class deliveries. *Patrick Eagar*

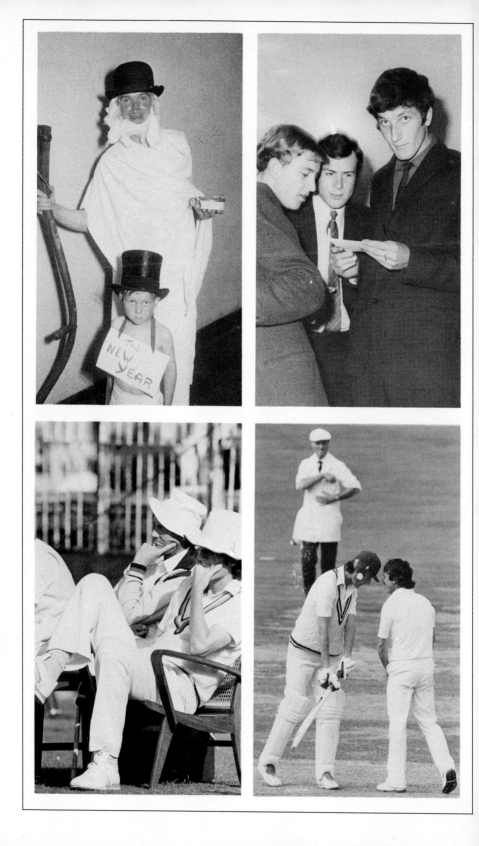

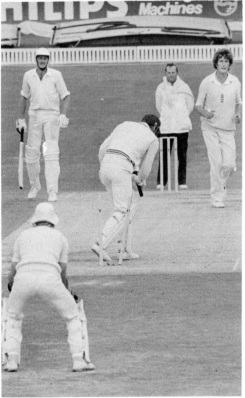

OPPOSITE
ABOVE LEFT R.G. Willis and Father Time (my father 'Tannoy') at a fancy dress party in 1952.

ABOVE RIGHT My first overseas tour: Surrey and Middlesex Young Cricketers to Pakistan, 1969. Standing next to me is Graham Barlow of Middlesex.

BELOW LEFT My last overseas tour: A.C. Smith and myself feeling the strain in Pakistan, 1984. It was Alan who persuaded me to join Warwickshire from Surrey in 1971. *Adrian Murrell/All-Sport*

BELOW RIGHT Robin Jackman, my rival for a first team place at The Oval, shares a word during the 1982 NatWest final. *Adrian Murrell/All-Sport*

THIS PAGE
ABOVE My first Test wicket: Ashley Mallett caught behind by Alan Knott, Sydney 1971. *The Sun*

RIGHT My 300th Test wicket: Jeff Crowe is the victim at Headingley, 1983. *Patrick Eagar*

ABOVE Two England captains sharing a joke? In fact, Tony Greig – whose comments after the match were to fire me with a new commitment to the game – has just brought off a spectacular catch during the Melbourne Centenary Test. Mike Brearley looks on with disbelief. *Patrick Eagar*

LEFT Dennis Lillee, without doubt the greatest bowler of my generation. *Patrick Eagar*

OPPOSITE
ABOVE Headingley, Fourth Test, 1977: champagne celebrations as the Ashes return to England during the summer of Brearley, Boycott and Botham – a series which launched me on a new stage in my career. *Patrick Eagar*

BELOW LEFT Headingley again, this time during the remarkable Ashes series of 1981: Bob Taylor catches Lawson on my way to 8 for 43. *Patrick Eagar*

BELOW RIGHT Giving encouragement to Norman Cowans during his match-winning spell at Melbourne, December 1982. *Adrian Murrell/All-Sport*

Three close friends from the world of cricket.

ABOVE LEFT Geoff Howarth, lodger in my parents' house in 1969 and opposing captain in two Test series. *Adrian Murrell/ All-Sport*

ABOVE RIGHT David Brown, stalwart of Warwickshire from 1961 to 1982 and cricket manager since 1980. *Patrick Eagar*

LEFT Ian Botham – the only Test player to achieve the double of 4000 runs and 400 wickets? I hope so. *Jan Traylen/Patrick Eagar*

OPPOSITE
ABOVE Messrs Jackman, Fowler, Marks and Botham join in celebrating our 2-1 victory over Pakistan in 1982. *Patrick Eagar*

BELOW Four seasoned campaigners show their concern at one of cricket's more unusual occurrences: a ball from Phil Edmonds has lodged in Bruce Edgar's helmet during the Second Test against New Zealand, 1983. *Patrick Eagar*

Moments from a 'glittering' Test batting career which somehow included a record 55 not outs. *Patrick Eagar/George Herringshaw (bottom left)*

of a common channel running down the corridor outside the doors of the rooms, perpetrating an indescribable smell. Geoff Miller once went up onto the roof of the Sangees to do some sunbathing during a free afternoon but quickly returned in some distress, having been attacked by thousands of mosquitoes who had set up camp there.

The hotel staff tried hard enough, and the food was quite good, which helped us through that leg of the tour. I still have grim memories of stumbling back to the hotel after the second of two long days in the field, desperate for a soak in the bath. There being neither bath, nor shower, nor even hot water, I had to make do with a dribble of cold water from the tap on the wall of the bathroom. For one whose joints suffer as mine do, this was sheer purgatory.

Most players expect to fall ill at some stage of an eastern tour, whether in India or Pakistan, but this particular trip seemed to feature an unusual amount of sickness, the worst of which was suffered by Ian Botham and Mike Hendrick in Lahore.

Without doubt they both had dysentery, each of them being desperately ill at times with diarrhoea and sickness with which the facilities of the bathroom were frequently not up to coping. The room which they shared was virtually a quarantine area to the rest of us. Very keen and ridiculously optimistic about playing in the Lahore Test, they pleaded with the selectors to delay their team announcement until both had undergone a fitness test.

Had it not been so pathetic, that fitness test would have been hilarious. As a warm-up, it was suggested that Ian and 'Hendo' should do a couple of circuits of the ground, just to shake off the lethargy of spending so long in bed. Hendo managed 300 yards before giving up while Ian staggered only about 15 yards before collapsing on the grass.

Many of us who were less than fully fit, though nowhere near as sick as these two, were obliged to play on, and no-one who has not done it can possibly comprehend what it is like to play cricket at the highest level, and in very high temperatures, when you are feeling wretched, longing to lie down on a welcoming bed rather than bowl another over. There is no easy route to escaping illness, either. Some players take excessive, almost obsessive precautions over what they eat and drink, even brushing their teeth with whisky rather than water to avoid germs – and still go down with some violent virus – while others float through the tour without a day's illness, despite eating and drinking everything available.

In adversity, there is always a spirit of togetherness which sometimes never develops in places such as Australia where social amenities and hotel facilities are so plentiful. For all the bad times suffered in Pakistan that winter, there were also many funny memories of the sort that seem better when looked back upon.

Ian Botham and Mike Gatting were both sent food-parcels from home, and although Ian had to pay a small fortune in duty to take possession of his, the bottle of very expensive cognac which was its main feature was well worth his expense! Ian, John Lever and myself sat down to drink it one long, lonely evening in Hyderabad, although the active drinkers were soon reduced to two as John, trying out a glass as a medicinal measure after a few days' illness, retired to the toilet following a single sip. In the course of the evening's conversation Ian – who had himself wed quite young – struck a bet with John and myself that we would both be married before the age of 30, the stake in each case being another bottle of this splendid cognac. I am pleased to report that both John and I remained bachelors into our thirties, even if we have since fallen!

We stayed for a one-day international in Sahiwal where, in stark contrast to most of Pakistan, it can become extremely cold at night. We were staying in a very spartan Rest House with three or four to a room, where most of us wore track suits in bed, with cricket socks worn on our hands as gloves. Mike Hendrick even found a bala- clava from somewhere. It was frequently difficult to get to sleep in such cold, uncomfortable conditions, and on one memorable night we seemed to have been sleeping only two or three hours when a banging on the door announced the arrival of the 'tea-wallah'. He was plainly under instructions from above to ensure that everyone was up, even though the hour turned out to be 6 a.m., and when some verbal abuse from the row of beds failed to get rid of him, Hendo emerged from under the covers long enough to hurl three pairs of cricket boots at the door.

We were later in another Rest House in Faisalabad and this time still more cramped. There were only four rooms allocated to the entire playing party, so most of us shared in rooms of five beds. Boycott, as vice-captain, was allocated a room at the very top of the house and was fairly happy until he discovered on the first night that his bed was directly under the loudspeakers from which the wailing noises so characteristic of Pakistan call the faithful to 4 a.m. prayers.

Played at slow pace on flat wickets and with little chance of posi- tive results, the cricket in Pakistan was almost all tedious. The intended course of the tour changed dramatically one morning at the Karachi Gymkhana Ground when Mike Brearley's arm was broken by a ball from the Test seamer Sikander Bakht. It was on a pitch that played perfectly well apart from one small spot – Sikander hit it, the ball took off and the crack which echoed around the ground left no-one in any doubt as to the extent of the damage.

Mike, inevitably, had to fly back to England for treatment, leaving Boycott in charge to fulfil another of his lifelong ambitions by captaining England. It was not the moment at which he would have chosen to take over, there being serious doubt over whether the final Test in Karachi would take place at all.

With the agreement of Kerry Packer, Pakistan's Board had flown back their three World Series players – Imran Khan, Mushtaq Mohammad and Zaheer Abbas – to play in the Test. To say this did not please us would be a gross understatement. Every one of our lads felt very strongly about the issue, even the most junior amongst us insisting that if the WSC men were chosen, we should refuse to play. This, of course, amounted to a strike threat and was potentially explosive. It was not something into which we entered lightly, but does emphasise the unanimous disgust at the Pakistan move. I might say at this point that even the Pakistani players felt strongly that it was wrong – and not just those who stood to lose their places if the trio returned.

Phone calls flashed between Pakistan and London at regular intervals and more than once I spoke to the TCCB at 2 a.m. to tell them of our views. Although – being vehemently anti-Packer themselves – they were full of sympathy, they could only take the official line, reminding us of our contracts and instructing us to go ahead with the game, leaving the respective Boards to sort out the problem. Our manager, Ken Barrington, naturally adopted a similar stance, leaving poor Boycott caught in the middle. Having himself turned down an approach from Packer, he was right behind the rest of us in our opinions on the matter, but was obviously keen that the game should go ahead so that he could captain the side.

The Pakistan Board eventually backed down, omitting the players who had returned from Australia, and the game went ahead. Boycott had his wish, even if it did take place in a nonentity of a match which was a predestined draw from the moment that Sarfraz's first delivery with the new ball bounced twice on its way to the wicketkeeper.

There was a spontaneous cheer from the lads as our plane took off for New Zealand, where more problems lay in store. In part, they stemmed from the relationship between Boycott and Barrington, which had no real chance of recovery following some thoughtless, unkind remarks Boycott had passed about administrative matters completely beyond Kenny's control, such as buses arriving late and food being below par. A manager's job in Pakistan can be trying enough without that kind of criticism.

The main drama, however, arose in the Test match we actually won, at Christchurch. We had gone into it 1–0 down, having been beaten on a rogue of a pitch at Wellington. Geoff's umpiring report stretched to several foolscap pages and went into quite fantastic detail about every one of the debatable decisions – of which there had been many – but in general, he handled the media well and accepted the defeat in better and more positive mood than I had anticipated.

At Christchurch we played our way into a commanding position, very nearly making New Zealand follow on. When we narrowly failed in this, midway through the fourth day, Geoffrey clearly felt that we had sacrificed all chance of winning the match. Along with many of the other lads I disagreed, feeling that we should hit out, score another 100 runs quickly, and leave ourselves a day in which to bowl them out again.

Boycott and Rose opened, which was probably the first mistake. Brian had been in terrible form all tour and Geoff seemed in no hurry, so that we had scored only 19 when Rose was out after 11 overs. Ewan Chatfield then ran out Derek Randall backing up, which incensed us all as a most unsporting gesture. Being the senior pro back in the dressing-room, I decided Ian Botham should go in to hurry things along. Ian's method of doing this was to run out Boycott by all of 17 yards, and he will tell you to this day that he did it deliberately. Being critical of the running between wickets of both men, I am not so sure, but the effect was to send our captain into a deep depression. He lay in the back of the dressing-room with a towel over his head, apparently taking no interest in the happenings on the field.

Ian hit out, then got out, and when Phil Edmonds went to ask Boycott if he should pad up, ready to go in ahead of Bob Taylor, the reply was apparently to the effect that the vice-captain seemed to be deciding the batting order.

At close of play we were 96 for four, with a lead of 279, which seemed quite enough with which to declare. Boycott, having spoken to no-one that evening, came down the following morning and asked various people, including myself, about the course of action we would recommend. When I told him I felt we should immediately declare, he moaned: 'You're just like the press. You want to see me lose another game.' Although I countered that this was far from being the case and that I regarded a declaration as being our best chance of winning the game and levelling the series, he was not instantly placated. None the less, a declaration was forthcoming, and we bowled New Zealand out inside three hours, largely through one of the most hostile spells I have ever bowled in Test cricket.

We came home from New Zealand with honour intact and Geoff passed the captaincy back to Mike without having lost face, although the lasting impression he gave to all of the players with him during that trip was of a terror of being beaten and having to face the consequences.

9

PITCHING IT SHORT

The outlook of the English sports fan has always struck me as being bewilderingly contrary. When England are doing badly, criticism becomes almost hysterical; so frequently are we termed the worst team in the world that the statement becomes preposterous. Yet when England are doing well, even very well, the reaction is rarely one of congratulatory acclaim but of either cynicism or sympathy towards the opposition.

Time after time I have seen this happening, and if cricket is the worst example it is by no means the only sport whose followers wallow in a self-denigratory shame. Even when England's footballers won the World Cup in 1966, there were many ready to demean the achievement: we were playing at home; the opposition was not up to much; we didn't play the best football – I read all the excuses for victory.

This irritating syndrome has rebounded on me more than once, but never more clearly or violently than in June 1978 when, on the Monday morning of the summer's first Test at Edgbaston, I hit the Pakistan nightwatchman, Iqbal Qasim, in the face with a bouncer and inadvertently caused a controversy which was to rage for weeks.

The first thing to be said is that I neither meant to hit Qasim, nor took any pleasure from the sight of his blood. That, I hope, puts the record straight on the most damaging of the slanderous remarks which came my way in the aftermath of the incident.

I did, however, bowl a short ball with the premeditated intention of unsettling him, which I maintain was a perfectly legitimate tactic. True, there had been a resolution from the International Cricket Conference instructing captains that bouncers should never be bowled at non-recognized batsmen (long since abandoned – witness the West Indian pace bowlers' treatment of anyone from one to 11 in the order!) but I did not consider this to apply to nightwatchmen, who would otherwise be able to plant their front foot down the pitch, smugly confident that every ball had to be pitched up to them, and achieve the dual purpose of seeing the shine off the ball and shielding the better batsmen. Qasim, who had come to the wicket on the Saturday evening and done his job well, had subsequently outstayed his welcome by hanging around for a further 40 minutes at a crucial stage of the game. To my way of thinking, he was no longer a tail-ender and had certainly sacrificed his right to be considered an unrecognised batsman – he was acting out the part of a number three, and as such, he qualified for a little softening up.

Over the 40-minute period I bowled him three short balls, the first two of which he avoided before deflecting the third into his face. It was a mess – blood everywhere, stitches and hospital the order of the day. I believe I committed my only sin in the whole affair by walking away, back towards my mark, while the rest of the England players went to Qasim's assistance. A great deal was made of this and I was widely accused of being a callous ogre. This was not the case, my reason for keeping my distance being the memory of what had happened in the Centenary Test, when I had rushed to Rick McCosker's aid after causing him a similar mishap. The sight of the injury, and its clear extent, had lessened my effectiveness as a bowler for the remainder of that game, and I was determined to prevent a repetition. In hindsight, of course, I was wrong. It did look bad, uncaring, and I regretted it later.

For bowling the ball which caused the damage I felt no real remorse. Much was made of the fact that I had switched to bowling round the wicket shortly before the incident, but there was nothing at all sinister in this. Anyone watching my tactics would have noticed that I very often went round the wicket to the left-handers, simply to alter the line of attack.

The fury in the general reaction surprised me, and there were two points on which I felt aggrieved. Firstly, only a few months earlier during the winter series in Pakistan, I had not complained when Sarfraz Nawaz, the Pakistan new-ball bowler, had made me duck and weave with a number of bouncers when I was batting as a true number 11, not even as a nightwatchman. One of the short balls which literally parted my hair could easily have landed me in hospital, and I wonder if the reaction of the Pakistan public would have been one of outraged accusation. I very much doubt it, because my second point is that it was typically English for so many people to work themselves into a lather over this affair. We were well on top in the match and looked likely to win it by an innings – which we eventually did. Pakistan being unlikely to prove much of a match for us in this series, the mood of the spectators (at least a large proportion of them) changed from one of support for their own side to sympathy for the opposition. All power to the underdogs, and woe betide any cad who should knock them about! If one of their quick bowlers had hit one of our tailenders in the mouth, I am certain it would have been passed off as 'just one of those things', without so much as an angry word. Sometimes, we are a very strange race.

Although my view of this episode is that neither reprimand, recrimination nor regret were necessary, there have been at least two instances in my career when I have deserved all three through a foolishly hot-headed delivery.

The first of these occurred in my first season at Edgbaston in 1972, when still young and impressionable, I was growing increasingly frustrated by my failure to induce any life from the slow, plumb Birmingham pitch. It was a macho reaction to something I considered an affront to my standing as a fast bowler, and did me no credit at all. The batsman was Barry Wood, later to be an England team-mate but at that stage a solid Lancashire opener. He was so confident of the pace and bounce of the wicket that he was advancing a pace or two down the pitch to play me – a cheeky tactic that so enraged me that I bowled him a beamer.

Now and again the ball can slip from any fast bowler's hand and turn into a beamer quite by accident. Not this one; it was deliberate, with malice aforethought. I actually wanted it to hit Wood, which it did, but fortunately only a glancing blow on his glove. It took me only a second or two to come to my senses and appreciate the stupidity of what I had done, and that was the first and last time I ever tried to injure a batsman.

Nine years later, however, I came close to a repeat performance during The Oval Test against Australia. It was the last match in a long and tiring, if exhilarating series, and I was on a short fuse. Umpire Dickie Bird was repeatedly calling me for the most marginal of no-balls. He was strictly correct, of course, but with a mentality typical of the martyred fast bowler I thought it characteristic that an umpire should pay pedantic attention to the bowling crease and – in my view – rather less to the business end of the action at the batsman's crease. What made it very much worse was the fact that the batsman was Dennis Lillee, who was enjoying himself hugely, stepping away to flat-bat the shorter balls over the slip cordon and successfully slogging the well-pitched-up variety through the leg side.

My 'revenge' was intended to satisfy my grievance against both Bird and Lillee. I was so fed up by the way things were going that I deliberately overstepped the crease by at least four feet and bowled a short ball off less than 21 yards. Dickie, predictably, flapped. 'What are you doing? What's going on here? You can't go doing that.' I knew it was a silly way to react and the moment was defused instantly.

The oddest thing about that little cameo was that it concerned two people for whom I have the greatest of admiration. Although I can find blemishes in the past history of them both (not difficult to do with anyone if you dissect carefully), Dickie Bird and Dennis Lillee typify the best of their respective worlds. Bird is the finest, fairest umpire of my era, Lillee unquestionably the greatest fast bowler, and now is a good time to reflect on the roles both have played during my time in the game.

As far back as my memory goes, English umpires have always been ranked top in the world league. The compliment still applies, despite the fact that in recent years almost all our better umpires have shown themselves susceptible to pressure at the very highest level. All, that is, except Dickie Bird.

The majority of our umpires have played a good deal of first-class cricket, which is vastly to their benefit when comparisons are made with overseas umpires, hardly any of whom have played the game at better than club standard. If one has to be critical to find the cause of faults, I would pinpoint the fact that our umpires, generally no more than county professionals who never aspired to the Test team, were unused to the very different and peculiar pressures which apply at that level.

Since 1977, the watershed of the game with the Packer explosion, nothing has been quite the same for anyone involved, simply because money has made it at least twice as important to everyone as it was previously. I include umpires in this, those on the Test panel now receiving fees which would have been undreamed of only a few years back, although it is the money the players are both receiving and fighting for which brings a new element of tension into the game and creates more exacting situations for the umpires to cope with. Many, all too aware that an enormous television audience is keen to act as judge and jury, do not react well.

The 1982 Pakistan touring team to England engaged in some cynical baiting of our umpires which plainly found the mark. I am convinced that complaints about decisions from both the captain, Imran Khan, and the manager, Intikhab Alam, were merely a try-on. They knew that if they ridiculed the umpires enough, they would probably want to have a go back, something which it is usually impossible to do in their job. Unfortunately, Ken Palmer and David Evans did, to a certain extent, crack under the scrutiny, and when Javed Miandad, who would not win my award for the most popular or sportsmanlike cricketer in the world for that or any other season, booted the ball petulantly away at Edgbaston having unsuccessfully claimed a 'catch' at slip when the ball had clearly bounced in front of him, Messrs Evans and Palmer felt the need to justify their decisions by talking to newspapermen.

Just as misguided, in my view, was Barrie Meyer's reaction to the controversial lbw verdict he gave at Lord's in 1984 to send Viv Richards on his way. Meyer, when questioned by journalists that evening, confessed he had made a mistake and revealed that he had already apologized to Richards. It was honest but foolish. He would have been far better to have said nothing publicly – apologizing to Richards if he felt he had to, but never allowing himself to be sucked so far into the media exposure as to openly discredit authority. This rare lapse by Meyer, whom I regard as the next-best umpire to Bird, underlined the fierce and merciless spotlight on the men who do such an onerous job.

Bird is in a different class because, despite his theatrical, idiosyncratic behaviour on the field, he is a tough and unyielding professional. His measures against the West Indian fast bowler Malcolm Marshall, when his short-pitched assault got out of hand in 1984, was a good example of his bravery. I have also been most impressed with the way he has progressed from being a compulsive 'not-out man' – better, probably than a compulsive finger-raiser but none the less unfair on the labouring bowlers – into someone whose pressure decisions can rarely be seriously questioned whether he gives them in or out.

I contrast this with my worst experience of decision-making in Brisbane, early in the 1978–79 tour of Australia, where my first delivery in my first match of the trip was a full toss with the sole merit of being straight. It hit the opening batsman, Wayne Broad, full on the pad and in my view would undoubtedly have flattened the middle stump, probably making contact no more than three inches off the ground. The appeal seemed a mere formality, but to my utter amazement the umpire adjudged it not out. Later that evening I had a chat with him, on very friendly terms, simply asking him what had been wrong with the appeal. 'Aw', he said, 'I never give a decision on the first ball of the game. I have to get my eye in, just like the batsmen.' I checked myself from making the justifiable observation that I might as well have saved my breath.

Although Dickie Bird and Dennis Lillee could not, in terms of character and temperament, be much further apart, there are certain striking similarities in the way they go about their respective business. Just as Bird is meticulous in his decision-making and quite scrupulously professional in his preparation and his knowledge, I have never known a cricketer more demanding of himself than Lillee. One needed only to watch his warm-up exercises for 20 minutes to see how fit the man was, and ten minutes' conversation would have been enough to convince anyone of how much success meant to him, right to the end of his career.

If I rank his Centenary Test efforts above all else, that may be because it was to become such a symbol of excellence for me to aim at. In truth, of course, the list of his achievements is as near endless as makes no difference, but if I must pick out one more individual game it would be the Melbourne Test on our three-Test trip down under in 1979–80.

Australia were already 2–0 up, the series settled, but at the same time they were enjoying very different fortunes against West Indies in one of those twin Test tours which were briefly popular in the wake of World Series cricket, taking as much of a pasting from the West Indians as they were handing out to us. They were being put through an absurdly rigorous schedule, yet here was Lillee turning in yet another match-winning performance on a Melbourne pitch fit to break the heart of any self-respecting fast bowler. Dennis reduced his pace on the slow, dead pitch, bowling off a shorter run and concentrating on cutting the ball off the seam. He bowled the lot – off-cutters and leg-cutters which would have done justice to Alec Bedser at his best – to take 11 wickets in the match as we were thumped again.

It was the end of a relatively brief trip for us, but I felt exhausted – just as I had during the Centenary Test on the same ground three years earlier – and found myself wondering yet again: 'What on earth keeps Lillee going?' Hardly knowing the man at the time, I could find no answer to my question, but in subsequent years, as our careers converged in their final stages and the flimsy barriers which had always prevented us getting on as individuals were broken down, I had many long conversations with Dennis, growing to understand him better.

He is an odd mix of a man, typically Australian in wanting to rile and provoke the opposition with taunts and insults, occasionally outrageous on the field to an unforgivable extent, yet not one to bear grudges. I discovered this in 1981, the year of those unforgettable Tests against Australia when we virtually came from the dead to take the Ashes. It was my benefit year, and on the evening after one of the incredible games had ended in another England victory at Edgbaston, I had arranged a dinner-dance in Birmingham, fittingly labelled a Kangaroo Ball. To be honest, I was not confident of seeing any of the Australian players at the function, but about half a dozen came, three staying on into the small hours. They were Kim Hughes the captain, Peter Philpott the assistant manager, and Lillee himself. They did not stay and sulk, either, but were so much the life and soul of the party that when everyone went home, Dennis came with me to another nightclub. It was 6.45 a.m. before we parted at the end of a riotously enjoyable night, during the course of which Dennis had pleased me no end by confiding that he had always admired my achievements . . . despite my having had a go at him in a previous book!

The subject of my attack had been his more undignified moments on the field – the aluminium bat incident and the kick aimed at Javed Miandad are but two incidents which spring to mind – and I shall never be shaken from my view that he has on these occasions betrayed both himself and the game of cricket.

While I was a constant admirer of his feats on the field, I therefore took a long while to learn to like Dennis, partly because one never quite knew what to expect from him. I counted Rod Marsh and Doug Walters as constants among the Australians of that era – win or lose, you could always guarantee their presence in the dressing-room afterwards with a beer and a yarn. I have often said that this practice of going instantly to share a drink with the opposition seems foreign and unnatural to me, but I would rather it was done all the time than only when it suits. Players are often conspicuous by their absence when they have been beaten, simply not socialising in the same numbers as when they win. That this is not just a failing of Test players, but is practised right down to the lower grade levels of club cricket, does not make it any more endearing. Australian humour also conflicts sharply with mine, for while I tend to make jokes at the expense of myself more than at the expense of others, their humour is based on biting sarcasm directed at others. Ian Botham could revel in the company of Australians for an unlimited period, but I always found them hard work, which is what kept Lillee at arm's length for so long.

One of the worst examples of Australian exhibitionism I ever came across was the crude way in which they celebrated the winning of the Ashes during the 1982–83 tour. The final Test in Sydney had ended in a predictable draw and, as captain, I paid my duty visit to the home dressing-room along with other members of our side. To my amazement, we were treated to an obviously rehearsed and acutely embarrassing spectacle of the Australian physio burning, or attempting to burn, two bails in a steel bucket. It plainly meant something to their players to do that in front of us, but I just shook my head at the childishness of it. Strangely, however, it was during that tour that I spent most time with D. K. Lillee, who was recovering from another injury when the series began. Catching him between sessions in the TV and radio commentary boxes and talks with his newspaper ghost writer, I chatted to him at length about knees – very much a mutual concern during our careers – fitness and remaining ambitions. It had been a long road, but I had learned to like as well as admire him. He might never be my greatest mate, but to me he would always be the greatest bowler.

Back in 1978, where this subject began, Dennis was to all intents and purposes on the opposite side of the fence to me, rather than just in the opposition dressing-room. He was a key figure in World Series Cricket, a hero for the propagandists to hype and a symbol for them to thrust before the public as apparent proof that they had attracted the best.

England were to come across this approach to promotion that winter, when we took on a full-scale Australian tour with the Packer programme in direct opposition. We went in good heart, as any side would who had just completed two comfortable victories in home series. Neither Pakistan nor New Zealand had proved to be a match for us in English conditions – the results: 2–0 and 3–0. Victory over Pakistan had been all the sweeter for the cheap dismissals inflicted on Miandad, whose infuriating antics both when batting and fielding were regarded by many English players as being very close to cheating. Victory over New Zealand emphasized my point that they were never likely to be a match for us on decent wickets; at Lord's, where the ball swung but the pitch was blameless, they collapsed humiliatingly to 37 for seven after Mike Brearley had told us, with considerable foresight, that if we bowled well we would have them out for under 100. Ian Botham took 11 wickets in the match (the first of several occasions on which he was to achieve the ten-wicket mark which eluded me throughout my Test career) and we won easily after trailing by 50 runs on first innings.

It was a successful, though hardly remarkable summer on the field; a surprising one off the field. On the last day of July I met the girl I was later to marry, brought together, you might say, by a combination of cricket, football and the fickle English weather.... On the rainy Monday of the Oval Test against New Zealand, bored with the dressing-room pursuits, the card-playing which I detest and the cacophony of music not always to my taste, I wandered into the Long Bar in search of some old friends from Corinthian Casuals FC who, I knew, had planned to be present. They were exactly where I expected to find them, accompanied by a girl who turned out to be a former secretary of the Casuals. Immediately regretting that she had not been at the club during my brief spell with them, I felt a strong urge to get to know her better. This I succeeded in doing over the following months, and by the time we set off for Australia, the bachelor status, which had been such a proud boast of mine while drinking cognac in Hyderabad less than 12 months earlier, did not seem quite so secure.

Meanwhile such momentous plans were pigeon-holed for the duration of what was to be an extraordinary, if not unique tour, with two cricketing camps making their way around Australia, each claiming to be the real thing, each bidding for the attention of the public.

Considering the controversy which was inevitably attached to the duel, it was for us a remarkably happy tour. Winning, as ever, was an enormous help, but I have the feeling that the group of players we had on that trip would have enjoyed themselves whatever the result. For one thing, they were united against World Series, and for another they belonged to what is now a bygone generation of players, perfectly able and willing to amuse themselves in free time.

That this party bore no resemblance in off-field character to the squad which visited the same place under my command four years later, I put down to a major change in the make-up of young people during that period. By the early eighties we were into the era of Walkman stereos, trendy clothes and demands for constant entertainment with the alternative of boredom, the greatest single enemy on modern cricket tours. In 1978–79, no-one needed telling what to do when they were not actually playing; no-one had to be persuaded to watch the cricket or instructed in the art of the 12th man's job. Things were just done naturally.

Certainly there were few raw youngsters in our side that winter, the fringe players involved in few of the major games including hardened professionals like Clive Radley and Roger Tolchard, who naturally had the ambition to play in the Tests, but were not the type to moan excessively of the tedium if they weren't picked.

Tolchard was the ideal man to have as number two wicket-keeper. It has long been a grouse of mine that England take two specialist wicketkeepers away on tour, because in most respects this is a place sacrificed. The touring captain usually leaves home with a very good idea of the 11 or 12 players who are going to be involved in most of the Test action, requiring of the others an ability to fill in and contribute. A third spinner and a second wicketkeeper should always be able to bat: Tolchard won a Test place on batting alone in India during the 1976–77 series and there was a time in Australia when it seemed the same could happen. Ian Gould played in all the one-day internationals on our Australian tour four years later, primarily because of his vigorous batting, and there was talk of his playing in the Tests for the same reason. Neither Tolchard nor Gould could seriously be ranked as the second-best 'keeper in England when they were chosen to tour, but they capably fulfilled the roles required of them.

As for Radley, I think being there at all was a bonus to him. He had been approaching his 34th birthday, all hopes of international honours probably discarded, when he was summoned to Pakistan the previous winter as a replacement for Mike Brearley. He had not wasted the chance, making a painstaking hundred in New Zealand and following it with another, against Pakistan, during the summer. 'Rad' was a self-made player, short on flair and grace but lacking nothing in application. He sold his wicket very dearly and I had high hopes that he would graft his way to one or two big scores against the Aussies. Sadly, it was not to be, for in the opening first-class match of the tour, Rad was hit on the head by a South Australian fast bowler of whom most of us knew precious little, the blow causing Clive to tread on his stumps, effectively wrecking his confidence for the rest of the tour. It was a dramatic way for the bowling star of the series, Rodney Hogg, to introduce himself.

At first sight, he does not look much. He runs in with his body thrown so far forward and his legs stuttering in such disarray that one always feels he is about to topple over – which he sometimes does. When he gets it right, he bowls very fast, very straight and very aggressively, although he has inevitably suffered a spate of injuries through bowling fast off such an unco-ordinated approach.

Yet the Australian attack is always better for his presence and, in this particular series, Hogg and his new-ball partner Alan Hurst were almost the only Australian successes. 'Hoggie' took 41 wickets, which was a startling achievement considering his side was beaten 5–1, and although he had the occasional contretemps with his captain, Graham Yallop, he retained a sense of humour which appealed greatly to many of us in the opposition. Hogg is adept at the dry one-liner, his personality attracting Mike Brearley and Ian Botham especially. Although he was a little flattered by taking quite so many wickets because we rarely distinguished ourselves with the bat, it remains a quite outstanding performance under the circumstances.

More often than not, our first four or five wickets would tumble quickly – usually to Hogg – and it would be left to the lower-middle-order men to drag us out of trouble. Ian Botham played his part in this direction, as did Geoff Miller and the other bowlers, but perhaps the innings of them all was played by Bob Taylor at Adelaide. After leading by only five runs on a low-scoring first innings, we were, as usual, in trouble, although for a change Hogg had not taken a wicket. When Chat went in at number eight we were 132 for six and Australia must have been fancying their prospects of a win which would have brought them back to 2–3 down with one to play. They were thwarted by Taylor and Miller, the Derbyshire pair inspiring each other in a century stand, with Bob falling only three runs short of the first hundred of his career. By then we were safe, and another big win put the series beyond doubt.

We had been well on top in the series from the time we reduced the Australians to 26 for six in the first Test at Brisbane. Our comfortable victory gave us a tremendous confidence boost, but I ended it in some pain from the old fast bowler's problem of blisters. I had some new boots made in Australia in an attempt to alleviate the problem, and sent for further supplies from England, so that in the end I probably had as many boots as the rest of the lads put together. Although I found a pair which did not rub in time to resume the fray in the second Test, the incident was not without its alarm and its retrospective humour.

Bernard Thomas took me to hospital in Perth, where I saw a doctor who came up with what seemed to me a horrifyingly extreme remedy, saying that the toe which was causing me the problem (next to the little toe on the left foot) was no good to me anyway. You might as well have it off and be done with it.' Believe it or not he was perfectly serious, and great was my relief when we decided to seek a second opinion!

Throughout the tour it was impossible to escape comparison with World Series Cricket. Their games were on TV as much as ours – the establishment version on ABC Channel Two and the Packer matches on his own Channel Nine – and, just as I have no doubt they watched us with some interest, so we switched on to them whenever we had a free day or evening.

There was a good deal of mickey-taking. WSC's marketing men had just come out with the song, 'Come on Aussie, Come on', which featured on all their TV commercials and rang out at the ground each time the Australians took a wicket. Our lads composed a different set of rather derogatory and possibly even slanderous lyrics to fit the catchy tune. There were those amongst us who remained convinced that certain WSC games were played less competitively than others. Perhaps we were wrong – there were certainly as many heads in the sand on our side of the fence as on theirs.

The Packer players felt they were pioneers. Proud of what they had joined, they tried to tell us that it was only a matter of time before we would all be involved in the same thing. We believed them to be victims of a mass indoctrination process and, while this was certainly no bad thing as it meant they identified with their team and believed in their jobs, it did nothing to lessen our distaste for the entire Packer circus.

We were dismissed in their eyes as an England team lacking a number of big names playing against an Australian third eleven. If there was a semblance of truth in the allegation it served only to harden attitudes. A number of players in our squad had, for their own reasons, rejected advances by WSC, so the inevitable feeling of 'them and us' predominated whenever the subject arose.

The two sets of players scarcely mixed at all. One evening at Sydney airport, when we came face to face with the Packer troupe while we were waiting for one plane and they for another, nods were exchanged, one or two going so far as to hold brief conversations with old friends, but there was no real warmth in the greetings. Later on our trip, Tony Greig invited a lot of us up to his splendid Sydney home for a barbecue and although a few went along, they were not many.

Looking back now I can readily concede the achievements of World Series Cricket. They came chiefly in the form of night cricket and advanced TV techniques, although at the time, we were probably as uncharitable about these facets as we were about the rest of the operation – mocking the 'pyjama-clad' players under the floodlights, scoffing at the insistence on TV of interviewing batsmen as they walked off after being out for nought. But when the dust settled, advances had been made and Australian cricket, for better or worse, was certainly never going to be the same again.

Channel Nine was revolutionary in much of what it attempted. Some of its features flopped, of course, but a lot of them have since been generally adopted, even by the BBC. Night cricket is a vivid and exciting spectacle, both on television and on the grounds themselves, the white ball, first introduced on that tour, being a great aid to ground spectators and TV viewers which could profitably be used in all one-day matches. The 50-overs-a-side games had their break of an hour between innings, with a time limit placed on the team batting first. This too, was a sensible development and, if employed in our domestic one-day competitions in England, could put an end to both the ludicrously early starts and the dusk finishes.

These things will not easily become part of our game because the stigma of being World Series ideas is still attached to them. When compromise was reached with Packer, the Australian administrators pandered to the new demands of their consumers, accepting that they now had in Australia what could accurately be termed 'the Macdonalds hamburger society' who would come to cricket as long as the action was snappy and the facilities glamourous. They gave them what they wanted in the way of one-day cricket in bulk and gimmicks a-plenty.

Our own establishment has been slow to see that English society has to some extent gone the same way. The cricket purists remain, and always will, so Test matches are not in danger; but there is a large new generation of cricket-watchers, if they can so be termed, who will attend one-day games as a social event where they can drink and be entertained as much off the field as by anything happening in the middle.

I don't altogether blame the English authorities for being so cautious. They suspected that PBL, the marketing company responsible for initiating WSC and later for promoting the plethora of one-day internationals in Australia, would drop cricket as soon as they considered the populace had had their fill, turning instead to water polo, ice hockey or anything else in which they saw potential. They also feared that such a preponderance of international matches was committing cricket to a process of overkill, taking it down the dangerous road already trodden by British soccer, in which it is now hard to distinguish the big game from the mundane.

Night cricket in England should never even have been dreamed about, as the random experiments in football grounds have disastrously proved. Climate and daylight hours are all-important and, however regrettable it may be, the English weather pattern just does not co-operate with the idea at all. Australia, though, are quite right to push the concept. It is justifiably big business there, and for that the Australian Board should be congratulated as well as the Packer promoters. They may not be globally popular within cricket but they have backed a winner, and backed it to the hilt.

Their advantage over our system is that they are able to make decisions so much more quickly. Although people tend to think of the Test and County Cricket Board as being made up of Donald Carr and a few figureheads, in reality the body embraces more than 20 organizations, each of whom has at least one, and usually two, representatives. They meet twice a year, for two days at a time, in an attempt to find some common ground. Even for 50 randomly selected people this would be a tall order, but when almost all the delegates come bearing instructions from their employers, decision-making is virtually impossible.

Far too many of the counties, whose representatives make up the majority of the TCCB, are selfish and parochial, interested only in their own balance sheets or success on the field rather than in what is best for the game as a whole. Some of us who had worked for years to achieve standard playing hours for the County Championship at last believed, a few seasons back, that uniformity had been reached. Everyone was to play from 11 a.m. to 6.30 p.m. with lunch at 1.15 and tea at 4.10. But within months of this agreement apparently being reached, three Midland counties – including my own – said they wanted the freedom to take lunch at 1.30 for the sake of their members who liked to come from work to watch an hour's play. I would guess that in each case the county was considering fewer than 50 people and a couple of dogs who might enjoy the walk!

Counties, especially the small and isolated, feel safety in the numbers of a committee such as the TCCB, and would object violently to any suggestion that decisions should be left to a few appointed individuals. In fact, a lot of them are at their happiest when they feel they can veto any decisions at all.

I have spent five years on the Overseas Tours committee of the

Board, slightly less than that on the Umpires committee. Many times have I been frustrated by this reluctance to change anything, but never have I been quite so alarmed by the attitude as when I was one of a dozen or so delegates sitting on a working party to investigate the structure of the first-class game in England.

My own views on this are widely known. I think we should be playing four-day Championship cricket, with one-day matches for each county every weekend, but I was quite prepared to be over-ruled as long as something positive was achieved. Instead, after 18 months and heaven knows how many lengthy meetings, the net result of the working party was a recommendation that no change should be made. There was clearly something wrong with the set-up for a working party to be needed in the first place.

The committee system will prevail in English cricket long after I have disappeared from the game and, while I am no supporter of selfish intransigence, there are many good, solid men at the head of our cricket. In recent years, since K. Packer took an interest in the game, they have needed to be tough.

10

HUMBLED BY WEST INDIES

A cricketer is fortunate indeed to emerge from his career with no regrets. Even someone who has played as long as I did will surely be troubled by something that was not quite achieved and something else which was not quite done properly. I have no illusions about the number of things I might have done a little differently, but of those I never managed to do at all, two stand out. The first is that I could not give Warwickshire the success they deserved, of which I will say more later. The second is that I never played in a World Cup final.

In years to come, the World Cup of cricket may achieve the status of its soccer equivalent – if, that is, the long-threatened division of black and white nations can be staved off and the game's international circuit preserved and expanded. But I was, at least, part of the formative years in which, with one-day cricket a new and thriving feature of the game, the idea of a world championship decided in limited-overs games was mooted and England pulled the whole operation together.

Three times the event was staged in this country with its final before a full house at Lord's on an atmospheric June Saturday. I was somewhere on the fringes every time, but the final, with all its glamour and its attendant memories, always just eluded me. In 1975, when I was recovering from surgery on my knees, the competition took place while I was still trying to perfect the art of walking and running again. Eight years later, I captained England in the 1983 tournament when, to my great disappointment, we were put out at the semi-final stage by the eventual winners, India, after playing with great purpose and efficiency early on. Between these years, in 1979, England made it to the final of the second World Cup under the sponsorship of Prudential Assurance, who supported one-day internationals in our country for so long. But I missed it.

I had played in every game leading up to the final for which we qualified easily, beating Australia, Pakistan and Canada to top our group, and pipping New Zealand by a mere nine runs in an exciting semi-final at Old Trafford. Late on in that match I twisted my knee landing awkwardly in a foothold and although I was able to complete my 12-over spell, it was soon clear that I would need some rest. With only two clear days available before the final against West Indies, I delayed my decision until the last possible moment, actually turning up at Lord's on the morning of the game still hoping to be fit to play. But when I bowled in the nets at the Nursery End, the knee still gave me considerable pain; so with great reluctance close to grief, I put aside foolish thoughts of trying to struggle through and told Alec Bedser that I had not recovered sufficiently to play.

To this day, I am not sure whether I could have completed my bowling and perhaps made a little difference, because the make-up of our squad dictated that we had to split my overs between three 'occasional' bowlers (Gooch, Boycott and Larkins), all of whom were hammered. In truth the batting of Vivian Richards and Collis King that day was so inspired that I doubt whether my figures would have made very good reading even if I had got through. We were beaten by a much better side. For the England team there was no disgrace in that, but for me there was plenty of sorrow and frustration.

Very quickly, however, the cricket spotlight moved from World Cup to Test series, when I suffered another minor injury which interrupted my long unbroken run of Test match appearances. India were the visiting side and England were expected to win. Sure enough we amassed 633 for five, batting first in the opening match of the rubber at Edgbaston, with 200 not out from David Gower and 155 from Geoff Boycott. The new generation and the old each dominated an Indian attack which, the redoubtable Kapil Dev apart, contained bowlers who were either below par or past their best. Three of the famous Indian spin quartet were on the tour, but Bedi, Chandra and Venkat between them could manage only 13 wickets in the series.

We duly made India follow on, and I think it was the effort of having to go straight out and bowl again, following 24 overs in the first innings, which caused my downfall. When I pulled up in obvious pain, Mike Brearley came across anxiously to ask: 'It's your knee again, isn't it?' But it wasn't. This time I had strained my stomach seriously enough to put me out for two or three weeks, so I was off the field when we completed the innings win at Edgbaston, and missed the Lord's Test, which threatened to go the same way until Vengsarkar and Viswanath scored centuries to salvage a draw for the Indians.

Extraordinarily, although we made all the running, that series could still have slipped through our fingers at the very last gasp. The Leeds Test having been a washout, with not even two innings completed, we came to The Oval one up, with no-one seriously expecting us to be extended to hang on to the advantage. Indeed, for three or four days it seemed likely that we could improve our position to 2–0, as we took a first-innings lead of 103 before another hundred from Boycott enabled us to set India the apparently impossible task of scoring 438 to win. Even when they ended the penultimate day of the game at 76 without loss I can't say there were any ripples of apprehension circling our dressing-room. Having been asked to climb a mountain, they were still in the foothills. We could not have foreseen the anxieties which awaited us.

India lost their first wicket at 213 and their second at 366. Neither of these were Sunil Gavaskar. On and on the little man batted, the improbable dream becoming more and more horribly possible from our point of view. Gavaskar passed 200, India approached 400. Then Botham took a hand. In the final 12 overs he played a part in the fall of five wickets, catching one, running out another and dismissing three, including Gavaskar, with his own bowling. India's requirement of 15 off the last over proved too much; they finished nine short with two wickets in hand as one of the most remarkable day's cricket I have ever experienced ended with the game drawn but the honours indisputably belonging to India.

Gavaskar, who averaged almost 80 in that series, would feature in any World XI I might choose from those I played with and against during my career. He rates so highly among the greatest because he was such a flawless judge of line. In batsmen's jargon, he always knew exactly where his off stump was, and had perfected the opener's art of selecting which balls to play and which to leave alone. Being so short, he was seldom obliged to play anything which was not of fairly full length and was rarely in any great danger from the authentic bouncer which would pass harmlessly over his head. It took bowlers around the world a very long time to work out the correct length to bowl to Gavaskar, and even when they did his supply of runs did not dry up. Events in India in 1984–85 may suggest that his appetite for batting is no longer as great as it always seemed to be when I bowled against him, but he already has the runs and records in the bag to prove his greatness. In many ways, he was similar to Boycott. Both wanted to bat for long periods, neither worried about being pinned down as long as they survived and occupied the crease, and both will probably be remembered more for their defensive techniques than for the flair of their strokeplay. In essence both were ideal openers and despite their idiosyncracies, which could sometimes be irritating, I would like tham to open the innings in any team of mine.

Ironically, my next Test after The Oval escape was to involve me in an incident with Boycott. We were being thoroughly out-played by the 'new' Australians, reinforced by the return *en masse* of their Packer players, and the final stages might have been no more than a formality but for the fact that 'Fiery' Boycott was close to yet another Test hundred. He had played well and deserved it, but it was up to me, at number 11, to ensure that he got there.

Geoff was on 97 when he tucked a ball through mid-wicket for what should have been an easy three. But it was the first ball of an over from Dennis Lillee and, on the pretext that a game should be put above an individual to the very end, I turned down the third run to let Geoff keep the strike. There was no chance of us winning the game, but far more hope – I thought – of surviving longer if Geoff took as much of the bowling as possible.

The plan went wrong because Geoff was left on 99. He was un-able to score off the remainder of the over and the first ball from left-armer Geoff Dymock was good enough to have me caught at slip by Greg Chappell. Boycott could not believe it, and instead of walking off with the rest of us he stood disconsolate and alone at the non-striker's stumps as if waiting for the bad dream to end.

I was to do almost the same thing in the second Test at Sydney, although this time the injured party was David Gower, stranded on 98 when I was again caught by Chappell. It was becoming a bad habit – and worse still, we were well beaten again. This, of course, was a very different Australian team from the one we had over-whelmed only 12 months previously. Only Derek Underwood had come back into our team after the peace treaty with Kerry Packer, but the Aussies restored the full, all-star cast. Both the Chappells, Lillee, Marsh, Mallett, Pascoe, McCosker, Laird and Bright all returned from the ranks of World Series to play against us in that series, which brought us three clear-cut defeats. Lillee took 23 wickets in the three games and Greg Chappell was outstanding with the bat, those two alone making an enormous difference.

Even leaving aside the defeat, this was not a tour I look back upon with any great affection. The itinerary was messy, with Australia obliged to play ourselves and West Indies in alternate Tests, fitting in a three-way limited-overs tournament at the same time to satisfy the demands of PBL Marketing. In the Tests, they were playing West Indies without a rest day and England with one; in the one-day series, the other two countries were wearing coloured stripes on their kit, while England insisted on white and also refused to play with the restrictive fielding circles. The whole affair was a confusion.

The return of Lillee undoubtedly improved the potential of the Australian side but did nothing for the standard of behaviour. The Perth Test was the scene for the now famous aluminium bat pantomime, which portrayed Dennis somewhere between John McEnroe and a persistent sales rep. Intent on squeezing the maximum publicity from the absurd notion, he refused to see sense despite the protestations of everyone around him and the eventual, if belated, pleas of his own captain. His final, petulant act of hurling away the tin bat was entirely unworthy of a great sportsman and the piffling fine meted out by the extraordinary Australian disciplinary system conducted by the players themselves was, I am afraid, symptomatic of a country in which the great advances made in cricket's commercial attraction have not all been handled with the necessary firmness.

As I have hinted previously, I felt the Australians were heading in this dubious direction ever since the accession of Ian Chappell to their captaincy. With frequently undesirable behaviour on the field, he continued to take on the cricket authorities of his country, head to head, no matter how many times they reprimanded, fined or suspended him. It was I. M. Chappell who brought 'sledging' into cricket in 1974. Later he undoubtedly played his part in the setting up and promotion of World Series Cricket but, rather than trying to show the doubters of the cricket world what a lot this brave, new concept had to offer, his whole outlook on life was summed up when he finished off the 1979 'Supertest Final' against Tony Greig's World XI by deliberately bowling such an outrageously wide ball that it went for four, neither batsman nor wicketkeeper able to get anywhere near it. He had never learned to lose with grace, something which Kim Hughes – patently inferior as captain and cricketer yet preferable as a character – carried off admirably under the most trying of circumstances in 1981.

Ian Chappell was never in the same class as his brother, Greg, as a batsman, but I have to say in mitigation of all the wrong he might have done the game, he most certainly proved himself an inspirational leader who shook Australia out of the doldrums, toughened up their cricketers and got them into the habit of winning. He has, with good reason, always been viewed as a bad lad by the establishment, but I wonder how many other people could have taken on the Australian side of the early seventies and made them so successful.

We discovered on this trip that time had not mellowed him. When we met up with him in the match against his state, South Australia, before the Tests began, he was returning to the game after a period of suspension for abusing an umpire. Far from being bowed by this, he disputed another decision when given out and came before the disciplinary committee once again. He also, pettily, bowled an over to Mike Brearley with every fielder on the leg side, having taken exception to our refusal to be bound by the Australian rule by which the number of leg side fielders is limited. This was pure Chappell – cheap exhibitionism, quite unworthy of a man with so much to give.

Ian Botham has often, understandably, found himself referred to as having many of the characteristics typical of the Australian, but I don't think he would thank anyone for comparing him with Ian Chappell. Their altercation in a Melbourne bar in 1976 has gone into cricketing folklore and needs no embellishment here; suffice it to say they never quite saw eye to eye. The comparison would, in any case, be extremely unfair, as one incident during the Test series on that tour proved.

Greg Chappell had batted Australia to the point of winning the Sydney Test, despite having survived a blatant catch behind when on 32. With four runs needed for victory, Chappell was on 94 and Botham was bowling. Had Ian Chappell found himself in Botham's position (possibly even if his brother was the batsman) he may well have repeated his 'Supertest' stunt of bowling the four wides just to deprive the man of any chance of reaching his hundred. Not 'Beefy' Botham. He tossed the ball up in a genuine attempt to give Greg the six he needed. The ball went only for four but the gesture had been appreciated, if not quite understood, by the hard-nosed Aussies.

Botham quite frequently throws up such anomalies in his behaviour. He will compete until he drops – but if he feels there is nothing left to compete for, he will throw in the towel in quite spectacular fashion. The schoolboy mentality still lurks within him and he loves to fool around.

Our third and final Test of that series, at Melbourne, featured a brilliant, unbeaten century by Botham, who then completely dominated the Jubilee Test we played against India in Bombay on the way home. It was one of the most astonishing all-round efforts I have ever seen by an individual in cricket, but was to take its toll in the following years. Botham had done a lot of bowling on the tour and now, in Bombay, he bowled virtually throughout. Of course, he was getting people out and it was not easy to take the ball off him, but the back problem which was to stay with him for years first occurred soon after that trip. I put it down to the amount he was being asked to do, for although he may have appeared super-human to many a fan, his body was no less vulnerable to strain than anyone else's.

No sooner had he returned home from his triumphs than he was made England captain. My opinion of this has never wavered – it was neither right for the England side, nor fair to Ian. While there was much to praise and applaud in the adventure of it, even a certain logic in choosing as captain the best player and one of very few automatic choices, no account was taken of the pressure he was already under to maintain his incredible standards, nor of a personality which did not mark him down as an ideal cricket skipper.

My views are not aided by hindsight, for I said exactly these things at the time. Early in the 1981 season I was interviewed on a local Warwickshire radio station, Mercia Sound, giving my opinion that the captaincy would seriously affect Ian's perform-ance with bat and ball. People wrongly construed what had been intended as constructive comment as a malicious criticism of Botham and I was fined by the Test and County Cricket Board under the rule which forbids players from making public state-ments about their colleagues. Perhaps I was misguided to speak so openly, but the fact remains that his game had been damaged.

This was nothing to be ashamed of, nor even a surprise. Anyone saddled with the burden of captaining a mediocre team against superior opposition is likely to suffer for it in terms of personal performance. More recently it has happened to David Gower and I think it also happened to me. Nobody had cause to say that my performances had fallen off, for I still took wickets, but on reflection I feel I should have bowled myself more than I did. Mental fatigue, however, took its toll of me.

Apart from the malaise it inflicted on his scoring of runs and taking of wickets the job was not made for Ian. He was fine on the field, where his brashness and confidence were often welcome and his underrated cricket brain could handle most tactical equations quite capably. But off the field, where so much of the cricket captain's best work has to be done, he was simply not mature enough to cope. The simple principles he had always applied to his own game – hit the ball as hard as you can and always bowl to attack and take wickets – no longer worked, now that he had the welfare of the entire side to consider. Ian was still the naughty schoolboy, trying hard but in vain to aspire to the job of headmaster.

There are always those players in a cricket team who need a degree of mollycoddling to bring out their best, to whom a few quiet, personal words of encouragement can mean a great deal. Chris Tavaré and Derek Randall were in this category, and so was I. Ian could never understand this mentality, playing cricket, to him, being perfectly straightforward. He did not like it cluttered with complications or anxieties, always getting on with the game uncomplainingly and imagining everyone else should do the same. A captain cannot afford to kid himself that everyone is the same.

Ian hardly ever spoke to the team about tactics. Oddly enough, he is not a very good talker in public, for all his gregarious nature and outrageous one-liners. To the best of my knowledge he never spoke to batsmen during an innings, either to encourage or advise. Fifteen years earlier this might have been acceptable, even sensible, the England side of the mid-sixties being so generously served with top-class batsmen mature enough to take care of themselves. In 1980, however, there were plenty of young or insecure players in the England side who wanted to be encouraged, told what was expected of them, and made to feel that the captain, at least, was living every minute of their anxieties with them. Unfortunately Ian could never respond to this need.

He was particularly at odds with Graham Dilley, and received some criticism from the media over it similar to that which I was to suffer three years later with regard to my handling of Norman Cowans. In both instances, the captain of the day was accused of ruining a young fast bowler's development because he did not rate him highly enough. In both instances the criticism was not entirely fair.

Botham and Dilley were, at the time, complete opposites. Graham, big and strong though he was, remained extremely short of confidence and during the 1980–81 trip to the West Indies he needed constant encouragement to believe that he was doing his job and might indeed take a wicket or two. Although Clive Lloyd was convinced Dilley had it in him to be an extremely effective fast bowler, Graham could not yet believe it himself. Where Botham, bowling badly, would respond to a sharp word and crude comment, Dilley would shrink further into himself and bowl still worse, needing the very type of handling that Botham could not give. Botham, meanwhile, longed for a fast bowler with his own outlook – like Graham Stevenson, who was also on the tour.

This undesirable impasse was not entirely Ian's fault. Certainly it could in part be put down to his immaturity and limitations as a captain, but it was also due to Graham's immaturity – something he later overcame to the extent that I was moved to give him a glowing report after the 1983–84 tour which I captained, despite the fact that he, like me, came home early.

Ian was made captain because of Mike Brearley's non-availability for further tours. One could understand the dilemma and the thinking behind getting the new man into the job at the earliest opportunity. Even if Ian had been the right man, though, I think it was muddled thinking. The 1980 home series pitted England against West Indies. Why subject any untried captain to the ordeal of a series we were not expected to win, but in which public interest and media scrutiny was bound to be fierce? It was, of course, an inconvenient time for Brearley to go, the next tour also being to the West Indies. But at least there, a new captain would have been away from the harshest glare of publicity, free to spend prolonged periods with his team, working out how best to approach the job without the constant distractions of a big series at home.

Brearley, I suggest, should have kept the captaincy for most of the 1980 summer. If it was felt the new man must at least be installed and inspected before the tour, he could have been appointed for the Lord's Centenary match with Australia, which followed the five-match series against the West Indies.

Clearly Botham had influential support among the selectors, much of it probably from his one-time Somerset skipper and mentor, Brian Close – someone so very like Ian in outlook that he would doubtless have pressed the theory that he was big enough and good enough to look after himself. Yet cricket had changed; the change had brought new pressures, and from the late seventies onwards there was more to the job of captaining England than even the selectors seemed to realize.

Although Ian was landed with a formidable set of fixtures with which to launch himself in the job, things might have turned out very differently for him had we won, as we should have, the first Test of his captaincy at Trent Bridge. It was a low-scoring game on a sporting wicket on which, in the frenetic final stages, we dropped at least two straightforward catches before Andy Roberts slogged the winning runs for a two-wicket victory.

This was to be the only positive result of a series which never quite lived up to its billing. Had we won at Trent Bridge and taken the series, Ian would have been a hero again and, who knows, might still be England captain today. As it was he did not even last another 12 months.

The second Test at Lord's was notable for three things – Graham Gooch made a fast and brilliant hundred for England, Viv Richards answered with another for West Indies, and Chris Tavaré batted four hours for 42 to be summarily dropped. I always thought this was terribly hard on a player with whom I have a great deal in common. We share the same traumas about the game of cricket, neither of us having learned to enjoy it very much at Test match level. Chris, like me, is a cloistered, complex character who found it physically and mentally hard to sustain the necessary concentration for Test cricket. Never part of the extrovert social set, he preferred to go to bed early – not because he was deliberately unsociable but because he was usually shattered. 'Tav' never felt very secure in the side, frequently suffering from an identity crisis in that he has never been sure what was required of him. The advice, which I have no doubt he sought from his Kent colleagues Alan Knott, Derek Underwood and manager Brian Luckhurst, would probably have been to make runs, no matter how long they took to come. It was sound advice, given England's need for a batsman who could stick around for hours at a time, occupying the crease and draining the fire from the West Indian quick bowlers. Being ideally equipped to do the job, Chris set his stall out to do just that and found himself dropped, without a word of explanation. He had probably taken the task too far, his determination to stay preventing him from keeping the score ticking over, but I had a great deal of sympathy with him, feeling that his sacking was the second selectorial mistake of the summer.

The third, it might be said, was their failure to drop me after the next Test at Old Trafford, in which I bowled as badly and ineffectually as I have ever done in all my years with England. I was thoroughly and mercilessly hammered, especially by Richards, and felt utterly helpless and depressed about it. It was then that Ian's loyalty, which he shows to all his friends and team-mates, came shining through. He took me out for a drink, cheered me up, and made sure I kept my place for the next game. It was more than I deserved, but I have always been grateful.

As things turned out, it was only a one-match stay of execution, for I bowled more rubbish at The Oval, crowning my frustrations by taking two wickets with no-balls. Although I played my part in saving the game with the bat during a long and unlikely partnership with Peter Willey, I was quite properly dropped from the side for the first time in five years. My unbroken four-year run in the side had begun against the West Indies at Leeds in 1976 and now, ironically, I was to miss the Leeds Test of this series.

I didn't feel bitter or mistreated, knowing it had been the right decision. I was more disappointed to find myself still omitted from the team for the Centenary Test at Lord's. County games had been programmed to coincide with this game, despite its apparent standing as a national celebration, so although all England cricketers who had played against Australia were invited to the event, David Brown and I were among those disgruntled souls who had to miss out on the parties, confining ourselves to Warwickshire affairs.

There was never any real doubt in my mind that I could get back in the side. My bowling problems were of a temporary nature, irritatingly minor yet quite sufficient to destroy my rhythm until I had gone back to basics to sort myself out. A few months later, however, I really did believe my career was over.

The West Indies tour, for which I was named vice-captain, did not start until after Christmas, beginning with a dreary and largely unproductive few weeks in which very little seemed to happen. What with bad weather, a patchy itinerary and our own decision to warm up quietly in Antigua at our own expense, the tour was a fortnight old before I even bowled a ball in a competitive situation. In my seventh over of the opening one-day fixture on the paradise holiday island of St Vincent, I landed awkwardly, twisting my knee. It was a familiar scenario, a familiar pain, and I immediately feared the worst, leaving the field to rest for some days before beginning my attempts to prove I was fit again. The injury refused to recover. I missed the first Test in Trinidad, and although I kept trying, ever more gingerly, ever more desperately, to bowl in the nets, I knew in my heart it was no good.

Towards the end of that Test, it was reluctantly agreed that I would not be fit enough to bowl for some considerable time. I was offered the chance to stay on as Ian's lieutenant, a non-playing senior professional, but was so depressed I could not envisage myself being of any benefit to the blokes. As they flew off to Guyana, where they expected to play the second Test, I prepared to fly home, convinced in my own mind that I was flying out of cricket forever. This time, I thought, the knee will be too bad to patch up. This time it really is all over.

LEEDS 1981 – THE GREATEST DAY

My Birmingham surgeon rescued my career for a second time in spring 1981, sending me out bursting with health for a season in which I was to bowl the most famous spell of my life . . . in a game for which I was originally not even chosen. He had put me right in 1975 when both my knees had given up on me. He had only one to cope with now, and had the aid of far more advanced technology than when I was last on the operating slab. Slowly, from the depths of the defeatism in which I had moped my way home from the Caribbean, I was made to realize that all was not lost.

I was approaching 32, almost elderly for a fast bowler, and the sensation of time running short filled me with panic. The brilliant surgeon restored my faith and ambition to play again, but had he told me I would have to spend as long a period in hospital and in painfully slow rehabilitation as I had endured six years earlier, I think my will to get back on the field would have evaporated.

Arthroscopy, which is basically surgery through a microscope, rendered the process so straightforward that I wondered why I had ever been in such doubt. As soon as I returned from the West Indies, I was taken in for the operation. A piece of cartilage was removed and, to my great surprise, I was on my feet within two days and starting light training within ten, prior to reporting back for pre-season practice with Warwickshire at the start of April with nothing more alarming than another in my collection of scars to betray the mental agonies I had been through.

England were still fighting it out under Botham against a palpably superior West Indian side. Andy Roberts might have been slightly past his best, but Joel Garner and the awesome Colin Croft were at their peak, Michael Holding was still silkily smooth and deadly, and there was a wiry young man named Malcolm Marshall trying very hard to break into the side. They were a formidable combination even before one mentions the likes of

Richards, Greenidge and the ageless skipper, Lloyd. I had thought it evident even before I left that we were in for a fearful hiding, leaving with the unhappy feeling of abandoning a sinking ship, although I knew there was absolutely nothing I could do to change the course of events. I was probably better off out of the way.

Robin Jackman, my mate, drinking partner and rival for a place in the Surrey team a decade earlier, won his first England trip as my replacement. That was the first irony of the situation. The second was a less happy one, for it was dear old Jackers who unwittingly caused one of cricket's most unpleasant political storms. He was deported from Guyana, and the rest of the England team left with him.

My sympathies went out to Robin, whose only 'crime' had been to play regular visits to South Africa to coach both black and white players. To think of him as a racist or a supporter of the apartheid system was absurd, but the Guyanan government saw it differently, the crisis erupting when the deportation order was served on Robin as he returned to his hotel room following a gruelling journey from a one-day international, up-country from Georgetown at Berbice. It must have been a terribly harrowing experience for someone who had waited so long to represent his country and now, surely, visualized it all being unfairly snatched back from him.

I sympathized, too, with Alan Smith, secretary of Warwickshire and now managing an England tour for the first time. What a baptism he was having – and how well he coped. It has always been a standing joke in cricket that A.C. relishes a crisis in which his exaggerated diplomacy can be seen to its best advantage, but I cannot imagine he enjoyed this one. The Navy, I believe, was on alert to sail in and pick up the team if it was thought their physical safety was in any way endangered, but in the event they were able to leave on a scheduled flight, having quite properly refused point-blank to play a Test match in a country which had just deported one of their players. They fled gratefully to the beaches of Barbados, staying there for days which must have seemed like weeks while discussions continued to decide the fate of the remainder of the tour.

Most of the players might privately have been hoping it would be abandoned, and I wouldn't blame them for that. It is a natural, human reaction when the already precarious equilibrium of a lengthy period away from home is disrupted in such an unpleasant way. Although cricket tours in recent years seem to have been plagued by problems utterly unconnected with the game itself, this was one of the worst, and even when the decision was taken in the small hours of a moonlit Barbados morning to continue with the rest of the schedule, the party's worries were far from over.

They manfully set about restoring form, fitness and an element of sanity before the Barbados Test, scheduled as the third of the series but now the second. It was with mixed feelings that I followed developments through the papers and the television from my Edgbaston home. I was not sorry to have missed the goings-on in Guyana (although I was acutely aware that if I had not come home they would never have happened), yet I missed the atmosphere of preparing for a big Test and the quite unique comradeship which can build up around a tour, particularly when things are going wrong. I remembered how everyone had rallied round the night before I flew home, throwing an impromptu party, and knew that there were strong characters in the side who would be whipping up the boys to forget the unpleasantness and get on with their cricket. I smiled when I remembered the laughs we had enjoyed in my brief spell on the trip, and decided to phone up on the eve of the Test to wish the boys luck.

The joke in Trinidad had concerned a disorganized taxi company called Bhattu Brothers, whose apparent monopoly on the island's cab services seemed to give them the right to turn up for orders as and when they pleased. Frequently they failed to turn up at all. One of the duties assigned to our assistant manager, Kenny Barrington, was the provision of transport to and from the ground, and I had a vivid mental picture of him standing with that massive jaw set, a familiar long-suffering expression on his face as the Bhattus let him down again. I thought it might amuse Kenny and the rest of the boys if I could get through and pretend to be representing Bhattu, so I put my call to the Holiday Inn and asked for the Barrington room.

His wife, Ann, answered the call and said that Ken was in a team meeting downstairs. The call was redirected to the team room, but instead of Ken, A.C. answered. I had quite a long chat with him about his recent problems and the prospects for the match, by which time my joke would obviously have fallen flat. I passed on my best wishes to the lads and never did get to speak to Kenny. Little did I think that I would never see him again.

Three days later, as I was driving to meet friends for Sunday lunch in a country restaurant, the one o'clock news came on the radio and as soon as I heard his name mentioned in the headline story, I knew instinctively that Kenny was dead. The tour which had gone through an awful battle to find some peace was now hopelessly upset again, with just about the worst tragedy imaginable. As far as I know no-one in cricket ever disliked Kenny. Popular all around the game's globe, to the England players he had helped to supervise since 1976 he was a friend and mentor, and would be missed terribly. Looked at clinically, though, I suppose one had to say that his death in this way was not a complete shock.

Kenny had retired from playing the game on doctor's orders. Having heart trouble he was advised to take things more easily, but this was never the Barrington style. He did spend a stretch of time out of cricket, concentrating on building up his garage business in Surrey, but when the chance arose to get involved at England level again, he jumped at it and, typically, threw himself wholeheartedly into the position. He travelled with the team on five consecutive tours, either as manager or assistant manager, and worked as a selector during the summer months. He was still plainly in love with the game, and the game was still in love with Kenny. Having been on all five of those tours, I recall the tremendous affection with which he was greeted everywhere he went, especially in India where he had become such a hero as a player. He took it all in his stride, laughing, joking and reminiscing. Perhaps not the archetypal administrator, he none the less was a players' manager, always showing he cared about their problems both on and off the field and always ready to listen and advise.

Although hindsight is hopelessly easy, I have often reflected since that Kenny should have been given more authority to help technically, for he had so much to offer, particularly to the batsmen. Most of his managerial duties were during the period of Mike Brearley's captaincy, and one of the matters on which I took issue with Mike was his reluctance to allow anyone, even Kenny, to step in and help a player who was struggling for form. Mike's theory was that a player who had proved himself good enough to play for England was perfectly capable of sorting out his own problems, but I can't help feeling this was a waste of Barrington's vast knowledge and experience.

Kenny was a kind-hearted man and very loyal. When I heard of his death my mind flashed back to the time when he visited my flat in Streatham Hill to try to persuade me that I still had a future with Surrey, the county where he had played all his cricket. He was an eternal worrier, and it was this, I suppose, which killed him. If it is possible, he cared too much about the game and about his players, becoming so involved in the problems of each one of the lads that, in a sense, he was suffering the traumas with them. In the West Indies, I can only imagine his concern as he watched our batsmen endure the now familiar nightmare of pace, ducking and weaving against bouncers on the lively Barbados pitch. When he died we were on the way to a second successive heavy defeat, and one of the pities of it was that he did not live to see Graham Gooch put some pride and respect back in the side by taking on the quick bowlers to score a hundred off them. He would have enjoyed that.

A memorial service was held at Southwark, in south London, at the end of the tour. England had returned with honour somewhat restored, having drawn the last two Tests in Antigua and Jamaica. It was an important revival, especially for Gooch, who made two centuries, and Gower, who saved the Jamaican game with another. They had always promised so much, but while no-one disputed their talent, they had too often flattered to deceive. Now they had proved they had the class and commitment to play big innings against the very best bowlers, and Kenny would have been proud of them.

I am not by nature an emotional person, yet on that April morning, as hundreds of his friends and relations remembered one of the nicest men I have ever known, tears ran uncontrollably down my face; and I was not alone in crying. It would have taken a very long time to count the tears shed in that cathedral.

Life had to go on, of course, and at least for me life had renewed purpose following the successful operation on my knees. I began the season with Warwickshire, intent on proving my complete recovery and on regaining my place in the England side for the summer Ashes series against Kim Hughes's Australians.

The Chappells had gone but with Lillee and Marsh, on their final tour of England, the Australian strength was not markedly different to the side of 18 months earlier which had beaten us 3–0. When they won the first Test at Trent Bridge, by a margin as frustratingly slender as that of West Indies on the same ground a year earlier, they extended our melancholy run to 11 Tests without a win under Ian Botham.

By now the job was plainly not only having a detrimental effect on Ian's cricket but on his whole life. The myth that he, or anyone else for that matter, has an indestructible temperament was quickly crumbling, the sparkle fading from 'Guy the Gorilla' so that I rued the day he was given the captaincy. The selectors, too, were showing signs of cold feet on the matter, appointing him not for the entire six-match summer series, nor even for a healthy period of three Tests, but retaining him on a game-by-game basis, which was doing very little for the peace of mind of anyone in the side and must have been tearing Ian apart. It was as if they were forcing him to walk the plank, a sword poised above his shoulder-blades. I envied him not one little bit.

It all came to a head at Lord's where, for the first time in his Test career, Botham bagged a 'pair'. Nought in each innings. One might suggest he was due for one, his style of batting being as likely to produce the odd catastrophe as it is the stunning century, but the timing was so appropriate to his situation that the coincidence could not easily be dismissed. He was miserable, and on the final morning of a game we were managing to draw, though not with any great conviction, he came to me in that famous old dressing-room where we had shared so many good times and bad with the news that he intended to resign the captaincy that very evening.

I don't for a moment suppose that Ian wanted me to try and talk him out of it, because once he makes a decision he normally abides by it. I certainly had no intention of trying to dissuade him. Frankly, I thought it was the only course open to him if he was to rescue his own career; I also thought it the best thing that could happen to the team, for as the results had become steadily more gloomy, and Ian's own form had plunged to unseen depths, we had undoubtedly lost our way. Ian was not an able enough captain to divorce himself from his own failings yet instil the sense of purpose that any team needs. To a significant degree, our results were inextricably tied to his individual form. I have often said that, for a period of several years, if Botham was playing well England would win, and if he failed they would fail. It was a needless agony to see the captaincy destroying such an important component.

So he quit. He did it in exactly the right way, first informing the chairman of selectors, Alec Bedser, and then, at the end of the game, making a formal announcement at the press conference, presumably dropping a bombshell which sent the journalists scurrying for the nearest phone. I hope they gave Ian due credit for the bravery and honesty of the decision, for he was not taking the easy way out, which would have been to bury his head in the sand and blunder on. He was being quite brutally honest with himself, making what amounted to a public confession that the job was getting him down and, incidentally, getting his family down too. What a pity that the selectors had to spoil it all. Instead of simply accepting his resignation and getting on with the job of finding a successor, they told the press later the same evening that they had already decided to replace Ian.

By appointing the wrong man at the wrong time, the selectors had now forced themselves into a tight corner. Their dilemma was this: four matches still remained of the Ashes series, followed by a winter tour of India and Sri Lanka. Mike Brearley was still around, and Ian himself had voiced the view that he should have the job back. But Mike had made it perfectly plain that he was not interested in going on any further tours, even to India, which he loves so much. Should they throw in yet another untried Test captain midway through a so far unsuccessful series? Or should they effectively admit that there was no-one else around who fitted the bill, turning back to Brearley while they cast around for the long-term answer?

They probably made the correct choice. As a reasonable alternative, they could have appointed Keith Fletcher, but suspicions seemed to persist concerning his ability to make runs against fast bowling. So back came Brearley and, as if by a magic formula known only to him, England came back from the dead to win the series and keep the Ashes. It was, of course, misleadingly simplistic of anyone to conclude that England's success was due entirely to the change of captain. That would be unfair on Ian and absurdly unrealistic regarding the admittedly excellent qualities of Mike. The victory owed something to the style and command of the captaincy and quite a lot to the rediscovered brilliance of Botham. I was one of several others to play significant roles in the most extraordinary sequence of exciting Test matches I ever took part in.

The first, and in some respects the most astonishing of them all, was at Leeds, where I very nearly didn't play. During the Lord's match I had developed a heavy cold which left me feeling pretty ropey. With a break of only nine days before the next Test, I was medically advised not to play in either of Warwickshire's County Championship matches, but was confident of being ready for Headingley. Imagine my surprise, then, when I was called to the phone while watching Warwickshire at The Oval that Saturday to be told by Alec Bedser that I had been left out.

The selectors had apparently assumed, without consulting me, that I was unlikely to make a complete recovery before Thursday and Mike, according to Alec, had been adamant that he did not want a half-fit bowler in the side. Although it took me some while to convince Alec that I had little doubt about my fitness for the game, I effectively talked my way back into the team. Alec phoned the other selectors, Mike Hendrick's invitation to play was intercepted before it could reach him, and the name of Willis was among those read out to the waiting world on the midday news the following day.

Quite rightly, the proviso on my inclusion was that I must play some cricket before the Test. I therefore captained Warwickshire in their John Player League match on the Sunday before driving back to Birmingham for a Second XI one-day match against Leicestershire at Edgbaston. Having satisfied myself and the selectors that I was restored to decent health, I drove on up to Leeds, checking in at the Post House hotel on the northern outskirts of the city. By Monday morning, with two further days of the game still scheduled, I was among the majority of England players who checked out again, certain of defeat before nightfall.

This might be thought defeatist but I would call it realist. We had been badly outplayed over the first three days, with Saturday a nightmare from start to finish. Forced to follow on, we started our second innings in gloomy light, in which poor Graham Gooch suffered the ultimate misery of being out twice for single figures in one day's play.

That night most of the team regrouped at Ian Botham's Humberside home. It had become a tradition for the Botham family to put on a barbecue party on the evening before the rest day of the Headingley Test, and it was always a thoroughly sociable event. Julie (by now my wife) and I stayed the night with the Bothams, enjoying a quiet, typically English Sunday – a couple of lunchtime pints in the local followed by a roast lunch and an afternoon nap. The Test was hardly discussed, although when the subject did arise we were unanimous in thinking that it would be over well before the end of Monday's play. So the following morning we packed our bags, handed in our room keys and prepared to drive back down the motorway later in the day.

By about five o'clock, the telephone in the Headingley dressing-room area was busy as we checked back in again. I understand the betting tent was also busy as Ladbrokes estimated the possible liabilities they had incurred by taking a few bets on England at 500–1, including – by their own admission – one from Messrs Lillee and Marsh. The cause of the commotion, of course, was a remarkable innings by Botham at his outrageously aggressive best.

I am convinced Ian began batting the way he did as little more than a bit of fun. It was not his style to hang around trying to block out the last day and a half, which was just as well, for had he tried to do so I am sure we would have lost heavily. Instead, he slogged. It was high-class slogging, but the description cannot be avoided. He was fortunate in having two partners, in Graham Dilley and Chris Old, who adopted very similar tactics and played above themselves. He was also fortunate that Kim Hughes chose to keep his spinners chafing in the outfield when they might have ended the spectacle long before it got out of hand. Ian was hitting almost everything in the air, the pace of the seam bowlers ensuring that the ball carried over the catchers to drop safely, even when he made only moderate contact. Against the slow bowlers, Ian might well have got 50 or 60 just as rapidly, but he would almost certainly have perished to a catch along the way.

By the time I was called upon to go in at number 11, our lead was over 100, which in itself seemed little short of miraculous following the dire position we had been in at the start of play. When I maintained my record of getting out at indecent moments, this time leaving Ian stranded on 149 not out, I still thought we had no chance of winning the game. Australia wanted 130 to win and, even allowing for the fact that they had spent a long and ultimately demoralizing spell in the field, our first-innings bowling had been so inadequate that I could see no prospect of bowling them out.

It might frequently be forgotten, whenever this incredible game is recalled, that my England place, and possibly my England career, was in considerable jeopardy. Although I had won back my position in the side at the start of the series, which gave great personal satisfaction after being written off so finally when I came home from the West Indies, I was very much aware of having done little to justify the selectors' faith. I had talked my way into the side for the Leeds Test, but was gloomily certain of being dropped unless I could salvage something from what remained of the game.

With so few runs to bowl at, my personal cause was not, I thought, assisted when Mike gave the new ball to Botham and Dilley. Ian, refusing to be kept out of the contest now that he had his teeth into it, dismissed Graeme Wood immediately. But even he is not inexhaustible. His batting marathon had left him weak, and Chris Old came on first change. The innings was out of its infancy by the time I was brought into the attack from the rugby league stand end, whence I bowled badly. Bowling uphill and into the wind, I could find neither rhythm nor pace, so virtually as a final shot I told Mike

I was too old for that sort of thing and asked if I could have a try from the top end.

In view of the way I was bowling, Mike could justifiably have refused, preferring to try someone else. One of cricket's great imponderables is what would have happened had he done so. Instead, he agreed to give me a go; I soon made a ball take off to get rid of Trevor Chappell and, quite suddenly, my adrenalin was pumping.

The secrets of my success that day were that I bowled a precise length, which was essential on that wicket, and that the fielders supported me with some quite outstanding catches. From 56 for one, cruising in carefree fashion to the target, Australia lost seven wickets in rapid succession, and until Ray Bright was joined by Dennis Lillee it seemed, preposterously, that we were about to win the game with a fair bit to spare. Bright then batted neatly while Lillee accumulated runs by flapping the rising ball over the slip cordon. It began to look frustratingly as though all the effort and the monumental recovery might have been in vain until I pitched the ball further up and Lillee obligingly chipped it aerially in the direction of mid-on, where Mike Gatting dived full-length for a brilliant catch. It was all over very quickly. We had won by 18 runs and I had taken eight for 43, the best figures of my Test career.

I ran off the ground unseeing, not really savouring the moment at all. I was delighted we had won, of course, delighted that we were back in the series, but my own part in it, and what it was to mean in terms of rescuing my international future, did not sink in at all in the immediate aftermath of the match.

Many people have told me, mostly with puzzlement and curiosity written on their faces, that I appeared to be in another world while bowling that spell. My eyes, they say, were glazed, my expression unnaturally severe, my entire demeanour suggesting I was in a trance of some kind. This is probably not far from the truth. Wrapped in a cocoon of concentration I could not afford to disturb, I knew exactly what I had to do and, once I had begun to bowl well, I believed it could be done. Throughout my career, I have bowled at my best when I have been left alone to operate in my own way. I don't appreciate being halted on my march back to the end of my run by a gesticulating captain, or anyone else, keen to change the field or give a word of advice. Mike Brearley, coming to know and respect this, never interfered once he could see I was in that frame of mind. Bob Taylor, always anxious to encourage, would usually sprint down the pitch at the end of an over to pat me on the back, but in truth I hardly noticed him during that spell at Leeds. Two years later, on the same ground, I was to reproduce that kind of bowling and concentration in the final innings against New Zealand, but on that occasion the match was too far gone for it to make any difference. It is inevitable that most people will think first of Leeds 1981 when they think of my bowling for England. I don't resent that at all, but I do feel that I probably bowled as well on certain other occasions without taking a wicket!

I can look back on the summer of 1981 with more pleasure than I felt at the time. Even after Leeds I was in my car and heading down the motorway within an hour of the game ending, drained of all emotion by the physical and mental energy I had expended. It was not until I heard my exploits described on the headlines of the radio news that I really took it all in, realizing what had happened and what it meant. Although I did not achieve such startling figures again in the series, the matches at Edgbaston and Old Trafford were both just as spectacular, just as exhausting, and the fact that I was simultaneously organizing my benefit year events did not help my efforts to relax.

This, I am sure, is why I cannot say I ever actually enjoyed playing Test cricket. I was never able to relax.

12

MALICE AND MISCHIEF
IN THE MEDIA

There are those, I am quite sure, who remember my performance on the final day of that 1981 Test at Headingley for more than just my eight wickets. Fleet Street cricket writers, in particular, are unlikely to have forgotten what happened immediately after the match when I was interviewed on BBC television by Peter West and, my face set in an expression of anger which must have bewildered many viewers, proceeded to vent my wrath on them.

There will be many even now unsure why I chose that particular moment, which by all known gauges should have been among the sweetest of my career, to sound off in such a furious manner about the way in which the game was being reported. It probably seemed a graceless act at best, yet I have no special regrets about it. The issue was one on which I felt so strongly that it soured my appreciation of a marvellous win and a notable personal milestone.

If I made a mistake, it was in not being specific enough about the subject of my resentment. Generalizations are always dangerous and it would be wrong to have assumed, either from that outburst on camera or the more detached words which follow here, that I wish to condemn journalists as a race. I have some good friends in the media. There are journalists for whom I have tremendous respect and admiration but, as I have written in a previous book before setting out on my final tour as England captain, there are some I like and trust, some I like but don't trust, a few I trust but don't like . . . and then there are those I can neither trust nor like.

It should also be made clear at this juncture that I am fully aware of the heightened pressures to which cricket writers have been subjected in recent years. The rapid and dramatic influx of money into the game, with all its commercial offshoots, has created difficulties for the writers as well as the players. Because the game has been given an importance it never previously attained, largely through the blanket coverage provided by television and the preponderance of generous but demanding sponsors, newspapers have taken to reporting the game in a new way. It is no longer considered adequate, in all but a few quality papers, to provide the readers simply with an account of the game; nor are the embellishments of comment and opinion sufficient to satisfy some Fleet Street editors. Back-up reporters are now sent out to all Tests, internationals and other important matches, with the sole brief of finding a 'quotes story'. Sometimes, their job is made relatively easy by an outstanding or unusual individual performance on the field. In such instances, they can interview the star of the day, extracting his story and his background to provide a satisfactory piece. It is on the quiet days that things can become unpleasant, the quotes men feeling they must offer their chiefs something newsy while nothing obvious presents itself. It is, I would be the first to admit, a dilemma.

Being only a player, I have never really understood the obsession with quotes. Although there are, naturally, exceptions, so many of these interview stories are fatuous in the extreme. Yet still the papers persist with them and still the quotes men are sent with instructions to produce a 'news story'. It is a difficult job which some do better than others, some, I am afraid to say, hiding behind something which hovers dangerously close to invention.

I always believed I had a good relationship with the press until the day in 1977 when it was revealed that I had decided not to join World Series Cricket. I deliberately avoided talking about the issue, not wishing to become embroiled in any controversy. This was clearly regarded as an unacceptable attitude by a Birmingham evening newspaper, whose cricket correspondent wrote a piece of some length in which I was widely quoted, giving my reasons for turning down the Packer approach and looking forward to my future with Warwickshire and England. The only thing was, I had never spoken about the matter to the journalist, nor to anyone else on that paper. The whole thing was a figment of the writer's imagination. He was duly sacked, but the incident set me more on my guard than I had ever thought necessary.

It was around this time that, in my view, the standard of cricket writing began to decline in many of our national papers, and before too long I stopped reading most of them to avoid getting angry. I just took *The Times*, which still confines itself chiefly to events on the field, but within the confines of a cricket dressing-room, papers inevitably get passed around. Someone will moan about something which has appeared in print, and soon everyone has read it. There is no escape, and in this pass-the-paper fashion I have discovered various other works of fiction under the by-lines of national cricket writers.

Perhaps my criticism of the press is too intolerant, for I do tend to see things either black or white, with precious few grey areas. If I am severe, my judgments are at least based on the experience of having had a journalist for a father; I do have a rudimentary knowledge of the job and its requirements, aware that whatever licence may sometimes be permissible to the writer, it can never include sheer invention.

I have already mentioned the Old Trafford Test of 1980. My bowling, you may recall, had gone to pot and I was crucified by Viv Richards. This in itself would have been enough to depress and frustrate me, although I am now phlegmatic enough to know that a good performance can very often follow a bad one as night follows day. What really upset me during that match was the inference – no, the 'revelation' – in at least one of our so-called 'popular' papers that there was a 'vendetta' between Messrs Willis and Richards.

If this sensational conclusion was drawn from the ferocity of Viv's shots it had better be admitted that my mother could probably have taken a few runs off me that day. If the vendetta seemed to emanate from our expressions, the writer obviously had not noticed before that Viv habitually wears a smouldering, smug look when batting and I frequently have a gaze of far-away anguish. There was nothing special in that. When I met Viv on the rest day of the match, he was as upset and mystified by the story as I had been; Richards, you see, is anything but a malicious character and the idea of his waging a vendetta against any bowler is rather worse than fanciful.

A year later, I had just come back from the latest of my knee injuries, suitably delighted to have proved the critics wrong to write me off for the umpteenth time. I held no resentment over this, for, having fully expected medical opinion to give me the red light on any future cricket, I could hardly blame the journalists for sharing my view. My anger, which exploded in front of TV viewers just as they were starting the celebrations of my bowling at Headingley, was directed at the clutch of writers who seemed intent on making utterly untenable the position of England captain – a post which should have brought honour and pestige.

Life had been made hard for Botham in his latter Tests as leader. The very writers who had been boldly campaigning for him to be given the job not many months earlier were now cruelly consigning him to the rubbish-patch. When Mike Brearley came back to take over, I kidded myself that things might be quieter for a while, but his first match back as skipper had not even begun when *The Sun* ran a back-page headline along the lines of 'Test War'. The reason for this slice of melodrama was that Brearley had mentioned he would be protesting if Dennis Lillee went on with his practice of leaving the field to change his shirt between bowling spells. No more, no less. Hardly the stuff for which wars are fought, I would have imagined.

Other, similar stories were printed around that time which can have had no other motive than mischief-making and, for better or worse, I blew my top about it at the post-match interview, surprising Mr West as much as anyone else. I did not feel contrite about my attack the following day, despite the fact that many laudatory things were written about my bowling at Leeds and my battle to get back to the top flight after injury. My anger was not aroused exclusively on my own behalf for I genuinely believed, and still do, that the game and its players are being badly served by this style of reporting.

My big blunder during this episode, and one I have lived to regret ever since, was accepting an offer from one of *The Sun*'s reporters to 'write' a first-person piece in his paper about my eight-wicket performance. What this means in effect is that the journalist asks the player a few questions before writing the story in what he imagines to be the player's words. It is quick and uncomplicated – but on that day of all days I should have turned it down flat.

I was approached immediately after giving a press conference, where I had not repeated my television tactics, instead answering all the writers' questions in reasonable humour. When I was offered the chance to do little more than say the same things in a different order so that *The Sun* could put an 'exclusive' tag on the page, I misguidedly agreed.

It might not have been so bad had it been any other paper, but *The Sun*, in my opinion, has taken cricket reporting further into the 'quotes and news' area, and further away from basic match reporting, than any of its rivals. I was foolish, and have been reminded of it by friends and foes in the press contingent whenever I have criticized their profession.

The next day, in a NatWest Trophy match against Sussex, I bowled poorly. I was still shattered from my efforts for England, a cross I am afraid my county had to bear far more often than I would have liked, and there could be no comparison with my efforts at Leeds. *The Sun*, who had included me among their 'star writers' that very morning, opted for more mischief-making. They published a picture of me with my face contorted as I struggled to get my bowling act together, with the headline: 'One Over the Eight'. Even the most unintelligent of *The Sun*'s five million readers must have caught the drift. What they were inferring, with a nudge and a wink, was that England's hero of the previous day had been out celebrating all night, waking with such a hangover that it was as much as he could do to run up to the stumps. There was nothing very subtle about the insinuation. Nothing very true, either. What had really happened the previous night was tediously simple – I had driven home in my wife's car, gradually realizing the enormity of the England victory and the great moment of my own performance. By the time I got back to Birmingham I was almost dead on my feet, and the 'wild celebrations' consisted of staying in, having an early teetotal supper and going to bed.

There was at least an attempt at humour in this particular tabloid effort. Drink, however, remained the theme, just as it has become an increasing obsession whenever such papers discuss the off-field habits of cricketers. I would never pretend that the modern cricketer is a paragon of virtue in his social life – indeed, I shall later discuss my considerable reservations about the way the young generation of players conduct themselves. I would make two points. The first is that a cricketer is entitled to some private life where he can have a drink without finding himself portrayed as a drunkard. The second is that I have noticed an increasing tendency for newspapers to seek the most absurd and insulting excuses for an England defeat – they seldom admit it was simply because the players were not good enough, but instead hint, suggest or baldly insist it must have been due to their social excesses.

In 1984 at least one tabloid Sunday paper revealed that certain England players had been drinking in a pub at Otley during the Headingley Test against West Indies. Some of them, it went on, had still been drinking in the pub long after normal closing time and, by inference, long after they should have been tucked up in bed. Apparently reliable witnesses were quoted on the matter, while the story contained an inevitable reference to the fact that England lost the Test match heavily. I have since discovered that this dubious tale was hawked around Fleet Street, a number of papers rejecting it out of hand. Once again, it was a story in which an acorn of truth had been transfigured to a tree of fantasy. I spent more than one evening in that Otley pub during the match in question, as did other England players, but there was nothing outrageous or reprehensible in anyone's behaviour. Most of us had made the pub a regular port of call during Leeds Tests for some years, including the 1981 match against Australia. Botham and Willis were among the patrons on both occasions, but I did not hear anyone complaining when Ian scored 149 not out, I took eight for 43, and England beat Australia!

This sort of thing has happened more than once. In Australia, Ian Botham was alleged by one paper to have been seen brawling with Rodney Hogg in a nightclub he had not even been near. On the same tour an English businessman, of all people, made a complaint to the *Daily Express* regarding the behaviour of certain players in a hotel bar. Worst of all, the following winter in Pakistan brought the dramatic allegations of drug-taking on our trip to New Zealand. It is not for me to discuss the rights and wrongs of this matter in public, but some papers indulged themselves with various smutty sexual insinuations about players, which apparently had nothing to do with the theme of their story, being included simply to paint the entire team in a disreputable light. Once again, it was a case of finding something to blame for being beaten, because the truthful explanations are not spicy enough.

When I was appointed England captain in 1982, I knew that one of my duties was to co-operate with the press. In recent years, cricket – in line with tennis, golf and other heavily exposed sports – has demanded more and more of its players in the way of press conferences. In cricket, it is usually the captain who accepts this responsibility, and although I had grave reservations about the place or value of such formal question-and-answer sessions, I could neither abdicate nor delegate. In two home seasons and two tours, I feel I bent over backwards to help the press, possibly even being too honest for my own good at times and certainly never cutting short a press conference if anyone wanted to raise any further points. It was sometimes a chore, sometimes quite an amusing diversion to a day, but sometimes I was let down so badly that all obligations I had felt towards the press became tarnished with resentment.

Oddly enough, Leeds was again the venue of an incident which left me thinking particularly badly of the cricketing scribes. We had just been beaten by New Zealand in 1983, our only defeat of the series. Ian Botham was having a bad run with bat and ball and in the 40 minutes I devoted to the press conference I was repeatedly pressed to confirm the majority press view that he should now be dropped. Representing only one fifth of the selection committee, I could not in fairness have done so even had I felt so inclined, but I was far from convinced that Ian should be left out and, when further quizzed about who should replace him, I attempted to explain why.

When Trevor Jesty was mentioned by someone I ventured the opinion that I could not imagine him taking 300 Test wickets. David Thomas's name was thrown in, to which I replied that surely no-one could seriously compare the all-round ability of Thomas with that of Botham. And so it went on. What I believed myself to be doing was marking cards – giving the day-by-day cricket writers an indication that we had not lost faith in Ian, still believing him to be the best all-rounder available, as plainly he was. The last thing I expected anyone to do was to pick up a phone to contact Jesty, Thomas and company, putting it to them each in turn that the England captain was being derogatory about him. Yet somebody did, and the whole thing appeared in a paper the next day – with me apparently sniping at perfectly capable county players and they, no doubt surprised by the phone call out of context, giving their replies. Perhaps I am naïve about these things, but that struck me as terribly cheap.

During the previous winter in Australia, *The Sun* suggested that Botham and I were at loggerheads. 'Rift' was the word they used, and Ian and I are still trying to fathom their evidence for it. It must have been another of those quiet days, like the one when a Sunday newspaper journalist telephoned Imran Khan and Clive Lloyd to ask some leading questions in an attempt to write a piece which would be strongly critical of my captaincy. To a degree he succeeded, but I have no idea whether the cheque-book was brandished on this occasion to assist the flow of quotes.

Some papers are willing to pay large sums of money to sportsmen, either for one-off articles or regular columns. It can be a lucrative sideline for the players involved, but I maintain it is unhealthy and should be stopped. As I readily admit I was wrong to do *The Sun*'s article in 1981, so I think Ian Botham and David Gower are treading on dangerous territory with their regular columns in national newspapers. Inevitably, controversy is the aim of the papers involved; just as inevitably David and Ian are occasionally going to upset people by commenting on other players or on current issues. It does the game and the personalities no good.

My other main bone of contention about the media is not really a criticism of the writers but more of the England selectors who, I am convinced, allow themselves to be influenced much too readily by what they read in their morning papers. Whether they take *The Times*, the *Daily Telegraph* or *The Sun* is not relevant; the point is that they are giving the writer credit for knowing an England player when he sees one, and I am not at all convinced by the selectorial qualifications of the majority of journalists.

Newspapers can, and do, play an important role in the promotion of cricket, some of them continuing to perform this and their other functions extremely well. There are, I must emphasize, a number of British sports writers whose offerings I admire, whose integrity I would never question and whose company I very much enjoy. But some of the others worry me. Fleet Street, I am sure, is a hard school, but I have wondered more than once whether one writer or another has slept easily after producing the latest piece of fabrication. The press have sometimes been good to me; at other times, I feel they have been extremely unfair. The modern trend of hounding the beaten captain and of hiding in the corner of bars hoping for gossip or scandal appalls me most. I wonder where it is all going to end.

13

SITTING ON THE FENCE

When Keith Fletcher finally became England captain at the end of the 1981 season, I cannot imagine there were many people in cricket less than delighted for him. 'The Gnome's' career had been long, distinguished but not always smooth and this was a welcome if belated recognition of his talents. He had done wonders at Essex, moulding a team of laughing cavaliers into a highly successful playing unit without detracting from their unique team spirit. Now at last he was to have the same chance with England.

Little did anyone know that the span of his captaincy was to be one of the briefest in England's history. He did just the one tour, an arduous and often tedious tour of India and Sri Lanka. But it was a tour on which, utterly unbeknown to Keith, the plans were secretly hatched for the South African expedition, the consequences of which are still reverberating around the cricket world.

South Africa. The mere mention of the place in cricketing circles is sufficient to start an argument. Everyone has a view on it and most people are quite intransigent in their views. My own opinion reflects the uncluttered outlook of a sportsman who feels instinctively that no nation should be stopped from playing games in international competition. I feel we should play against everyone, without prejudice or politics entering the argument – and that does not indicate any perverse approval for apartheid on my part. The system stinks. Of course it does. Having visited South Africa and seen the divisions for myself I can speak with first-hand knowledge of the subject, and am convinced that there are practices at least equally abhorrent in several other countries with whom we retain, unquestioningly, regular sporting contact. South Africa is singled out for special attention with sport the zealots' easiest target.

The upshot of all this is that when the possibility of a trip to South Africa involving a party of English Test players was mentioned, I was by no means set against the idea. Although I did not eventually join the team sponsored by South African Breweries and captained by Graham Gooch, it was very much an eleventh-hour decision to stay at home. Had I gone on the trip, it would have been me, and not Gooch, in charge. It would also, of course, have been the end of my Test career.

Throughout the summer of 1981 there were intermittent rumours and rumblings about South Africa. The first I heard of any possible contact was when I met Derrick Robins socially at a Test match. Derrick, you may recall, is the English businessman who, during the early seventies, took international teams out to South Africa and subsequently went to live there himself, although by 1981 he had moved his home to France, retaining many contacts in the outlawed country. He told me that the South African cricket authorities were desperate to attract the top English players there and were quite prepared to talk money in figures like telephone numbers.

I was also one of several England players approached by John Edrich on the subject. John made no offer in financial terms, and I am not sure whether he was acting on behalf of the official South African Union or, as seems more likely, a private promoter. As John was an England selector at the time, I imagine he was caused considerable embarrassment when the story of his private approaches found its way into a Sunday newspaper. In any case, I heard no more about it and set off for India as vice-captain to Fletcher, not giving South Africa another thought.

It was during the first Test in Bombay, which ended for us in disastrous defeat and consigned us to four further games of wretched stalemate, that it became plain that an 'England' tour to South Africa might be rather more than the pipedream of a promoter. An envoy from the country arrived in Bombay and certain of the touring players were asked to come along to discuss South Africa. This was the end of the red herrings and the start of the authentic trail which led to the South African Breweries tour in the spring of the following year.

It was immediately apparent that secrecy would be the major obstacle because at that stage, out of a tour party of 16, the South Africans were interested in only seven players – Boycott, Gooch, Botham, Gower, Emburey, Dilley and Willis – and the problems of keeping such a dramatic project from the other nine can readily be imagined.

Fletcher might have interested the South Africans, but it was felt that it would be both unfair to Keith and dangerous to the required secrecy for an England captain to be approached. So he was deliberately kept in the dark and, although I know some people have difficulty in believing it, I can state that he knew nothing at all about the planned trip until it was virtually under way.

The rest of us heard little more for some weeks after the initial Bombay meeting at which we had all said we were provisionally interested. This was my first contact with any such proposals, although the others, I discovered, had been aware of the possibility of a tour back in the West Indies, long after I had gone home.

Pretty soon the numbers showed signs of dwindling. Botham and Gower voiced some reservations on commercial grounds, probably believing they could make more money by staying in Test cricket. Ian's agent and solicitor flew out to Madras to discuss it with him, and by the time they left he had made up his mind not to go. So then there were five.

Dilley seemed very apprehensive – understandably so for such a young player – and I considered him a very doubtful starter. Gooch appeared wavering; Emburey warmed ever more to the idea when he found himself left out of most of the Tests in India; Boycott was committed, and I was quite keen. We all waited for further developments, dragging ourselves from one boring Test match to another.

The next major development was quite unconnected with the South African tour, despite the construction that many suspicious minds may have put upon it. Geoff Boycott went home. He plainly could not cope with the Indian environment, neither enjoying the country nor getting on with the food or the people. Once he had achieved his major objective of breaking the all-time record for aggregate Test runs, his appetite for cricket, and especially for the current tour, appeared to wane day by day. His behaviour became steadily more unpredictable, culminating in the strange incident of his pinning a note to the tea-room table with a knife to apologize for his extraordinary decision to play golf in Calcutta, when he should either have been in bed or out on the field helping our efforts to level the series.

There are few captains easier to get along with than 'Fletch', both he and Raman Subba Row, the manager, going out of their way to accommodate Boycott's idiosyncrasies to keep him going as a part of the squad. Eventually it became impossible; he had to go, and there were very few in the side who mourned his going.

People who have not had close dealings with Geoffrey refuse to accept the stories cricketers relate about him. Probably, some of them are apocryphal, others are certainly exaggerated, but it cannot be denied that there have been episodes throughout his career which mark him out as a man of unusual temperament. From the towel put over his head in New Zealand when he was supposed to be captaining the team; to his habit of lying under a table during team meetings in the West Indies, and to his attitudes in India – none of it seemed likely to endear a player to his team-mates.

The Indian series was lost 1–0 and gladly buried by all who had taken part, on our side at least. The umpiring had been bad and the over-rate a farce, negating any tactics 'Fletch' could devise for us. Poor Keith knocked off a bail when he was given out in Banga-lore as the ultimate symbol of a captain's helpless frustration. It cost him dear, but I do not think it was his worst mistake of the trip. He was wrong to let the umpiring undermine him so much in the opening Test in Bombay, because his negative feelings permeated the rest of the team. He was also misguided to come down to the Indians' level by slowing our own over-rate to around ten an hour in Madras, achieving nothing except bad feeling.

None the less, I felt sympathy for Keith, rating him a fine cricketer and a very shrewd captain who was thrown into Test leadership in circumstances which would have tested the patience of a saint. Until one has been to India it is not possible to com-prehend the differences between playing the Indians in England, where they have never done well, and in their own country, where everything is stacked in their favour. The problems often seem endless, and to come from behind to win a series there, as England managed under David Gower three years later, is an enormous achievement.

Not only was that beyond us in 1982, it even looked for a time as though the tour was going to end on a thoroughly ignominious note with defeat in the inaugural Test against Sri Lanka. This was a part of the trip I had been dreading, the place having agreed with me not at all on my only previous visit in 1977. I was surprised and delighted to find a great deal of changes for the better. The hotel and its food was outstanding, I met a lot of friendly, hospit-able people, and found it a pleasant stay, certainly brightened by our eventual win in the Test.

My own part in that victory received a good deal of publicity. Too much was made of it. The fact is we were in a hole at tea-time on the third day, with the Sri Lankans more than 100 runs on with seven second-innings wickets standing, and I sensed that we needed a jolt to wake everyone up. We were playing the game in slow-motion, as if anaesthetised by the cricket we had endured in India, no-one, apparently, reacting to the imminent danger of humiliating defeat.

It has never been Keith's way to shout at players. At Essex, they play their cricket in such a way that there is guaranteed to be an occasional disaster, when they will be bowled out for next to nothing or the opposition will make 600. 'Fletch' accepts this as a hazard of the side, amply compensated for by their recent success, and he will lose his cool only if they let him down in two or three games in succession. Similarly, I never saw Mike Brearley bawl out his team collectively. Nor Ian Botham. But in Colombo in 1982 someone had to do it before it was too late.

It was an impromptu rollicking, rather than something I had planned to any extent. I simply said my piece, making it very plain what I thought of the performance so far and what would await us in the way of a welcome at home if we got beaten. It happened to work. We took the last seven wickets in exceptionally quick time, five of them going to John Emburey in one inspired spell, before knocking off the runs without any great traumas.

When we returned with honour redeemed, I walked out of Gatwick airport without knowing that two of the organizers of the South African trip were waiting to speak to some of the lads in a nearby hotel. They soon caught up with me at home, and when I went to meet them two days later they told me that the trip was due to start within 72 hours and that they wanted me to captain the English side. The invitation took me completely by surprise as I had always assumed that Boycott was to be captain, though it made very little difference to my thinking on the issue. I asked for more time to decide, promising to let them know the following day.

My interest in the tour had, I think, suffered from false foundations. In India, among players becoming steadily more disgruntled, it was easy to get enthusiastic about touring a place like South Africa . . . the grass certainly looked greener . . . but, as I had done in the case of World Series Cricket, I intended to weigh up the options carefully, seeking the advice of a few trusted people.

I had a long talk with my wife, who did not think I should go. Others said the same thing, so that my resolve, such as it had been, weakened further. From my point of view there was still a lot to be said for going. It being almost five years later in my career than the Packer affair, I had less to lose through a ban from Test cricket.

The financial offer was extremely attractive, the organizers even offered the services of tax-avoidance specialists. South Africa was also a country I was certain to enjoy touring and I had no moral reservations about the validity of such a trip.

On the other side of the argument was the damage the tour could cause. I already had a big toe in the establishment through being on two Test and County Cricket Board committees and, much as the cautious outlook of many in this organisation often dismayed me, I could appreciate their dilemma over South Africa. If a tour there meant the future series with the West Indies, India and Pakistan were cancelled, the financial structure of the Board would be wrecked. They could not even be sure of the support of Australia, so vehemently anti-South African that they will not allow their players to go there as individuals and even prevent their national airline from flying there. The thought of falling out with the oldest enemy was anathema.

This tour had to be viewed in a different light from World Series Cricket because it did not deliberately set out to oppose and disrupt traditional Tests. It was simply one country's exasperated attempt to try to end more than a decade of standing on the boundary watching everyone else play. I did not think they should be condemned for that.

From the time I arrived back in England to the time I informed the organizers of my decision, my mind was in a turmoil. It was an important decision, possibly the last one I would make in accepted cricket, and I agonized over it at tremendous length. Finally I turned it down for the same reasons that I turned down World Series Cricket. I had become establishment minded and could still not imagine being sufficiently motivated by international matches which were not what they claimed to be.

When I phoned to say I would not be going, there were no recriminations; from start to finish my dealings with the men who set up the tour were cordial and professional. I have no idea when they told the other players I had dropped out or whether they were aggrieved that I had made that decision after spending so much time sitting on the fence. My conscience was clear because I kept faith with those who went, never trying to influence any other player either to go or not to go, believing it to be a personal decision. Equally, when the leak occurred as I suppose it had to, I refused to 'shop' anyone.

Donald Carr, secretary of the Test and County Cricket Board, phoned me on the Friday of that longest week, the day before the party was scheduled to fly out, word of what was happening having reached official ears. Donald's information amounted to nothing more than an awareness that a tour was being hatched. He asked me if I was going and I said no. To his question whether I knew which players had agreed to go, I admitted I knew of some but was not prepared to tell him who they were. It seemed the least I could do.

Presumably his efforts elsewhere were equally unproductive, because the party left for South Africa on the Saturday evening. By Sunday, when they arrived in Johannesburg, it was headline news in England, and was to stay that way for at least a week. I was astonished at the level of interest and the extent of the outrage. I suppose the guys were unlucky that they happened to go in a week when there was no major world news to occupy the media. This unauthorized sortie to an outlawed land was just what the editors needed to get their teeth into, and they made the most of it.

If I felt sorry for the players over the uproar they had caused, I was astonished by their reaction to the suspension imposed upon them. Shock and dismay, mingled with a clear feeling that they had been punished for the wrong reasons, came across in everything they said about the matter. Frankly, I think they were being naïve and unrealistic if they expected anything else.

On the face of it, a three-year ban was harsh. Most people in the game would admit that and, with the exception of the few who hysterically demanded a life ban, I think most people in the TCCB would agree. Yet they had very little option. It did not need the sharpest of brains to conclude from the schedule for future Test series that 1985 was the earliest the so-called 'rebels' could be allowed back without putting established Test rivalries at risk.

There will be those who say the TCCB are weak-minded and indecisive, sheltering in the safe route when, if every delegate put hand on heart, the majority might well elect to tour South Africa. There may be some remnants of truth in this, but we come directly back to the fact that the TCCB is an amalgam of the counties, whose priorities are financial security. The day may come when we have a right-wing establishment anxious to play South Africa regardless of the consequences; then and only then would we know whether the black countries would carry out their threat to divide the Test circuit into two. Until that day, if it ever arrives, political expediency will be pursued and measures taken to ensure the smooth running of the current seven-nation Test programme.

The three-year ban was not applied maliciously, nor was it done without some heart-searching. It eventually came down to considerations of the pocket, the counties being understandably unprepared to risk bankruptcy by condoning the tour. Immediate action was required and although the sentence might seem savage, there was no real alternative.

Looking, at the time, at the players who went on the tour, I felt that Gooch was likely to be the only major casualty. He was approaching his peak as an opening batsman but probably still had seven or eight years of Test cricket ahead of him. He had sacrificed a lot for his month abroad and England would assuredly miss him. Of the rest, there had to be a doubt about whether Boycott would ever again play for England following the circumstances of his homecoming from India; Emburey was worried about a niggling back injury and disheartened by his inability to hold down a regular England place; John Lever and Derek Underwood, two who had accepted an offer late in the Indian tour, could doubtless see the end of the road in Test cricket looming large anyway and regarded South Africa as a bonus payout.

The same probably applied to Alan Knott, Mike Hendrick, Chris Old and Bob Woolmer, all of whom had been tracked down during the winter by the South African agents. Although Peter Willey and Les Taylor had possibly thrown away some Test cricket, I thought the worst decision of anyone but Gooch was taken by the Yorkshire all-rounder, Arnie Sidebottom, when he joined up with the party much later. I assume he was paid less and, the furore having already erupted, he had the benefit of hindsight. He still received the same ban, though, and had he not signed I think he would probably have played for England by now. Both Sidebottom and Geoff Humpage of my own county, Warwickshire, joined the tourists around the same time, presumably attracted by the considerable razzamatazz they could see going on around them as they went about their coaching duties in the provinces of South Africa.

When the boys returned from South Africa, they all attended the annual meeting of the Cricketers' Association, held each April at Edgbaston, where Gooch led the speeches asking for the support of the Association members as they challenged the ban. Although considerable sympathy was expressed, the hoped-for support was not forthcoming.

I am glad to say they accepted that nothing could be done and reluctantly settled down to see their sentence through. It must have been hard for someone like Graham Gooch to sustain a decent level of motivation through three years without any incentive of Test cricket. It also occurred to me at the time that it was not going to make the England captain's job any easier. What never occurred to me was that the England captain might be me.

14

THE ULTIMATE HONOUR

To say I was surprised to be offered the England captaincy would be a rank understatement. I was flabbergasted. Until the moment when I answered the phone at my home on a Friday afternoon in mid-May 1982 to find myself speaking to Peter May, the new chairman of selectors, I had not given the prospect more than a passing thought. I simply assumed Keith Fletcher would be reappointed.

Keith may not have emerged from the Indian tour covered in glory but there had, after all, been extenuating circumstances. It never occurred to me that he might be sacked for the manner of defeat, nor even for his unwise burst of temper in Bangalore. The win in Sri Lanka can surely have done his position no harm and I thought he must have removed any remaining doubts about his future in the job when he rejected a late but attractive offer from South Africa. When I dropped out of the tour the organizers were without a captain and they sought the consensus of their players and came up with the name of Fletcher.

When he was made skipper of the MCC side to play the champion county, Middlesex, in the traditional early-season game, it seemed the selectors were endorsing their faith in him. I expect he thought the same. Instead, it turned out to be a thank-you-and-goodbye gift. David Gower captained MCC against the touring Indians, fuelling a little press speculation that the selectors were prepared to gamble on giving him the job, but on the final day of that match they announced their choice which shocked everyone in the game.

'Are you sitting down?' asked Peter May. 'I would like you to captain England against India this summer.' I can't remember my exact reply but am quite sure it expressed something close to amazement. Although I had been captain of Warwickshire for the past couple of years, and vice-captain of England on a number of winter tours, I had never considered myself a potential captain in Test cricket, largely because it is unfashionable to give the job to a fast bowler. For all my astonishment, though, I did not have to think twice before accepting the offer.

When Peter May told me he had already phoned Keith Fletcher to inform him of the decision, I could well imagine that he had encountered similar surprise there, without the added pleasure. I immediately called Keith myself, but his wife, Sue, told me he had gone for a drive to think things over. He phoned me back later and I was genuinely sympathetic. But what could I say? Regrets sound so insincere when offered by the haves to the have-nots.

One of my first thoughts was that I would not exactly have the strongest England side of recent times at my disposal. No Gooch, Boycott, Emburey, Underwood etc. And now, obviously, no Fletcher either. To some degree, it was going to resemble the task Graham Yallop had in captaining the official Australian Test side during the WSC split.

I had no grand illusions. I knew that, at best, I was helping the selectors out of a tight corner at a time when the candidates for captaincy could easily be counted on the fingers of one hand. Brearley had gone, Fletcher had not been re-appointed and Botham could hardly be invited back, having resigned only a year earlier. Of the other current members of the Test side, only Gower and Taylor picked themselves; one was too immature for the job, the other had never shown any liking for it. Outside the team, Roger Knight of Surrey seemed the most popular media choice, but he really would have been a shot in the dark.

Captaining England had never been an ambition of mine, even in boyhood. While I had always yearned to play for my country, to bowl fast and take a lot of wickets, skippering had never been part of the dream.

Naturally when I look back on it all now, I have to say it was a highlight of my career. Far from glamorous, often painfully frustrating and always hard work, it still represented the pinnacle of all my years in the game. I know I will not be remembered as England's greatest captain and I also know that sections of the media were anxious to get me out of the job almost before I had started. But the record books will show that I led England to seven Test victories during my two years in charge, including at least one against every country we met in that period. I don't think that is anything to be ashamed of.

From the start, I had a good relationship with Peter May, which was obviously important if I was to make anything of the job. He had taken over from Alec Bedser with some very clear priorities mapped out for English cricket, having strong views about the way the game should be played and about discipline among players. These views largely coinciding with my own, we were able to communicate on a man-to-man footing rather than as chairman and player. He supported me in everything I did, and no captain can ask for more than that.

Selection was a hazardous business. Shorn of so many of our better-class players, we still had to apply the traditional process of writing down 12 names and then selecting a standby to cover for injury or illness in each position. Some may believe we picked some unexpected players in the Test teams; the names on the standby list were often far more improbable.

More than one of those who got a game under me had probably never even dreamed of playing Test cricket and would not have played in any other era. We made what I still feel were some positive, adventurous selections, partly forced upon us by the shortage of competition at the highest level but also because we wanted to use the opportunity to blood younger players who could be of service to England for years to come. There were disappointments, as we knew there had to be, and Derek Pringle was probably the biggest of these, so obviously possessing a rare degree of natural ability yet seldom able to reproduce it in the international arena. Others, such as Tony Greig's younger brother, Ian, lacked for nothing in effort or commitment but proved to be short of that indefinable class which separates the successful Test players from the pack.

I went about the job in what I consider to be a conscientious manner. As a fast bowler, and one who has always engulfed himself in the details of his own performance, I anticipated certain difficulties on the field, never hesitating to encourage the involvement and advice of my vice-captain and senior players. I know I was accused of 'captaining by committee' but, as long as I was able to retain overall command of any situation, I always believed that two or three sets of eyes were more likely to spot something useful than I might have done when bowling.

Off the field I did a lot of talking. More, certainly, than my predecessors were accustomed to do, but then I had always believed in voicing my thoughts in my days as vice-captain and before. Captains of strong, settled and successful sides need to say far less to their players than a captain in my relatively parlous position.

I had at my command a good number of inexperienced and insecure cricketers, and felt they would benefit more from being told too much than from thinking they were being neglected.

We lost only one Test during my first summer in the job, and it happened to be the only one I missed through injury – at Lord's against Pakistan. I would not venture to blame my deputy, David Gower, in any way for the setback, but I did find it interesting to see the different ways in which we approached a crisis. There was a time in that match when the follow-on threatened and an all-out attritional effort was demanded. I would have spent some time cajoling the players to greater things, but David's style was much more laid-back, being that of the passive leader rather than the active.

Poor David suffered a desperate summer with the bat, and with Allan Lamb making virtually no runs against Pakistan after starting his England career with such promise against India, and Ian Botham below his brilliant best, there was some serious misfiring in the engine-room of our side.

This was distressing enough for the players concerned, but what made it worse was that it began to affect other people in the team. Because Gower, Lamb and Botham were considered the prime batsmen, the selectors were reluctant to disturb them from their favoured positions at three, four and five. This meant we often had three out-of-form players coming in to bat in succession while others, who might have strengthened the often fragile nature of our batting, were being played out of position.

Mike Gatting and Chris Tavaré both suffered from this, but no-one was messed around more often than Derek Randall. I don't suppose even he can recall exactly how many positions he has filled for England. It would probably be easier for him to name the rare occasions on which he played at the same number in the order for more than two consecutive games. It was horribly unfair on someone who unfailingly gave of his best for England and who, on a number of occasions, played the decisive innings of a Test match. He had good cause to complain at his lot, and many players would have done so. But not 'Arkle'. Blessed with a simple philosophy which owed much to patriotism, he just regarded himself as fortunate to be in the England side, never once moaning about what he was being asked to do.

Perhaps I developed an exaggerated sense of loyalty to those who did a good job while I was captain, yet I cannot help thinking that both Tavaré and Randall have been unlucky over the years, and had they been given the preferential handling afforded to some, England could have had far more from them.

Randall has always been a good man to have in and around the side because of his jovial, bubbling nature and his unfailing loyalty. As a batsman he is terrible to watch early in an innings, when one has the awful feeling he might well be out to every single delivery, but if he gets past this nervy opening period he seldom throws away his wicket. In 1982 we had lost so many of our best openers to the South African ban that we had to ask him to go in first, and despite often looking awkward against the speed of Imran Khan, he battled through to a hundred against Pakistan at Edgbaston which set us up for victory.

To my mind, he has frequently been a victim of muddled thinking by the selectors. Not a great player against the fastest of bowling, he is now a very fine player of spin, so I was incredulous when he was chosen in the first Test team against West Indies in 1984 and then overlooked for the tour of India which followed.

Having sat on a few selection committees, I would never pretend that the job is straightforward. In England we have five selectors, including the captain, each one coming to the meetings with his own idea of the team written down. Inevitably, after the debates and disagreements, there has to be a measure of compromise.

As captain, I used to have a major say in selection and strongly believe that this should be the entitlement of the man who has to lead the side and take the ultimate responsibility for their performances. When discussing this very issue with Greg Chappell during a recent visit to Australia, I found he took a completely different stance, asserting that it was invidious for the captain to be a selector at all. Greg has been through the mill of Australian cricket and is now a Test selector himself, but I wonder whether he held that view when he was captain.

I became much more conversant with the system of selection after a couple of years as captain and on the whole I think it is a good one. With 17 first-class counties and cricket being played every day of the week, it is not practical to think of having fewer selectors; the counties would very soon claim that they never saw one at their games and that their players were being neglected. I am among those in favour of a full-time manager being appointed to the England side, though not in the guise of an all-powerful supremo such as the national football manager. The games are essentially different, in that a cricket captain has so many more critical decisions to take in a day's play than his soccer counterpart would make in a game; a cricket captain is director and stage-manager on the field, a football captain is often little more than head of the chorus line. In our game, therefore, it is the captain who must always be answerable for what has happened on the field. He is the real decision maker of the side. But the peripheral pressures on the modern cricket captain are such that he needs a figure of authority with him to ease the load. I envisage the manager's job as being that of a wide-ranging co-ordinator, an active member of the selection committee, certainly dealing with media enquiries whenever it is not absolutely essential to involve the captain, and always organising team practices both at home and abroad.

Those who are against such an appointment contend that there would not be enough for a manager to do. Having observed managers in county cricket, especially the excellent David Brown at Warwickshire, as well as experiencing the frantic demands on the Test team, I am convinced it is a worthwhile position which should be adopted as soon as possible.

A manager might also help maintain a competitive atmosphere around his team. This is chiefly the captain's duty but I don't think it is a bad thing to have someone outside the eleven players, watching all the time, who can add a voice when some chivvying-up is called for. When we played Pakistan in 1982, for instance, I was impressed by the excellent team efforts which brought us victory over a strong side. After that, I am afraid, things were never again as competitive, and the winter tour of Australia represented one of the low points of my entire career.

It was not just that we lost the Test series 2–1 and relinquished the Ashes, nor even that we played so abysmally in the limited-overs matches which followed, both in Australia and New Zealand. I was concerned more by the manner of our defeats – Australia were the better side, with some match-winning fast bowlers, but we had too many players in our party who neither did themselves justice nor appeared to be too worried about it.

All who know me well are only too aware of how tense I become at Test time and how acutely I feel defeat. In Australia, I had the added responsibility of being in charge for the first time abroad. We did not have a brilliant side and I was enough of a realist to embark with the clear realization that we were worthy underdogs. But still I took it all to heart, literally worrying myself sick.

We achieved a perfectly respectable draw in a high-scoring first Test in Perth, before losing the next match badly in Brisbane.

When we came to Adelaide for the third Test, every bone in my body told me we should bat first if I won the toss. Yet I allowed myself to be talked out of it by batsmen who simply did not fancy going in against the Australian fast bowlers. When we lost the game, I did not know whether I was more upset at the reluctance of my batsmen, or the fact that I had been weak enough to make a decision I knew to be wrong.

In the next Test at Melbourne I was physically ill with worry, although Doug Insole, managing his second tour of Australia, restored my sanity by drumming into me that I had done everything I could and that the opposition was simply better than we were. Fate stepped in at the perfect time in that game. Australia were within four runs of going 3–0 up and putting the series beyond dispute when Chris Tavaré fumbled a slip catch but contrived to flap the ball over his head. Geoff Miller ran around behind him to complete the catch and we had won the game. I ran off feeling only blind relief that something had been salvaged and, although we could only draw the final game in Sydney, I did not consider the outcome of the series was in any way a disgrace.

What struck me most forcibly was the rapid change which had taken place in the lifestyle and the outlook of Test cricketers on tour. World Series Cricket was probably a contributory factor; certainly, the 1978–79 tour of Australia was the last on which England players behaved in the manner that I had been brought up to believe was expected of a touring side. From then on, whether through the intensity of the cricketing merry-go-round, the growing familiarity of the places or – as I would choose to think – the dramatic increase in the money available to Test players, the attitude of players altered, and not for the better. For the past few years now, things have not been conducted as I think they should be on tours, and I eventually came to realise that I was at the top end of a dangerously widening generation gap.

The Centenary Test in Melbourne in 1977 signposted the changes to come. It was a game surrounded by commerce; suddenly sponsors were everywhere, and for a set of cricketers accustomed to staying in either traditional old hotels or modern motels where convenience outstrips comfort, it came as something of a surprise to be billeted in the Hilton. It was quite luxurious and extremely expensive. A beer in their main bar costing around three dollars, none of us drank there, finding our way instead to the more familiar surroundings and modest prices of the MCG pub just up the road. I remember, too, that a large number of ex-players from around the world who had been invited out for the game were put up free at the Hilton but their terms were room only, without breakfast. So, in common with many others of their generation, they bought juice and cereal from the local delicatessen, eating it in their room, rather than paying £5 a head in the Hilton restaurant. This was not a sign of meanness; it was the way they had been brought up in the game, living on a tight budget.

All that has long since changed. The England tourists of later years are paid the equivalent of almost £100 a day. They have grown up in the game with money and have become accustomed to lavishing some of it on the luxuries of touring life. They don't think twice about spending that three dollars (it may well now be four) on a beer in the hotel's most expensive bar, and no-one should pompously condemn them for that. What worries me is the trend to spend three or four hours in a hotel bar, drinking for the sake of it because they cannot be bothered to do anything else.

It is usually in Australia that this has been most noticeable and the reasons are obvious enough. Every hotel is of decent standard with at least one good bar, the country has a vibrant social atmosphere and young players tend to get a little heady on it. It has happened to me, but now I can view it objectively, feeling that it has been allowed to go too far.

On the complicated post-Packer tour of 1979–80, on which I was vice-captain to Mike Brearley, I voiced my first anxieties about the 'wasters' in the party who seemed to me to be spending all their spare time, and a fair proportion of their money, in the bars. It was considerably worse three years later, when I took the side there as captain. Norman Gifford, returning to the England scene as assistant manager after almost a decade away, was startled by the social behaviour of some of the players; Bernard Thomas, omnipresent on recent tours, was openly appalled; I was frustrated. Only Doug Insole, the manager, probably prepared by his dealings with the off-beat Essex players and with his own growing family, managed to remain thinking straight about the matter – and that should have told us all something.

There is absolutely no point in preaching to players of today about how things were done 20 or 30 years ago. For one thing, they will probably laugh, and for another it is simply not realistic to hark back to the times when we had a couple of pounds a day to live on. They are not, in most cases, deliberately flaunting their new-found wealth or abusing the privileges they have as England players, but are behaving just as they would away from the game.

They are part of a different generation, having been brought up in a different way with more money.

Where I took issue with the younger players during the 1982–83 tour was over their apparently blasé acceptance of results. They may quite probably have slogged their guts out on the field, but if it was all in vain and the game was lost, they would emit nothing more tangibly remorseful than a shrug before discussing the evening's socialising. It grated especially on me because, having through the years endured so many wakeful nightmares about the performances of England and myself, I found it hard to reconcile this with any hint of indifference from my team-mates. Ian Botham has always behaved in this way, of course, yet no-one could accuse him of lacking the correct attitude on the field. But Botham is unique; any lesser man trying to copy his ways is likely to fall flat on his face.

Drinking has always been an accepted facet of the cricketer's life, just as it is wholly unacceptable in that of a professional footballer. To him, a few pints after the match on Saturday (providing there is no match on Monday or Tuesday) is about the limit of his manager's tolerance, whereas cricketers are somehow expected to drink most nights, if not every night. There are, however, degrees of acceptability.

The players of past generations always had a beer together at the end of a day's play, whether their background was in the landed gentry or the working classes. Cutting through the class system, cricket was a great social leveller, so that in passing on their cricketing philosophies to a new generation these old-timers have always encouraged players to drink socially and enjoy a cameraderie with the opposition. Sadly, the wheels of the social bandwagon have come off. The five cans of ale that the old-timers might have enjoyed before a civilised dinner each night have turned into prolonged, boredom drinking in public. Many of today's players, I fear, drink for the discreditable reason that they won't read a book or go to the cinema and would rather avoid accepting an invitation to a cocktail party or a dubious dinner. They just trail into the hotel bar for three or four hours and, if there is no match the next day, they will in some cases scorn the importance of nets, turning up for practice in a condition not worthy of highly paid international sportsmen.

Those same old-timers will inevitably claim that cricket is no longer the fun it was when they were playing and they are almost certainly right. The life of the top-flight cricketer of today may

not be much tougher on balance than in their day – indeed physically, with the preponderance of one-day games, shorter tours and
easier travelling, it may be more comfortable – but the mental
strain is incomparably greater now than it has ever been before.

Television, and the media in general, has a good deal to do with
this, both directly and indirectly. Their spotlight falls unremittingly
on the leading stars in all their waking hours, so that the man in the
street is encouraged to take more notice of cricketers to a point
where Ian Botham, for one, has now found he can't do anything
or go anywhere without being instantly recognized, his every move
being monitored. The pressure can be almost intolerable, hence
the fall from grace of soccer superstars such as George Best, and
I cannot imagine it was remotely similar in the days of the pros
and amateurs and the long, leisurely tours under the management
of someone like the Duke of Norfolk.

The modern cricketer is not an ogre, nor is he deliberately ob-
structive. Although in most cases it would be unfair to dismiss him
as a spoiled brat, he is too often lazy, ill-disciplined and reluctant
to put in the effort and dedication commensurate with the wages
he is earning. He has a very low boredom threshold with a constant
need to be told what to do with his free time.

Touring, of course, can be a very boring business. There are
long days of relative inactivity with nothing planned but the
morning net session, coupled with long nights, especially in
countries like India and Pakistan, when one needs a bright initiative
or a good hobby to get through. The seasoned tourist comes to
know what he must expect each day, experiencing rather like the
man on the dole, a constant fight to keep the brain awake when he
is not actually being called upon to play cricket. The younger
players don't seem to have much of this fight in them, and on the
last couple of tours I undertook, old-stagers like Bob Taylor found
it increasingly difficult to bridge the generation gap and relate to
the attitudes and outlook of his younger team-mates.

It would be wrong to say I returned from that long tour in
1982–83 feeling entirely disillusioned. I was certainly reflective
about the directions in which the game was heading, realizing for
the first time that, partly through having gravitated to the captaincy and partly through the simpler process of advancing years,
I was now of a generation older than most of the England players.
Many of my contemporaries were no longer around at that level
and I was uncomfortably aware that I saw things in a different
light from many members of my team.

Towards the end of that tour my own limitations as a captain were being raised both in my own mind and, mercilessly, by the press. Having failed to qualify for the finals of the three-way limited-overs series in Australia, we had a few days to hang around before trying to reactivate enthusiasm for three more one-day internationals in New Zealand. It was never going to be easy and we failed. Looking back now on my diary entry for the day of 19 February (in the first *Captain's Diary*) I can instantly relive the depression.

'My worst fears were realized today. We not only lost against a side missing both Hadlee and Wright but lost in a manner which indicates an absence of motivation. Sub-consciously, the guys have all accepted that they are on a short, last leg of the trip and they have let themselves go, mentally if not physically. It is un-professional and unacceptable, however understandable it may seem. I have failed too, because the buck stops with me and it was primarily my job to lift them for this game. But I can't do that unless they give some sort of professional response and that, un-fortunately, has been sadly absent.'

It was scathing but heartfelt criticism, more poignant because I knew only too well that we would be considered outright failures back in England, on the strength of having played so badly in the one-day games. The Test series, which to my mind was much more important, had gone against us although not by much, and there were times in the series when we competed extremely well. The public, fired by the media, has short sporting memories and we had flopped in their minds.

From all the quizzing I received about my future as captain it was plain that some people expected me to resign, although I had no such intention, feeling that I was still learning the job and was improving. Moreover, I was looking forward to leading the side in the World Cup, also hoping to extract some revenge from the New Zealanders in the four-Test series to follow. For all my in-hibitions about various aspects of the tour, and for all the worries I put myself through, I still wanted to be captain.

Peter May having duly confirmed my reappointment, I settled down to plan the campaign. My wife, Julie, and I had moved into a new house in Edgbaston, still handy for the county ground but pleasantly secluded, and I found myself planning not only for cricket but planning a home too, in a thoughtful domestic way I had never believed possible. All too soon it was April again. The rest between tours and home seasons seemed to get shorter every year, and I needed to whip up my own enthusiasm in order to pass it on to the players at Warwickshire. I still wanted to help them win something more before I eventually gave up the game.

England's efforts in the World Cup somehow summed up the way we have played in recent years. We showed, albeit within the confines of one-day cricket, that we were capable of beating everyone except the all-powerful West Indies. We were playing very efficiently, the lads were enjoying the day-to-day involvement and I think our acting-manager Peter May was enjoying his first prolonged contact with the side. I had high hopes that we could at least go all the way to the final, but at the final hurdle we collapsed. Old Trafford provided a poor pitch for our semi-final with India, and I would certainly have fancied us rather more to beat them on any other surface. But the fact remains that when it mattered most we played badly, the opposition played well, and we were out. One more black mark.

With a single hiccup at Headingley, we went on to win the Test series very convincingly and, I thought, did the job as capably as anyone could have asked. Yet we received precious little credit for it. It was the old, timeless English habit of denigrating the opposition whenever we happen to win. Sometimes that jars on me, and I long for the Australian brand of support with the thousands of partisan, one-eyed ockers. But then again . ..

15

INTO RETIREMENT

If I had wanted to retreat quietly, without shame or scandal, from the firing-line of being England captain, I could easily have done so at the end of the 1983 season. Taking me aside after our third and final Test win over New Zealand, Peter May asked if I had had enough of the job, telling me he knew all about the extraneous pressures, having captained the side himself in both good times and bad, and assuring me that nobody would think any the worse of me if I stood down.

I don't think that was his wish and it certainly wasn't mine. My reasons for wanting to keep the job may have been slightly selfish, for I wanted to go on playing for at least another year and feared I would be far less enthusiastic about the game if ever I lost my close contact with the management of the England side. There is, as I am constantly repeating, a lot of time on players' hands when away on tour and handling the duties of the captain is certainly one excellent way of filling it in. I had done only one tour as skipper, but three more as vice-captain, and had reached the time of life when I could not easily imagine returning to the ranks. So to throw in the towel was not something I found at all appealing; thanking Peter for his concern, I reiterated that I was available to lead the team to New Zealand and Pakistan.

Retirement had, it is true, been in my mind for some while, but only in the general sense of knowing something is imminent and must be dealt with sooner rather than later. I had made no definite provision for life after cricket, having no trade in which I was qualified, nor any previous profession to fall back upon. I did not want to be an umpire and feared I would not enjoy being a full-time coach. The thought of staying in cricket in a role which might combine administration and management was attractive, but I had no clear idea of the job I wanted nor even if anyone was likely to think me suitable.

It was a growing problem. Cricket had given me a good living, particularly in the later years of my career, and although I had turned down substantial sums from both World Series Cricket and South Africa, the combination of playing for England during five lucrative years, and a generous benefit year granted by Warwickshire, meant that I would not exactly starve for a while when the day came. Equally, I was not in a position to put my feet up for ten years.

I devoted a lot of time and thought to considering my future but came to the conclusion that, as I was physically as fit as I had been for some years, there was nothing to be gained by quitting prematurely. While accepting the probability that New Zealand and Pakistan would be my final tour, I had no way of knowing it would end quite as sadly and controversially as it did.

It was a bad tour in many ways. On the field we contrived to lose both the Test series, New Zealand beating us for the first time ever. Off the field I became still more dismayed by the lack of professionalism shown by some players in our side. To cap it all in a way I would have considered inconceivable only a few years earlier, a sequence of newspaper stories culminated in the unquestionably sensational allegations in the *Mail on Sunday*, naming Ian Botham in connection with drugs parties, one of which is supposed to have taken place in the Christchurch dressing-room while we were being beaten by New Zealand in the second Test.

To deal with the cricket first, I said at the time and I will say again that I refuse to believe New Zealand were the superior team. We outplayed them for most of the first game but failed to turn it into victory; they then beat us, humiliatingly, on a bad pitch where we managed to be bowled out twice for under 100; the final game, hardly surprisingly, was a pre-ordained stalemate. In Pakistan, we never looked likely to recover after being beaten by three wickets in the first Test at Karachi.

There is no escaping the fact that we were a poor side. We set off with certain well-established shortcomings, received little of the available luck, and ended the tour with the three senior fast bowlers – Botham, Dilley and myself – all prematurely back in England with various ailments. Botham was in hospital for surgery on his knee, Dilley was having urgent tests for a worrying loss of feeling in his leg, and I had fallen victim to the old, familiar tour illness which has plagued me for years, though this time with the symptoms sharpened and the suspicion prevailing that I might have hepatitis.

I flew home during the final Test, not sorry to leave Pakistan, which has never been among my favourite holiday spots, but depressed at leaving with the team under such pressure both on and off the field. Moreover, although I would not publicly have admitted it, I knew I had captained England for the last time. We had been beaten twice, the team had been caught up in an unprecedented scandal and I had not even completed the tour. Such evidence was overwhelming and I faced the inevitability of the decision.

If I had possessed a crystal ball, I might, perhaps, have accepted Peter May's offer to stand down, after all. I would certainly not have chosen to bow out at the end of an eminently forgettable tour, with the public wondering if they really dare believe the juicier slices of gossip about us in the press. If there was a saving grace, it was that I was left with no great regrets. I had led my country, won a few games, and now it was coming to an end I could not summon any feeling of bitterness or resentment. In a sense, I suppose, it was a relief, a load taken off my back, and I know how much more I relaxed as soon as the change was made official.

These things are rarely done in quite the way one would like, and I was disturbed to find from speaking to various people when I got home that the decision to replace me was well on the way to being taken. I would have appreciated the chance to sit down with the relevant administrators, giving them my version of what happened on that tour, which might have varied considerably from any second-hand versions they may have heard. In cricket, at least in English cricket, this is never the procedure. The captain files his tour report, which I completed late owing to my illness, and waits to hear whether he has been reappointed. I was not.

I cannot look back on my final tour with any great sense of achievement. More than anything, I found myself bemoaning the absence of remorse on the part of our players when things went wrong. I would never be an advocate of the near-hysterical soccer-style inquests in a locked dressing-room, but there must be a happy medium between that and the opposite extreme of casual acceptance followed by getting drunk in the bar.

Our problems stemmed at least partly from a lack of competition in the batting department, the leading players knowing they would be chosen for every big game because we had virtually no-one else to turn to. Subconsciously, lazy instincts took over so that, try as I might to drum home the importance of occupying the crease, the message never got through. Just as a fast bowler must be physically fit to do his job properly, so a batsman must be mentally fit in order to concentrate for long periods, and my growing conviction was that some of our prime players were not.

The circumstances in which English cricket found itself meant that there were players on the trip to whom a Test tour must have been as unexpected as winning the pools; maybe it was understandable that they felt they were only on a honeymoon before things got back to normal. Others, who should have known better, were carried away by the social opportunities in New Zealand to the point of sadly neglecting their cricket commitments. The attitude of 'It's only nets tomorrow, it doesn't matter if I have a hangover' can never be acceptable within any professional, national team.

None the less, the players in general responded admirably to the crisis which confronted us in the shape of the drugs allegations. Alan Smith, the manager, and I had to bear the brunt of the inquisition, it is true, but a lot of characters among the party shone through in a situation which must rank among the most peculiar any touring side has ever faced. It often needs adverse circumstances to show the true colours of any group of people, and the spirit of togetherness which was engendered by the slur was quite remarkable to witness.

The underlying, ominous message of the newspaper stories is that Fleet Street had changed the unwritten rules which had previously governed the reporting of a foreign sporting tour. Whether it be rugby or cricket (these being the two games in which the national side regularly spends long periods abroad) the players have always been accompanied by journalists. There are probably more now than ever before but still, for the sake of tidy arrangements and their preference for proximity to any news, they usually stay in the same hotels as the players and, by the nature of such existence, they witness and often share in the social life. Players will have a drink with journalists of an evening; occasionally, they might get drunk with them. Those players would understandably feel cheated if the same journalists were to write in the following day's papers of disgraceful, drunken and unprofessional behaviour by the England cricketers/rugby players. Until recently, this had never happened, the cricket writers accepting that they were in a privileged position which they did not abuse. They wrote about the games and, naturally, any news – sensational or otherwise – connected with the cricket, but did not write about the players' private lives, respecting, in other words, their right to have one.

All that has changed. Whether through a heightened circulation war in Fleet Street, different editors with fewer moral principles, or simply a symbol of changing times, it would seem that anything goes in the reporting of events on and off the field during a tour. I don't blame the majority of cricket writers for this, rather their superiors who have taken to sending the sharpshooting news-gatherers to dig out the dirt in the happy knowledge that they will never have to meet or deal with the 'victims' again. All they have succeeded in doing is driving a wedge between the players and press which will need very careful removing if the long-term relationship of fully mutual trust is ever to be restored.

After all my previous comments about the laziness and unpro-fessionalism of a proportion of younger players, I am not now about to paint them in saintly light or suggest they are beyond reproach. Of course things have happened on tours which do the players no credit, and maybe there have even been times when it would not have been a bad thing for a respected cricket journalist to write about them in a constructive fashion. But it can do no good at all, with the possible exception of the paper's short-term circulation, to indulge in cheap smut and fanciful innuendo. I felt sorry for my players over the drugs story; I also felt sorry for a few of the genuine cricket writers.

For Botham, the man at the centre of the controversy, it was an extension of a dilemma which had been setting traps for him for some time and which has ensnared pop stars in plenty as well as the occasional sportsman with genius to match Botham's. I believe Ian is the greatest all-round cricketer of my generation with whom no other playing today can fairly be compared. His personality is so charismatic and his lifestyle so attractive to those who live more humdrum existences that he is never out of the news. Ian is not a natural escapee and because he insists on living his life exactly how he wishes, ignoring the spotlight, he is bound to attract attention when, as is his way, he does something outrageous or extravagant. At present he cannot go through a tour, or a home season, with the privacy expected by normal human beings or even normal sports-men. I think he was well-advised to take the winter of 1984–85 off from touring and hope it may have benefited both Ian himself and English cricket as a whole. Although it would be mis-stating the facts to say he enjoyed a quiet winter, he was at least able to spend more time at home, with his wife and family, taking an objective look at his life in cricket. I hope he can put things more into perspective and go on playing for England for a few years yet, preferably free from the more undesirable elements of publicity he has sometimes attracted.

Ian and I had both apparently recovered from our respective ailments in time to begin the 1984 county season. I say apparently, because in reality I don't think I completely recovered at all. It was obvious to me quite early in the season that I was short of energy and unable to recharge my batteries after bowling as rapidly as I used to. At first I thought I was 'short of a gallop', to use the parlance of a racing trainer describing a horse not yet quite race-fit, but the problem refused to go away.

Despite having lost the England captaincy I did have great incentives for the season. I wanted to put up a good performance against the West Indies – whether we beat them was an entirely different matter – and I wanted Warwickshire to win something. It was to be my last chance, because quite early in the season, probably influenced by the clinging virus and the accompanying depression, I made up my mind to retire in September.

I have never been one for records, and although the taking of 300 Test wickets and the subsequent overhauling of Fred Trueman's record English aggregate of 307, was naturally an achievement to savour with some satisfaction in years to come, I had no burning ambition to drag myself on in Test cricket in an effort to pass Dennis Lillee's all-time record. It would prove nothing; I know Dennis was a better bowler than I and my taking one more wicket would not change that. With my worrying habit of falling ill in tropical climates, I was also less than keen to prolong my career into a winter tour of India. But the overriding reason was that, at 35, I felt I had done enough.

I was never likely to be the type of player happy to go on bowling as he drops down in levels – first out of Test cricket, then down into the county Second team and so on. I have a sneaking admiration for some who have done it, but it is not in my character; I would no longer feel any motivation to play. I had always felt I would know instinctively when the time was right to retire and in May 1984 I knew.

Although I now know that the decision was taken while I was far from well, I have never regretted it. In the three Tests I played against West Indies I was more relaxed than I have felt for years in such an environment. For a while, too, it seemed as though at least some of my remaining ambitions were to be granted. Although we were taking a fearful beating from the best team in the world, I had bowled with spark on a few occasions, picking up some wickets; in county cricket, Warwickshire reached the final of the Benson and Hedges Cup, and confidence within the side was such that few would even contemplate defeat against Lancashire.

The semi-final of that competition, against Yorkshire at Headingley, had been the beginning of the end for my season. Physically, it drained me; I was no use either to Warwickshire or England after that. Like any cricketer in such a position, I was determined to play in the final, but at our team dinner on the eve of the match at Lord's, I felt so rough that I said to David Brown: 'I'm either very ill or very nervous – and I don't think it's nerves.'

Brownie tried to reassure me, as he has done so often, but I felt no better the next morning. If anything I deteriorated while watching our batsmen lay the foundations for a big score only to throw it all away. We had convinced ourselves that we could not play as badly as we had done in our previous Lord's final – against Surrey in the NatWest Trophy two years earlier. But we managed it. With Lancashire bowling straight and fielding brilliantly, we simply did not set them enough runs. Oh, there were valid excuses; we lost the toss and were inevitably put in on a pitch which started scandalously damp. But the fact is, we had done the hard bit, overcoming the first session before the wickets began to tumble.

I got through my overs. Just. We kept a fingertip hold on the game for a while, but Neil Fairbrother, whom I rate among the best of the young batsmen now on the county circuit, played a mature and impressive innings to make absolutely sure that Lancashire would win.

Back in the dressing-room, surrounded by the familiar furnishings, the smells and the atmospheres I had come to know so well during a decade and a half of playing at the game's headquarters, there was no longer any doubt in my mind. I was ill. The rest of our lads went across to the Westmoreland Hotel opposite, where we were due to stay that night, and no doubt they drowned their considerable sorrows. I asked Julie to drive me home.

The Warwickshire players had put a lot into that competition and I was as sick at heart for them as I was sick in body myself. Pretty soon, I knew I would not play again, for although my condition gradually improved, I was still lacking strength and energy. I was forever putting back the deadline as the medical men kept advising me I would be foolish to put my health at risk again. England lost another Test. I watched it on TV at home. Then Warwickshire won their quarter-final in the NatWest Trophy. There was still hope, I thought, of a last chance in a cup final.

It was semi-final day – against Kent at Edgbaston. With Andy Lloyd, who had fought his way into the England side, batting well before being cruelly struck down by a bouncer from Malcolm Marshall, I watched from the roof of the Edgbaston pavilion; two crocks willing their team-mates to get through. They didn't make it, and possibly with that defeat both Andy and I were spared the risk of trying to hasten the recovery process. Neither of us played again during the season.

Enforced idleness was not something I remotely enjoyed. It was sheer frustration feeling a need and a desire to retain contact with the team of which I was still nominally captain, yet knowing that I could do little except get in the way. My situation was not eased by the knowledge that some people probably thought I was malingering. It came to the stage where I was ticking off the days to 11 September, and when it arrived and everyone packed their bags prior to dispersing to their winter employments, I felt no great sense of loss, just overwhelming relief that it was over.

To many people, my Warwickshire epitaph will probably be that I never took the wickets of which I was capable. I cannot dispute the facts, but merely point to the similarities with Test fast bowlers through the years. It is simply not possible, especially with the new, increased volume of international cricket, for a fast bowler to perform at his peak day after day. Sadly, it is usually his county which suffers for the syndrome. I put a lot of time and effort into the Warwickshire club and hope the relationship was mutually beneficial. Certainly I could not have chosen better in 1971 when I left Surrey. Thirteen years later, at the end of my career, the club surprised me enormously by electing me an honorary life member, a privilege accorded to very few, and in the years to come I trust I can continue to put something back into the county after all their loyalty to me.

One of the ways in which I find Warwickshire an impressive club is through its broad, universal view of the English game. Far too many counties are narrow and parochial in their outlook, content to do no more than ensure their own solvency for the conceivable future. Warwickshire have always taken whatever line they consider will be of the most value to the game as a whole.

It is in this respect that the Test and County Cricket Board could be thought to be democracy gone mad. Because all seventeen counties and various affiliated bodies have a say in the running of the game, there is so much self-interest expressed that sometimes few things get done. It was one of my major frustrations during my latter years as a player that I could win no overall support for a complete revision of our first-class cricket structure. Appointed to a working party set up to investigate what could be done to improve the structure, I kidded myself that at long last some changes might be adopted. But nothing was done.

My own view, and one which has long been shared by Warwickshire and Surrey, is that we should play four-day Championship cricket in midweek. Each county would play all the others once, making an authentic and absolutely fair 16-match programme. The weekend would then be devoted to one-day competitions, the very popular John Player League continuing on Sundays (possibly with an earlier start) and two other events sharing the Saturdays. If crowds are going to watch county games they are going to come at weekends and, apart from the hard core of members, most will want to see a game with a finish. Let us give the audience what they want by staging the limited-overs games at weekends, at the same time encouraging the development of Test cricketers by playing four-day matches in which the batsmen have time to build an innings and the spinners, it is to be hoped, will be better employed.

To me it seemed an ideal solution. To many counties it seemed repellent. There were some sound financial reasons put forward by certain of the dissenters, but nothing, I would have thought, that could not have been overcome, given the right amount of foresight. I went to the extent of planning a full fixture programme which proved that the Test players would be able to appear in the majority of their county's Championship matches, improving the competition still further. But the arguments fell on a lot of deaf ears.

The question of overseas players is another perennial issue occupying the minds of TCCB members and the voices of virtually every cricket follower. Many people believe we should put a permanent block on imported stars; others think they should be unlimited. The Board have tried to tighten the regulations for the general good of cricket, restricting each club to one overseas player, but the counties strive to find loopholes in the law to suit their own ends. My own view is that although the top overseas players do have a part to play in our game, attracting the crowds and often improving standards, they can also stunt the development of young English players by their presence in vital positions. So I would restrict them to one-day matches, where they will play in front of big audiences, leaving the Championship entirely to English-qualified players. Again, it is a theory which has advanced no further than the drawing-board.

I played long enough and, through sitting on various committees, saw enough of the game from different angles to have formed some strong opinions on the way it should be played. My views tend to harden with passing time for I am a black and white person with little patience for hiding in the grey areas of indecision.

On Test match over-rates, for instance, I feel the only way to solve the problem is for every country to agree to a statutory minimum of 90 overs per six-hour day – or 15 overs an hour. In India and Pakistan, where daylight hours are short, Tests should be played over six five-hour days to achieve a uniformity in playing time. I would go further, suggesting that the International Cricket Conference should agree to a fining system to be imposed on any side falling short of the required over-rate. It will not be universally popular – England have been fighting a lonely battle in this regard for some time now – but a threat to the pocket is the one sure way to ensure professionals get through their overs at a respectable rate. The alternative method, tried recently in England, of simply continuing play until the overs are complete is not satisfactory because spectators tend not to be interested in staying at a cricket match long after the scheduled close. West Indies insist, tongue in cheek, that over-rate rules should not apply to them because if they bowled them any quicker they would finish each game inside three instead of four days. Their superiority will not last for ever, and a rule such as this can be effective only if it embraces every country playing the game at Test level.

I have often made known my opinion that rest days in Test matches should be statutory. Only recently have certain countries, notably Australia, introduced five straight days – and, in Australia, it is not a cricketing decision but a promotional one. I can see the argument of the marketing men that the momentum and appeal of a game can be lost with a break in the middle, but from the players' viewpoint, and perhaps more particularly from the fast bowlers', a Test is already quite demanding enough without taking away the one opportunity to wind down, recharge and rest those niggling injuries which so often occur in the five-day game.

Being a long-serving member of the fast-bowlers' 'union', I might be expected to have no firm opinions on the excessive amount of short-pitched bowling in modern Tests, but that is not the case. All through my career I insisted that the bouncer was a legitimate part of the pace bowlers' armoury, and am not about to alter that view now I am on the outside looking in. As I have mentioned earlier in this book, the West Indians have recently escalated the bowling of bouncers to unacceptable levels and, on the very rare occasions when an umpire has taken steps to curb them, their reaction has been one of outraged innocence.

I always bowled my fair share of bouncers, but whenever an umpire told me I was overdoing it I simply stopped bowling them. The West Indians seem to believe they have *carte blanche* in the matter – licence to bowl six bouncers an over if they choose, simply because it is a Test match.

The old chestnut of neutral umpires has recently been raised again and it has its attractions. An international panel of Test umpires might at least obviate the feeling now experienced by virtually every touring side that they are receiving the rough end of decisions from home officials. The practicalities of such an innovation are bewildering, though. What, for instance, do the umpires do between Tests? And would the same two umpires be appointed to stand in every Test of a particular series? Would inexperienced umpires from, shall we say, Sri Lanka, be joyfully welcomed to umpire in a series in England, where we consider our own officials to be the finest in the world?

The best thing that could happen to the standard of umpiring would be if a great deal more former Test players were to take up the white coat. Many of the current crop have never played top cricket at all, and simply don't know what it is like to be a batsman getting a faint edge or a bowler convinced he has an lbw. No amount of reading the rules will ever replace that instinct which accrues only from playing the game at its highest level. I am not optimistic in this direction. We will continue to get a trickle of good English players turning to umpiring, but in Australia that progression is inconceivable. There is no rapport between the player and the umpire – the players never argue; they simply treat the umpires as they would a traffic cop, no more thinking of taking on one of those jobs than the other.

If a batsman is being intimidated, it is the duty of the umpire to protect him with firm action. As batsmen, in practice, receive precious little protection from umpires, they have had to come to terms with protecting themselves. Hence the controversial arrival of the helmet and all the arguments about whether, aesthetically, it has any place in what should be a characterful game. Aesthetics should not come into it when a man's life is at stake and it is by no means melodramatic to labour the risk of a fatality. The curious thing is that someone has not been killed already, because heaven knows how many times we have come close to it. In the summer of 1984, for instance, Andy Lloyd's life was saved by the fact that he was wearing a helmet – an inadequate one, admittedly, but a helmet none the less. He will never open the batting again without such protection, and the injuries he suffered surely render all arguments against the helmet absurd. How can you justify risking death just to look more appealing to the spectator?

Similarly, I have no objection to helmets being worn by close fielders, with the important proviso that their use should not permit the fielder to stand any closer to the batsman than he would otherwise feel able to do. The time may have come for a line to be drawn past which the silly-point and short-leg must not venture.

My greatest concern as I packed my cricket bag for the last time was for the England team. After playing almost 100 Tests it is natural that I should feel an affinity with the team, whatever its current make-up, and if they are to flourish in the future I feel the generation gap which I have already discussed must be closed. There is currently a lack of understanding at both ends of the spectrum, both from the people running the side at the top end of the age scale and the players whose young ideas can cause anxiety. The players need a certain amount of pulling into line so that they concentrate more on the playing of cricket rather than the twin attractions of social opportunities and commercial ventures outside the game. Equally, the administrators should probably strive to show a greater degree of understanding.

Ian Botham and David Gower have both recently strayed too far in the direction of money-earning to the possible slight neglect of their cricket. It would be a pity if this were to damage either career, for they are without doubt England's most naturally talented players. It is for this reason that I have always opposed the appointment of each in turn as England captain. It did nothing for Ian and, judging by his batting form since getting the job, it has also done nothing for David. People will naturally jump to the conclusion that I am maliciously keen to do David down because he relieved me of the job, but this is not so. I like him enormously and admire his batting ability, but don't think he should have been compromised by the burdens of captaincy just as he was beginning to establish himself among the world's premier players. He is to be heartily congratulated on the result he achieved in India during the winter of 1984–85, where he steered England to a 2–1 series win despite making very few runs himself. For his own sake, I hope he can regain his batting form and prove my fears ungrounded.

For myself, I cannot imagine ever disappearing entirely from the game which has given me my life. I will continue to follow it closely while enjoying the freedom which retirement has given me from the sleepless nights and the taut, tense days which were never less frequent, no matter how long I played. I wish England well every time they take the field, glad that I no longer find my patience and temper shortening on the first morning of each new Test.

I will enjoy a day at the races without wondering how long it will be before some boorish person berates me for my latest bowling effort; spend a night at the cinema, an opera or in a restaurant without worrying about being in bed by ten in order to snatch sleep when it comes; have a drink too many now and then without the fear that someone might be around the corner on the phone to Fleet Street. I shall be relaxed where before I could be hopelessly tetchy. I shall enjoy life.

The chance to manage the England Under-19 side in the West Indies, early in 1985, was something I eagerly accepted. It was an opening for me to use my experience in the game and pass on some of my knowledge to young players.

I would like to think I could make a success of that type of job, but in the meantime, while I sort out my long-term future, I am content to do what for me is strikingly unusual – spend plenty of time at home with my wife, Julie, my daughter, Katie-Anne, and my friends.

Cricket has been good to me. Sometimes I will look back to that faraway day when I almost quit after six weeks of my apprenticeship with Surrey, and wonder what on earth might have become of me had I done so. Being totally honest, I cannot claim that 15 years of top-class cricket has been non-stop fun and pleasure. It has been hard work, rewarding yet demanding. But I would not have changed it.

STATISTICAL APPENDIX

R. G. D. Willis in first-class cricket 1969 to 1984
Compiled by Simon Wilde

All matches overseas were played for either MCC or England teams on tour with the exception of six matches in South Africa in 1972–73, five of which were for D. H. Robins' XI and one for Northern Transvaal. Willis also began England's tour of West Indies in 1980–81 but returned home because of injury before playing in a first-class match.

Willis played for Surrey from 1969 to 1971 and for Warwickshire from 1972 to 1984.

* Signifies not out.

† Eight-ball overs were in use in Australia in 1970–71, 1974–75, 1976–77 and 1978–79; in New Zealand in 1970–71 and 1977–78; in Sri Lanka in 1976–77; and in Pakistan in 1977–78.

First-class Cricket	M	I	NO	Runs	HS	50	Avge	Ct	Overs	Mdns	Runs	Wkts	Avge	BB	5wI	10wM
1969	6	6	4	11	8*	—	5.50	2	151	29	379	22	17.23	5-78	1	—
1970	14	12	8	61	25	—	15.25	4	373.3	67	1135	40	28.38	4-57	—	—
1970–71 (A/NZ)	9	8	3	74	27	—	14.80	4	†182	29	738	23	32.09	4-81	—	—
1971	16	16	8	156	33	—	19.50	9	370	83	1011	35	28.89	4-57	1	—
1972	11	8	2	47	12	—	7.83	5	297.1	66	901	29	31.07	8-44	1	—
1972–73 (SA)	6	7	3	72	34	—	18.00	2	159.2	36	424	13	32.62	6-26	1	—
1973	19	23	11	223	32	—	18.58	9	470.1	133	1164	58	20.07	5-42	—	—
1973–74 (WI)	6	6	5	30	10*	—	30.00	8	140	27	526	15	35.07	4-91	1	—
1974	19	22	16	159	24	—	26.50	10	471.2	92	1369	62	22.08	5-85	—	—
1974–75 (A)	9	15	6	108	21	—	12.00	5	†223.7	29	811	26	31.19	5-61	1	—
1975	4	5	1	39	19	—	9.75	3	129.5	33	338	18	18.78	5-82	1	—
1976	8	10	4	80	43	—	13.33	3	239.2	41	757	32	23.66	6-55	3	—
1976–77 (I/SL/A)	11	10	4	62	37	—	10.33	5	191.1 †63.5	36 †5	740	37	20.00	6-53	4	—
1977	16	15	5	124	29	—	12.40	5	399	94	1183	58	20.40	8-32	5	1
1977–78 (P/NZ)	11	11	6	50	14	—	10.00	3	†241.6	58	658	39	16.87	5-32	1	1
1978	18	16	5	117	23*	—	10.64	10	474.2	116	1197	65	18.42	7-63	5	—
1978–79 (A)	10	13	4	115	24*	—	12.78	3	†210.3	34	696	34	20.47	5-44	1	—
1979	12	8	5	98	42*	—	32.67	1	261	68	699	21	33.29	5-41	1	—
1979–80 (A)	4	6	0	21	11	—	3.50	—	113	30	252	3	84.00	1-26	—	—
1980	19	21	6	185	33	—	12.33	8	457.2	118	1366	49	27.88	5-65	1	—
1981	13	18	5	149	33*	—	11.46	3	391.1	85	1037	42	24.69	8-43	2	—
1981–82 (I/SL)	10	6	3	26	13	—	8.67	3	242.1	62	687	24	28.63	4-35	—	—
1982	18	22	9	351	72	2	27.00	7	446	89	1444	51	28.31	6-45	2	—
1982–83 (A)	7	13	5	65	26	—	8.13	7	225	41	656	28	23.43	5-66	1	—
1983	17	20	9	183	37	—	16.64	6	376.5	98	1058	41	25.81	5-35	1	—
1983–84 (NZ/P)	7	8	3	28	6	—	5.60	5	188.5	53	495	19	26.05	4-51	—	—
1984	8	8	5	56	22	—	18.67	3	213	42	747	15	49.80	2-19	—	—
TOTALS	308	333	145	2690	72	2	14.31	134	6780.3 and †921.5	1539 and †155	22,468	899	24.99	8-32	34	2

Test cricket		M	I	NO	Runs	HS	Avge	Ct	Overs	Mdns	Runs	Wkts	Avge	BB	5wI
1970–71	Australia	4	5	3	37	15*	18.50	3	†88	16	329	12	27.42	3-58	—
1970–71	New Zealand	1	2	0	10	7	5.00	0	†20	3	69	2	34.50	2-54	—
1973	West Indies	1	2	1	5	5*	5.00	2	35	3	118	4	29.50	4-118	—
1973–74	West Indies	3	5	4	25	10*	25.00	3	73	15	255	5	51.00	3-97	—
1974	India	1	1	0	24	24	24.00	1	36	8	97	5	19.40	4-64	—
1974	Pakistan	1	1	1	1	1*	—	0	35	4	129	2	64.50	2-102	—
1974–75	Australia	5	10	5	76	15	15.20	1	†140.4	15	522	17	30.71	5-61	1
1976	West Indies	2	4	2	5	5*	2.50	1	57.3	11	234	9	26.00	5-42	1
1976–77	India	5	7	2	19	7	3.80	3	135	25	335	20	16.75	6-53	2
1976–77	Australia	1	2	2	6	5*	—	1	†30	0	124	2	62.00	2-33	—
1977	Australia	5	6	4	49	24*	24.50	2	†166.4	36	534	27	19.78	7-78	3
1977–78	Pakistan	3	3	1	27	14	13.50	1	†59	8	190	7	27.14	2-26	—
1977–78	New Zealand	3	4	3	15	6*	15.00	0	†103.6	27	255	14	18.21	5-32	1
1978	Pakistan	3	1	0	18	18	18.00	1	88.4	16	233	13	17.92	5-47	1
1978	New Zealand	3	3	3	11	7*	—	0	99.2	33	229	12	19.08	5-42	—
1978–79	Australia	6	10	2	88	24	11.00	3	†140.3	23	461	20	23.05	5-44	1
1979	India	3	2	2	14	10*	—	0	102	23	298	10	29.80	3-53	—
1979–80	Australia	3	6	0	21	11	3.50	0	98	26	224	3	74.67	1-26	—
1980	West Indies	4	6	3	61	24*	20.33	0	110.1	27	407	14	29.07	5-65	1
1981	Australia	6	10	2	43	13	5.38	2	252.4	56	666	29	22.97	8-43	1
1981–82	India	5	4	2	26	13	13.00	0	129.1	29	381	12	31.75	3-75	—
1981–82	Sri Lanka	1	1	0	0	0	0.00	2	28	10	70	3	23.33	2-46	—
1982	India	3	3	1	35	28	17.50	0	88	11	330	15	22.00	6-101	1
1982	Pakistan	2	3	3	29	28*	—	3	74	14	222	10	22.20	3-55	—
1982–83	Australia	5	9	3	63	26	10.50	4	166.3	26	486	18	27.00	5-66	1
1983	New Zealand	4	7	2	67	25*	13.40	4	123.3	38	273	20	13.65	5-35	1
1983–84	New Zealand	3	4	1	14	6	4.67	0	115.1	28	306	12	25.50	4-51	—
1983–84	Pakistan	1	2	0	8	6	4.00	1	19	6	46	2	23.00	2-33	—
1984	West Indies	3	5	3	43	22	21.50	1	85	15	367	6	61.17	2-48	—
TOTALS		90	128	55	840	28*	11.51	39	2117.2 and †581.5	460 and †92	8190	325	25.20	8-43	16

Test Cricket *continued*

Season	Opponents	Venue	Batting 1st	2nd	Bowling 1st	2nd
1970–71	AUSTRALIA	Sydney	15*	–	9-2-26-0	3-2-1-1
		Melbourne	5*	–	20-5-73-3	10-1-42-1
		Adelaide	4	–	12-3-49-2	13-1-48-1
		Sydney	11	2*	12-1-58-3	9-1-32-1
1970–71	NEW ZEALAND	Auckland	7	3	14-2-54-2	6-1-15-0
1973	WEST INDIES	Lord's	5*	0	35-3-118-4	–
1973–74	WEST INDIES	Port-of-Spain	6	0*	19-5-52-1	4-1-6-0
		Kingston	6*	3*	24-5-97-3	–
		Bridgetown	10*	–	26-4-100-1	–
1974	INDIA	Old Trafford	24	–	24-3-64-4	12-5-33-1
1974	PAKISTAN	Oval	1*	–	28-3-102-2	7-1-27-0
1974–75	AUSTRALIA	Brisbane	13*	3*	21.5-3-56-4	15-3-45-3
		Perth	4*	0*	22-0-91-2	2-0-8-0
		Melbourne	13	15	21.7-4-61-5	14-2-56-1
		Sydney	2	12	18-2-80-0	11-1-52-1
		Adelaide	11*	3	10-0-46-1	5-0-27-0
1976	WEST INDIES	Headingley	0*	0	20-2-71-3	15.3-6-42-5
		Oval	5*	0	15-3-73-1	7-0-48-0
1976–77	INDIA	Delhi	1	–	7-3-21-0	9-3-24-1
		Calcutta	0*	–	20-3-27-5	13-1-32-2
		Madras	7	4*	19-5-46-1	13-4-18-3
		Bangalore	7	0	17-2-53-6	18-2-47-2
		Bombay	0	–	13-1-52-0	6-1-15-0
1976–77	AUSTRALIA	Melbourne	1*	5*	8-0-33-2	22-0-91-0
1977	AUSTRALIA	Lord's	17	0	30.1-7-78-7	10-1-40-2
		Old Trafford	1*	–	21-8-45-2	16-2-56-2
		Trent Bridge	2*	–	15-0-58-1	26-6-88-5
		Headingley	5*	–	5-0-35-0	14-7-32-3
		Oval	24*	–	29.3-5-102-5	–
1977–78	PAKISTAN	Lahore	14	–	17-3-67-0	7-0-34-2
		Hyderabad	8*	–	16-2-40-2	11-2-26-2
		Karachi	5	–	8-1-23-1	–
1977–78	NEW ZEALAND	Wellington	6*	3	25-7-65-2	15-2-32-5
		Christchurch	6*	–	20-5-45-1	7-2-14-4
		Auckland	0*	–	26.6-8-57-2	10-3-42-0
1978	PAKISTAN	Edgbaston	–	–	16-2-42-2	23.4-3-70-2
		Lord's	18	–	13-1-47-5	10-2-26-2
		Headingley	–	–	26-8-48-2	
1978	NEW ZEALAND	Oval	3*	–	20.2-9-42-5	13-2-39-1
		Trent Bridge	1*	–	12-5-22-1	9-0-31-0
		Lord's	7*	–	29-9-79-1	16-8-16-4
1978–79	AUSTRALIA	Brisbane	8	–	14-2-44-4	27.6-3-69-3
		Perth	2	3*	18.5-5-44-5	12-1-36-1
		Melbourne	19	3	13-2-47-0	7-0-21-0
		Sydney	7*	0	9-2-33-2	2-0-8-0
		Adelaide	24	12	11-1-55-1	12-3-41-3
		Sydney	10	–	11-4-48-1	3-0-15-0
1979	INDIA	Edgbaston	–	–	24-9-69-3	14-3-45-1
		Headingley	4*	–	18-5-42-2	–
		Oval	10*	–	18-2-53-3	28-4-89-1
1979–80	AUSTRALIA	Perth	11	0	23-7-47-0	26-7-52-1
		Sydney	3	1	11-3-30-1	12-2-26-1
		Melbourne	4	2	21-4-61-0	5-3-8-0

Test Cricket *continued*

Season	Opponents	Venue	Batting 1st	Batting 2nd	Bowling 1st	Bowling 2nd
1980	WEST INDIES	Trent Bridge	8	9	20.1-5-82-4	26-4-65-5
		Lord's	14	–	31-12-103-3	–
		Old Trafford	5*	–	14-1-99-1	–
		Oval	1*	24*	19-5-58-1	–
1981	AUSTRALIA	Trent Bridge	0	1	30-14-47-3	13-2-28-1
		Lord's	5	–	27.4-9-50-3	12-3-35-1
		Headingley	1*	2	30-8-72-0	15.1-3-43-8
		Edgbaston	13	2	19-3-63-0	20-6-37-2
		Old Trafford	11	5*	14-0-63-4	30.5-2-96-3
		Oval	3	–	31-6-91-4	10-0-41-0
1981–82	INDIA	Bombay	1	13	12-5-33-1	13-4-31-1
		Delhi	–	–	26-3-99-2	–
		Calcutta	11*	–	14-3-28-2	6-0-21-0
		Madras	1*	–	28.1-7-79-2	7-2-5-1
		Kanpur	–	–	23-5-75-3	–
1981–82	SRI LANKA	Colombo	0	–	19-7-46-2	9-3-24-1
1982	INDIA	Lord's	28	–	16-2-41-3	28-3-101-6
		Old Trafford	6	–	17-2-94-2	–
		Oval	1*	–	23-4-78-3	4-0-16-1
1982	PAKISTAN	Edgbaston	0*	28*	15-3-42-2	14-2-49-2
		Headingley	1*	–	26-6-76-3	19-3-55-3
1982–83	AUSTRALIA	Perth	26	0	31.5-4-95-3	6-1-23-2
		Brisbane	1	10*	29.4-3-66-5	4-1-24-0
		Adelaide	1	10	25-6-76-2	8-1-17-1
		Melbourne	6*	8*	15-2-38-3	17-0-57-0
		Sydney	1	–	20-6-57-1	10-2-33-1
1983	NEW ZEALAND	Oval	4	–	20-8-43-4	12-3-26-2
		Headingley	9	4	23.3-6-57-4	14-5-35-5
		Lord's	7	2*	13-6-28-1	12-5-24-3
		Trent Bridge	25*	16	10-2-23-0	19-3-37-1
1983–84	NEW ZEALAND	Wellington	5*	–	19-7-37-3	37-8-102-2
		Christchurch	6	0	22.1-5-51-4	–
		Auckland	3	–	34-7-109-3	3-1-7-0
1983–84	PAKISTAN	Karachi	6	2	17-6-33-2	2-0-13-0
1984	WEST INDIES	Edgbaston	10*	22	25-3-108-2	–
		Lord's	2	–	19-5-48-2	15-5-48-0
		Headingley	4*	5*	18-1-123-2	8-1-40-0

AUSTRALIA   35 Tests, 58 innings @ 10.35, 128 wickets @ 26.14
INDIA   17 Tests, 17 innings @ 11.80, 62 wickets @ 23.24
NEW ZEALAND 14 Tests, 20 innings @ 10.64, 60 wickets @ 18.87
PAKISTAN   10 Tests, 10 innings @ 16.60, 34 wickets @ 24.12
SRI LANKA   1 Test,   1 innings   3 wickets @ 23.33
WEST INDIES   13 Tests, 22 innings @ 15.44, 38 wickets @ 36.34

In all, Willis delivered 17,357 balls in Test cricket, taking a wicket every 53.41 balls and conceding 47.19 runs per 100 balls.

Willis, with 325 wickets, stands as the leading wicket-taker for England in Test cricket. He took the record from F. S. Trueman (307 wickets in 67 Tests) on 20 January 1984 against New Zealand at Wellington, when he dismissed B. L. Cairns in his 84th Test. As at 31 May 1985 I. T. Botham has taken 312 wickets in 73 Tests for England.

Willis also holds the wicket-taking record for England against Australia, with 128 wickets in 35 Tests. He took the record from W. Rhodes (109 wickets in 41 Tests) on 28 August 1981 at the Oval, when he dismissed D. K. Lillee. It was his 30th Test against Australia, though he had bowled more deliveries than Rhodes.

Willis headed England's Test bowling averages in the following series: v West Indies, 1976; v Australia, 1977; v New Zealand, 1977–78; v India, 1982; v Pakistan, 1982; v Australia, 1982–83; v New Zealand, 1983; v New Zealand, 1983–84 (the last five being in consecutive series).

His 325 Test wickets were taken in the following manner: Bowled 68; lbw 33; Caught by wicketkeeper 67 (R. W. Taylor 38, A. P. E. Knott 28, P. R. Downton 1); Caught-and-bowled 4; Caught by other fielders 151 (I. T. Botham 22); Hit wicket 2.

Willis dismissed the following batsmen in Test cricket: **Australia:** 11 times – K. J. Hughes; 9 – G. S. Chappell, R. W. Marsh; 7 – R. B. McCosker, G. N. Yallop; 6 – J. Dyson, K. D. Walters; 5 – I. M. Chappell, G. F. Lawson, J. R. Thomson, G. M. Wood; 4 – D. K. Lillee, M. H. N. Walker, B. Yardley; 3 – A. R. Border, R. J. Bright; 2 – G. J. Cosier, I. C. Davis, W. J. Edwards, J. W. Gleeson, R. M. Hogg, D. W. Hookes, A. G. Hurst, W. M. Lawry, K. J. O'Keeffe, I. R. Redpath, C. S. Serjeant, K. C. Wessels; 1 – T. M. Alderman, T. M. Chappell, R. Edwards, T. J. Jenner, T. J. Laughlin, A. A. Mallett, C. G. Rackemann, K. R. Stackpole, P. M. Toohey, D. M. Wellham, M. R. Whitney. **India:** 5 – S. M. Gavaskar, R. J. Shastri; 4 – C. P. S. Chauhan, S. Madan Lal, B. P. Patel; 3 – S. M. H. Kirmani, E. A. S. Prasanna, D. B. Vengsarkar, G. R. Viswanath, Yashpal Sharma; 2 – M. B. Amarnath, B. S. Chandrasekhar, A. D. Gaekwad, K. D. Ghavri, Kapil Dev, A. Malhotra, E. D. Solkar, K. Srikkanth; 1 – S. B. Amarnath, B. S. Bedi, F. M. Engineer, G. A. Parkar, S. M. Patil, P. Sharma, S. Venkataraghavan, N. S. Yadav, Yajurvindra Singh. **New Zealand:** 7 – J. G. Wright; 6 – B. A. Edgar, G. P. Howarth; 4 – S. L. Boock, B. L. Cairns, M. D. Crowe, R. J. Hadlee; 3 – M. G. Burgess, B. E. Congdon, J. J. Crowe; 2 – R. W. Anderson, B. P. Bracewell, E. J. Chatfield, J. M. Parker; 1 – J. G. Bracewell, J. V. Coney, R. O. Collinge, T. J. Franklin, W. K. Lees, I. D. S. Smith, M. C. Snedden, K. J. Wadsworth. **Pakistan:** 4 – Mohsin Khan, Mudassar Nazar, Sadiq Mohammad; 3 – Wasim Raja; 2 – Haroon Rashid, Imran Khan, Iqbal Qasim, Javed Miandad, Shafiq Ahmed, Wasim Bari; 1 – Anil Dalpat, Liaqat Ali, Mansoor Akhtar, Salim Malik, Sikander Bakht, Talat Ali, Zaheer Abbas. **Sri Lanka:** 1 – R. L. Dias, B. Warnapura, S. Wettimuny. **West Indies:** 5 – C. G. Greenidge; 4 – D. L. Murray; 3 – D. L. Haynes, I. V. A. Richards; 2 – S. F. A. Bacchus, R. C. Fredericks, V. A. Holder, M. A. Holding, A. I. Kallicharran, C. H. Lloyd, M. D. Marshall, L. G. Rowe; 1 – E. A. E. Baptiste, A. G. Barrett, K. D. Boyce, J. Garner, R. B. Kanhai, A. M. E. Roberts, G. S. Sobers.

Six or more wickets in an innings:
8-32 Warwickshire v Gloucestershire, Bristol, 1977
8-43 England v Australia, Headingley, 1981
8-44 Warwickshire v Derbyshire, Edgbaston, 1972
7-63 Warwickshire v Gloucestershire, Edgbaston, 1978
7-78 England v Australia, Lord's, 1977
6-26 D. H. Robins' XI v Natal, Durban, 1972–73
6-44 Warwickshire v Middlesex, Edgbaston, 1978
6-53 England v India, Bangalore, 1976–77
6-55 Warwickshire v West Indians, Edgbaston, 1976
6-101 England v India, Lord's, 1982

Ten or more wickets in a match:
11-72 Warwickshire v Gloucestershire, Bristol, 1977
11-83 Warwickshire v Middlesex, Edgbaston, 1978
Willis's match return of 9-92 for England v New Zealand, Headingley, 1983, is a record for a Warwickshire bowler in a Test for England.

Hat-tricks:
Warwickshire v Derbyshire, Edgbaston, 1972
Warwickshire v West Indians, Edgbaston, 1976

50 or more runs in an innings:
72 Warwickshire v Indians, Edgbaston, 1982 (adding 175 for seventh wicket with A. M. Ferreira)
63* Warwickshire v Gloucestershire, Nuneaton, 1982
For England v West Indies, Oval, 1980, Willis (24*) added 117 unbroken for the 10th wicket with P. Willey, one of only three century stands for England's last wicket in Tests. Willis has a share in the 10th-wicket partnership records for England against both India and Pakistan: 70 with P. J. W. Allott, Lord's, 1982 and 79 with R. W. Taylor, Edgbaston, 1982.
Willis is the only batsman in Test cricket to have achieved over 50 not-out innings (55).
Willis captained England in 18 Tests from 1982 to 1983–84, winning seven, losing five and drawing six. He also captained Warwickshire from 1980 to 1984.